THE ART OF HORROR MOVIES

THE ART OF HORROR MOVIES

AN ILLUSTRATED HISTORY
EXPANDED EDITION

EDITED BY STEPHEN JONES
FOREWORD BY JOHN LANDIS

APPLAUSE
THEATRE & CINEMA BOOKS

An Imprint of Rowman & Littlefield Publishing Group, Inc

LEFT: *Creature from the Black Lagoon* (2001), acrylic and oils on gessoed board by American artist Drew Struzan, produced as a limited edition giclée print. "We weren't actually selling the movie," explains Struzan. "What we were doing was a reprise, celebrating an experience that we all loved from our childhood. I had to honor that."

FEATURED ARTISTS

Ivan Albright	Rolf Armstrong	Anselmo Ballester	Nicky Barkla
Bryan Baugh	John Becaro	Richard Bernal	Randy Broecker
Harley Brown	Reynold Brown	Jeff Carlson	Frederick Cooper
Glenn Cravath	Steve Crisp	Sara Deck	Guillermo del Toro
Frank Dietz	Vincent Di Fate	Jason Edmiston	Les Edwards
Bob Eggleton	Brian Ewing	Christopher Franchi	Frank Kelly Freas
Gary Gianni	Thomas Gianni	Godmachine	Basil Gogos
Mark Hammermeister	Alex Horley	Graham Humphreys	Scott Jackson
Daryl Joyce	Christopher Jones	Douglas Klauba	Mark Maddox
Malleus Rock Art Lab	Jack Manning	Dave McKean	Rick Melton
Uli Meyer	Micah Lee Mowbray	Lee Moyer	Marcelo Neira
Christian Pacheco	Anthony Petrie	Doug P'gosh	Jeff Preston
Andrei Riabovitchev	Roberto Ricci	Sanjulián	Joseph "Joe" Smith
Patrick Carson Sparrow	Scott Spillman	Jeff Stahl	William Stout
Drew Struzan	Darren Tan	Darren Taylor	Jack Thurston
Bruce Timm	Pete Von Sholly	Paul Watts	Woody Welch

Copyright © Elephant Book Company Limited 2017, 2022

www.elephantbookcompany.com

All rights reserved. No part of this book may be reproduced in any form, without written permission, except by a newspaper or magazine reviewer who wishes to quote brief passages in connection with a review.

Applause Books
An imprint of Globe Pequot, the trade division of
The Rowman & Littlefield Publishing Group, Inc.
4501 Forbes Blvd., Ste. 200, Lanham, MD 20706

www.rowman.com

Distributed by NATIONAL BOOK NETWORK

Trade Book Division Editorial Offices
246 Goose Lane, Suite 200, Guilford, Connecticut 06437

Editorial director: Will Steeds
Project manager: Adam Newell
Book design: Paul Palmer-Edwards
Picture researcher: Sally Claxton

Printed in China

Library of Congress Cataloging-in-Publication Data is available upon request.

ISBN 978-1-4930-6325-3

www.applausebooks.com

FRONT ENDPAPERS: Detail of pre-production trade announcement by artist Károly Grósz for *Bluebeard* to be scripted by Bayard Veiller and star Boris Karloff, from the Universal Studios exhibitor book for 1935–36. PRC eventually made another film with that title in 1944, starring John Carradine.

HALF-TITLE PAGE: *Ardeth Bey* (2004), ink on paper portrait of Boris Karloff from *The Mummy* (1932) by British artist Les Edwards. "This started out as a sketchbook drawing," explains Edwards. "Karloff's face is endlessly fascinating to draw and is absolutely iconic to people of my generation."

FRONTISPIECE: Original pastel portrait of Boris Karloff from *Bride of Frankenstein* (1935) painted by American artist Rolf Armstrong. "The Frankenstein art hung over the head of my bed like a guardian angel as I grew up," recalls artist Woody Welch, whose mother owned the picture.

BACKGROUND THIS SPREAD: Detail of the cover for the German production book for Prana-Films' *Nosferatu, eine Symphonie des Grauens* (Dir: F.W. Murnau, 1922) illustrated by producer and production designer Albin Grau, a lifelong student of the occult and a member of the hermetic order Fraternitas Saturni.

CONTENTS

Foreword: The Iconography of Horror ... 8
By John Landis

Introduction: Painting with Light and Shadows ... 10
By Stephen Jones

1
THE SINISTER SILENTS
Silent Screams and German Expressionism ... 16
By Sir Christopher Frayling

2
THE THRILLING THIRTIES
The Kings of Horror and Universal Studios ... 42
By Tom Weaver

3
THE FRIGHTENING FORTIES
Noir Nightmares and Poverty-Row Horrors ... 80
By Barry Forshaw

4
THE FEARSOME FIFTIES
Atomic Aliens and Technicolor Terrors ... 116
By David J. Schow

5
THE STYLISH SIXTIES
AIP, Hammer, Amicus, and Tigon ... 152
By Kim Newman

6
THE SATANIC SEVENTIES
Vivacious Vampires and Demonic Damsels ... 188
By Jonathan Rigby

7
THE EVIL EIGHTIES
Freddy, Michael, Jason, and Friends ... 220
By Lisa Morton

8
THE NASTY NINETIES
Remakes, Re-imaginings, and Retribution ... 252
By Anne Billson

9
THE 2000s MANIACS
Hand-Held Horrors and Foreign Frights ... 282
By Ramsey Campbell

Contributor Bios ... 314

Index ... 316

Art Credits / Acknowledgments ... 320

FOREWORD
THE ICONOGRAPHY OF HORROR

John Landis

"The films I have made were made for entertainment, maybe with the object of making the audience's hair stand on end, but never to revolt people."
Boris Karloff

ACCORDING TO THE *Oxford Dictionary*, the definition of the word "horror" is "an intense feeling of fear, shock, or disgust."

It is not difficult to horrify an audience watching a movie. All you have to do is show them something horrific. However, to get the audience invested in the story, and emotionally involved with the people in the story, is another matter entirely.

Boris Karloff, Christopher Lee, Peter Cushing, and Vincent Price are four famous actors who were typecast in "horror pictures." All four disliked the term "horror" to describe their movies. Karloff, Lee, Cushing, and Price much preferred to call them "fantasy" or "terror" films.

All motion picture stories require the viewer's "suspension of disbelief." These gentlemen took pride in their efforts to create people (or monsters) who, though they were often grotesque and twisted, were fully realized characters. Of course, sometimes they played magic, evil, or undead characters, but they always invested them with an emotional inner life.

From the earliest days of cinema, advertising art was produced to persuade the public to purchase tickets for the movie being marketed. Illustrators and graphic artists depicted images either from the movie or inspired by the movie to capture the eye, and hopefully the purse. The image on the poster must not just inform, but also entice.

Movie posters are often misleading, especially when it comes to genre films. Many times the fantastic creatures on the posters outside the cinema were not *quite* as fantastic when seen on the screen inside. The lurid advertising art for Roger Corman's *The Wasp Woman* (1959) shows the hideous body of a giant wasp with a human head, when in fact the title creature in the film is a normal-sized woman with a big wasp's head!

Film posters through the years reflect the advertising fashions of the time when they were produced, not only in style but also in graphic design. James Whale's *Frankenstein* (1931) was depicted in both Deco and Gothic styles when originally released, and it is interesting to see how many different styles of *King Kong* (1933) posters have been created over its many years of re-release.

Different countries can produce very divergent advertising for the same film. Many of the sleaziest exploitation pictures have rather elegant Czech and Polish posters.

It is surprising how often just a simple image can inspire dread: the small baby carriage superimposed on Mia Farrow's face on the one-sheet for *Rosemary's Baby* (1968), or the upstairs window throwing the shaft of light onto *The Exorcist* (1973) on its evocative poster.

The image on the poster must not just inform, but also entice.

However, the posters for so-called "Grindhouse Cinema" are often more outrageous. I saw Lucio Fulci's *Zombie* (aka *Zombie Flesh Eaters*, 1979) on Hollywood Boulevard, having been lured into the theater by the extremely effective poster outside. It was a gigantic close-up of a particularly disgusting zombie with the memorable tagline, "WE WILL EAT YOU!"

The iconography of horror—the dismembered bodies, the skulls, the eyes, the moon, the screaming woman, the dolls, the knives, axes, and chainsaws all have become a kind of shorthand instantly identifying the genre of the movie being sold. When you see the poster for *Werewolves on Wheels* (1971) you know exactly what you're getting into when you buy that ticket, and sometimes the creepy factor of just the illustration itself is enough to prevent someone from going to see the movie.

My five-year-old son Max was terrified by the billboard for Tom Holland's *Child's Play* (1988)—a very large image of the leering demonic doll Chucky holding a very big knife —and made me promise not to take him to see it. I do not believe that was the result the studio was hoping for.

Many horror film posters have become iconic and valuable collector's items. The posters for *The Mummy* (1932), *King Kong*, *Creature from The Black Lagoon* (1954), and (perhaps my favorite) *Attack of the 50 Foot Woman* (1958) are all not only artistically pleasing, but act as moments remembered and treasured—souvenirs of the cinematic experience itself.

RIGHT: *Meatloaf Jack* (2017), pen and ink with digital colors by Canadian artist Patrick Carson Sparrow. "The original piece was created back in 2012," he recalls, "It has been great fun to revisit and re-do for this book, and to really pay homage to one of my favorite films."

INTRODUCTION
PAINTING WITH LIGHT AND SHADOWS

Stephen Jones

"I knew nothing but shadows and I thought them to be real."
The Picture of Dorian Gray (1890) by Oscar Wilde

"In a horror film, lighting is 70 percent of the effectiveness. It's essential in creating the atmosphere."
Mario Bava

THE MOVIES BEGAN at the end of the nineteenth century. It was only then, when pioneers such as the French brothers Auguste and Louis Lumière (1862–1954 and 1864–1948, respectively) developed the "Cinematograph" and American Thomas A. Edison (1847–1931) produced his rival "Kinetoscope" process that photography finally came to life.

Because of the limits of the technology at the time, most of these early films ran for under a minute and were black and white and silent. They were usually projected by traveling exhibitors or as part of a vaudeville program.

As the novelty of moving pictures grew, so the filmmaking process moved from productions created by a handful of people to the establishment of a full-scale entertainment industry. The first film studios started to appear in 1897, and around the same time special effects, story continuity, and rudimentary editing techniques began to be used.

Perhaps the best-known pioneer of these various procedures was another Frenchman: Georges Méliès (Marie-Georges-Jean Méliès, 1861–1938) was an illusionist and filmmaker whose innovative use of multiple exposure, substitution editing, and time-lapse photography helped establish him as one of the leading innovators of technical and narrative developments in the early days of motion picture history.

Méliès's studio in Montreuil, just outside Paris, had a glass roof and three glass walls, along the same design as those used for still photography, and thin cotton cloths could be stretched below the roof to diffuse the direct rays of the sun. The property also included a shed that was used as dressing rooms and a hangar for constructing sets. Because of the way colors would change when photographed in black and white, the hand-painted backdrops, costumes, and actors' makeup were crafted in different shades of gray.

Between 1896 and 1913 Méliès would produce, direct, and distribute more than 500 short films, the majority of these being one-shot productions completed in a single take and utilizing in-camera effects. Although he worked in almost every genre of film, today Méliès is best remembered for such science fiction and fantasy subjects as *A Trip to the Moon* (1902), *The Damnation of Faust* (1903), *The Impossible Voyage* (1904), and *The Conquest of the Pole* (1912), before bankruptcy put an end to his career.

The first film studios started to appear in 1897, and around the same time special effects, story continuity, and rudimentary editing techniques began to be used.

However, Méliès was not the only originator of special effects cinema. George Albert Smith (1864–1959) was a British stage hypnotist, psychic, and magic lantern lecturer based in Hove, near Brighton. Smith's first film was *The Haunted Castle* (1897), a one-minute comedy set in an inn run by ghosts. It was based on the longer *Le Château hanté* (aka *The Devil's Castle/The Haunted Castle*) made by his friend and correspondent Méliès that same year.

In fact, it was G.A. Smith who had pioneered the basic technique of double exposure in July 1898, using a set draped in black and, after taking the main shot, re-exposing the negative to produce an overlaid scene. He also initiated the technique of reverse motion by filming the action a second time using an inverted camera and then joining the tail of the second negative to that of the first. The earliest surviving example of this effect can be seen in Smith's short *The House That Jack Built* (1900).

Although D.W. Griffith is often credited as having invented the close-up shot, again it was Smith who originated the technique in the 1900 films *As Seen Through a Telescope* and *Grandma's Reading Glass*, although there is some debate over the authorship of the latter title, which

TOP LEFT: French artist Marcellin Auzolle created the first poster to advertise a specific scene in a film for Louis Lumière's *L'Arroseur arrosé* (1895), which is widely regarded as the earliest known comedy film and also the first to portray a fictional story.

BOTTOM LEFT: 1891 *affiche* for *Les farces de la lune ou les mésaventures de Nostradamus* (The Moon's Pranks or the Misadventures of Nostradamus), one of many "fairy plays" performed by Georges Méliès at the Paris theater once owned by renowned French magician Jean Eugène Robert-Houdin (1805–71).

BOTTOM MIDDLE: French *affiche* for Georges Méliès's *Le Manoir du diable* (aka *The Haunted Castle/The Devil's Castle*, 1896), in which a cavalier encounters the Devil and attendant specters in a medieval castle.

ABOVE RIGHT: Fantastical French *affiche* for Georges Méliès's 1912 film *À la conquête du pôle* (aka *The Conquest of the Pole*), which was loosely based on the works of Jules Verne. An international expedition travels to the North Pole in a flying machine, where they discover a man-eating Giant of the Snows.

INTRODUCTION

some sources credit to British film pioneer Arthur Melbourne-Cooper (1874–1961).

Starting with *The Little Doctors* in 1901, Smith became one of the first people to create a coherent narrative or "film grammar" by developing such techniques as breaking up a scene into shots taken from different camera angles, presenting objective and subjective point of view shots, and using dream sequences. *Mary Jane's Mishap; or, Don't Fool with the Paraffin* (1903) is a somewhat gruesome comedy short which has been described as "the first modern film." After the titular maid (played by Smith's wife, Laura Bailey) is blown to pieces, she returns from the grave as a superimposed ghost who scares a group of schoolgirls.

As the film business grew in popularity, competing exhibitors regularly copied or illegally exhibited each other's films. In an attempt to better protect the copyright to his work, Thomas Edison began to deposit prints of his films on long strips of photographic paper with the U.S. Copyright Office.

During this first decade of movie making, Europe and America were also gripped by a new method of advertising that soon developed into an art form in itself. The illustrated color poster quickly replaced the dull, promotional broadsheets of old and brightened up the streets of towns and cities all over the world.

Often called the "Father of the Modern Poster," Parisian painter and lithographer Jules Chéret (1836–1932) combined both of his skills to design more than a thousand vivid posters for the Folies Bergère, the Moulin Rouge, the Théâtre de l'Opéra, and other clients that epitomized the period in art that later became known as *La Belle Époque* ("The Beautiful Era").

The movement spread across Western Europe and the United States during the years running up to the First World War, and among the many poster artists who embraced this time of optimism and artistic prosperity were Henri de Toulouse-Lautrec, Maxfield Parrish, Eugène Grasset, Dudley Hardy, the Beggarstaffs (William Nicholson and James Pryde), and Leonetto Cappiello.

Beautiful women in beautiful settings enticed from billboards selling everything from laundry soap, cigarettes, bicycles, and even alcoholic drinks. However, when the Czech-born *Art Nouveau* ("New Art") painter Alphonse Mucha met Parisian actress Sarah Bernhardt in 1894, their first professional collaboration—a lithographed advertisement for her stage production *Gismonda*—revolutionized poster design and established the cult of "star" status.

The world's first film poster produced to advertise a specific production was for Louis Lumière's *L'Arroseur arrosé* (1895). Created by Marcellin Auzolle (1842–1942), the poster depicted a French audience laughing at a scene from the film being projected on a screen. In the first example of its kind, the colorful image was used by the Lumière brothers to beguile audiences into seeing their forty-five second slapstick comedy.

It should be remembered that the earliest motion picture stocks at this time were orthochromatic, which meant that they were sensitive to blue and green light, but not red. This obviously caused problems when recording color photography. As a result, the first color films either utilized aniline dyes to create artificial color or were hand-tinted.

One of the first hand-colored films was Thomas Edison's *Annabelle Serpentine Dance* (1895), created for his hand-cranked "Kinetoscope" process. Georges Méliès also offered his films in hand-painted versions at a higher cost than the black and white prints. For example, sections of *A Trip to the Moon* were painted frame-by-frame by 21 women working on a production line in his Montreuil studio.

The first commercially successful color stencil process, Pathé Color (later Pathéchrome), was introduced in 1905 and ran the entire film at sixty feet per minute through a stencil that came into contact with six dye-soaked rollers in a staining machine. By 1910 Pathé had more than 400 women employed as stencilers in their factory in Vincennes, on the outskirts of Paris.

As the film business grew in popularity, competing exhibitors regularly copied or illegally exhibited each other's films.

A more common technique used around this time was tinting, where the film emulsion was dyed a uniform color to create a specific narrative effect (blue for night, yellow for daylight, red for fire, etc.).

In 1902, the pioneering British inventor and cinematographer Edward Raymond Turner (1873–1903) tested a simplified additive color system that utilized a rotating disk of three primary color filters to photograph and project a black and white film through. Following Turner's sudden death from a heart attack, his financial backer turned to G.A. Smith to develop the method. However, Smith concluded that the process was commercially unviable and instead created "Kinemacolour," the first successful additive two-color process using alternating red and green filters.

The Nickelodeon became the first permanent theater showing only films when it opened in Pittsburgh in 1905. There was now enough material available to fill at least a half-hour program, which was changed on a weekly basis. Recognizing the commercial potential, other exhibitors quickly followed suit, and within a couple of years there were thousands of purpose-built nickelodeons operating across the United States, Britain, and France.

The world's first full-length narrative feature film, *The Story of the Kelly Gang*, opened in Melbourne in December 1906. Running for over an hour, the movie told the story of Australian bushranger Ned Kelly and was accompanied by live sound effects at some screenings.

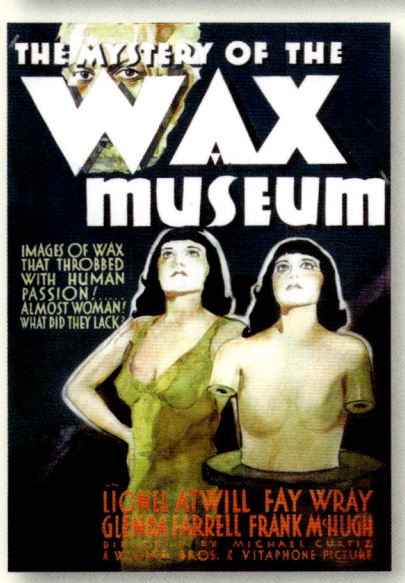

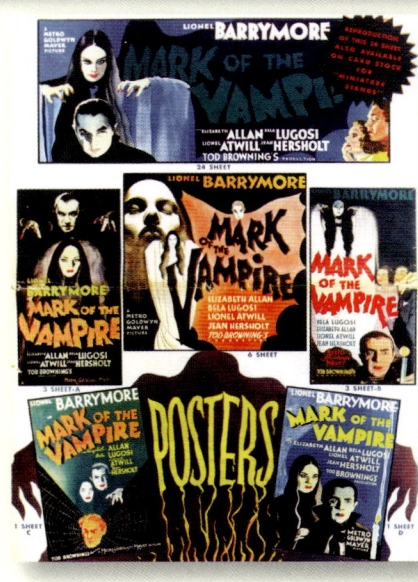

TOP: Stunning 24-sheet poster for *The Mysterious Island* (Dir: Lucien Hubbard, 1929), based on the 1874 novel by Jules Verne, filmed by Metro-Goldwyn-Mayer in two-strip Technicolor with partial sound and synchronized music and sound effects.

BOTTOM MIDDLE: Press advert for Universal's 1930 reissue of the silent *The Phantom of the Opera* (Dir: Rupert Julian, 1925), which included a newly recorded synchronized music score and sound effects.

BOTTOM LEFT: Window card for Warner Bros.' *Mystery of the Wax Museum* (Dir: Michael Curtiz, 1933), which was the last dramatic film made in the two-color Technicolor process. Thought to be lost for decades, a color print was discovered in the collection of Jack L. Warner in the late 1970s.

BOTTOM RIGHT: A page from Metro-Goldwyn-Mayer's color pressbook for *Mark of the Vampire* (Dir: Tod Browning, 1935) showing just some of the range and variety of materials that theater owners could use to promote the movie in their neighborhood.

As films grew longer and began to feature proper stories, writers were employed by the studios to create scenarios from popular novels or plays that would fit on one reel. Although the movies were still silent, from 1908 onward intertitles, often containing lines of dialogue, became commonplace. Within a few years, when these dialogue captions were edited into a scene of someone speaking on the screen, they basically transformed the narrative of the medium.

It wasn't until 1910 that actors started to receive screen credit for their roles, and the concept of "film stars" began to evolve. Up until this time many actors—who had come from a "legitimate" stage background—felt embarrassed about appearing in this new medium and did not want to be credited on movie posters. However, this soon began to change.

Having initially opposed the promotion of their actors out of a fear of rising wages, the studios eventually embraced the concept of promoting a popular leading man or woman, which would bring more people into the theater and increase their profits. As a result, posters started predominantly giving credit to the stars of the movie.

As the nickelodeons gave way to movie theaters, so the type of advertising materials began to change as well. Thomas Edison had set the standard size for film posters (27" x 41"), and this became known as the one-sheet, which was prominently displayed in glass cases inside and outside the movie theater. However, a bewildering array of other poster sizes also became available to exhibitors, including the half-sheet, insert, three-sheet, and six-sheet, while the 24-sheet poster (which was exactly 24 times the size of a one-sheet) was used for advertising on billboards.

Lobby cards (which, as their name implies, were used in the theater lobby) became smaller in size and were printed in sets of eight, while window cards (which had a blank space at the top to write on), midget window cards, and heralds were used to promote forthcoming titles.

Overseas, Britain had the quad and double crown, Australia had the daybill, France had the *affiche*, and Italy had the *foglio*, *locandina*, and *photobusta*. In 1917, the studios also started issuing "pressbooks" to help promote the movie to newspapers and other media.

Up until 1913 most American films were still made in and around New York City, due to the monopoly of Edison's film patents. This began to change in 1909, when many filmmakers started moving to Southern California, and by the 1920s most of the industry was based in what came to be known as "Hollywood." At that time the United States was producing an average of 800 feature films a year, or 82 percent of the world total.

During the First World War there had been an important shift away from shorts to feature-length films, as the exhibition venues grew in size. Movie theaters were replaced by luxurious movie palaces, and this aesthetic was reflected in the posters used to advertise the films.

Unfortunately, American studios never allowed the illustrators to sign their work, as commercial artists were often permitted to do on European movie posters.

Many of these early advertising posters were created using the complicated process of stone lithography, which had been around since the early 1800s. Although this technique produced superior results in both terms of detail and color saturation, it was eventually replaced by the use of zinc plates, which resulted in a slightly grainier image.

Despite Thomas Edison having experimented with exhibiting his films with a mechanically synchronized soundtrack recorded on a cylinder, up until this time most films were still projected silent and usually accompanied by live music—either using an orchestra or a theater organ—to enhance the mood on the screen. This all changed in October 1927 when Warner Bros. released *The Jazz Singer* with the first synchronized sound in a feature film.

The studios rushed to add sound.

The studios rushed to add sound to their previously silent productions. Having scrapped the idea of making a sequel, in February 1930 Universal re-issued *The Phantom of the Opera* (1925) with a synchronized music score, sound effects, and new dialogue sequences directed by Ernst Laemmle and Frank McCormick.

Within two years the early sound on disc process had been superceded by sound on film and, despite some initial reluctance from the studios, movies became "talking pictures." This rapid transition was a difficult one for some silent movie stars who were unable to adjust to the new sound medium, and many found their careers abruptly curtailed.

Meanwhile, convinced that there was no commercial future in additive color processes, Technicolor had been experimenting with new methods of creating color photography using red and green filters that transferred the colors physically on to the print and therefore required no special projection equipment.

When originally released, *The Phantom of the Opera* had contained around 17 minutes of color, although only the "*Bal Masqué*" sequence survives today. Over at Metro-Goldwyn-Mayer, *The Mysterious Island* (1929) was filmed entirely in two-strip Technicolor and released as a "part-talkie" with synchronized music and sound effects.

Warner's *Doctor X* (1932) and *Mystery of the Wax Museum* (1933) were among the last films to be released in the two-color process, and in 1935 RKO's *Becky Sharp* became the first feature film photographed entirely in three-strip Technicolor.

By the end of the 1930s the movie industry had firmly established itself as the premier art form and entertainment medium around world—a dominance it would maintain until the advent of the television boom of the 1950s.

OPPOSITE: *Stephen Jones and Friends* (2003), oils on board by Les Edwards. "Some horror icons," explains the British artist. "This was painted for Mr. Jones's 50th birthday. Like many of us, Steve is a long-time fan of *Famous Monsters of Filmland* magazine, so I tried to give the painting that sort of feel. I am no Basil Gogos however."

THE SINISTER SILENTS

SIR CHRISTOPHER FRAYLING

"The trick, intelligently applied, today allows us to make visible the supernatural, the imaginary, even the impossible."

GEORGES MÉLIÈS

> "Adding sound to movies would be like putting lipstick on the Venus de Milo."
> Mary Pickford

ONE OF THE best-known intertitles in the whole of silent cinema appears during Hutter's/Harker's journey to Count Orlok's remote castle in the first *Dracula* film, the silent German production *Nosferatu* (1922): "And when he crossed the bridge, the phantoms came to meet him."

Parisian Surrealist artists saw the film in its 1926 French version, and immediately adopted this intertitle as their catchphrase. André Breton wrote about it several times, and called it "The sentence I have never been able to see without a mixture of joy and terror." "Crossing the bridge" became shorthand for entering a parallel universe of fantasies, dreams, transgressions, and nightmares. But F.W. Murnau's horror film was not in fact influenced by early Surrealism. Its landscapes were instead inspired by the German Romantic painter Caspar David Friedrich; individual sequences echoed a variety of Northern European artists from Rembrandt (*The Anatomy Lesson of Dr. Nicolaes Tulp*) to Arnold Böcklin (*The Isle of the Dead*); and some of its most celebrated moments (the performance of Knock/Renfield, the estate agent; the voyage on the death ship; the opening high-angle shot from a church tower) were fashionably Expressionist. As were the original posters and published production drawings by the producer, designer, and occultist Albin Grau—featuring the distorted face of Count Orlok, the Dracula figure, with pointy ears, rodent teeth, and bald head (a convincingly undead corpse for once), and diagonal rats carrying the plague running over the Count's great-coated legs to match the diagonal shadows of the film itself.

Because, as has often been noted, between 1919 and 1927 a series of horror films made in the Germany of the unstable Weimar Republic grew out of the earlier Expressionist movement in painting, literature, and theater—a remarkable example of an advanced art movement being thoroughly absorbed, after a short time-lag, into commercial cinema.

The craze began with *The Cabinet of Dr Caligari* (1920), coinciding with the delayed post-war staging of Expressionist plays in Berlin. *Caligari*'s fusion of painted, light-reflecting sets; jagged buildings and cracked walkways; perpendicular lines replaced by diagonals; broad gestural performances (Werner Krauss's shuffling walk; Conrad Veidt's sleepwalking—their makeup and costumes matching the scenery), and the sense of a visual world which is an outward sign of inner turmoil; all became associated with horror and fantasy for the first time. One of the film's designers, Hermann Warm, called them "drawings brought to life," and that is what they were.

Posters added vivid colors, rather than tinting, to the mix. Expressionist art had not shown much interest in the supernatural: it was the distorted cityscapes of painters Lyonel Feininger and Alfred Kubin which were primary influences—to the point where critics thought these artists must surely have been employed on the film. Kubin was in fact approached, but declined the offer. Feininger thought the designers had borrowed his ideas.

Not everyone was convinced by this aesthetic approach. Sergei Eisenstein called it "a barbaric carnival," full of "monstrous chimeras," and other commentators thought the film un-cinematic and retrograde with its static camera pointing at painted canvases. In some ways, *Caligari* was an aesthetic dead-end. But in more important ways, it was one of the most influential horror films of all time,

---

Between 1919 and 1927 a series of horror films made in the Germany of the unstable Weimar Republic grew out of the earlier Expressionist movement in painting, literature, and theater.

---

if not the most influential. Its fusion of Gothic and Romantic traditions with a style best described as Expressionist—as the most effective way of giving visible form to the old stories—exported to Hollywood, came to define the look of horror in the early sound era and how it was best to be performed by over-the-top (usually) British actors. 1919 was also the year when Sigmund Freud published the first version of his essay on "The Uncanny," centered on an analysis of E.T.A. Hoffmann's eerie short story "The Sandman." Familiar things presented in unfamiliar or heightened or off-center ways, he wrote, were particularly unsettling. And the old stories still had the power to reach dark places.

Other German films which immediately got the message, in one way or another, and which saw the advantages of product differentiation, included: *Madness* (1919, with Conrad Veidt); *Genuine* (1920) and *Raskolnikow* (1923) both helmed by *Caligari*'s director Robert Wiene; Paul Wegener's *The Golem, How He Came Into the World* (1920); *The Head of Janus* (1920—a version of *Dr. Jekyll and Mr. Hyde*—again with Conrad Veidt); Fritz Lang's *Destiny* (1921); *Nosferatu* (1922); *Warning Shadows* (1923); Paul Leni's *Waxworks* (1924—the Jack the Ripper, or "Spring-Heeled Jack" segment); *The Student of Prague* (1926 version); Murnau's *Faust* (1926); and Fritz Lang's *Metropolis* (1926) which owed a lot to a trio of

PREVIOUS SPREAD: *The Phantom of the Opera* (1994), acrylic on board by American artist Basil Gogos. "I painted this character with an eye to make a limited edition print of the image," explains the artist, "and then it was used for one of the covers on Vanguard Productions' book *Famous Monster Movie Art of Basil Gogos* (2005)."

ABOVE LEFT: German poster for Decla-Bioscope's *Genuine* (Dir: Robert Wiene, 1920) by artist Josef Fenneker (1895–1956), considered to be one of Germany's most important stage designers.

TOP RIGHT: 1926 Russian poster for Paul Leni's *Das Wachsfigurenkabinett* (aka *Waxworks*, 1924) by brothers Vladimir Stenberg (1899–1982) and Georgii Stenberg (1900–33).

BOTTOM MIDDLE: German poster for Sokal-Film's *Der Student von Prag* (aka *The Student of Prague*, 1926), scripted by Hanns Heinz Ewers and director Henrik Galeen and loosely based on the story "William Wilson" by Edgar Allan Poe.

BOTTOM RIGHT: French *affiche* for Gainsborough Pictures' *The Lodger: A Story of the London Fog* (Dir: Alfred Hitchcock, 1927), based on the novel by Marie Belloc Lowndes (1868–1947).

THE SINISTER SILENTS

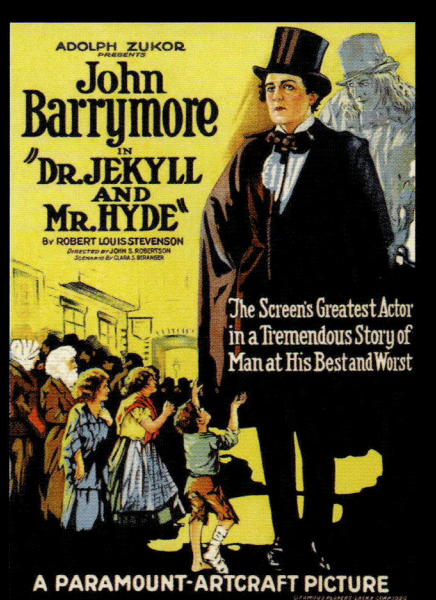
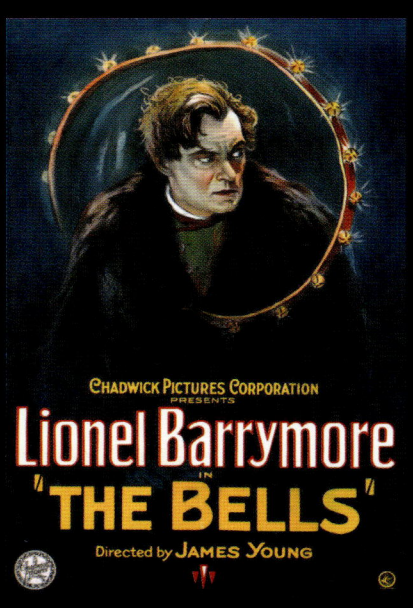

TOP LEFT: The only known press sheet advertisement for Ocean Film Corporation's *Life Without Soul* (Dir: Joseph W. Smiley, 1915), the second movie inspired by Mary Shelley's *Frankenstein* and now considered to be lost.

BOTTOM LEFT: American stone litho window card for Paramount-Artcraft's *Dr. Jekyll and Mr. Hyde* (Dir: John S. Robertson, 1920), based on the novella *Strange Case of Dr Jekyll and Mr Hyde* (1886) by Robert Louis Stevenson.

BOTTOM MIDDLE: Stone litho one-sheet poster for Chadwick Pictures Corporation's *The Bells* (Dir: James Young, 1926) based on the 1871 play *The Bells* by Leopold Davis Lewis. The film is remembered today for an early role by Boris Karloff.

ABOVE RIGHT: Note the misspelling of the author's name on this *Art Nouveau*-style one-sheet poster for Eclair Films' two-reel *The Raven* (1912), the first film to be inspired by the 1845 narrative poem by Edgar Allan Poe (1809–49).

THE ART OF HORROR MOVIES

Expressionist plays by Georg Kaiser called *Gas*, and to its stage performance styles.

This may seem a lot but, in fact, Expressionist films represented only a tiny fraction of commercial releases in the 1920s, and were in a radically different style to the mainstream. Their significance lies in their profound influence on other filmmakers. Alfred Hitchcock, for example, always acknowledged the importance of the time he spent in Berlin in the mid-1920s, and viewing of the films of Murnau and Lang, on his own work starting with *The Lodger: A Story of the London Fog* (1927).

In the United States, it took until 1920 for a major studio, Paramount-Artcraft, to make a horror film which was feature-length—John Barrymore playing urbane Jekyll and leering, clawed Hyde in *Dr. Jekyll and Mr. Hyde* (1920), which also brought together American barnstorming stage-acting

> This one-reel Frankenstein has been called the first-ever American horror film, with a story, worthy of the name.

and horror, a marriage which would last a long time. Lionel Barrymore took on that old chestnut *The Bells* in 1926, with Boris Karloff as a hypnotist in Caligari-style makeup.

Before that, there had been assorted short versions of other classics: including the Edison *Frankenstein* (1910), which based the makeup of the Creature (Charles Ogle) on the 1826 stage version rather than the novel, added an alchemical theme by having the obsessed scientist create him in a huge bubbling pot, and which ended on the Creature dissolving into a mirror—a surprisingly subtle touch which suggested that creator and created were two sides of the same person. This one-reel *Frankenstein* has been called the first ever American horror film, with a story, worthy of the label.

Then there was *Life Without Soul* (1915), another version of *Frankenstein*, the climax of which was a chase across Europe to catch the (less grotesque) "Brute Man" who has murdered the scientist Frawley's sister; and *The Raven* (1912 and 1915), based on Edgar Allan Poe's 1845 poem, billed in 1912 as "an American classic."

It was as if horror was only palatable in the early days of cinema if it was based on an acknowledged, respectable classic—a form of cultural legitimation. *Caligari* opened in New York and Los Angeles, April–May 1921, distributed by Goldwyn, and was immediately met by angry demonstrations about paying "war tax to see German-made pictures." The popular press panned it as morbidly un-American, but serious critics immediately noted its possible lessons for "native products" which badly needed an aesthetic shot in the arm.

Most commentators insisted on calling the film "Cubist" (= modern art). *The Moving Picture World* advised the distributor to "play on the novelty of the picture and keep quiet about the German origin of the work." Although Goldwyn regretted the decision to import the film, *Caligari* was followed by limited art house-style releases of *Nosferatu*, *Waxworks*, and others. But before the arrival in the later 1920s of émigrés to Hollywood in significant numbers, from Germany, Austria, France, and Britain—as directors, actors, and designers—who brought with them a Northern European aesthetic, other more American traditions dominated.

Such as the carnival tradition. As historian David J. Skal has pointed out, the culture of horror in the USA has always had almost as much to do with carnival-style promotional gimmicks as with the films themselves: not quite respectable, a guilty pleasure, a glimpse of another world where transgressive things can happen, and (let's face it) often a bit tacky.

Director Tod Browning, responsible for some of the most interestingly perverse Hollywood horror films of the 1920s (including *The Unholy Three* and *The Unknown*, both with a circus setting, and the lost *London After Midnight*, Hollywood's first vampire film now reconstructed from stills) actually started his professional career working on traveling carnivals and freak shows.

In *London After Midnight* (1927), as in all Hollywood horrors of the 1920s, the horror is explained away in the last reel as having natural causes: the vampire is really an elaborate hoax to trap a murderer. Another tradition was the comedy-mystery, a staple of the Broadway stage, in which disguised criminals known as "The Bat" or "The Cat" or some other creature stalked the passageways of cobwebby haunted houses, with spooky and funny results, before being unmasked.

Paul Leni, shortly after his arrival in Hollywood, made the most celebrated of them, *The Cat and the Canary* (1927), based on a hit play of 1922, which has been called "a key work in the transition from Weimar Germany to the American terror-film."

A third tradition—another bid for respectability—was the "big European set" as a selling point in the mid-1920s—most notably in the Universal pictures *The Hunchback of Notre Dame* (1923), with its huge "plaza in front of the cathedral," and *The Phantom of the Opera* (1925), with its equally gigantic version of the Paris Opéra and catacombs below. The publicity for these Lon Chaney vehicles emphasized the staggering statistics (scale, craft skills, dollars) as much as the horror.

By the arrival of sound on film, most of the elements were in place for the Hollywood horror renaissance of the early 1930s. The strange brew of Expressionism (domesticated), comedy, grotesquerie, over-acting, irreverent adaptations of classics preferably in the public domain, European actors and visualizers—and carnival—was about to transmute into an American genre. All it needed to succeed was a Great Depression.

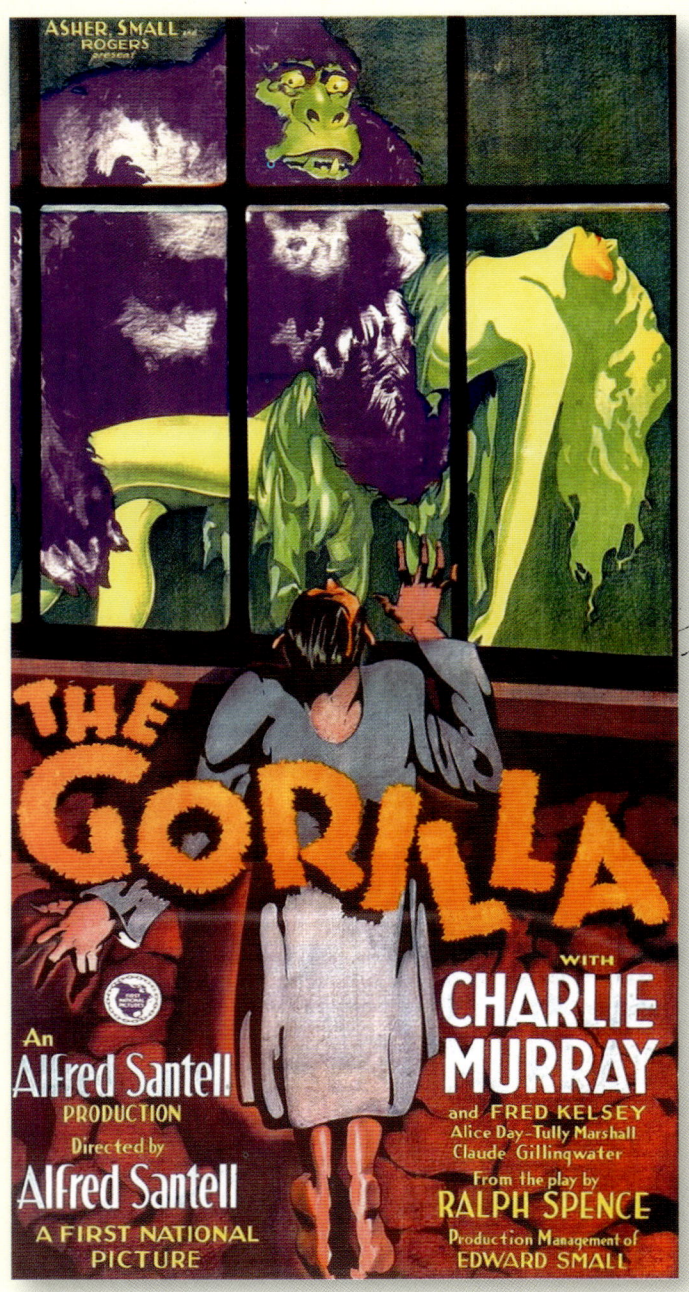

TOP LEFT: Three-sheet litho poster for First National Pictures' *The Gorilla* (Dir: Alfred Santell, 1927), the first movie adaptation of Ralph Spence's 1925 Broadway play. A murderer in a gorilla suit stalks a spooky old mansion.

BOTTOM LEFT: Exhibitor's manual advertisement for Universal's *The Man Who Laughs* (Dir: Paul Leni, 1928), based on the 1869 novel *L'Homme qui rit* by Victor Hugo. The illustration is by prolific Austrian-born poster and magazine artist A. (August) M. (Maria) Froehlich (1880–1950).

ABOVE RIGHT: *The Man Who Laughs* (2008), ink and acrylic on board by British artist Les Edwards. "I was aware of the image of Gwynplaine long before I watched the movie thanks to *Famous Monsters of Filmland* magazine," the artist explains. "When I finally saw the film I found it quite disturbing."

PREVIOUS PAGE: *The Silver Scream* (2016), mixed media by American artist Thomas Gianni. "In 1925 my father, who was ten years old at the time, saw Lon Chaney in *The Phantom of the Opera*, the likes of which had never been seen before," recalls Gianni. "Decades later, he acted out to my brother and me the unmasking scene. This one is for you, Dad."

TOP LEFT: Double-page German magazine advertisement for *Nosferatu, eine Symphonie des Grauens* (Dir: F.W. Murnau, 1922) created by the film's art director, Albin Grau (1884–1971).

BOTTOM LEFT: German art deco poster for G.W. Pabst's *Die Büchse der Pandora* (US: *Pandora's Box*, 1929) by Hungarian artist and typographer József Bottlik (1897–1984).

ABOVE RIGHT: *Nosferatu* (2014), ink on board with digital color by American artist William Stout, published as a limited edition serigraph print. "I was eager to do this classic horror film visual justice," he explains. "I tried to include all the most fantastic elements in my design, and ended up with what I consider one of the best pieces of my career."

OPPOSITE, TOP LEFT: *Cesare* (2009), ink on paper illustration by British artist Les Edwards for the 1969 story "Amber Print" in *Darkness, Mist & Shadow: The Collected Macabre Tales of Basil Copper* (2010). "Conrad Veidt from *The Cabinet of Dr. Caligari*, of course," reveals the artist. "He just has one of those memorable faces."

THE ART OF HORROR MOVIES

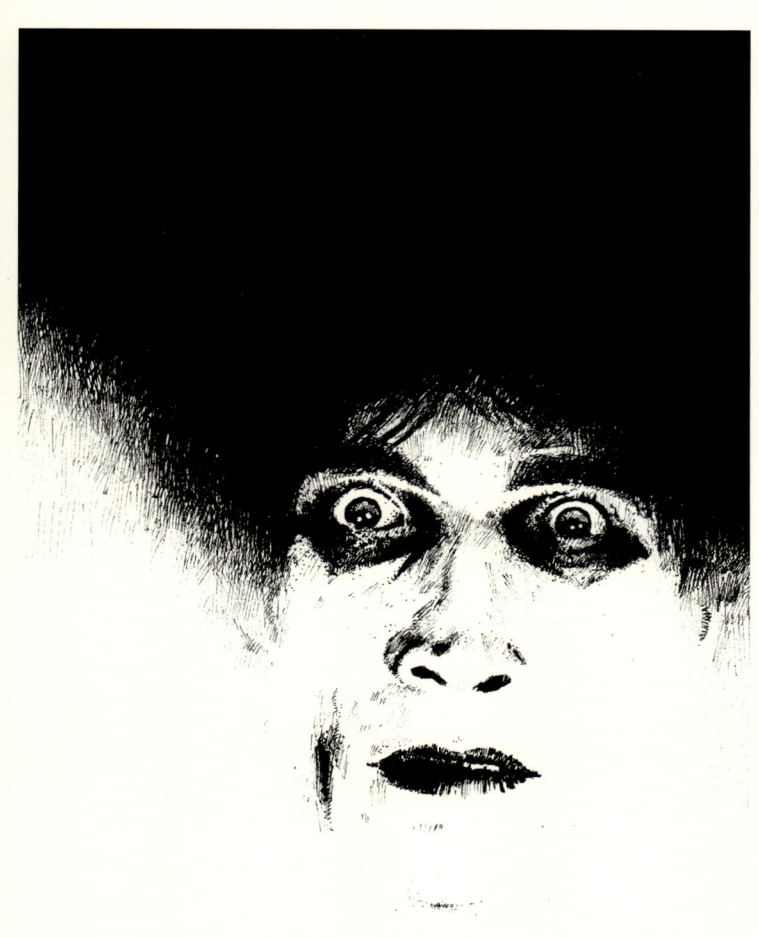

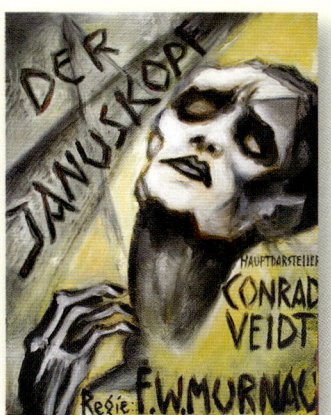

TOP RIGHT: *Unheimliche Geschichten/Weird Tales* (2009), acrylic, ink, papers and copper on collage by British artist Dave McKean, inspired by the 1919 German silent film. "This was done for *Nitrate*, my forthcoming art book inspired by silent cinema," McKean says. "It was one of the few films that played with Expressionist images at the time."

BOTTOM LEFT: Expressionist poster for UFA's *Der Golem wie er in die Welt kam* (1920), in which German co-director Paul Wegener also starred as a magical man of clay.

BOTTOM MIDDLE, LEFT: Conrad Veidt and Béla Lugosi both appeared in the now lost *Der Januskopf* (Dir: F.W. Murnau, 1920).

BOTTOM MIDDLE: Conrad Veidt starred as a pianist with the transplanted hands of a murderer in *Orlac's Hände* (Dir: Robert Wiene, 1924).

BOTTOM MIDDLE, RIGHT: MGM's poster for UFA's *Faust* (Dir: F.W. Murnau, 1926), which exists in multiple versions, including the US print prepared by Murnau himself.

BOTTOM RIGHT: One of a colorful and stylized series of early 1920s British posters created for the release of *The Cabinet of Dr. Caligari* (Dir: Robert Wiene, 1920).

THE SINISTER SILENTS

THE MAN OF A THOUSAND FACES

"When I am working on a story for Chaney, I never think of the plot. That follows itself after you have conceived a characterization."
Tod Browning

LON, OR LEONIDAS, Chaney (1883–1930) "The Man of a Thousand Faces"—many of them grotesque—was the first superstar of Hollywood horror cinema, although most of his films did not in fact belong to that developing genre.

In his heyday, between 1920 and 1930, he was a one-man repertory company playing detectives, criminals, assorted ethnic "types" (several Chinese)—and seriously disabled or disfigured characters: an industry one-liner was "Don't step on it, it might be Lon Chaney." Chaney learned mime, body language, and how to use his expressive face while being brought up by deaf-mute parents; and how to make professional use of his skills on the stage in vaudeville. He entered the film industry in 1913, and appeared as a character actor in scores of movies before making his name with *The Miracle Man* (1919) as a phony cripple who pretends to be cured through faith, and with *The Penalty* (1920), as a crime boss who has, through a medical error, had both of his legs removed in childhood and who is understandably very angry about it.

A punishing regime of elaborate facial makeup, and distortions of the body, characterize his best work—he portrayed disabilities of various kinds in nine films of the 1920s—and his distinctive talent was to encourage morbid curiosity from his vast audience ("freak show" style) while also encouraging sympathy for the inner human being beneath the skin, a winning combination in America just after the carnage of the First World War.

"There is no Lon Chaney," he liked to say, "I am the character I am creating. That is all." He seldom socialized, wore dark glasses in public (a first), and by all accounts was totally dedicated to the self-imposed discomforts of his work. Directors and actors who collaborated with him noted how tense he could be while on the set, how much he suffered for his art—and how there was a perverse element of self-martyrdom about him. The inevitable Hollywood biopic, with James Cagney as Chaney (*Man of a Thousand Faces*, 1957), captured the grotesquerie and suffering of the makeup while missing the humanity.

In Tod Browning's *The Unholy Three* (1925), Chaney played a dishonest ventriloquist dressed up as a grandmother; in *The Blackbird* (1926), he was a conman who snaps his spine after posing as his paralyzed twin brother; in *The Unknown* (1927), he was Alonzo the armless knife-thrower who amputates his arms because his beloved Estrellita/Nanon (Joan Crawford) cannot bear to be touched—only to discover that she has got over her phobia after all; in *London After Midnight* (1927), to judge by stills, he pretended to be a vampire complete with two rows of razor-sharp teeth and bulging eyes surrounded by black makeup—suggesting that he needed a good night's sleep.

"There is no Lon Chaney," he liked to say, "I am the character I am creating. That is all."

After portraying both a mad doctor and his hunchbacked, ape-like assistant—the collateral damage of an earlier experiment—in *A Blind Bargain* (1922), and a lunatic waxworks curator in *While Paris Sleeps* (1923), Chaney played the two parts for which he is now best known, both for Universal: Quasimodo the bell-ringer in *The Hunchback of Notre Dame* (1923) for director Wallace Worsley, and Erik the hideously disfigured composer in *The Phantom of the Opera* (1925), which he partly directed himself.

For *Notre Dame*, he wore a rubber mask and a plaster hump weighing 50 pounds, a leather harness that prohibited him from standing upright, and a dental device that prevented him from closing his mouth. The filming took a grueling three months.

For *The Phantom*, partly shot in early Technicolor, he wore a wire contraption to pull back the nose in his skull-like face, with the wires disguised under layers of putty. The key scene in the film involved his shock unmasking by Christine (Mary Philbin), his protégé, a moment that has been called by author Robert Bloch "The most memorable horror image that emerged from the entire silent era."

Tod Browning invited him to play Dracula in 1931, but had to fall back on Bela Lugosi instead when Chaney died unexpectedly of throat cancer at the age of 47.

No doubt Lon Chaney's sufferings were exaggerated by the writers of press releases, but still his was a unique form of celebrity: he was famous for his chameleon qualities, his courageous changes of image, his reclusiveness, his relish at playing villains, his many faces, and his masochism. Not many Hollywood celebrities, then or now, would dare to promote themselves in these ways. CF

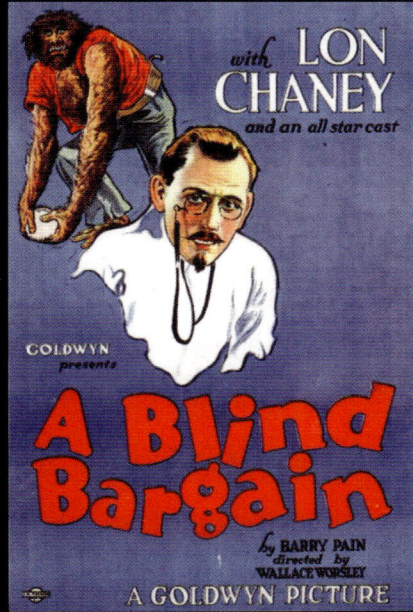

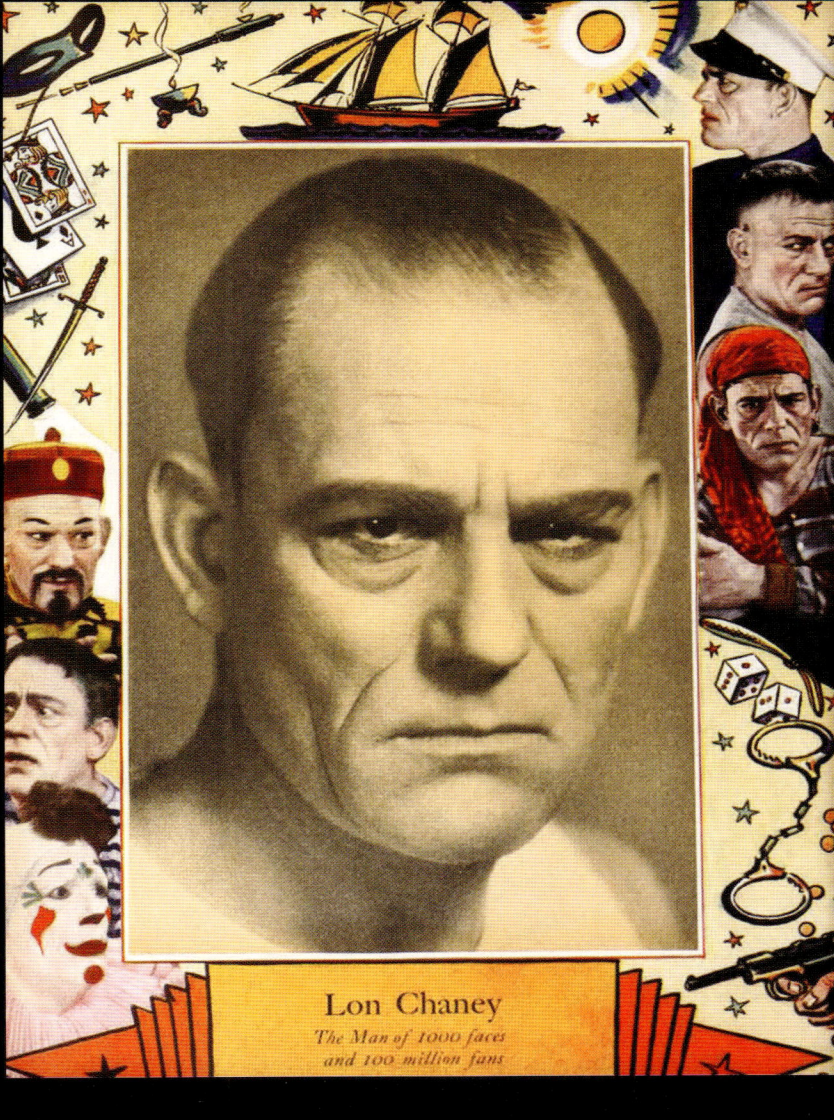
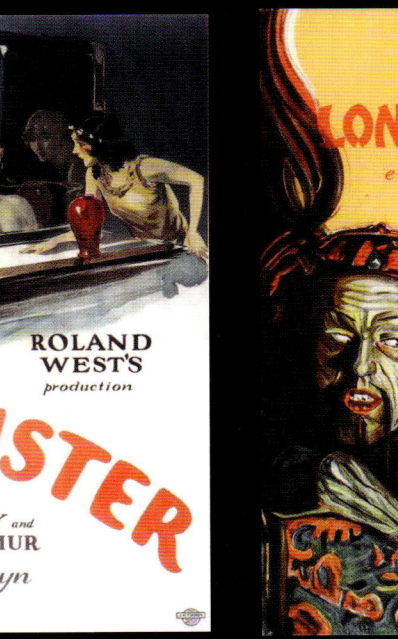

TOP LEFT: American stone litho one-sheet poster for Goldwyn Pictures' *A Blind Bargain* (Dir: Wallace Worsley, 1922), based on the 1897 novel *The Octave of Claudius* by Barry Pain. The last surviving print was apparently destroyed in the MGM vault fire of 1967.

TOP MIDDLE: Dutch poster for Metro-Goldwyn's *He Who Gets Slapped* (Dir: Victor Seastrom aka Victor Sjöström, 1924) by artist Franz Bosen (1891–1949), who specialized in the linocut technique to achieve such vivid colors.

BOTTOM LEFT: American one-sheet poster for Metro-Goldwyn's horror-comedy *The Monster* (Dir: Roland West, 1925), based on the 1922 stage play by actor and future screenwriter Crane Wilbur (1886–1973).

BOTTOM MIDDLE: Based on the American one-sheet, this design for Metro-Goldwyn-Mayer's *Mr. Wu* (Dir: William Nigh, 1927) is by Dolly Rudeman (1902–80), the only female Dutch movie poster artist of the 1920s.

ABOVE RIGHT: Late 1920s magazine page depicting Lon Chaney, "The Man of 1000 faces and 100 million fans." "Don't step on it; it might be Lon Chaney!" was a popular joke of the time.

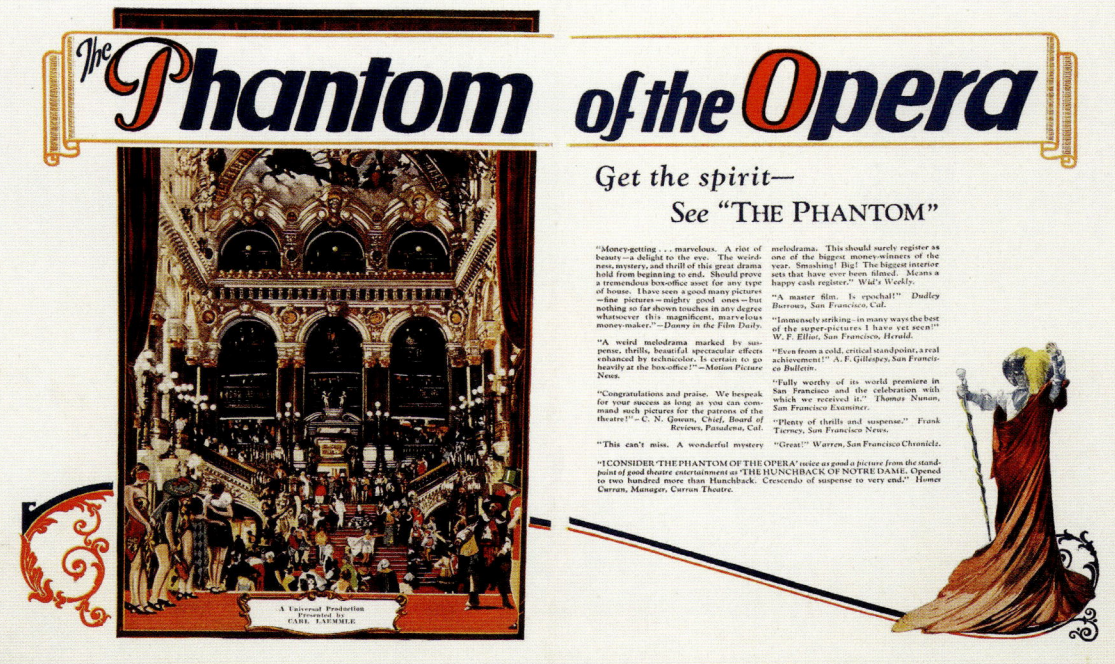

BOTTOM MIDDLE: The cover of No. 149 of the British weekly newsprint magazine *Picture Show* (March 4, 1922) featured "seven studies of Lon Chaney, who can change his face as easily as the average man can change his collar." This issue carried a feature on the actor and his "small makeup box" inside.

BOTTOM RIGHT: Two months after the movie's New York City premiere, the studio's campaign magazine, *Universal Weekly*, trumpeted the continuing success of *The Hunchback of Notre Dame* (Dir: Wallace Worsley, 1923) on the back cover of its November 17, 1923 (Vol. 18, No. 14) edition.

TOP: Double-page campaign advertisement for *The Phantom of the Opera* (Dir: Rupert Julian, 1925), from a special "54 from Universal" edition (Vol. 21, No. 14) of the exhibitor's magazine *Universal Weekly*, May 16, 1925, following the movie's San Francisco premiere three weeks earlier.

ABOVE LEFT: Back cover advertisement from the July 26, 1930 edition of the British magazine *The Film Weekly* (Vol. 4, No. 93) for the now-lost 1929 re-release version of *The Phantom of the Opera* (1925), featuring newly synchronized sound sequences and selected scenes in color.

OPPOSITE: *Lon Chaney, Sr. in The Hunchback of Notre Dame* (2018), marker and pencil on Bristol board by Frederick Cooper. "Chaney's performance as Quasimodo remains a reminder of the love and humanity that still exists in those we call monsters," explains the American artist.

THE ART OF HORROR MOVIES

ABOVE LEFT: The only known American three-sheet stone litho poster to exist for the lost Metro-Goldwyn-Mayer mystery movie *London After Midnight* (Dir: Tod Browning, 1927), depicting Lon Chaney in his iconic vampire makeup. A partial version of this poster, with only the top two panels original, sold at auction in 2015 for $71,700.

TOP MIDDLE: The only known US stone litho one-sheet poster for *London After Midnight* (1927) surfaced in 2014. Very similar to the design of the previously discovered Argentinean version, it sold in November of that year for $478,000, the all-time highest auction price realized for any movie poster to date.

TOP RIGHT: This stone litho Belgian *affiche* for *London After Midnight* (1927) is illustrated with a skulking Lon Chaney by artist G. Rader, who produced many other posters. The last surviving print of the film was reportedly destroyed in an electrical fire at the MGM vault in May 1967.

BOTTOM MIDDLE: British artist J. (John) Morton-Sale (1901–90) painted the evocative dust jacket art for the UK tie-in of *London After Midnight* by Marie Coolidge-Rask, published in hardcover by The Readers Library Publishing Company Ltd.

BOTTOM RIGHT: Metro-Goldwyn-Mayer's pressbook for *London After Midnight* (1927) came in the form of a newsprint broadsheet that consisted of eight pages, and even included a crossword puzzle!

TOP LEFT: *London After Midnight* (2013), acrylic on Bristol board and digital by American artist Scott Jackson, produced for the collector's card set *Monster Masterpieces: The Painted History of the Horror Film Vol.1* (2013). "This was a great opportunity to describe the film title itself inside a single image," recalls Jackson.

ABOVE RIGHT: *Lon Chaney—London After Midnight* (2016), acrylic and ink on collage by British artist Dave McKean. "This was a private commission," explains the artist, "a portrait of the most famous of 'lost' films."

BOTTOM LEFT: Hand-colored lobby card for *London After Midnight* (1927).

RIGHT: Two-column advertising cut for *London After Midnight* (1927), from a contemporary theater herald.

THE SINISTER SILENTS

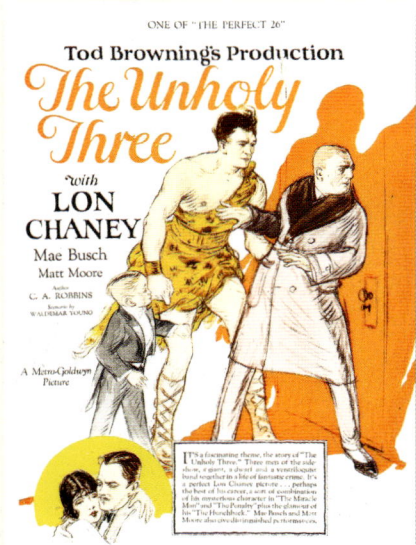

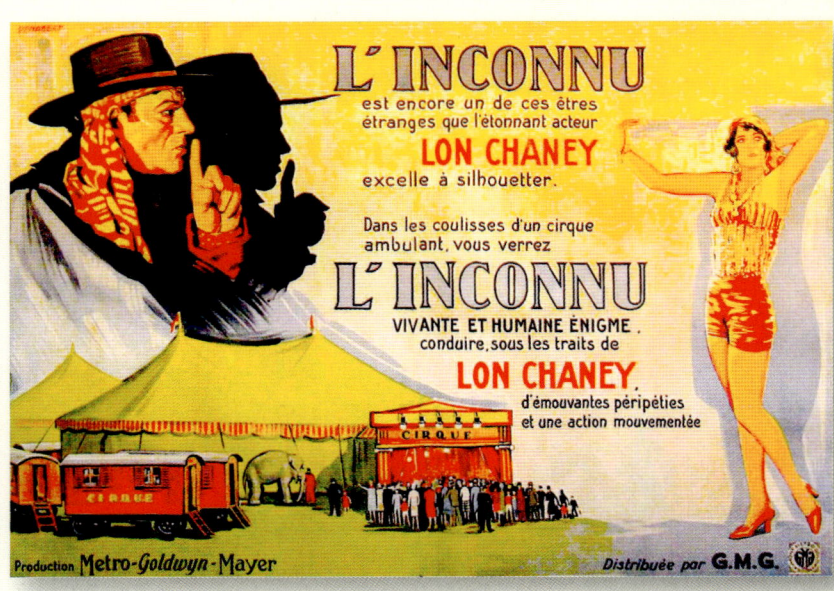

The Browning Version

Although he directed the film which launched the Universal horror cycle, the surprisingly restrained *Dracula* (1931); the unlikeable if well-intentioned *Freaks* (1932), a film which was buried for 30 years, and put Lionel Barrymore in drag as an avenger who mobilizes miniaturized colleagues in *The Devil-Doll* (1936), Tod Browning (Charles Albert Browning, 1880–1962) is today celebrated much more for his strange silent horrors—especially the ones he made with Lon Chaney between 1925 and 1930, which usually brought together disability and confidence tricks. Browning ran away from home in his mid-teens to work variously as a barker, a clown, a contortionist, and a prematurely buried corpse in carnival, then vaudeville. Having directed some early shorts and mysteries in Hollywood, he suffered a serious car crash in 1915 and was subsequently sidelined in the industry because of alcoholism. His comeback film was *The Unholy Three* (1925), which combined his own circus experience with Chaney's flair for makeup and dressing up. Increasingly perverse follow-ups (including *The Unknown* and *London After Midnight*, both 1927) made his name and caused alarm among some newspaper critics. His obsession with amputation below the waist has caused recent commentators to wonder what exactly happened to him in that car crash. He retired in 1942. CF

TOP LEFT: Trade advertisement for Metro-Goldwyn's *The Unholy Three* (Dir: Tod Browning, 1925), based on the 1917 novel by Clarence Aaron "Tod" Robbins (1888–1949). Lon Chaney starred in dual roles.

TOP MIDDLE: Rotogravure one-sheet for Metro-Goldwyn-Mayer's *The Thirteenth Chair* (Dir: Tod Browning, 1929), based on the 1916 play by Bayard Veiller. Bela Lugosi played a police detective who attempts to trap a murderer at a séance.

TOP RIGHT: French lobby card for Metro-Goldwyn-Mayer's *The Unknown* (1927). Lon Chaney portrayed Alonzo, a criminal circus knife-thrower so hopelessly in love with a young woman (Joan Crawford) that he has his arms amputated.

BOTTOM LEFT: Glass slide used to promote Metro-Goldwyn-Mayer's *The Road to Mandalay* (Dir: Tod Browning, 1926) to movie theater audiences. Lon Chaney used the first full-sclera white glass contact lens to simulate blindness in a scratched-out eye.

OPPOSITE: *Tod Browning and Some of His Characters* (1995), acrylic on board portrait by American artist Basil Gogos. "This is the story of Count Mora and his daughter Luna, or *London After Midnight*," explains the artist. "The image was painted as a commission for the cover of *Monsterscene* #6 (Fall, 1995)."

Women in Horror: The Silents

As the screen's first Christine Daaé, Mary Philbin (1902–93) dared to rip away Lon Chaney's mask in *The Phantom of the Opera* (1925), and she was the object of Conrad Veidt's twisted obsession in both *The Last Performance* (1927) and *The Man Who Laughs* (1928). Director Paul Leni had Laura La Plante (1904–96) menaced by maniacal murders in both *The Cat and the Canary* (1927) and *The Last Warning* (1929). Patsy Ruth Miller (1904–95) starred as Chaney's object of devotion in *The Hunchback of Notre Dame* (1923), while German actress Brigitte Helm (1906–96) is remembered for her portrayals of cold-hearted synthetic women in *Metropolis* (1927) and two versions of *Alraune* (1928 and 1929), based on the novel by Hanns Heinz Ewers.

ABOVE LEFT: American one-sheet for Universal's *The Man Who Laughs* (Dir: Paul Leni, 1928). German-born Conrad Veidt (1893–1943) starred as the disfigured Gwynplaine, who falls in love with a blind girl (Mary Philbin). Veidt's grotesque makeup was the inspiration for Batman's arch-villain, The Joker.

TOP MIDDLE: American insert card for Universal's *The Phantom of the Opera* (Dir: Rupert Julian, 1925). Mary Philbin's Christine Daaé removed the mask of the Phantom (Lon Chaney).

TOP RIGHT: Swedish poster for *The Phantom of the Opera* (1925) by artist and actor Eric Rohman (1891–1949).

BOTTOM MIDDLE: Trade advertisement for Universal's *The Cat and the Canary* (1927), the first screen adaptation of John Willard's influential 1922 stage play, filmed in the Expressionist style by German émigré Paul Leni (1885–1929).

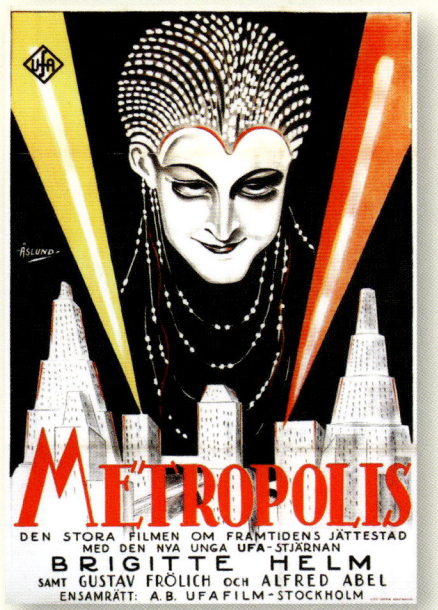

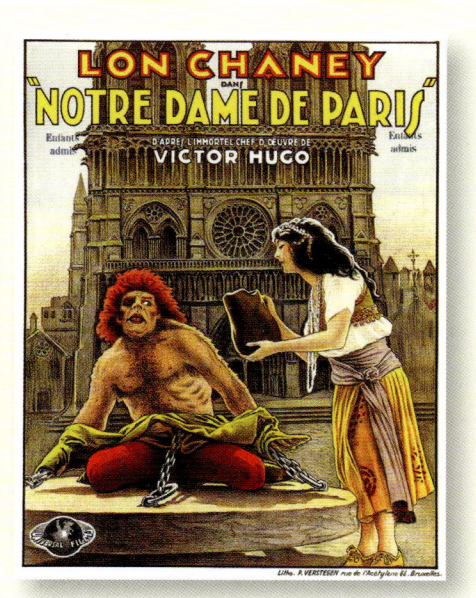

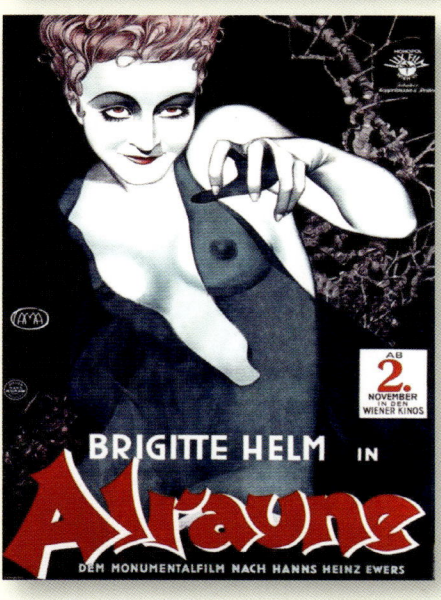

OPPOSITE, BOTTOM RIGHT: Window card for Paul Leni's final film, *The Last Warning* (1929), released by Universal just eight months before the director died of blood poisoning. Based on the 1922 Broadway play by Thomas F. Fallon, it was a re-run of *The Cat and the Canary* set in an old theater.

TOP LEFT: The cover of the July 26, 1925 issue of the Hollywood trade paper *The Film Daily* promoting Universal's *Lorraine of the Lions* (Dir: Edward Sedgwick, 1925). Patsy Ruth Miller starred as the survivor of a circus troupe washed up on a desert island, where her only companion is a gorilla.

BOTTOM LEFT: Swedish poster for UFA's *Metropolis* (Dir: Fritz Lang, 1927) by artist and set designer John Mauritz "Moje" Åslund (1904–68). This German Expressionist science fiction epic starred 18-year-old Brigitte Helm in her first film.

BOTTOM MIDDLE: Brigitte Helm portrayed another artificially created woman in Henrik Galeen's *Alraune* (aka *A Daughter of Destiny*, 1928), based on the 1911 novel by Hanns Heinz Ewers.

TOP MIDDLE: Belgian poster for Universal's *The Hunchback of Notre Dame* (Dir: Wallace Worsley, 1923), based on the 1831 novel by Victor Hugo.

ABOVE RIGHT: One of two American one-sheet poster designs for *The Hunchback of Notre Dame* (1923). Patsy Ruth Miller portrayed the dancing gypsy girl Esmeralda.

THE SINISTER SILENTS

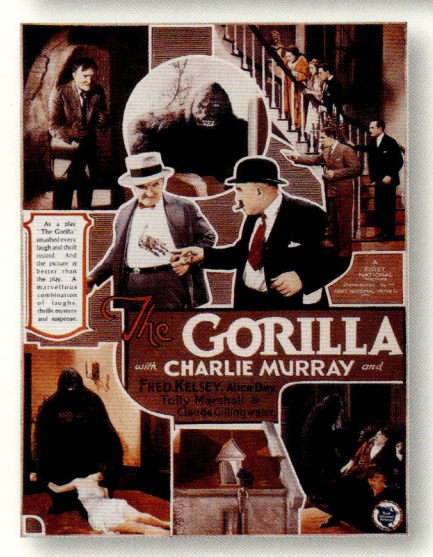

ABOVE RIGHT: Campaign advertisement by American poster illustrator Burton Rice (Dynevor Rhys, 1894–19??) from the February 23, 1918 issue of *The Moving Picture World* (Vol. 35, No. 8) for Pathé's 20-chapter old dark house serial *The House of Hate* (Dir: George B. Seitz, 1918), starring Pearl White.

TOP LEFT: Trade advertisement from *The Film Daily* Vol. XLVII, No. 14 (January 17, 1929) for Fox's now-lost talkie, *The Ghost Talks* (Dir: Lewis Seiler, 1929), based on a 1924 play by Edward Hammond and Max Marcin. Stepin Fetchit played a character named "Christopher Lee"!

BOTTOM LEFT: Campaign advertisement from the hardcover *Pathé 1928–1929* exhibitor's book for First National Pictures' now-lost *The Gorilla* (Dir: Alfred Santell, 1927), based on the 1925 play by Ralph Spence. It was remade in 1939 by Twentieth Century-Fox, starring The Ritz Brothers.

BOTTOM MIDDLE: Trade advertisement for Universal's *The Last Warning* (Dir: Paul Leni, 1928) from *Exhibitors Herald and Moving Picture World* Vol. 91 No. 4A, April 28, 1928. Filmed on the same sets as *The Phantom of the Opera* (1925) in both part-sound and silent versions, only the latter now exists.

THE ART OF HORROR MOVIES

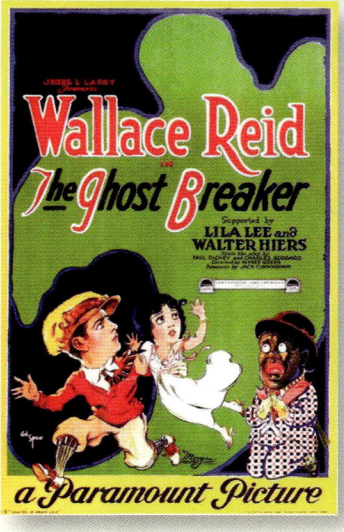

ABOVE LEFT: Argentinean poster signed "A. Wagener" for Metro-Goldwyn-Mayer's *The Magician* (Dir: Rex Ingram, 1926), based on a 1908 novel by W. Somerset Maugham that was loosely inspired by the life of British occultist Aleister Crowley. The film was thought lost for many years.

BOTTOM MIDDLE: Poster by [Adrian] Gil Spear (1885–1965) for the now-lost *The Ghost Breaker* (Dir: Alfred E. Green, 1922). Based on a 1909 play by Paul Dickey and Charles W. Goddard, it starred tragic Hollywood leading man Wallace Reid. Paramount remade it in 1940 as a vehicle for Bob Hope.

TOP RIGHT: Lobby card for First National Pictures' part-sound *The Haunted House* (1928), based on the 1926 stage play by Owen Davis. This apparently lost film was remade by director Benjamin Christensen the following year with the same two stars, Chester Conklin and Thelma Todd, as *House of Horror*.

BOTTOM RIGHT: Stone litho poster for First National Pictures' *Seven Footprints to Satan* (1929), which was also directed by Benjamin Christensen and starred tragic Hollywood actress Thelma Todd. Based on the 1928 novel by Abraham Merritt, it was released in both part-sound and silent versions.

THE SINISTER SILENTS

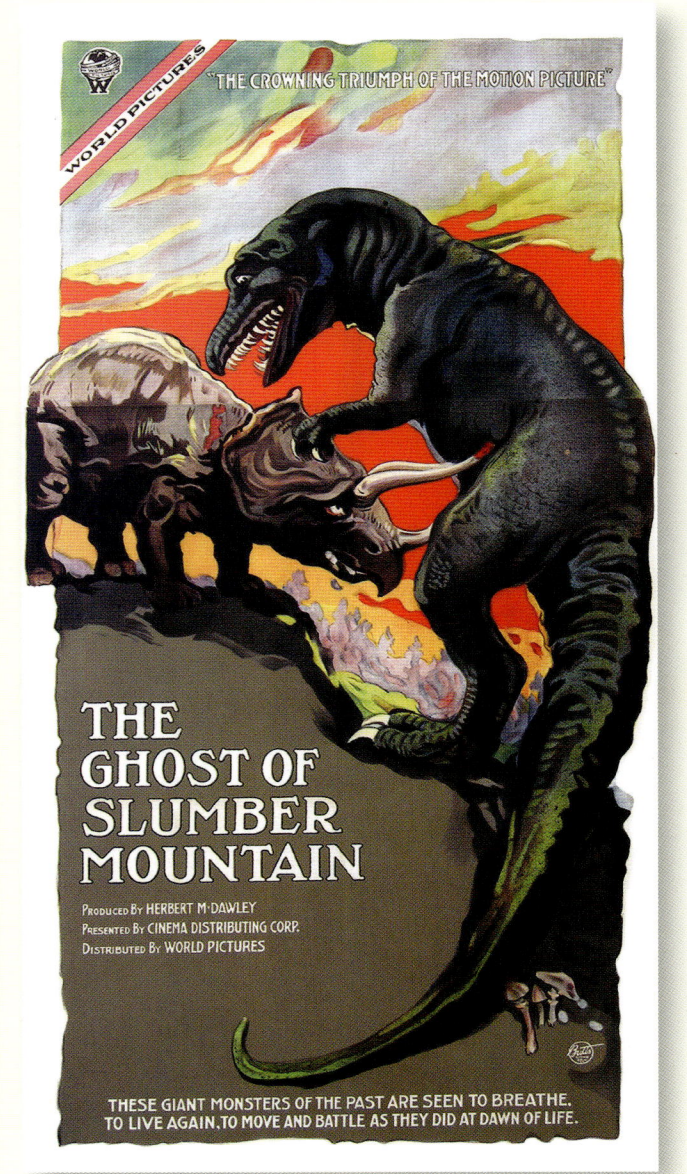

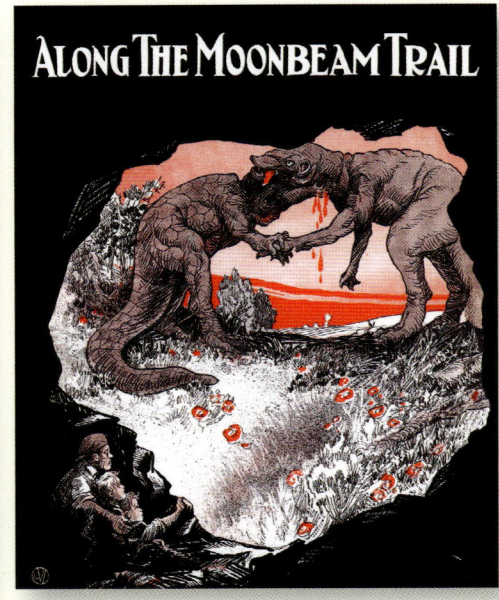

ABOVE LEFT: American litho three-sheet poster for *The Ghost of Slumber Mountain* (Dir: Willis H. O'Brien, 1918), the first film to show live actors on the screen with stop-motion dinosaurs.

TOP MIDDLE: Pressbook cover for *Along the Moonbeam Trail* (1920). Thought lost for many decades, the often inferior stop-motion animation appears to have been created by producer and director Major Herbert M. Dawley himself and not his former collaborator, Willis H. O'Brien.

TOP RIGHT: American trade advertisement trumpeting the box office success of First National's *The Lost World* (Dir: Harry O. Hoyt and William Dowling, 1925), based on the 1912 adventure novel by Sir Arthur Conan Doyle (1859–1930).

BOTTOM RIGHT: Promotional advertisement for *The Lost World* (1925) from a November 1925 issue of the French magazine *Mon Ciné*.

OPPOSITE, ABOVE LEFT: *Häxan* (2014), acrylic, ink, and papers on collage by British artist Dave McKean, inspired by the silent 1922 Swedish-Danish co-production. "This was done for *Nitrate*," explains the artist, "a forthcoming book of paintings and drawings inspired by silent cinema. Director Benjamin Christensen himself played the Devil in this strange semi-documentary full of startling images."

They Call It Witchcraft

Partly inspired by the *Malleus Maleficarum*, a fifteenth century German treatise on witchcraft by Catholic clergyman Heinrich Krämer (as "Henricus Institoris"), *Häxan* (aka *Heksen*, 1922) is a Swedish-Danish co-production written and directed by Benjamin Christensen (1879–1959). Filmed only at night as a four-part documentary with dramatized sequences, it explores how medieval beliefs in witchcraft and demonology may be explained as a result of mental illness and features the director himself playing a jolly Satan. After decades of languishing in obscurity, the film was finally reissued in an abbreviated version as *Witchcraft Through the Ages* in 1968 for the psychedelic generation, with an added deadpan commentary by American counterculture author William S. Burroughs which actually reduced the emotive power of Christensen's dazzling original.

FOLLOWING SPREAD: *London After Midnight* (2012), gouache on watercolor paper by British artist Graham Humphreys. "The publication of the screenplay for this lost film required a wraparound artwork for a collector's hardback edition," explains the artist. "Using the best-known portrait image of Lon Chaney, I had to use my imagination to extend the image as required."

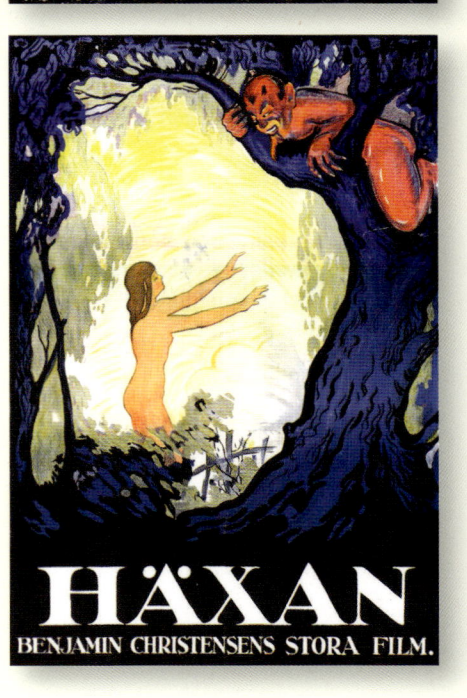

THE SINISTER SILENTS

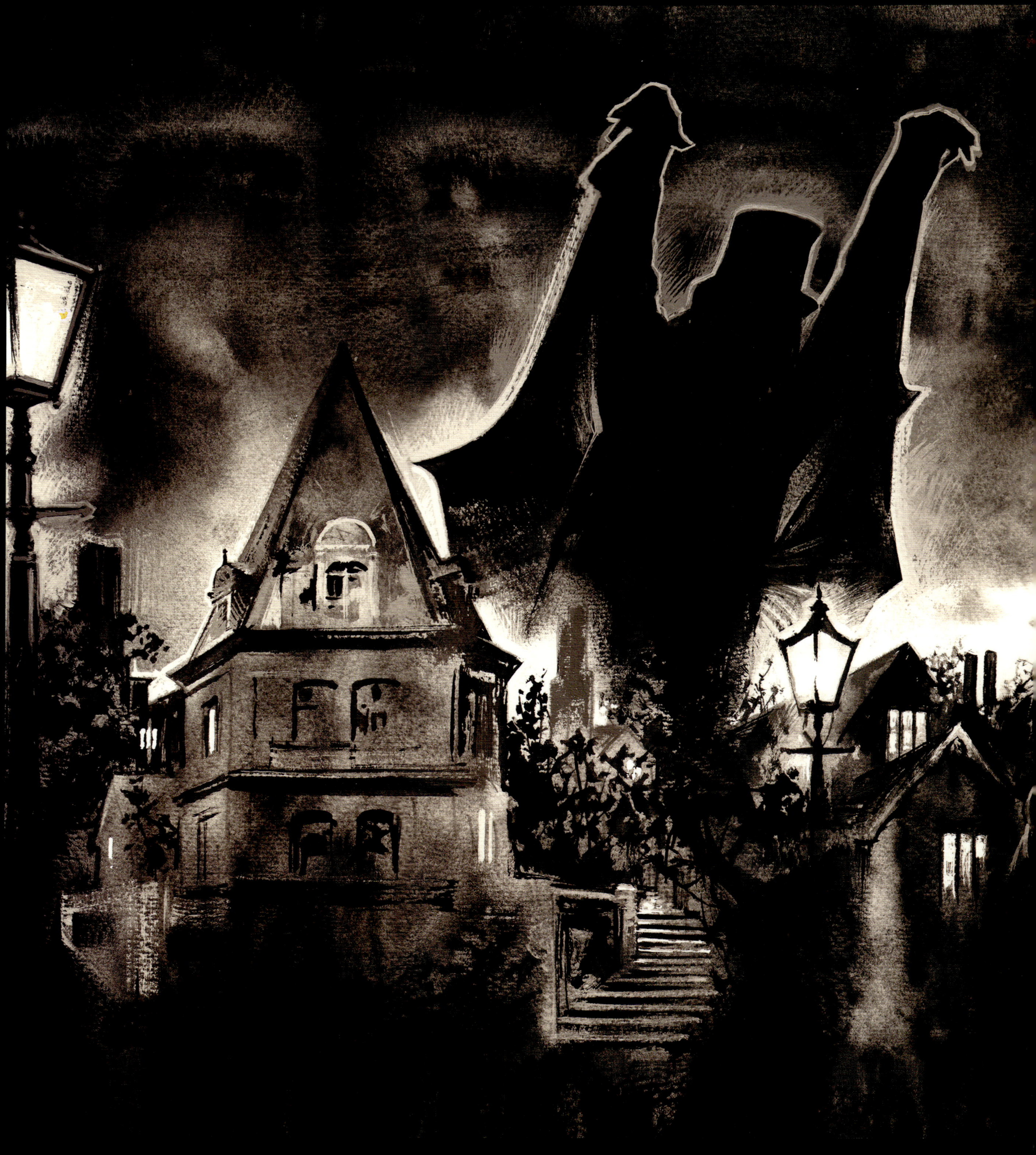

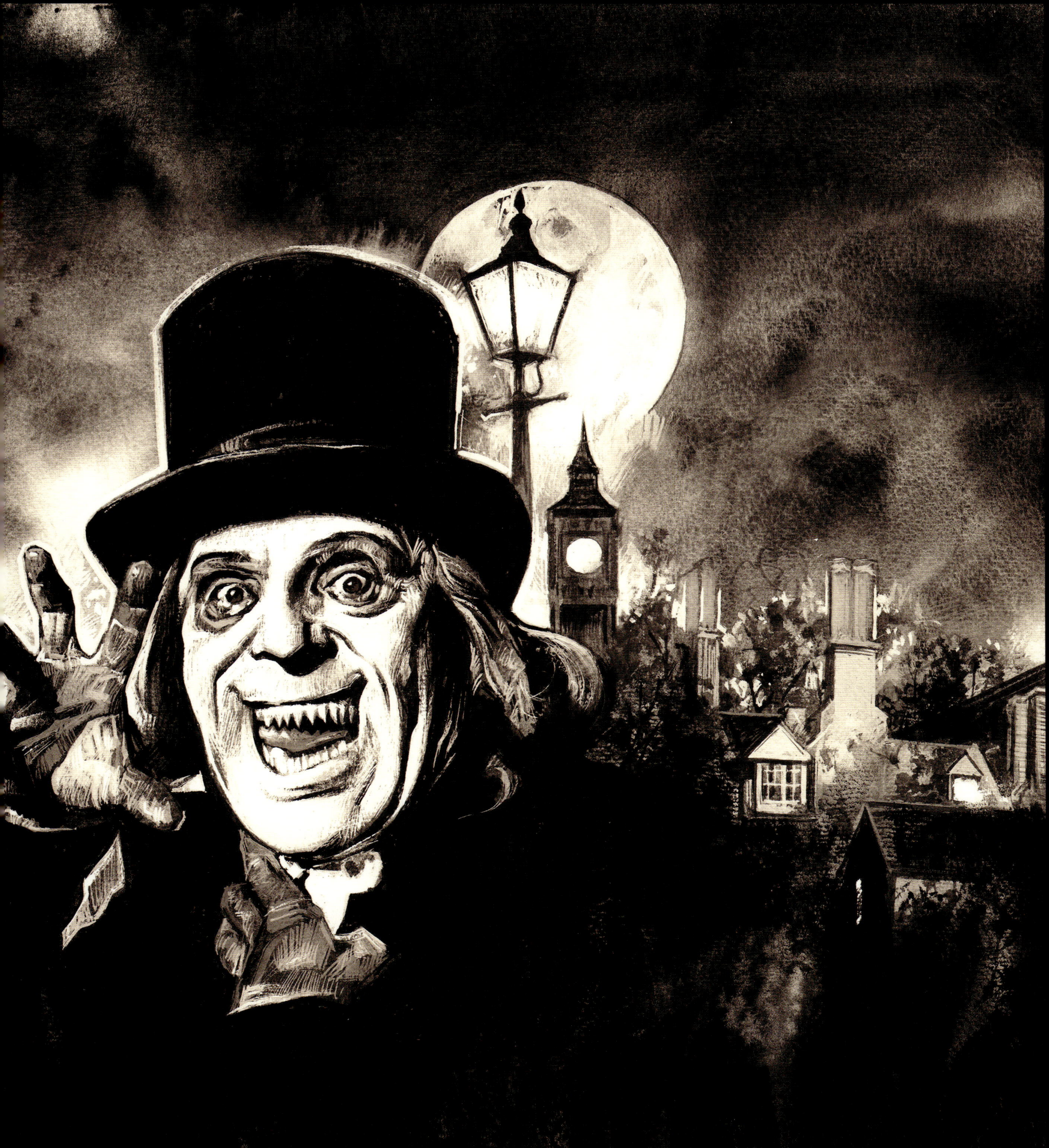

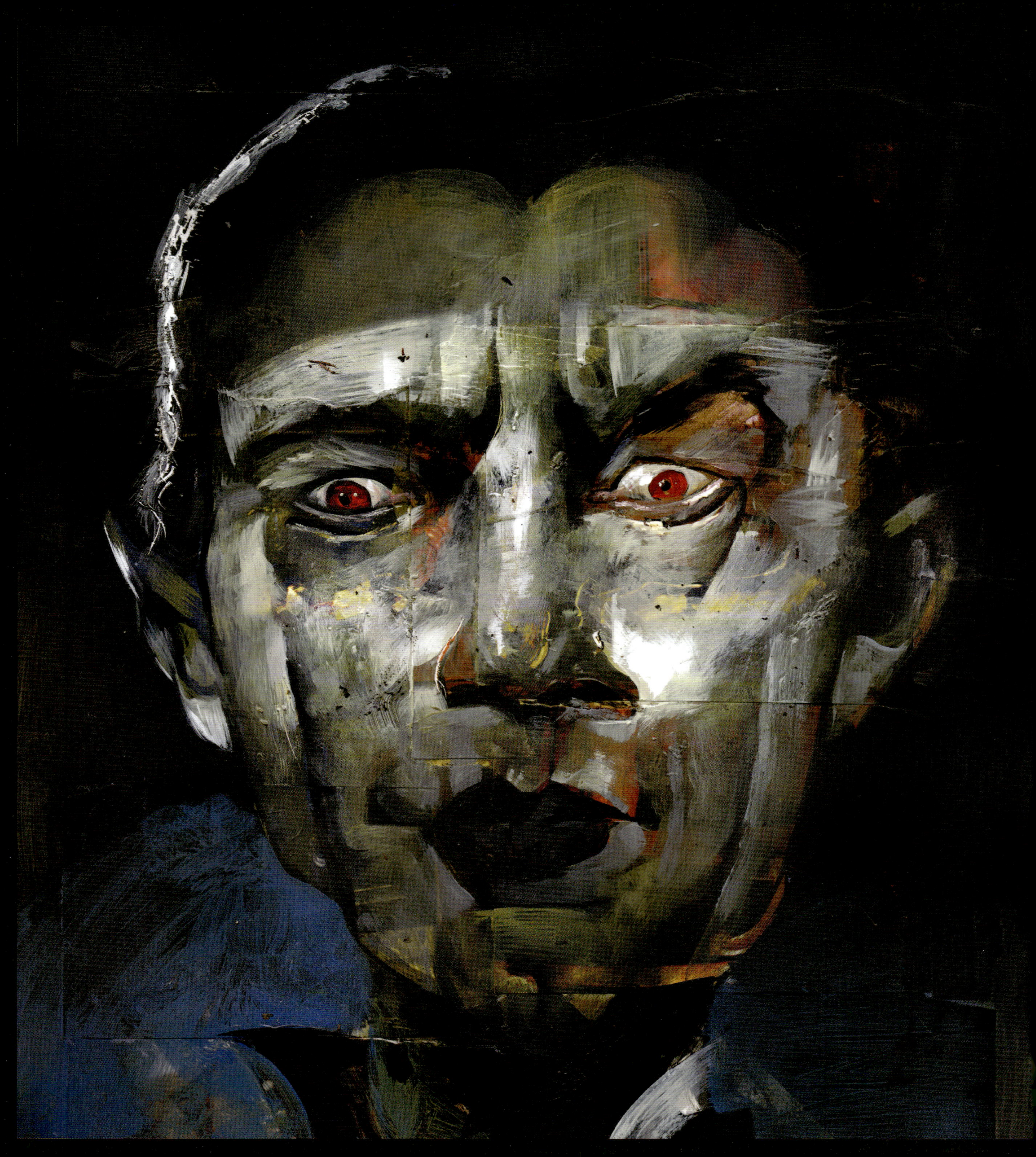

THE THRILLING THIRTIES

TOM WEAVER

"This great Nation will endure as it has endured, will revive and will prosper. So, first of all, let me assert my firm belief that the only thing we have to fear is fear itself."

FRANKLIN D. ROOSEVELT

> "There's a parallel between time, history, and horror pictures... In times of peace, there's no place for horror films; times of fear—like now—bring out the need for violence in people. This reflects, in my opinion, a fear of the people of *tomorrow*."
> Curt Siodmak

THE FIRST WORLD War had a devastating effect on post-war Europe—but an ocean away, it was a whole 'nuther story. Almost a full century before the current crop of U.S. politicians' grand promises, Presidents Harding and Coolidge had proceeded to Make America Great Again. New jobs. Rising wages. New thinkers.

The '20s roared. There had been no need for escapism into horror-fantasy as there was in, say, Germany, where Doktor Caligari and Cesare and other nightmares took *Die Bürgers*' minds off the fact that their country was drenched in blood. Who needs Nos-fer-a-tu when you've got vo-de-oh-doe?

In America, there was prosperity—families to raise, Foxtrots to dance, Babe Ruth, babes to boff, enough bootleg beer to bathe in, and no outstanding need for Boogie Men on film, on stage, or in fiction.

The 1929 stock market crash put the shoe (the one with the hole in the sole) on the American foot. Black Friday led to the century's greatest financial crisis—bankruptcies, mass unemployment, and worse. And entertainment-wise, people who had a few coins to spend on things other than food and shelter found themselves making Hollywood's newest genre—the horror film—the Next Big Thing. Times were hard and the future promised to be even harder, in ways that some probably hesitated to even try to imagine. That was the worst of it—any horror is preferable to the horror of utter uncertainty.

In America, it was in the hills of Universal Studios, in California's San Fernando Valley, that the horror genre first flowered. History was made in 1930 when the studio produced *Dracula*, based on the Bram Stoker novel and the 1927–28 Broadway play. Eight years earlier, in happier days, Universal president Carl Laemmle had rejected the suggestion that the studio produce *Dracula* ("We [consider it] a little too gruesome to screen well," he wrote at the time), but in 1930 the bloom was on the wolfbane. The Broadway Dracula, Bela Lugosi, reprised his undead role in director Tod Browning's adaptation, joined by the stage cast's Edward Van Sloan and Herbert Bunston as Prof. Van Helsing and Dr. Seward, respectively.

The movie represented a major shift in how Hollywood screen horrors were presented: fright-flicks from the silent days rarely featured supernatural monsters. Even Lon Chaney's vampire in Browning's *London After Midnight* (1927) turned out to be a mortal. Lugosi's Dracula was the real deal, with artwork of a bat (behind the opening credits) bracing the audience for a genuine vampire and amped-up horror content.

Next, courtesy of director James Whale, came the studio's version of Mary Shelley's *Frankenstein* (1931), again with artwork behind the title providing an early warning to audience members: a pair of wide, staring eyes with rays (the ultraviolet ray?) emanating from both, plus clawed hands. Weirder and more frightening: under the subsequent credits, the image of a demonic, inscrutable, mask-like face, with eyeballs kaleidoscopically circling.

The role of "The Monster," according to the opening credits, was played by "?," but he wouldn't remain a question mark for long: With *Frankenstein*, Boris Karloff—an actor who'd spent years on the down-low in Hollywood—did a one-movie leap to stardom on the silver scream.

Hollywood's pre-Motion Picture Production Code era offered moviemakers a window of opportunity to make the kind of horror pictures that couldn't have been made by major studios before or after. Some of them couldn't even be made today, in our politically correct modern age.

Universal's third monsterpiece again set a mood with images behind the titles, but this time the honors went to the artists in the prop shop: atop a sand-covered turntable, they created a diorama of the Sphinx and Egyptian pyramids—and one pyramid had the letters spelling out THE MUMMY looming off of its sloped surface.

At first Universal had the horror cycle to itself, as other studios searched for horror tales "squeamishly" (according to *Variety*), while also trying to determine if "nightmare pictures" would continue to have box office pull.

In 1931, Paramount dusted off Robert Louis Stevenson's *Dr. Jekyll and Mr. Hyde*, one-upping Universal when the stylish Fredric March-starrer earned Best Writing and Best Cinematography Academy Award nominations, and an Oscar for March.

The same year at Warner Bros., John Barrymore brought chills into the art world as a sinister singing teacher—and hypnotist—in *Svengali* (Best Cinematography and Best Art Direction nominations) and as the warped, club-footed ballet master in *The Mad Genius*.

Sculptor Lionel Atwill fashioned wax figures in *Mystery of the Wax Museum* (1933), first the conventional way and then, after being maimed in a fire, by coating corpses in wax.

PREVIOUS SPREAD: *Bela Lugosi —Dracula* (2015), acrylic and ink on collage portrait by British artist Dave McKean. "More recently, I've moved back to pen, brush, and pencil much more," explains the artist. "I just prefer drawing than staring into a monitor all day. I would rather do something that's a bit more personal."

THE ART OF HORROR MOVIES

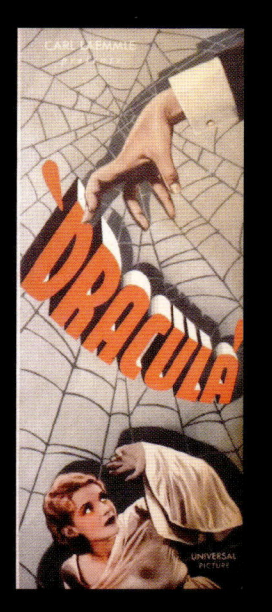

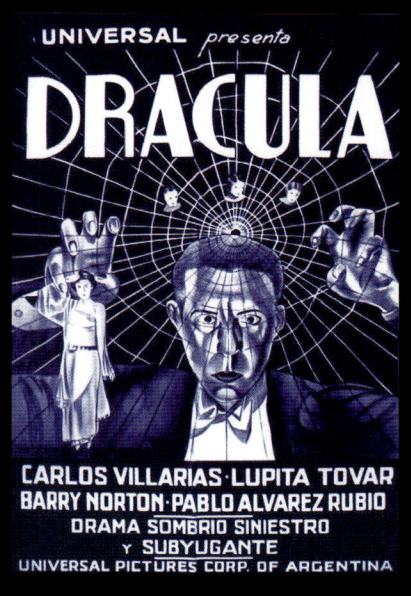

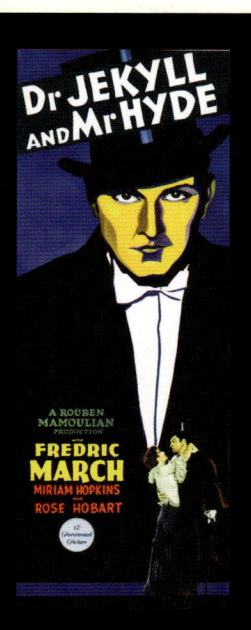

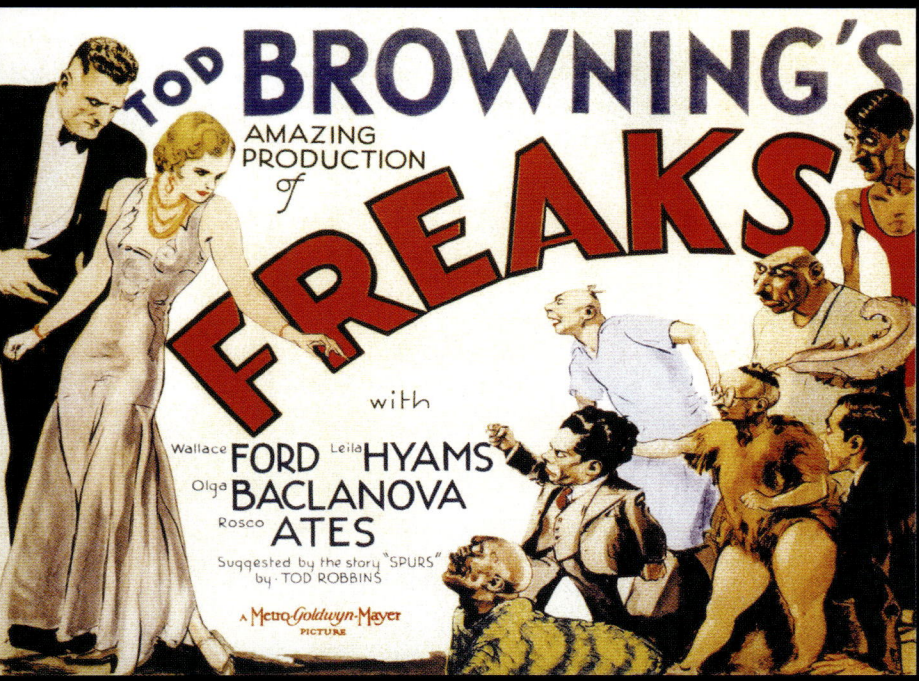

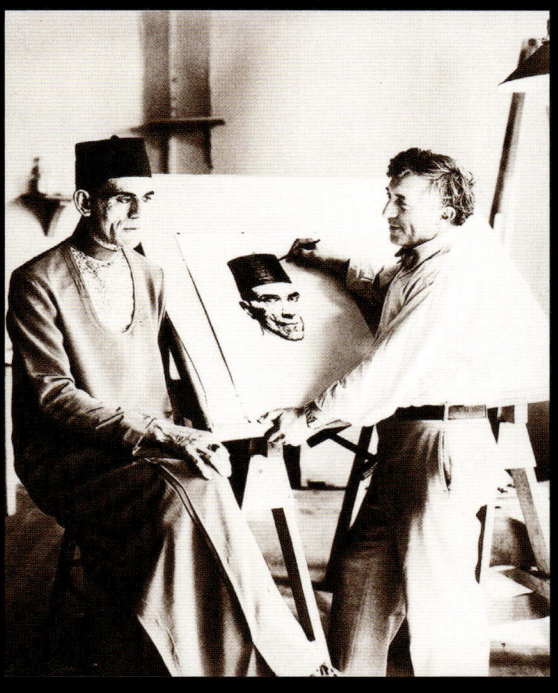

TOP LEFT: Front cover of the herald for Universal's 1931 horror hit *Dracula* (Dir: Tod Browning).

TOP MIDDLE, LEFT: Argentinean one-sheet poster for Universal's Spanish-language version of *Drácula* (Dir: George Melford, 1931), starring Carlos Villarías and Lupita Tovar.

TOP MIDDLE, RIGHT: Art deco-style American insert card for Paramount's *Dr. Jekyll and Mr. Hyde* (Dir: Rouben Mamoulian, 1931), thought lost for 30 years until it was reissued in the early 1970s.

BOTTOM LEFT: Half-sheet poster for Metro-Goldwyn-Mayer's controversial *Freaks* (Dir: Tod Browning, 1932), suggested by Tod Robbins's 1923 short story "Spurs." Pulled from domestic release before it completed its initial run, it was banned in the UK for 30 years, severely damaging Browning's subsequent career.

TOP RIGHT: Title lobby card for the 1951 Realart re-release of Universal's *The Mummy* (Dir: Karl Freund, 1932), which starred Boris Karloff as a reanimated Egyptian sorcerer-priest.

BOTTOM RIGHT: This publicity shot from *The Mummy* (1932) shows Hungarian-born artist William Andrew ("Willy") Pogány (1882–1955) working on a pen-and-ink sketch of Boris Karloff. The drawing's present whereabouts are unknown.

THE THRILLING THIRTIES

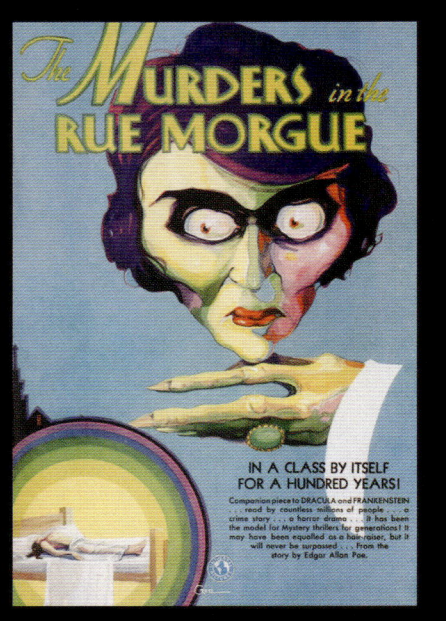

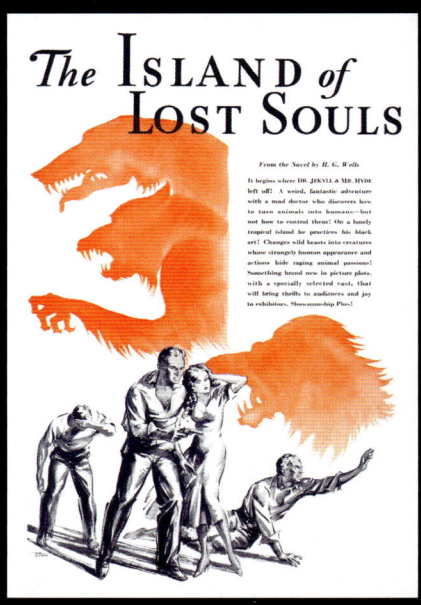

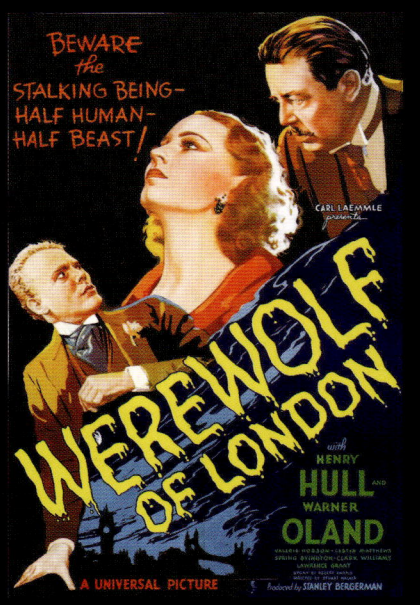

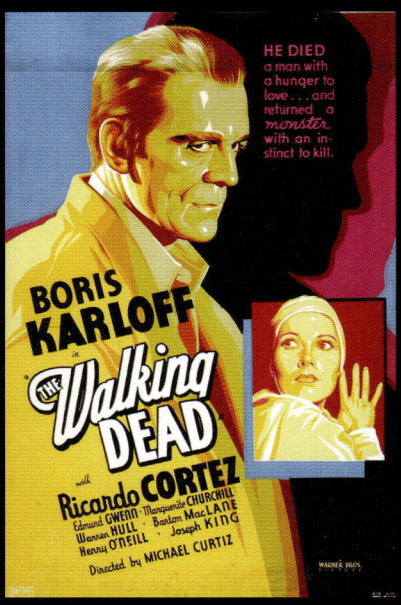

TOP LEFT: Publicity still of American "pin-up" artist Rolf Armstrong (1889–1960) working on the pastel portrait of Boris Karloff during the filming of *Bride of Frankenstein* (1935) that appears as the frontispiece to this volume.

TOP RIGHT: British quad poster for the 1950 re-release of Universal's *Son of Frankenstein* (Dir: Rowland V. Lee, 1939). Note the "H" (for "Horrific") certificate, which was introduced in January 1937 by the British Board of Film Censors.

BOTTOM LEFT: Pre-production trade advertisement by Hungarian-born artist Károly Grósz for *Murders in the Rue Morgue* (1932), from *The Big Book from Universal 1931–1932* exhibitor's manual.

BOTTOM MIDDLE, LEFT: Pre-production advertisement signed "Graven" for Paramount's *Island of Lost Souls* (Dir: Erle C. Kenton, 1932). The movie was based on the 1896 novel *The Island of Dr. Moreau* by H.G. Wells, and was banned in the UK until July 1958 due to its (implied) vivisection scenes.

BOTTOM MIDDLE, RIGHT: American one-sheet poster for Universal's *WereWolf of London* (Dir: Stuart Walker, 1935). After star Henry Hull complained that the werewolf makeup overshadowed his character, Jack P. Pierce finally got to use his original design on Lon Chaney, Jr. six years later.

Hollywood's pre-Motion Picture Production Code era offered moviemakers a window of opportunity to make the kind of horror pictures that couldn't have been made by major studios before or after. Some of them couldn't even be made today, in our politically correct modern age.

"Dirty, slimy freaks! Freaks, freaks, freaks!" were the stars of, you guessed it, MGM's *Freaks* (1932); cities around the country and countries around the world laid out the un-welcome mat for that Tod Browning shocker. Human heads adorned mad hunter Count Zaroff's walls in RKO's *The Most Dangerous Game* (1932), and a walking corpse in her wedding dress haunted the halls of *houngan* Bela Lugosi's castle in the indie *White Zombie* (1932).

Dr. Mirakle (Lugosi again) wanted his pet ape to do the horizontal hustle with a mousy mademoiselle in Universal's Edgar Allan Poe-inspired *Murders in the Rue Morgue* (1932). H.G. Wells's literary creation Dr. Moreau (Charles Laughton) was similarly resistant to the idea of keeping one's penis in their genus, seeking to mate man and Panther Woman in Paramount's *Island of Lost Souls* (1932).

> Two years of chills was enough for audiences to go cold on horror pictures. In February 1933, just days short of the second anniversary of the release of *Dracula*, *Variety* reported that some exhibitors were no longer playing up horror movies *as* horror movies.

Two years of chills was enough for audiences to go cold on horror pictures. In February 1933, just days short of the second anniversary of the release of *Dracula*, *Variety* reported that some exhibitors were no longer playing up horror movies as horror movies, instead accentuating other angles in these films. Theaters whose advertisements featured *Island of Lost Souls*' Panther Woman did better than ones that stressed its horror content.

Universal stuck to its ghoulish guns, turning again to Poe for *The Black Cat* (1934). As seen in the opening credits, it starred...

KARLOFF
And
Bela Lugosi

...making horror film fans aware which of the two stars of *The Black Cat* was Alpha Dog. The budget was kept low, but there was no cap on the imagination of its 29-year-old director Edgar G. Ulmer. It boasted a morbid plot; some of Boris and Bela's best acting; the novelty of Bela as a sympathetic character and Boris as the blackest of archfiends; a classical music score, and a unique setting—Karloff's Hungarian hilltop mansion: above, sleek and ultra-modern in architecture and furnishings; below, a diabolical dungeon where the devil-worshipping Hjalmar Poelzig stores women's corpses in lighted display cases.

The horror parade continued at Universal in 1935 with the quirky and magnificent *Bride of Frankenstein* and the talking screen's first lycanthrope in *WereWolf of London*. But now civic groups were turning up the heat on horror moviemakers, and other countries began hanging out their DO NOT ENTER signs. The few studios that still made horror movies sought to cope by making them scientific rather than supernatural: Warner's *The Walking Dead* (1936) with Karloff, and Universal's *The Invisible Ray* (1936) with Karloff and Lugosi.

This new approach reached heights of ridiculousness with *Dracula's Daughter* (1936). Script drafts which featured Dracula in early scenes were scrapped so that science could play a larger part in the proceedings: Countess Zaleska (Gloria Holden) claims to be Dracula's Daughter—and a vampire—and feels she can be cured of vampiric tendencies by sympathetic psychiatric treatment. Unlike her dad, she never becomes a bat or wolf; she avoids mirrors but we never see whether she casts a reflection or not; and she's done in by a wooden arrow through the heart, which would kill *any*body.

While audiences everywhere took her at her word that she was indeed undead, probably never even noticing that she performed none of her father's fearsome feats, Universal could pass it off in horror-phobic precincts as a movie about a woman who *thought* she was a vampire, and was not the real McCoy.

Dracula's Daughter ends at Castle Dracula, where the 1931 *Dracula* began, which brought the 1930s horror cycle full circle. This sequel also revived the idea of artwork behind the opening credits—this time weird images which (later in the movie) we find are examples of the outré output of Countess Zaleska, a painter. By the end of the classic 1930s horror cycle, the monster herself was providing her own macabre images for the opening credits!

By this time, it had gotten to the point where horror pictures were more toil and trouble than they were worth to the Hollywood production plants, so the monsters went into mothballs, and the stars too-closely associated with them—Karloff and Lugosi—onto Poverty Row and/or the unemployment line.

Their hibernation was brief however, as news (again) from Europe caused quite the worldwide *Führer*. Another conflict was brewing. The death toll of this war would be the greatest in human history.

In 1938 Universal turned again to horror, endowing life into its Monster series: with the genre's power couple Karloff and Lugosi again paired, *Son of Frankenstein* was produced on a grand (for Universal) scale. Would audiences again "take" to a monster movie, in these tumultuous times?

In *Son of Frankenstein*'s key city openings the following year, it did the biggest box office business in the history of horror pictures.

OPPOSITE, BOTTOM RIGHT: The only known copy of an art deco-style poster for Warner Bros.' *The Walking Dead* (Dir: Michael Curtiz, 1936), featuring Boris Karloff as reanimated corpse of a former convict framed and executed for a murder he didn't commit.

THE THRILLING THIRTIES

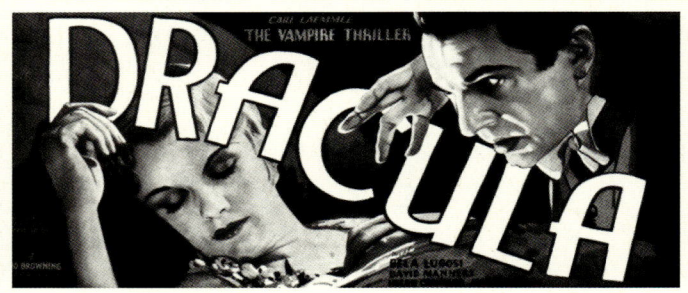

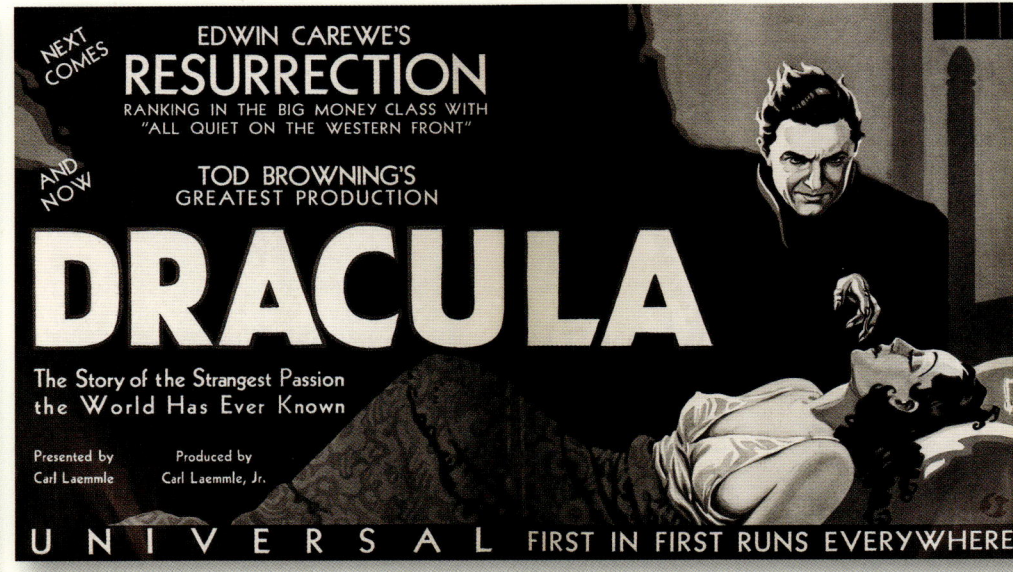

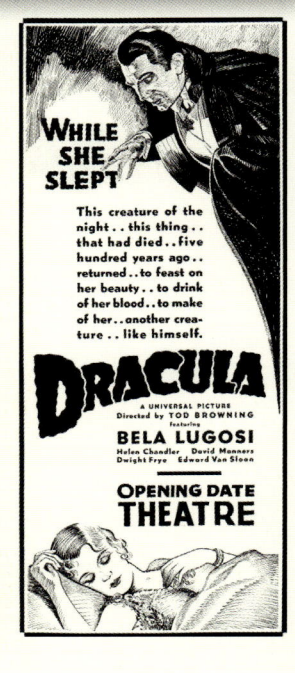

TOP LEFT: Advance campaign advertisement for *Dracula* (Dir: Tod Browning, 1931) from Universal's 1930–31 exhibitors' book. Based on the 1897 novel by Bram Stoker, the 1927 stage play by Hamilton Deane and John L. Balderston was a huge hit on Broadway starring Bela Lugosi.

TOP RIGHT: Double-page preview advertisement for Universal's *Dracula* (1931) that ran in such motion picture trade journals as *Exhibitors Herald-World*, *Motion Picture News*, and *Variety* in November 1930. Bela Lugosi was forced to accept just $3,500 for seven weeks of work.

BOTTOM LEFT: 24-sheet poster for *Dracula* from Universal's 1931 exhibitors' campaign book. No copies of this poster are known to have survived. Reportedly, a now-lost silent version of the movie with inter-titles was released to theaters that had not yet been wired for sound by the early 1930s.

BOTTOM MIDDLE, LEFT: Also from the studio's 1931 exhibitors' campaign book, no copies of this "Style D" three-sheet poster for *Dracula* are known to exist. There is little doubt that the studio would have tried to cast Lon Chaney in the title role, had the actor not died prematurely of a hemorrhage of the throat in 1930.

BOTTOM MIDDLE, RIGHT & BOTTOM RIGHT: Following the premiere of *Dracula* at the Roxy Theatre in New York City on February 12, 1931, the Fox West Coast Theatres chain created these stylish pen-and-ink ad mats for newspapers to promote the release of the movie on America's West coast.

THE ART OF HORROR MOVIES

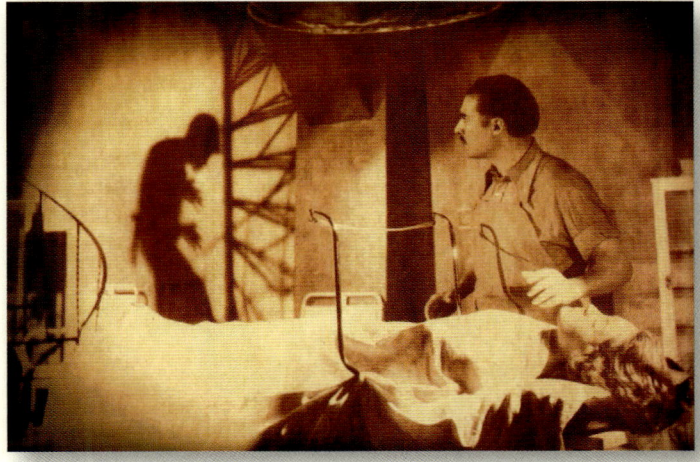

TOP LEFT: Generally considered to be the first Mexican sound horror movie, Eco Films' *La Llorona* (Dir: Ramón Peón, 1933) was loosely inspired by the myth of "The Crying Woman"—a banshee-like ghost whose melancholy lament for her dead children is considered a portent of death.

BOTTOM LEFT: Argentinean poster for the Mexican *El fantasma del convento* (The Phantom of the Convent, 1934). Fernando de Fuentes, who was one of three writers on *La Llorona* (1933), went on to co-script and direct this haunted monastery movie for Producciones FESA.

BOTTOM RIGHT: Directed by Miguel Zacarías for Producciones Pezet, *El baúl macabro* (The Macabre Trunk, 1936) starred Ramón Pereda (the hero of *La Llorona*) as a mad doctor who kidnaps young women and then transfuses their blood into his terminally ill wife in an attempt to cure her.

TOP RIGHT: Chano Urueta directed *El signo de la muerte* (The Sign of Death, 1939) for Cinematografica Internacional S.A. It featured comedians "Cantinflas" (Mario Moreno) and (Manuel) Medel, and some surprising nudity, as a sacrificial Aztec cult attempts to resurrect its ancient god.

THE THRILLING THIRTIES

Monstrous Movie Marquees

Although the advertising and marketing of movies began in earnest in the early 1900s, it reached its zenith during the first half of the 20th century with the growth of the movie palaces. Studios would often literally rebuild the exterior and interior of theaters to produce eye-catching exhibits designed to tell the public what film was playing. For these "event" movies, distributors would create large displays using electric or neon signs and enormous cutouts based on the advertising to entice passersby into the building to see the picture.

TOP LEFT: Following their successful first runs in 1931, Universal's *Dracula* and *Frankenstein* were first paired together in August 1938 to become box office hits again, much to the studio's surprise. This marquee display at Brandt's Victory Theatre on New York's West 42nd Street is for Realart's record-breaking reissue in April 1952.

TOP RIGHT: Manager Eddie Helwig created an impressive Egyptian façade and giant cutout heads for the early 1933 release of Universal's *The Mummy* at Warner Bros.' Rivoli Theatre in Paterson, New Jersey.

BOTTOM LEFT: Front-of-house ballyhoo for *Doctor X* (1932) clearly utilizing an identical image of Bela Lugosi used to promote *White Zombie* the same year.

BOTTOM RIGHT: A "doctor" and his "patient" promote a pairing of *The Walking Dead* (1936) and *Revolt of the Zombies* (aka *Revolt of the Demons*, 1936).

THE ART OF HORROR MOVIES

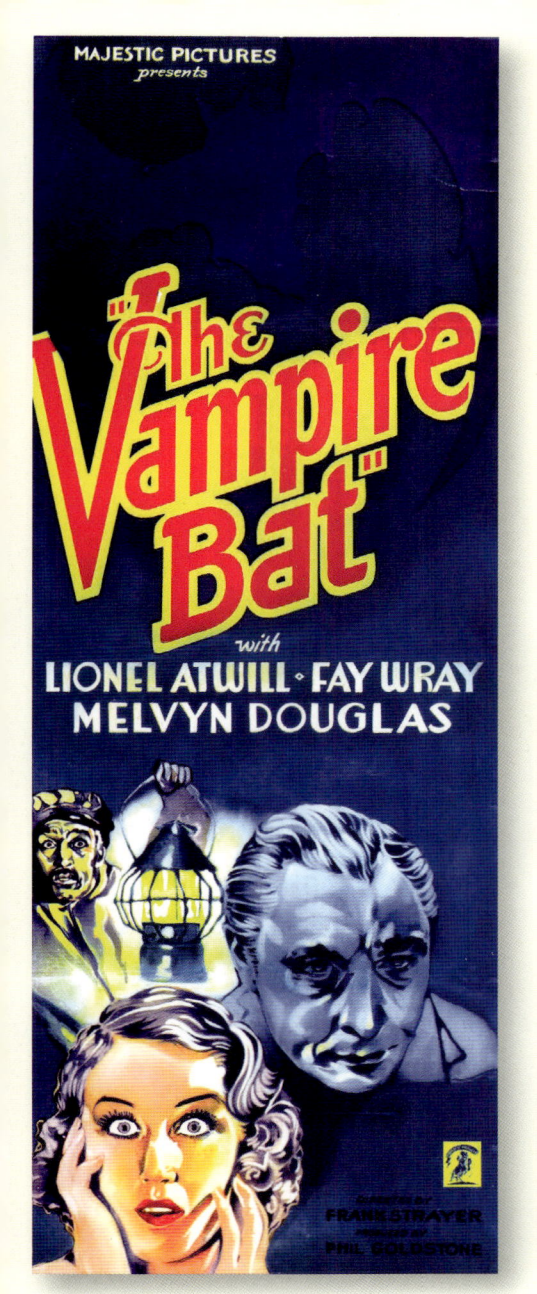

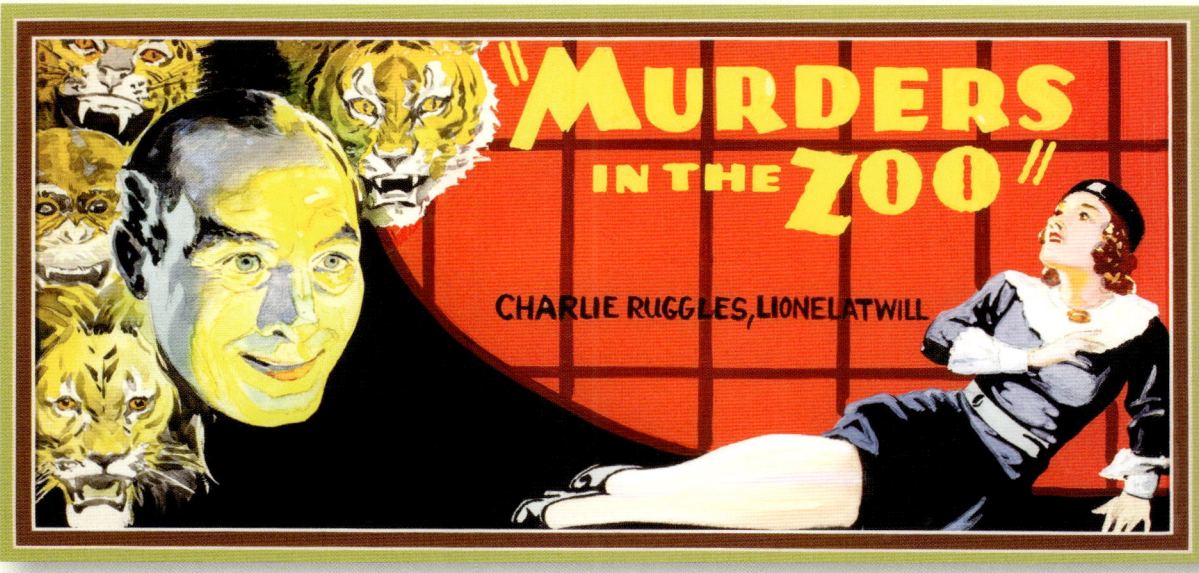

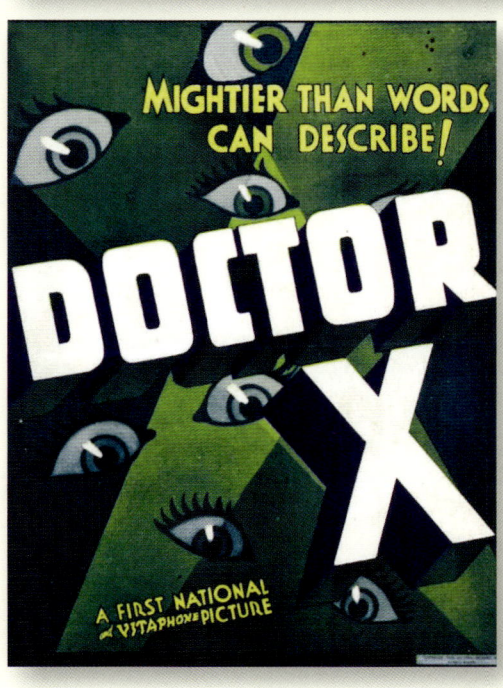

ABOVE LEFT: British-born Lionel Atwill (1885–1946) co-starred with Canadian actress Fay Wray in three Hollywood horror movies of the early 1930s. This insert card is for Majestic Pictures' poverty row *The Vampire Bat* (Dir: Frank R. Strayer, 1933), the last of their on-screen collaborations.

TOP RIGHT: Original gouache on illustration board preliminary poster art for the Paramount *conte cruel Murders in the Zoo* (Dir: A. Edward Sutherland, 1933). Lionel Atwill played an insanely jealous big game hunter who sews up the mouth of a rival.

BOTTOM MIDDLE: The first time that Lionel Atwill and Fay Wray were paired together was in First National Pictures/Warner Bros.' two-color Technicolor mystery *Doctor X* (Dir: Michael Curtiz, 1932).

BOTTOM RIGHT: Lionel Atwill and Bela Lugosi were reduced to playing comic foils in Twentieth Century-Fox's old dark house mystery *The Gorilla* (Dir: Allan Dwan, 1939), based on Ralph Spence's 1925 stage play.

THE THRILLING THIRTIES

BRIDE OF FRANKENSTEIN

Out of the ruins of shattered box-office records rises the Frankenstein monster — to claim himself a bride, and to work further havoc with record theatre grosses!... Can you imagine the advertising you can do on this one?... The mere thought of the monster seeking a bride makes a showman's fingers fairly itch to write the flaming lines that will pack any theatre in the world!... The original Frankenstein proved what could be done with exploitation. NOW ADD THE BRIDE IDEA TO ALL YOU'VE HAD BEFORE, AND YOU'VE GOT A "TREMENDOUSITY" OF APPEAL—and in plain English, THAT'S PLENTY!

A JAMES WHALE Production

A CARL LAEMMLE JUNIOR PRODUCTION

MORE SENSATIONAL THAN HER UNFORGETTABLE FATHER!

DRACULA'S DAUGHTER

DIRECTED BY JAMES WHALE

ISLAND OF LOST SOULS

He took them from his mad menagerie…nights were horrible with the screams of tortured beasts…from his House of Pain they came re-made… Pig-men…Wolf-women… thoughtful Human Apes and his masterpiece—the Panther Woman throbbing to the hot flush of love.

ISLAND OF LOST SOULS

From H. G. Wells' surging rhapsody of adventure, romance and terror, "The Island of Dr. Moreau" with CHARLES LAUGHTON BELA LUGOSI RICHARD ARLEN LEILA HYAMS, AND THE PANTHER WOMAN

A Paramount Picture

ISLAND · OF · LOST · SOULS

They came from gloomy caves and slimy puddles, neither humans nor animals, these insane misfits of nature. Trembling with animal fury and ignoring the god who made them, they stormed the House of Pain, seeking the girl who was All-Human. The moonlit night was hideous with their snarls, roars, and screams. It seemed as if the whole world paused in terror.

C'EST avec une légitime fierté que PARAMOUNT est en mesure d'annoncer aujourd'hui la sortie prochaine de ce film, tiré du drame immortel de STEVENSON. Chef d'œuvre en regard duquel toutes les autres incursions dans le terrifiant domaine de l'inconnu semblent choses enfantines…

— Le DOCTEUR JEKYLL, — aimé par les plus jolies femmes et recherché par tous — MISTER HYDE — un démon criminel, ne sont qu'un même homme. Nul n'échappera à la hantise qui se dégage de cette œuvre hallucinante. Les rôles les plus énigmatiques, les plus sensationnels que l'écran ait jamais connu. Une distribution digne de ces rôles et qui sera publiée d'ici peu.

Le Dr. Jekyll et Mr. Hyde

OPPOSITE, TOP: Double-page campaign advertisement for *The Bride of Frankenstein* (Dir: James Whale, 1935) from Universal Pictures' 1934–35 exhibitor book. House artist Frederick "Fred" Bennett Kulz left the studio in November 1936, after the Laemmle family lost control of it in April that same year.

OPPOSITE, BOTTOM: Advance campaign advertisement for *Dracula's Daughter* (1936), from Universal Pictures' 1934–35 exhibitor book. The image of the Countess seems to be modeled on bit-player Geraldine Dvorak (who was in the 1931 *Dracula*), while credited director Whale was replaced by Lambert Hillyer.

TOP LEFT & RIGHT: Three pages from the Paramount 1932–33 exhibitor book promoting *Island of Lost Souls* (Dir: Erle C. Kenton, 1932). Although Bela Lugosi is listed second on this promotional material, he received fourth billing on the movie itself and earned just $800 for his role as the "Sayer of the Law."

BOTTOM: The French market was deemed so important to the American studios in the early 1930s that Paramount issued its own *La nouvelle production 1931–1932* exhibitor book, which included this campaign advertisement for *Dr. Jekyll and Mr. Hyde* (Dir: Rouben Mamoulian, 1931).

THE THRILLING THIRTIES

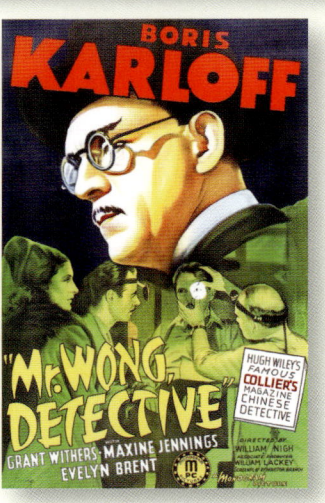

TOP LEFT: One-sheet poster for Fox Film Corporation's *Chandu the Magician* (Dir: William Cameron Menzies and Marcel Varnel, 1932), which featured Edmund Lowe (1890–1971) as the eponymous mystical hero from the popular radio series.

TOP RIGHT: This stone litho six-sheet poster for Twentieth Century-Fox's *The Adventures of Sherlock Holmes* (Dir: Alfred L. Werker, 1939) depicts Basil Rathbone in his second of 14 film appearances as Sir Arthur Conan Doyle's iconic consulting detective.

BOTTOM LEFT: Fox's *The Black Camel* (Dir: Hamilton MacFadden, 1931) was the second film to star Swedish-born actor Warner Oland as Honolulu detective Charlie Chan.

BOTTOM MIDDLE, LEFT: Spanish poster for *Charlie Chan at the Opera* (Dir: H. Bruce Humberstone, 1936) by Josep Soligó Tena.

BOTTOM MIDDLE, RIGHT: Stone litho one-sheet poster for *Thank You, Mr. Moto* (Dir: Norman Foster, 1937), the second of eight films from Twentieth Century-Fox starring Peter Lorre as author John P. Marquand's wily Japanese law enforcement agent.

BOTTOM RIGHT: One-sheet poster for *Mr. Wong, Detective* (Dir: William Nigh, 1938), the first of five movies from Monogram Pictures starring Boris Karloff as Hugh Wiley's fictional Chinese-American detective, James Lee Wong.

THE ART OF HORROR MOVIES

— 54 —

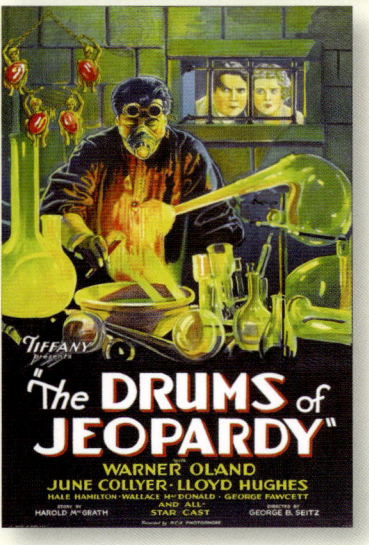

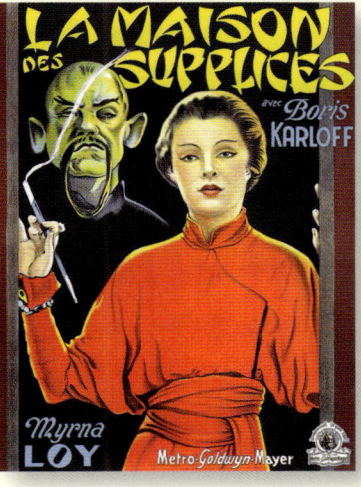

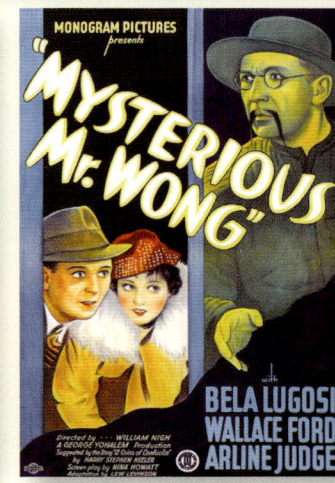

TOP LEFT: Pre-production trade advertisement by artist Károly Grósz from Universal's *The Box Office Book 1932–33* for the unproduced *Cagliostro*, set to star Boris Karloff. Author Nina Wilcox Putnam wrote a nine-page treatment about a 3,000-year-old scientist-magician who creates a death ray. It eventually became *The Mummy* (1932).

TOP RIGHT: Warner Oland played Sax Rohmer's Oriental villain Fu Manchu in three films for Paramount. *Daughter of the Dragon* (Dir: Lloyd Corrigan, 1931) was the last in the series.

BOTTOM LEFT: Tiffany's *The Drums of Jeopardy* (Dir: George B. Seitz, 1931) starred Oland as Russian scientist "Boris Karlov."

BOTTOM MIDDLE, LEFT: Window card for Warner Bros./Vitaphone's *Svengali* (Dir: Archie Mayo, 1931), based on the 1894 novel *Trilby* by George Louis du Maurier and starring John Barrymore as the eponymous evil musical maestro.

BOTTOM MIDDLE, RIGHT: Belgian litho poster for MGM's epic *The Mask of Fu Manchu* (Dir: Charles Brabin, 1932), based on the novel of the same name by Sax Rohmer.

BOTTOM RIGHT: Béla Lugosi portrayed a scheming Chinatown shopkeeper searching for the Twelve Coins of Confucius in Monogram Pictures' poverty row *The Mysterious Mr. Wong* (Dir: William Nigh, 1934), based on a 1928 story by Harry Stephen Keeler.

THE THRILLING THIRTIES

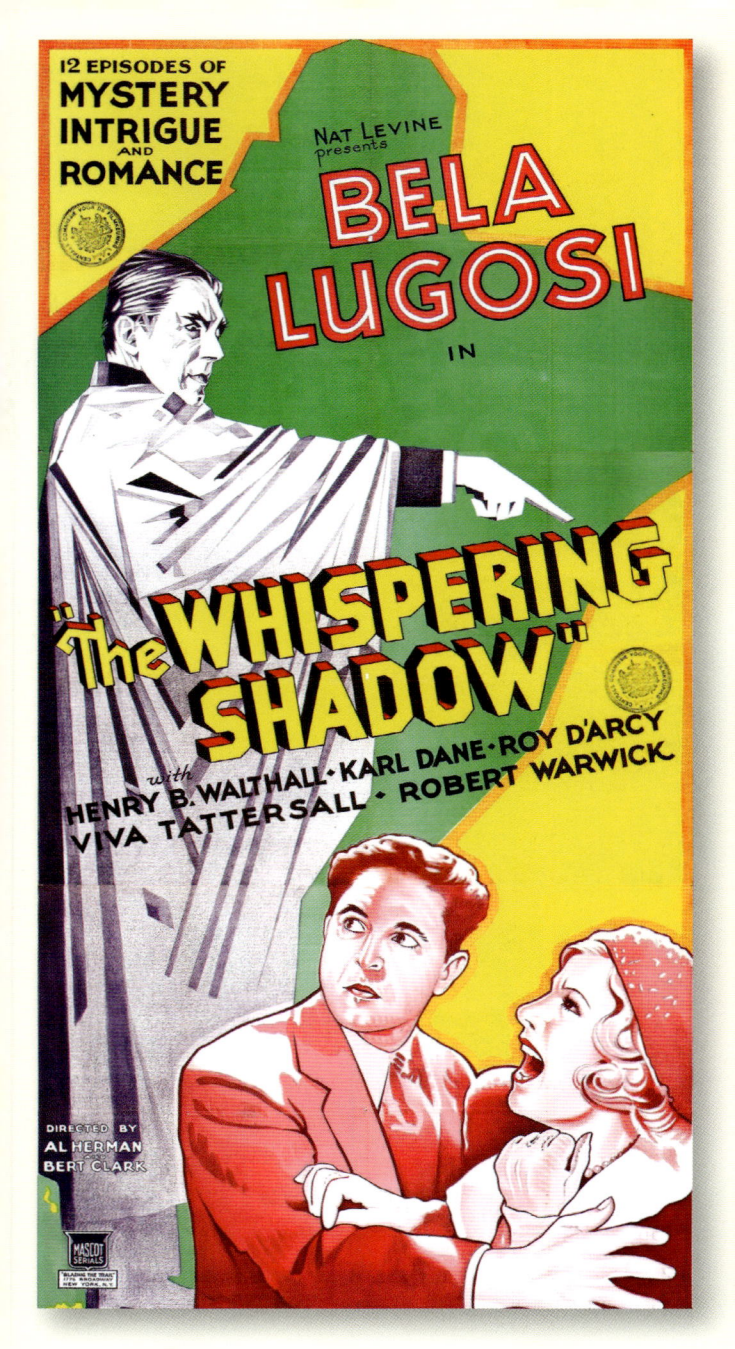

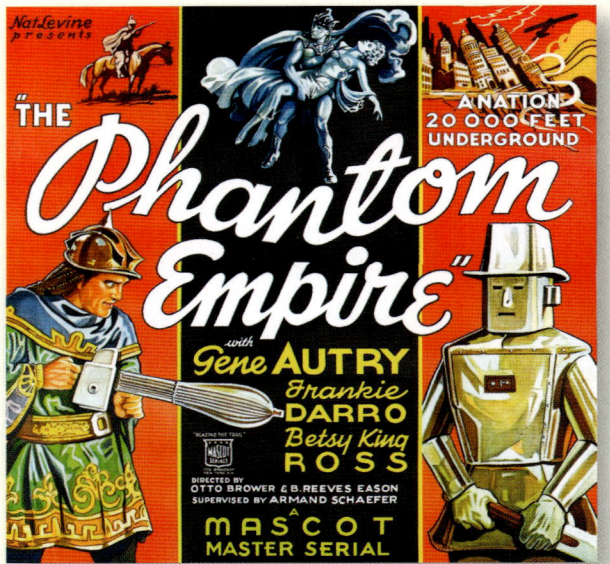

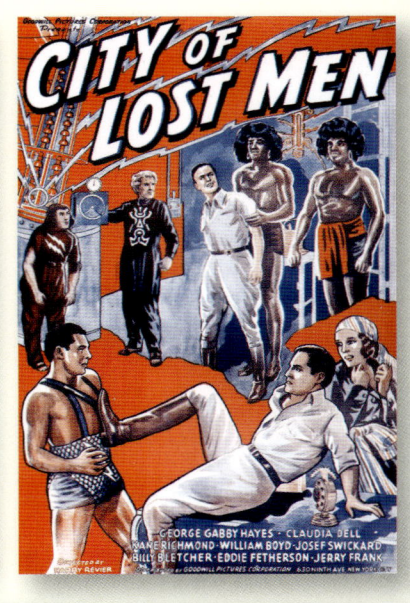

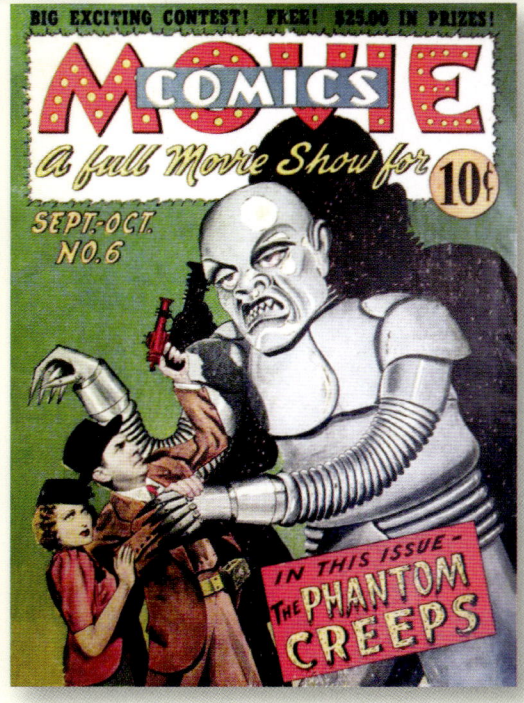

ABOVE LEFT: Stone litho three-sheet poster for Mascot Pictures' 12-chapter *The Whispering Shadow* (Dir: Colbert Clark and Albert Herman, 1933), about a criminal mastermind who has invented a radio death ray.

TOP MIDDLE: Stone litho six-sheet poster for Mascot Pictures' 12-chapter serial *The Phantom Empire* (Dir: Otto Brower and B. Reeves Eason, 1935). Singing cowboy Gene Autry discovers an advanced super-science civilization 20,000 feet below his dude ranch.

TOP RIGHT: Famed pulp artist Frank R. Paul possibly illustrated this 1940 poster for an apparently now lost feature-length reissue of Super Serial Productions' 12-chapter *The Lost City* (Dir: Harry Revier, 1935), re-titled *City of Lost Men*.

BOTTOM MIDDLE: One-sheet poster for Victory Pictures' 15-chapter *Shadow of Chinatown* (Dir: Robert F. Hill, 1936), which starred Bela Lugosi. Producer Sam Katzman also simultaneously released an edited-down feature-length version.

BOTTOM RIGHT: The September-October 1939 edition of All-American Publications' *Movie Comics* was the sixth and final issue. It featured an eight-page photo-strip adaptation of Universal's 12-chapter serial *The Phantom Creeps* (Dir: Ford Beebe and Saul A. Goodkind, 1939).

THE ART OF HORROR MOVIES

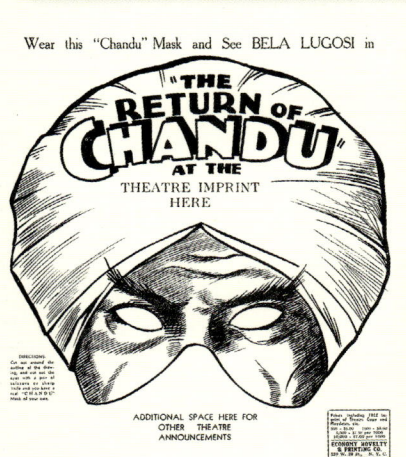

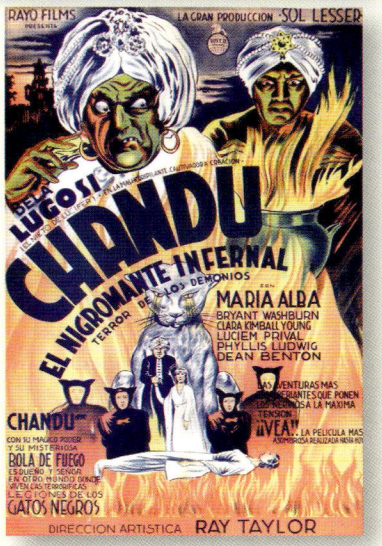

Lugosi's Chandu

Two years after he played megalomaniac madman Roxor in Fox's *Chandu the Magician* (1932), Bela Lugosi was back in his second serial as the mystical radio show hero himself in the 12-chapter *The Return of Chandu* (Dir: Ray Taylor, 1934). Produced for the poverty row Principal Pictures Corporation, Lugosi's miscast romantic protagonist has to rescue Egyptian Princess Nadji (Maria Alba) from the clutches of the sorcerer-priests of the mysterious sect of the cat god Ubasti, who have taken her to the magic island of Lemuria. To maximize box office potential, it was released in serial form and as two edited-down feature films, *The Return of Chandu* (1934) and *Chandu on the Magic Island* (1935).

ABOVE RIGHT: Pressbook cover for Principal Pictures Corporation's 12-chapter serial *The Return of Chandu* (1934).

BOTTOM LEFT: To promote the release of *The Return of Chandu* (1934), the Economy Novelty & Printing Co. of New York City produced this paper mask.

TOP LEFT: Stone litho six-sheet poster for the edited-down feature-length version of *The Return of Chandu* (1934), comprising the first four episodes of the serial, which theaters could either run as a stand-alone movie or then follow with the remaining eight chapters in serial format.

BOTTOM MIDDLE: Spanish poster for the feature-length *Chandu on the Magic Island* (1935), which was an edited-down version of the remaining eight chapters of the serial.

THE THRILLING THIRTIES

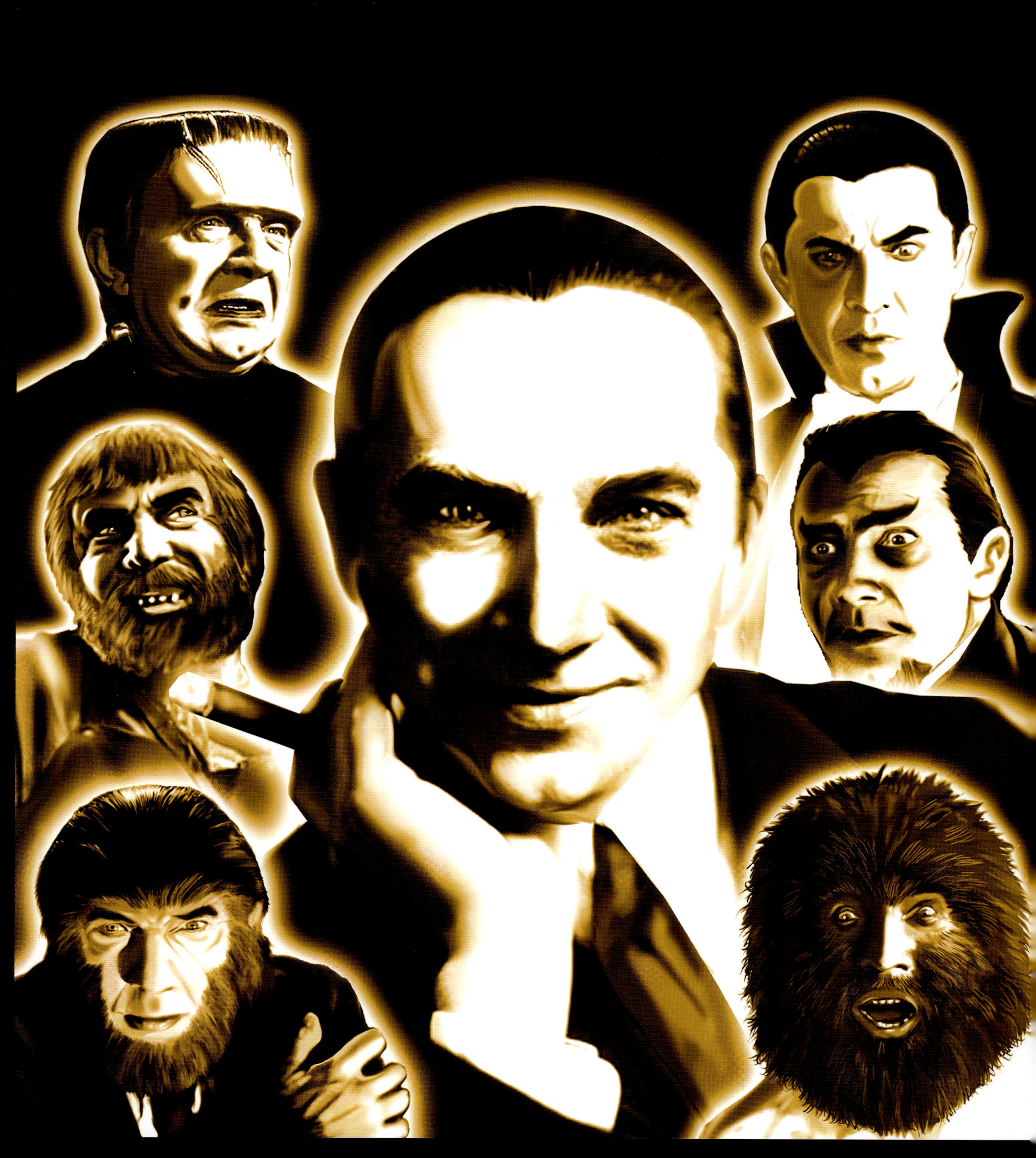

OPPOSITE: *Lugosi Montage* (2017), digital portrait by American artist Pete Von Sholly done for the forthcoming book *Fantastic Fictioneers*. "These are the many faces of the great Bela Lugosi," says the artist.

RIGHT: *Mummy–Halloween* (2013), signed and numbered screen print limited to 30 copies by American artist Brian Ewing. "This was originally created for a Queens of the Stone Age gig poster," recalls the artist. "I always loved movie stills from old horror films, and wondered what would happen if I drew anatomy on top of them. Would it change the way people look at them?"

THE THRILLING THIRTIES

TITANS OF TERROR

"My dear old Monster, I owe everything to him. He's my best friend."
Boris Karloff

"If I had one percent of the millions *Dracula* has made, I wouldn't be sitting here now."
Bela Lugosi

REMOVE COMEDY DUOS (Laurel and Hardy, Abbott and Costello, etc.) from the equation and it would be difficult to name two Golden Age actors more closely linked in the public mind than Boris Karloff and Bela Lugosi. It would also be difficult to name a screen team whose relationship was surrounded by more drama. How much of it was real, how much publicity, how much fan speculation? At this point, a full answer may be too obscured by the gauze of time.

We do know that after *Dracula* (1931), the Hungarian-born Lugosi was Hollywood Horror's MVP (on a team with no other players) until he created his own competition. *Dracula* gave him fame, and fame gave him an ego (if he didn't have one already), and his ego gave him the notion that the non-speaking, buried-in-makeup role of the Monster in *Frankenstein* (1931) was something he needed like Dracula needed sunglasses.

But then the actor hired Frank-instead, Boris Karloff, also catapulted to stardom. The English-born Karloff would go on to become the Sceptered Isle's gift to horror pictures: he had more range than Lugosi and could play a wider assortment of roles, even sympathetic ones. Lugosi tended always to come across as a creature of pure evil, and sometimes talked like he had a mouthful of goulash.

In all their screen pairings, Karloff was billed one slot above Lugosi... even when Lugosi should have been third- or fourth-billed (*The Invisible Ray*). Or tenth-billed (*Black Friday*, *The Body Snatcher*).

Their first film together, *The Black Cat* (1934), was a fine vehicle for both, and it went against expectations by making Karloff a too-bad-to-be-true villain and Lugosi halfway sympathetic as a past victim of Karloff's cruelty.

For the first and last time, Lugosi had the bigger, better part in *The Raven* (1935) as a sadistic, Edgar Allan Poe-obsessed physician; surgically transforming Karloff's face into a mask of horror is just the tip of his not-so-niceberg.

In *Son of Frankenstein* (1939), Karloff was again the Monster, comatose half the movie and semi-wasted in the rest. Meanwhile, Lugosi had a wonderful ham holiday as Ygor, the broken-necked, snaggle-toothed blacksmith who has made himself the Monster's keeper. Beneath Jack Pierce's makeup, it's hard to see that it is Lugosi—he doesn't sound like Lugosi; and, full of simple-minded malicious mischief, he doesn't act like Lugosi. It's funny, but sad, that the first time Lugosi didn't look, sound, or act like Lugosi, he gave his best performance!

From here it was downhill (for Bela) in their shared films. They have no scenes together in *Black Friday* (1940),

In all their screen pairings, Karloff was billed one slot above Lugosi.

and in *The Body Snatcher* (1945) Boris acts up an Oscar-worthy storm around Bela as he sits and watches, mute and morose. And with this, their eighth team-up, their association sputtered to an end.

In interviews granted after Lugosi's death, the one remaining pillar of the classic horror pantheon (Boris) spoke respectfully if not fondly of Bela, sometimes referring to him as "Poor Bela."

Letting down his hair in an early 1960s interview with Colin Edwards, Karloff said that Lugosi had led a "tragic, tragic life," adding: "I've always felt extremely sorry for him. In a way, he was his own worst enemy."

Producer Richard Gordon, who worked with and was befriended by both men, has provided a telling anecdote that reveals how Lugosi felt about the actor who had eclipsed him. Hanging in Gordon's New York office were autographed photos of many of the people with whom he had been associated—and office visitor Lugosi "got very upset" that his picture was hanging next to Karloff's. From then on, to keep the peace, Gordon made it a point to take down Karloff's photo when he knew Lugosi would be dropping by. And hang it up again after Lugosi left.

Karloff died in 1969, and in the years since fan appreciation of their work has grown tremendously. And in the Monster Kids' pit, the pendulum seems to be moving away from St. Boris to Blasphemous Bela. Far enough that when Gregory William Mank's 1990 book *Karloff and Lugosi* was expanded and reprinted, smart marketing called for a title change to *Bela Lugosi and Boris Karloff*. TW

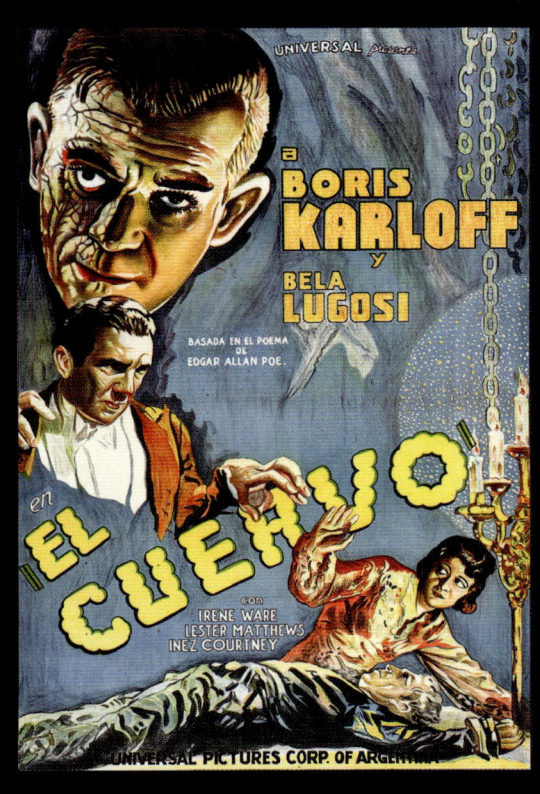

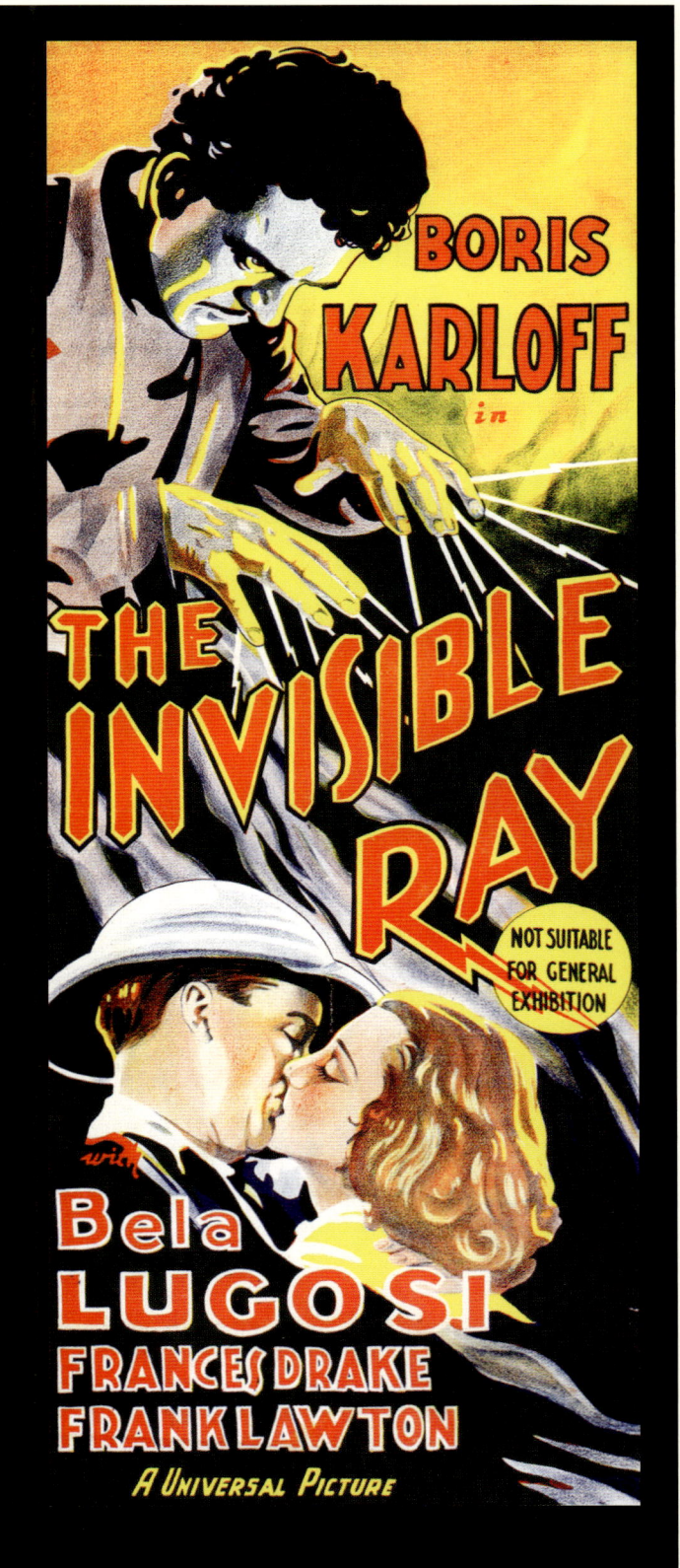

TOP LEFT: One-sheet poster for Universal's *The Black Cat* (Dir: Edgar G. Ulmer, 1934), the first movie to pair the studio's top two horror stars.

TOP MIDDLE: Boris Karloff's name is already bigger than Bela Lugosi's on this Argentinean one-sheet poster for their second major pairing from Universal, *The Raven* (Dir: Louis Friedlander, 1935).

ABOVE RIGHT: Australian daybill for Universal's *The Invisible Ray* (Dir: Lambert Hillyer, 1936), the duo's third major collaboration.

BOTTOM LEFT: The January 1936 edition of Street & Smith Publications, Inc.'s pulp *Movie Action Magazine* contained a 22-page "Full Length Novel" of *The Invisible Ray*, illustrated with stills from the Universal release.

BOTTOM MIDDLE: Spanish poster for Universal's *Son of Frankenstein* (Dir: Rowland V. Lee, 1939). A box office hit, it ushered in the next great cycle of horror films.

THE THRILLING THIRTIES

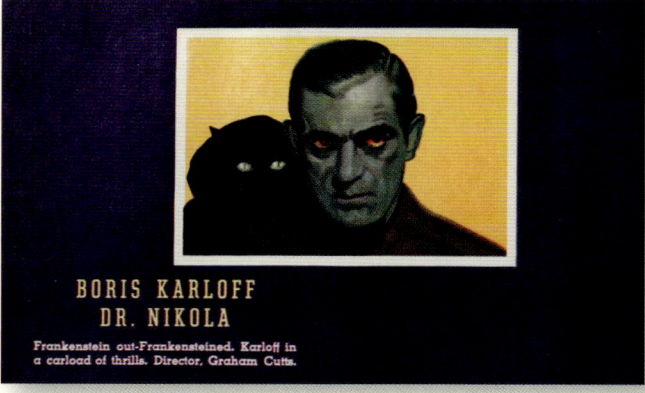

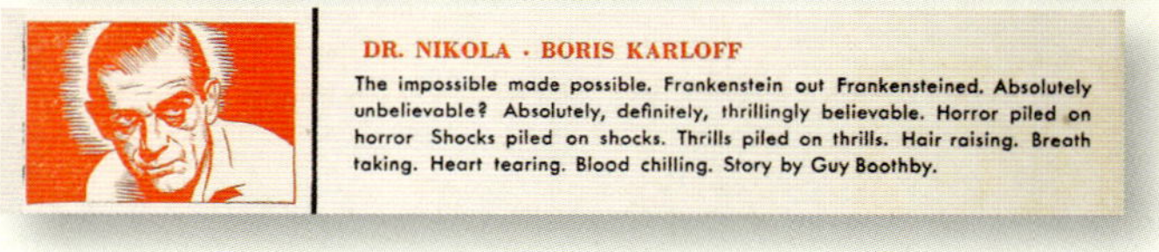

TOP LEFT: American trade publicity for the Gaumont-British movie *The Ghoul* (Dir: T. Hayes Hunter, 1933) from the Vol. 115, No. 2 edition of *Motion Picture Herald* (April 7, 1934). A success in the UK, box office returns were disappointing in the US despite the hullabaloo of this advertisement.

MIDDLE LEFT & BOTTOM LEFT: Gaumont-British announced "Sixteen Star Spangled Specials" with an eight-page color spread in the October 22, 1935 issue (Vol. 68, No. 95) of the US trade magazine *Film Daily*. This included an advertisement for *Dr. Nikola*, to be directed by Graham Cutts and starring Boris Karloff as the occultist criminal mastermind seeking the secret of immortality. Based on a series of five books by Australian-born writer Guy Boothby (1867–1905), the project never got off the ground, and instead Karloff returned to the UK in 1936 to make *The Man Who Changed His Mind*.

ABOVE RIGHT: American one-sheet for *Juggernaut* (Dir: Henry Edwards, 1936), a "quota quickie" crime movie that Boris Karloff filmed for independent German-born producer Julius Hagen (1884–1940) in the UK after he finished work on *The Man Who Changed His Mind* (1936).

THE ART OF HORROR MOVIES

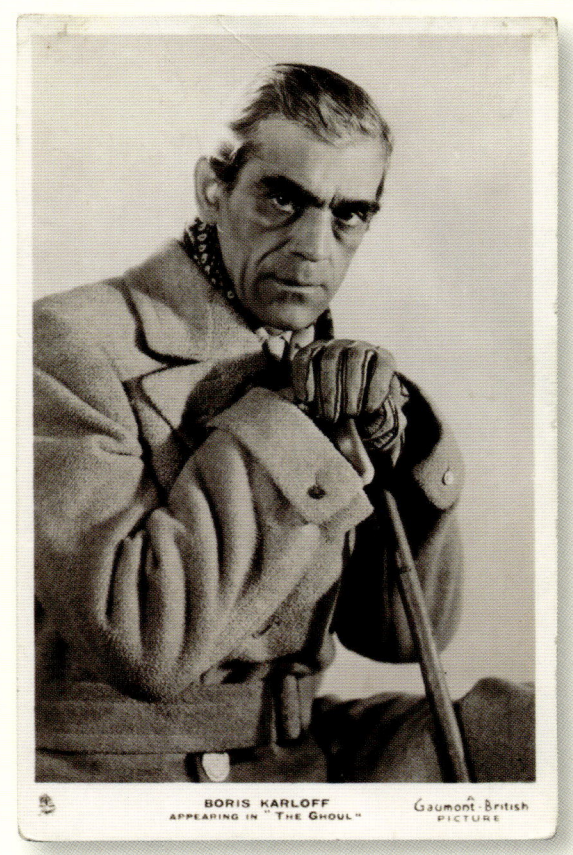

THIS PAGE: During the 1920s and '30s, pasteboard arcade cards or photographic postcards were often considered a cost-effective method by the studios and theaters to promote their movies and stars to the general public. Rarely saved, some of these cards are now highly collectible today.

TOP LEFT: Penny Arcade picture card promoting MGM's *London After Midnight* (1927) under its pre-release title, *The Hypnotist*. Manufactured by the Exhibit Supply Company of Chicago, the same cards were available for many years in weight or fortune-telling vending machines.

TOP RIGHT: Founded by Nazi refugee Heinrich Ross (1870–57), Ross-Verlag was a German postcard publisher (1912–41) that licensed its film star images directly from the studios. Dating from the late 1920s or early '30s, this hand-tinted postcard depicts Lon Chaney from MGM's *Mr. Wu* (1927).

BOTTOM LEFT: Issued by British postcard manufacturer Raphael Tuck & Sons in its "Real Photographs" series, this behind-the-scenes publicity photo of Boris Karloff (#109-S) promoted the Gaumont-British movie *The Ghoul* (1933), which marked the actor's return to the UK after nearly 25 years.

BOTTOM RIGHT: This rare promotional postcard for Columbia Pictures' *The Black Room* (Dir: Roy William Neill, 1935) was probably sent out by theaters to publicize the movie's release to their regular patrons. British author and journalist Graham Greene was a big fan of the film.

THE THRILLING THIRTIES

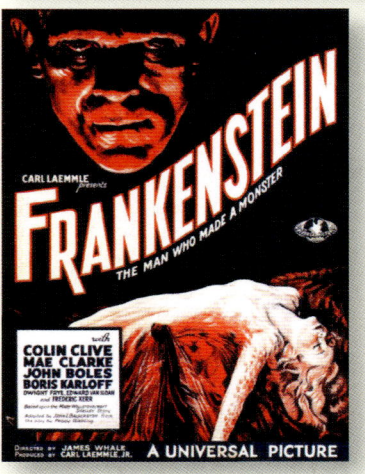

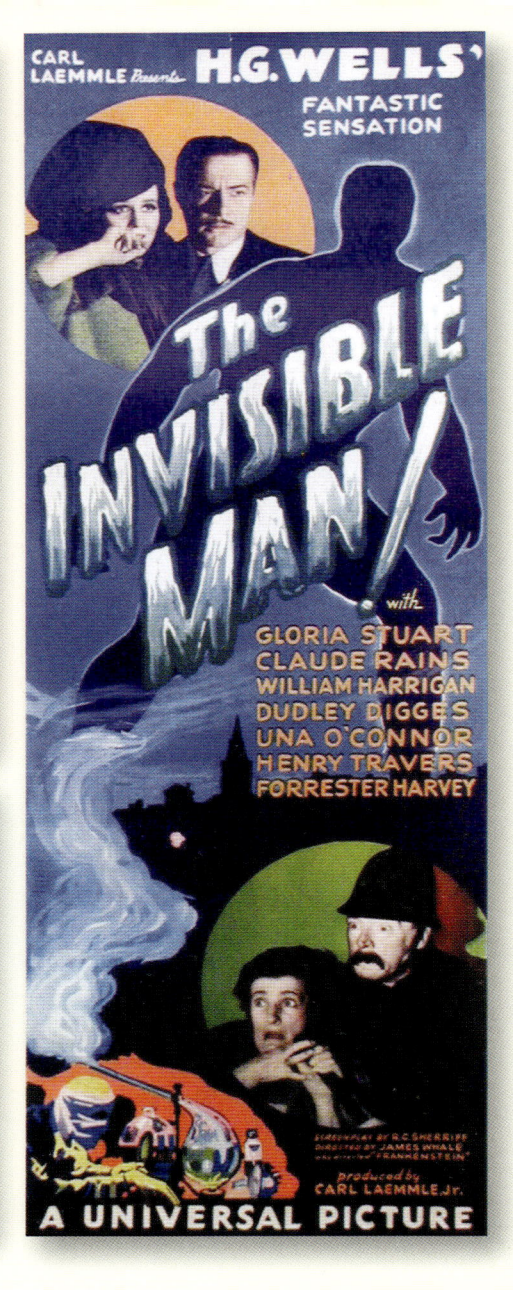

A Whale of a Director

In the 1930s, Universal became the abysm from which Hollywood nightmares crawled, and no director rode herd on their horrors like James Whale (1889–1957), a former graphic artist and newspaper cartoonist. After his blood-freezing *Frankenstein* in 1931, his subsequent shockers (*The Old Dark House* [1932], *The Invisible Man* [1933], *Bride of Frankenstein* [1935]) were as much quirky humor as horror, done in a sophisticated style that the directors of sequels couldn't match—or even approach. After Whale's Hollywood years, painting and occasional work in theater became his life—and in 1998, his life became the biopic *Gods and Monsters* with Ian McKellen as the director who raised fantastic cinema to its apex. It was shot in the summer of 1997, the 40th anniversary of Whale's death-by-drowning swimming pool suicide. TW

TOP LEFT: In an attempt to capitalize upon the box office success of Hammer's color remake, Rank Film Distributors reissued the original *Frankenstein* (1931) in the UK in 1957 with this gory quad poster.

BOTTOM LEFT: One of a very small number of American window cards for *Frankenstein* (1931) known to still exist. This sold for $89,625 at auction in 2015.

ABOVE RIGHT: The only known original insert card for Universal's *The Invisible Man* (Dir: James Whale, 1933), based on the 1897 novel by H.G. Wells. Saved by a former Iowa movie usher, this insert sold at auction in 2007 for $80,500.

BOTTOM MIDDLE: Glass slide produced by Consolidated Film Industries, Inc., to promote *The Invisible Man* (1933). These slides were projected on to the screen of a movie theater to inform patrons about forthcoming attractions.

ABOVE LEFT: *Boris Karloff—Frankenstein* (2015), acrylic and ink on collage by British artist Dave McKean. "I always make notes in sketchbooks first for almost everything," explains the artist. "It helps to see it represented on paper—I can judge it then. While it's only swimming around my head, it's too insubstantial. It feels like I'm clutching at remembering a dream until I commit to paper."

ABOVE RIGHT: *Karloff: The Monster* (2008), oils on canvas board portrait by British artist Les Edwards of the actor in *Bride of Frankenstein* (1935). "You don't often see the Monster from the side," the artist points out. "I was fascinated with the highlight that outlines his profile. It really defines the whole image. The art of lighting."

RIGHT: Pre-production design sketch for *Frankenstein* (1931) by British-born art director Charles D. Hall (aka Daniel Hall, 1888–1970). With the ousting of studio founder Carl Laemmle in 1936, Hall left Universal for Hal Roach Studios, and he later became well-known for his watercolor paintings.

THE THRILLING THIRTIES

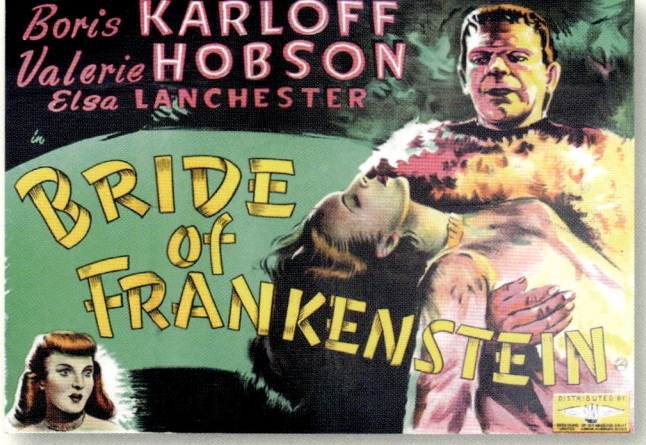

FAR LEFT: Magazine column "written" by Universal president Carl Laemmle promoting *The Bride of Frankenstein* (1935) with a heading illustration probably by studio artist Fred Kulz.

LEFT: Late 1940s or early '50s British reissue quad for *The Bride of Frankenstein*, displaying an "H" certificate.

ABOVE RIGHT: *To a New World of Gods and Monsters* (2016), stained glass window by American artist Micah Lee Mowbray. "Delicate glass chips and threads are ladled over with molten glass and rolled into sensuous lines and translucent shapes," reveals the artist. "Fracture-Streamer glass enhances the hauntingly beautiful Bride in all her patchworked glory!"

THE ART OF HORROR MOVIES

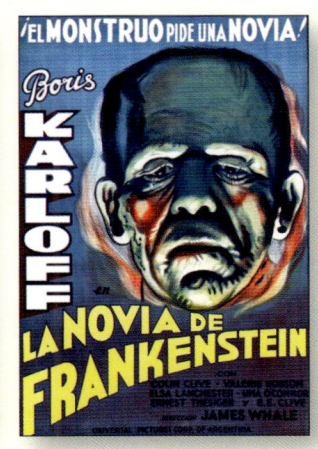

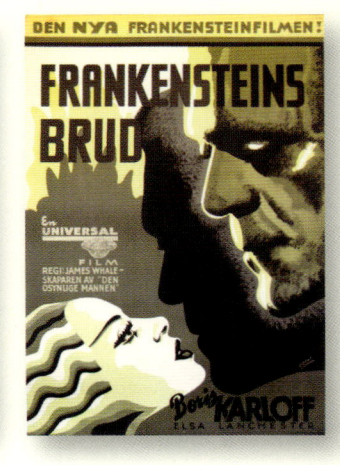

TOP LEFT: American window card for Universal's *The Bride of Frankenstein*. Window cards were overprinted with additional information and displayed by the local community in the windows of restaurants and stores.

BOTTOM LEFT: American publicity herald for *The Bride of Frankenstein*. Movie heralds were usually a folded, single-sheet flyer, printed on both sides and over-printed with the name of the movie theater.

BOTTOM MIDDLE, LEFT: Modernistic French *affiche* for *The Bride of Frankenstein* by Ukraine-born French artist Constantin Belinsky (1904–99).

BOTTOM MIDDLE, RIGHT: This Argentinean poster for *The Bride of Frankenstein* uses an image of Karloff, but totally ignores the Bride herself!

BOTTOM RIGHT: This Swedish poster by Walter Fuchs for *The Bride of Frankenstein* is also painted in a flat, modernistic style.

TOP RIGHT: *The Bride* (2008), pencil on paper by British artist Les Edwards. "The Universal monster movies produced any number of iconic images," he explains, "and I think this is one of the most striking. It started out as a preliminary drawing for a painting, but it ended up as a much more finished image than I originally intended."

THE THRILLING THIRTIES

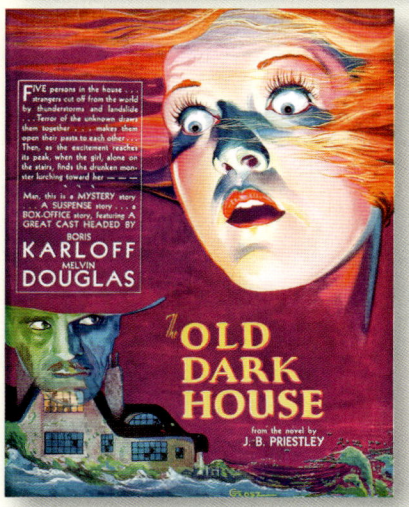

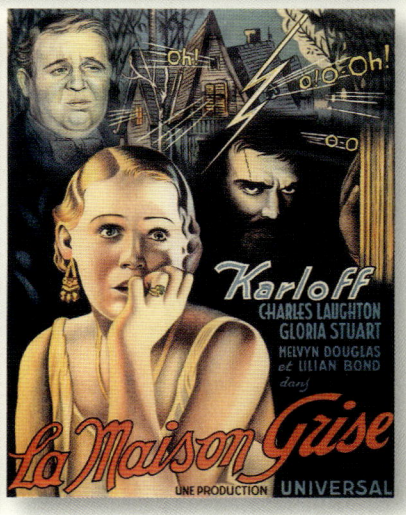

The Old Dark House

Based on the 1927 novel *Benighted* by British author J. (John) B. (Boynton) Priestley, director James Whale's sardonic follow-up to *Frankenstein* (1931) was the blackly comic *The Old Dark House* (1932). Although Boris Karloff is wasted as the menacing mute butler Morgan (an opening caption assures us that it really is the same actor from the earlier film), the wonderful family of potentially homicidal Welsh eccentrics includes Ernest Thesiger's cadaverous Horace Femm, Eva Moore as his religious fanatic sister Rebecca, Brember Wills as mad pyromaniac Saul, and Elspeth Dudgeon (billed as "John Dudgeon") as the bedridden 102-year-old Sir Roderick Femm. Melvyn Douglas, Raymond Massey, Gloria Stuart, Charles Laughton, and Lilian Bond play the unlucky travellers trapped overnight by a storm in the foreboding abode of the title. Thought lost for many years, a print was discovered by director Curtis Harrington in 1968.

TOP LEFT: American half-sheet poster for Universal's *The Old Dark House* (1932). For this black comedy, James Whale was reunited with cinematographer Arthur Edeson and set designer Charles D. Hall from *Frankenstein* (1931).

BOTTOM LEFT: Károly Grósz's artwork for this trade advertisement for *The Old Dark House* (1932), from Universal's *The Box Office Book 1932–33*.

BOTTOM MIDDLE: This original Belgian poster for *The Old Dark House* (1932) emphasized Charles Laughton's name in the billing.

ABOVE RIGHT: Original brush and ink on board artwork by prolific Belgian movie poster artist "Wik." This was produced for the 1947 re-release of *The Old Dark House*.

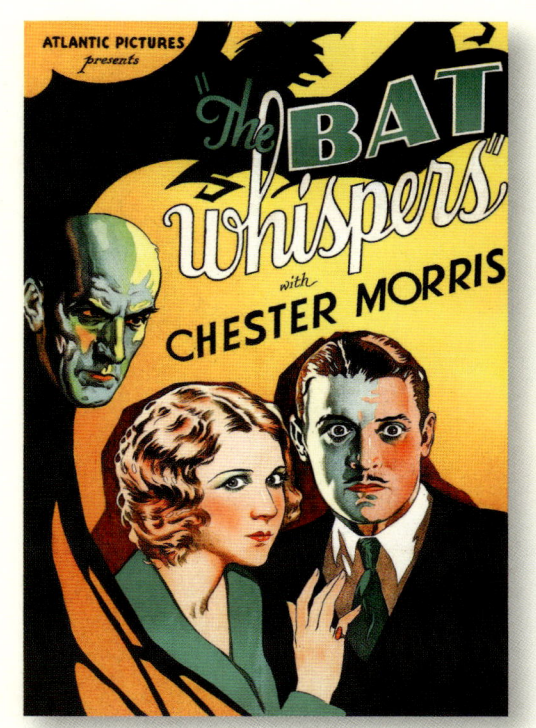

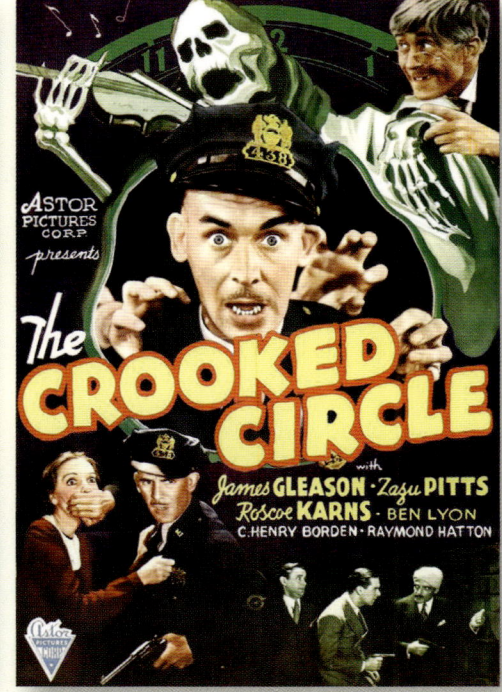

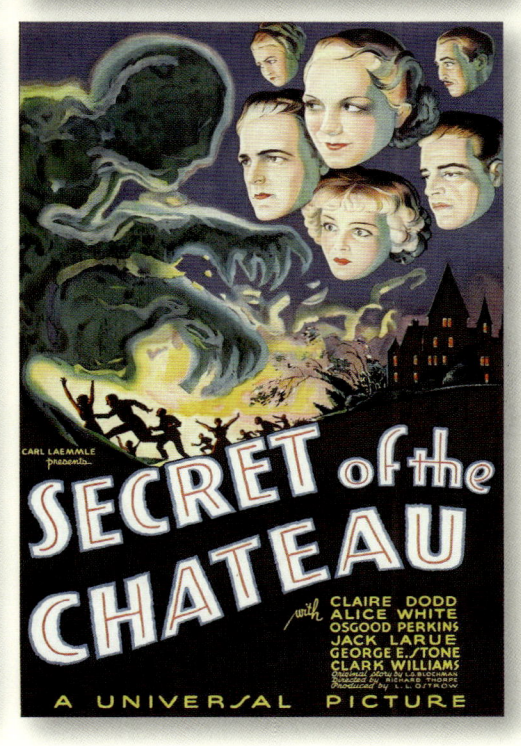

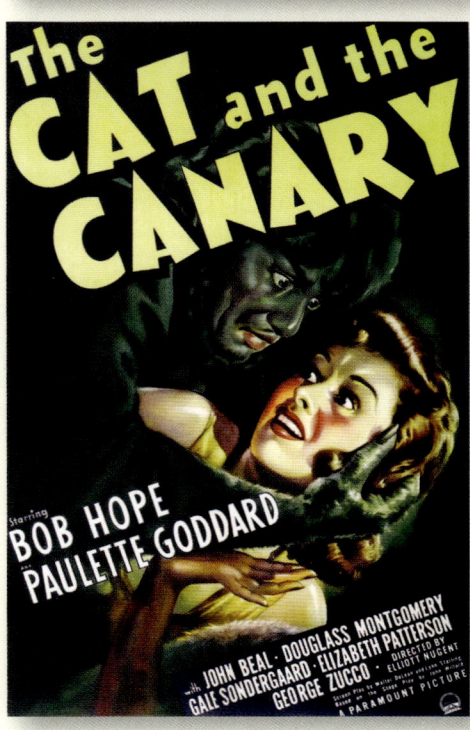

TOP LEFT: One-sheet poster for the 1938 Atlantic Pictures reissue of *The Bat Whispers* (1930) by American artist and actor Alvan Cordell "Hap" Hadley (1895–1976).

TOP MIDDLE: One-sheet poster for the Astor Pictures Corp. reissue of the creaky horror-comedy *The Crooked Circle* (Dir: H. Bruce Humberstone, 1932). This became the first film shown on television in March 1933.

TOP RIGHT: Midget window card for Columbia Pictures' *Night of Terror* (Dir: Ben[jamin] Stoloff, 1933). At the end, a crazed lunatic warns the audience not to reveal the identity of the killer.

BOTTOM LEFT: Swedish poster by Walter Fuchs for Universal's *Secret of the Blue Room* (Dir: Kurt Neumann, 1933).

BOTTOM MIDDLE: A wily French police detective attempts to capture his old nemesis in Universal's *Secret of the Chateau* (Dir: Richard Thorpe, 1934).

BOTTOM RIGHT: One-sheet poster for Paramount's *The Cat and the Canary* (Dir: Elliott Nugent, 1939), a comedy remake based on the 1922 play by John Willard.

THE THRILLING THIRTIES

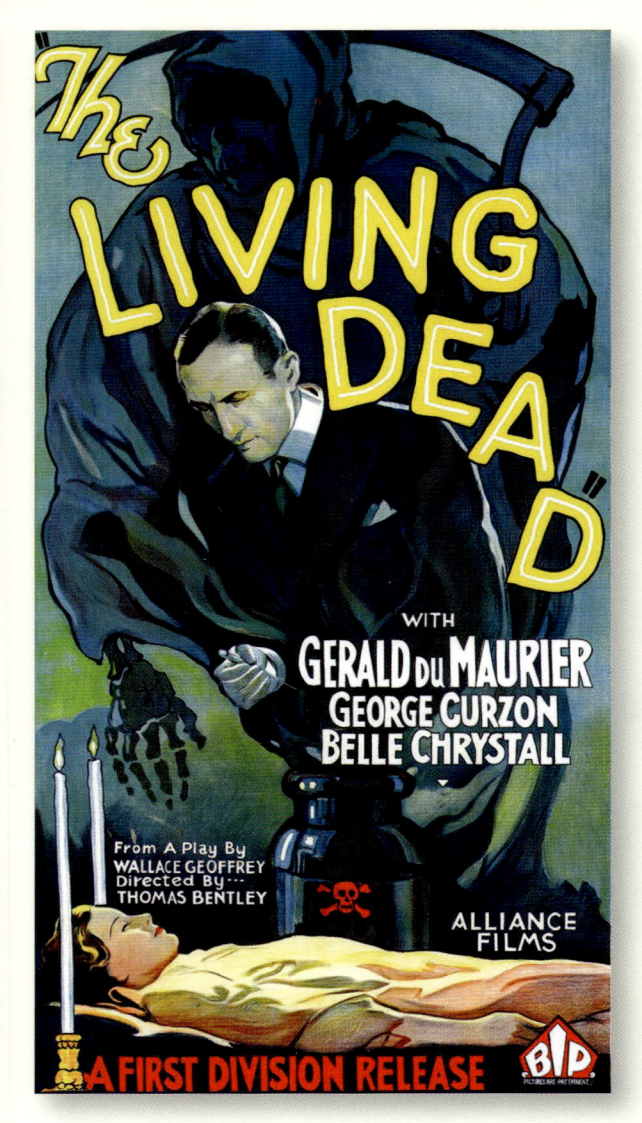

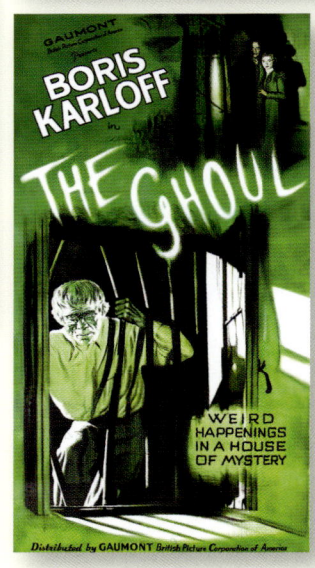

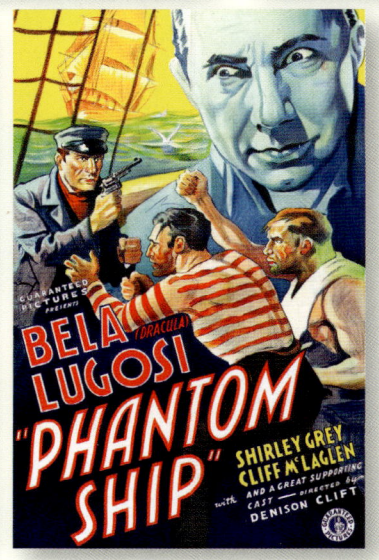

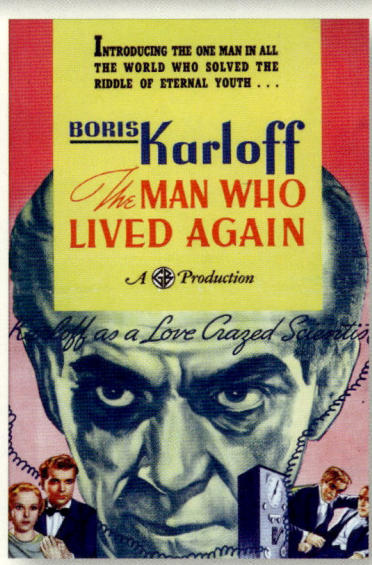

BOTTOM MIDDLE, LEFT: 1934 American three-sheet poster for *The Ghoul* (Dir: T. Hayes Hunter, 1933), Boris Karloff's first British movie since he found success in Hollywood. Loosely based on the 1928 novel by Frank King, the film was lost for many years, until a print was discovered in 1968.

ABOVE LEFT: American stone litho three-sheet poster for the 1936 reissue of the British film *The Scotland Yard Mystery* (1934), re-titled *The Living Dead*.

TOP MIDDLE: Stylized Swedish poster by John Mauritz "Moje" Åslund (1904–68) for Gaumont-British Picture's *The Clairvoyant* (aka *The Evil Mind*, 1935).

BOTTOM MIDDLE, RIGHT: Bela Lugosi's first British film, *The Mystery of the Mary Celeste* (Dir: Denison Clift, 1935), was re-titled *Phantom Ship* when released in the US.

BOTTOM RIGHT: Boris Karloff starred in *The Man Who Changed His Mind* (Dir: Robert Stevenson, 1936), re-titled *The Man Who Lived Again* for its US release.

TOP RIGHT: 1940 Turkish poster by Tarik Uzmen for Pathé's *The Dark Eyes of London* (Dir: Walter Summers, 1939), re-titled *The Human Monster* in America.

THE ART OF HORROR MOVIES

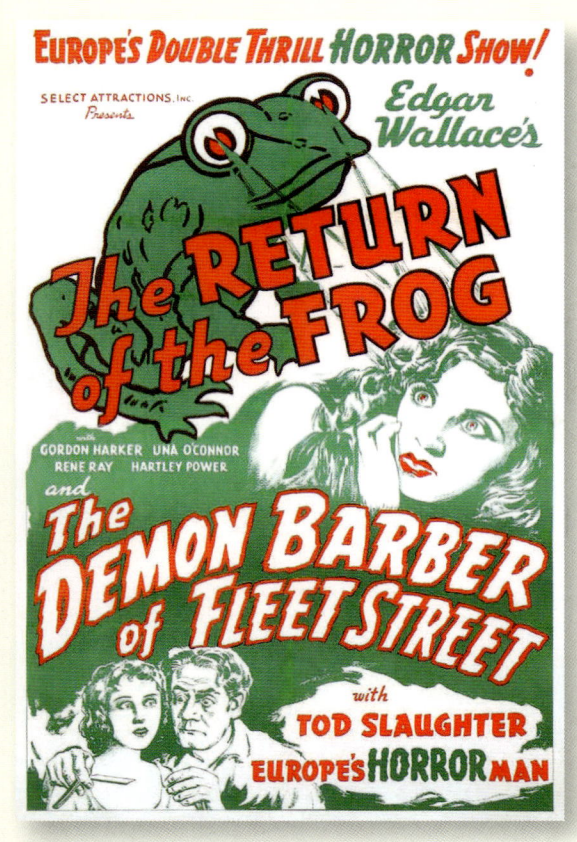

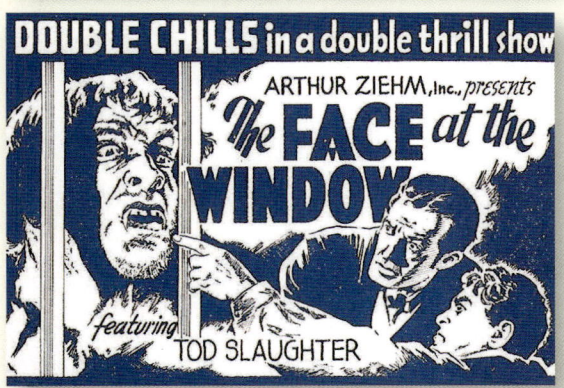

"The Horror Man of Europe"

Tod Slaughter (Norman Carter Slaughter, 1885–1956) was born in Newcastle upon Tyne, England. He began his career as a barnstorming stage actor-manager, touring the UK in revivals of "blood-and-thunder" Victorian melodramas. During the 1930s and '40s, a number of these productions were cheaply filmed as "quota quickies" by theatrical agent turned producer and director George King (1899–1966), including *The Crimes of Stephen Hawke* (1936), *The Ticket of Leave Man* (1937), *Sexton Blake and the Hooded Terror* (1938), and *Crimes at the Dark House* (1940), with Slaughter usually cast as the cackling villain. His most famous role was as Sweeney Todd, the Demon Barber of Fleet Street, whom he portrayed on stage an estimated 2,000 times, in King's 1936 movie of the same name, and in an obscure 1954 short film.

TOP LEFT: American one-sheet poster for the 1939 double bill release of the Edgar Wallace adaptation *The Return of the Frog* (1938) and Tod Slaughter's best-known film, *Sweeney Todd* (Dir: George King, 1936), slightly re-titled for US audiences.

BOTTOM LEFT: 1940 press advertisement for the American release of *The Face at the Window* (Dir: George King, 1939), based on the "famous melodrama" by F. Brooke Warren.

BOTTOM RIGHT: Poster by R. Mancinelli for the 1947 Italian release of *Crimes at the Dark House* (Dir: George King, 1940), loosely based on the 1859 novel *The Woman in White* by Wilkie Collins.

TOP RIGHT: *Tod Slaughter* (2016), oils on board portrait by Les Edwards of the actor in *The Face at the Window* (1939). "I watched several of Tod Slaughter's movies to research this portrait," reveals the artist. "His acting style was certainly theatrical by modern standards, but he brought a kind of insane glee to the screen which I rather liked."

THE THRILLING THIRTIES

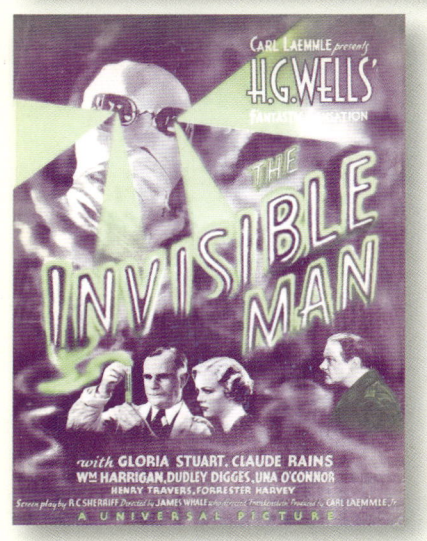

Women in Horror: 1930s

From the moment she was told to "Scream Ann, scream for your life!" in *King Kong* (1933), Fay Wray (1907–2004) became the archetypal scream queen of 1930s cinema, whether she was being hunted through the jungle by a madman in *The Most Dangerous Game* (aka *Hounds of Zaroff*, 1932) or menaced by Lionel Atwill's crazed creators in *Doctor X* (1932), *The Vampire Bat* (1933) or *Mystery of the Wax Museum* (1933). Director James Whale had Gloria Stuart (1910–2010) threatened by Boris Karloff's mute butler in *The Old Dark House* (1932) and Claude Rains's see-through psycho in *The Invisible Man* (1933), while Gloria Holden (1903–91) turned up as a distant relative of the Count's in *Dracula's Daughter* (1936) and British-born Elsa Lanchester (1902–86) was the made-to-order *Bride of Frankenstein* (1935), created as a mate for Karloff's lovesick Monster.

ABOVE RIGHT: Joel McCrea and Fay Wray's shipwreck survivors were hunted by the mad Count Zaroff (Leslie Banks) in RKO Radio Pictures' *The Most Dangerous Game* (aka *Hounds of Zaroff*, 1932), based on the 1924 short story by Richard Connell.

BOTTOM LEFT: This window card for Universal's *The Invisible Man* (Dir: James Whale, 1933) sold for more than $5,000 at auction in 1992.

BOTTOM MIDDLE: Elsa Lanchester not only appeared as the mate for the Monster in Universal's *Bride of Frankenstein* (1935), but also as author Mary Shelley.

TOP LEFT: American half-sheet poster for *Dracula's Daughter* (Dir: Lambert Hillyer, 1936), which ended Universal's first great cycle of horror movies.

THE ART OF HORROR MOVIES

RIGHT: *Blood and Black Velvet* (2016), stained glass window by American artist Micah Lee Mowbray. "Tattooing pales in comparison to my love of stained glass," she explains. "Still, I enjoy cross-pollinating these chosen art forms. I collected this brilliant 'blood glass' ten years ago, waiting for just the right window. My own tattoo parlor is located in the middle of nowhere, where no one can hear you scream."

THE THRILLING THIRTIES

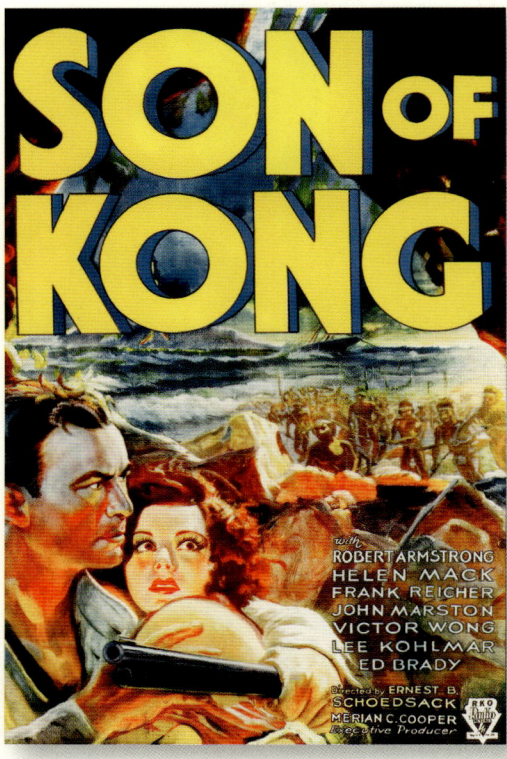

TOP RIGHT: This oversized Swedish stone lithographic poster for RKO Radio Pictures' *King Kong* (Dir: Ernest B. Schoedsack and Merian C. Cooper, 1933) is based on the design of the American Giant Upright Six-Sheet ("twice as tall as a man!"). It sold at auction in 2015 for just over $31,000.

TOP LEFT: To promote *King Kong* (1933), RKO Radio Pictures came up with a promotional campaign that included this die-cut lithographic door hanger (with theater details to be stamped on the reverse). Originally available for $7.50 per 1,000, an example sold at auction in 2009 for $1,434.

BOTTOM RIGHT: Part of RKO's promotional campaign for *King Kong* (1933) was a series of six, five-column daily strips by artist Glenn Cravath to run for free in local newspapers. This original ink-on-board artwork for the first strip in the sequence sold at auction in 2007 for $17,925.

TOP MIDDLE: This "Style A" one-sheet poster for RKO Radio Pictures' *Son of Kong* (Dir: Ernest B. Schoedsack, 1933) by American artist Glenn Cravath (1897–1964) doesn't even feature the titular character but instead concentrates on the two leading actors, Robert Armstrong and Helen Mack.

BOTTOM LEFT: At least this dynamic fold-out campaign advertisement for *Son of Kong* (1933) by Canadian-born commercial artist Karl Godwin (1893–1962), from the RKO Radio Pictures 1933–1934 exhibitor book, features an image of the 12-feet-tall white ape in the background.

THE ART OF HORROR MOVIES

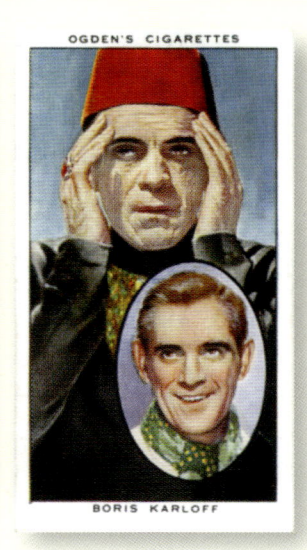

Stars on Cards

Long before the advent of bubble gum cards, there was the less healthy hobby in Europe of collecting cigarette or tobacco cards. These cards were originally issued by cigarette manufacturers in 1880s America to stiffen their paper packaging and advertise a particular brand. When they proved incredibly popular with the public, cards soon evolved into a marketing ploy to encourage people to buy more cigarettes. The hobby of collecting tobacco cards is known as "Cartophily". The 1938 "Actors: Natural & Character Studies" series of 50 cards from British brand Ogden's included cards #25 [TOP LEFT] and #27 [TOP MIDDLE LEFT] depicting actors Sir Seymour Hicks and Boris Karloff as both themselves and their respective characters in Twickenham Film Distributors' *Scrooge* (1935) and Universal's *The Mummy* (1932). Another British manufacturer, Gallaher, issued the 48-card "Film Episodes" series in 1936 that included #10: Universal's *The Raven* (1935) [TOP MIDDLE] and #39: MGM's *Hands of Orlac* (aka *Mad Love*, 1935) [TOP MIDDLE RIGHT]. Lon Chaney, "der Meister der Filmmasks," was popular with German smokers, with Salem Bilder including a number of cards featuring the Hollywood actor in its 124-card "Die Welt in Bildern," (The World in Pictures) series of 1928, including #78/3: MGM's *Mr. Wu* (1927) [MIDDLE LEFT] and #78/1: *The Unholy Three* (1925) [MIDDLE MIDDLE]. The latter movie was also represented [TOP RIGHT] in the second series of Salem's premium "Goldfilm" series from 1933, which had gold-foiled backgrounds. Another actor featured in Salem's "Die Welt in Bildern" series was German star Paul Wegener, who appeared on card #76/1 in Terra-Filmkunst's *Svengali* (1927) [MIDDLE RIGHT]. Tobacco cards could be collected and glued into albums, as was the case with this page of John Player & Sons' *An Album of Film Stars: Third Series* (1938) from the UK [BOTTOM RIGHT], featuring "autographed" cards of Conrad Veidt and Anton Walbrook.

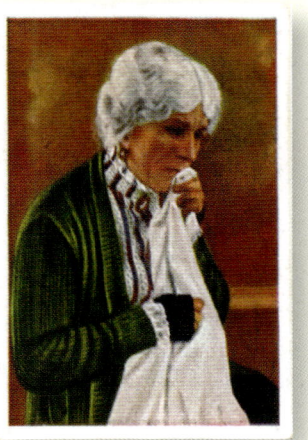

THE THRILLING THIRTIES

LEFT: *White Zombie* (1994), Prismacolor markers by American artist Jeff Preston, done for *Monsterscene* #3 (Fall, 1994). "A single-page illustration of Madge Bellamy as Madeline Short Parker," explains the artist, "an ethereal beauty that I wanted to juxtapose with the hypnotic eyes of Bela Lugosi in the background. This was my first illustration for *Monsterscene* magazine."

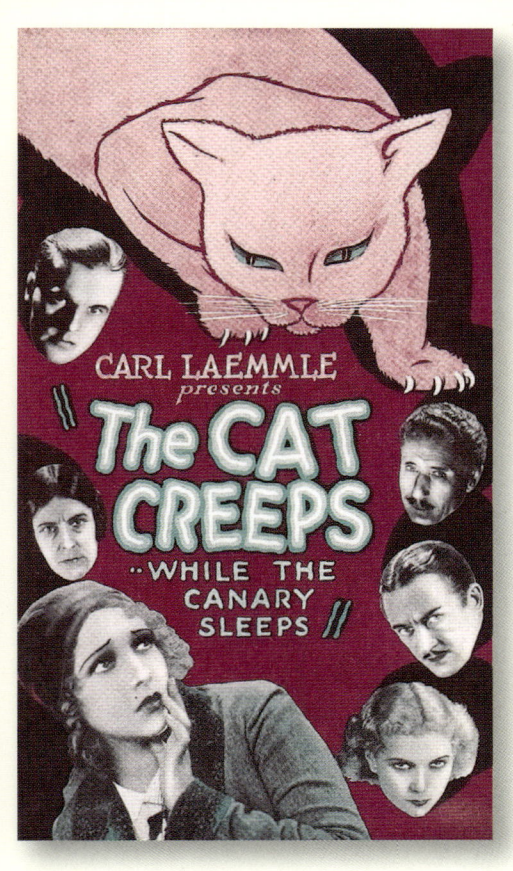

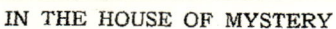

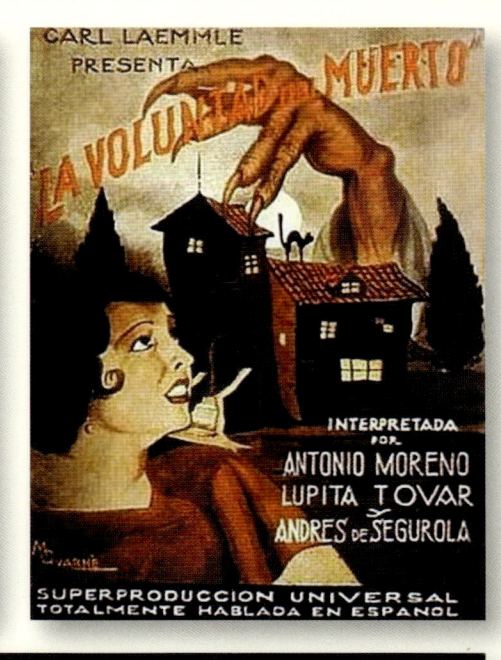

The Mislaid Moggy

The last film directed by Rupert Julian (*The Phantom of the Opera*, 1925), based on John Willard's 1922 stage play *The Cat and the Canary*, *The Cat Creeps* (1930) was Universal Pictures' first full sound horror movie and featured an impressive cast that included former theater star Helen Twelvetrees, Jean Hersholt, Neil Hamilton, Montagu Love, and Lawrence Grant. The American version is long thought lost, although a few clips appear in the 1932 short *Boo*, and the sound discs are known to survive. As they did with other movies (including *Dracula*, 1931), Universal filmed a Spanish-language version (*La voluntad del muerto*), which directors George Melford and Enrique Tovar Ávalos shot at night on the same sets. Starring Antonio Moreno and Lupita Tova, it also no longer exists, and the studio used the title again in 1946 for an unrelated horror thriller.

TOP LEFT: Front cover of the promotional herald for Universal's now-lost old dark house mystery *The Cat Creeps* (1930).

TOP MIDDLE: This inside spread of *The Cat Creeps* herald references the original play with the tagline: "The Cat Creeps . . . While the Canary Sleeps."

BOTTOM LEFT: Press advertisement for *The Cat Creeps*.

BOTTOM MIDDLE: The February 28, 1931 issue of the British comic *Boy's Cinema* featured a photoplay adaptation *The Cat Creeps*.

BOTTOM RIGHT: Title lobby card for *The Cat Creeps*. Supporting actress Elizabeth Patterson reprised her role in the remake, *The Cat and the Canary* (1939).

TOP RIGHT: Poster for George Melford and Enrique Tovar Ávalos's now-lost Spanish-language version of Universal's *The Cat Creeps*.

THE THRILLING THIRTIES

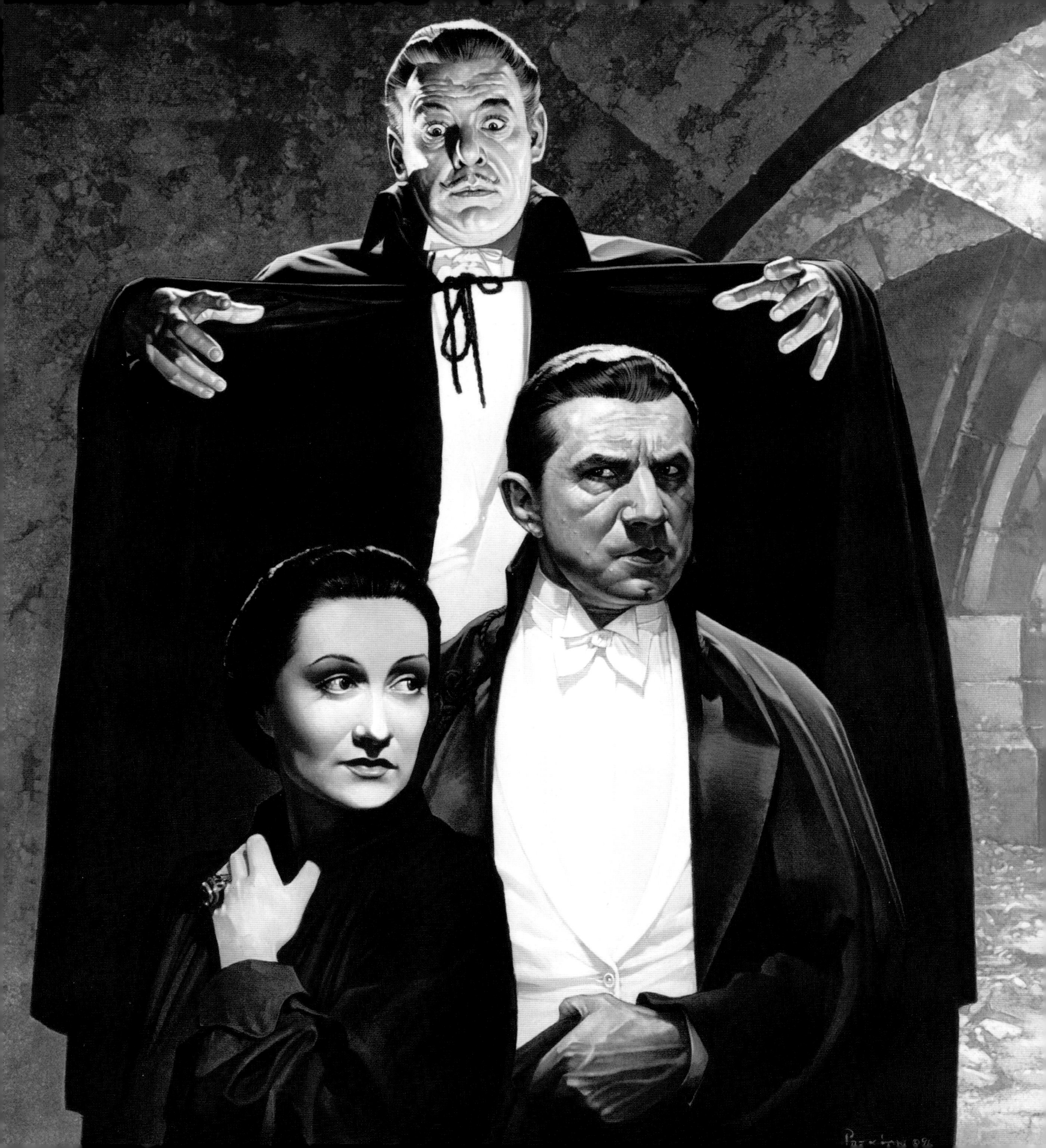

LEFT: *Family Dracula* (1996), Prismacolor markers by American artist Jeff Preston. "This was done for *Monsterscene #7* (Spring, 1996) as a double-page spread," he recalls. "These are always a challenge—you want your art to stand alone, but you also have to keep in mind copy will print over most of the illustration. On a personal note I feel this illustration, above all others, stands as the pinnacle of what I was able to achieve with my marker technique."

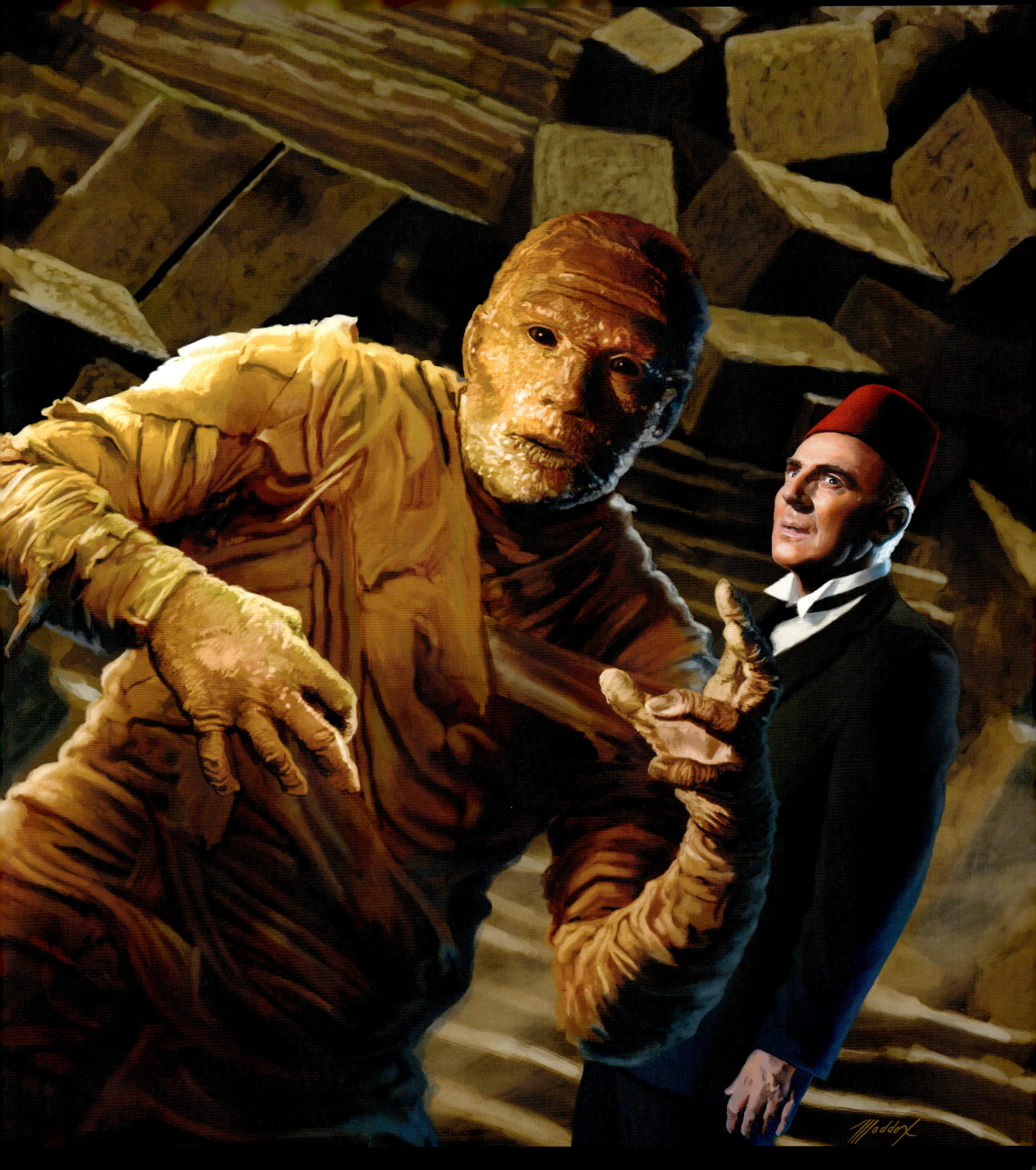
Maddox

3

THE FRIGHTENING FORTIES

BARRY FORSHAW

"What is America but beauty queens, millionaires, stupid records, and Hollywood?"

ADOLF HITLER

> "I wrote always. And it saved my life. When the Nazis forced me to leave Germany, who wanted an engineer? But a writer can work anywhere… Today, nobody lives better than I do. I have an estate, fifty acres overlooking the mountains, and every night I say 'Heil Hitler!' because without that son of a bitch I wouldn't be in Three Rivers, California, I'd still be in Berlin!"
> Curt Siodmak

GIVEN THE DRACONIAN limitations of what could be shown in terms of the gruesome and macabre within the strict film censorship of the 1940s, it is amazing just how unsettling and disturbing many of the horror films made in that era were—possibly because directors were forced by these restrictions to use their ingenuity. They became adept at conveying the sensations of horror to the audience by using (but subverting) the permissible. Some producers, of course, even made a virtue of the power of suggestion—notably the celebrated Val Lewton.

Monster mashes were the order of the day, with a motley collection of creatures shoe-horned into the same film (often with diminishing—but still entertaining—returns), from Roy William Neill's *Frankenstein Meets the Wolf Man* (1943), to the crowded *House of Frankenstein* (1944) and *House of Dracula* (1945), both directed by Erle C. Kenton.

Trends in horror cinema are always cyclical: the iconic monsters of the movies—notably Count Dracula, the Frankenstein Monster (and his creator), the Wolf Man, and the Mummy—all stalked cinema screens in the 1930s, and this cadre of the ghastly and the grotesque were subsequently revived by Hammer Films in the 1950s and '60s, with filmic life still being pumped into the reinvigorated corpses of these creations even today.

But this recycling process also produced another syndrome, which first became apparent in the 1940s—genre exhaustion. The terrifying tropes that were so effective in their debuts became shopworn with overuse or (even worse) credibility shredding parody, as in the series of films in which Bud Abbott and Lou Costello met all the great movie monsters. Ironically, this series, despite the presence of the above-the-title comedians, is still cherished by horror aficionados for the opportunities it gave the actors who helped shape the genre (including Boris Karloff and Bela Lugosi) to play iconic monsters once again, in relatively non-parodic fashion.

But before mockery and cliché set in, some memorable contributions to the horror field continued to appear during the 1940s—and not just from the important studios such as Universal (the spiritual home of the monster movie)—but also from poverty-row outfits such as Republic, PRC, and Monogram. Films from the latter studios may have been made on budgets that would not have covered the cost of Bette Davis's hairdresser, but some gems were to be found among the many cheap, forgettable items churned out by these studios. They may have paid directors less, but they still utilized such reliable merchants of menace as Karloff and Lugosi, while Republic Pictures even managed to employ the once A-list Erich von Stroheim in *The Lady and the Monster* (1944).

But this recycling process also produced another syndrome, which first became apparent in the 1940s—genre exhaustion. The terrifying tropes that were so effective in their debuts became shopworn with overuse or (even worse) credibility shredding parody, as in the series of films in which Bud Abbott and Lou Costello met all the great movie monsters. Ironically, this series, despite the presence of the above-the-title comedians, is still cherished by aficionados.

However, a particular low-rent nadir was reached by William "One-Shot" Beaudine—so named for his speedy set-ups—in *The Ape Man* (1943), with Bela Lugosi's scenery-chewing performance unable to redeem this desperate piece of filmmaking.

The supernatural reigned in the horror and fantasy genre of the period, especially in a slew of whimsical comedies. But most fondly remembered are the more serious efforts, notably from Universal. Well aware just how lucrative the creations of Mary Shelley and Bram Stoker had been for the studio, they began looking around for new franchises, such as the hirsute monster created by Curt Siodmak, the writer who came up with *The Wolf Man* (1941), in which Lon Chaney, Jr. played the tormented lycanthrope. Also added to the canon were the series of "Inner Sanctum Mysteries," most of them produced largely by rote, but with the odd splash of imagination.

And then there was the army of mad scientists. This breed ran wild in the 1940s in a dizzying succession of failed attempts to create monsters and sexually seductive beast women. Even today, the real pleasure of this sub-genre is the authority and command given to a series of

PREVIOUS SPREAD: *The Mummy's Hand* (2012), pencil and digital by American artist Mark Maddox, created for *Mad Scientist* #25 (Summer, 2012). "My first Universal Monster cover!" exclaims the artist. "I had waited to do one for so long."

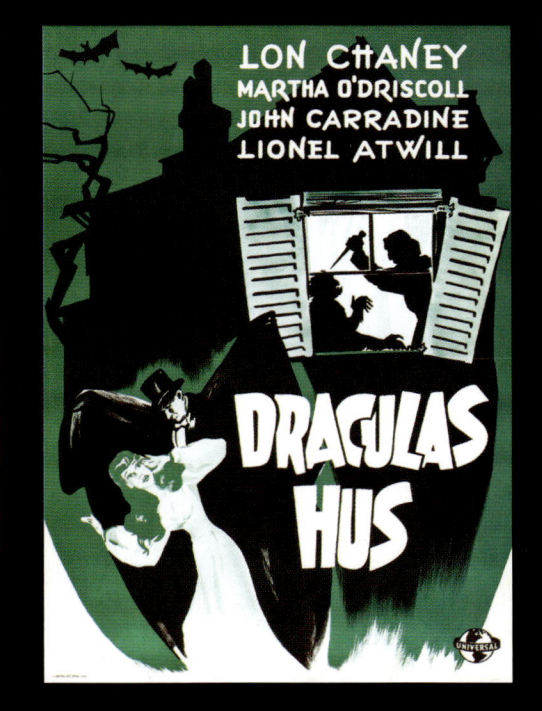

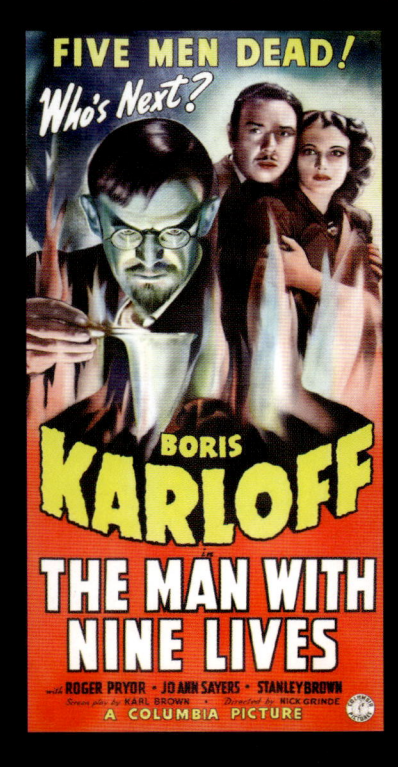

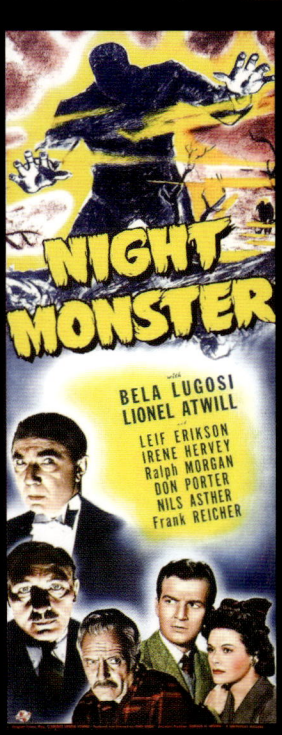

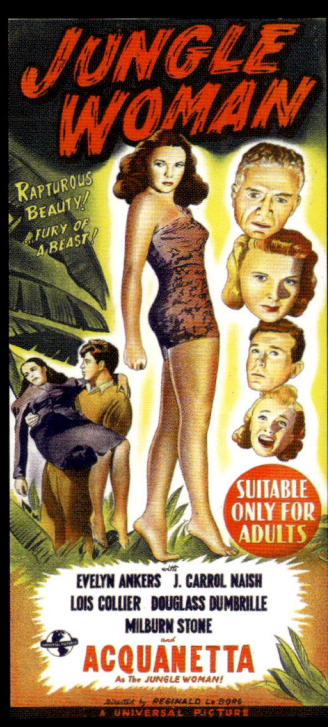

TOP LEFT: British quad reissue poster for Universal's *House of Frankenstein* (Dir: Erle C. Kenton, 1944) with "X" certificate.

TOP RIGHT: 1946 Swedish poster for *House of Dracula* (Dir: Erle C. Kenton, 1945), the last serious entry in the classic monster cycle dating back to *Dracula* (1931).

BOTTOM LEFT: American three-sheet poster for Columbia's *The Man with Nine Lives* (Dir: Nick Grindé, 1940). Boris Karloff's obsessed Dr. Leon Kravaal is awakened from an accidental cryogenic sleep and soon begins experimenting again.

BOTTOM MIDDLE, LEFT: Insert card for Universal's *Night Monster* (Dir: Ford Beebe, 1942), which wasted the talents of top-billed Bela Lugosi and Lionel Atwill in a neat little B movie involving a paraplegic murderer (Ralph Morgan) prowling an isolated mansion.

BOTTOM MIDDLE, RIGHT: Australian daybill for *Jungle Woman* (Dir: Reginald Le Borg, 1944), the brief middle entry in Universal's trilogy about "Paula, the Ape Woman" (here played for the second and final time by the exotic Acquanetta).

BOTTOM RIGHT: Trade advertisement for Republic's *The Lady and the Monster* (Dir: George Sherman, 1944), based on the 1942 novel *Donovan's Brain* by Curt Siodmak.

THE FRIGHTENING FORTIES

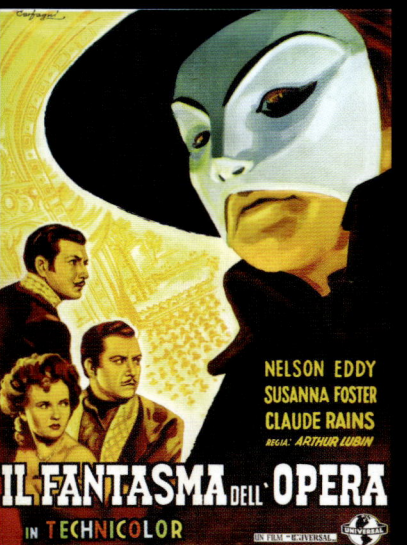

TOP LEFT: Six-sheet poster for Columbia's *The Return of the Vampire* (Dir: Lew Landers, 1943), which saw Bela Lugosi's return to playing a vampire after *Dracula* (1931).

BOTTOM LEFT: Italian *duo-foglio* for Universal's *Phantom of the Opera* (Dir: Arthur Lubin, 1943) by F. Carfagni. Filmed in lavish Technicolor, this remake of the 1925 Lon Chaney classic is the only Universal monster movie to earn Academy Awards.

BOTTOM MIDDLE: Original 1948 artwork by Anselmo Ballester (1897–1974) for the Italian *quattro-foglio* for *The Face Behind the Mask* (1941). Ballester became the pioneer and founder of the *Pittori del cinema* (Cinema Artists) movement from the end of the silent era through to the early 1960s.

ABOVE RIGHT: Anselmo Ballester's *quattro-foglio* for Columbia's *The Face Behind the Mask* (Dir: Robert Florey, 1941), a crime drama given a nihilistic twist by Peter Lorre's horrifically burned criminal, who hides his face behind a lifelike mask.

THE ART OF HORROR MOVIES

— 84 —

underwritten demented boffins by such impeccable character actors as the British Lionel Atwill and George Zucco. The latter glowered in James P. Hogan's *The Mad Ghoul* (1943), while Atwill enlivened Ford Beebe's *Night Monster* (1942), and both actors—when not conducting dangerous experiments in these types of films—were facing down Basil Rathbone's Sherlock Holmes in a frequently macabre series directed by Roy William Neill. *The Pearl of Death* (1944), for instance, featured a memorable but largely unseen monster, the "Hoxton Creeper," played by the acromegalic actor Rondo Hatton, a fixture from this era who played his back-breaking monster *sans* makeup.

Another reliable toiler in the mad scientist genre was the New York-born actor J. Carrol Naish, perceived by the

> Ealing Studios was best known for its gentle comedies, but its uncharacteristic portmanteau chiller *Dead of Night* (1945) brilliantly exploited the film's recurring nightmare scenario. Its most famous sequence was the one directed by Alberto Cavalcanti: the ventriloquist dummy segment in which a disturbed Michael Redgrave had a bizarre battle of wills (or does he?) with an evil, wise-cracking piece of wood called Hugo.

studios as an all-purpose foreigner who could be a politically incorrect Japanese villain in the 1943 *Batman* serial, or the creator of the shape-shifting *Jungle Woman* (1944). That film featured no overt horror, and the sense that this was a more restrained era might also be said to be encapsulated by a sumptuous remake of *The Phantom of the Opera* (1943), with Claude Rains as the (mildly) acid-scarred Erique in a production that substituted plush production values (in luxuriant Technicolor) and ersatz opera sequences for the unforgettable shocks of the original Lon Chaney, Sr. film. Forged from the same template was the similarly horror-free but equally colorful *The Climax* (1944), with a silver-maned Karloff as the principal reason for watching it.

Further evidence of the playing down of gruesome elements was to be found in Victor Fleming's remake of Robert Louis Stevenson's *Dr. Jekyll and Mr. Hyde* (1941) for MGM, with the sexual degradation of the Hyde character more strongly suggested in Spencer Tracy's alter ego (considerably less hideous than Fredric March a decade earlier), rather than any overt horror elements. A striking version of another literary classic for the same studio was Albert Lewin's take on Oscar Wilde's *The Picture of Dorian Gray* (1945), in which the final shot of the eponymous portrait revealing a grotesquely decayed Dorian was shown as the one color shot in an otherwise monochromatic movie.

Heavier and jowlier in this era, Bela Lugosi demonstrated that he was not as flexible an actor as his one-time rival Boris Karloff by once again playing a vampire in Lew Landers's *Return of the Vampire* (1943), in which his final disintegration was one the few explicitly horrific moments of the period.

Robert Florey, initially in the frame to helm *Frankenstein* (1931), made an imaginative contribution to the genre with *The Beast with Five Fingers* (1946), in which the severed hand of a pianist committed a variety of murders as a terrified Peter Lorre looked on. It featured such unforgettable scenes as Lorre trying to nail the hand to a table or throwing it into the fire—neither of which, of course, succeed in dealing with the crawling horror.

Although Lorre was to become one of the great notables of horror cinema, the 1940s might be said to belong to Boris Karloff, no longer hidden behind the dead features and bolted neck of the Frankenstein Monster, but proving himself to be an exemplary character actor in such Val Lewton films as *The Body Snatcher* (1945), *Isle of the Dead* (1945), and *Bedlam* (1946). In fact, a measure of his skill was how well he came out of his dispiriting appearance in (Abbott and Costello) *Meet the Killer* (1949), playing a suspicious swami without any overt parody.

However, in more serious fare, mad scientists and dismembered body parts were not the only things called upon to do service in scaring audiences. The understated Val Lewton series of nine films apart, much subtler horror was also to be found in Lewis Allen's atmospheric *The Uninvited* (1944), set in a very Americanized Cornwall but featuring an unpleasant ghost making itself felt to jocular brother and sister Ray Milland and Ruth Hussey in a variety of ephemeral ways. The modern psychopathic killer made an early appearance too, in Robert Siodmak's terrifying noir nightmare *The Spiral Staircase* (1946), its picture of deranged evil still deeply unsettling today.

England still fought shy of the horror genre in the 1940s, but made a consummate contribution to the field. That contribution may have been a relatively lonely one, but it was among the most impressive of the era on either side of the Atlantic. Ealing Studios was best known for its gentle comedies, but its uncharacteristic portmanteau chiller *Dead of Night* (1945) brilliantly exploited the film's recurring nightmare scenario. Its most famous sequence was the one directed by Alberto Cavalcanti: the ventriloquist dummy segment in which a disturbed Michael Redgrave had a bizarre battle of wills (or does he?) with an evil, wise-cracking piece of wood called Hugo.

For a time, the moody black and white chiaroscuro cinematography in both the noir crime films and the horror movies of the period showed them to be blood brothers, but that ended with the decade. More graphic horror was to creep into the genre, but the 1940s—for all the maladroit, cheapjack product the era threw up—still produced some of the best-remembered bone-chillers in the history of the genre.

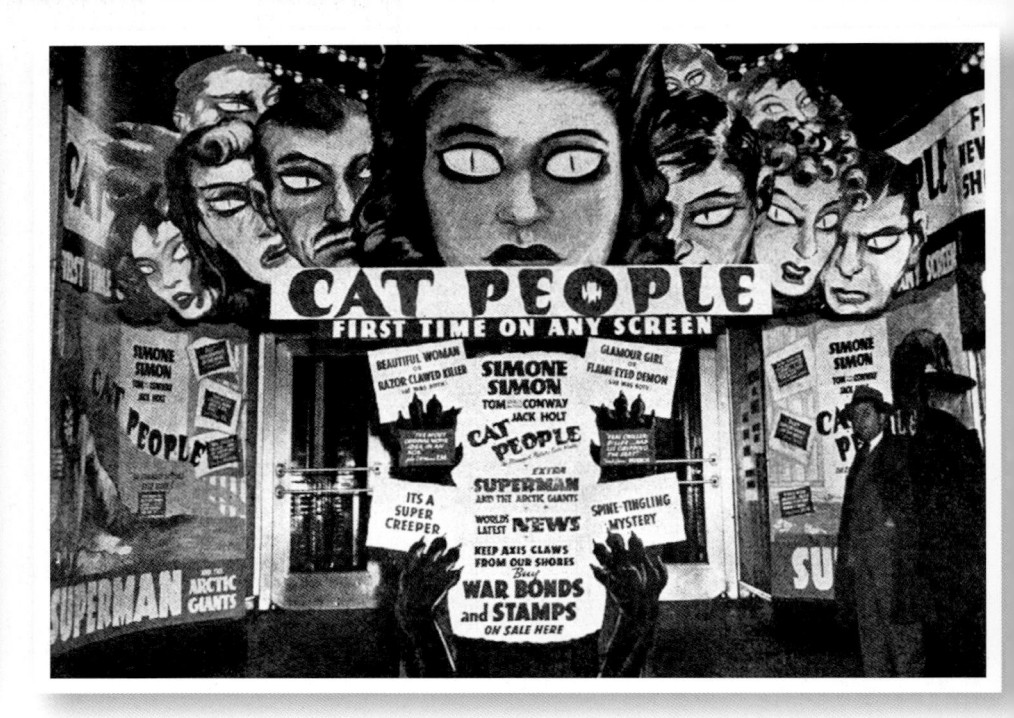

TOP LEFT: American movie theater marquee for *The Ghost of Frankenstein* (Dir: Erle C. Kenton, 1942), the fourth in the series that began back in 1931. Universal's marketing campaign encouraged theaters to place a spare chair in the lobby with a sign reading: *Will You Loan Me Your Brain?*

TOP RIGHT: Impressive movie theater façade to promote RKO Radio Pictures' *Cat People* (Dir: Jacques Tourneur, 1942). Studio executives were reportedly concerned that the finished movie was too subtle and could not compete with the type of horror movies Universal was turning out.

BOTTOM LEFT: Front-of-house marquee for the multi-monster reunion *House of Dracula* (Dir: Erle C. Kenton, 1945), the fifth in the diminishing *Dracula* series. Universal's publicity material suggested theater managers erect a "First Aid for Shock" booth with a white-garbed "nurse" in their lobby.

BOTTOM RIGHT: Although Boris Karloff declined to reprise his role as the Monster in *Abbott and Costello Meet Frankenstein*, as a favor to Universal he agreed to pose for some publicity photos during its New York City opening in 1948—just so long as he didn't have to watch it!

THE ART OF HORROR MOVIES

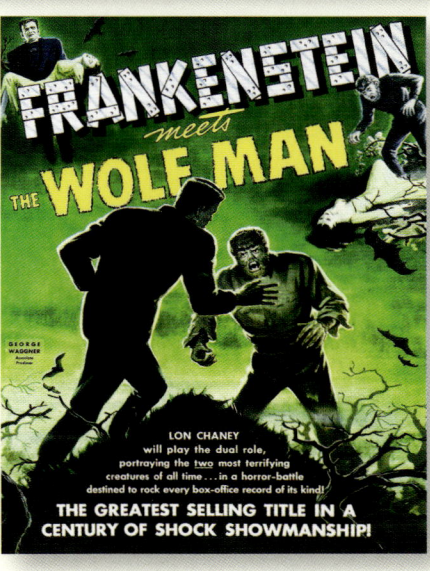

TOP LEFT: British trade advertisement for Universal's gangster-horror movie *Black Friday* (Dir: Arthur Lubin, 1940). Prior to filming, Boris Karloff took the role of the brain-swapping scientist meant for Bela Lugosi, who was relegated to a minor supporting role, and the two actors share no scenes.

TOP RIGHT: The 1940–41 Universal exhibitor book contained this campaign advertisement for *The Monster of Zombor*, to co-star Boris Karloff and Bela Lugosi. Unfortunately, the movie was never made and *Black Friday* (1940) marked their fifth and final horror pairing for the studio.

BOTTOM LEFT: Campaign advertisement for Universal's belated sequel, *The Invisible Man Returns* (Dir: Joe May, 1940), from the studio's 1940–41 exhibitor book. With Vincent Price forced to remain invisible for most of the running time, it was Sir Cedric Hardwicke who received the top billing.

BOTTOM MIDDLE: Campaign advertisement for *Frankenstein Meets the Wolf Man* (Dir: Roy William Neill, 1943) from Universal's 1942–43 exhibitor book. It claims that Lon Chaney (Jr.) would play *both* roles, before Bela Lugosi was miscast as Frankenstein's Monster (and had all his dialogue cut).

BOTTOM RIGHT: Universal's Spanish exhibitor book for 1944 featured these campaign advertisements for *Son of Dracula* (1943) and three of Basil Rathbone's Sherlock Holmes movies: *Sherlock Holmes Faces Death* (1943), *The Spider Woman* (1944), and *The Scarlet Claw* (1944).

THE FRIGHTENING FORTIES

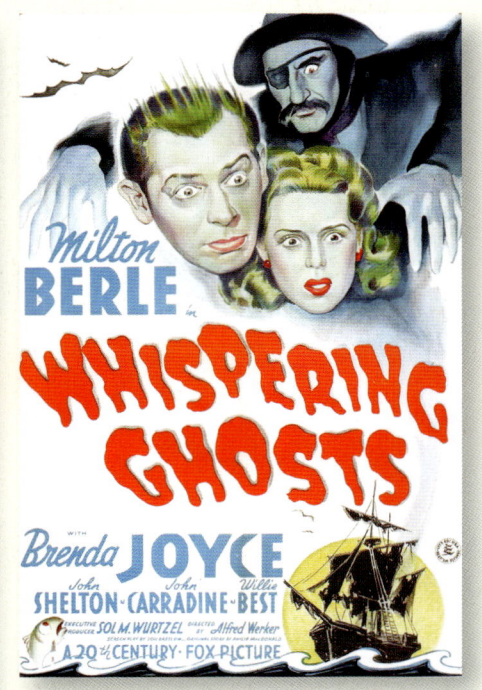

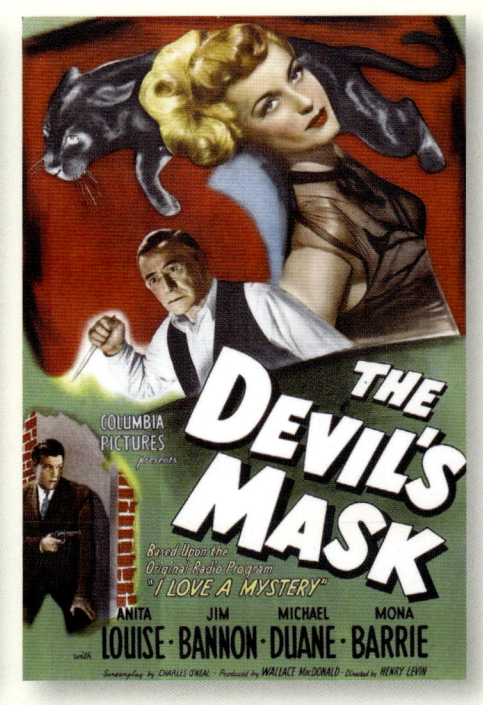

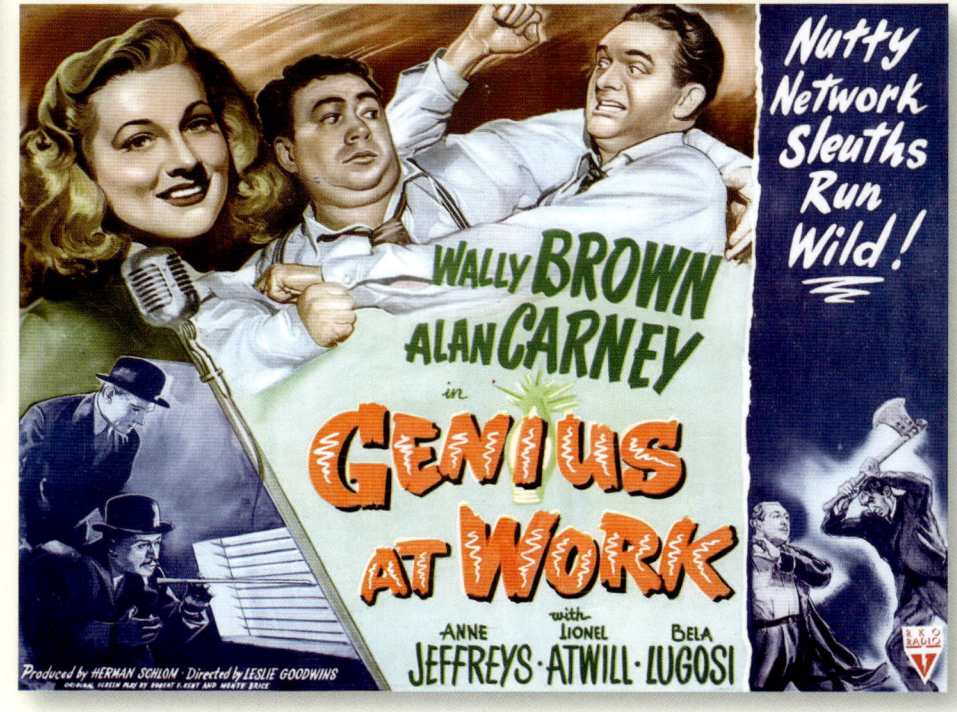

TOP LEFT: One-sheet poster for RKO Radio Pictures' horror-comedy *You'll Find Out* (Dir: David Butler, 1940), in which radio bandleader Kay Kyser finds himself menaced in a spooky house by Peter Lorre, Boris Karloff, and Bela Lugosi.

BOTTOM LEFT: Giant 24-sheet poster for *You'll Find Out* (1940).

TOP MIDDLE: Milton Berle played a radio detective in Twentieth Century-Fox's enjoyable mystery-comedy *Whispering Ghosts* (Dir: Alfred L. Werker, 1942).

TOP RIGHT: Columbia's *The Devil's Mask* (Dir: Henry Levin, 1946) was the second of three B movies based on Carlton E. Morse's popular radio series *I Love a Mystery* (1939–44).

BOTTOM RIGHT: Title lobby card for RKO Radio Pictures' *Genius at Work* (Dir: Leslie Goodwins, 1946). In their last film together, comedy duo Wally Brown and Alan Carney play radio detectives on the trail of a criminal genius.

OPPOSITE, TOP LEFT: Three-sheet poster for *Calling Dr. Death* (Dir: Reginald Le Borg, 1943), the first in Universal's series of six "Inner Sanctum Mysteries" based on Himan Brown's popular radio series (1941–52) and all starring Lon Chaney.

THE ART OF HORROR MOVIES

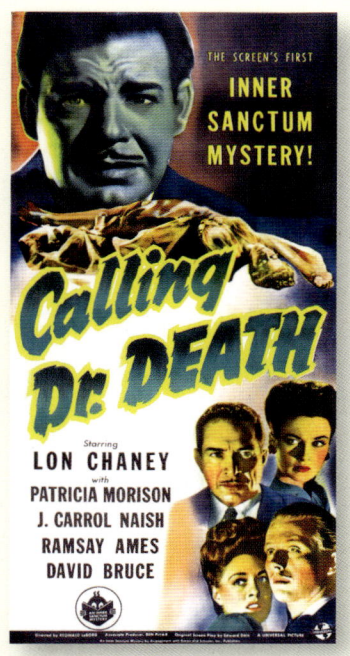

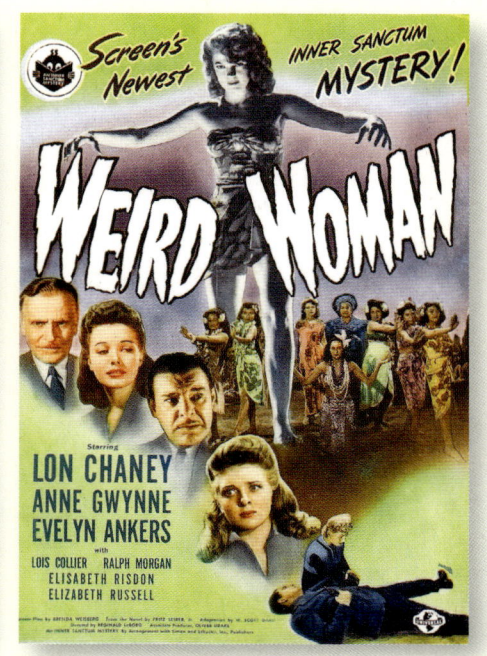

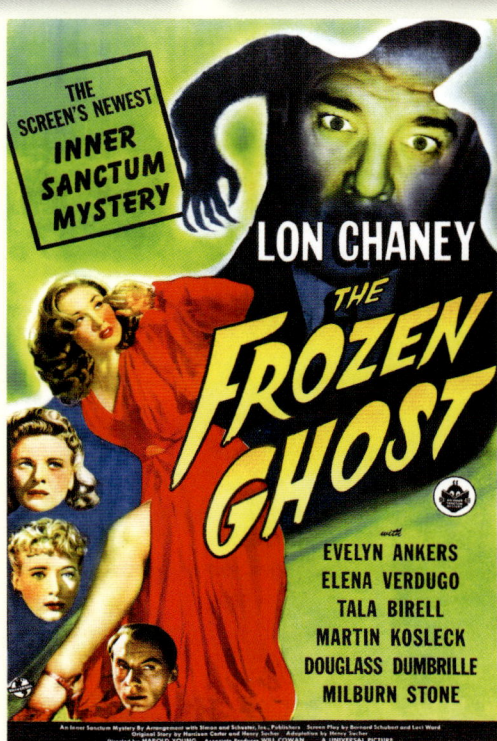

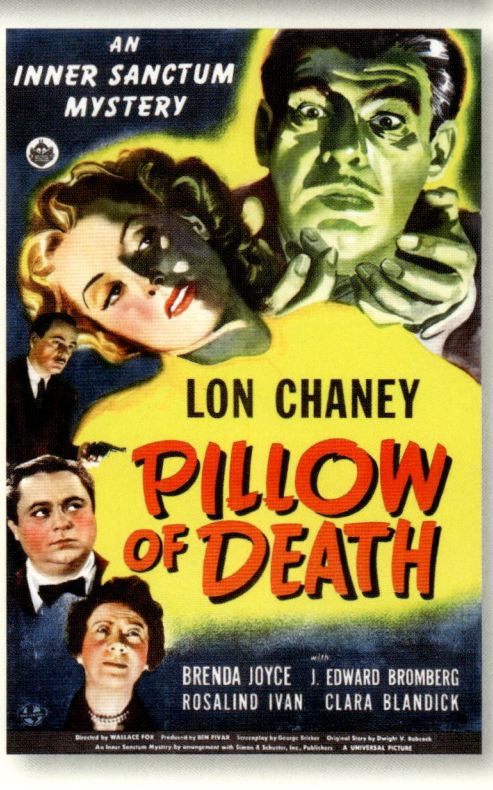

TOP MIDDLE: Possibly the best of all Universal's "Inner Sanctum Mysteries," *Weird Woman* (Dir: Reginald Le Borg, 1944) was based on Fritz Leiber, Jr.'s 1943 contemporary witchcraft novel *Conjure Wife*.

TOP RIGHT: Title lobby card for Universal's *Dead Man's Eyes* (Dir: Reginald Le Borg, 1944), the third "Inner Sanctum Mystery" based on the radio show and mystery novel imprint from Simon & Schuster.

BOTTOM LEFT: The fourth "Inner Sanctum Mystery" from Universal, *The Frozen Ghost* (Dir: Harold Young, 1945) found Lon Chaney's tortured stage mentalist reduced to working in a creepy wax museum.

BOTTOM MIDDLE: Lon Chaney's browbeaten chemist discovers that he has been betrayed by his unscrupulous boss (J. Carrol Naish) in *Strange Confession* (Dir: John Hoffman, 1945), which was reissued by Realart in 1953 under the title *The Missing Head*.

BOTTOM RIGHT: *Pillow of Death* (Dir: Wallace Fox, 1945) was the sixth and last of Universal's "Inner Sanctum Mysteries," all but this one introduced by a disembodied head (David Hoffman) in a crystal ball.

THE FRIGHTENING FORTIES

"THE WAY YOU WALKED WAS THORNY...

"...through no fault of your own, but as the rain enters the soil, the river enters the sea, so tears run to a predestined end. Now you will have peace for eternity."

The gypsy Maleva (Maria Ouspenskaya) in *The Wolf Man* (1941)

LATE IN HIS film career, the actor Lon Chaney, Jr. would cheerfully advise his directors to get what they needed from him before midday, as he knew that his prodigious drinking would reduce his acting options as the day wore on. By the 1950s, Chaney's imposing physique and almost-handsome looks had deserted him; he had become an unkempt, overweight figure given to over-the-top performances. The actor knew that his directors (in a series of increasingly woebegone films) would feel they'd got their money's worth, but in the 1940s—from his star-making role in George Waggner's *The Wolf Man* (1941) onward—Chaney was box office gold.

He may not have been the equal of his father, celebrated for such silent classics as *The Phantom of the Opera* (1925), nor, for that matter, in the same league as the more versatile Boris Karloff, but he was a charismatic and extremely watchable presence, and a performer who could convey great vulnerabilities as well as menace in his horror roles. What's more, he had already proved himself a considerable actor, as *Of Mice and Men* (1939), with Chaney as the physically powerful but mentally challenged Lennie, showed beyond doubt. Unfortunately, that career best moment overshadowed his later work, but his was a career that had more than its share of highs as well as lows.

Lon Chaney, Jr. is famous for being the only actor to have played all four of the most iconic movie monsters: the Wolf Man (a part he originated), the Frankenstein Monster, the mummy, and (in one egregious piece of miscasting) a version of Dracula. Chaney was always a blue-collar, rough-hewed figure, and singularly lacked the aristocratic demeanor that Bela Lugosi and Christopher Lee brought to the latter part.

Born in Oklahoma in 1906, his success in the Steinbeck film was something of a blind alley; it was as the lycanthropic Larry Talbot that Chaney conveyed a genuinely tragic dimension, however difficult it was to believe that this quintessentially American figure was the son of the very British Claude Rains in the movie.

The actor had watched on in dismay at the troubled marriage of his famous father and mother, a singer. The latter had attempted suicide by swallowing poison, and after the couple divorced, Chaney, Jr. had an unhappy childhood in various boarding schools. After trying to avoid emulating his father's acting career, he made his way to Hollywood, initially as a stuntman and bit part player. After being persuaded to change his given name of "Creighton" to "Lon" (to inform audiences of his lineage and finesse his marketability), Chaney's first film in the horror genre was Waggner's *Man Made Monster* (1941), a movie that utilized his imposing bulk but little else.

Lon Chaney, Jr. is famous for being the only actor to have played all four of the most iconic movie monsters: the Wolf Man (a part he originated), the Frankenstein Monster, the mummy, and (in one egregious piece of miscasting) a version of Dracula. Chaney was always a blue-collar, rough-hewed figure, and singularly lacked the aristocratic demeanor that Bela Lugosi and Christopher Lee brought to the latter part.

As the Frankenstein monster in Erle C. Kenton's *The Ghost of Frankenstein* (1942), Chaney managed to recapture some of the pathos that Karloff had brought to the part. Although he had authority in the role, Chaney was the weak link in Robert Siodmak's otherwise interesting *Son of Dracula* (1943), and he was unable to make much of the mummy in the first of his multiple assumptions of the role in Harold Young's *The Mummy's Tomb* (1942), presenting merely a shambling, bandaged threat.

After leaving the Universal studio, he began to gratefully accept smaller roles that suited his diminished energy levels as his alcoholism took hold. In this new phase of his career, he blossomed as a character actor, and was a reliable performer in several non-genre films directed by Stanley Kramer, also enlivening such outrageous fare as Roy Del Ruth's *The Alligator People* (1959), playing a deranged alcoholic—a standard role for him as the years rolled on.

Although Chaney's last few films were unworthy of his talent, his period of grace in the 1940s enshrined him as one of the great horror stars—not in the first rank, perhaps, but in the upper echelons of the second. BF

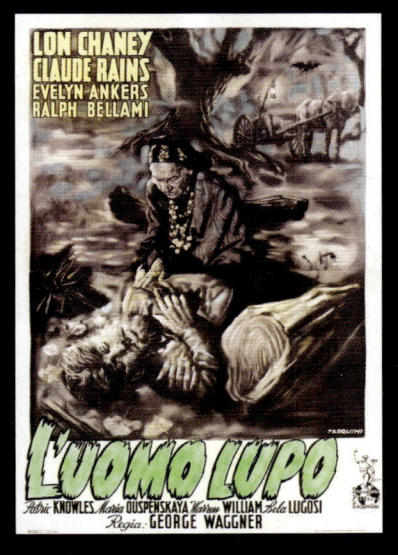

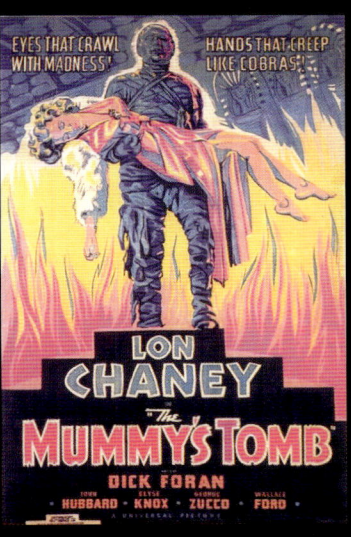

TOP LEFT: Stunning *quattro-foglio* for the 1949 Italian release of Universal's *The Wolf Man* (Dir: George Waggner, 1941), executed in pastels by Paolo Tarquini (1918–2011). Lon Chaney recreated his definitive role as doomed lycanthrope Larry Talbot in four sequels.

TOP MIDDLE: 1949 poster for the first Japanese release of Universal's *The Ghost of Frankenstein* (Dir: Erle C. Kenton, 1942), the fourth in the series. Lon Chaney replaced Boris Karloff as the Monster under Jack P. Pierce's makeup.

BOTTOM LEFT: Belgian poster for Universal's *Son of Dracula* (Dir: Robert Siodmak, 1943), the third in the series. Lon Chaney took over the role of "Count Alucard" (try spelling it backward).

BOTTOM MIDDLE: 1948 reissue poster for Universal's *The Mummy's Tomb* (Dir: Harold Young, 1942), in which Lon Chaney took over the role of living mummy Kharis for this sequel to *The Mummy's Hand* (1940).

ABOVE RIGHT: *Beware the Autumn Moon* (2016), stained glass window by American artist Micah Lee Mowbray. "'Wolf hair' glass border, eerie mist, and a full moon of Vaseline/Uranium glass," explains the artist. "This handmade yellow jewel fluoresces radioactive green under ultraviolet light. It's harmless, but can set off a sensitive Geiger counter."

THE FRIGHTENING FORTIES

TOP LEFT: One-sheet Mexican poster by Spanish-born artist "Juanino" (Juan Renau Berenguer, 1900–89), for Jaime Salvador's obscure old dark house comedy *Yo dormí con un fantasma* (I Slept with a Ghost, 1947) starring comedy actor "Resortes" (Adalberto Martínez Chávez).

TOP MIDDLE: This 1953 Mexican reissue poster by artist "Vargas" (Juan Antonio Vargas Ocampo) for Carlos Hugo Christensen's voodoo melodrama *La balandra Isabel llego esta tarde* (The Yacht Isabel Arrived This Afternoon, 1949) re-titled the movie *Mariposas negras* (Black Butterflies).

TOP RIGHT: Mexican poster by Spanish Civil War artist Josep Renau Berenguer (1907–82) for Juan Bustillo Oro's proto-*giallo* thriller *El hombre sin rostro* (The Man Without a Face, 1950), in which a troubled detective hunted wrestler Wolf Rubinsky's faceless serial killer of young women.

BOTTOM LEFT & RIGHT: Mexican lobby cards often feature colorful artwork by indigenous artists that has little or no relation to the American movies they are supposed to be promoting. This is the case with the examples here by [Rodolfo] Aguirre Tinoco (b. 1927), promoting the later release of two Monogram titles. The card for *Invisible Ghost* (Dir: Joseph H. Lewis, 1941) depicts Bela Lugosi as a totally unrelated vampire and incorporates a still from *Voodoo Man* (Dir: William Beaudine, 1944), while the card for that film claims that Lugosi is portraying the Count in *Dracula's Revenge*!

THE ART OF HORROR MOVIES

Creator of Kong

Born into poverty in London in April 1875, [Richard Horatio] Edgar Wallace worked as a journalist and war correspondent before turning his hand to writing novels in the early 1900s to alleviate his debts. After the failure of his first book, *The Four Just Men* (1905), his collection of African adventure stories, *Sanders of the River* (1911), became a bestseller and was filmed in 1935. Wallace, who claimed he could write a 70,000-word novel in three days, recorded his words onto wax cylinders, which his secretaries would then type up. He rarely edited the manuscripts afterward. By the 1920s he was known as the "King of Thrillers," and in 1928 it was claimed that one in four books being read in the UK was written by him. During a prolific career, Wallace wrote more than 170 novels, 18 stage plays, and nearly 1,000 short stories, and his work was translated around the world. However, despite his success, the author wrote mainly to repay his many creditors—a result of gambling debts and an extravagant lifestyle. He also scripted movie adaptations of his own work, including the ten-chapter serial *Mark of the Frog* (1928), *The Valley of Ghosts* (1928), and *The Squeaker* (1930). Wallace continued to be burdened by debt and, after writing the screenplay for the first sound version of *The Hound of the Baskervilles* (1932), he moved to Hollywood, where he was employed as a "script doctor" at RKO Radio Pictures. He was working on the initial drafts of what would later become *King Kong* (1933) when he died, at the age of 56, of complications of diabetes and double pneumonia on February 10, 1932. During the late 1950s and '60s, Wallace's stories and novels—and those of his eldest son, Bryan Edgar Wallace (1904–71)—formed the backbone of West Germany's popular genre of *krimis* (thriller) films.

TOP RIGHT: Based on a 1927 mystery play by Edgar Wallace, Film Alliance of the United States, Inc. released the British-made *The Terror* (Dir: Richard Bird, 1938) in the early 1940s. It had previously been filmed in 1928 by Warner Bros. in an "all talking" sound version and a now-lost silent version.

BOTTOM LEFT: Filmed in England as *The Dark Eyes of London* (Dir: Walter Summers) in 1939 and based on a 1924 novel by Edgar Wallace, this movie was distributed in America the following year as *The Human Monster*, the first in a series of titles starring Bela Lugosi from Monogram Pictures.

BOTTOM RIGHT: A man suffering from hereditary madness uses an Indian scarf to strangle his victims in the old dark house thriller *The Case of the Frightened Lady* (Dir: George King, 1940), based on a 1931 play by Edgar Wallace. The title was shortened for its American release the following year.

THE FRIGHTENING FORTIES

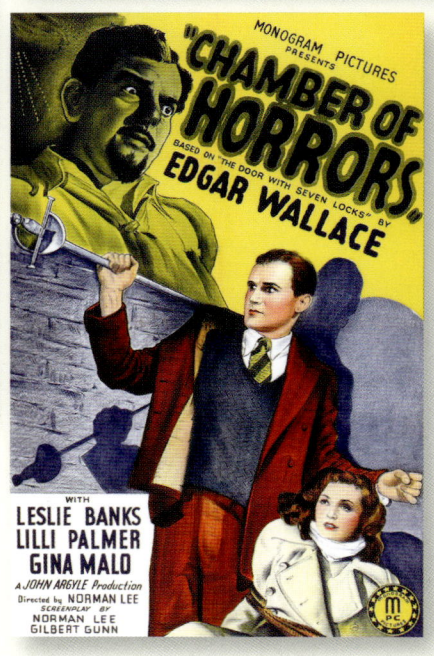

ABOVE LEFT: Australian stone litho poster for Ealing Studio's multi-director portmanteau *Dead of Night* (1945), featuring Michael Redgrave as the ventriloquist who believes his dummy Hugo is actually alive.

TOP RIGHT: British quad poster for *Dead of Night* (1945) by artist Leslie George Hurry (1909–78).

BOTTOM MIDDLE: Based on a novel by Edgar Wallace, Pathé Pictures' *The Door with Seven Locks* (Dir: Norman Lee, 1940) was retitled *Chamber of Horrors* for its release in America.

BOTTOM RIGHT: 1946 Danish poster for ABC/Pathé Pictures' *The Night Has Eyes* (Dir: Leslie Arliss, 1942), which was originally released in America under the title *Terror House* and later reissued as *Moonlight Madness*.

OPPOSITE, TOP LEFT: Insert card for *The Mummy's Hand* (Dir: Christy Cabanne, 1940), the first entry in Universal's new series about Kharis, the living mummy (played here for the only time by cowboy actor Tom Tyler).

OPPOSITE, TOP MIDDLE: Stone litho one-sheet for PRC Pictures' poverty-row murder mystery *The Black Raven* (Dir: Sam Newfield, 1943), a remake of the 1936 movie *The Rogues' Tavern*.

THE ART OF HORROR MOVIES

— 94 —

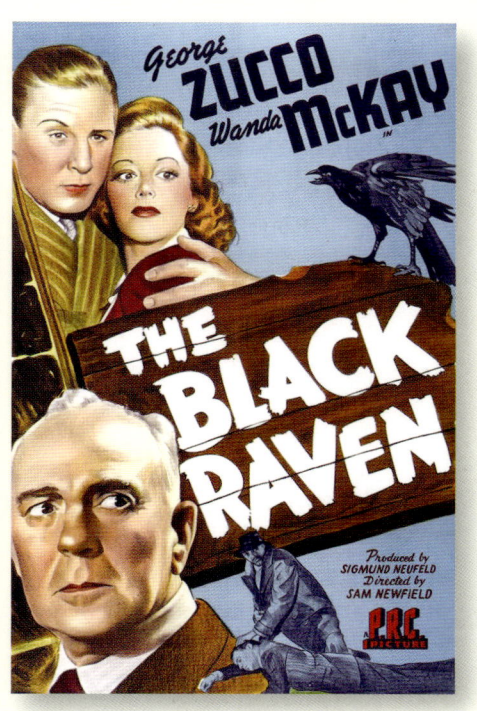

BOTTOM LEFT: One-sheet poster for PRC Pictures' *The Flying Serpent* (Dir: Sherman Scott [Sam Newfield], 1945). This was basically a remake of *The Devil Bat* (1940).

BOTTOM MIDDLE: Insert card for Golden Gate Pictures' *Scared to Death* (Dir: Christy Cabanne, 1946). This was the only film starring Bela Lugosi to be made in color.

ABOVE RIGHT: *George Zucco from The Mummy's Hand* (2002), pencil portrait by American artist Frank Dietz, created for *Frank Dietz's The Things Remain Sketchy* convention sketchbook. "George Zucco was always a perfectly erudite villain," observes the artist. "Diabolical intent rendered with perfect diction."

The Second Maddest Doctor

After Lionel Atwill, British-born actor George Zucco (1886–1960) was perhaps Hollywood's second maddest doctor of them all. He began acting on the stage, and appeared in a number of films, culminating with *The Man Who Could Work Miracles* (1936), before moving to America. He varied his Hollywood career between appearing in such prestige productions as *The Adventures of Sherlock Holmes* (1939, as Professor Moriarty) and *The Hunchback of Notre Dame* (1939), and "Poverty Row" horrors like *The Mad Monster* (1942) and *Voodoo Man* (1944). However, whatever the size of his role, Zucco always gave it his best shot.

THE FRIGHTENING FORTIES

"My Feets Ain't Gonna Stand Around..."

During the 1930s and '40s, African-American actors invariably appeared in subservient or comedic roles in horror movies. As demeaning as these parts often were, a number of actors stood out in these supporting roles. Lincoln Theodore Monroe Andrew Perry (1902–85) made his movie debut in the mid-1920s as "Stepin Fetchit," a name he claimed he took from a racehorse. His stereotypical performance as a slow-witted, eye-rolling comedy relief in such films as *The Ghost Talks* (1929, as a character named "Christopher Lee"!) and *Charlie Chan in Egypt* (1935) made him the first African-American actor to become a millionaire, but he was bankrupt by 1947. Willie Best (1916–62) started his career in the early 1930s as "Sleep 'n' Eat" with movies like *The Monster Walks* (1932), but by the middle of the decade had reverted to his real name. The actor honed his scared, stuttering performance in *Mummy's Boys* (1936), *The Ghost Breakers* (1940), *The Smiling Ghost* (1941, in which he utters the immortal line: "I ain't afraid, but my feets ain't gonna stand around and see my body abused"), *The Hidden Hand* (1942), and many other titles before a drug arrest ended his career.

TOP LEFT: Rare poster for the obscure comedy-horror "race picture" *Comes Midnight* (1940) starring lugubrious comedian Eddie Green (1896–1950), who also produced the movie for his own Sepia-Art Pictures Co.

TOP MIDDLE: Stone litho three-sheet poster for Astor Pictures' 1938 reissue of the poverty-row mystery *The Monster Walks* (Dir: Frank Strayer, 1932).

TOP RIGHT: Half-sheet poster for Paramount's *The Ghost Breakers* (Dir: George Marshall, 1940), the studio's follow-up to the previous year's *The Cat and the Canary*.

BOTTOM RIGHT: Six-sheet stone litho poster for Monogram Pictures' *Invisible Ghost* (Dir: Joseph H. Lewis, 1941). A pioneer of the "Black Theatre" movement, Clarence Muse brought a rare touch of quiet dignity to his portrayal of Bela Lugosi's loyal butler.

OPPOSITE, ABOVE LEFT: Insert card for Monogram's *The Scarlet Clue* (Dir: Phil Rosen, 1945), the fifth of 15 "Charlie Chan" mysteries to co-star Mantan Moreland as the cowardly chauffeur, Birmingham Brown.

THE ART OF HORROR MOVIES

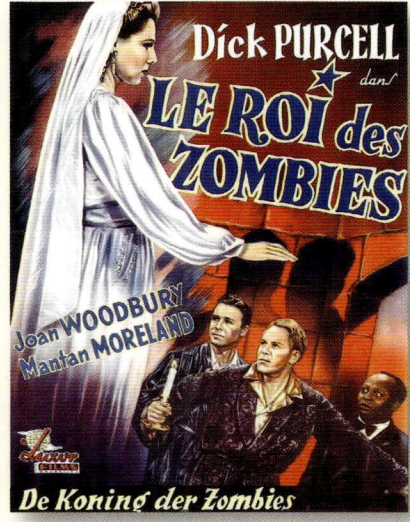

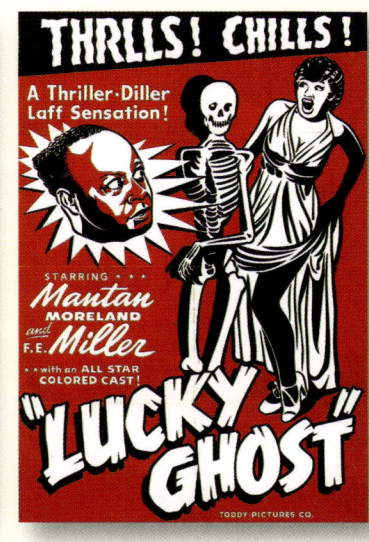

Clarence Muse (1889–1979) was the first African-American actor to "star" in a movie and the first black actor to direct a Broadway show. A songwriter and playwright, who was considered a pioneer of the "Black Theatre" movement, Muse brought a dignified gravitas to supporting roles in such films as *White Zombie* (1932), *Black Moon* (1934), and *Invisible Ghost* (1941). Undoubtedly one of the most successful African-American actors in Hollywood was Mantan Moreland (1902–73), who was best known for playing Charlie Chan's skittish chauffeur "Birmingham Brown" in 15 Monogram mysteries during the second half of the 1940s. Moreland's long career not only encompassed supporting roles in such movies as *King of the Zombies* (1941), *The Strange Case of Doctor Rx* (1942), *Revenge of the Zombies* (1943), and *Spider Baby or, The Maddest Story Ever Told* (1967), but he also starred in his own "All Colored" comedies like *Lucky Ghost* (aka *Lady Luck*, 1942). With the benefit of hindsight we can now see how racially stereotyped these and other African-American performers were during this period, but there is no denying that they often made significant contributions to the movies they appeared in and, arguably, paved the way for those actors of color who followed in their footsteps.

TOP MIDDLE: Belgian poster for Monogram Pictures' *King of the Zombies* (Dir: Jean Yarbrough, 1941), in which Mantan Moreland's manservant Jefferson "Jeff" Jackson is turned into a "zombie" by Henry Victor's foreign spy.

TOP RIGHT: Re-release poster for Dixie National Pictures' *Lucky Ghost* (Dir: William X. Crowley [William Beaudine], 1942) which co-starred the comedy team of "Miller and Mantan" (F.E. Miller [1885–1971] and Mantan Moreland).

BOTTOM RIGHT: Title lobby card for PRC's *The Ghost and the Guest* (Dir: William Nigh, 1943). Busy character actor Sam [Samuel Rufus] McDaniel (1886–1962) turned up in this screwball "haunted" house comedy.

THE FRIGHTENING FORTIES

ABOVE: Italian *locandina* by F. Carfagni for Universal Pictures' first Technicolor horror film, *Phantom of the Opera* (Dir: Arthur Lubin, 1943).

RIGHT: American trade advertisement for the studio's equally colorful follow-up, *The Climax* (Dir: George Waggner, 1944).

KARLOFF · TURHAN BEY

WAX

in Technicolor

DOLENZ
GOMEZ
TOSSEL

BOTTOM RIGHT: One-sheet poster for *Sherlock Holmes and the Voice of Terror* (Dir: John Rawlins, 1942), the first in Universal's series of 11 horror-tinged B movies re-teaming Basil Rathbone as Sherlock Holmes and Nigel Bruce as Doctor Watson.

BOTTOM MIDDLE: Spanish poster for *The Spider Woman* (Dir: Roy William Neill, 1943) by artist José Peris Aragó (1907–2003). In the fifth entry in Universal's contemporary B movie series, Basil Rathbone's Holmes matches wits against Gale Sondergaard's "female Moriarty."

BOTTOM LEFT: Spanish herald for Universal's *The Scarlet Claw* (Dir: Roy William Neill, 1944), the sixth and probably best in the series, based around a series of gruesome murders attributed to a legendary 100-year-old marsh monster.

TOP RIGHT: Half-sheet poster for *The Pearl of Death* (Dir: Roy William Neill, 1944), the seventh in the low-budget Universal series. Acromegalic actor Rondo Hatton appeared as the monstrous "Hoxton Creeper."

TOP LEFT: Trade advertisement for Universal's *The House of Fear* (Dir: Roy William Neill, 1945), the eighth in the series, involving a series of mysterious mutilation deaths in an old Scottish mansion.

THE ART OF HORROR MOVIES

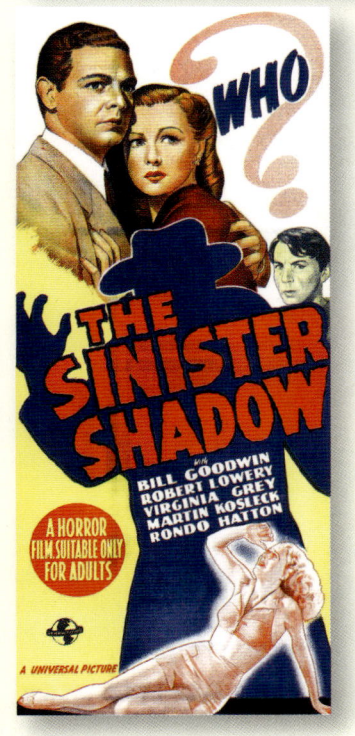

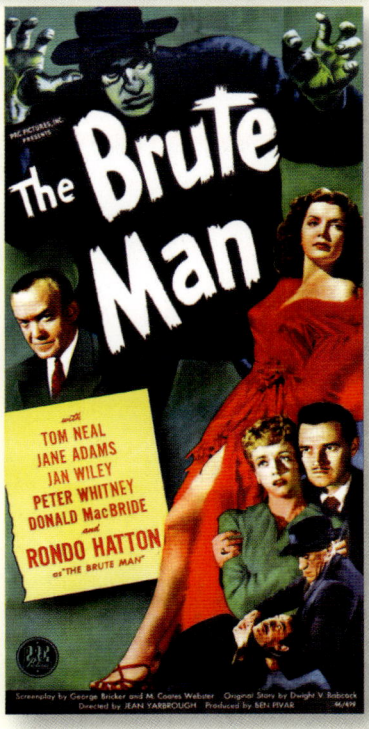

The Brute Man

A respected high school athlete and later newspaper reporter, studio publicity would claim that exposure to poison gas in France during the First World War led to Rondo Hatton (1894–1946) developing acromegaly, a progressive and disfiguring bone disease. After appearing in small roles in movies including *The Hunchback of Notre Dame* (1939), Universal put him under contract and exploited his arresting looks in such films as *The Jungle Captive* (as "Moloch the Brute," 1945) and *The Spider Woman Strikes Back* (as "Mario the Monster Man," 1946). Hatton was cast as various "Creepers" in *The Pearl of Death* (1944), *House of Horrors* (1946), and *The Brute Man* (1946) before his premature death from a heart attack.

TOP LEFT: 1952 Realart re-release half-sheet poster for Universal's *House of Horrors* (Dir: Jean Yarbrough, 1946), "introducing" audiences to Rondo Hatton's spine-crusher, The Creeper.

BOTTOM LEFT: Australian daybill for *House of Horrors* (1946), retitled *The Sinister Shadow* in that country.

BOTTOM MIDDLE: Insert card for *The Brute Man* (Dir: Jean Yarbrough, 1946), which Universal sold on to poverty-row distributor PRC. Rondo Hatton recreated his character of The Creeper for the third and final time.

ABOVE RIGHT: *Rondo Hatton as The Brute Man* (2005), acrylic on board by American artist Basil Gogos. "This piece was never used for anything other than its appearance in my book *Famous Monster Movie Art of Basil Gogos* (2005)," reveals the artist. "I really love this painting—I love the beauty of his ugliness—and I still own it."

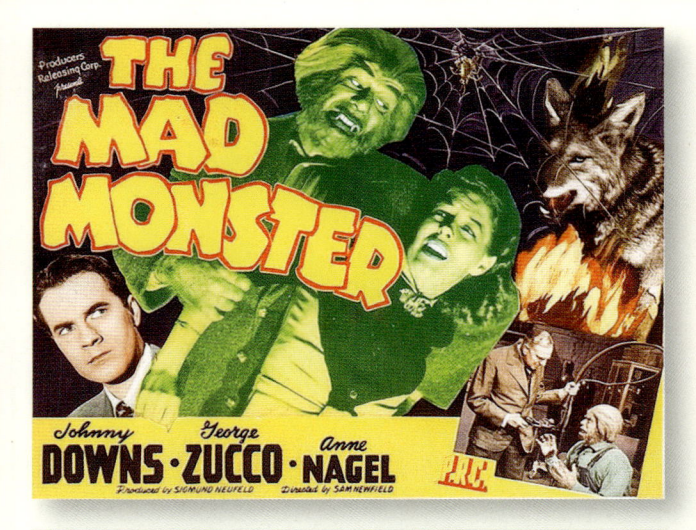

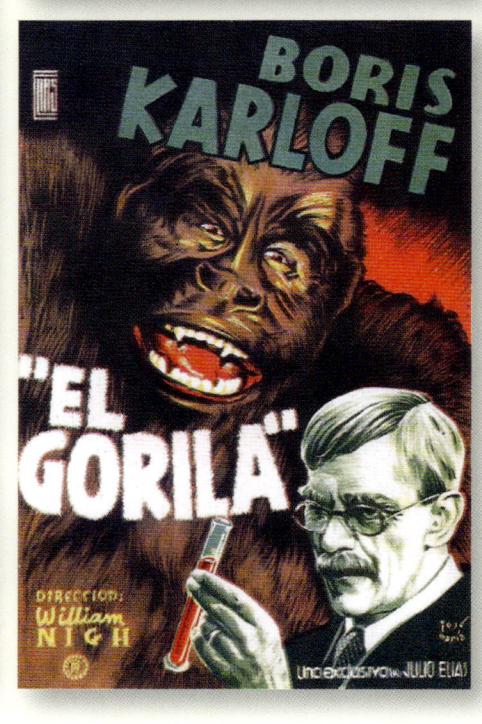

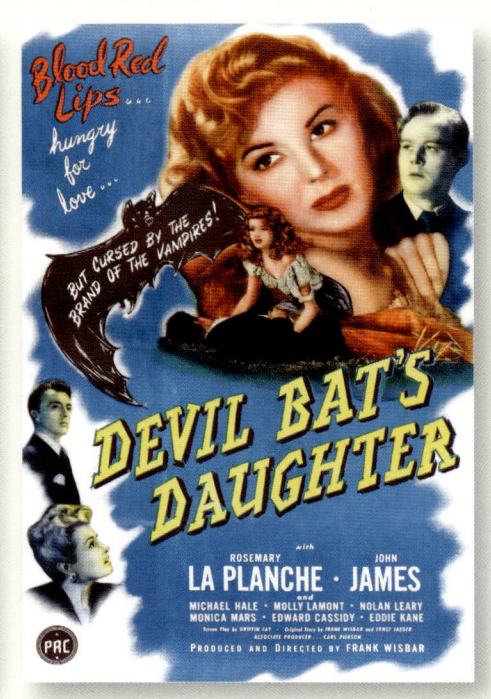

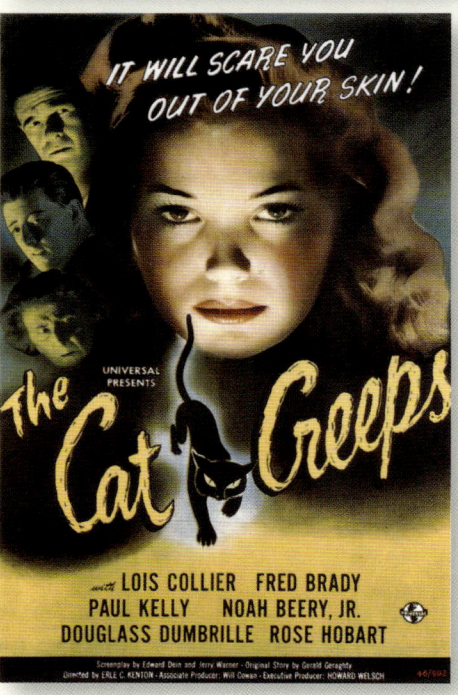

TOP LEFT: Title lobby card for PRC's *The Mad Monster* (Dir: Sam Newfield, 1942), in which George Zucco's crazy Dr. Cameron injects his gentle handyman (Glenn Strange) with his wolf-blood serum and turns him into a prototype for his army of wolf-men.

TOP MIDDLE: Argentinean reissue poster for PRC's poverty row entry *The Devil Bat* (Dir: Jean Yarbrough, 1940).

TOP RIGHT: One-sheet poster for PRC's sequel *Devil Bat's Daughter* (Dir: Frank Wisbar, 1946), which exonerated the original killer.

BOTTOM LEFT: 1950 British pressbook cover for Monogram Pictures' *Return of the Ape Man* (Dir: Philip Rosen, 1944), which actually wasn't a sequel to *The Ape Man* (1943).

BOTTOM MIDDLE: 1945 Spanish herald for Monogram's Pictures' *The Ape* (Dir: William Nigh, 1940) by artist José María. Based on a 1927 play by Adam Hull Shirk, Boris Karloff plays a kindly scientist who disguises himself as an escaped circus ape to obtain human spinal fluid for his experiments.

BOTTOM RIGHT: One-sheet poster for Universal's *The Cat Creeps* (Dir: Erle C. Kenton, 1946), which wasn't a remake of the lost 1930 movie but an old dark house mystery in which a black cat was said to be possessed by the spirit of a murdered woman.

THE ART OF HORROR MOVIES

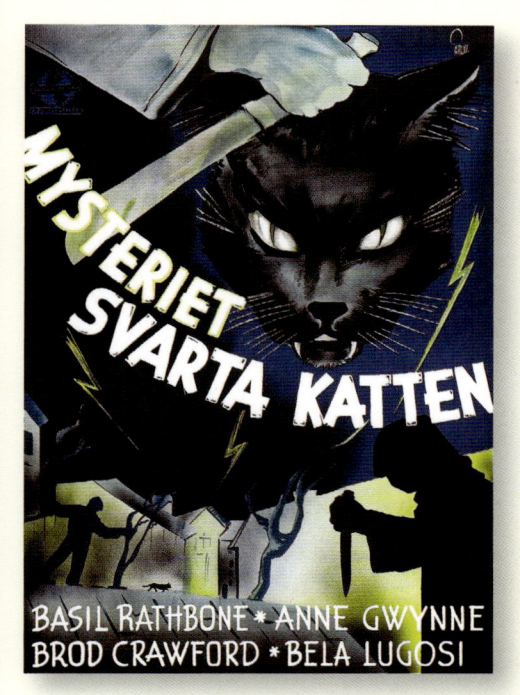

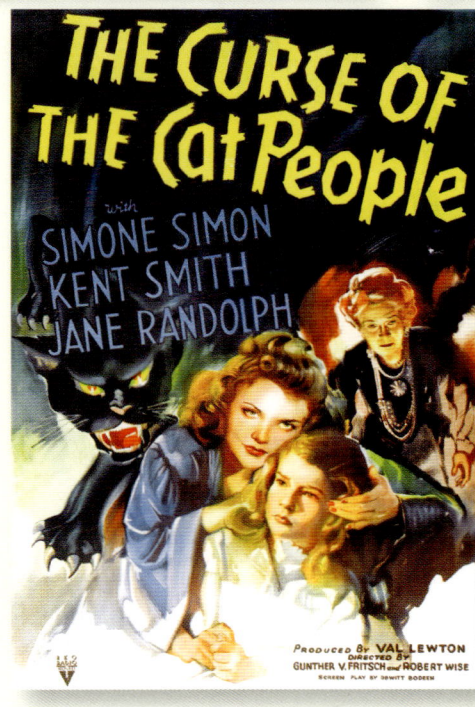

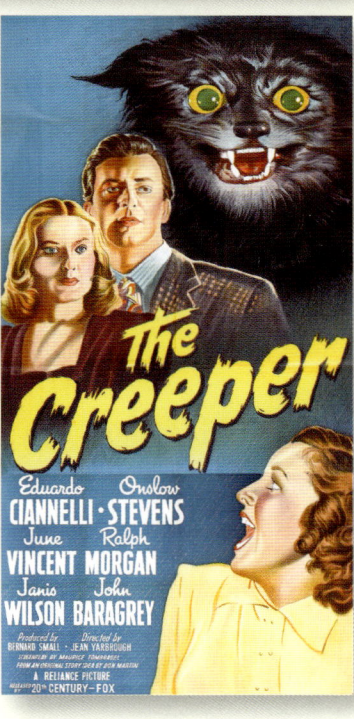

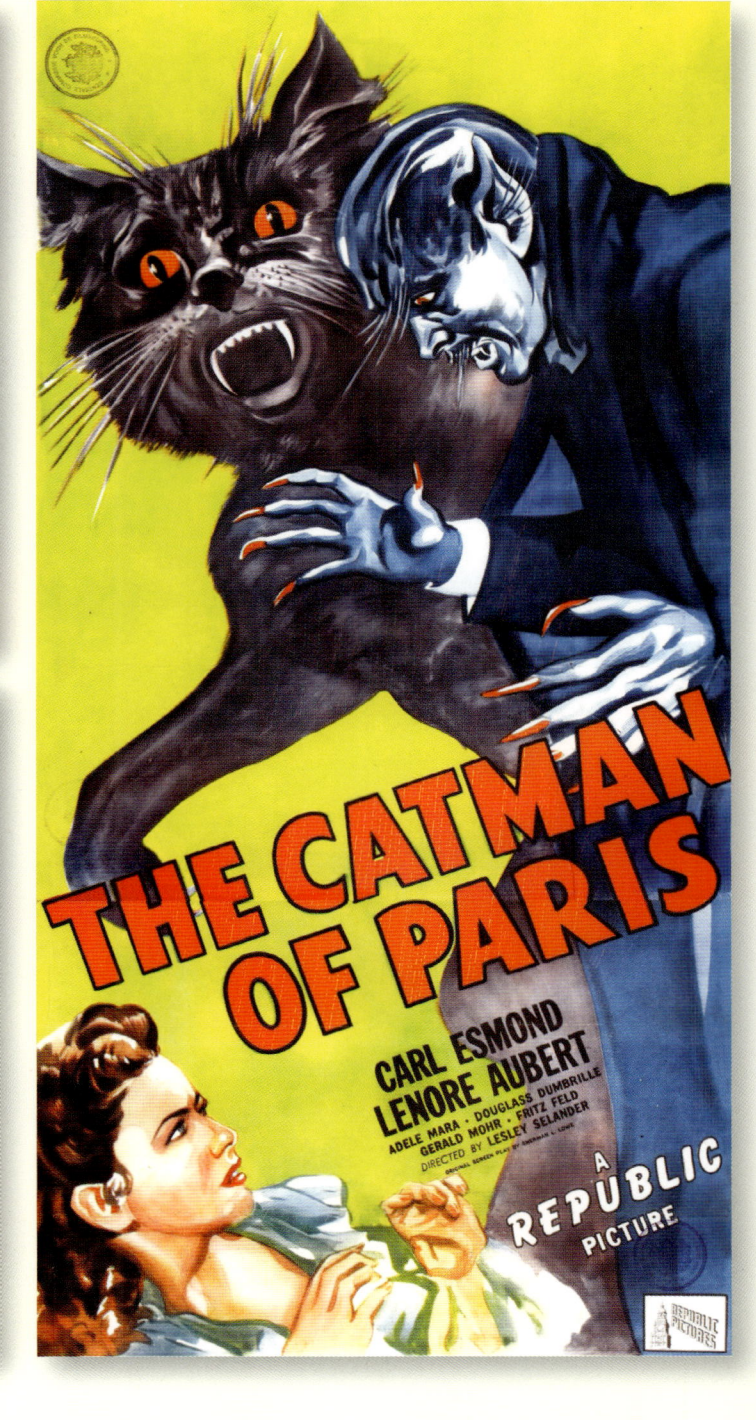

TOP LEFT: Swedish poster for Universal's *The Black Cat* (Dir: Albert S. Rogell, 1941) by artist Gösta Äberg (1905–81). This old dark house comedy-mystery has little to do with Edgar Allan Poe's original story.

TOP MIDDLE: 1947 Spanish poster for RKO's *Cat People* (Dir: Jacques Tourneur, 1942) by artist Emilio "Chapí" Rodríguez (1911–49), depicting Simone Simon's Irena Dubrovna, who believes she is descended from a race of cat-women.

BOTTOM LEFT: One-sheet poster for RKO's *The Curse of the Cat People* (Dir: Gunther von Fritsch and Robert Wise, 1944). Producer Val Lewton's semi-sequel to *The Cat People* (1942) turned the story into a dark fairy tale.

BOTTOM MIDDLE: Three-sheet poster for *The Creeper* (Dir: Jean Yarbrough, 1948), Twentieth Century-Fox's attempt to rival the success of Val Lewton's films.

ABOVE RIGHT: Three-sheet poster for Republic Pictures' *The Catman of Paris* (Dir: Lesley Selander, 1946), in which an author suffering from blackouts believes he may be a 300-year-old top-hatted were-creature.

THE FRIGHTENING FORTIES

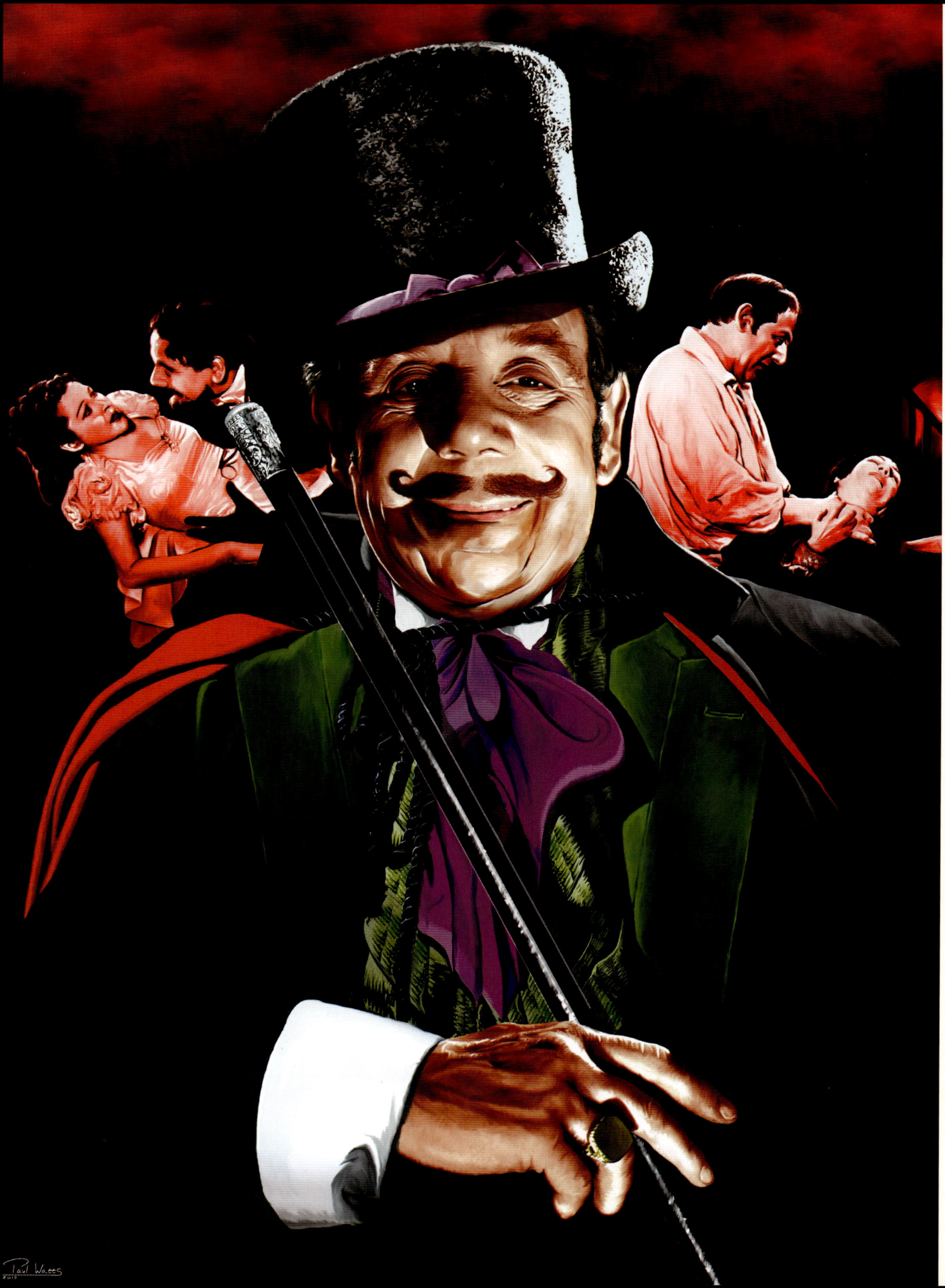
Paul Watts

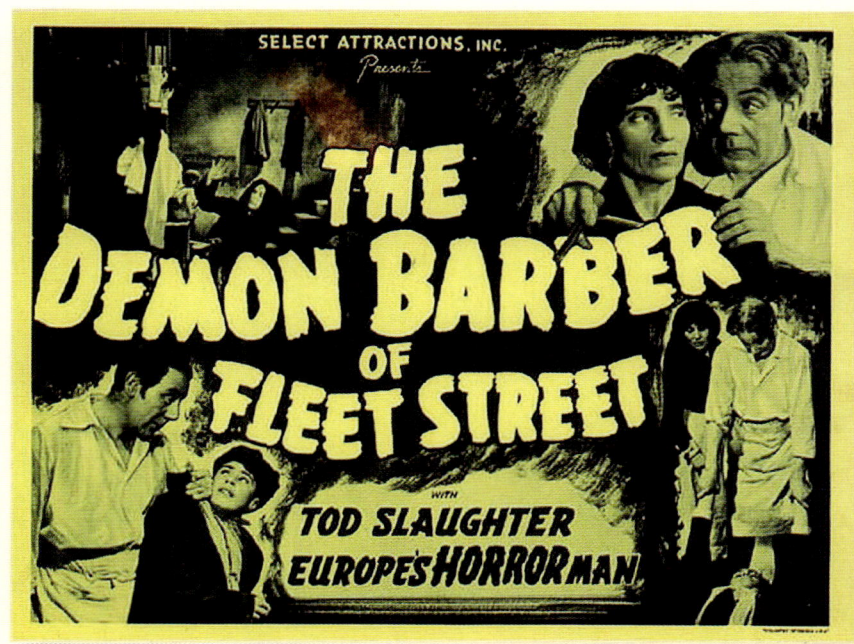

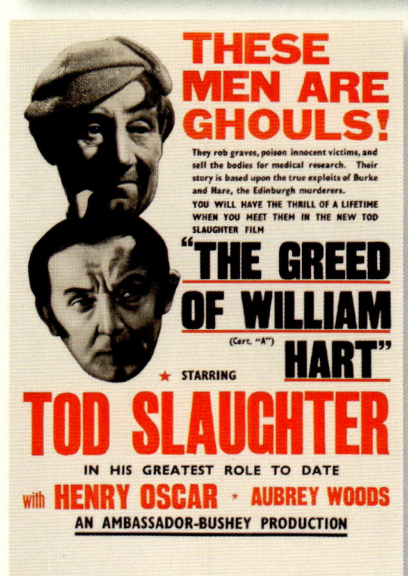

OPPOSITE: *Mr. Murder— The Life and Times of Tod Slaughter* (2019), ink and digital portrait of the British stage and screen star of Victorian melodramas by artist Paul Watts. "This was a commission from Denis Meikle of publisher Hemlock Books to produce the front cover of their prestigious biography," explains the artist, "as well as a poster and promotional artwork."

TOP RIGHT: British horror star Tod Slaughter never really managed to break into the American market. As this lobby card shows, the title of his most famous and iconic film, *Sweeney Todd: The Demon Barber of Fleet Street* (Dir: George King, 1936), was shortened for the American market when it was finally released there by Select Attractions, Inc. three years after it was made.

ABOVE LEFT: Originally a huge hit on the British stage for Tod Slaughter, the film of the Victorian melodrama *The Face at the Window* (Dir: George King, 1939) was released in America in 1940 by Arthur Ziehm, Inc. Set in 1880 Paris, Slaughter's scheming serial killer "The Wolf" uses the monstrous visage of his foster brother (Harry Terry) to distract his intended victims.

BOTTOM MIDDLE: British double-crown poster for *The Greed of William Hart* (Dir: Oswald Mitchell, 1948). Inspired by the real-life exploits of nineteenth century Scottish body snatchers Burke and Hare, it starred Tod Slaughter as "Hart" and Henry Oscar as "Moore" after the UK Censors insisted that the film's soundtrack be rerecorded to avoid upsetting the nation's sensitivity.

BOTTOM RIGHT: *The Greed of William Hart* (1948) and *The Curse of the Wraydons* (Dir: Victor M. Gover, 1946) were released in America by New York's J.H. Hoffberg Company on a 1953 "roadshow" double-bill that changed their titles to the more exploitative *Horror Maniacs* and *Strangler's Morgue*, respectively, with some of the most amateurish publicity artwork ever seen.

THE FRIGHTENING FORTIES

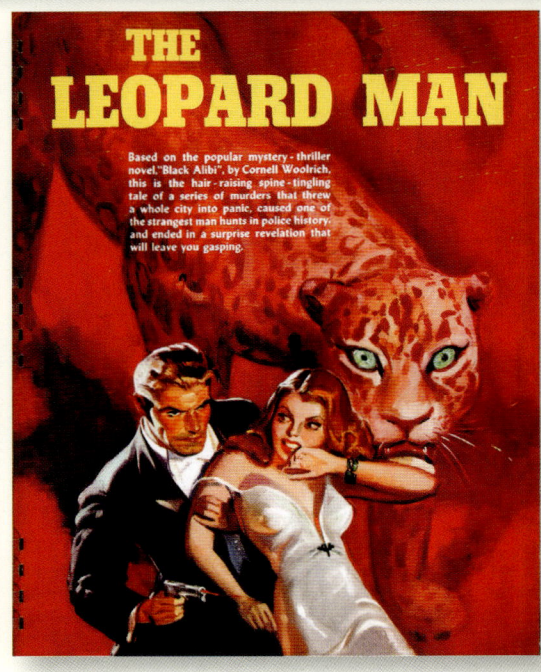

The Poetry of Horror

In the field of the horror film, one man is customarily referenced as someone who injected depth, complexity, and intelligence into his work: the producer Val Lewton (1904–51). Born in Yalta, Russia, Lewton took the awful titles handed to him by RKO (most famously *Cat People* and *I Walked with a Zombie*) and turned out movies attached to them which were much more ambitious and atmospheric than the more straightforward horror fare that was the industry standard in the 1940s. He used psychological horror to scare his audiences, and those much-mocked titles have now acquired a classical sheen that makes them sound genuinely poetic. BF

ABOVE LEFT: One-sheet poster for *The 7th Victim* (Dir: Mark Robson, 1943), possibly the most subtle of all Val Lewton's low-budget horror films for RKO Radio Pictures.

TOP RIGHT: Six-sheet poster for RKO's *Isle of the Dead* (Dir: Mark Robson, 1945), the most underrated of Boris Karloff's three movies with producer Val Lewton.

BOTTOM MIDDLE: Insert card for RKO's *I Walked with a Zombie* (Dir: Jacques Tourneur, 1943), loosely based on the 1847 novel *Jane Eyre* by Charlotte Brontë (1816–55).

THE ART OF HORROR MOVIES

— 106 —

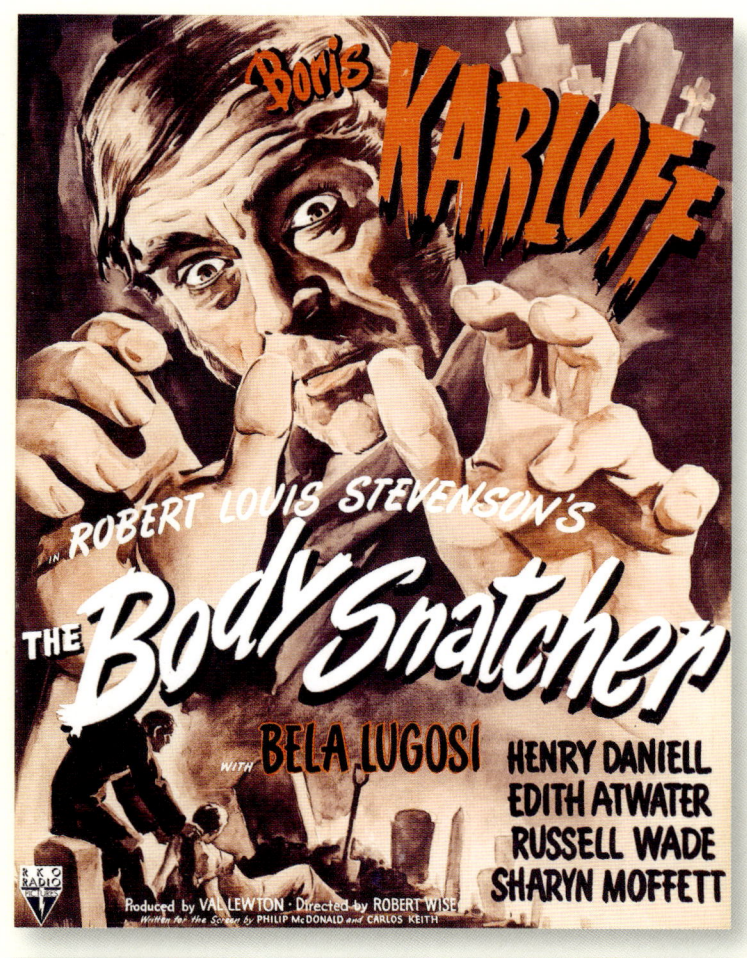

OPPOSITE, BOTTOM RIGHT: This advance trade advertisement for *The Leopard Man* (Dir: Jacques Tourneur, 1943) from the *RKO Radio Pictures 1942–1943* exhibitor book plays up Cornell Woolrich's source novel.

TOP LEFT: American window card for *The Body Snatcher* (Dir: Robert Wise, 1945) by RKO Radio Pictures' staff artist, William Rose. Based on a short story by Robert Louis Stevenson (1850–94), it marked the final on-screen pairing of Boris Karloff and Bela Lugosi.

BOTTOM LEFT: Half-sheet poster for RKO's *Bedlam* (Dir: Mark Robson, 1946), Boris Karloff's third and final collaboration with producer Val Lewton, suggested by William Hogarth's series of paintings *A Rake's Progress* (1732–33).

ABOVE RIGHT: *I Walked with a Zombie* (2014), digital poster by Canadian artist Sara Deck. "This piece was one of the first digital poster designs that I ever created," observes the artist. "I have a real admiration for Val Lewton's films, and so I was inspired to dive into one of my favorites of his titles."

THE FRIGHTENING FORTIES

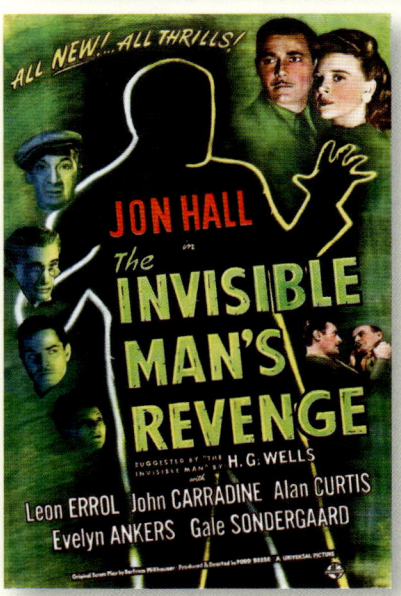

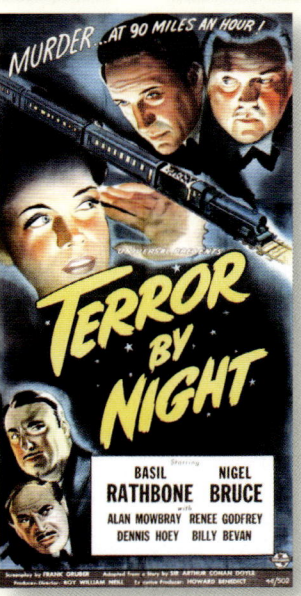

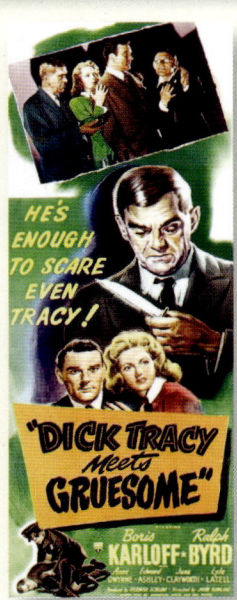

The Little Man of Horror

The natural successor to Dwight Frye during the 1940s, the emaciated-looking English-born actor Skelton [Barnaby] Knaggs (1911–55) began his career performing Shakespeare plays on the London stage, before appearing in a handful of "quota quickies." Moving to Hollywood in the late 1930s, he brought sinister support with a number of small but memorable roles in horror movies, often as a disgruntled villager or menacing assistant. Beginning with the poverty row *Torture Ship* (1939), he appeared in supporting roles in such films as *The Invisible Man's Revenge* (1944), *Isle of the Dead* (1945), *House of Dracula* (1945), *Terror by Night* (1945), *Bedlam* (1946), and *Dick Tracy Meets Gruesome* (1947). Perhaps his most memorable part was as the mute seaman Finn who narrates the Val Lewton production *The Ghost Ship* (1943), and he ended his horror career as a mad doctor's assistant in the Bowery Boys comedy *Master Minds* (1949). He died of cirrhosis of the liver.

TOP LEFT: One-sheet poster for RKO Radio Pictures' *The Ghost Ship* (Dir: Mark Robson, 1943) by William Rose. This was probably the most obscure of Val Lewton's productions for the studio, after it was withdrawn from distribution following a plagiarism lawsuit.

BOTTOM LEFT: One-sheet poster for *The Invisible Man's Revenge* (Dir: Ford Beebe, 1944), the fifth and final serious entry in Universal's unconnected series.

BOTTOM MIDDLE: Three-sheet poster for *Terror by Night* (Dir: Roy William Neill, 1946), the eleventh and penultimate entry in the Universal "Sherlock Holmes" series.

BOTTOM RIGHT: Insert card for *Dick Tracy Meets Gruesome* (Dir: John Rawlins, 1947), the last of R.K.O.'s series of four films starring Ralph Byrd as the eponymous detective, based on the comic strip by Chester Gould (1900–85).

TOP RIGHT: *Skelton Knaggs* (2016), oils on board portrait by Les Edwards of the British-born character actor in RKO Radio Pictures' *Dick Tracy vs. Cueball* (Dir: Gordon M. Douglas, 1946). "Not only an amazing face," says the artist, "but a wonderful name to go with it. I thought the glasses were beautifully creepy."

THE ART OF HORROR MOVIES

Forties Shades of Gray

Based on the 1890 novel by Oscar Wilde, Metro-Goldwyn-Mayer's elegant adaptation of *The Picture of Dorian Gray* (Dir: Albert Lewin, 1945) stars American actor Hurd Hatfield (1917–98) as the narcissistic young man of the title who remains youthful while his portrait reflects the evil he commits. The terrific supporting cast includes George Sanders, Donna Reed, Angela Lansbury, Peter Lawford, Miles Mander, Billy Bevan, and Skelton Knaggs, with Cedric Hardwicke as the uncredited narrator. Filmed mostly in black and white, the horribly ravaged portrait is revealed in a series of three-strip Technicolor inserts. To create the hideous oil painting [RIGHT], the studio commissioned Magic Realist artist Ivan Albright (1897–1983) for a fee of $75,000. Albright was reportedly supposed to paint four portraits, revealing Gray's progressive dissolution, but the artist only had time to finish one. For the uncorrupted portrait of Gray seen earlier in the film, MGM originally chose Albright's identical twin brother Malvin (seen ABOVE with Ivan, apparently working on the unfinished painting alongside a dummy of the decayed Dorian Gray), although the final portrait shown in the film is credited to the Portuguese artist Henrique Medina (1901–88). Albright's painting hangs in the Art Institute of Chicago, while Medina's portrait was originally sold for $25,000 at the MGM Auction in 1970 and, at some point, was gifted to Hurd Hatfield himself. In March 2015 it was sold during an auction at Christie's, New York, for $149,000. However, the question remains, what happened to Malvin Albright's painting, if it ever existed?

THE FRIGHTENING FORTIES

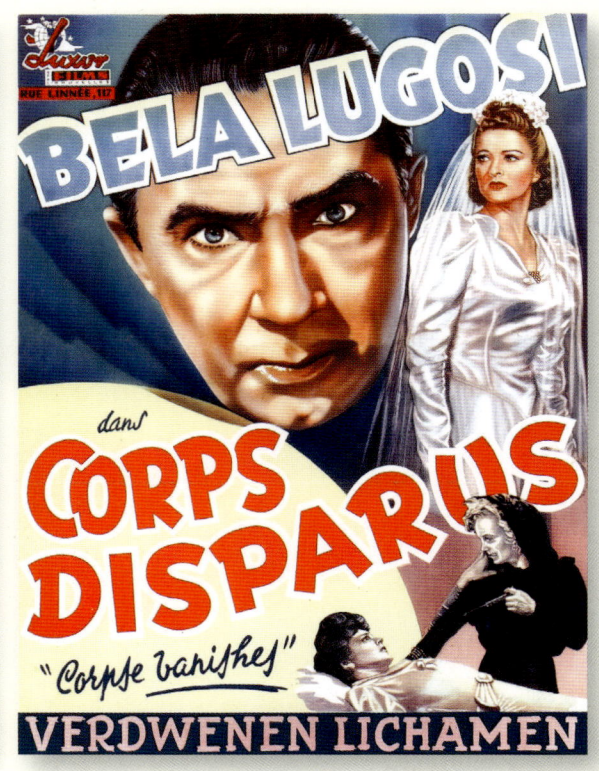

Women in Horror: 1940s

If ever there was the epitome of a 1940s "Dragon Lady" it was Gale Sondergaard (Edith Holm Sondergaard, 1899–1985), who portrayed menacing—yet always alluring—*femme fatales* in numerous Hollywood movies. Perhaps her finest roles were as the scheming Adrea Spedding in Universal's *The Spider Woman* (1944) and as Zenobia Dollard in the sequel-in-name-only *The Spider Woman Strikes Back* (1946). Born to British parents in Chile, Evelyn Ankers (1918–85) was an archetypal Universal leading lady in such films as *The Wolf Man* (1941) and *The Ghost of Frankenstein* (1942), but she revealed her range as an actress in another Sherlock Holmes mystery, *The Pearl of Death* (1944). Louise Currie's (1913–2013) sassy heroine brightened up the Monogram programmers *The Ape Man* (1943) and *Voodoo Man* (1944), while Minerva Urecal (Minerva Holzer, 1894–1966) was invariably cackling away in the background in such titles as *The Corpse Vanishes* (1941) and *Ghosts on the Loose* (1943) for the same studio.

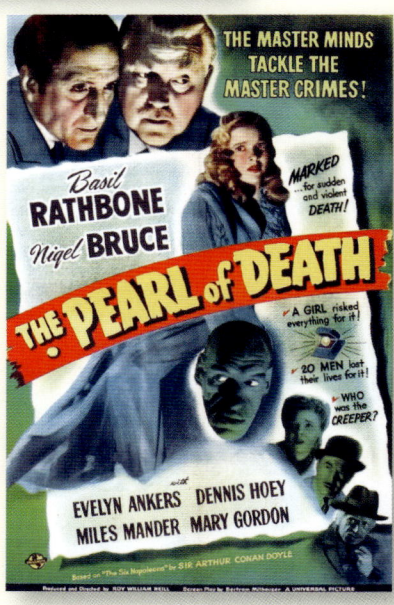

TOP LEFT: Title lobby card for *The Spider Woman Strikes Back* (Dir: Arthur Lubin, 1946), a spin-off of sorts from Universal's "Sherlock Holmes" series.

TOP RIGHT: Belgian Poster for Monogram Pictures' *The Corpse Vanishes* (Dir: Wallace Fox, 1942), in which Bela Lugosi's mad doctor kidnaps "dead" society brides at the altar and extracts a fluid from their glands to keep his wife eternally young.

BOTTOM LEFT: Three-sheet poster for Monogram's *The Ape Man* (Dir: William Beaudine, 1943), in which Bela Lugosi's missing mad scientist steals human spinal fluid to prevent himself from turning into a hairy ape-man.

BOTTOM MIDDLE: Insert card for Monogram's *Voodoo Man* (Dir: William Beaudine, 1944), in which Louise Currie can't resist Bela Lugosi's hypnotic powers.

BOTTOM RIGHT: One-sheet poster for *The Pearl of Death* (Dir: Roy William Neill, 1944), in which Evelyn Ankers shines as a villain.

OPPOSITE: *Frankenstein Meets the Wolf Man* (2015), oils on canvas by Spanish artist Sanjulián (Manuel Pérez Clemente). "Being a lover of classic horror movies," says the artist, "I could not refuse to work on this painting."

THE ART OF HORROR MOVIES

— 110 —

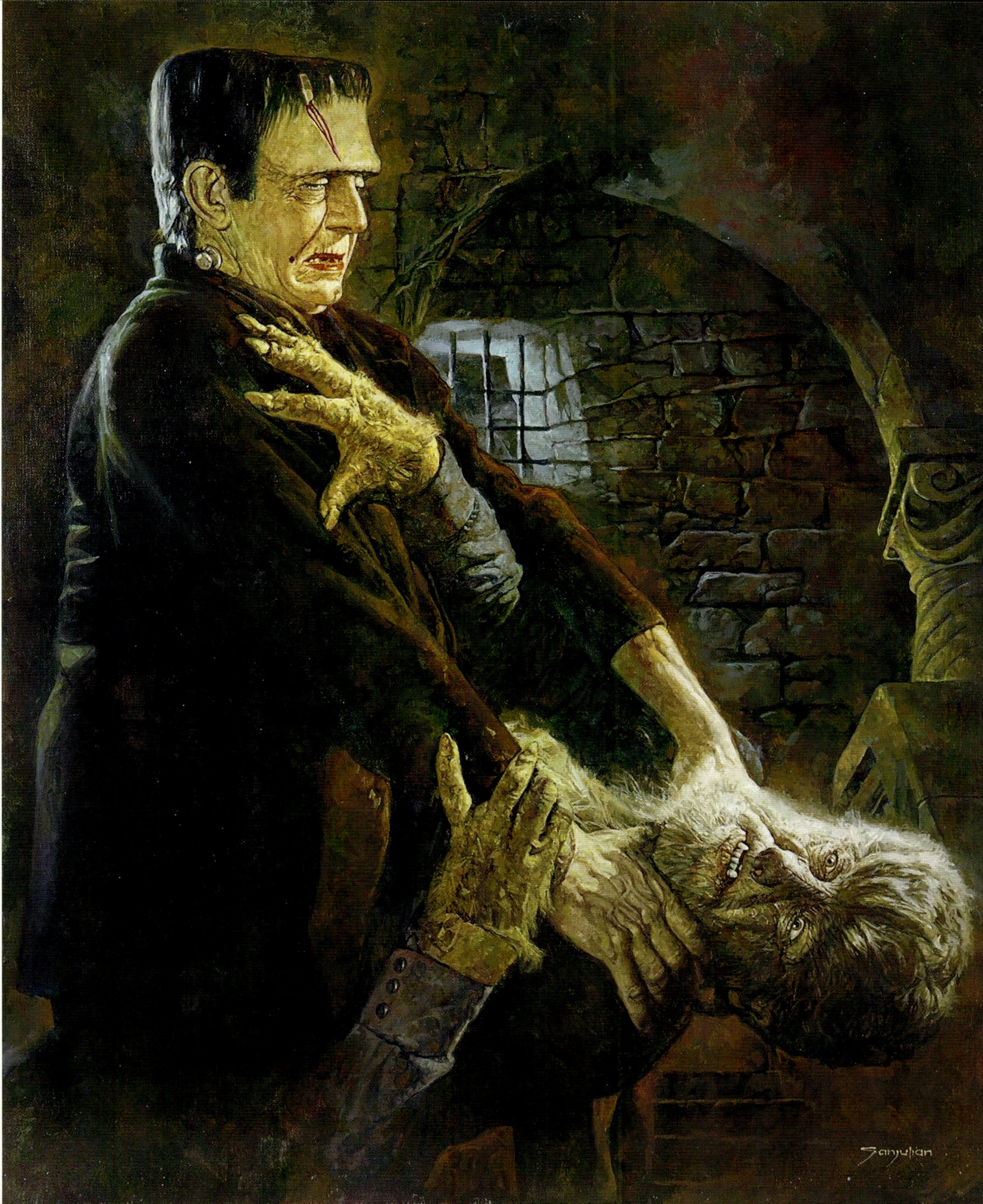
Sanjulian

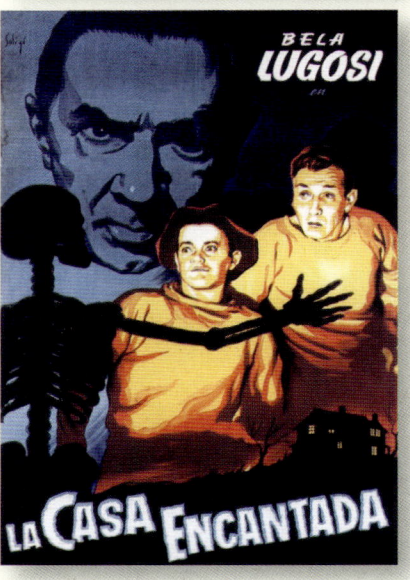

TOP LEFT: Belgian poster for Columbia Pictures' comedy *The Boogie Man Will Get You* (Dir: Lew Landers, 1942), inspired by the success of the stage play of *Arsenic and Old Lace*, which was running on Broadway at the time.

TOP MIDDLE: One-sheet poster for RKO Radio Pictures' *Mexican Spitfire Sees a Ghost* (Dir: Leslie Goodwins, 1942) starring Mexican-born comedian and dancer Lupe Vélez (María Guadalupe Villalobos Vélez).

BOTTOM LEFT: Spanish poster for "The East Side Kids" comedy *Ghosts on the Loose* (Dir: William Beaudine, 1943) by artist Josep Soligó Tena (1910–94). 19-year-old Ava Gardner made her first credited appearance in this movie.

BOTTOM MIDDLE: One-sheet poster for "The Bowery Boys" comedy *Master Minds* (Dir: Jean Yarbrough, 1949), in which Alan Napier's mad scientist transfers the brain of "Sach" (Huntz Hall) into his monstrous creation, Atlas (Glenn Strange).

ABOVE RIGHT: 1950 *grande affiche* for Universal's (Abbott and Costello) *Meet the Killer* (Dir: Charles T. Barton, 1949) by French artist Jacques Bonneaud (1898–1971), who produced more than 2,000 movie posters from the 1920s until 1958, when offset printing eventually replaced the lithography technique.

THE ART OF HORROR MOVIES

Meet Frankenstein

With Universal's 1940s cycle of horror movies drawing to a close, the studio squeezed one last drop of profit out of their classic Monsters by teaming them up with their most successful comedic duo in the surprisingly entertaining *Abbott and Costello Meet Frankenstein* (Dir: Charles Barton, 1948). Originally intended to be a serious entry in the series entitled *The Brain of Frankenstein*, comedians Bud Abbott and Lou Costello helped Lon Chaney's Lawrence Talbot/Wolf Man prevent Dr. Lahos/Count Dracula (Bela Lugosi) from transplanting Lou's brain into the Frankenstein Monster (Glenn Strange). Chaney stood in for an injured Strange during the laboratory climax, and an uncredited Vincent Price is heard at the end reprising his role as the Invisible Man. The on-screen title is actually *Meet Frankenstein* (with the comic duo billed separately above), and in the UK it was released as *Abbott and Costello Meet the Ghosts*.

TOP LEFT: 1954 Japanese poster for Universal's *Abbott and Costello Meet Frankenstein* (1948).

TOP MIDDLE: 1965 Spanish reissue poster for *Abbott and Costello Meet Frankenstein* (1948) by artist Alvaro.

BOTTOM LEFT: American half-sheet poster for *Abbott and Costello Meet Frankenstein* (1948).

ABOVE RIGHT: *Bela Lugosi* (2000), oils on canvas board portrait by British artist Les Edwards of the actor's second and final screen appearance as Count Dracula in Universal-International's *Abbott and Costello Meet Frankenstein* (1948). "This is one of a number of experimental paintings I did in black and white," explains Edwards. "The lighting in old studio photos is often very beautiful, and I find it a source of inspiration."

FOLLOWING SPREAD: *Frankie's Got a New Ride* (2015), acrylic on illustration board by Doug P'gosh. "Frankie and friends go for a ride in his new custom-built hot-rod," explains the artist. "Frankenstein's Castle looms in the deep background; King Kong can be seen waving from the distance; Boris Karloff gets a second nod as the Body Snatcher crossing the road behind the car, and the tentacles behind the Creature are a tribute to Ray Harryhausen and *It Came from Beneath the Sea* (1955)."

THE FRIGHTENING FORTIES

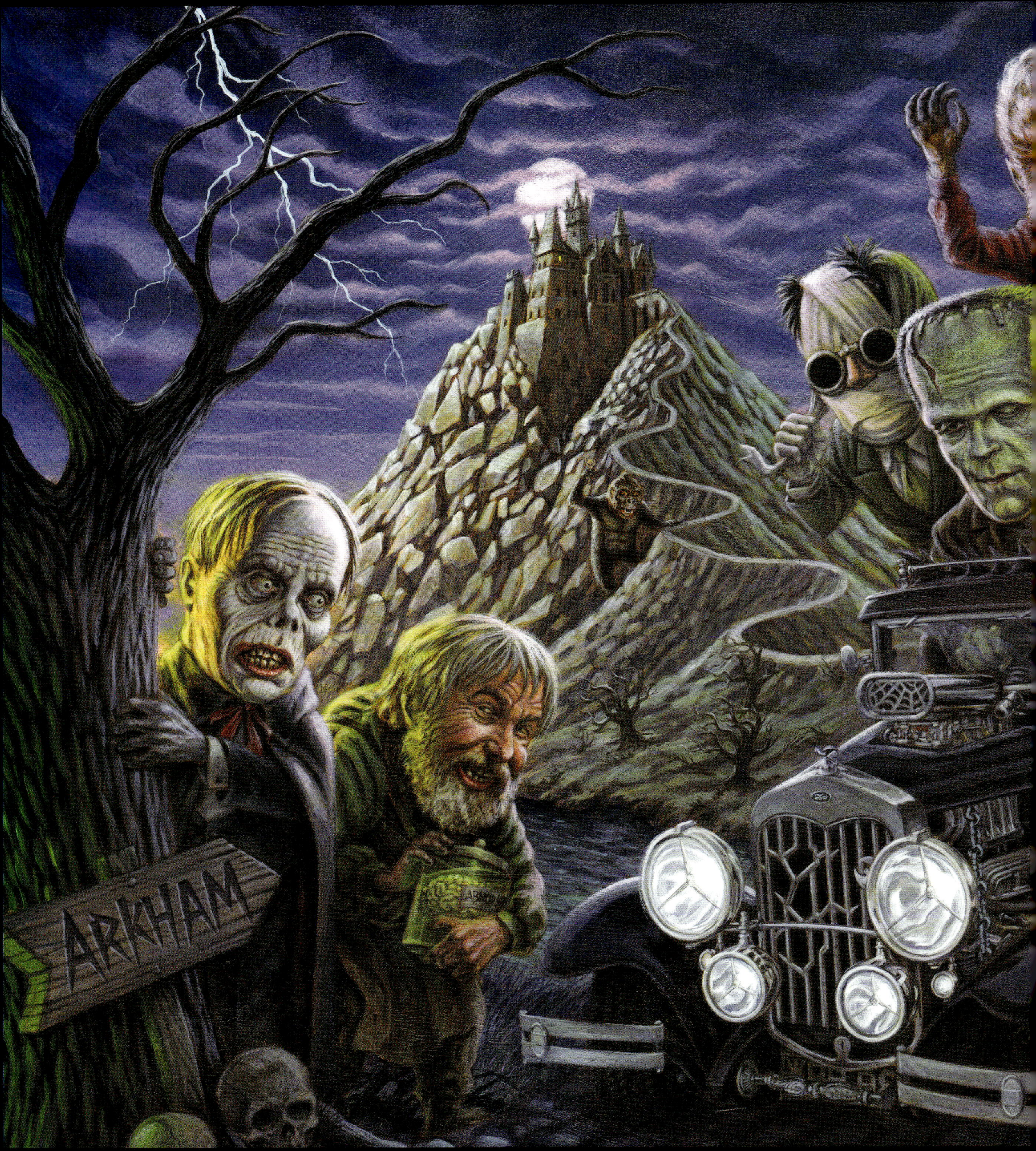
ARKHAM

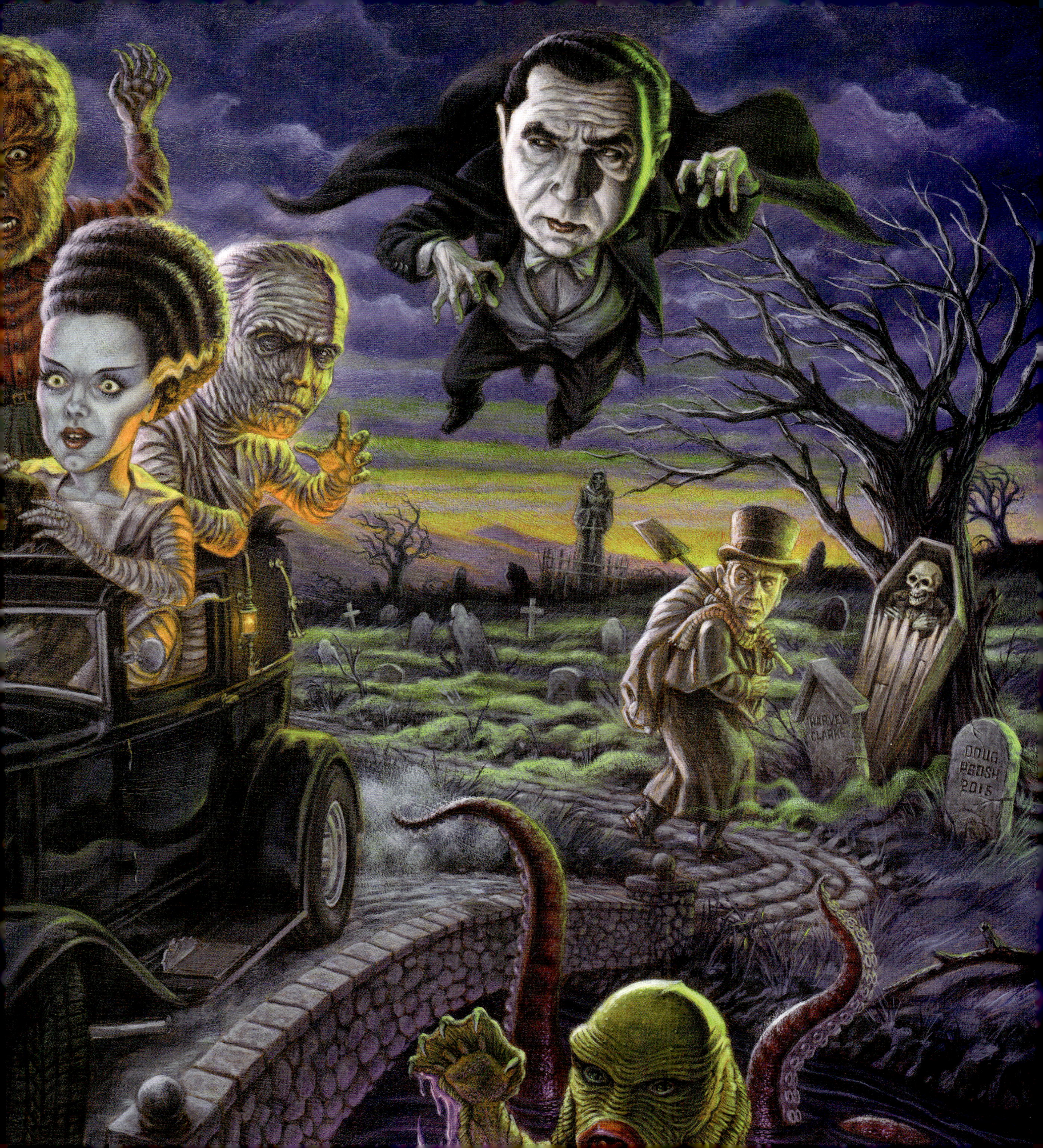

HARVEY CLARKE
DOUG POTOSH 2015

PLEASE STAND BY

THE FEARSOME FIFTIES

DAVID J. SCHOW

"Now I am become Death,
the destroyer of worlds."

KRISHNA

> "When you see something that is technically sweet, you go ahead and do it and you argue about what to do about it only after you have had your technical success. That is the way it was with the atomic bomb."
>
> J. Robert Oppenheimer

TRENDS RARELY HEW to the boundaries of specific decades, but we can broadly say that the 1950s were the age when science fiction and horror films graduated from the previous idiom of mad scientists (who had become comfy and predictable in their be-smocked craziness) to science that was itself insane—particularly when it waxed nuclear. The impingement on monster movies by the brand of lurid color once reserved for more "important" films helped refresh the thrill factor not only for moviegoers, but for studios already quaking in fear at another invasion—television.

As electricity was the sorcery of choice for the prior era's mad doctors, so did atomic radiation become the go-to fuel for a new generation of invaders from outer space and supersized creatures. Living dinosaurs were no longer the big beasts on the block; in order to compete during the 1950s, they had to virtually glow in the dark with poisonous emissions. The radium and X-rays of previous science-gone-berserk melodramas also thrived in their updated incarnations—fallout and (best of all) *atomic mutation*, which basically made *anything* possible. Low-budget filmmakers in particular could not have asked for a sweeter catchall.

As Kim Newman has pointed out, if the Gothic monstrosities of the 1930s and 40s were analogous to the Beatles, then the cultural warhead power of an Elvis Presley accompanied landfall by the Creature from the Black Lagoon—a prehistoric man-phibian throwback older than *all* his predecessors, and better yet, *not* just another resurrected dead guy. Simultaneously, the post-war bugaboo of atomic bomb tests unleashed a wave of gigantism across the animal kingdom even as Godzilla was cinematically born to level Japan as a cautionary callback to Hiroshima and Nagasaki.

Once Klaatu's pie-plate spaceship touched down in *The Day the Earth Stood Still* (1951) it became open season for anyone or anything else piloting a flying saucer—a term that had been around since the 1930s (as seen on many a pulp magazine cover), but which captivated the zeitgeist in the wake of the Air Force's Project Blue Book investigations and the public thirst for any and all shapes of Unidentified Flying Objects—newly coined as "UFOs" amid the furor over the so-called Roswell Incident and speculations about the United States government's enigmatic Area 51.

The threat of the intergalactic Outsider swiftly amplified from the lone, green-blooded plant-man of *The Thing from Another World* (1951)—individual, localized terror in black and white—into an entire armada of indestructible ships from Mars in *The War of the Worlds* (1953), laying waste to the entire planet. They came for our kids (*Invaders from Mars*, 1953), our women (*I Married a Monster from Outer Space*, 1958), our corpses (*Invisible Invaders*, 1959), and even returned to their vegetable roots to consume and replace us with plant pod simulacra (*Invasion of the Body Snatchers*, 1956). And for each of these, there came a secondary invasion of cheaper knockoff movies, the very word "invasion" serving as a hot-button paranoia cue during the age of McCarthyism and the Red Scare.

> The impingement on monster movies by the brand of lurid color once reserved for more "important" films helped refresh the thrill factor not only for moviegoers, but for studios already quaking in fear at another invasion—television.

Worst of all, *teenagers* became newly perceived as a consumer market that needed pandering to, just as drive-in theaters needed double-bills to support all that groping and smoking and hanging out beyond parental supervision. Hence, modernization—the werewolf archetype got a letterman's jacket and a trigger based not in myth but pseudoscience (*I Was a Teenage Werewolf*, 1957); a descendant from reliable European mad scientist stock got Americanized and created a resurrected patchwork man from the corpses of high school athletes (*I Was a Teenage Frankenstein*, 1957); and a female vampire decimated a school for wayward girls (*Blood of Dracula*, 1957). On the plus side stood a ready horde of "ordinary" adolescents who knew the straight dope and were prepared to intercede against every threat from *Teenage Cave Man* (1958) to *Teenagers from Outer Space* (1959); you have but to re-watch *The Blob* (1958) for the basic story template—plucky teens save the day when the authorities won't believe them.

And if improbably interpreted, hot-rodding high schoolers were not in the vanguard, Nigel Kneale's brilliant and cantankerous Professor Bernard Quatermass certainly was, slamming down the cold, hard facts to a constituency

PREVIOUS SPREAD: *B-Movie Nightmares* (2013), acrylic on illustration board by American artist Doug P'gosh. "A tribute to the midnight movies I watched as a youth," the artist explains. "A nightmare fueled by too much soda, junk-food and staying up way past my bedtime. Early TV horror hostess Vampira from *Plan 9 from Outer Space* (1959) presents her menagerie at the front of the saucer, while the elder statesmen of horror, Boris Karloff, Bela Lugosi, and Lon Chaney, Jr., way past their prime, float above the scene."

TOP LEFT: 1954 reissue half-sheet poster for RKO Radio Pictures' *The Thing from Another World* (Dir: Christian Nyby, 1951), based on the novella "Who Goes There?" by Don A. Stuart (John W. Campbell, Jr.) originally published in the August 1938 issue of *Astounding Science-Fiction*.

BOTTOM LEFT: British trade show advertisement for the Anglo Amalgamated Film Distributors' 1958 double-bill release of American International Pictures' *I Was a Teenage Frankenstein* and *Blood of Dracula* (both Dir: Herbert L. Strock, 1957) under the revised titles *Teenage Frankenstein* and *Blood is My Heritage*.

ABOVE RIGHT: Stylized French *grande affiche* for Hammer Films' *Quatermass 2* (aka *Enemy from Space*, 1956) by Clément Hurel (1927–2008), considered one of the most important French movie poster artists of the twentieth century.

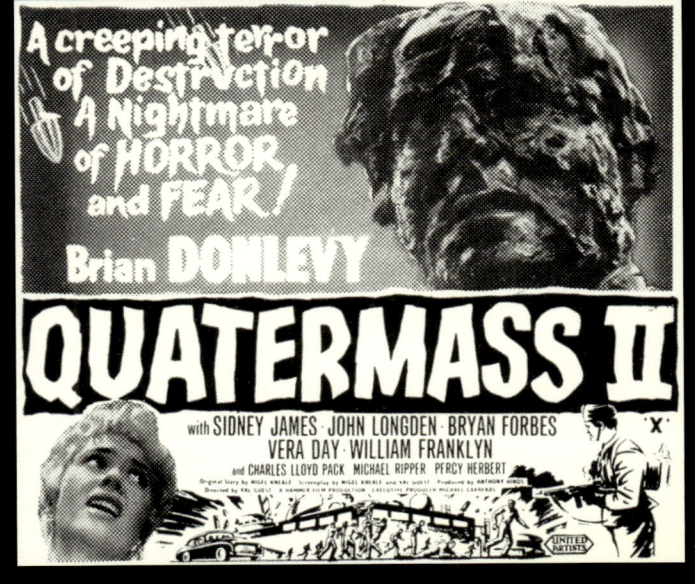

THE FEARSOME FIFTIES

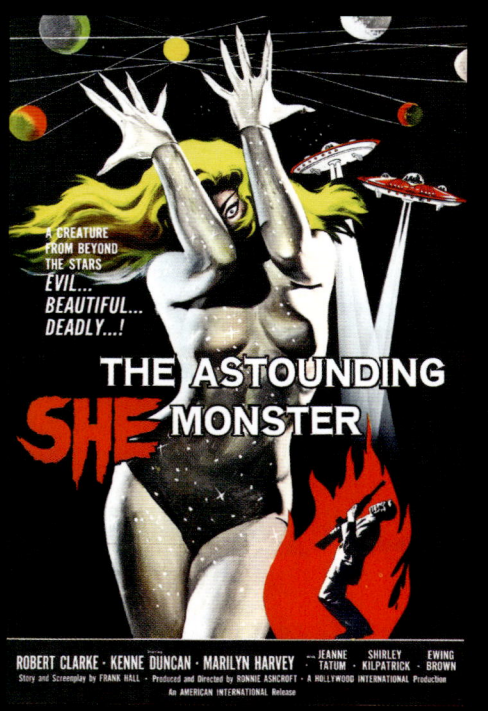

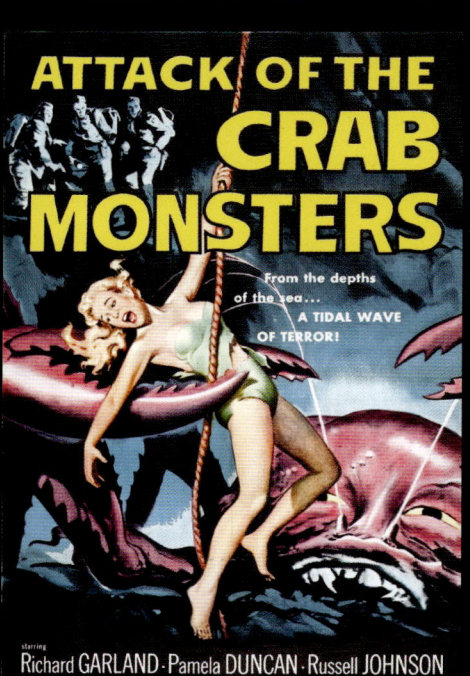

TOP LEFT: Title lobby card for American Releasing Corporation's *The Beast with a Million Eyes* (Dir: David Kramarsky and an uncredited Roger Corman, 1955) by designer Albert [James] Kallis.

TOP RIGHT: Half-sheet poster for Universal-International's American release of *Blood of the Vampire* (Dir: Henry Cass, 1958) by artist Joseph "Joe" Smith (1912–2003). "If I liked the art," recalled Smith, "I worked my signature somewhere into the poster. Universal never argued with me on that."

BOTTOM LEFT: Albert Kallis's one-sheet poster design for American International's *The Astounding She-Monster* (Dir: Ronnie Ashcroft, 1957). "Jim [Nicholson] and I would make up most of the titles and kick around what the advertising approach would be," explained the artist. "Then, I'd make up an ad campaign."

BOTTOM MIDDLE: Six-sheet poster for Allied Artists' *World Without End* (Dir: Edward Bernds, 1956) by Peruvian-born pin-up artist Alberto Vargas (1896–1982), who was paid $1,500 to create full-length watercolor paintings of actresses Nancy Gates, Lisa Montell, and Shawn Smith.

BOTTOM RIGHT: One-sheet poster for *Attack of the Crab Monsters* (Dir: Roger Corman, 1957) by Albert Kallis, who recalled: "I told Roger, 'I'm doing stuff with Saul Bass and the best studios . . . If, after general conversations, you'd leave all the decisions to me, I might be interested—*and* I'd give you a fixed price.' That appealed to Roger greatly."

of inferiors and naysayers in Hammer Films' feature versions of the popular BBC serials: *The Quatermass Xperiment* (aka *The Creeping Unknown*, 1955) and *Quatermass 2* (aka *Enemy from Space*, 1956).

Low- and no-budgeters thrived in this loam, and today the likes of Roger Corman, Jack Arnold, Bert I. Gordon, and Herman Cohen are remembered mostly for their efforts during the 1950s heyday of anything goes sci-fi and horror—which categories had themselves become conflated, intertwined, and remain so to this day.

Metro-Goldwyn-Mayer's bid for respectability in such "low" forms was realized in the widescreen Technicolor spectacle of *Forbidden Planet* (1956), which grandeur Universal attempted to mimic with the hilarious *This Island Earth* (1955)—"Two and a half years in the making!" went the ballyhoo. MGM had sourced its film—loosely—from Shakespeare, while Universal's near-nonsensical pageant was pure *Thrilling Wonder Stories*.

Old-school monsters had been rumped out the exit with a comedy bang in 1948 via *Abbott and Costello Meet Frankenstein*, which was nothing compared to the insult and injury yet to befall them throughout the 1950s. Bad horror is comedic; bad comedy is likewise horrific, but bad horror comedy is the death rattle of a genre gasping its last.

In 1956, Hammer Films picked up the torch summarily discarded by Universal—which by then was grinding out B-features like *The Mole People* (1956)—and rebirthed the classic monster canon by ramping up the sex and violence (or "romance and adventure," for those with finer sensibilities) in dynamic, action-packed, vibrant Technicolor. Now the Frankenstein monster was uglier than ever before, the pink of his burn tissue and scars hideously present; now, when Count Dracula attacked, he was on you like a wolverine; the revamped Mummy now towered over his victims and erased them with relentless Terminator speed.

The 1950s were the Golden Age of monster movie posters, and the heyday of Saul Bass protégé Albert Kallis, who for 17 years produced nearly all of the flamboyant, hard-sell poster art for American Releasing Corporation, which evolved into American International Pictures. His arresting style imparted a sultry muscularity to often impoverished subjects—he made *The Beast with a Million Eyes* (1955) and *The Astounding She-Monster* (1957) seem better than you already knew they could possibly be. As writer Stephen Rebello observed, Kallis "helped elevate naked hustle to an art form."

Nobody embodied the platinum standard for 1950s monster movie poster art more than acclaimed artist Reynold Brown. Perpetually underpaid and overworked, with an uncanny knack for depicting actors' faces, his minutely detailed scenarios bridled against the tired montage style of most movie advertising, and often presented crowds of urbanites fleeing from some titular menace. His magic palette could lend a rocket-powered kick in the pants to the likes of *World Without End* (1956), or help boost a monster directly into cinema history, as with *Creature from the Black Lagoon* (1954). What is possibly one of the most iconic movie posters of all time, *Attack of the 50 Foot Woman* (1958), was completed by Brown when Albert Kallis got caught under deadline pressure.

Fortunately, the heyday of Brown cohort Joseph Smith arrived simultaneously with the influx of British films to be distributed by Universal Studios—having done *It Came from Outer Space* (1953) and *The Mole People*, he handily executed the American sell-art for such titles as *Blood of the Vampire* (1958) and Hammer's *Dracula* (aka *Horror of Dracula*, 1958), and *The Mummy* (1959).

Other studio illustrators for this period included Bob Totten (shared with Brown on *Touch of Evil*, 1958), Ken Sawyer, Ruth Corbett, Sy Mezerow, and Harry Timmins.

The premier "astronomical artist" of this timeframe was the venerable Chesley Bonestell, whose illustrations not only informed and inspired actual space exploration, but gilded films from George Pal's *Destination Moon* (1950) to the schlock perennial *Cat-Women of the Moon* (1953).

Stop-motion animator Ray Harryhausen's work was not on the posters, but up on the silver screen, a confluence of graphic design, sculpture, modeling, and laboriously realized optical effects (back when special effects were still "special") that without doubt also classifies as representative art of those times, which saw the release of *The Beast from 20,000 Fathoms* (1953), *Earth vs. The Flying Saucers* (1956), *20 Million Miles to Earth* (1957), and *The 7th Voyage of Sinbad* (1958).

A modest hat-tip is also due to Warner Bros. animator Paul Julian, who conceived striking title backdrops for such Corman quickies as *Attack of the Crab Monsters* and *Not of This Earth* (both 1957). Julian also designed and colored the Oscar-nominated 1953 animated version of Poe's *The Tell-Tale Heart*.

What we have come to remember as "1950s monster movies" actually kept chugging through to the mid-1960s at least, by which time the looming competitor of television had already delivered a classic salvo of its own: 1959 was the premiere year for Rod Serling's *The Twilight Zone*.

> In 1956, Hammer Films picked up the torch summarily discarded by Universal—which by then was grinding out B-features like *The Mole People* (1956)—and rebirthed the classic monster canon by ramping up the sex and violence (or "romance and adventure," for those with finer sensibilities) in dynamic, action-packed, vibrant Technicolor.

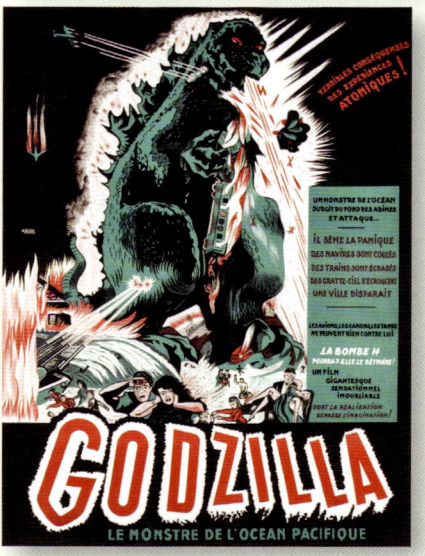

TOP: Japanese banner poster for Toho Film Company's most iconic and enduring example of 1950s monster movies, *Gojira*, aka *Godzilla* (Dir: Ishirô Honda, 1954). When the concept of using stop-motion was rejected, special effects director Eiji Tsuburaya (1901–70) used a man in a suit (Haruo Nakajima).

BOTTOM LEFT: 1957 French *petite affiche* for *Godzilla* (1954) by artist A. Poucel. The look of the atomic-breathing creature in the movie was actually inspired by the paintings of Czech paleo-artist Zdeněk Burian (1905–81).

BOTTOM MIDDLE, LEFT: Exploitative insert card for Lippert Pictures' *Monster from the Ocean Floor* (Dir: Wyott Ordung, 1954), which was the first solo producing credit for Roger Corman.

BOTTOM MIDDLE, RIGHT: Australian daybill for Columbia Pictures' *The Giant Claw* (Dir: Fred F. Sears, 1957). The poster artists were reportedly not shown any footage of the giant alien bird, which is why the image on the advertising material looks nothing like the laughable puppet that was eventually used in the movie.

BOTTOM RIGHT: Half-sheet poster for the Italian-made *Caltiki, il mostro immortale* (1959), released in America by Allied Artists in 1960 as *Caltiki, the Immortal Monster*. When director Riccardo Freda (credited as "Robert Hamton") walked off the project, cinematographer and special effects director Mario Bava took over.

THE ART OF HORROR MOVIES

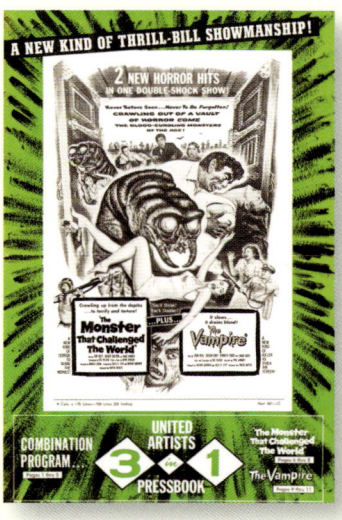

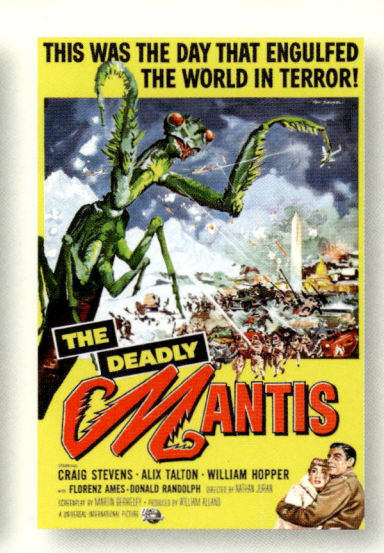

ABOVE LEFT: Original pencil on illustration board artwork for United Artists' "Double Shock Show" of *The Monster That Challenged the World* (Dir: Arnold Laven, 1957) and *The Vampire* (Dir: Paul Landres, 1957).

TOP MIDDLE: The cover of United Artists' combination pressbook for *The Monster That Challenged the World* and *The Vampire* (both 1957).

TOP RIGHT: One-sheet poster by Ken Sawyer (1896–1960) for Universal-International's *The Deadly Mantis* (Dir: Nathan Juran, 1957). Unusually for an American movie poster of this period, the artist boldly signed his work in the top right-hand corner.

BOTTOM RIGHT: Original gouache on board artwork (with lettering on an acetate overlay) by Reynold Brown (1917–91) for Universal-International's *The Land Unknown* (Dir: Virgil Vogel, 1957).

THE FEARSOME FIFTIES

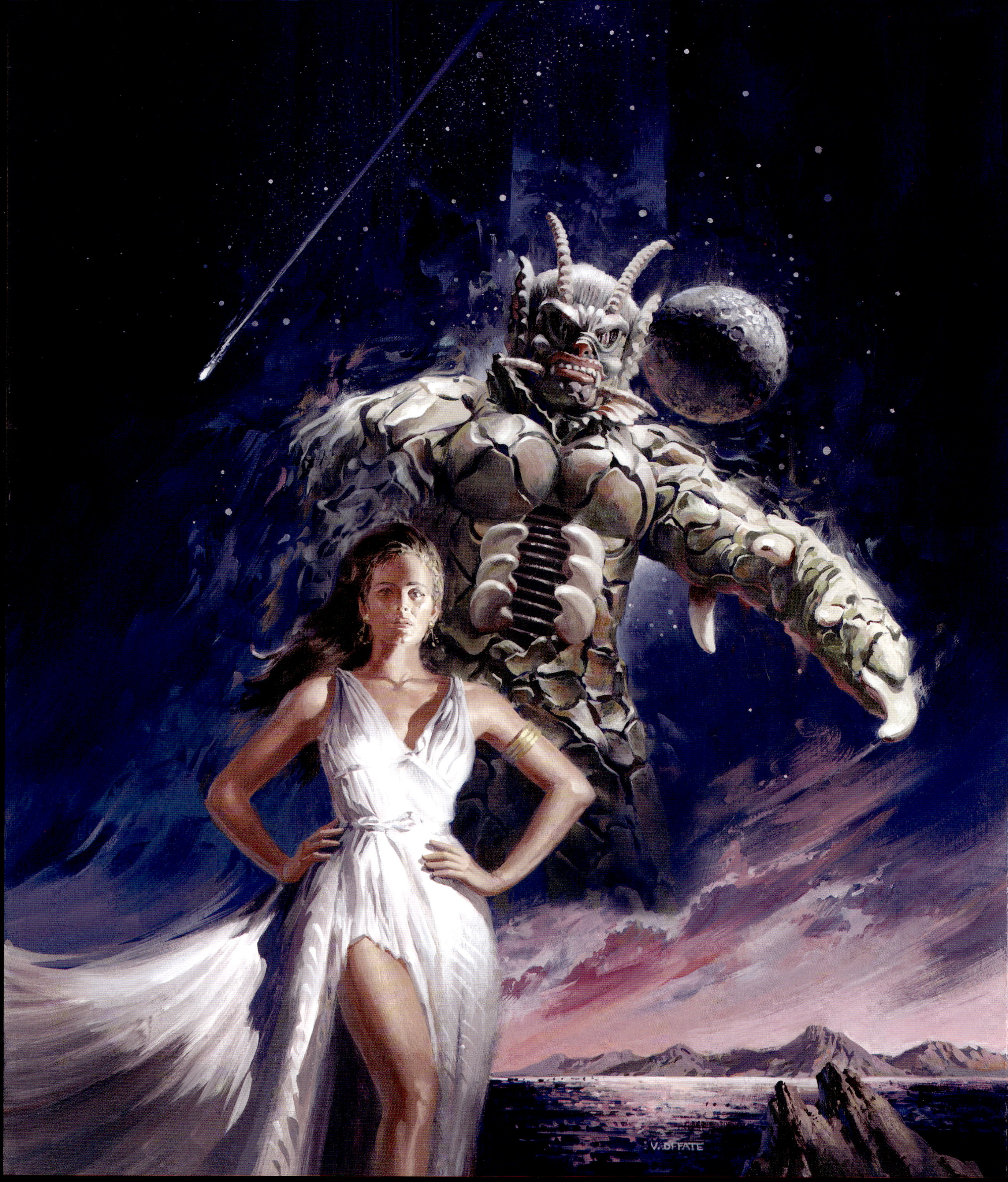
V. DI FATE

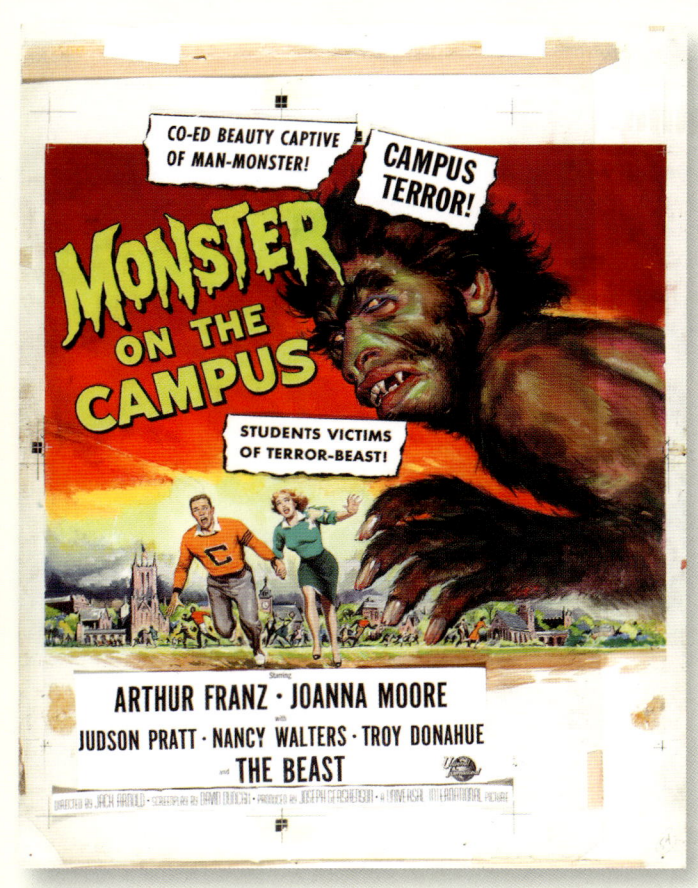

OPPOSITE: *The She-Creature* (2005), acrylic on hardboard, produced by American artist Vincent Di Fate as a commemorative limited edition print. Based on the 1956 American International movie of the same name, the artist describes this as "A homage to the artistry of monster-maker Paul Blaisdell."

TOP LEFT: Original gouache on board artwork (with tape residue from the acetate lettering overlay) by Reynold Brown for Universal-International's *Monster on the Campus* (Dir: Jack Arnold, 1958). "Over the years, monsters became more vicious and ill-mannered," recalled the artist, "but not yet."

BOTTOM LEFT: American half-sheet poster for *The Abominable Snowman of the Himalayas* (Dir: Val Guest, 1957), based on the live BBC-TV play *The Creature* by Nigel Kneale.

ABOVE RIGHT: *The Mole People* (2016), a pen and ink, wash, and graphite personal piece on board by American artist Randy Broecker. "You had to feel sorry for them," explains Broecker, "the 'last gasp' of Universal's Monsters, and, like several of their earlier 'relations,' *not* really monsters . . . just misunderstood."

THE FEARSOME FIFTIES

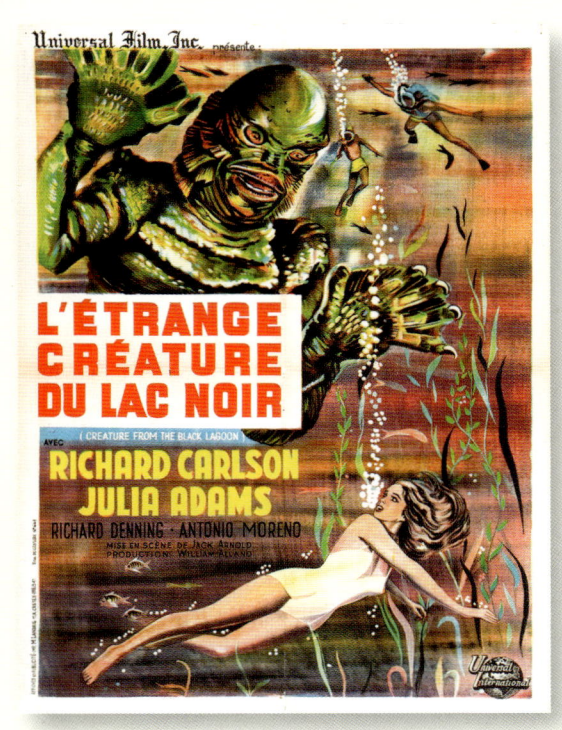

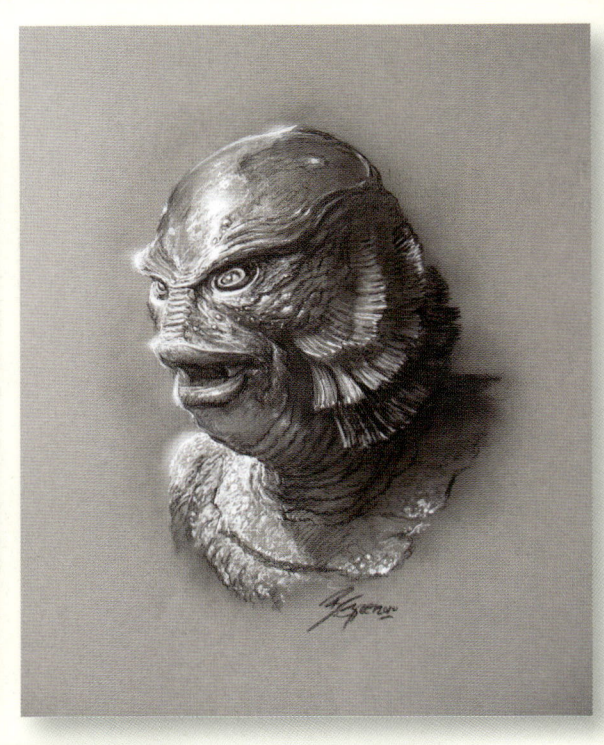

TOP LEFT: 1962 French reissue *affiche* for Universal-International's *Creature from the Back Lagoon* (Dir: Jack Arnold, 1954). For this first entry in the trilogy, actress and illustrator Milicent Patrick (1915–98) actually "visualized" the Gill Man, but Universal's head of makeup, "Bud" Westmore, took credit for the design.

BOTTOM RIGHT: Half-sheet poster for Universal-International's *Revenge of the Creature* (Dir: Jack Arnold, 1955). For this sequel, Tom Hennesy and Ricou Browning put on the Gill Man suit.

TOP MIDDLE: 1960 Italian *foglio* for Universal-International's *The Creature Walks Among Us* (Dir: John Sherwood, 1956), in which Don Megowan and Ricou Browning wore the Creature suit for the third and final entry in the series.

TOP RIGHT: *Creature from the Black Lagoon* (2011), Conté crayon on gray paper by American artist Bob Eggleton. "This was a study for a more ambitious work," explains the artist. "Studies sometimes wind up more fun than the finished work. I like the black and white medium because I'm forced to capture things in a more basic sense."

BOTTOM LEFT: *The Creature* (2016), oils on panel by American artist Richard Bernal. "The Creature from the Black Lagoon was a childhood favorite of mine," recalls the artist, "and it was fun to try to capture him in paint."

THE ART OF HORROR MOVIES

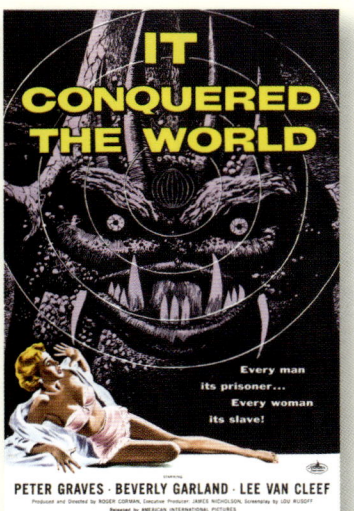

TOP LEFT: Original charcoal on board illustration for United Artists' *It! The Terror from Beyond Space* (Dir: Edward L. Cahn, 1958). This image was used on various poster formats, with color added during the production process.

ABOVE RIGHT: Insert card for *It! The Terror from Beyond Space* (1958). Set in a futuristic 1973, the crew of the first manned expedition to Mars are killed by an alien creature that has stowed away on their vessel.

BOTTOM LEFT: One-sheet poster for *It Conquered the World* (Dir: Roger Corman, 1956) by American International Pictures' art director Albert Kallis. "This was the heyday of the drive-in theater," noted the artist, "most of these pictures were sold from newspaper ads or posters."

BOTTOM MIDDLE: British quad poster for Universal-International's first 3-D movie, *It Came from Outer Space* (Dir: Jack Arnold, 1953), based on five draft treatments by Ray Bradbury (1920–2012). Milicent Patrick once again created various concept sketches for the film's one-eyed alien xenomorph.

THE FEARSOME FIFTIES

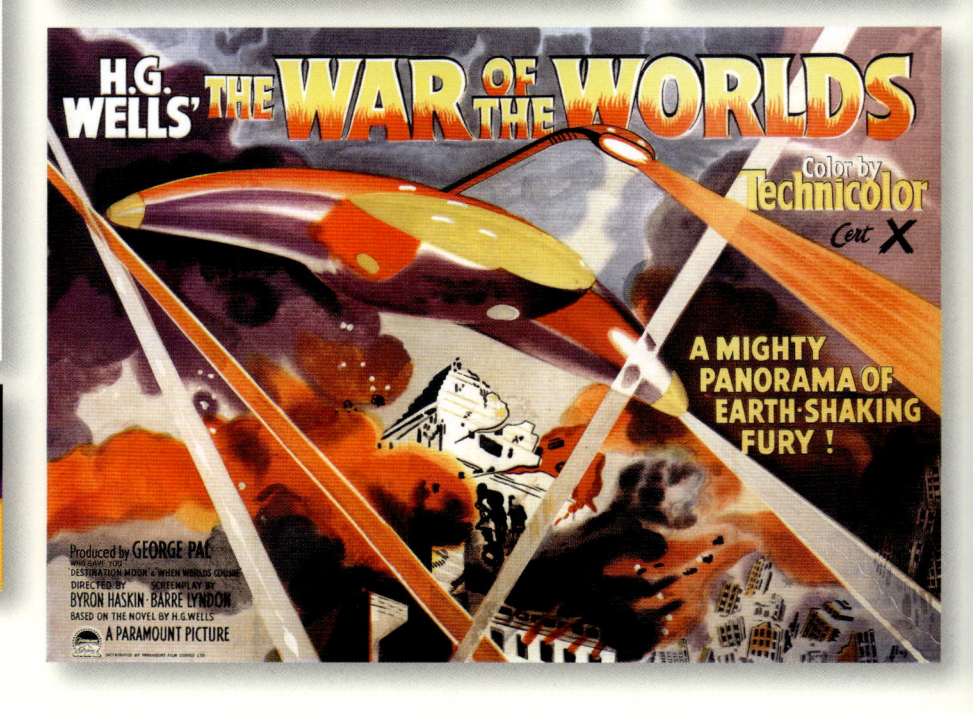

TOP LEFT: 1960 Italian *duo-foglio* for Columbia Pictures' *20 Million Miles to Earth* (Dir: Nathan Juran, 1957) by Anselmo Ballester (1897–1974). The first spaceship to Venus returns to Earth carrying an alien creature (stop-motion effects created by Ray Harryhausen).

BOTTOM LEFT: Banner poster for Twentieth Century-Fox's *Invaders from Mars* (Dir: William Cameron Menzies, 1953) depicting the Martian Intelligence played by former "Munchkin" Luce Potter (1914–2005).

TOP MIDDLE: Original pencil on vellum conceptual art for advertising United Artists' *Invisible Invaders* (Dir: Edward L. Cahn, 1959). Invisible aliens (a clever cost-cutting measure) from the Moon invade the Earth by taking over the bodies of the recently dead.

TOP RIGHT: Albert Kallis's insert card for American International Pictures' *Invasion of the Saucer Men* (Dir: Edward L. Cahn, 1957). "Our problem was to make the artwork leap off the newspaper page or poster," recalled the artist about working for AIP, "to create that compelling sense, 'I've gotta see it *now*!'"

BOTTOM RIGHT: British quad poster for Paramount's *The War of the Worlds* (Dir: Byron Haskin, 1953), based on the novel by H.G. Wells (1866–1946). Cecil B. DeMille and Alfred Hitchcock were both linked with earlier attempts to film Wells's book.

THE ART OF HORROR MOVIES

RIGHT: *The Nancy Monster* (2002), acrylic on stretched canvas by American artist Woody Welch, based on the AIP movie *Blood of Dracula* (1957). "I've been painting and drawing dinosaurs and pretty girls all of my life," admits the artist. "This was done quite a while ago, and is still hanging on the door of my storage closet."

THE FEARSOME FIFTIES

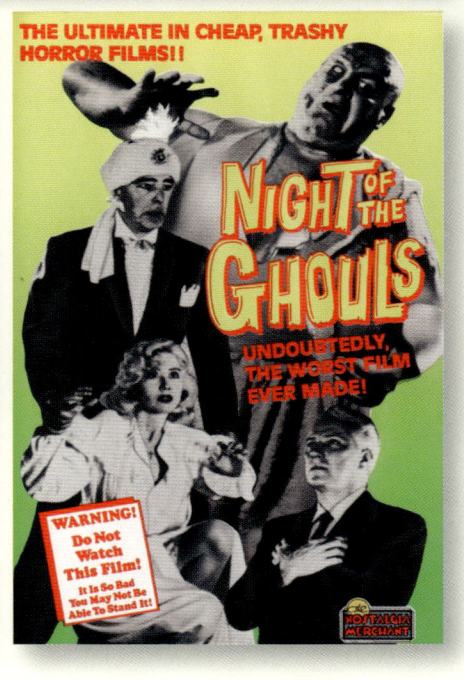

TOP LEFT: American half-sheet poster for *Bride of the Monster* (aka *Bride of the Atom*, 1955) the first of a trio of science fiction/horror movies Edward D. Wood, Jr. (1924–78) wrote and directed on minuscule budgets in the late 1950s. It starred Wood's friend, Bela Lugosi (who reportedly earned $1,000 in cash), as a mad scientist attempting to create a race of atomic supermen.

TOP RIGHT: Legend Films brought Ed Wood's infamous *Plan 9 from Outer Space* (1958) back to Japanese movie theaters for the first time in 60 years in a digitally colorized version in 2020.

BOTTOM RIGHT: Two-column newspaper ad mat for *Plan 9 from Outer Space* from the original 1958 Distributors Corporation of America (DCA) pressbook.

BOTTOM LEFT: Ed Wood's screenplay (originally titled *Queen of the Gorillas*) for Allied Artists Pictures' *The Bride and the Beast* (Dir: Adrian Weiss, 1958) was based on the real-life Bridey Murphy case, in which an American housewife claimed to be reincarnated. The case caused a sensation and also inspired the 1956 movies *The Search for Bridey Murphy* and *I've Lived Before*.

BOTTOM MIDDLE: Video box cover for The Nostalgia Merchant's 1984 Beta tape release of Edward D. Wood, Jr.'s *Night of the Ghouls* (1983), which had originally been filmed in 1957 as *Revenge of the Dead*, a semi-sequel to *Bride of the Monster*. It remained unreleased until Wade Williams acquired the rights because Wood was unable to pay the film laboratory fees.

THE ART OF HORROR MOVIES

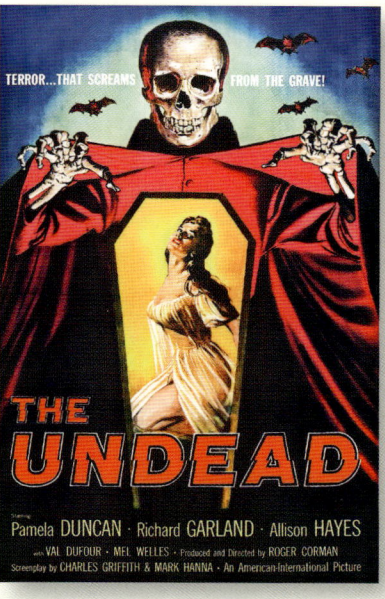

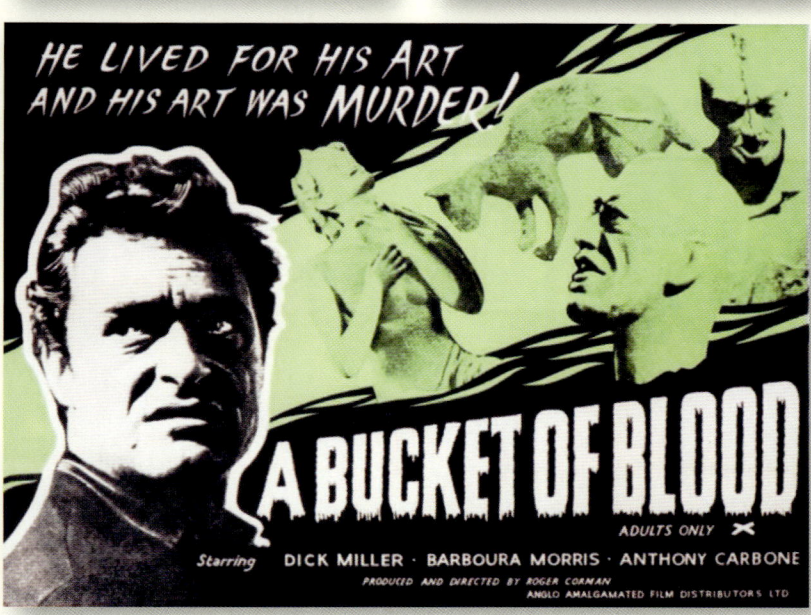

ABOVE RIGHT: 1961 Italian *quattro-foglio* for American Releasing Corporation's *Day the World Ended* (1955). It was Roger Corman's fourth movie as a director and shot over ten days. The mutated monster menacing Lori Nelson on the poster was created and played by the inventive Paul Blaisdell (1927–83), who achieved wonders on minuscule budgets.

TOP LEFT: American one-sheet poster for Allied Artists Pictures' *Not of This Earth* (1957), produced and directed by Roger Corman. Star Paul Birch (who walked off the movie before shooting was completed) portrays a blood-seeking alien trying to save his home world. The drive-in double-bill of this movie and *Attack of the Crab Monsters* (1957) made a 400% profit in its first week.

TOP MIDDLE: Albert Kallis's one-sheet poster for American-International Pictures' *The Undead* (1957). Produced and directed by Roger Corman, it was one of a number of reincarnation movies made in the late 1950s that was inspired by hypnotist Morey Bernstein's book *The Search for Bridey Murphy*. Charles B. Griffith's original script was titled *The Trance of Diana Love*.

BOTTOM LEFT: British quad poster for American-International Pictures' *A Bucket of Blood* (1959), producer/director Roger Corman's black comedy about Walter Paisley (Dick Miller), a talentless beatnik artist who becomes the darling of the Bohemian set when he starts killing people, covering their bodies in plaster, and passing them off as his own sculptures.

THE FEARSOME FIFTIES

HORROR'S DIABOLICAL DUO

"For virtually all my teen years, the intense adoration I felt for Hammer horror films, Peter Cushing's Van Helsing, and Chris Lee's Dracula, was based entirely on black-and-white photographs!"

Peter Jackson

THE RESURRECTIONIST FACE-LIFTS lent to the Dracula and Frankenstein myths by Britain's Hammer Films during the 1950s made horror superstars out of actors Peter Cushing and Christopher Lee, who arguably trumped the classic triumvirate of the earlier wave—Boris Karloff, Bela Lugosi, and Lon Chaney, Jr. As principal players, Cushing and Lee became the "face" of what came to be called "Hammer horror," and it all started with *The Curse of Frankenstein* (1957), a worldwide success that anchored the studio's dominance of the genre for the next decade.

As Baron Victor Frankenstein, Cushing logged an iconic performance—a driven, diabolical genius who was by turns cold, aloof, dismissive, hyper-focused, and haughtily superior. Cast mainly for his height and presence, Lee was a mute and stubbornly un-killable Creature who successfully reinterpreted the classic role away from what Universal Studios had turned into a flat-headed robot.

Almost immediately, Lee got his chance to shine in *Dracula* (aka *Horror of Dracula*, 1958), presenting a more statuesque, imposing, and dangerous Count. Barely seven minutes into the film, we see the unforgettable image of Lee gliding down his imperial castle stairway like a dark wraith to greet his "guest," Jonathan Harker, in a commanding yet deceptively civil basso voice. This was no coy, operatic, or foppish Dracula—this was a barely tethered predator whose gaze would go crimson with animalistic bloodlust; one immediately got the sense that he deeply resented even the (occasionally necessary) pretense of humanity.

While the real monster of *Curse* was the megalomaniacal Baron, Cushing proved to be an equally dynamic and fiercely dedicated Van Helsing in *Dracula*, a hero devoted to science as much as respecting superstition, dominating the film and offering hope with his razor-sharp intellect and keen righteousness.

Hammer horror was off to a rousing start.

However, Cushing's first role in a Hammer film was for *The Abominable Snowman* (aka *The Abominable Snowman of the Himalayas*, 1957), which filmed slightly prior to *Curse*. Sans Lee, he next reprised both his signature roles for *The Revenge of Frankenstein* (1958) and *Brides of Dracula* (1960)—two canonical monster movies that share the rare distinction of being superior sequels to their progenitors. Thereafter, the Baron would be mostly doomed to father a progression of reanimated hulks who repeatedly frustrate his quest for perfection (with the notable exception of *Frankenstein Created Woman*, 1967). His biggest success, fittingly, was *himself* in *Revenge*, in which he transmutes into an entirely new body.

> As principal players, Cushing and Lee became the "face" of what came to be called "Hammer horror," and it all started with *The Curse of Frankenstein* (1957).

Lee forsook Dracula until *Dracula Prince of Darkness* (1966), with the conditional exception of an Italian one-off comedy, *Uncle Was a Vampire* (aka *Hard Times for Dracula*, 1959). The typecasting had taken hold and proved difficult for Lee to shake for most of the following decade. Like Cushing, he came to be known primarily as a "horror star" in the wake of his turn as grave-robber Resurrection Joe (co-starring with Karloff) in *Corridors of Blood* (1958) and *The Man Who Could Cheat Death* (1959), amid a plethora of sequels and new Hammer horrors yet to come.

Before the 1950s closed out, Cushing and Lee were teamed again by Hammer in *The Mummy* (1959) and, the same year, *The Hound of the Baskervilles*. Cushing played Sherlock Holmes in *Hound*—the first Holmes film shot in color—opposite Lee's Sir Henry, and both men went on to portray the consulting detective in movies and on TV. Lee also appeared as Sherlock's cantankerous brother, Mycroft, in Billy Wilder's *The Private Life of Sherlock Holmes* (1970).

Fast friends in real life, Cushing and Lee would appear in more than 20 films together, often as antagonists, usually biased toward horror. Cushing received an O.B.E. (Officer of the Order of the British Empire) in 1989 and Lee was knighted in 2009. Cushing's final collaboration with his nearly lifelong friend consisted of voice-over narration for the documentary *Flesh and Blood: The Hammer Heritage of Horror* in 1994, before his death in August that year at age 81.

Sir Christopher Lee was truly the Last Man Standing in the annals of horror. He died in June 2015 at age 93. DJS

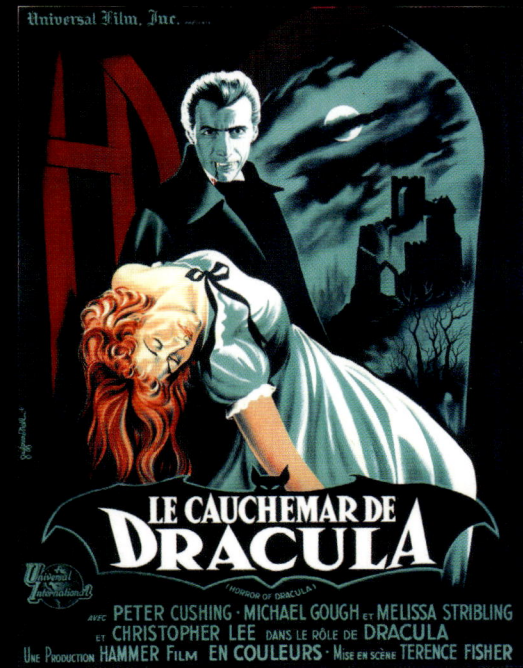

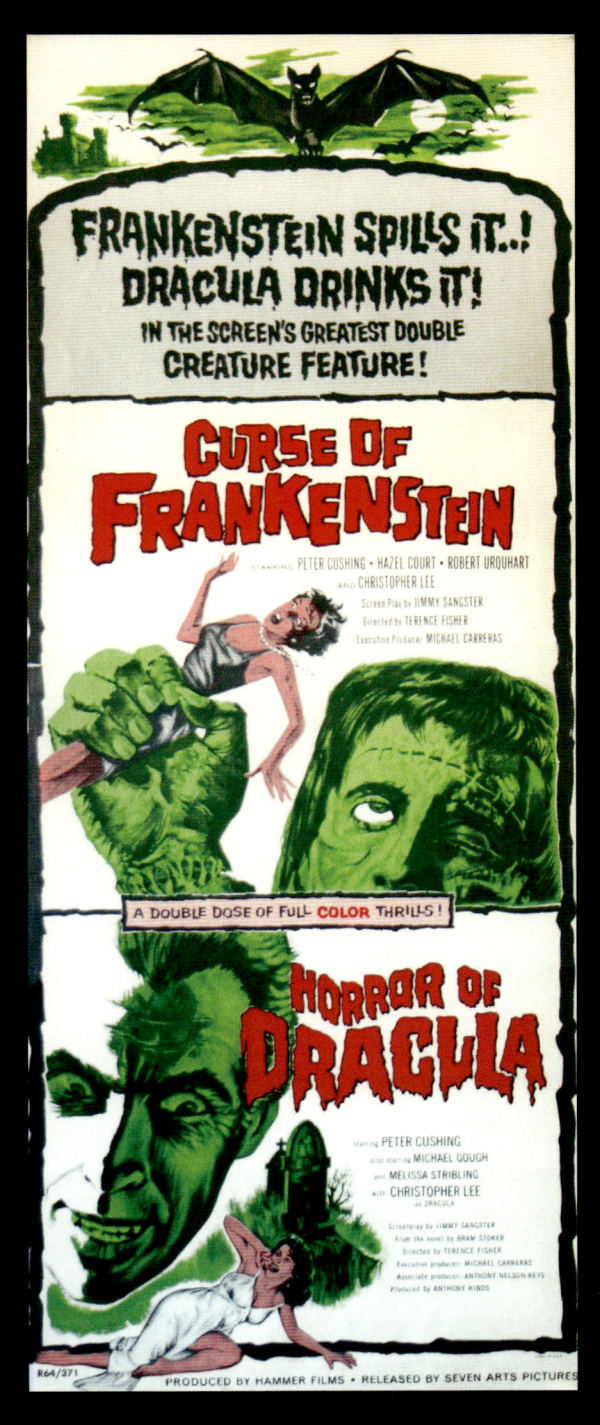

TOP LEFT: 1970s *grande affiche* for the French reissue of *The Curse of Frankenstein* (Dir: Terence Fisher, 1957), the film that established the "Hammer horror" franchise of Gothic cinema and made international stars of Peter Cushing and Christopher Lee.

TOP MIDDLE: French *grande affiche* for Hammer Films' *Dracula* (aka *Horror of Dracula*, 1958), the second of two designs artist Guy Gérard Noël (1912–94) produced for the film.

BOTTOM LEFT: French *affiche* for Hammer Films' *The Hound of the Baskervilles* (Dir: Terence Fisher, 1959), done very much in the style of Guy Gérard Noël.

BOTTOM MIDDLE: The second of two poster designs French artist Guy Gérard Noël did for Hammer Films' *The Mummy* (Dir: Terence Fisher, 1959). Notable for his use of lurid colors, Noël, who had to audition throughout his career, started designing movie posters in 1948 and retired in the mid-1960s after offset printing replaced lithography.

ABOVE RIGHT: American insert poster for Seven Arts Pictures' hugely successful 1964 reissue double-bill of Hammer Films' *The Curse of Frankenstein* (1957) and *The Horror of Dracula* (1958), which reintroduced the movies and their stars to a whole new generation of "Monster Kids" growing up on *Famous Monsters of Filmland* magazine.

THE FEARSOME FIFTIES

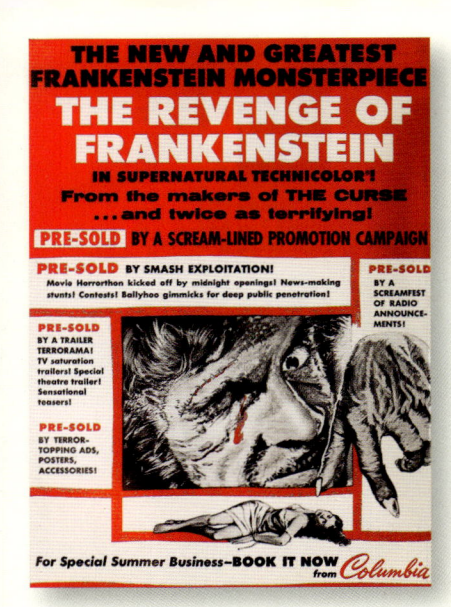

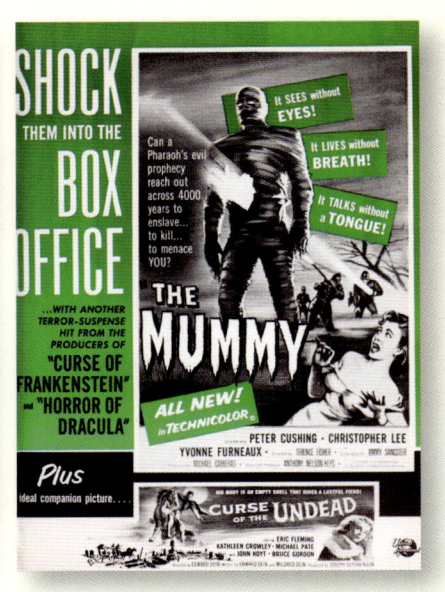

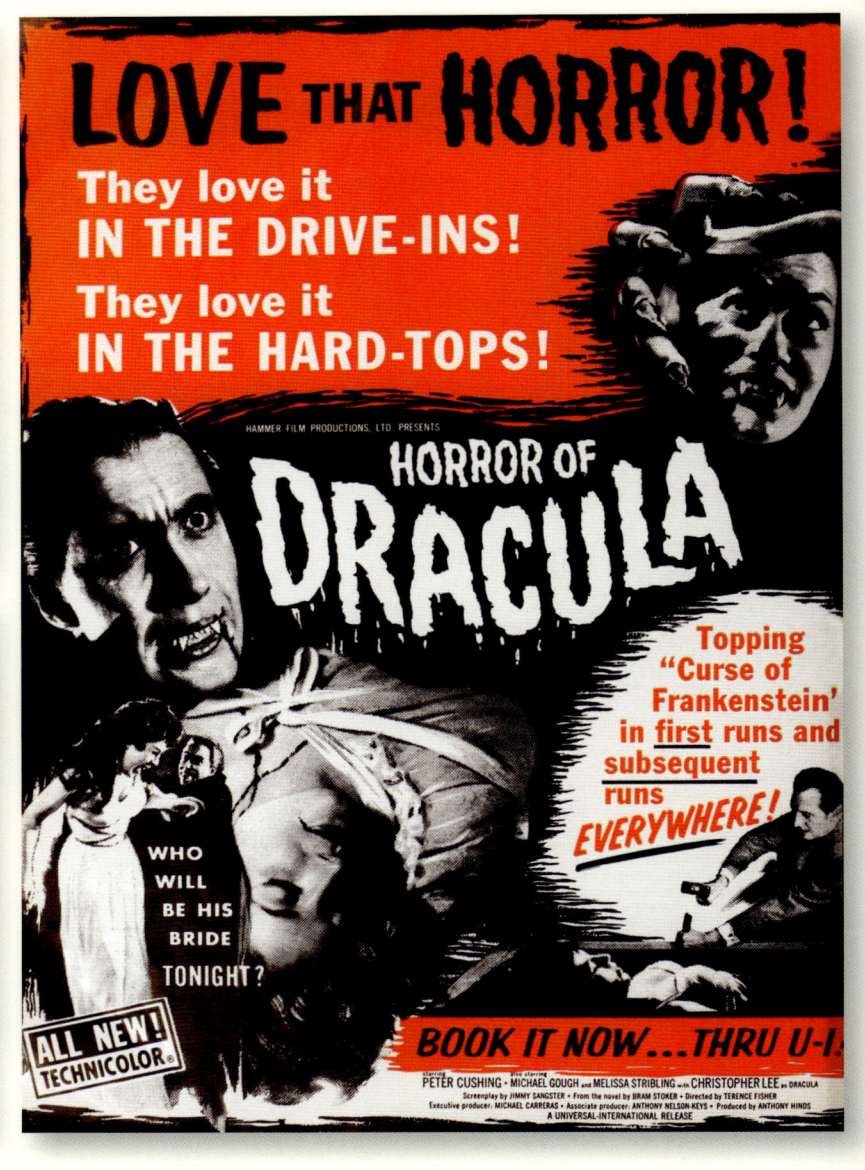

TOP LEFT: American trade advertisement from Vol. 83, No. 112 of *Motion Picture Daily* (June 10, 1958) for Columbia Pictures' release of Hammer's first horror sequel, *Revenge of Frankenstein* (1958), which marked the return of Peter Cushing's Baron.

ABOVE RIGHT: US Trade advertisement for Hammer's *Horror of Dracula* (1958) from the July 21st, 1958 issue of *Film Bulletin* (Vol. 26, No. 15). The film was re-titled in America to avoid confusion with the 1931 version, which was still in re-release from Realart Pictures.

BOTTOM LEFT: British trade advertisement for Hammer's *The Man Who Could Cheat Death* (1959) from *Kinematograph Weekly*, April 30 1959. Anton Diffring's starring role was intended for Peter Cushing, who turned it down shortly before filming began.

TOP MIDDLE: American trade advertisement from the June 22nd, 1959 issue of *Film Bulletin* (Vol. 27, No. 13) for Hammer Films' *The Mummy* (1959), which Universal-International released on a double-bill with the vampire Western *Curse of the Undead* (1959).

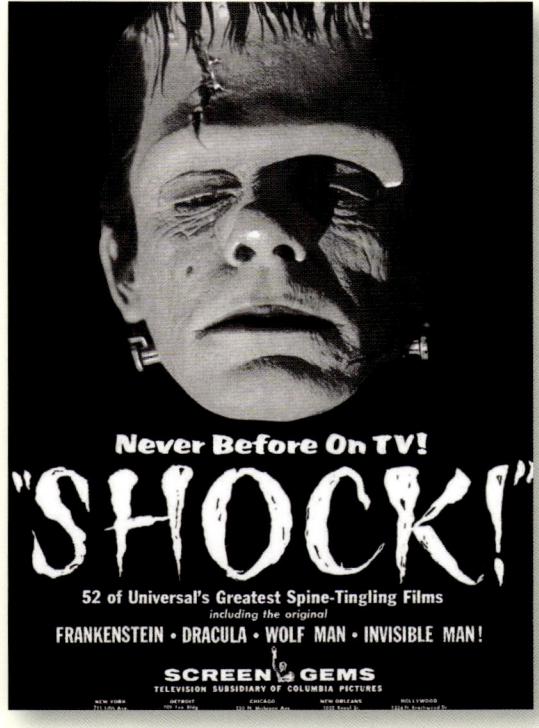

Shock! Around the Clock

In 1957, the same year that Britain's Hammer Films released *The Curse of Frankenstein* and revitalized the genre with a new cycle of horror pictures on both sides of the Atlantic, Universal Pictures sold its first syndicated package of horror movies to American television. Released under the umbrella title *Shock!* (aka *Shock Theater*) by Screen Gems, the television subsidiary of Columbia Pictures, and backed by an extensive publicity campaign, the 52 titles that comprised the initial catalog quickly became a surprise late-night ratings success nationwide. Although the original package included classics like *Dracula* (1931), *Frankenstein* (1931), *The Mummy* (1932), *The Black Cat* (1934), *The Raven* (1935), and *The Wolf Man* (1941), it also featured such obscure non-horror titles as *Chinatown Squad* (1935) and *Danger Woman* (1946). For a post–World War II audience that had never seen these films before—especially in their own homes—the reaction was immediate, as a whole new subculture of TV horror hosts, monster magazines, and horror movie collectibles started appearing almost overnight. So well received was the first record-breaking *Shock!* package, that the following year Screen Gems released the aptly titled *Son of Shock* ("a sequel without equal"), consisting of a downsized list of 20 titles (some sources claim 21). This not only featured a number of Universal films that should have been included in the original batch—*Bride of Frankenstein* (1935), *The Ghost of Frankenstein* (1942), *House of Frankenstein* (1944), *The Mummy's Curse* (1944), and *House of Dracula* (1945)—but also several horror titles from Columbia Pictures, including the studio's quintet of "mad doctor" movies (1936–42), all starring Boris Karloff.

BOTTOM: Cover of Screen Gems' 1957 *Shock!* exhibitor book, detailing the first 52 Universal horror movies released to American television. The spiral-bound brochure also included a pop-up image of the studio's Frankenstein Monster [TOP LEFT].

TOP MIDDLE: Syndication advertisement for Screen Gems' *Shock!* package of "52 of Universal's Greatest Spine-Tingling Films," distributed in October 1957 to television stations across America. The release led to a resurgence of interest in the classic horror films.

TOP RIGHT: Trade advertisement from *Broadcasting* (May 19, 1958) for *Son of Shock*, Screen Gems, Inc.'s follow-up package of 20 horror movies that included a mixture of classic titles from both Universal and Columbia Pictures.

THE FEARSOME FIFTIES

Bel-Air Productions

Co-founded in 1953 by producer Aubrey Schenck (1908–99), director Howard W. Koch (1916–2001), and theater chain executive Edwin F. Zabel, Bel-Air Productions turned out more than 20 low-budget Westerns and crime thrillers for distribution through United Artists. In 1956, the company made its first entry in the revivified horror market with *The Black Sleep*, which was filmed for an estimated $235,000 and starred an impressive lineup of horror stars whose careers were no longer at their peak. Given a major release on a double-bill with Hammer's *The Creeping Unknown* (aka *The Quatermass Xperiment*), *The Black Sleep* did well enough for Bel-Air to release two further horror films the following year.

TOP LEFT: Original pencil on paper conceptual art for four-column ad mat for United Artists' *The Black Sleep* (Dir: Reginald Le Borg, 1956). The final version did not include the syringe.

BOTTOM LEFT: Unused pencil on paper conceptual art for an ad mat for *The Black Sleep* (1956).

ABOVE RIGHT: Belgian poster for *The Black Sleep* (1956) portraying Basil Rathbone's crazed Dr. Cadman administering to his cataleptic wife (Louanna Gardner), while his horde of hideous failed experiments gaze on.

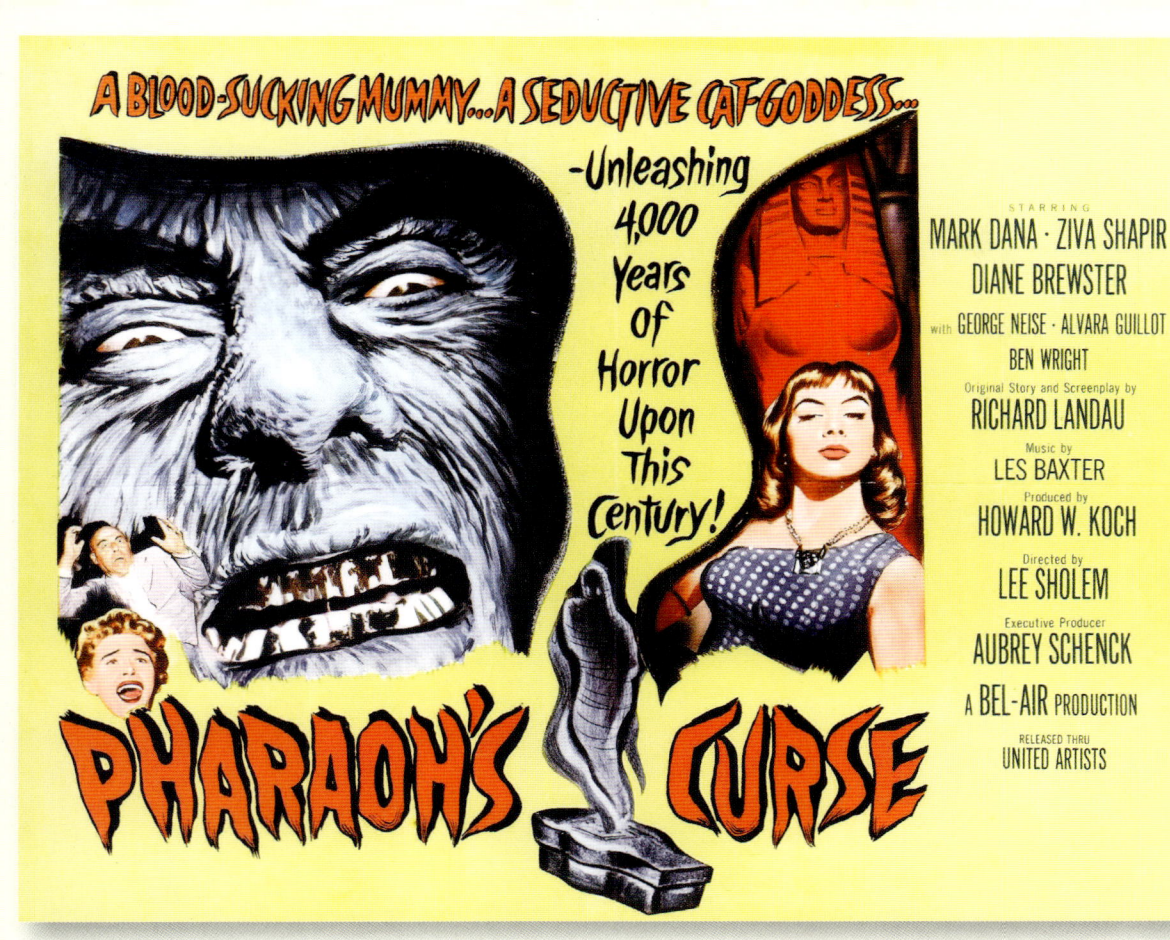

Having done a solid job with *The Black Sleep*, director Reginald Le Borg was retained for *Voodoo Island*. Shot on the island of Kauai, Hawaii, on a budget of around $150,000, it marked Boris Karloff's return to movies after three years in television and included some surprising lesbian undertones for its time. *Pharaoh's Curse*, which was filmed in just six days by director Lee Sholem for an estimated $116,000, may have lacked the star presence Bel-Air brought to its other horror projects, but at least it featured a 4,000-year-old blood-drinking mummy. In 1962, *Voodoo Island* and *The Black Sleep* and were reissued on an exploitation double-bill under the titles *Silent Death* and *Dr. Cadman's Secret*, respectively.

TOP LEFT: American half-sheet poster for United Artists' offbeat mummy movie *Pharaoh's Curse* (Dir: Lee Sholem, 1957), in which a local Egyptian is possessed by the vengeful spirit of a tomb's 4,000-year-old blood-sucking guardian.

TOP RIGHT: 1959 Italian *foglio* for United Artists' *Voodoo Island* (Dir: Reginald Le Borg, 1957), featuring a spurious image of Boris Karloff as The Mummy.

BOTTOM LEFT: The September, 1962 issue of the French magazine *Jungle Film* adapted *Voodoo Island* (1957) as a photo-strip.

BOTTOM RIGHT: Cari Releasing Corporation's one-sheet poster for the 1962 double-bill reissue of *Voodoo Island* (1957) and *The Black Sleep* (1956) under the revised titles *Silent Death* and *Dr. Cadman's Secret*.

THE FEARSOME FIFTIES

TOP RIGHT: Mexican lobby card for *Il monstruo resucitado* (The Resurrected Monster, 1953), loosely inspired by the Frankenstein story. Produced by actor Abel Salazar, Chano Urueta's film is widely regarded as reviving Mexico's Gothic cinema of the 1950s.

ABOVE LEFT: Abel Salazar not only produced, but also starred in Fernando Méndez's seminal Mexican Gothic *El vampiro* (The Vampire, 1957). Germán Robles played the titular bloodsucker, Count Karol de Lavud, in this and the sequel, *El ataúd del vampiro* (1958).

BOTTOM MIDDLE: Rafael Portillo's *La maldición de la momia azteca* (The Curse of the Aztec Mummy, 1957) was the second in a trilogy of movies co-written by Alfredo Salazar and starring Mexican actor Ramón Gay as the scientist hero pitted against the evil Dr. Krupp.

BOTTOM RIGHT: *La momia azteca contra el robot humano* (The Aztec Mummy Against the Humanoid Robot, 1958) was the final entry in the trilogy directed by Rafael Portillo. Star Ramón Gay was shot to death in 1960 by Evangelina Elizondo's former husband.

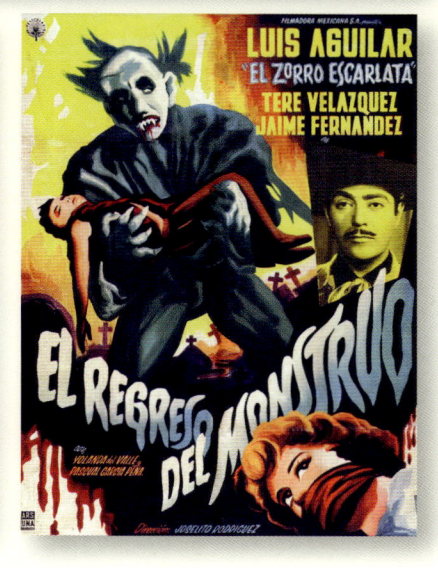

TOP LEFT: Evangelina Elizondo co-starred with comedian "Clavillazo" (Antonio Espino) in Julián Soler's horror comedy *El castillo de los monstruos* (Castle of the Monsters, 1958), which featured Germán Robles spoofing his role as El Vampiro.

BOTTOM LEFT: Credited to a story by Alfredo Salazar, Alfredo B. Crevenna's *El hombre que logró ser invisible* (The Man Who Was Invisible, 1958) was yet another reworking of H.G. Wells's story, as Arturo de Córdova's scientist was falsely accused of murder.

BOTTOM MIDDLE: Joselito Rodríguez's *Il regreso del monstruo* (Return of the Monster, 1959) was one of four serial-like Westerns starring Luis Aguilar as El Zorro Escarlata (The Scarlet Fox) who, with his singing charros, battles a monster created by a skeletal witch.

ABOVE RIGHT: 1961 American one-sheet poster for Fernando Méndez's occult thriller *Misterios de ultratumba* (Mysteries from Beyond the Tomb, 1959), featuring Abel Salazar. The US pressbook described it as "One of the most hair-raising suspense stories ever filmed."

THE FEARSOME FIFTIES

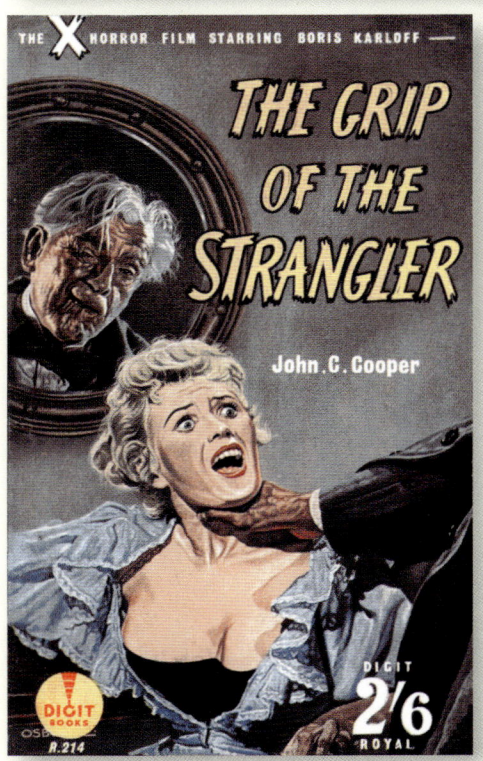

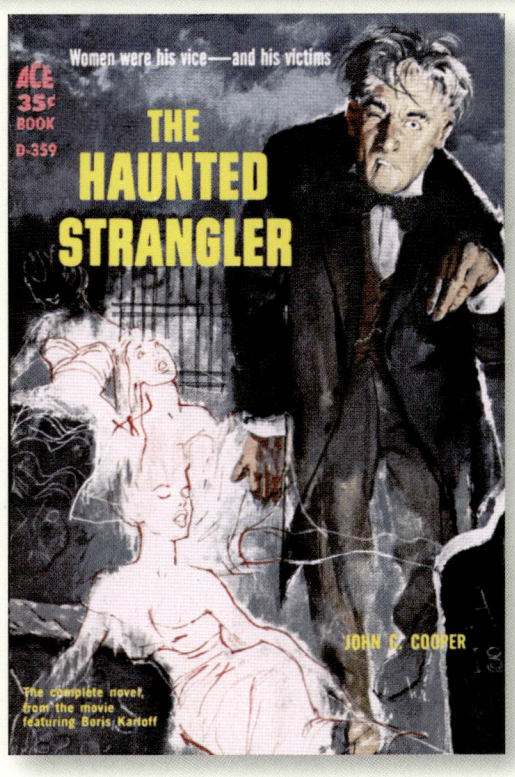

Amalgamated Productions

Much like its American counterpart, Bel-Air Productions, Amalgamated Productions was founded in 1956 by British-born producer and financier Richard Gordon (1925–2011) and screenwriter/producer Charles F. "Chuck" Vetter, Jr. to churn out a series of low-budget programmers for various distribution companies. Amalgamated's first seven films were crime dramas usually featuring an American star imported to England. In 1958, following a financing deal negotiated with the UK's Eros Films and a US distribution agreement with Metro-Goldwyn-Mayer, the company brought 70-year-old Boris Karloff back from Hollywood to make his first British movie in more than 20 years.

TOP: Belgian poster for Metro-Goldwyn-Mayer's British production, *The Haunted Strangler* (Dir: Robert Day, 1958), which starred Boris Karloff. The original UK title was *Grip of the Strangler*.

LEFT: Credited to co-writer and producer John Croydon under his "John C. Cooper" alias, the paperback tie-in was published as *The Grip of the Strangler* in the UK by Digit Books (1958) and as *The Haunted Strangler* by Ace Books (1959) in the USA. The striking cover art for the British edition was by Robert A. Osborne (1898–1974).

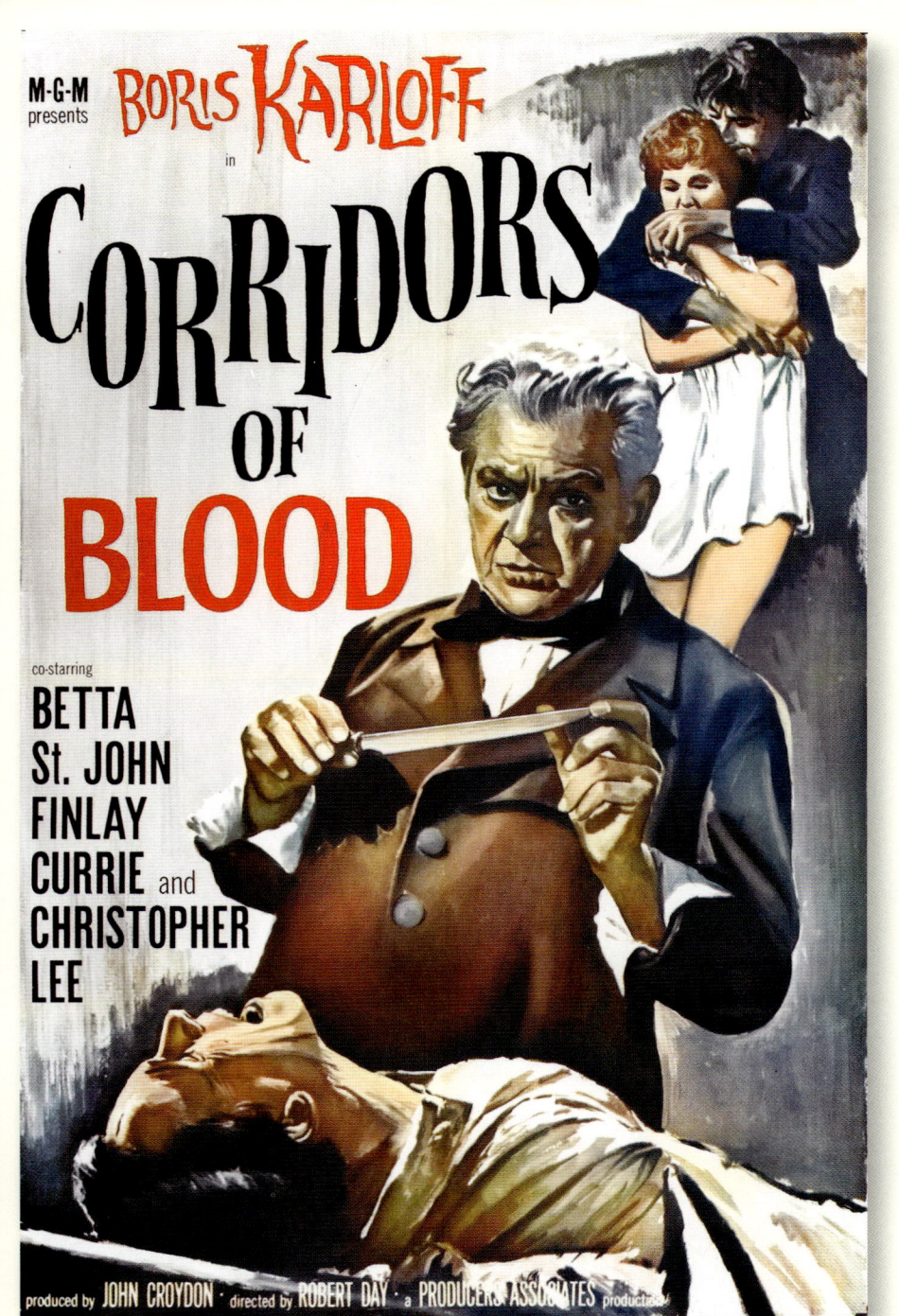

Grip of the Strangler (aka The Haunted Strangler) was co-scripted (as "John C. Cooper") by producer by John Croydon (1907–94) and filmed at Walton Studios, Walton-on-Thames, for an estimated £70,000. The company's second collaboration with Karloff, Corridors of Blood (1958) teamed the veteran actor with Christopher Lee, but was not released in America for another five years. Amalgamated's final two productions starred American leading man Marshall Thompson in a pair of science fiction films, Fiend Without a Face (1958) and First Man Into Space (1959).

ABOVE LEFT: One-sheet poster for Metro-Goldwyn-Mayer's Corridors of Blood (Dir: Robert Day, 1958), which was not released in America until 1962. It marked the first movie pairing of Boris Karloff and Christopher Lee.

TOP RIGHT: Half-sheet poster for Metro-Goldwyn-Mayer's Fiend Without a Face (Dir: Arthur Crabtree, 1958), based on the pulp story "The Thought-Monster," by Amelia Reynolds Long (1904–78), originally published in the March 1930 issue of Weird Tales.

BOTTOM RIGHT: Two-column ad mat for Metro-Goldwyn-Mayer's First Man Into Space (Dir: Robert Day, 1959), an example of the limited amount of advertising material to actually show the film's blood-drinking monster.

THE FEARSOME FIFTIES

LEFT: *The Curse of Frankenstein* (2008), Prismacolor markers by American artist Jeff Preston. "I honestly feel the early Hammer films, with such a rich palette of color, superb art direction, and impeccable design, opened my young eyes to the wonder of art on the screen," says Preston. "I've tried to translate that 'Hammer feel' to my work."

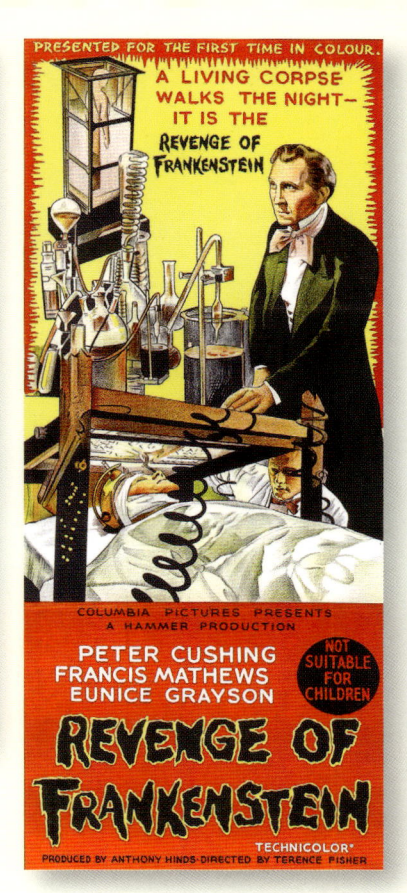

The Fisher King

Director Terence Fisher (1904–80) infused vibrant new electricity into the dormant category of Gothic frightmares with his opening trifecta for Hammer Films of *The Curse of Frankenstein* (1957), *Dracula* (aka *The Horror of Dracula*, 1958), and *The Mummy* (1959)—vividly re-imagining the old tropes in widescreen Technicolor with then-unprecedented lashings of sex and grue, creating lasting series franchises from the ground up, and transforming Peter Cushing and Christopher Lee into enduring horror stars in the process. His re-energization of *Dracula* cannot be underestimated as an influence on all that followed, culminating in the nihilistic masterpiece *Frankenstein Must Be Destroyed* (1969), and although he suffered a stormy relationship with the studio, he is now remembered as the prime architect of "Hammer horror." DJS

TOP LEFT: Australian daybill for Gainsborough Pictures' *So Long at the Fair* (Dir: Terence Fisher and Antony Darnborough, 1950). Based on an urban legend, Jean Simmons's English visitor to the 1889 Paris Exhibition awakens to find that her brother (David Tomlinson) has disappeared, and nobody will believe that he actually existed.

TOP MIDDLE: 1953 half-sheet poster for the American release of *Spaceways* (Dir: Terence Fisher, 1952). Produced by the UK's Exclusive Films (a forerunner to Hammer) for Lippert Pictures, this science fiction murder mystery was based on the BBC radio play by Charles Eric Maine (David McIlwain, 1921–81).

TOP RIGHT: Australian daybill for *The Revenge of Frankenstein* (Dir: Terence Fisher, 1958), the second in Hammer's series starring Peter Cushing as the eponymous Baron, who ends up becoming his own Monster when his brain is transplanted into another body.

BOTTOM LEFT: Belgian *affiche* for Hammer Films' *The Man Who Could Cheat Death* (Dir: Terence Fisher, 1959), a remake of the play and 1944 movie *The Man in Half Moon Street*, written by Barré Lyndon.

BOTTOM RIGHT: Italian poster for *The Stranglers of Bombay* (Dir: Terence Fisher, 1959), Hammer Films' disappointing historical horror movie about the murderous Thuggee cult devoted to the goddess Kali in India during the early nineteenth century.

ABOVE LEFT: Australian stone-litho daybill for Renown Pictures Corporation's *Svengali* (Dir: Noel Langley, 1954), based on George Du Maurier's much-filmed 1894 novel *Trilby*. After a few weeks' shooting, stage actor-manager (Sir) Donald Wolfit was brought in to replace an erratic Robert Newton as the evil genius who hypnotizes Hildegard Knef's ingénue into becoming a successful concert singer. German actress Knef's singing voice as artist's model Trilby O'Ferrall was dubbed by Elisabeth Schwarzkopf, one of the greatest sopranos of her generation.

THE ART OF HORROR MOVIES

OPPOSITE, RIGHT: Founded in Bradford, W.E. Berry Ltd. (1888–2004) became one of Britain's most significant producers and printers of film posters. This original hand-painted artwork from the company was for the J. Arthur Rank Overseas Film Distributors Ltd. one-sheet for *Svengali* (1954).

TOP: Original hand-painted poster artwork from Bradford printer W.E. Berry Ltd., based on the original American half-sheet design [RIGHT], for the release of *Abbott and Costello Meet the Mummy* (1955) in the UK by General Film Distributors Ltd. Note how the mummy is only shown in silhouette.

It's a Wrap!

The American vaudeville team—straight-man Bud Abbott (1897–1974) and comic Lou Costello (1906–59)—first started mixing humor and horror at Universal Pictures in the 1941 haunted house comedy *Hold That Ghost*. They returned to the genre with *The Time of Their Lives* (1946), but it was with *Abbott and Costello Meet Frankenstein* (1948) that they hit upon a winning formula. Over the next few years they "met" the Killer (Boris Karloff), the Invisible Man, and Dr. Jekyll and Mr. Hyde (Karloff again), and even went to Mars. The series (and their association with the studio) ended with *Abbott and Costello Meet the Mummy* (Dir: Charles Lamont, 1955), in which a sacred medallion led the pair to a lost Egyptian tomb, where they were chased around by stuntman Eddie Parker's living mummy, Klaris.

THE FEARSOME FIFTIES

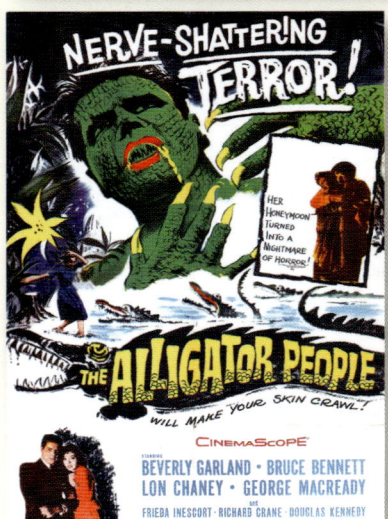

Women in Horror: 1950s

Although her biggest role was in *Attack of the 50 Foot Woman* (1958), during the 1950s Allison Hayes (1930–77) brought her undeniable sex appeal to such movies as *Zombies of Mora Tau*, *The Undead*, *The Unearthly*, and *The Disembodied* (all 1957). Beverly Garland (1926–2008) made an unusually feisty heroine in *It Conquered the World* (1956), *Curucu, Beast of the Amazon* (1956), *Not of This Earth* (1957), and *The Alligator People* (1959), while sultry Faith Domergue (1924–99) also held her own in *Cult of the Cobra*, *This Island Earth*, *It Came from Beneath the Sea*, and *The Atomic Man* (all 1955). Demure Gloria Talbott (1931–2000) had her own problems in *Daughter of Dr. Jekyll* (1957) and *I Married a Monster from Outer Space* (1958), but bounced back in *The Cyclops* (1957) and *The Leech Woman* (1960).

ABOVE LEFT: Italian *quattrofoglio* poster for Columbia Pictures' *Zombies of Mora Tau* (Dir: Edward L. Cahn, 1957) by Anselmo Ballester. A group of treasure hunters encounter a cursed treasure's zombie guardians.

ABOVE RIGHT: Six-sheet poster for Universal-International's *Cult of the Cobra* (Dir: Francis D. Lyon, 1955), in which Faith Domergue's shape-changing High Priestess hunts down five American soldiers who trespassed on a secret religious ceremony.

BOTTOM MIDDLE: One-sheet poster for Twentieth Century-Fox's *The Alligator People* (Dir: Roy Del Ruth, 1959), featuring Beverly Garland, Lon Chaney, and a missing mutated husband.

BOTTOM RIGHT: Argentinean poster for Allied Artists' *The Cyclops* (Dir: Bert I. Gordon, 1957), with Gloria Talbott, Lon Chaney, and a lost mutated fiancé.

THE ART OF HORROR MOVIES

Reynold Brown's Beast

Filmed in Eastmancolor on location in Brazil, writer/director Curt Siodmak's *Curucu, Beast of the Amazon* (1956) was just a jungle potboiler featuring John Bromfield, Beverly Garland, and Tom Payne, along with a silly looking man-in-a-bird-monster suit (pronounced "Koo-Ruh-Soo"). However, when it came to doing the poster art for Universal-International, American artist Reynold Brown (1917–91) decided it needed something special to draw the crowds in. Although his first attempt at a one-sheet design in gouache on illustration board [ABOVE] was rejected, Brown came up with a central image that utilized oblique elements of the feathery monster costume—a staring eye, a wickedly clawed hand—and painted them in a perspective that, when compared to the human figures, gave the impression of a gigantic monster emerging from the jungle foliage. "Basically, I had pretty much control in doing what I wanted—except stylistically," recalled Brown. "As years went by, I was given more freedom to use my own judgements as to the color, composition, and style of the rendering... My job was to make a movie seem better than it was—to make people think a movie was *really* going to be good." The studio's posters for *Curucu* proclaimed that it was "Like Nothing Your Eyes Have Ever Seen Before!" and, after comparing the monster in the movie to that depicted by Brown on the publicity art, audiences most probably agreed with the hype...

TOP LEFT: Half-sheet poster for Universal-International's *Curucu, Beast of the Amazon* (1956) by Reynold Brown. "I'd see from the script where the action scenes were," explained the artist. "I'd usually do the artwork on 22" x 30" Whatman board and the actual work was done on cardboard 1/16" thick, so you could cut around figures with a razor blade and move things if they wanted."

BOTTOM LEFT: Belgian *affiche* for *Curucu, Beast of the Amazon* (1956). Filmed on location in the Brazilian municipality of Belém, the gateway to the Amazon River, star Beverly Garland later told Tom Weaver: "It was probably one of the most exciting things that I ever did."

BOTTOM RIGHT: Six-column ad mat for Universal-International's double-bill of *Curucu, Beast of the Amazon* and *The Mole People* (Dir: Virgil Vogel, 1956). In the latter movie, John Agar's archaeologist discovers a lost 5,000-year-old Sumarian civilization beneath a mountain plateau in Asia.

THE FEARSOME FIFTIES

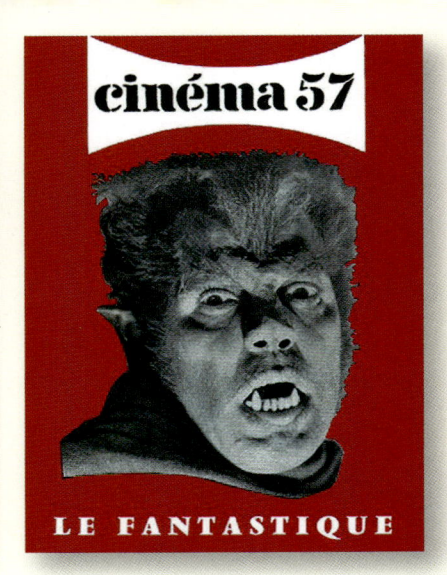

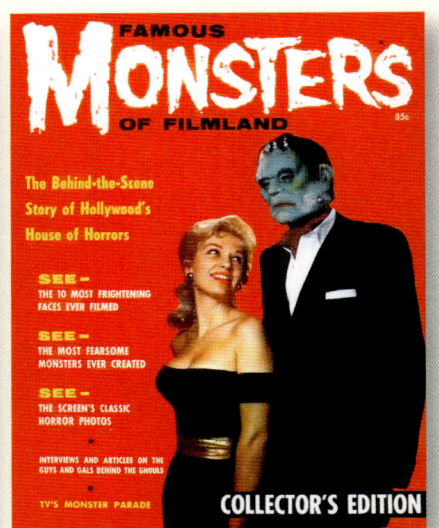

The First Monster Magazines

Published by the French Federation of Ciné Clubs in July–August 1957, issue #20 of the annual digest-sized *Cinéma 57* (the title changed each year), edited by Pierre Billard, was a 144-page special devoted to the *ciné fantastique*. Although undated, but probably published a few months later by Pep Publishers and Printers of Croydon, England, the one-off digest *Screen Chills* featured fiction and film reviews, including adaptations of *I Was a Teenage Werewolf* and *Zombies of Mora Tau*. In October 1957, Screen Gems released a package of pre-1948 horror films, mostly from Universal, to American television under the *Shock Theater* (aka *Shock!*) banner. For many post-World War II "baby boomers" it was their first exposure to such classic movies as *Dracula* (1931) and *Frankenstein* (1931). Inspired by this resurgence of interest among teenagers and a copy of the French *Cinéma 57* that he had picked up on a recent trip to Europe, editor and science fiction super-fan Forrest J Ackerman launched the pun-filled *Famous Monsters of Filmland*, possibly the most influential of all monster magazines, for publisher James Warren in February 1958. It ran for 191 issues, before folding in March 1983. The first magazine to follow *FM* onto the newsstands was editor M. J. Shapiro's *Monster Parade*. Irwin Shaw's Magnum Publications produced four issues between September 1958 and March 1959, and added a companion title, *Monsters and Things*, in January 1959. Under the editorship of L.T. Shaw, it published just one further issue in April that same year. Edited by M. Leon Howard for Magsyn Publications, *World Famous Creatures* produced four issues between October 1958 and June 1959, along with a UK reprint of the first edition. The single issue of publisher/editor Myron Fass's *Shock Tales* also appeared in January 1959 and used film stills to illustrate its fiction. Like Forry Ackerman, another long-time fan working in the publishing business was Calvin T. Beck, who issued the one-shot *The Journal of Frankenstein* in 1959. It would soon lead to bigger things.

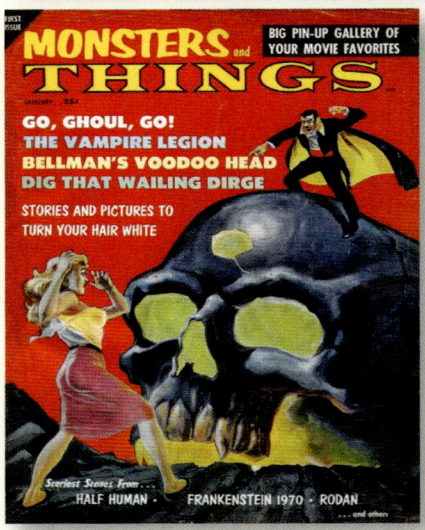

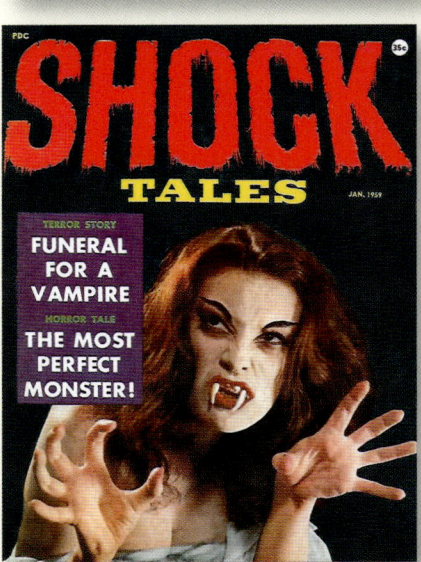

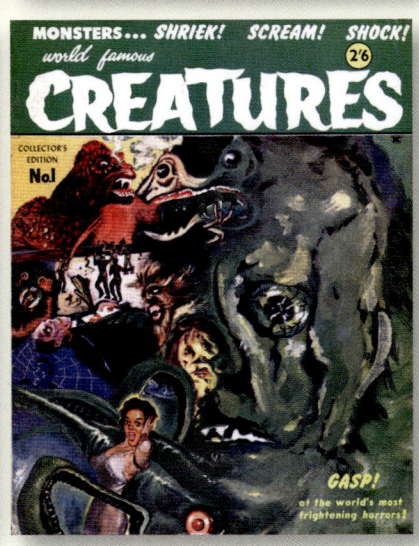

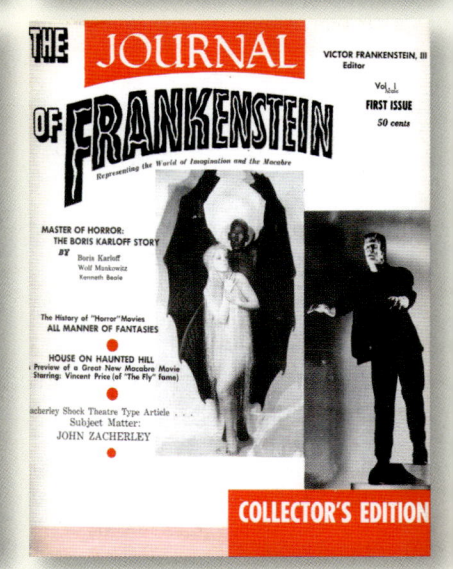

THE ART OF HORROR MOVIES

RIGHT: *House of Wax* (1970), acrylic on board portrait of Vincent Price's fire-scarred sculptor in the 1953 movie by American artist Basil Gogos, used as the cover for *Famous Monsters of Filmland* #64 (April, 1970). "It took a little longer to do because his features are so distorted and badly treated," recalls the artist, "but that gives you a chance to, you know, put your fingers in it and really build that face."

RIGHT: *1954 Godzilla* (2004), acrylic on canvas by American artist Bob Eggleton, "I produced this painting to celebrate the fiftieth Anniversary of the original *Gojira/Godzilla*," explains the artist. "I did it primarily for myself, and it was used as a wraparound cover for a special issue of *Japanese Giants* #10 (September, 2004). I wanted to work in greens and create a sense of underwater depth."

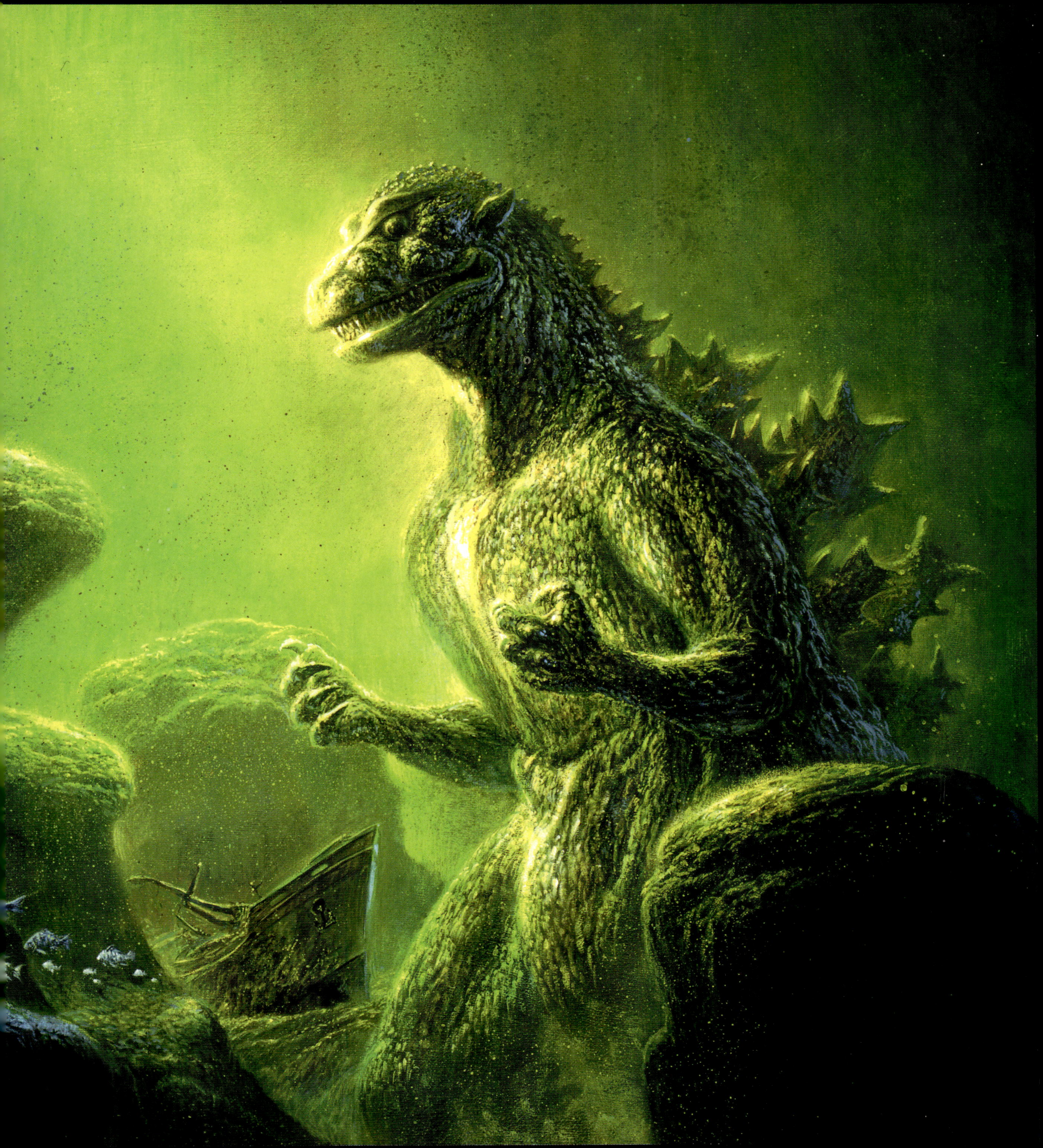

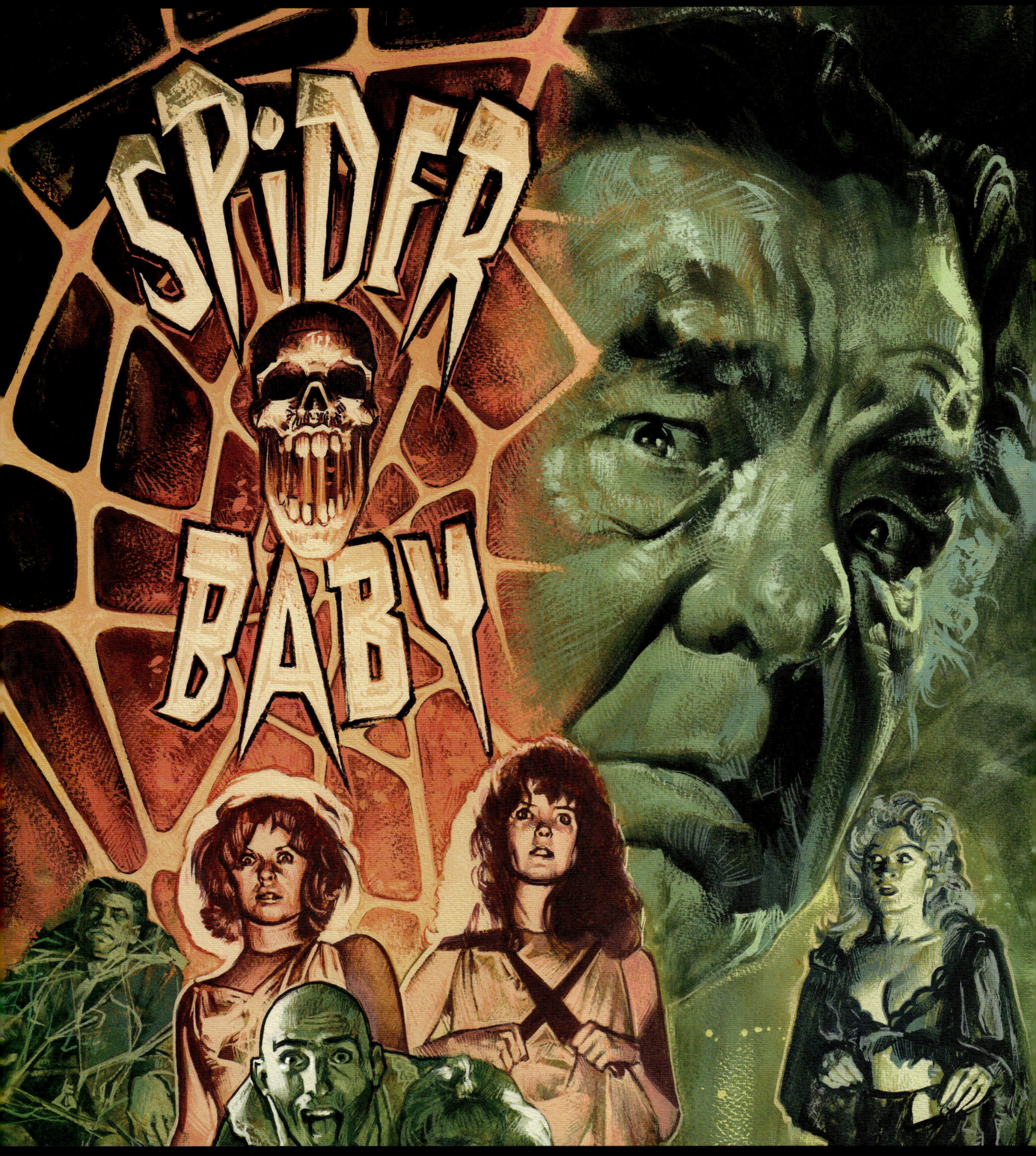
SPIDER
BABY

THE STYLISH SIXTIES

KIM NEWMAN

"You know, a long time ago being crazy meant something. Nowadays everybody's crazy."

CHARLES MANSON

> "Oh, Sammy, what's the use? 'Mr. Boogey Man,' 'King of Blood' they used to call me. 'Marx Brothers make you laugh, Garbo makes you weep, Orlok makes you scream'... You know what they call my films today? Camp! High camp!"
>
> Byron Orlok (Boris Karloff) in *Targets* (1967)

THE 1960s WAS the era of the generation gap. The horror films of the decade obsessively literalize the theme with stories of corrupt, evil, decadent old people—often played by stars held over from earlier times, like Vincent Price or Joan Crawford, stuck in cluttered Gothic mansions always on the point of falling down or going up in flames—exerting malign influence over with-it youth, who rebel at the risk of becoming monstrous themselves.

The four key horror films of 1960 all fit this template: Alfred Hitchcock's *Psycho*, with sensitive young Norman Bates (Anthony Perkins) murdering in the guise of his rotted-to-a-skeleton-in-the-fruit-cellar mother; Roger Corman's *The Fall of the House of Usher*, with neurasthenic Roderick Usher (Vincent Price) deliberately burying his generations-younger sister Madeline (Myrna Fahey) alive and destroyed along with his rotten mansion when she emerges maddened from the tomb; Mario Bava's *La maschera del demonio* (*Black Sunday*), with innocent Katia (Barbara Steele) replaced by her lookalike vampire-witch ancestress Princess Asa (also Steele), who has bare-bone ribs under her velvet bodice; and Michael Powell's *Peeping Tom*, with young filmmaker Mark Lewis (Carl Boehm) warped into a serial killer by sadistic experiments carried out when he was a child by his psychologist father (played by Powell himself).

Hitchcock and Powell were established talents venturing into new, shocking territory—the Englishman in California prospered from a shower murder, while his stay-at-home countryman was vilified for unhealthy fixations. Corman and Bava were newer talents, but looked to nineteenth century Gothic tales rather than Freud's casebook and true crime.

All of these films—even *Peeping Tom*, which fed into the disreputable Off-Wardour Street horrors of Michael Reeves and (later) Peter Walker—were hugely influential, and set off cycles of follow-ups and imitations. Corman and Price found a formula with Edgar Allan Poe and refined it in a series of increasingly sophisticated, widescreen charades which gave genre cinema its first taste of the psychedelia that would wash over pop culture later in the decade. It's no accident that Corman, hooked up with American International Pictures, went from *The Masque of the Red Death* (1964) and *Tomb of Ligeia* (1964) to the LSD-themed *The Trip* (1967). *Psycho* encouraged a run of *grande dame* Gothics—most notably Robert Aldrich's *What Ever Happened to Baby Jane?* (1962)—with faded stars competing with the dead Mrs. Bates to slash out at the pretty young things rising up to take their place at the box office.

Mario Bava spearheaded a revival of the Gothic in mainland Europe, encouraging extraordinary, personal work from busy, prolific, hit-or-miss talents like Riccardo Freda (*L'orribile segreto del Dr. Hichcock/The Horrible Dr. Hichcock*, 1962), Jesús Franco (*Gritos en la noche/The Awful Dr. Orloff*, 1962), Jean Rollin (*Le viol du vampire/Rape of the Vampire*, 1967), and writer-star Jacinto Molina/Paul Naschy (*La marca del hombre lobo/Frankenstein's Bloody Terror*, 1967). All these creators would turn out impressive filmographies, revisiting the old monsters in

> Critics who condemned their late 1950s Gothics now held them up as a standard for newer, rougher, stranger films.

mod, daring manners—taking advantage of relaxing censorship standards around the world, but also riding the zeitgeist of an era of consumption to the point of excess.

In America, Herschell Gordon Lewis carved out a niche with *Blood Feast* (1963) and *Two Thousand Maniacs!* (1964)—sloshing more gore than any studio picture would dare to compensate for semi-amateurish production values and performances. Bava's *Sei donne per l'assassino/Blood and Black Lace* (1964) is as violent, but far more stylish—exquisitely mounting murder set pieces with fetishist glee.

Hammer Films kept apace, periodically adding new blood to their product—or at least bringing in younger women to be bitten by Christopher Lee or rescued by Peter Cushing—but quickly came to be seen as almost respectable. Critics who condemned their late 1950s Gothics now held them up as a standard for newer, rougher, stranger films.

Terence Fisher had a shaky period, with ambitious but uncertain takes on classic stories (*The Two Faces of Dr. Jekyll*, 1960; *The Phantom of the Opera*, 1962), but re-established himself with *Dracula Prince of Darkness* (1965)—which significantly elevated Christopher Lee's star status—and turned out perhaps his finest works, *The Devil Rides Out* (1967) and *Frankenstein Must Be Destroyed* (1969).

Even in Britain, Hammer no longer held a monopoly on horror. Classy, literary efforts like Jack Clayton's *The Innocents* (1961) and Robert Wise's *The Haunting* (1963) were Hammer Films for the carriage trade, but Amicus's

PREVIOUS SPREAD: *Spider Baby* (2013), gouache on watercolor paper by British artist Graham Humphreys. "One of the joys of my work is discovering a film for the first time," he explains. "*Spider Baby* (1967) features the legendary Lon Chaney, Jr., and I felt the oranges and greens captured the mood perfectly."

TOP LEFT: Italian *duo-foglio* for Hammer Films' *The Two Faces of Dr. Jekyll* (Dir: Terence Fisher, 1960) by Luigi Martinati (1893–1983), who co-founded the BCM agency with fellow artists Anselmo Ballester and Alfredo Capitani, which was renowned for its "realist" style of movie poster artwork.

BOTTOM LEFT: American three-sheet poster for Twentieth Century-Fox's *The Innocents* (Dir: Jack Clayton, 1961), based on the 1898 novella *The Turn of the Screw* by Henry James (1843–1916). Future director Freddie Francis was the cinematographer.

ABOVE RIGHT: *Psycho Blood Red* (2014), signed and numbered screen print by American artist Brian Ewing. "I was working for *Hustler* on the magazines, handling scheduling and printers," he recalls. "When I quit my job in porn to freelance as an artist full-time, I swore that'd be my last day job."

THE STYLISH SIXTIES

TOP LEFT: Belgian poster for Mario Bava's *6 donne per l'assassino* (aka *Blood and Black Lace*, 1964), the archetypal "*giallo*," which helped popularize that cinematic movement in Italy. The word, which translates as "yellow," was used to denote a popular series of pulp paperback crime mystery novels with yellow covers.

TOP RIGHT: 1968 Italian *foglio* for 23-year-old Michael Reeves's *The Sorcerers* (1967), which reflected the "swinging London" scene of the 1960s.

BOTTOM LEFT: 1970 Italian *foglio* for George A. Romero's highly influential *Night of the Living Dead* (1968), which erroneously credits the director as "George A. Kramer."

BOTTOM MIDDLE: Japanese poster for Roman Polanski's *Rosemary's Baby* (1968), a hugely influential mainstream horror movie based on the 1967 novel by Ira Levin (1929–2007).

BOTTOM RIGHT: Spanish poster for Gordon Hessler's *Scream and Scream Again* (1969) by artist Montalban. Produced by AIP/Amicus and based on the 1966 novel *The Disorientated Man* by "Peter Saxon" (Stephen D. Frances), it marked the first screen teaming of Vincent Price, Christopher Lee, and Peter Cushing in the same movie.

THE ART OF HORROR MOVIES

Dr. Terror's House of Horrors (1964)—directed by Freddie Francis, cameraman on *The Innocents* and director of several of Hammer's *Les diaboliques*-flavored psycho-horrors—was an attempt by writer-producer Milton Subotsky to usurp Hammer's market dominance (with Cushing and Lee hired as insurance) by bringing vampires, werewolves, and other classic fiends into a contemporary setting.

Like William Castle in America, Subotsky drew on writer Robert Bloch, a brand-name thanks to *Psycho*, for material and scripts. Alongside anthologies on the pattern of *Dr. Terror*, Amicus made unsettling, almost-art films like Francis's *The Skull* (1965), from Bloch's short story "The Skull of the Marquis de Sade," which opened up a new avenue for British horror.

> The other significant hit of 1968 was initially almost unnoticed—George A. Romero's *Night of the Living Dead*, shot well away from Hollywood in Pittsburgh, in budget-dictated black and white (but as gruesome as anything H.G. Lewis could envision). Herk Harvey's *Carnival of Souls* (1962), made in Kansas, was a precedent for regional American art-horror, but Romero's movie, which invented a new mythology for flesh-eating zombies that would become insanely dominant over the next four decades, was a tougher, more ruthless effort.

Hammer and Amicus were paradoxically staid, and much of the power of their films comes from seeing respectable, trustworthy figures like Peter Cushing (or light entertainment refugees like Roy Castle) reduced to quivering terror. The next wave came from shadier outfits, like Compton-Cameo and Tigon, and chancers like Tony Tenser, who picked up where Herman Cohen left off.

Tenser let Polish emigré Roman Polanski make *Repulsion* (1965), which crawls inside the mind of a female psychopath (Catherine Deneuve) who cracks up inside a London flat that becomes haunted by phantasms of her own imagining. Polanski's example opened the way for British-born, short-lived Michael Reeves to deliver radical, upsettingly violent genre-stretching fare with *The Sorcerers* (1967) and *Witchfinder General* (1968), which dwell on the gnarled faces of horror stars Boris Karloff and Vincent Price respectively as they leer and sneer at a younger generation personified in both films by Ian Ogilvy.

Gordon Hessler's *Scream and Scream Again* (1969), scripted by critic Christopher Wicking, is a co-production between Amicus, Tigon, and AIP which assembles many strains of 1960s horror into one mosaic with name stars (Cushing, Lee, Price), science fiction and horror, *The Avengers*/Bond-style surreal action, political upheaval, youth revolt (and many disco scenes), and a dunking in the acid bath for anyone who gets in the way.

Polanski followed *Repulsion* with the surreal, menacing *Cul-De-Sac* (1966)—as influenced by Samuel Beckett and Harold Pinter as Corman and Amicus—and the Hammer spoof pastiche *Dance of the Vampires* (1967). In America, he made *Rosemary's Baby* (1968) for Paramount and producer Robert Evans. The cool, disturbing adaptation of Ira Levin's breakout horror bestseller redefined big studio horror for decades to come. Another story of corrupt age (Ruth Gordon's eccentric coven) exploiting youth (Mia Farrow's fragile young thing) for dark ends (the birth of the Antichrist), *Rosemary's Baby* was a commercial blockbuster, earning the sort of profits Hammer could never imagine. Levin conquered bestseller lists with a book that might have been a paperback throwaway in the 1950s—setting a precedent for William Peter Blatty, Stephen King, Peter Straub, and others.

The other significant hit of 1968 was initially almost unnoticed—George A. Romero's *Night of the Living Dead*, shot well away from Hollywood in Pittsburgh, in budget-dictated black and white (but as gruesome as anything H.G. Lewis could envision). Herk Harvey's *Carnival of Souls* (1962), made in Kansas, was a precedent for regional American art-horror, but Romero's movie, which invented a new mythology for flesh-eating zombies that would become insanely dominant over the next four decades, was a tougher, more ruthless effort.

Informed by Vietnam news footage and the simmering racial and political tensions of a decade of assassinations and riots, *Night of the Living Dead* is a stark, suspenseful siege-horror (influenced by Richard Matheson's novel *I Am Legend*, 1954, and Alfred Hitchcock's *The Birds*, 1963). It breaks with convention at every point, from a heroine (Judith O'Dea) who retreats into catatonia during a crisis, to a black hero (Duane Jones) who survives the zombies but is shot by the Sheriff's posse. A few earlier films, including *Dance of the Vampires*, go with ambiguous or downbeat endings, but *Night of the Living Dead* upset the cart to the point when, in the 1970s, an unhappy, cynical twist became almost mandatory in horror.

Like *Psycho*, *Night of the Living Dead* changed not only the way horror films looked and their subject matter, but how they were financed, marketed, and franchised—even where they were made. Romero's example was noted by filmmakers struggling with underground or student projects well away from even the Hollywood connections of Roger Corman. They would follow him by making their own rule-breaking pictures in Texas, Toronto, upstate New York, or farther afield.

The key word of the late 1960s was escalation, and *Night of the Living Dead* was the film that took horror away from the old people—even if they remained a baleful, constant presence, as stars and producers—and opened up possibilities that would be thoroughly explored in the 1970s.

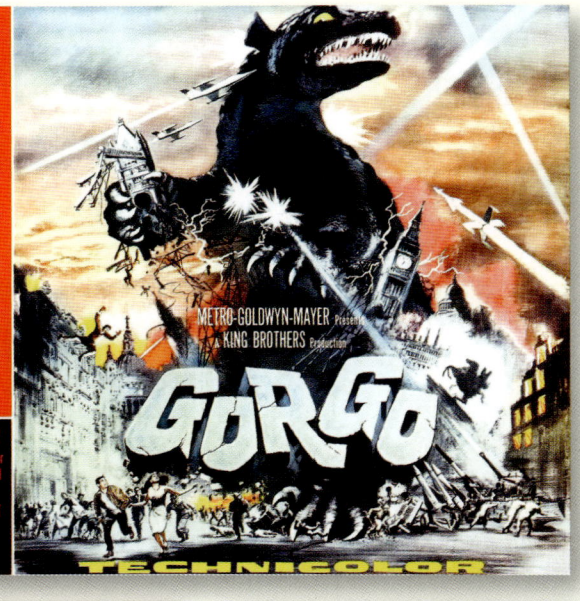

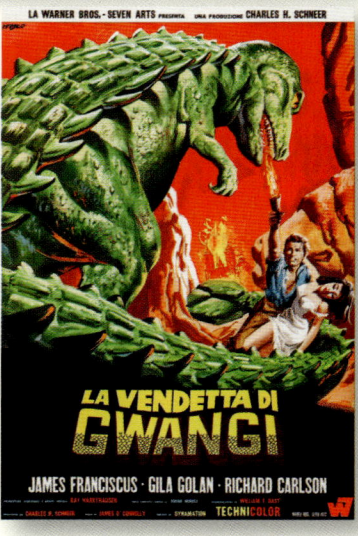

ABOVE LEFT: Original charcoal and gesso "rough" on illustration board by Joseph "Joe" Smith (1912–2003) for the American poster for *Gorgo* (Dir: Eugène Lourié, 1961). Although Metro-Goldwyn-Mayer used a different poster design by the artist, Smith preferred this version.

TOP RIGHT: This American half-sheet poster for MGM's British monster movie *Gorgo* (1961) featured another concept by Joseph "Joe" Smith, who was asked to add a "chiseled stone" logo. "I did letters for *Ben-Hur* that looked like stone," recalled Smith. "Then everybody asked for that look."

BOTTOM MIDDLE: Italian *duo-foglio* signed "Bart" for Universal-International's juvenile fantasy/adventure *Dinosaurus!* (Dir: Irvin S. Yeaworth, Jr., 1960), in which a young boy and a friendly Neanderthal helped save a Caribbean island from two reanimated dinosaurs (created by Marcel Delgado).

BOTTOM RIGHT: Italian *duo-foglio* for Warner Bros.-Seven Arts' *The Valley of Gwangi* (Dir: James O'Connolly, 1969) by Picchioni Franco (1942–2002). Based on an unrealized project by the late Willis H. O'Brien, Ray Harryhausen created the stop-motion special effects.

THE ART OF HORROR MOVIES

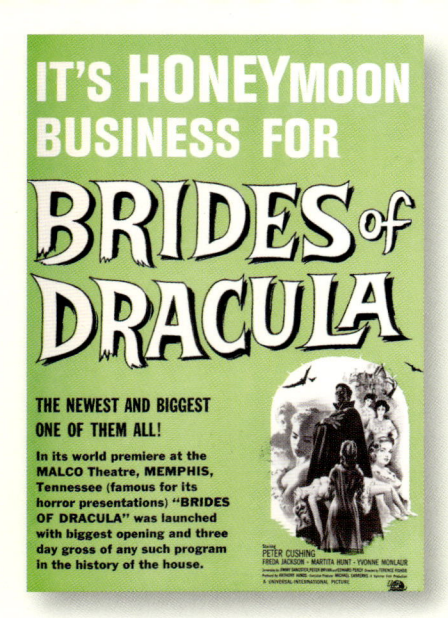

TOP LEFT: Advertisement from the June 8, 1960 trade magazine *Motion Picture Daily* for Universal-International's American release of Hammer Films' *The Brides of Dracula* (Dir: Terence Fisher, 1960). Despite the title, this sequel to *Dracula* (1958) didn't even feature the Count!

TOP MIDDLE: Trade advertisement from *The Film Daily* (April 28, 1961) for Universal-International's American release of Hammer's *The Curse of the Werewolf* (Dir: Terence Fisher, 1961) which, due to its combination of horror and sex, was censored on both sides of the Atlantic.

ABOVE RIGHT: Inspired by the success of Universal's *Shock!* packages in the late 1950s, in 1964 Hammer Films created a spiral-bound brochure to promote *The Hammer TV Playhouse of Shock and Suspense*, not realizing that the TV rights to their movies were owned by the American distributors.

BOTTOM LEFT: Cover of a 1963 draft treatment by former camera operator Peter Bryan (later revised by Anthony Hinds) for the Hammer film that would be released three years later as *The Plague of the Zombies* (Dir: John Gilling, 1966). At least they increased the number of zombies.

BOTTOM MIDDLE: As this brochure aimed at potential distributors for Hammer's *The Reptile* (Dir: John Gilling, 1966) shows, the opposite was apparently true of the synopsis written by Anthony Hinds under his "John Elder" pseudonym, which ended up featuring only the one monster.

THE STYLISH SIXTIES

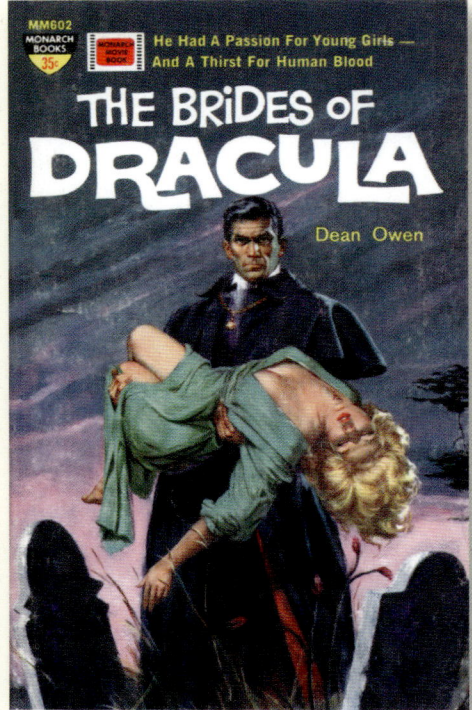

ABOVE LEFT & TOP RIGHT: Original gouache on illustration board painting used for the cover of the 1960 Monarch Books tie-in of *The Brides of Dracula* by "Dean Owen" (Dudley Dean McGaughey, 1906–86).

BOTTOM RIGHT: French *affiche* for *Brides of Dracula* (1960) by Joseph Koutachy.

THE ART OF HORROR MOVIES

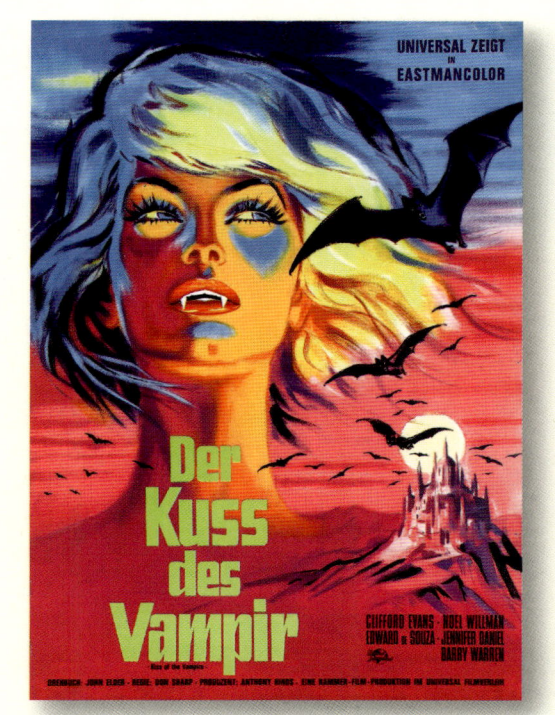

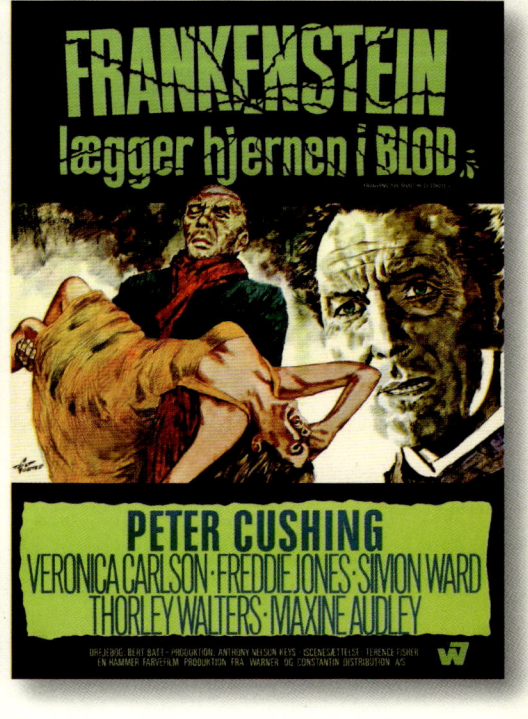

TOP LEFT: German poster for Hammer Films' *The Kiss of the Vampire* (Dir: Don Sharp, 1963). When shown on American TV as *Kiss of Evil*, additional footage was shot to replace the material cut out.

TOP RIGHT: UK double-bill quad poster for Hammer's *The Evil of Frankenstein* (1964) and *Nightmare* (1964), which were both directed by Academy Award-winning cinematographer Freddie Francis (1917–2007).

BOTTOM LEFT: French *grande affiche*, the second of three versions printed for Hammer Films' sequel *Dracula Prince of Darkness* (Dir: Terence Fisher, 1965), with art by Guy Gérard Noël (1912–94), who also produced posters for the 1958 original.

BOTTOM MIDDLE: 1968 Italian *duo-foglio* for Hammer Films' *Quatermass and the Pit* (aka *Five Million Miles to Earth*, 1967), director Roy Ward Baker's version of Nigel Kneale's third and final "Quatermass" TV serial, broadcast by the BBC in 1958.

BOTTOM RIGHT: Danish poster for Hammer Films' *Frankenstein Must Be Destroyed* (Dir: Terence Fisher, 1969) by Rolf Goetze, who produced around 800 movie posters between the late 1940s and the early 1970s.

THE STYLISH SIXTIES

The Face of Hammer

Prolific British character actor Michael [George] Ripper (1913–2000) began his film career in the 1930s appearing (usually uncredited) in such "quota quickies" as *Old Mother Riley's Jungle Treasure* (1951) and *The Anatomist* (1956). However, he is best known for his long association with Hammer Films. Between 1949 and 1972 he appeared in more than thirty movies for the studio, usually cast in small but significant supporting roles as policemen, innkeepers, gravediggers, and assorted comedic characters. He gave standout performances in *The Plague of the Zombies* and *The Reptile* (both 1966), but perhaps his most substantial role was as the cowardly assistant Longbarrow in *The Mummy's Shroud* (1967). He also appeared in several films for Hammer's would-be rivals Amicus Productions, World Film Services, and Tyburn Film Productions, but no matter how large or small the part was, Michael Ripper always indelibly made it his own.

ABOVE LEFT: *Michael Ripper* (2016), oils on board portrait by British artist Les Edwards of the hard-working character actor in his role as the police sergeant in *The Plague of the Zombies* (1966). "Apparently he appeared in more Hammer Films than anyone," reveals the artist. "He has a great face to paint, full of character."

TOP RIGHT: American half-sheet poster for Hammer Films' *The Curse of the Werewolf* (Dir: Terence Fisher, 1961), probably by artist Ruth Corbett. Based on the 1933 novel *The Werewolf of Paris* by Guy Endore, the story was moved to Spain.

BOTTOM RIGHT: Six-sheet poster for Hammer Films' *Captain Clegg* (Dir: Peter Graham Scott, 1962), which was re-titled *Night Creatures* and given a more horror-orientated publicity campaign in America.

THE ART OF HORROR MOVIES

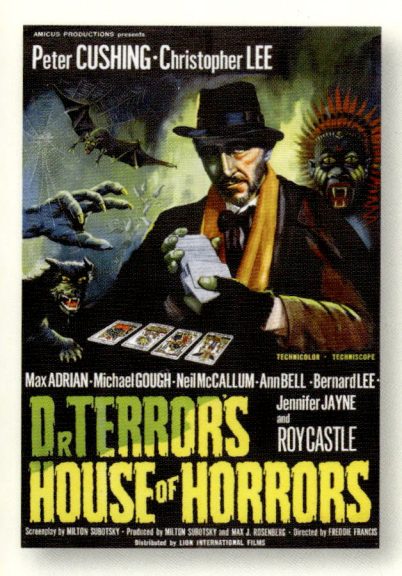

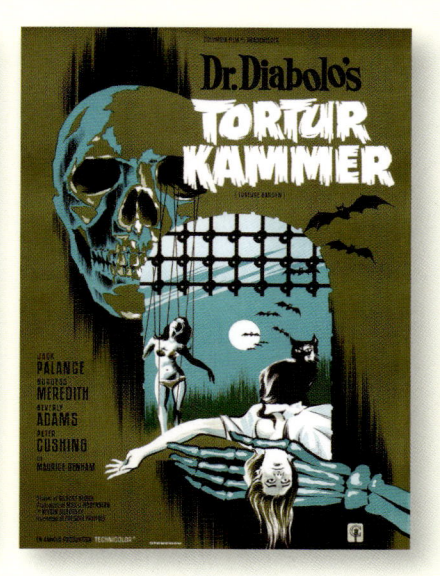

TOP LEFT: British poster for Amicus Productions' first portmanteau film, *Dr. Terror's House of Horrors* (Dir: Freddie Francis, 1965), signed simply "R.T." Five railway travelers have their Tarot cards read by Peter Cushing's mysterious Dr. Terror, with predictably horrific results.

TOP MIDDLE: Stylized Danish poster for Amicus Productions' *Torture Garden* (Dir: Freddie Francis, 1967) by the reclusive John Stevenov. It was scripted by Robert Bloch, from his own stories.

BOTTOM LEFT: American half-sheet poster for Amicus Productions' *The Psychopath* (Dir: Freddie Francis, 1966), also scripted by Robert Bloch (1917–94).

ABOVE RIGHT: Original French *grande affiche* for Amicus Productions' *The Skull* (Dir: Freddie Francis, 1965), based on Robert Bloch's story "The Skull of the Marquis de Sade" from the September 1945 issue of the pulp magazine *Weird Tales*.

THE STYLISH SIXTIES

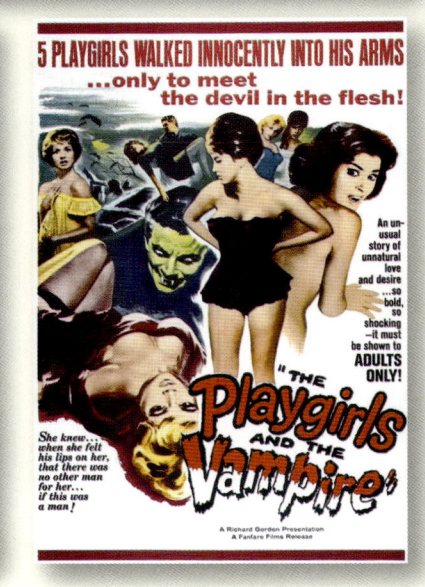

ABOVE LEFT: 1965 Spanish poster for Mario Bava's *I tre volti della paura* (aka *Black Sabbath*, 1963), by the prolific "Mac" (Macario Gómez Quibus, b. 1926).

TOP RIGHT: American half-sheet poster for the 1967 exploitation double-bill from Pacemaker Pictures of the Italian movies *Il boia scarlatto* (aka *Bloody Pit of Horror*, 1965) and *5 tombe per un medium* (aka *Terror-Creatures from the Grave*, 1965), both of which were directed by Massimo Pupillo under pseudonyms.

BOTTOM MIDDLE: American one-sheet poster for the 1962 United Artists' release of Renato Polselli's influential European Gothic, *L'amante del vampiro* (aka *The Vampire and the Ballerina*, 1960).

BOTTOM RIGHT: American one-sheet poster for the "Adults Only!" 1963 Fanfare Films release of Piero Regnoli's *L'ultima preda del vampiro* (aka *The Playgirls and the Vampire/Curse of the Vampire*, 1960).

OPPOSITE, TOP LEFT: British ad mat for Tigon Pictures' 1968 double-bill of *Il castello dei morti vivi* (aka *The Castle of the Living Dead*, 1964), directed by Warren Kiefer and Luciano Ricci, with some uncredited input by Michael Reeves, and Massimo Pupillo's *5 tombe per un medium* (aka *Terror-Creatures from the Grave*, 1965).

THE ART OF HORROR MOVIES

RIGHT: *The Castle of the Living Dead* (2011), gouache on watercolor paper by British artist Graham Humphreys. "This film was made in black and white," explains the artist. "I added some color, though was careful not to suggest full color by avoiding natural hues. It was a wonderful opportunity to portray Christopher Lee in a Gothic setting that was not a Hammer horror."

THE STYLISH SIXTIES

— 165 —

BEWARE THE EYES THAT PARALYZE...

"Ah! Barbara Steele... her eyes are metaphysical, unreal, impossible, like the eyes of a Chirico painting. There are times, in certain conditions of light and color, when her face assumes a cast that doesn't appear to be quite human, which would be impossible for any other actress."
Riccardo Freda

THE PERCEPTIVE CRITIC Raymond Durgnat described Barbara Steele (b. 1937) as "the only gal in film whose eyelids can snarl." She was also—setting aside shrinking, shrieking ingénues like Fay Wray and Evelyn Ankers—the first real female horror star. In the 1960s, she looked like a live-action Disney cartoon villainess. Her raven hair, wide eyes, and expressive mouth evoke Charles Addams's Morticia (or Vladimir Nabokov's Vivian Darkbloom), while her pin-up figure added sex appeal to the sort of sinister roles once taken by Gale Sondergaard or Judith Anderson.

If Brigitte Bardot was a sex kitten, Barbara Steele was a sex panther. She could play beleaguered innocents but was best as monstrous, scheming women—unfaithful, murderous wives or staring, thirsty vampires.

The Cheshire-born English actress was striking enough to be signed up by The Rank Organisation in the UK and Twentieth Century Fox in Hollywood, but was too exotic-looking and unpredictable to be best used by aging, conventional English-language film industries. In Britain, she had only tiny bits in films from *Bachelor of Hearts* (1958) to *Upstairs and Downstairs* (1959); as a former art student, she's probably best cast (albeit uncredited) in the Soho bohemian milieu of *Sapphire* (1959). In America, she walked off the set of Don Siegel's Elvis Presley Western *Flaming Star* (1960) and was replaced by Barbara Eden. Ordinarily, that would have been the end of a career but Italian cinematographer Mario Bava, looking for a leading lady for his film debut, noticed Steele in a magazine layout and summoned her to Rome.

Bava's *La maschera del demonio* (aka *Black Sunday*, 1960) was a startling debut, with Steele playing both the depraved, ravening Princess Asa Vajda and her innocent lookalike descendant. It's a lush, black and white Gothic confection—most of Steele's star vehicles are monochrome—steeped in folklore, and Steele is its centerpiece. It was impressive enough to earn her a brief stopover in Hollywood to be the supposedly dead wife in Roger Corman's *Pit and the Pendulum* (1961), but she was drawn back to Italy to become the preferred leading lady of a cycle of costume dramas built entirely around her haunting eyes and sinister smile.

Oddly, she did not reunite with Bava but was cast by the new master's rivals, Riccardo Freda: *L'orribile segreto del Dr. Hichcock* (aka *The Horrible Dr. Hichcock*, 1962) and *Lo spettro* (aka *The Ghost*, 1963), and Antonio Margheriti: *Danza macabra* (aka *Castle of Blood*, 1963) and *I lunghi capelli della morte* (aka *The Long Hair of Death*, 1964).

She could play beleaguered innocents but was best as monstrous, scheming women.

Her presence is undimmed, but away from Bava and Freda her vehicles became more conventional. Despite working for Federico Fellini (*8½*, 1963), she found horror offered her a narrower range of roles than that allowed her male co-stars.

Mario Caiano's *Amanti d'oltretomba* (aka *Nightmare Castle*, 1965) is unusual only in that her actual voice appears on the English-language version, *Night of the Doomed*. Massimo Pupillo's *5 tombe per un medium* (aka *Terror-Creatures from the Grave/Cemetery of the Living Dead*, 1965) and Camillo Mastrocinque's *Un angelo per Satana* (aka *An Angel for Satan*, 1966) entertainingly go over old ground.

She was unhappy as a work-for-one-day-only guest star in Michael Reeves's Italian-made *The She Beast* (1965), and painted green under a goat-horn hat as yet another evil ancestress in Vernon Sewell's *The Curse of the Crimson Altar* (1968). Her cult lingered, and filmmakers sought her out for interesting supporting sexy maniac roles—Jonathan Demme (*Caged Heat*, 1974), David Cronenberg (*Shivers*, 1975), Joe Dante (*Piranha*, 1978), and Denny Harris (*The Silent Scream*, 1979). Gradually, she shifted focus to production, working with Dan Curtis on the epic miniseries *War and Remembrance* (1988), which led to her taking a regular role in the TV revival of Curtis's *Dark Shadows* (1991), though demoted from *grande dame* menace to family doctor.

In the twenty-first century, she is active again in horror—taking a star role in Jonathan Zarantonello's *The Butterfly Room* (2012) and a significant supporting turn in Ryan Gosling's *Lost River* (2014). KN

OPPOSITE, TOP LEFT: Italian *quattro-foglio* for Mario Bava's *La maschera del demonio* (aka *Black Sunday*, 1960) by artist Giuliano Nistri (b.1929). The movie made a star out of Barbara Steele and set the template for Italian horror.

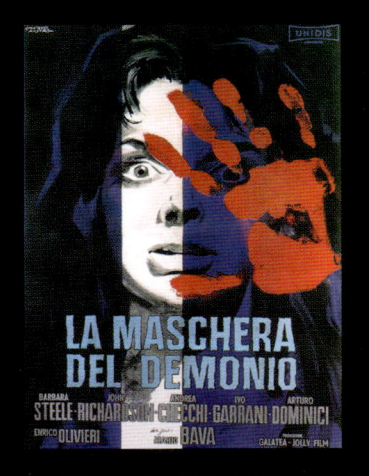

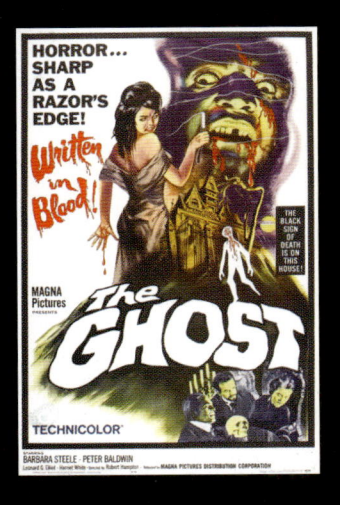

TOP MIDDLE: Japanese trade advertisement for AIPs' second Edgar Allan Poe adaptation, *Pit and the Pendulum* (Dir: Roger Corman, 1961).

MIDDLE LEFT: Half-sheet poster for the 1964 American release of Riccardo Freda's *L'orribile segreto del Dr. Hichcock* (aka *The Horrible Dr. Hichcock/The Terror of Dr. Hichcock*, 1962).

BOTTOM LEFT: 1965 American one-sheet poster for Riccardo Freda's *Lo spettro* (aka *The Ghost*, 1963), which has a plot twist worthy of *Les diaboliques* (1955).

BOTTOM MIDDLE: Italian *foglio* for Massimo Pupillo's *5 tombe per un medium* (aka *Terror-Creatures from the Grave*, 1965), which was supposedly based on a story by Edgar Allan Poe.

ABOVE RIGHT: *Curse of the Crimson Altar* (2013), pencil with digital color by Filipino *komiks* artist John Becaro. "I like to draw beautiful and sexy women," he admits. "This was a private commission to depict Barbara Steele from the classic 1968 movie."

THE STYLISH SIXTIES

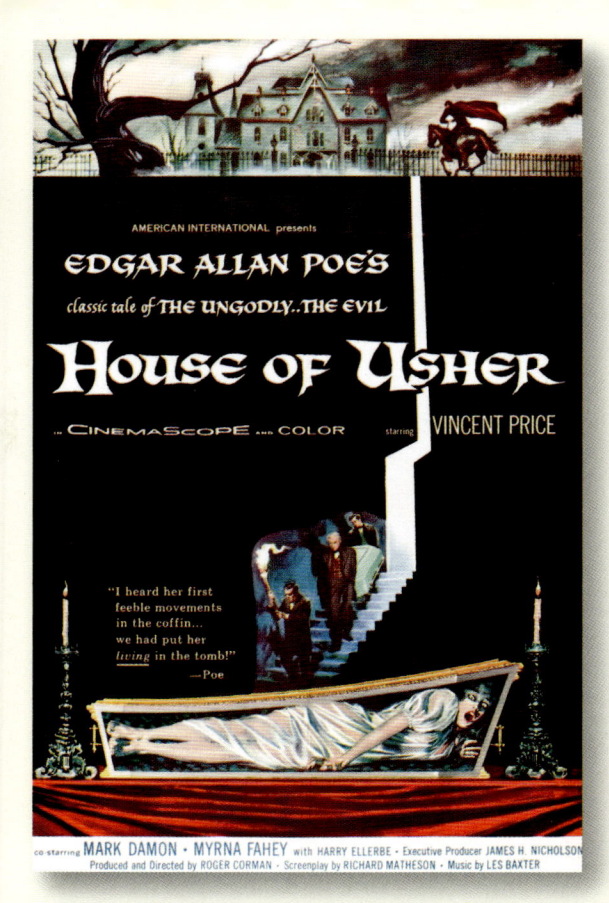

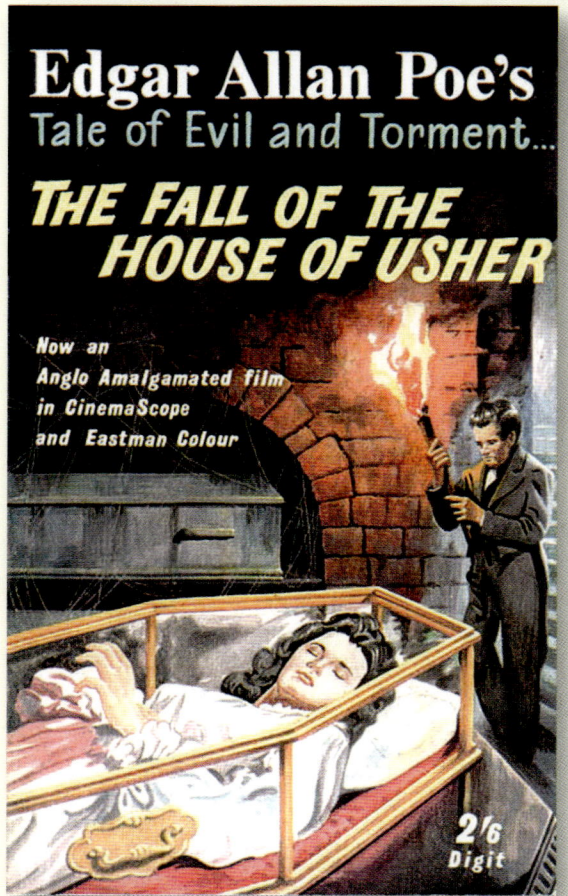

TOP LEFT: American one-sheet poster by Reynold Brown (1917–91) for Roger Corman's first Edgar Allan Poe adaptation for American International Pictures, *The Fall of the House of Usher* (1960). At the time, AIP would often come up with the poster design before making the film.

BOTTOM LEFT: The British tie-in paperback to Roger Corman's film was published in 1961 by Digit Books, the genre imprint of independent London publisher Brown, Watson Ltd.

ABOVE RIGHT: *The Fall of the House of Usher* (2013), gouache on watercolor paper by British artist Graham Humphreys. "Roger Corman's Poe adaptations are examples of imaginative, if lurid, budget filmmaking, inspiring future filmmakers and artists alike," observes the artist. "The film is still a mini-library of visuals for the inquisitive mind and, 55 years later, clearly a touchstone for Guillermo del Toro's *Crimson Peak*."

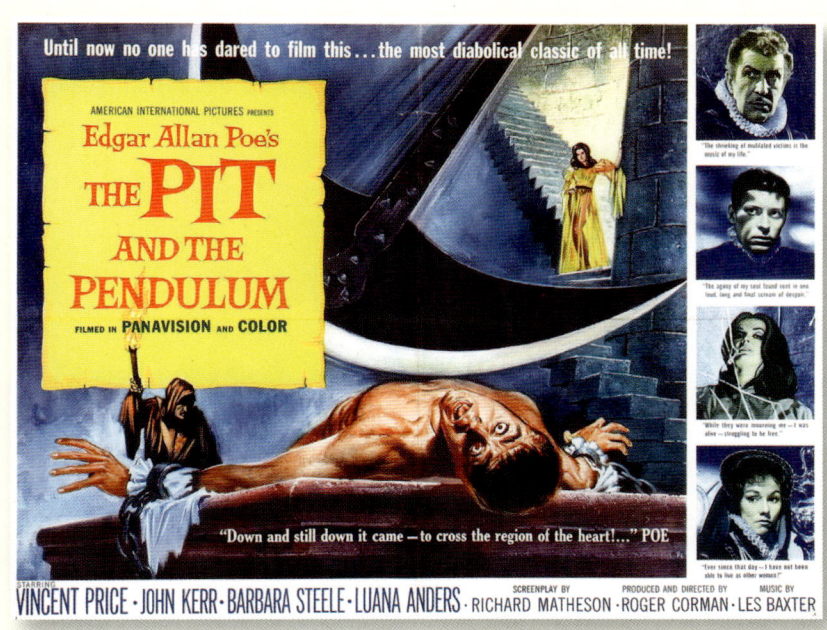

TOP LEFT: Half-sheet poster for American International Pictures' second Edgar Allan Poe adaptation, *Pit and the Pendulum* (Dir: Roger Corman, 1961), by Reynold Brown.

BOTTOM LEFT: For Roger Corman's third Poe adaptation, *Premature Burial* (1962), Reynold Brown's uncharacteristic duo-tone poster may have been a contributing factor to why this movie was not as successful as the previous two from AIP.

TOP RIGHT: Spanish poster for Roger Corman's fourth Edgar Allan Poe movie for American International Pictures, *Tales of Terror* (1962), by Catalan painter Josep Soligó Tena (1910–94).

BOTTOM MIDDLE: This striking 1967 Polish poster for Roger Corman's final Edgar Allan Poe adaptation for American International Pictures, *The Tomb of Ligeia* (1964), was designed by acclaimed graphic artist Maciej Hibner (b. 1931).

BOTTOM RIGHT: British artist Graham Humphreys's 2016 bottle label for Vincent Price Black Cat Ale pays tribute to the Master of Menace's encounters with frightening felines in *Tales of Terror* and *The Tomb of Ligeia*. Brewed in Kent, England, by Hopdaemon, the beer is a crisp, hoppy American IPA.

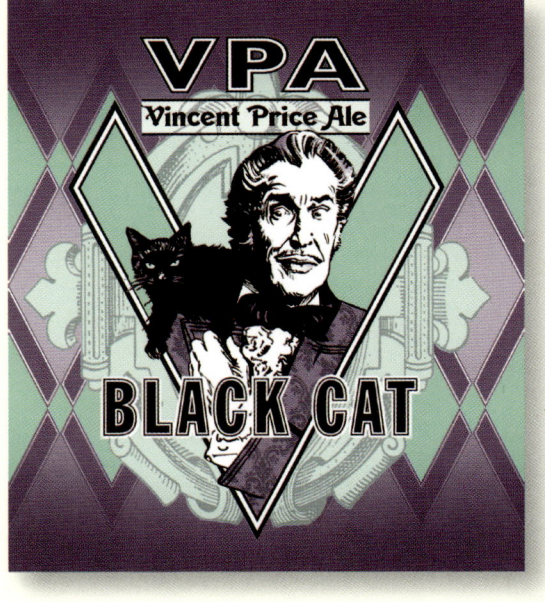

THE STYLISH SIXTIES

Horror on a Budget

Roger Corman (b. 1926) began a prodigious career as a producer/director in the 1950s, venturing into a variety of drive-in genres—his early work might be summed up by *Teenage Cave Man* (1958), which features youth revolt, atomic war, a monster, and nude bathing. He pioneered knowing, blackly comic horror with *A Bucket of Blood* (1959) and *The Little Shop of Horrors* (1960), but hit his stride with *The Fall of the House of Usher* (1960), a colorful Edgar Allan Poe adaptation starring Vincent Price. In the first half of the 1960s, he directed a series of increasingly sophisticated follow-ups, which remain a touchstone for the horror of the period. KN

TOP LEFT: American half-sheet poster for Filmgroup's *The Little Shop of Horrors* (1960).

TOP RIGHT: Belgian poster for American International Pictures' *X: The Man with the X-Ray Eyes* (Dir: Roger Corman, 1963).

BOTTOM LEFT: Original half-sheet poster artwork for American International Pictures' *The Raven* (Dir: Roger Corman, 1963), screenwriter Richard Matheson's comedy version of Edgar Allan Poe's 1845 poem.

BOTTOM RIGHT: 1965 Italian *duo-foglio* for American International Pictures' *The Tomb of Ligeia* (Dir: Roger Corman, 1964), filmed in Britain and adapted from Poe's 1838 story by Robert Towne.

THE ART OF HORROR MOVIES

RIGHT: *Masque of the Red Death* (1993), acrylic on board by American artist Frank Kelly Freas, done for the Fall 1993 edition of the revived *Famous Monsters of Filmland* #201, a special obituary issue paying homage to Vincent Price.

TOP ROW: By the early 1960s, the post-war "baby boomer" generation had re-discovered the classic monster movies, thanks to their syndication on TV in America via the "Shock Theater" packages and the popularity of monster magazines such as Famous Monsters of Filmland. In 1963 the Jaymar Specialty Co. of Brooklyn, New York, began issuing in various formats four licensed interlocking picture puzzles "for little fingers" based on the Universal monsters Frankenstein [LEFT, which also features the Wolf Man and, oddly, "Jake" from The Human Monster (1939)], Dracula [RIGHT], the Mummy, and the Wolf Man.

BOTTOM ROW: On television, ABC launched cartoonist Charles Addams's macabre The Addams Family (1964–66) as a half-hour weekly comedy series created by David Levy, while over at CBS the network did the same thing with the classic Universal monsters in The Munsters (1964–66), created by Allan Burns and Chris Hayward. Both shows debuted within a week of each other, and both lasted only two seasons (although there have been various revivals and movie versions since). It wasn't long before tie-in toys from both shows were being marketed to children: The Milton Bradley Company released two The Addams Family Mystery Jigsaw Puzzles in 1965 ["Cleopatra's Plight" shown LEFT], which came with a "Solution to the Mystery" story booklet that was only revealed by cutting open the back cover. Whitman's two 100-piece The Munsters Jigsaw Puzzles [RIGHT] were also issued in 1965, and depicted America's first family of fright having fun.

THE ART OF HORROR MOVIES

Dell's Movie Classic Comics

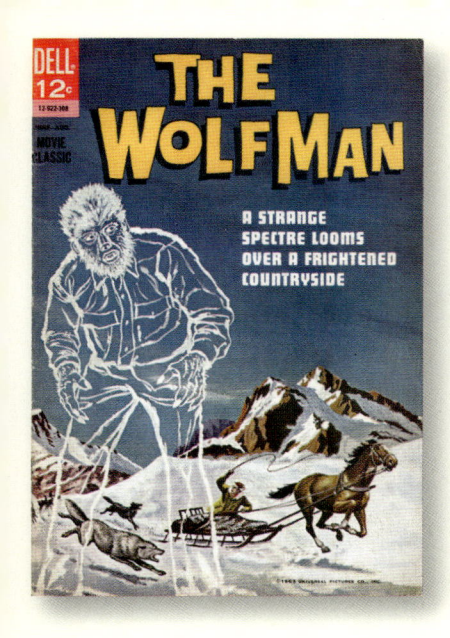

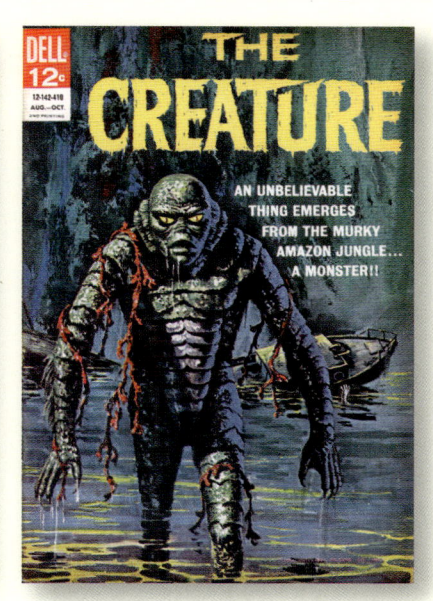

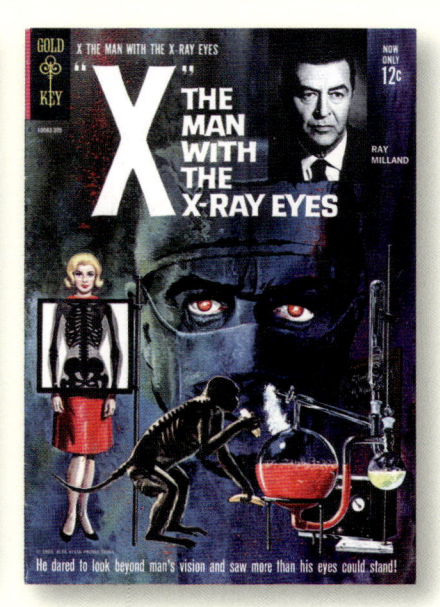

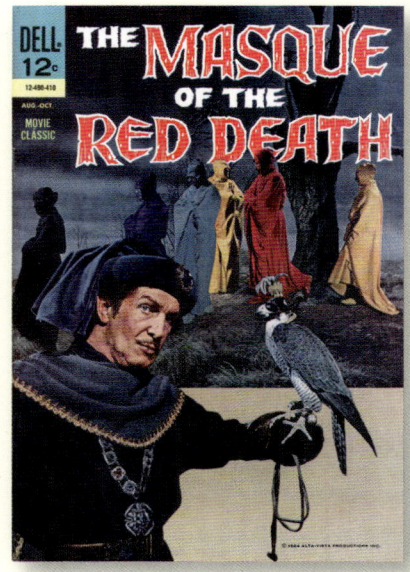

During the 1950s and '60s, Dell Comics produced a wide range of one-shot movie and television tie-in titles, many of them based on classic or contemporary horror movies. Up until 1962, Western Publishing had controlled the licensing, editorial, and publishing process on behalf of Dell, and this creative partnership reportedly accounted for a third of the millions of comics sold each year in America. After that time, the Dell Publishing Co., Inc. continued producing tie-in "Movie Classic" comics under its own banner. Along with official adaptations of Universal's *Dracula*, *Frankenstein*, and *The Mummy*, there were also loose versions of *The Wolf Man* (June–August, 1963; cover artist unknown) and *The Creature* (December–February, 1963; cover art by Vic Prezio). Although the slightly re-titled *"X" The Man with the X-ray Eyes* (1963; cover art by George Wilson) appeared from Western's newly formed Gold Key imprint, other comic adaptations of Alta-Vista Productions/American International Pictures, including *The Masque of the Red Death* (August–October, 1964), *Tomb of Ligeia* (April–June 1965; cover art by John Tartaglione and Vince Colletta), and *Die, Monster, Die!* (March 1966), were published by Dell. The movie studios were apparently very aware of the company's market share, sending them multiple scripts to choose from, and they viewed these comic book adaptations as a cost-effective method to build advance publicity for forthcoming releases. United Artists was another distributor who took advantage of the graphic medium by licensing an adaptation of *Twice Told Tales* (November–January 1964) to Dell, while Warner Bros. Pictures went the same route with *Two on a Guillotine* (April–June, 1965; cover art by John Tartaglione and Vince Colletta). Dell continued to turn out these four-color film and television tie-ins until the company ceased publishing them in 1973, and many of these comic book adaptations were among the company's bestselling titles.

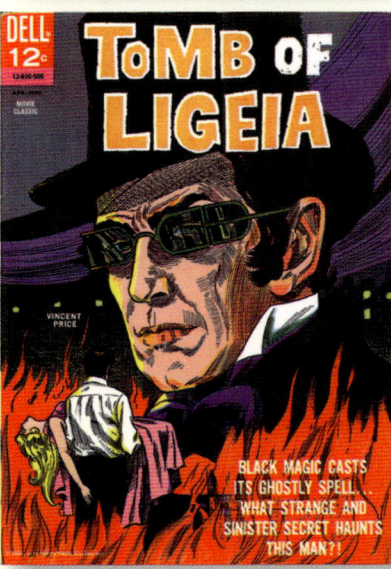

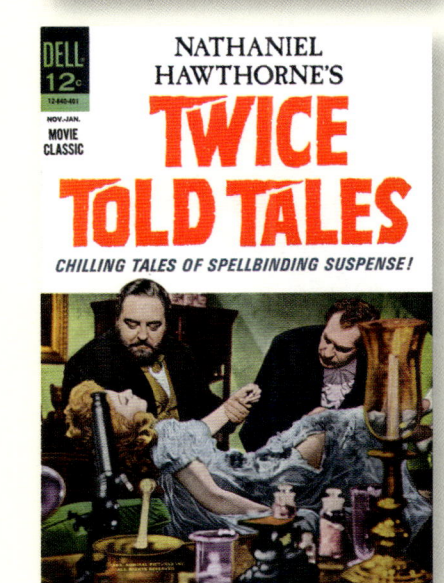

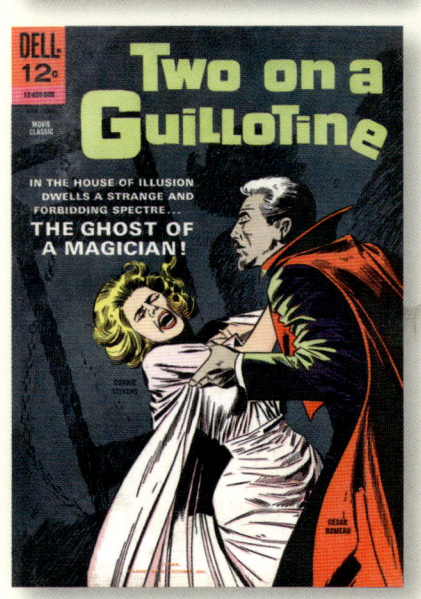

THE STYLISH SIXTIES

LEFT: *The Reptile/The Plague of the Zombies* (2009), markers and colored pencil on paper by American artist Bruce Timm, done for the front cover of *Little Shoppe of Horrors* #23 (October, 2009). "I'm almost completely self-taught," admits Timm. "I never actually went to formal art school or anything."

THE ART OF HORROR MOVIES

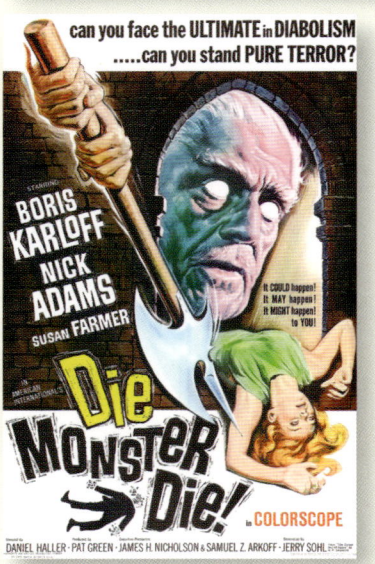

TOP LEFT: American half-sheet poster for American International's British-made *The Masque of the Red Death* (Dir: Roger Corman, 1964), based on Edgar Allan Poe's 1842 short story of the same title and the author's 1849 tale "Hop-Frog." Reynold Brown's original painting, comprising the figures of Prospero's victims, was reworked for the key advertising art as a line drawing by Ken Sawyer.

ABOVE RIGHT: Belgian *affiche* for Hammer Films' *The Gorgon* (Dir: Terence Fisher, 1964). "The whole thing fell apart because the effect of the snakes on Megaera's head was not sufficiently well done," complained star Christopher Lee. "It could have been terrific."

BOTTOM LEFT: Reynold Brown's one-sheet poster for American International Pictures' *Die, Monster, Die!* (Dir: Daniel Haller, 1965), filmed in Britain as *Monster of Terror* and based on H.P. Lovecraft's 1927 story "The Colour Out of Space."

BOTTOM MIDDLE: Italian *foglio* for Hammer Films' *The Reptile* (Dir: John Gilling, 1966), which starred Jacqueline Pearce as a scaly snake-monster in makeup created by Roy Ashton.

Women in Horror: 1960s

After co-starring in *Doctor Blood's Coffin* (1961), British-born Hazel Court (1926–2008) dabbled with the dark side in Roger Corman's Poe adaptations *Premature Burial* (1962), *The Raven* (1963), and *The Masque of the Red Death* (1964). Barbara Shelley (b. 1932) battled the alien offspring of *Village of the Damned* (1960) before also finding herself seduced by evil in Hammer's *The Gorgon* (1964), *Dracula Prince of Darkness* (1965), and *Rasputin The Mad Monk* (1965). At least Suzan Farmer's (b. 1942) ingénue heroine was able to resist Christopher Lee's seductive charms in both those latter films, while also surviving Boris Karloff's Lovecraftian mutant in *Monster of Terror* (aka *Die, Monster, Die!*, 1965). Poor Jacqueline Pearce (b. 1943) had her head chopped off in Hammer's *The Plague of the Zombies* (1966), before giving in to her scaly side in *The Reptile* (1966) for the same studio.

THE STYLISH SIXTIES

BOTTOM LEFT: Spanish poster by comics artist Josep Martí Ripoll for Tigon's *The Sorcerers* (1967). 23-year-old co-writer/director Michael Reeves gave Boris Karloff's career a late boost portraying a scientist who invented a device that allowed him to live vicariously through the minds of others.

TOP RIGHT: US half-sheet poster for the Tigon British production *The Blood Beast Terror* (Dir: Vernon Sewell, 1968), re-titled for America.

BOTTOM RIGHT: Renato Casaro's Italian *locandina* for *The Blood Beast Terror* (1968) depicted Christopher Lee instead of Peter Cushing.

TOP LEFT: A Tigon British/American International Pictures co-production, *Witchfinder General* (Dir: Michael Reeves, 1968) was re-titled *The Conqueror Worm* in America to tie in with AIP's Edgar Allan Poe series. This version included a new opening and closing narration by Vincent Price.

BOTTOM MIDDLE: American one-sheet poster for Tigon's *Curse of the Crimson Altar* (Dir: Vernon Sewell, 1968), which AIP re-titled *The Crimson Cult* in the US. Boris Karloff's last British film was very loosely based on H.P. Lovecraft's 1932 story "The Dreams in the Witch House."

THE ART OF HORROR MOVIES

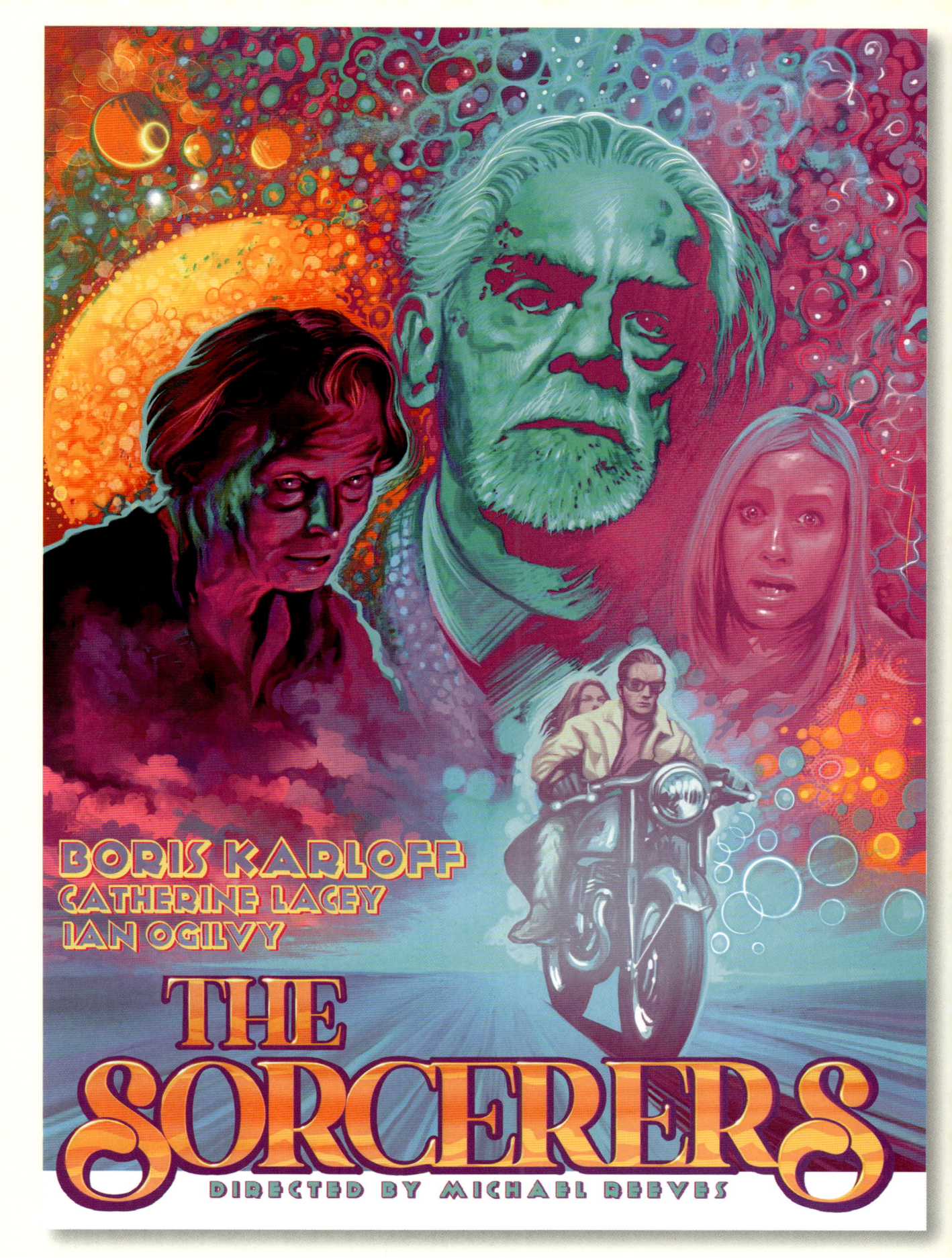

RIGHT: *The Sorcerers* (2019), digital art by Daryl Joyce, who reveals: "This was done to express some of psychedelic aspects of the transference process that sees Boris Karloff and Catherine Lacey reliving their lives, and freeing their inhibitions, through the troubled young man played by Ian Ogilvy."

THE STYLISH SIXTIES

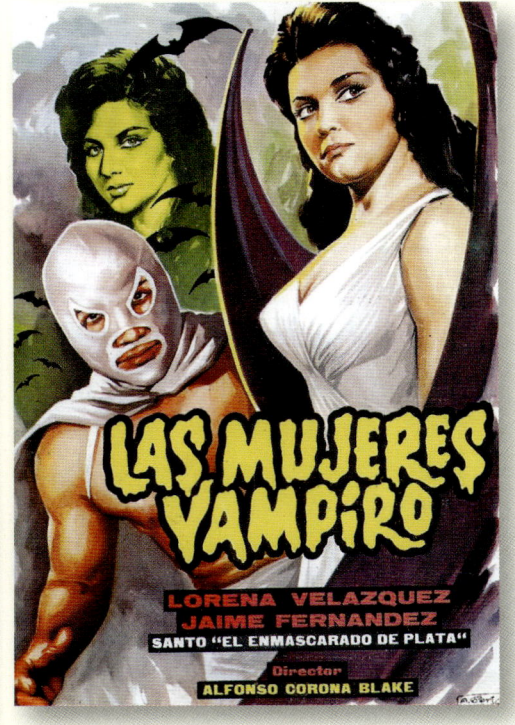

ABOVE LEFT: *Enmascarado de Plata* (2012), digital portrait by Mexican graphic designer Christian Pacheco "Kimbal" of the silver-masked *Luchador*, Santo. "He is the greatest Mexican hero," says the artist. "Defender of the world in his comics and movies, and a symbol of good and justice every Sunday in the arena."

TOP RIGHT: Spanish poster for Alfonso Corona Blake's *Santo vs. las mujeres vampiro* (aka *Samson vs. the Vampire Women*, 1962) by artist A. Perís.

BOTTOM RIGHT: Mexican poster for Alfonso Corona Blake's *Santo en el museo de cera* (aka *Samson in the Wax Museum*, 1963) by artist Francisco Cerezo.

RIGHT: Ad mat for *Santo contra los zombies* (1961).

THE ART OF HORROR MOVIES

— 178 —

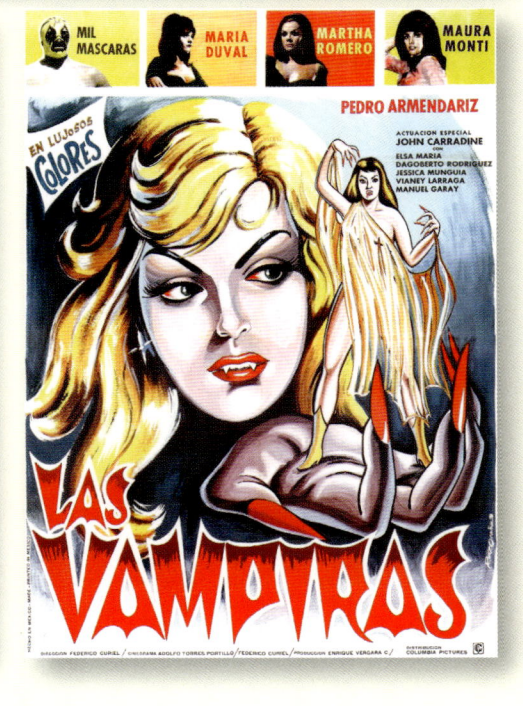

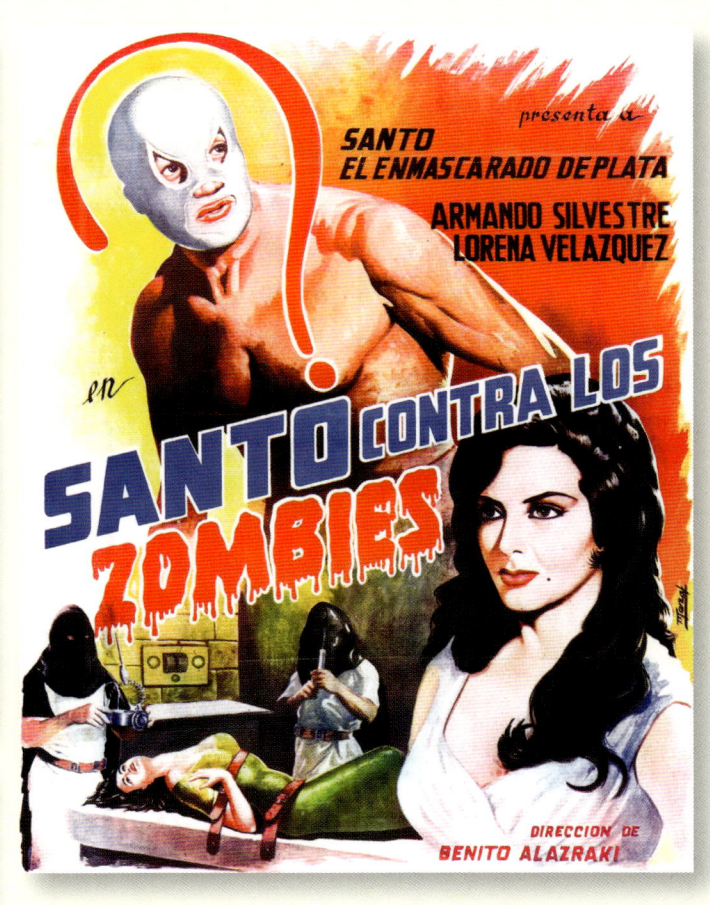

TOP LEFT: Mexican lobby card by artist Roberto Ruiz Ocaña for *Arañas infernales* (Dir: Federico Curiel, 1968), featuring Alejandro Muñoz Moreno as Santo's biggest rival, Mexican masked wrestler Blue Demon.

TOP RIGHT: 1964 Spanish poster signed "Marzal" for Benito Alazraki's *Santo contra los zombies* (aka *Invasion of the Zombies*, 1961), the silver-masked wrestler's third movie and his first starring vehicle.

BOTTOM LEFT: Mexican reissue poster for René Cardona's *Las luchadoras contra la momia* (aka *Wrestling Women vs. the Aztec Mummy*, 1964), the second movie featuring the female wrestling team.

BOTTOM MIDDLE: Mexican poster for *Las vampiras* (Dir: Federico Curiel, 1968) by artist Roberto Ruiz Ocaña. Aaron Rodriguez Arellano's wrestler Mil Máscaras ("1,000 Masks") appears in his third movie.

BOTTOM RIGHT: Mexican lobby card for *El barón Brákola* (Dir: José Díaz Morales, 1967), in which Santo's *el Enmascarado de Plata* ends up wrestling in the ring with the eponymous vampire (real-life *luchador* Fernando Osés, who also co-scripted).

THE STYLISH SIXTIES

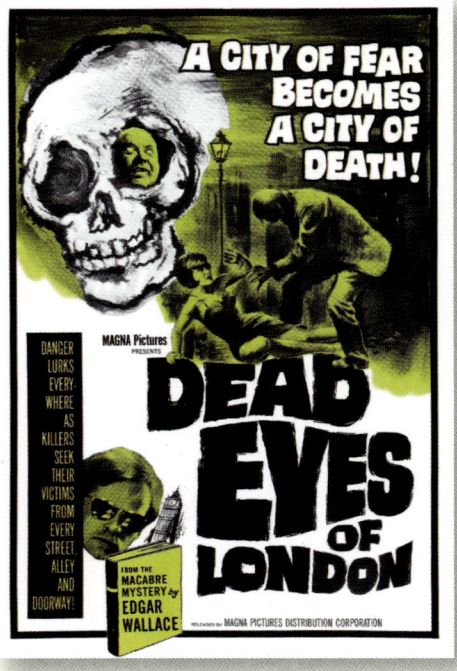

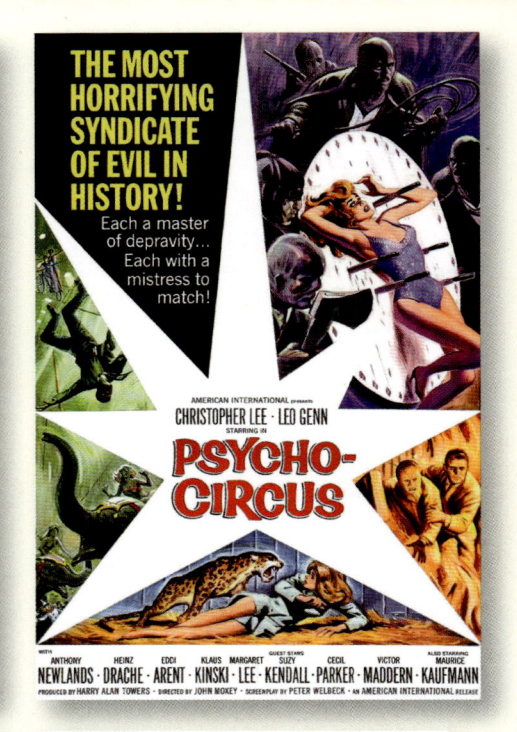

TOP MIDDLE: American one-sheet poster for Alfred Vohrer's West German *krimi* ("thriller") film *Die toten Augen von London* (aka *Dead Eyes of London*, 1961), which was based on the same 1924 Edgar Wallace novel that inspired *The Dark Eyes of London* (1939), starring Bela Lugosi.

TOP RIGHT: Filmed in Britain as *Circus of Fear* (Dir: John [Llewellyn] Moxey, 1966) and re-titled *Psycho-Circus* in America, this *krimi* was based on a 1928 novel by Edgar Wallace. Werner Jacobs is credited as the director on the West German version, *Das Rätsel des silbernen Dreiecks*.

BOTTOM MIDDLE: This striking French *affiche* for Alfred Vohrer's *Der Bucklige von Soho* (aka *The Hunchback of Soho* 1966), the first in Rialto Film's Edgar Wallace *krimis* series to be shot in West Germany in color, reused the Italian poster art by Renato Casaro (b. 1935).

ABOVE LEFT: Renato Casaro also created the art for this Italian *locandina* for Alfred Vohrer's *Der Hund von Blackwood Castle* (aka *The Monster of Blackwood Castle*, 1968), the 25th film in Rialto's Edgar Wallace series. Overseas posters were invariably superior to the West German versions.

BOTTOM RIGHT: Renato Casaro firmly established himself as the Italian poster artist for Rialto's Edgar Wallace *krimis* series, as with this *duo-foglio* for Alfred Vohrer's *Im Banne des Unheimlichen* (aka *The Zombie Walks*, 1968), based on the 1927 novel *The Hand of Power*.

THE ART OF HORROR MOVIES

THIS PAGE: Having released a number of foreign movies in Britain, Tom Blakeley of Planet Film Distributors Ltd. decided to get involved in production. The trio of horror/science fiction movies he produced in the late 1960s compare favorably to those made by Hammer and Amicus.

TOP LEFT: Italian *locandina* by Renato Casaro for *Devils of Darkness* (1965), a modern-day occult thriller in which William Sylvester's American tourist found himself involved with a French vampire-cult led by Hubert Noël's Count Sinistre. It was director Lance Comfort's last film.

TOP MIDDLE: Italian *locandina* by Basilio Morini for the 1973 reissue of *Island of Terror* (Dir: Terence Fisher, 1966), which was filmed under the title *Night of the Silicates*. On a remote island off the Irish coast, Peter Cushing's pathologist encounters tentacled, bone-dissolving creatures.

ABOVE RIGHT: Italian poster for *Night of the Big Heat* (Dir: Terence Fisher, 1967), in which Christopher Lee and Peter Cushing's scientists are caught up in an alien invasion on an isolated island. It was based on a 1959 novel by "John Lymington" (John Richard Newton Chance).

BOTTOM LEFT: *Night of the Big Heat* (1967) was re-titled *Island of the Burning Damned* in the US when finally released on the lower half of a double-bill with a Godzilla movie in 1971 by Maron Films Limited. The title was further changed to *Island of the Burning Doomed* for American TV.

THE STYLISH SIXTIES

ABOVE LEFT: Original tempera on illustration board painting for Warner Bros.-Seven Arts' *It!* (Dir: Herbert J. Leder, 1966), created by Canadian-born book cover and movie poster artist Jack LeRoy Thurston (b. 1919) for the B.G. Charles Agency.

ABOVE RIGHT: Jack Thurston's original tempera on illustration board painting for the co-feature, *The Frozen Dead* (Herbert J. Leder, 1966), produced for the advertising agency founded by Bill Gold and his brother.

LEFT: As this four-column ad mat shows, Jack Thurston's artwork was used for the poster and advertising material for the US double-bill release of *The Frozen Dead* and *It!* in 1967.

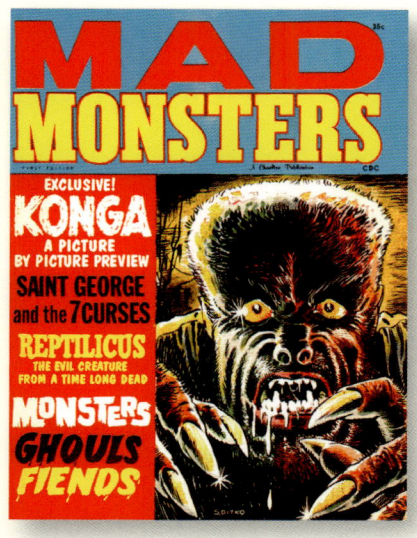

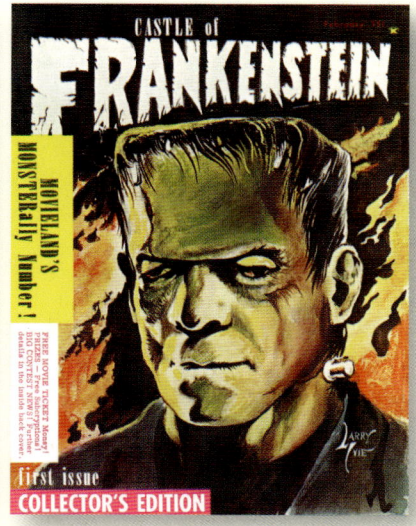

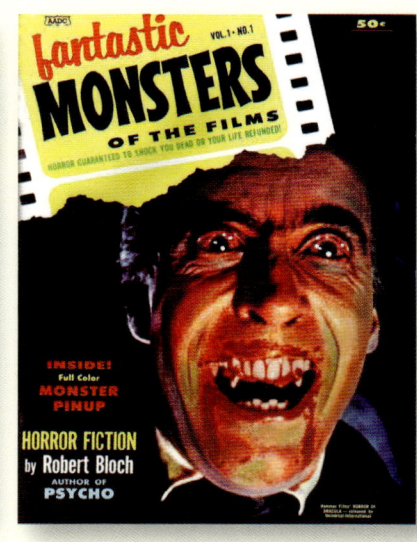

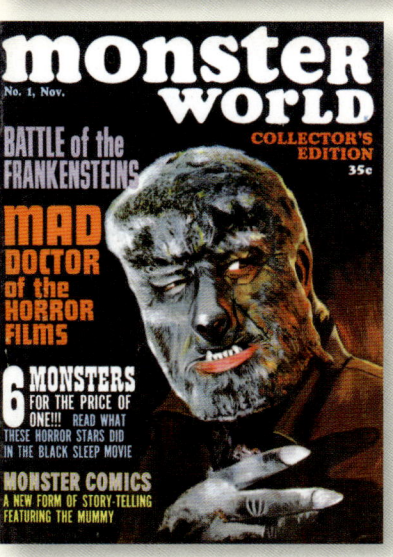

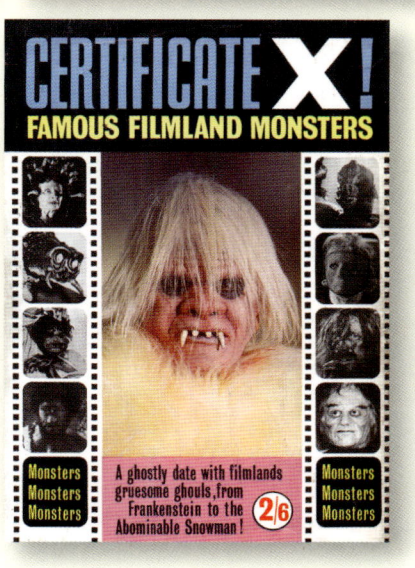

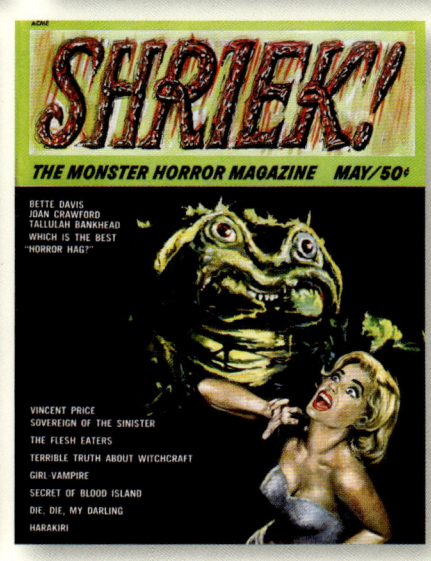

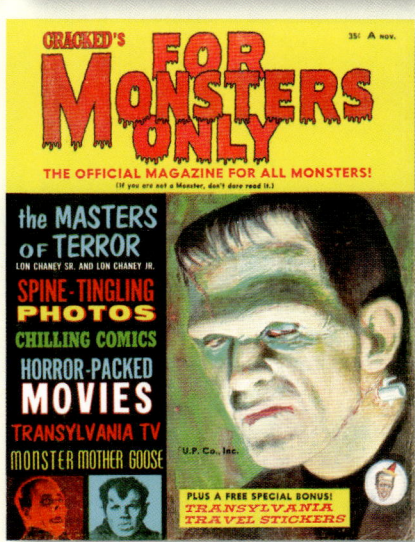

Sons of *Famous Monsters*

During the 1960s, the success of *Famous Monsters of Filmland* led to a rash of imitators trying to cash-in on the monster-boom. Charlton Publications launched the anonymously edited *Horror Monsters* in 1961, along with companion title *Mad Monsters* with a cover by Steve Ditko. Both magazines each ran for ten issues. That same year, Calvin T. Beck was back publishing the first critical monster magazine, *Castle of Frankenstein*, which ran for 25 issues and an annual under various editors until June 1975. The French *Midi-Minuit Fantastique*, launched in May–June 1962 by anti-establishment publisher Eric Losfeld, was another serious film journal, edited by Michel Caen and Jean-Claude Romer. It lasted for 24 issues before ceasing publication in 1971. Publishers Paul Blaisdell and Bob Burns had experience in the movie industry when they produced *Fantastic Monsters of the Films* under the editorship of Ron Haydock in 1962. An attempt to produce a more mature American monster magazine, it ended its run with issue #7 in 1963.

Editor Forrest J Ackerman and publisher James Warren decided to compete with themselves when they launched *Monster World* in November 1964 with a cover by Russ Jones. It lasted for ten issues before the title was folded into *Famous Monsters of Filmland* in 1966. The one-shot *Certificate X! Famous Filmland Monsters* appeared from Britain's World Distributors Ltd. in January 1965, while the first issue of *Shriek!* from Acme News Co., Inc. debuted in America four months later. It lasted just four issues before ceasing publication with its Winter 1967 edition. With the newsstands now glutted with monster magazines, it was inevitable that the industry would eventually descend into self-parody. In November 1965, *MAD* magazine imitator *Cracked* launched *For Monsters Only* under the editorship of Lorraine Zuckerman. A mixture of articles and satirical comic strips (by EC's John Severin, among others), it lasted for ten issues and a 1967 "Gigantic Annual" before coming to an end in June 1972. But by now, the readers were growing up . . .

THE STYLISH SIXTIES

"WHO PUT PEPPER IN MY BUBBLE GUM?"

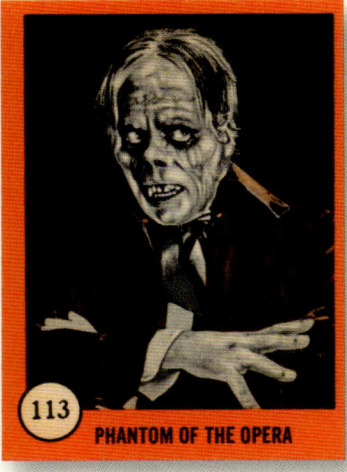

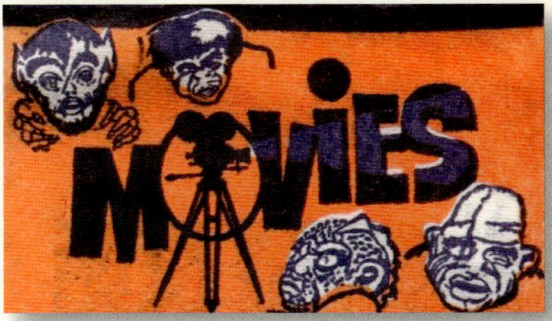

KING KONG

113 PHANTOM OF THE OPERA

MAY I HAVE THE NEXT DANCE?
©UNIVERSAL PICTURES CO., INC., PRINTED IN U.S.A.

The Golden Age of Monster Cards

Inspired by the "monster boom" of the late 1950s, in 1959 Bubbles, Inc. issued the first series of monster bubble gum cards in America. *You'll Die Laughing* (or *Funny Monsters* according to the wax paper wrapping) consisted of 66 full-color pasteboard cards illustrated by veteran EC comics artist Jack Davis [TOP LEFT]. Two years later, Nu-Cards, Inc. created two series of *Horror Monster* cards with green (#1–66) and orange (#67–146) borders [TOP MIDDLE LEFT, TOP MIDDLE RIGHT & ABOVE] featuring photographs from mostly recent horror movies, some printed in duo-tone color. *Spook Stories* from Leaf Brands, Inc. [TOP RIGHT & ABOVE RIGHT] used images of the classic Universal monsters. Although copyrighted 1961, they were issued between 1962–63 in two sets of 72 cards apiece plus stickers. Sold through Forrest J Ackerman's magazine of the same name, the Rosan Printing Corporation's *Famous Monsters* set from 1963 [MIDDLE LEFT] included 64 cards with photos from American International Pictures. Rosan's series of *Terror Monster* cards from that same year also featured images from AIP movies and was issued in two sets, with green (#1–64) and purple (#67–132) borders [MIDDLE RIGHT], along with two unnumbered "bonus" cards. In 1973 T.C.G. released a 128-card variation on the *Spook Stories* series as *You'll Die Laughing*, with different numbering and captions, and the faces of the actors replaced by those of employees [BOTTOM LEFT]. Topps issued yet another variant set of 88 cards in 1980 as *Creature Feature* [BOTTOM RIGHT]. Each packet contained 12 photo cards, a sticker, and a stick of hard bubble gum.

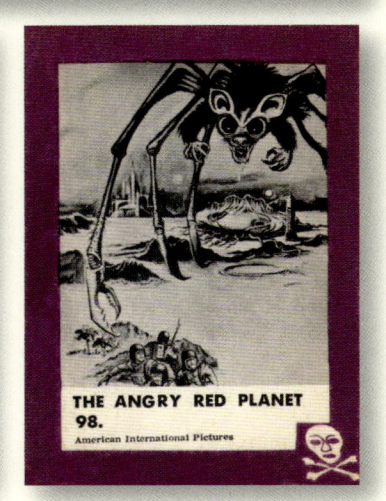

11 WAR OF THE COLOSSAL BEAST

THE ANGRY RED PLANET
98.
American International Pictures

PLEASE... NOT ON OUR FIRST DATE!

CREATURE FEATURE
12 PHOTO CARDS
1 STICKER • 1 STICK BUBBLE GUM

THE ART OF HORROR MOVIES

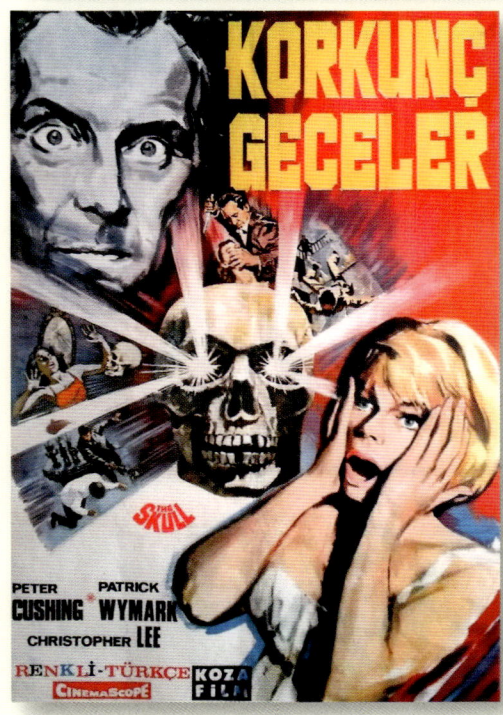

THIS PAGE: Turkey's *Yeşilçam* movie industry—named after a street in Istanbul filled with numerous film production companies—flourished from the 1950s through the 1980s, turning out more than 300 movies a year. One-sheet posters were originally hand-drawn by local artists, but from the mid-1950s onwards, thanks to advances in photo-offset printing and color separation, they started utilizing photographs or adapting existing publicity artwork, often creating hallucinogenic collages that did not always incorporate images from the foreign movies they were supposed to be advertising.

TOP LEFT: Turkish poster for *The Hypnotic Eye* (1960), which starred French actor Jacques Bergerac as a crazed hypnotist disfiguring women.

TOP MIDDLE: The Turkish one-sheet for Hammer's *The Curse of the Werewolf* (1961) used the poster art to better effect than in the US.

TOP RIGHT: Slightly misleading Turkish poster for the British-made *Konga* (1961), about a giant ape rampaging through London.

BOTTOM LEFT: This Turkish poster for the Italian production *Horror Castle* (1963) featured completely original artwork.

BOTTOM MIDDLE: The Turkish one-sheet for Amicus's *The Skull* (1965) skilfully reworked the American poster design.

BOTTOM RIGHT: The Turkish poster for the British *Theatre of Death* (1966) used a collage of existing artwork and photographs.

THE STYLISH SIXTIES

DONALD
SUTHERLAND
CHRISTOPHER
LEE
ROY
CASTLE
NEIL
McCALLUM
ALAN
FREEMAN

LEFT: *Dr. Terror's House of Horrors* (2016), gouache on watercolor paper by British artist Graham Humphreys, who explains: "Designed as a wraparound for a SteelBook® Blu-ray release of this familiar Amicus classic, the client had already suggested their ideal requirements—using the tarot cards as a device to portray the key casting. This was an opportunity to paint some characterful and familiar faces. For the featured portrait of Peter Cushing, I photographed a friend's gloved hands with a real tarot pack. The title was always conceived as integral to the layout and is retained here in the form intended."

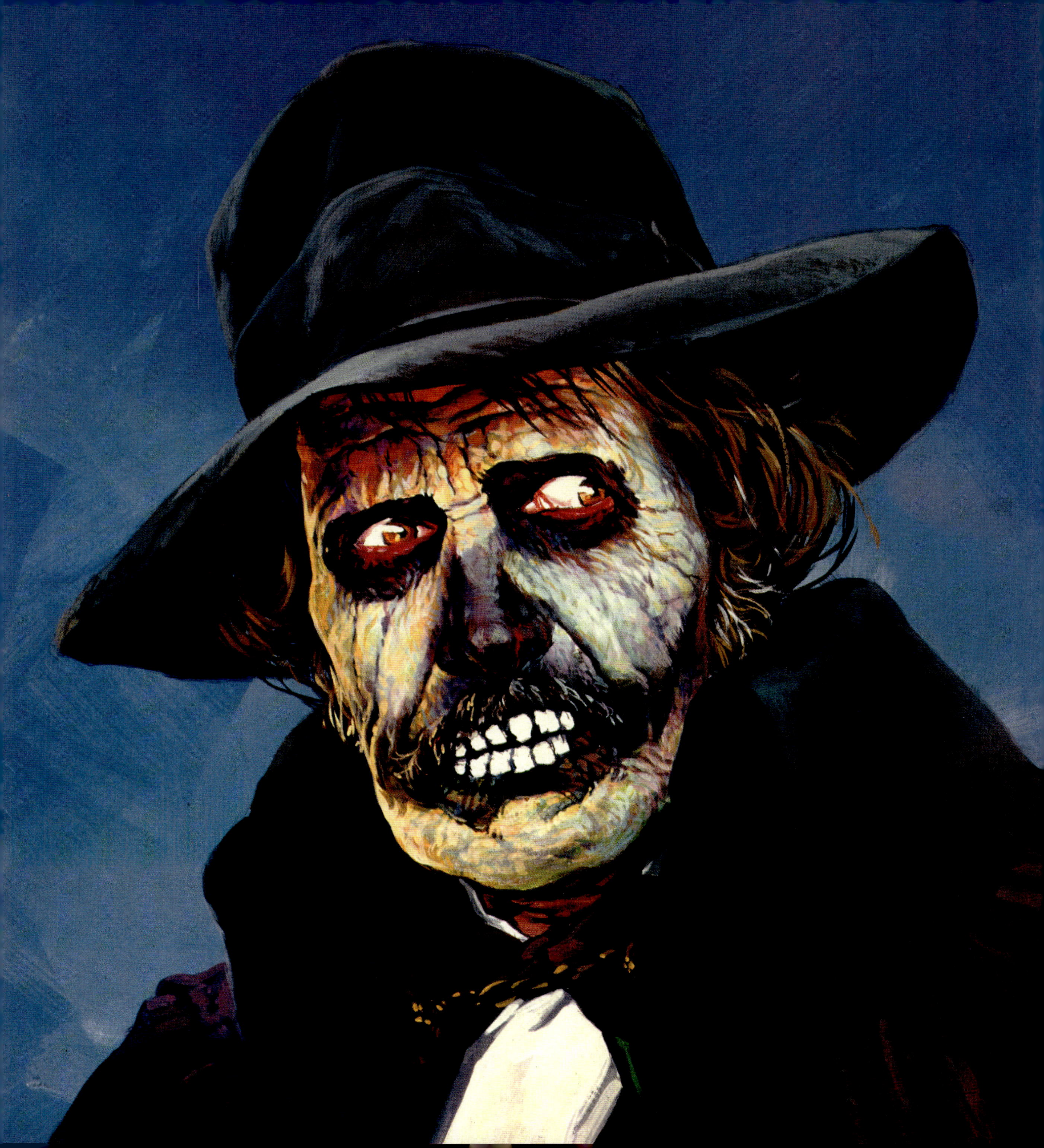

6
THE SATANIC SEVENTIES

JONATHAN RIGBY

"I'm not thriving off a career slagging
off the Queen. I think I have something valid to say.
My words are my bullets."

JOHN LYDON (AKA "JOHNNY ROTTEN")

> "I trust people who are violent about art, as long as they aren't closed-minded."
> Vincent Price

THE 1970s WERE the years, in horror cinema, when the gloves came off. Bloodletting and body parts became crucial selling points, reflecting the grim and uncompromising nature of a strife-torn decade. And, in holding the proverbial mirror up to nature, horror films became more than ever obsessed with the dehumanizing effects of possession by outside forces, whether the soul being fought over was that of a pampered Georgetown pre-teen (in William Friedkin's *The Exorcist*, 1973) or a gauche expat Pole in Paris (Roman Polanski's *The Tenant*, 1976), or even the compromised souls of various self-absorbed San Franciscans (Philip Kaufman's modernized *Invasion of the Body Snatchers*, 1978).

The euphoric optimism of the 1960s had been extinguished at the turn of the new decade by the Charles Manson murders, the violence at Altamont, the Kent State shootings, and, above all, the ongoing trauma of the Vietnam War. As a result, cynicism, paranoia, and pessimism became as much hallmarks of the horror genre as they were of society at large.

Yet the seeds of 1970s horror cinema had been planted a little earlier by a couple of films made in the summer of 1967. The Manhattan diabolists of Polanski's *Rosemary's Baby* and the flesh-eating corpses of George A. Romero's *Night of the Living Dead* were to have innumerable heirs.

Although not released until the 1970s, the arcane rituals of Daniel Haller's *The Dunwich Horror* (1970) and Bernard McEveety's *The Brotherhood of Satan* (1971) were in the can before the decade even got started, while the "undead siege" scenario of *Night* was quickly replicated in numerous films, notably Robert Kelljan's *The Return of Count Yorga* (1971) and Jorge Grau's brilliant Spanish-Italian co-production *No profanar el sueño de los muertos* (1974). (The latter's title—"Do Not Profane the Sleep of the Dead"—became *Let Sleeping Corpses Lie* in America and, amusingly, *The Living Dead at Manchester Morgue* in Britain.)

In addition to these spirited zombie stand-offs, traumatized Vietnam vets got their very own undead representative at the end of 1972, when the Canadian director Bob Clark went to Florida to shoot the quietly harrowing *Deathdream* (aka *Dead of Night*).

In the midst of all this, Britain's sometime market leader, Hammer Film Productions, struggled to stay relevant but nevertheless produced some startling late works prior to effectively collapsing mid-decade.

The coyly titillating lesbian bloodsuckers of Roy Ward Baker's *The Vampire Lovers* (1970) gave the company a sizable commercial hit, but were rapidly outclassed by such genre-bending curios as Baker's *Dr. Jekyll & Sister Hyde* (1971) and *The Legend of the 7 Golden Vampires* (1974), Peter Sasdy's *Hands of the Ripper* (1971), Robert Young's *Vampire Circus* (1972), Alan Gibson's *Dracula A.D. 1972* (1972), and the gore-strewn Gothic farewell that was Terence Fisher's final film, the 1974 release *Frankenstein and the Monster from Hell*.

The advertising for these and other titles was the work of Arnaldo Putzu, Mike Vaughan, Vic Fair, Tom Chantrell, and Bill Wiggins, with the lurid artwork aptly complementing the meticulous art direction of the films themselves. The cool grandeur of Roy Stannard's Pinewood sets for *Twins of Evil* (1971), for example, was balanced by the empurpled gloom of Vaughan's poster design.

The euphoric optimism of the 1960s had been extinguished at the turn of the new decade by the Charles Manson murders, the violence at Altamont, the Kent State shootings, and, above all, the ongoing trauma of the Vietnam War. As a result, cynicism, paranoia, and pessimism became as much hallmarks of the horror genre as they were of society at large.

Elsewhere in the UK, Amicus scored their biggest portmanteau hit with *Tales from the Crypt* (1972), whose staring-eyeball poster was censored for use on the London Underground, and Arnaldo Putzu created a memorable demonic embrace to advertise Piers Haggard's chilling Tigon production *Blood on Satan's Claw* (aka *Satan's Skin*, 1971). The prolific Tom Chantrell, meanwhile, interleaved commissions for the British releases of *Night of the Living Dead* and its 1978 follow-up, *Dawn of the Dead*, with such home-grown shockers as the Norman J. Warren trio *Satan's Slave* (1976), *Prey* (1977), and *Terror* (1978).

The previously reticent Spain enjoyed its own horror boom in the first half of the 1970s. Kicked off in 1968 by Enrique López Eguiluz's *La marca del hombre lobo* (aka *Frankenstein's Bloody Terror*), which introduced the quixotic local horror star Paul Naschy, the boom was consolidated by the phenomenal success of the January 1970 release *La residencia*; exported as *The House That Screamed*, this classy period chiller was written and directed by TV's horror king, Narciso Ibáñez Serrador.

Spain, too, could boast an iconic poster artist in "Jano" (Francisco Fernández-Zarza Pérez), whose unmistakable style graced first *La marca del hombre lobo* and then a whole range of Spanish horrors, including several for the company that advertised itself as "the Spanish Hammer"—Profilmes.

PREVIOUS SPREAD: *Madhouse* (1974), acrylic on board portrait by American artist Basil Gogos of Vincent Price from the eponymous British movie, used for the cover of *Famous Monsters of Filmland* #109 (August, 1974). "It looks like a touch of death," says the artist. "It's a grayish-bluish dark color that's quite unpleasant, but it makes an attractive cover."

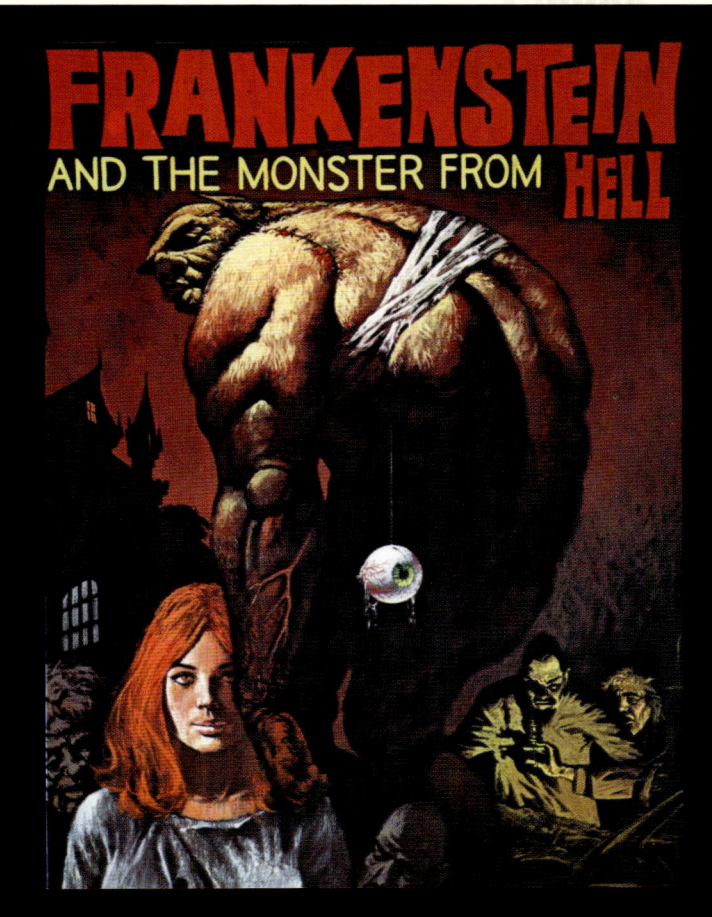

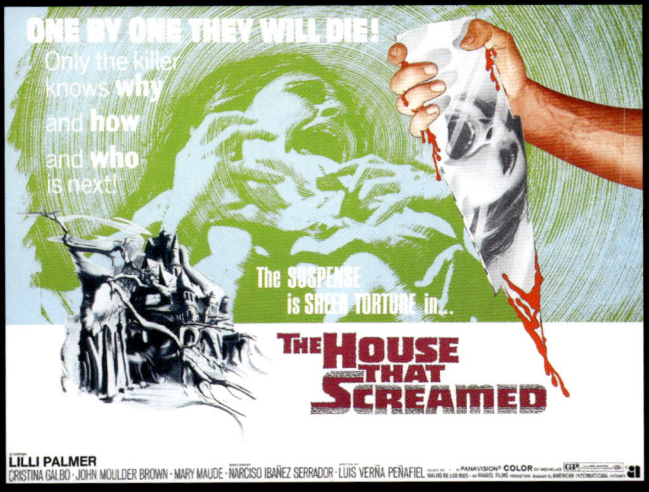

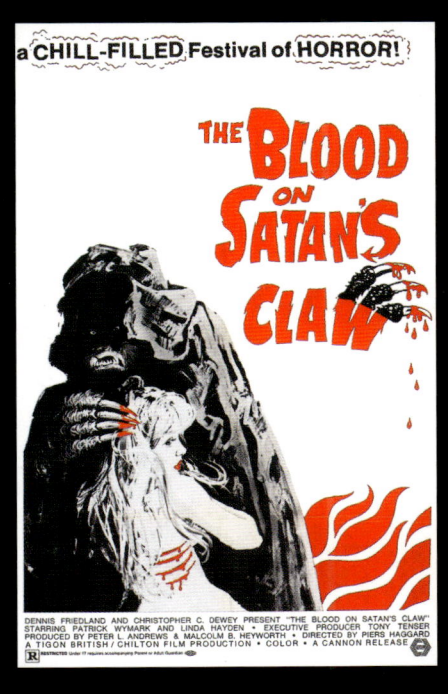

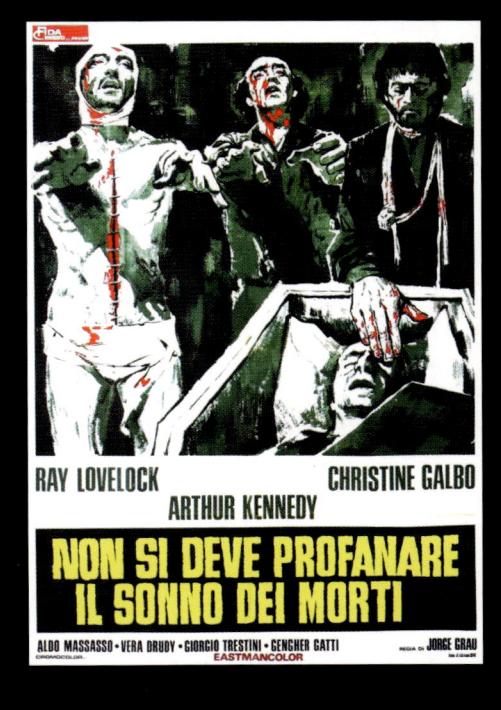

TOP LEFT: Pre-production promotional poster for Hammer Films' *Frankenstein and the Monster from Hell* (1974) by Keenan Forbes. This was director Terence Fisher's fifth and final Frankenstein movie for the studio, and Peter Cushing's sixth and last appearance in the role.

TOP RIGHT: American International Pictures' half-sheet poster for the 1973 US release of *Death Line* (Dir: Gary Sherman, 1972), exploitatively re-titled *Raw Meat*.

BOTTOM LEFT: AIP's half-sheet poster for the Spanish-made *La residencia* (Dir: Narciso Ibáñez Serrador, 1970), re-titled *The House That Screamed* in 1971 for its US exploitation release.

BOTTOM MIDDLE: American one-sheet poster for Tigon British-Chilton Film Productions' *The Blood on Satan's Claw* (Dir: Piers Haggard, 1970) by Italian artist Arnaldo Putzu (1927–2012). An example of the "folk horror" subgenre in British cinema of the late 1960s and early '70s.

BOTTOM RIGHT: Original Italian poster for *No profanar el sueño de los muertos* (aka *Don't Open the Window*, *The Living Dead at Manchester Morgue*, and numerous other titles, 1974), Spanish director Jorge Grau's entry in the European zombie genre.

THE SATANIC SEVENTIES

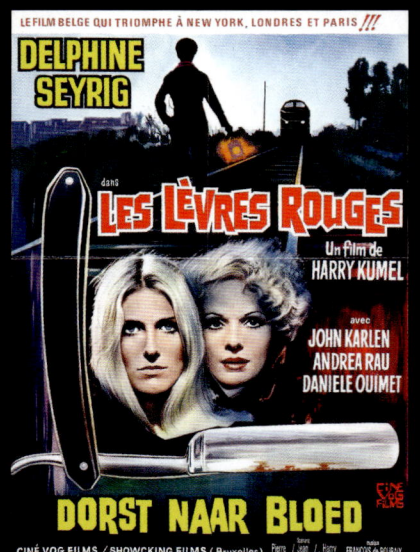

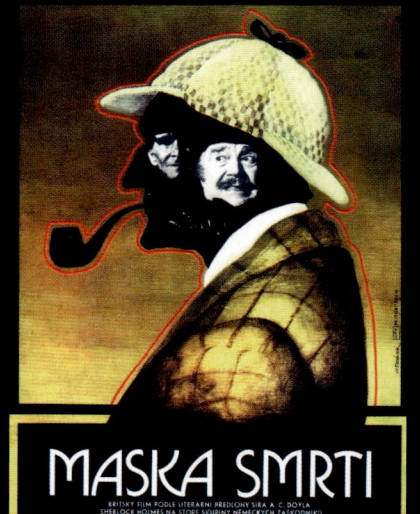

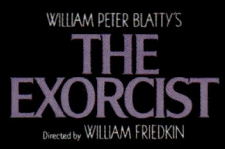

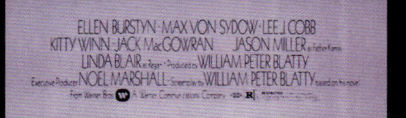

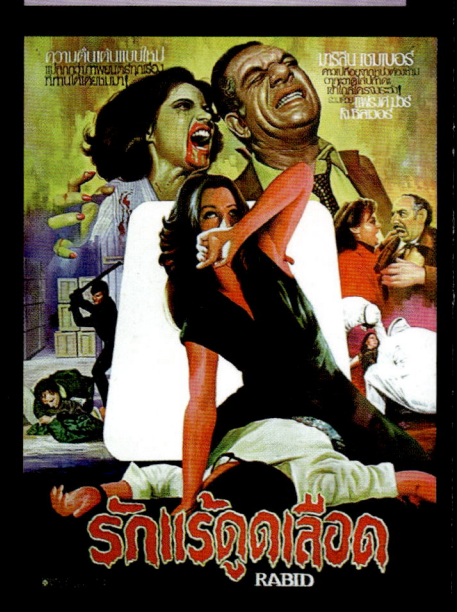

ABOVE LEFT: Colorful Spanish poster for José Luis Madrid's *El Vampiro de la autopista* (aka *The Horrible Sexy Vampire*, 1970) by artist "Jano" (Francisco Fernández-Zarza Pérez, 1922–92), who began his career illustrating movie posters in the 1940s.

TOP MIDDLE: Original Belgian *affiche* for *Les lèvres rouges* (aka *Daughters of Darkness*, 1971), director Harry Kümel's erotic vampire film set in a desolate, winter-bound seaside hotel in Ostend.

TOP RIGHT: The iconic American one-sheet for Warner Bros.' *The Exorcist* (Dir: William Friedkin, 1973), created by graphic designer Bill Gold (b. 1921), who began working on movie posters in the early 1940s. This was the first horror film to be nominated for the Best Picture Oscar.

BOTTOM MIDDLE: Czechoslovakian poster for Twentieth Century-Fox's *The Omen* (Dir: Richard Donner, 1976). The movie was a huge commercial success around the world, and was followed by three official sequels, a 2006 remake, and the inevitable TV series.

BOTTOM RIGHT: Taiwanese poster for the Canadian-made *Rabid* (1977), director David Cronenberg's slice of "body horror" starring former adult film star Marilyn Chambers.

For maverick director Jesús Franco, Jano created the advertising art for the provocative 1970 film *Vampyros Lesbos* (known in Spain as *Las vampiras*), while for Amando de Ossorio he painted the splendidly ghoulish Knights Templar of the 1972 release *La noche del terror ciego*, which was exported as *Tombs of the Blind Dead*. *Vampyros Lesbos*, incidentally, was the most famous title in a vogue for Sapphic vampires kicked off by Hammer and, more generally, by the sudden loosening of censorship restraints.

Much the cleverest and most sumptuous product of this trend was Belgian director Harry Kümel's *Les lèvres rouges*, which made plenty of export dollars in 1971 as *Daughters of Darkness*.

Richard Donner's *The Omen* bust box offices worldwide with a masterfully contrived story aggravating the exposed nerve of the Watergate scandal, in which the US Ambassador to the UK inadvertently fostered a Satanic tyke that, in the cynical closing shot, had its eyes set firmly on the White House.

The real game-changer in the new decade reached US screens on Boxing Day 1973. Based on a bestseller by William Peter Blatty, *The Exorcist* stirred up unprecedented levels of hysteria in the tabloids and broadsheets and indeed in cinemas themselves; as one sorely tried Chicago exhibitor complained: "My janitors are going crazy wiping up the vomit."

The film's blasphemous utterances and unflinchingly gruesome special effects announced a sea change in the attitude of major studios (in this case Warner Bros.) to the kind of graphic material previously reserved for independents. Bile-spattered *Exorcist* clones rose up in abundance almost as soon as the film appeared, the most notorious coming from Italy. Indeed, Ovidio G. Assonitis's *Chi sei?*, exported as *Beyond the Door*, and Alberto De Martino's *L'anticristo* (aka *The Antichrist*) started shooting just a week apart in May 1974.

The Exorcist itself was advertised with one of the decade's most indelible images—a strikingly queasy use of chiaroscuro by designer Bill Gold, emphasizing the traditional battle between Light and Dark that ensues when Father Merrin arrives at little Regan MacNeil's Georgetown home.

Proceeding in a direct line from *Rosemary's Baby*, the natural big-studio successor to *The Exorcist* was in production by the autumn of 1975. With the full might of Twentieth Century-Fox behind it, Richard Donner's *The Omen* bust box offices worldwide with a masterfully contrived story aggravating the exposed nerve of the Watergate scandal, in which the US Ambassador to the UK inadvertently fostered a Satanic tyke that, in the cynical closing shot, had its eyes set firmly on the White House.

Tom Jung's poster, though replicating the chiaroscuro of *The Exorcist*, was otherwise a hokier affair, with the frightened faces of Gregory Peck and Lee Remick surmounting a lycanthropic double silhouette of the cherubic Damien.

Other large scale responses to *The Exorcist* included unashamed schlock like Michael Winner's *The Sentinel* (1976) and William Girdler's *The Manitou* (1978), films that were made to look even less interesting by the emergence of a confrontational new breed of independent filmmakers.

Shot in the broiling summer of 1973 and released the following year, Tobe Hooper's *The Texas Chain Saw Massacre* reconfigured the real-life Ed Gein case into a hair-raising saga of five guileless young trippers and the demented cannibal family they stumble across. As well as Robert A. Burns's art direction (a marvel of plucked feathers and rattling bones), the film also boasted the classic poster tagline: "Who will survive and what will be left of them?"

So intense it conjures the ghastliest of disembowelments with recourse to virtually no on-screen blood, and so insanely funny it perfects a kind of hillbilly version of the Theatre of the Absurd, *Chain Saw* endures as a genuine masterwork of horror.

The collapse of the old verities surrounding the all-American family unit was subsequently underlined by the feral Arizona mutants of Wes Craven's 1977 shocker *The Hills Have Eyes*, while, up in Canada, David Cronenberg crafted a wholly original species of venereal horror in such strikingly intelligent films as *Shivers* (1975), *Rabid* (1977), and, arguably his best work, *The Brood* (1979).

In addition to an explosion of low-budget exploiters aimed at the Grindhouse, the decade also saw the meteoric rise of the young novelist Stephen King as a *bona fide* horror brand name; the 1976 film of his debut novel *Carrie*, dazzlingly directed by Brian De Palma, is distinguished by a piercingly truthful performance, in the telekinetic title role, by Sissy Spacek.

Another new horror brand name emerged in Italy, where Dario Argento's *Profondo rosso* (aka *Deep Red*, 1975) and *Suspiria* (1977)—lurid thrillers as cruelly ingenious as they are eye-poppingly gruesome—had a truly shattering effect in a depressed local market given over to sleazy Nazisploitation, Mondo-style cannibal shockers, and the occasional Gothic throwback.

But it was a small film shot in Pasadena in the spring of 1978 that set the scene for the slasher pictures that would predominate in the following decade. Made by John Carpenter on a $320,000 budget and raking in a whopping $55 million, *Halloween* was a model of suspense filmmaking and scored extremely high in the "whole audience screams collectively" department.

Rival filmmakers could hardly fail to take notice; indeed, Sean S. Cunningham had *Friday the 13th* in production by September 1979. But that's another story...

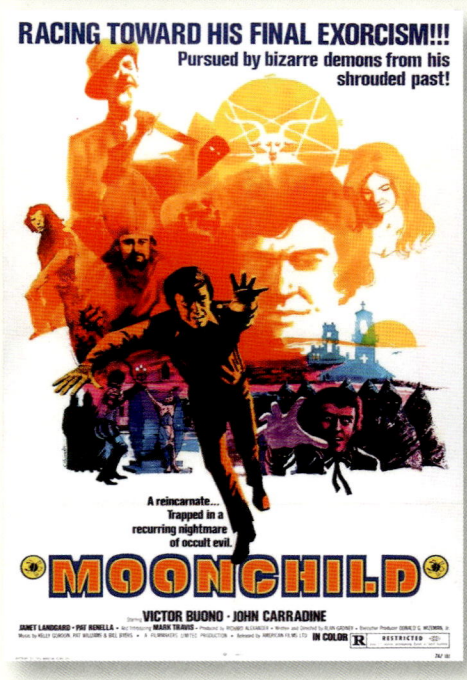

ABOVE LEFT: Insert poster for *Equinox* (Dir: Jack Woods, 1970). Started as a student film in 1967 and filmed on location in southern California, author Fritz Leiber, Jr. shows up clutching the *Necronomicon*, while David Allen, Jim Danforth, and Dennis Muren created the special effects.

BOTTOM MIDDLE: *Moonchild* (1972) also started out as a student film and was released theatrically in 1974. Shot in Riverside, California, the trippy occult mystery was director Alan Gadney's only movie credit, but he was lucky enough to get cameos by genre veterans Victor Buono and John Carradine.

BOTTOM RIGHT: The deliriously offbeat *Shriek of the Mutilated* (1974) was filmed in Croton-on-Hudson, New York. 39-year-old independent filmmaker Michael Findlay was decapitated in a helicopter accident three years later on top of the Pan Am Building in New York City.

TOP RIGHT: Filmed cheaply around California's scenic Huntington Lake, *The Crater Lake Monster* (Dir: William R. Stromberg, 1977) still managed to use stop-motion effects created by David Allen, Randall William Cook, Jim Danforth, Phil Tippett, and others to create its revived dinosaur.

THE ART OF HORROR MOVIES

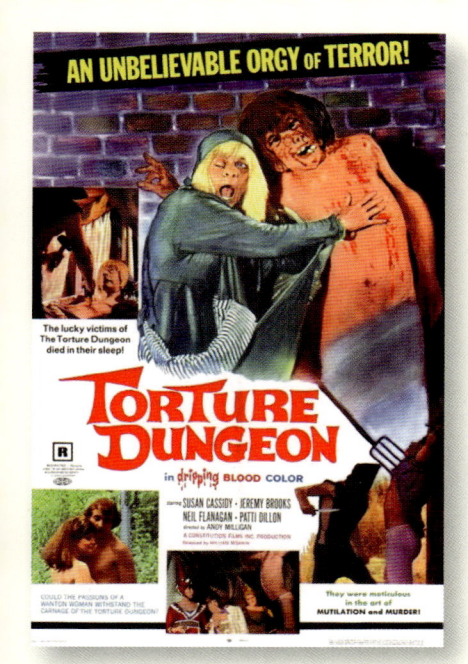

TOP LEFT: Set in Medieval England but filmed for an estimated $15,000 on New York City's Staten Island with a cast of mostly non-professional actors, *Torture Dungeon* (1970) was just one of 27 movies shot on the cheap between 1965 and 1988 by American *auteur* Andy Milligan (1929–91).

ABOVE RIGHT: Andy Milligan traveled to the UK in 1969 to film *Bloodthirsty Butchers* (1970) on location (with additional scenes shot on Staten Island). Made for an estimated $18,000, John Miranda starred as the Demon Barber of Fleet Street in this updated version of the "Sweeney Todd" story.

TOP MIDDLE: Andy Milligan's *Guru, the Mad Monk* (1970), the director's first movie shot on 35mm, was filmed for an estimated $11,000 around St. Peter's Episcopal Church in Manhattan, New York City. Neil Flanagan played the deranged fifteenth century prison chaplain of the title.

BOTTOM LEFT: Despite an estimated $18,000 budget, the director had to play two different roles himself in *The Rats Are Coming! The Werewolves Are Here!* (1972), another of Andy Milligan's movies shot in London in 1969 (with additional sequences filmed later on Staten Island).

BOTTOM MIDDLE: Filmed in the director's Staten Island home for an estimated $25,000, Andy Milligan's *Blood* (aka *Black Nightmare in Blood*, 1973)—a tribute to the classic Universal horror movies— was released on the lower half of a double-bill with Gerard Damiano's *Legacy of Satan* (1974).

THE SATANIC SEVENTIES

ABOVE LEFT: *Prince Mamuwalde* (2013), acrylic on wood panel portrait by American artist Jason Edmiston. "This was created for my Mondo Gallery solo show, entitled 'A Rogues Gallery,'" recalls the artist. "I've always been fascinated by the antagonistic or evil characters in horror."

TOP RIGHT: French *affiche* for American International Pictures' *Blacula* (Dir: William Crain, 1972), part of the wave of American "blaxploitation" films of the early 1970s.

BOTTOM RIGHT: One-sheet poster for AIP's sequel *Scream Blacula Scream* (Dir: Bob Kelljan, 1973), in which William Marshall's dignified Prince Mamuwalde is raised from the dead in modern-day Los Angeles.

THE ART OF HORROR MOVIES

— 196 —

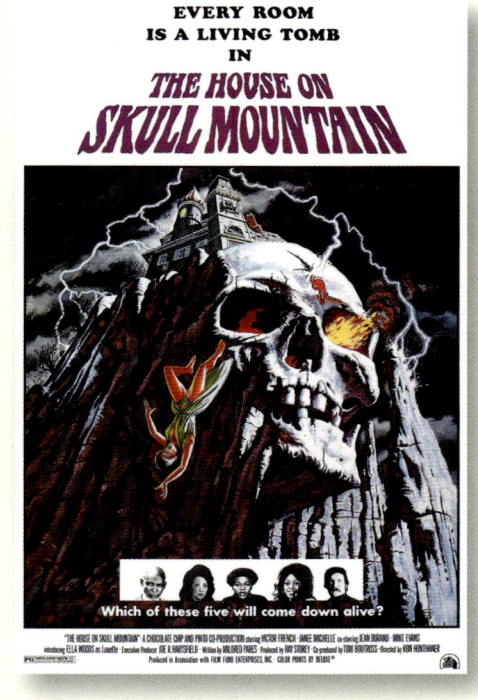

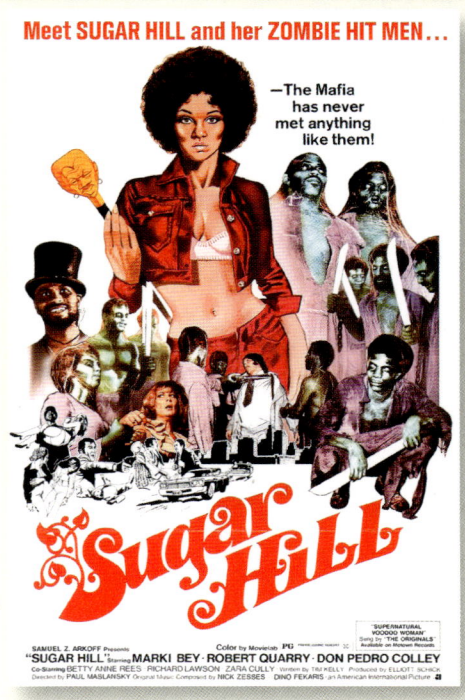

TOP LEFT: Following the relative highs of the *Blacula* movies, blaxploitation horror soon descended into feeble efforts such as Exclusive International's *Blackenstein* (Dir: William A. Levey, 1972).

TOP MIDDLE: One-sheet poster for Twentieth Century-Fox's old dark house mystery *The House on Skull Mountain* (Dir: Ron Honthaner, 1974) by Robert Tanenbaum (b. 1936), who went on become a renowned portrait artist.

TOP RIGHT: American International Pictures' blaxploitation version of *The Exorcist*, *Abby* (Dir: William Girdler, 1974), was withdrawn from distribution after Warner Bros. sued.

BOTTOM LEFT: In AIP's *Sugar Hill* (Dir: Paul Maslansky, 1974), Marki Bey's voodoo queen uses her zombies to get revenge on a mob boss (Robert Quarry).

BOTTOM MIDDLE: The spirit of a 1940s hustler possesses the body of a young college student in AIP's *J.D.'s Revenge* (Dir: Arthur Marks, 1976).

BOTTOM RIGHT: One-sheet poster by Joseph J. "Joe" Smith (1912–2003) for Dimension Pictures' *Dr. Black Mr. Hyde* (Dir: William Crain, 1975), which starred Bernie Casey as an inner-city doctor who develops a drug that transforms him into an albino monster.

THE SATANIC SEVENTIES

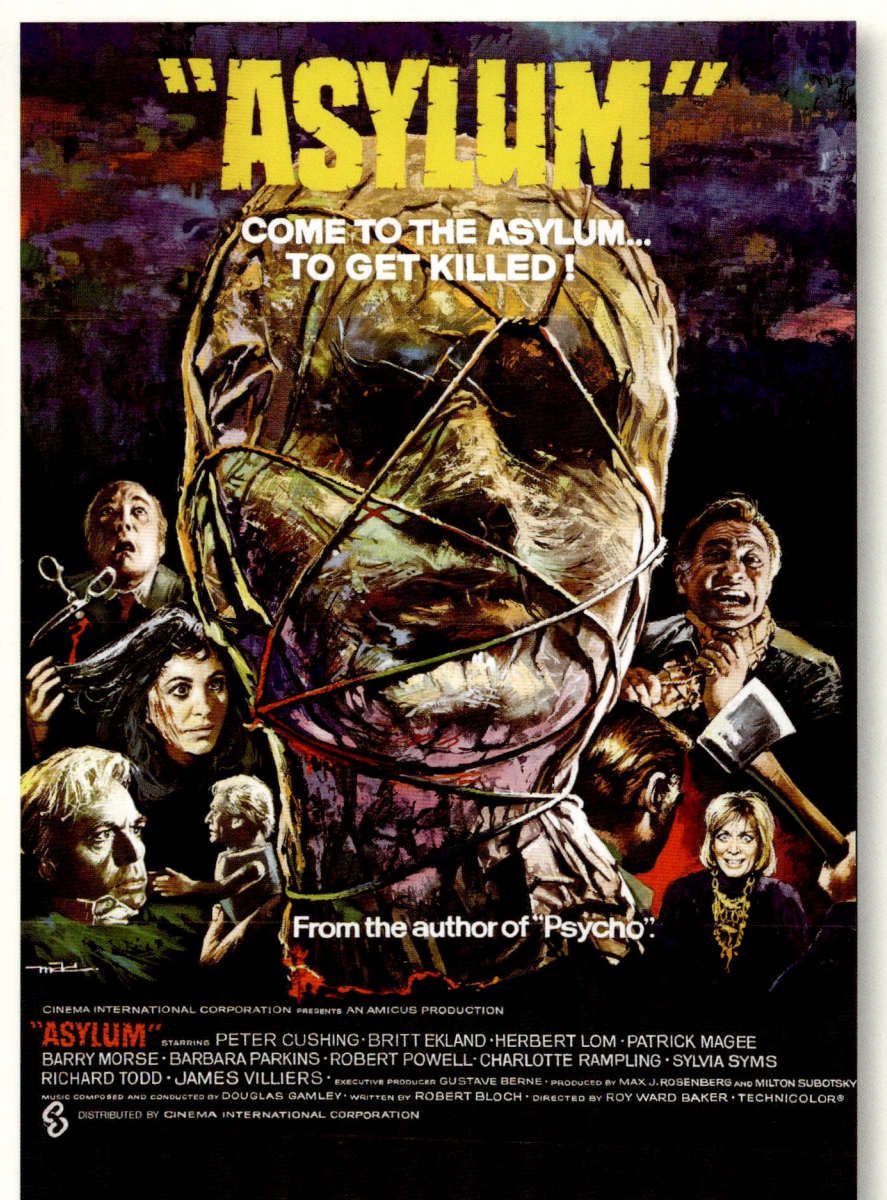

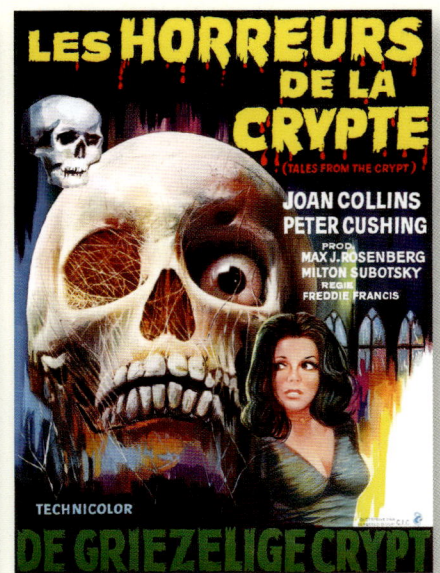

ABOVE LEFT: This British poster for the Amicus production *Asylum* (Dir: Roy Ward Baker, 1972) is one of two designs for the film created by Spanish artist Macario "Mac" Gómez Quibus (b. 1926).

TOP MIDDLE: Belgian *affiche* for Amicus's episodic movie *Tales from the Crypt* (Dir: Freddie Francis, 1972), which was based on five stories from the titular 1950s EC horror comic, along with its companion titles *The Vault of Horror* and *The Haunt of Fear*.

TOP RIGHT: This American one-sheet poster for Amicus Productions' anthology movie *The House That Dripped Blood* (Dir: Peter Duffell, 1971) misspells scriptwriter Robert Bloch's name as "Block."

BOTTOM RIGHT: Rare British quad by Italian artist Arnaldo Putzu (1927–2012) for *Vault of Horror* (Dir: Roy Ward Baker, 1973), the second and final all-star Amicus portmanteau film based on five stories from the EC horror comics of the 1950s.

OPPOSITE, TOP LEFT: Preliminary pencil on paper sketch by Les Edwards for the cover of *The Mammoth Book of Vampire Stories by Women* (2000).

RIGHT: *Ingrid* (2000), oils on board by British artist Les Edwards. This painting depicts Polish-born actress Ingrid Pitt (1937–2010) as the vampiric "Carla" from Amicus Productions' *The House That Dripped Blood* (1971). "Painting beautiful women can be tricky at the best of times," reveals the artist, "and if it's someone well-known you have the added problem of nailing the likeness. Good reference is essential and the drawing needs considerable care."

THE MERCHANT OF MENACE

"In Vincent, I found a man of cultural refinement for Usher. This was partly his reputation and partly his persona as I had seen it in many of his films. He was a first-rate actor and handsome leading man who had a distinguished career."

Roger Corman

IN 1963–64, Vincent Price was in Britain to make the last two entries in a seven-film sequence sold, not just on his name, but also those of Edgar Allan Poe and producer-director Roger Corman.

The press response to these final Price-Poe-Corman collaborations said a lot about Price's appeal as America's post-war master of Gothic horror. Reviewing *The Masque of the Red Death*, the British trade paper *Daily Cinema* noted that "With that striking Gothic face of his and air of supercilious fanaticism, Vincent Price is ideally cast." Some six months later *Time* magazine greeted *The Tomb of Ligeia* with the observation that "the cream-centered menace is Vincent Price, an actor who appears to be swooping around in a cape even when he stands perfectly still."

Unlike his British contemporaries Peter Cushing and Christopher Lee, Price (1911–93) was inclined to season his performances with a pinch of self-aware humor. As a result he could suggest "supercilious fanaticism" one minute while seeming "to be swooping around in a cape" the next.

But he gained his best effects when going the Lee-Cushing route and cutting out all hint of irreverence. This was the case in his first Corman picture, *The Fall of the House of Usher* (1960), where his spectral, neurasthenic Roderick Usher is confined to a lushly upholstered Hollywood soundstage, and also when he played Matthew Hopkins in Michael Reeves's *Witchfinder General* (1968), in which his parchment-faced, government-sanctioned sadist roams freely across East Anglia.

Hopkins, especially, showed a steel and controlled ferocity that took Price fans by surprise; this historical villain could never be described, to use *Time*'s somewhat pointed phrase, as "cream-centered." As American International Pictures co-head Samuel Z. Arkoff put it, "Michael really brought out the balls in him. I was surprised how terrifying Vincent was in that."

Born in St. Louis, Missouri, this supremely cultivated actor—whose horror output, between *The Masque of the Red Death* in 1963 and the egregious *Bloodbath at the House of Death* twenty years later, emerged exclusively from British studios—began his film career as a Universal contract player. This entailed early brushes with a rather neutered form of horror in the 1939 productions *Tower of London* and *The Invisible Man Returns*; more tellingly, the 1946 film *Dragonwyck*, a gorgeous Gothic potboiler made by Joseph L. Mankiewicz for Twentieth Century-Fox, allowed him to anticipate his later Poe protagonists in every particular.

But it wasn't until his barnstorming performance in André de Toth's 1953 smash *House of Wax* that he was marked out as a possible new horror star, though Hollywood's unwillingness to indulge in any further Gothic revivals hampered his potential for a few years.

Unlike his British contemporaries Peter Cushing and Christopher Lee, Price was inclined to season his performances with a pinch of self-aware humor.

When a new strain of Hollywood horror finally emerged, Price proved natural casting for such films as Kurt Neumann's *The Fly* (1958) and the hokey William Castle double *House on Haunted Hill* (1958) and *The Tingler* (1959). There followed Corman's remarkable Poe sequence, which, after *The Fall of the House of Usher*, encompassed *Pit and the Pendulum* (1961), *Tales of Terror* (1962), *The Raven* (1963), and *The Haunted Palace* (in reality an elaborate H.P. Lovecraft adaptation, 1963), followed by the above-mentioned British entries.

Again, *Daily Cinema*'s critic had a pithy phrase for *Pit and the Pendulum*, noting that "Such a film calls for a certain kind of acting: i.e., Vincent Price acting." Indeed it did, and Price gave his all to the entire series.

In 1970 Price was in Britain again for *The Abominable Dr. Phibes*, an archly self-reflexive AIP divertissement with strong echoes of *Ligeia* and *House of Wax*. Two years later, after dashing off a workaday Phibes sequel, Price was gifted with a film that, though made outside his imprisoning AIP contract, perfected the Phibes theme of a methodical vendetta conducted by a mad and wounded aesthete.

Edward Lionheart, Price's vengeful Shakespearean actor-manager in Douglas Hickox's exceptional *Theatre of Blood* (1973), was as meaty a showcase as any actor could desire. There were a few more horror subjects in its wake, but essentially Lionheart represented an apotheosis that was unrepeatable. And Price rose to the challenge in grand style. JR

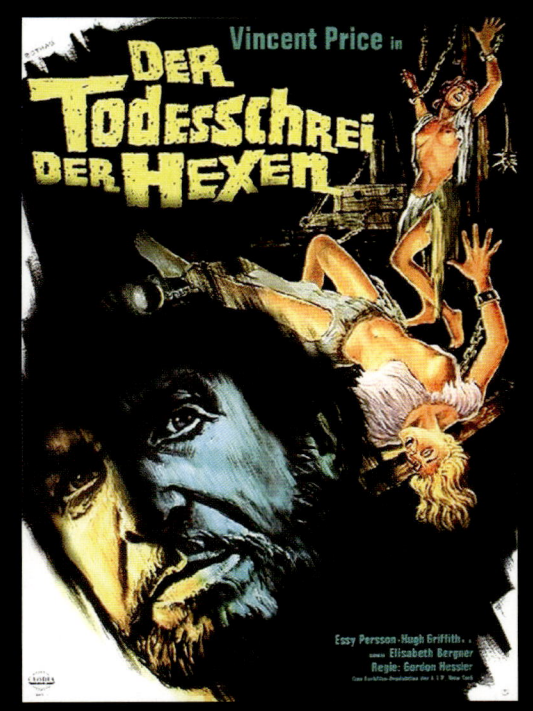

TOP LEFT: 1971 German poster for *Cry of the Banshee* (Dir: Gordon Hessler, 1970) signed "Bothas." American International Pictures marketed this British-made production about sixteenth century witchcraft as an Edgar Allan Poe adaptation and Vincent Price's 100th film (it was neither).

BOTTOM LEFT: Italian *duo-foglio* for American International Pictures' *The Abominable Dr. Phibes* (Dir: Robert Fuest, 1971) by Renato Casaro (b. 1935). Vincent Price created his one genuine contribution to the pantheon of horror characters in this movie and its sequel, *Dr. Phibes Rises Again* (1972).

ABOVE RIGHT: *The Possession of Charles Ward* (2015), acrylic, markers, and colored pencils by American artist Jeff Carlson. "This was a private commission," explains the artist, "the latest in an ongoing series of Vincent Price portraits."

THE SATANIC SEVENTIES

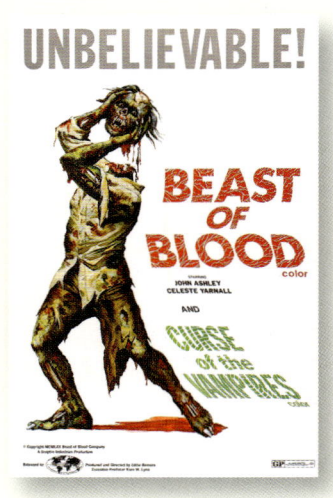

ABOVE LEFT: American insert poster for United Artists' "His and Her Horror!" double-bill of Filipino movies *Daughters of Satan* (Dir: Hollingsworth Morse, 1972) and *Superbeast* (Dir: George Schenck, 1972).

TOP RIGHT: Original gouache on board conceptual poster art for United Artists' *Daughters of Satan* (1972), one of many low-budget American co-productions shot in the Philippines during the late 1960s and '70s.

BOTTOM MIDDLE, LEFT: Iconic American one-sheet poster by artist Charles Copeland (1924–79) advertising Hemisphere Pictures' Filipino double-bill of Eddie Romero's sequel *Beast of Blood* (aka *Blood Devils*, 1970) and Gerardo de Leon's *Curse of the Vampires* (*Ibulong mo sa hangin*, aka *Creatures of Evil*, 1966).

BOTTOM MIDDLE, RIGHT: New World Pictures' double-bill of the Filipino *Beast of the Yellow Night* (Dir: Eddie Romero, 1971), and the West German Edgar Wallace *krimis*, *Die blaue Hand* (Dir: Alfred Vohrer, 1967), as *Creature with the Blue Hand*.

BOTTOM RIGHT: One-sheet poster for Dimension Pictures' *Twilight People* (1972), an uncredited Philippines-shot version of H.G. Wells's 1896 novel *The Island of Doctor Moreau*.

THE ART OF HORROR MOVIES

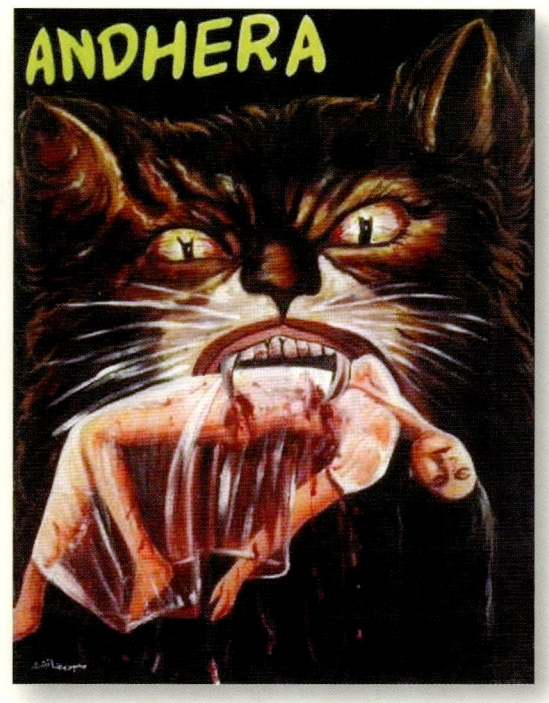

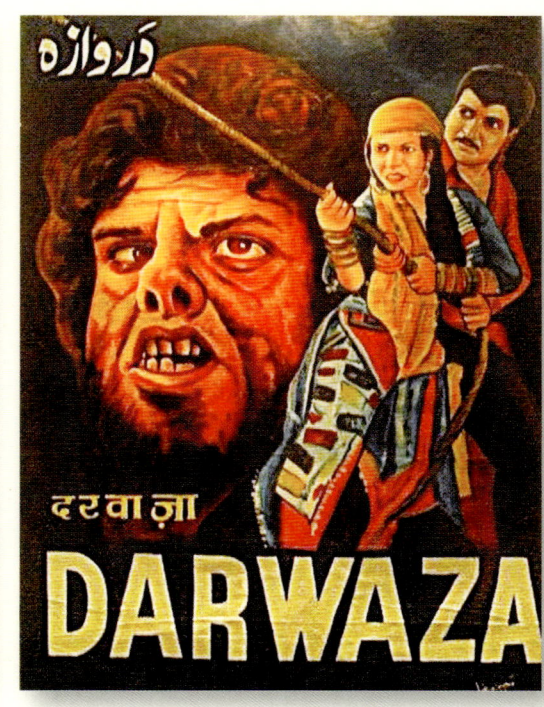

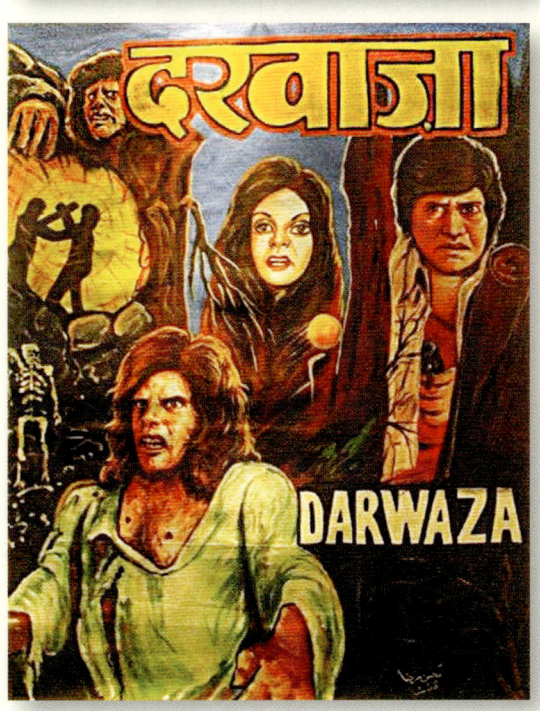

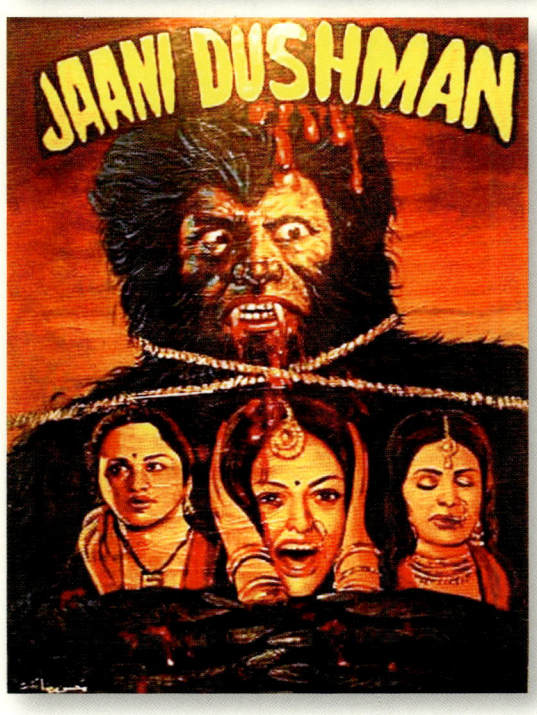

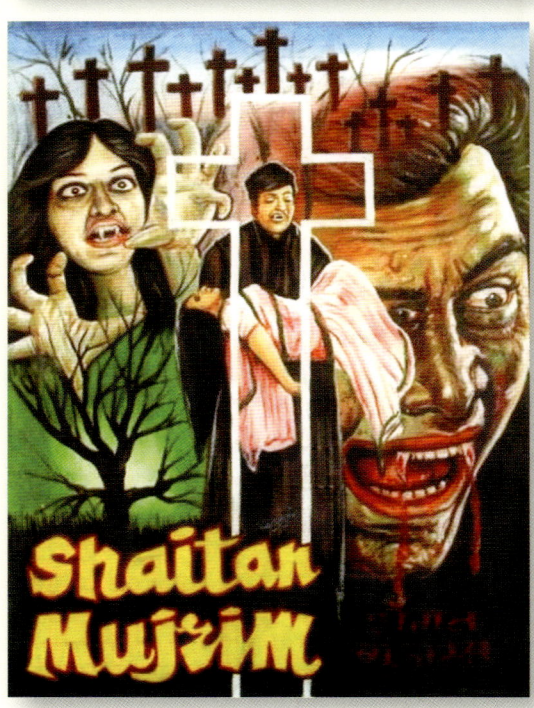

TOP LEFT: Hand-painted oils-on-canvas Indian movie posters were usually lithographically printed in Bombay on low-quality paper, as in the case of this design for Juno Jupiter Movies' obscure Hindustani horror film *Bhoot Mera Saathi* (Dir: Shahid Lal, 1974).

TOP MIDDLE: Indian poster for Ramsay Films' Hindi horror movie *Andhera* (aka *The Darkness*, 1975). This revenge drama with songs was an early collaboration between directors Tulsi Ramsay (b. 1944) and his brother Shyam Ramsay (b. 1952).

TOP RIGHT & BOTTOM LEFT: Two different Indian posters for Ramsay Brothers' influential Hindi horror film *Darwaza*, aka *The Door* (Dir: Tulsi Ramsay and Shyam Ramsay, 1978).

BOTTOM MIDDLE: Indian poster for Shankar Movies' Hindi horror *Jaani Dushman*, aka *Beloved Enemy* (Dir: Raj Kumar Kohli, 1979), in which a man reading *The Pan Book of Horror Stories* turns into a hairy monster.

BOTTOM RIGHT: Indian poster for Irk Films' Hindi horror movie *Shaitan Mujrim* (Dir: Nazar Khan, 1979), about a doctor who ends up creating a bloodsucking vampire.

THE SATANIC SEVENTIES

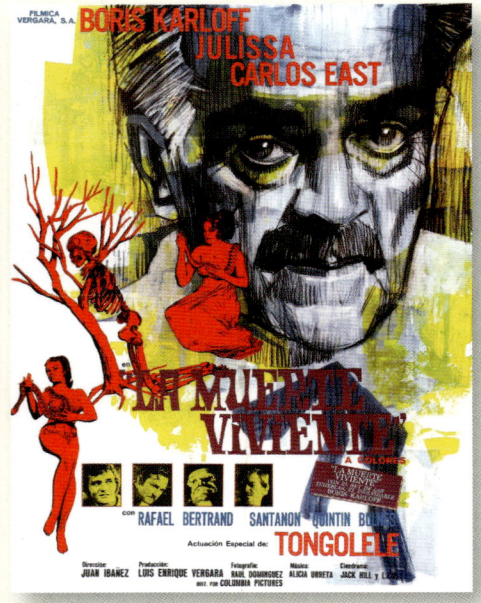

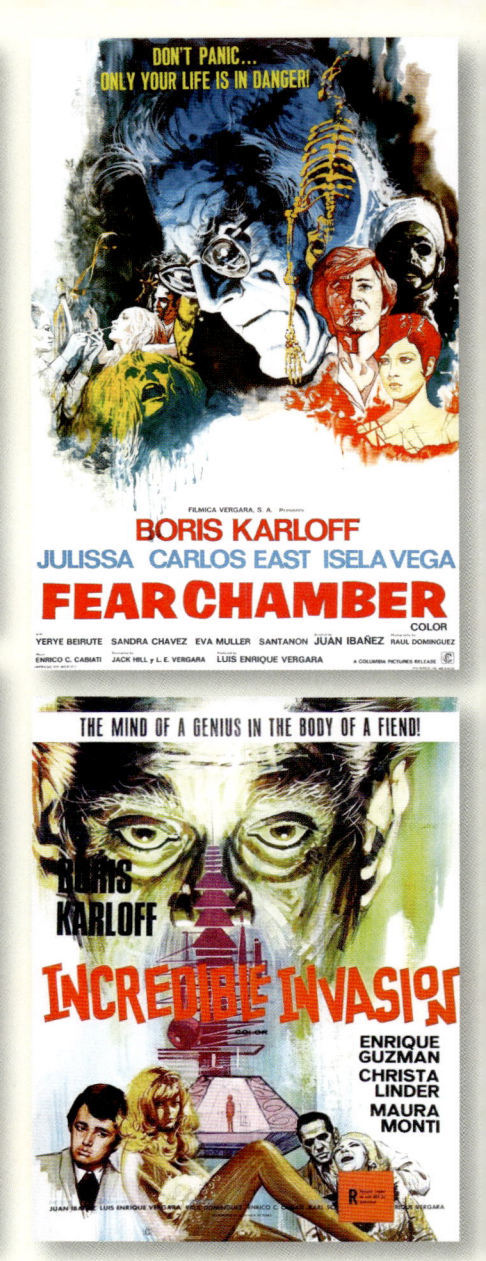

ABOVE LEFT: Front cover detail from the original painting of Boris Karloff for the 1969 third printing of the paperback book *Tales of the Frightened* (Belmont Books, 1963). A companion to the two-volume set of albums issued by Mercury Records in 1963, prolific American author Michael Avallone (1924–99) collected 26 of his stories.

TOP MIDDLE: In the spring of 1968, an ailing 81-year-old Boris Karloff was hired by producer Luís Enrique Vergara to shoot scenes in Hollywood for four movies that would subsequently be completed in Mexico. The first of these to eventually be released was Columbia Pictures' *La muerte viviente* (Dir: Juan Ibáñez and Jack Hill), which appeared in 1971 as *Snake People*.

TOP RIGHT: Also released in 1971 as *Fear Chamber*, Columbia Pictures' *La cámara del terror* (Dir: Juan Ibáñez and Jack Hill) starred Boris Karloff as an obsessed scientist who discovers a living rock creature near the center of the Earth.

BOTTOM MIDDLE: Released as *House of Evil* in 1972 and supposedly credited to a story by Edgar Allan Poe, Columbia Pictures' *Serenata macabra* (Dir: Juan Ibáñez and Jack Hill) featured Boris Karloff as a nineteenth century recluse who believes that one of his relatives has inherited the family's curse of insanity.

BOTTOM RIGHT: Columbia Pictures' *Invasión siniestra* (Dir: Juan Ibáñez and Jack Hill) was Boris Karloff's final film. Released as *Incredible Invasion* in 1971, disembodied aliens tried to sabotage a molecular death ray invented by Karloff's kindly scientist.

THE ART OF HORROR MOVIES

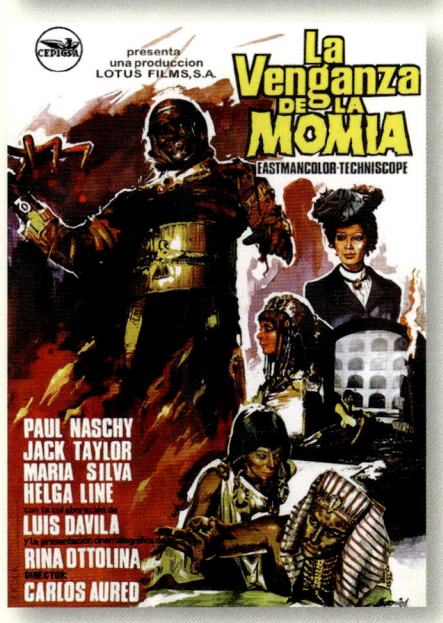

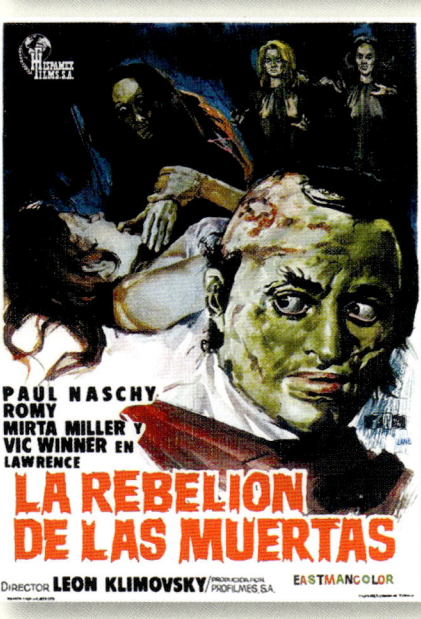

TOP LEFT: Spanish poster for Tulio Demicheli's Spanish-West German-Italian co-production *Los monstruos del terror/Dracula jagt Frankenstein/Operazione terrore* (aka *Assignment Terror*, 1970). This was Paul Naschy's third movie as reluctant werewolf Waldemar Daninsky.

TOP MIDDLE: Italian poster for León Klimovsky's Spanish-West German co-production *La noche de Walpurgis/Nacht der Vampire* (aka *The Werewolf vs. the Vampire Woman/Werewolf Shadow*, 1971), Naschy's fifth outing as Waldemar Daninsky.

BOTTOM LEFT: 1975 Spanish poster for Carlos Aured's *La venganza de la momia* (aka *The Mummy's Revenge*, 1973) signed "Hermida." Paul Naschy (1934–2009) appears in dual roles in this reworking of Universal's *The Mummy* (1932).

BOTTOM MIDDLE: Spanish poster for León Klimovsky's *La rebelión de las muertas* (aka *Vengeance of the Zombies*, 1973) by "Jano" (Francisco Fernández-Zarza Pérez). In one of three roles, Paul Naschy played an East Indian mystic who murders his female victims and brings them back from the dead to join his zombie army.

ABOVE RIGHT: Belgian *affiche* for Carlos Aured's Spanish-Mexican co-production *El retorno del Walpurgis/La noche del asesino* (aka *Curse of the Devil*, 1973), the seventh in the series of 12 films about werewolf Waldemar Daninsky, played by Paul Naschy.

THE SATANIC SEVENTIES

The Night Horror Came Home

The wit, elegance, and restraint of *Halloween* (1978) set it apart from the majority of its copycat followers, and all three qualities owed much to the film's director, John Carpenter (b. 1948). Carpenter followed *Halloween* with a chilling coastal ghost story, *The Fog* (1980), and a stupendously effective re-imagining of *The Thing* (1982); rejected by audiences at the time, the latter has since been accepted as a classic. His subsequent genre credits range from the Stephen King adaptation *Christine* (1983) to *Prince of Darkness* (1987), *They Live* (1988), *In the Mouth of Madness* (1994), *Vampires* (1998), and *The Ward* (2010). JR

TOP LEFT: American one-sheet poster for Columbia Pictures' *Eyes of Laura Mars* (Dir: Irvin Kershner, 1978), based on the spec script *Eyes* by John Carpenter, which was extensively re-written by others.

BOTTOM LEFT: German video cover for the NBC-TV movie *Someone's Watching Me!* (1978), a psychological thriller written (as *High Rise*) and directed by John Carpenter.

ABOVE RIGHT: 1979 Danish poster for Compass International Pictures' low-budget *Halloween* (Dir: John Carpenter, 1978) by artist Jørgen Hansen. The time frame of Carpenter's original script, titled *The Babysitter Murders*, was changed to a single day for budgetary reasons.

THE ART OF HORROR MOVIES

RIGHT: *Michael Myers* (2013), acrylic on wood panel by American artist Jason Edmiston. "This was also created for my Mondo Gallery solo show," he explains. "The style is indicative of the art I've built my career upon: high contrast, dynamic, and saturated with color."

THE SATANIC SEVENTIES

LEFT: *The Exorcist* (2019), acrylics, gouache, dyes and Prismacolor pencils on cold press illustration board by Christopher Franchi. "I always hated the original poster for the film," explains the artist. "The lack of anything frightening made it boring for me, so I decided to make my own."

TOP LEFT: Just as the popularity of traditional horror films began to decline in the early 1970s, so too did that of Mexico's *lucha libre* genre of masked wrestlers, which responded by upping the sex and monster content in films such as *La venganza de las mujeres vampiro* (Dir: Federico Curiel, 1970).

TOP RIGHT: Following the same trajectory as Abbott and Costello's movie career, El Enmascarado de Plata teamed up with his cinematic rival to defeat a mad scientist (Jorge Rado) and his army of reanimated monsters in *Santo y Blue Demon contra los monstruos* (Dir: Gilberto Martínez Solares, 1970).

BOTTOM LEFT: The two masked Mexican *luchadors* had to deal with yet more resurrected monsters—Aldo Monti's Drácula and Agustín Martínez Solares's Rufus Rex and his army of fellow werewolves —in *Santo y Blue Demon vs Drácula y el Hombre Lobo* (Dir: Miguel M. Delgado, 1973).

BOTTOM MIDDLE: The silver-masked *luchador* and his azure friend had to stop Frankenstein's grandson, Dr. Irving Frankenstein (Jorge Russek), from following in his ancestor's evil brain-swapping experiments in *Santo y Blue Demon contra el Dr. Frankenstein* (Dir: Miguel M. Delgado, 1974).

BOTTOM RIGHT: Santo teamed up with Cuban welterweight boxing champion, José Mantequilla Nápoles, to battle one of Mexico's most famous/tragic supernatural entities, "The Crying Woman" (Kikis Herrera Calles), in *La venganza de la Llorona* (Dir: Miguel M. Delgado, 1974).

THE SATANIC SEVENTIES

LEFT: *Carrie* (1995), acrylic on board with airbrush by British artist Steve Crisp, who explains: "Originally painted with red blood, I was asked to change this to black because the UK government decided that blood could not be shown on video covers following a mass-murderer being influenced by the graphic and gory 'video nasty' images of the time."

RIGHT: *'Salem's Lot* (1990), gouache on board book cover by Steve Crisp. "As the Stephen King novel was about the gradual spread of vampires through the town of 'Salem's Lot, started by the undead Kurt Barlow," recalls the artist, "I decided to use him as the main figure with a trail of hapless victims enveloped in mist disappearing behind him."

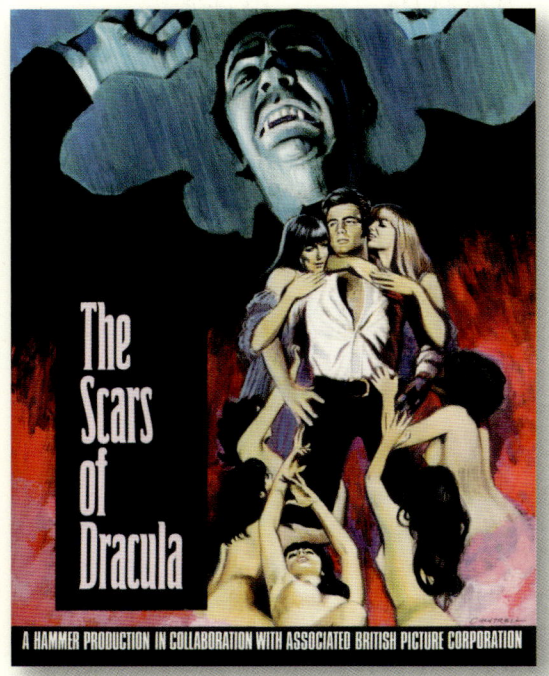

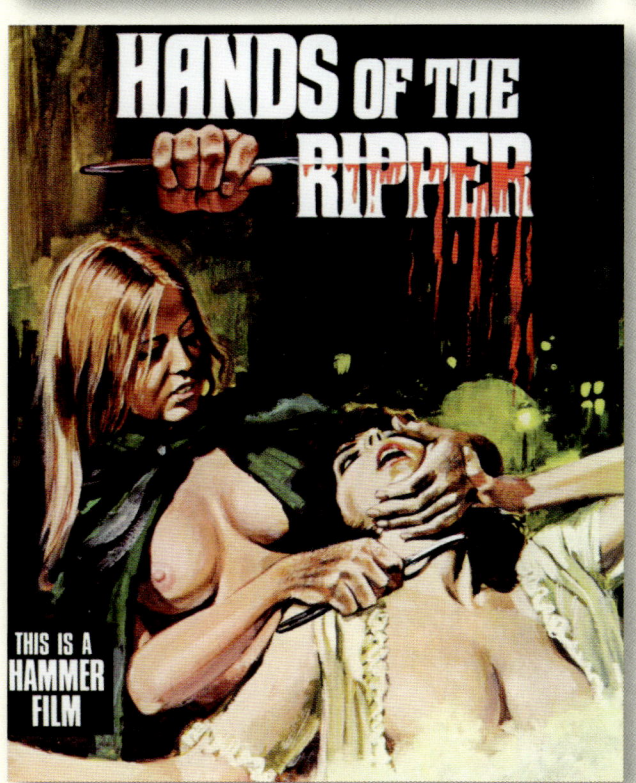

THIS PAGE: Prolific British movie poster artist Tom Chantrell (1916–2001) was best known for his work on the *Carry On* comedy series and Hammer horror films. As a "house artist" for the latter studio, Chantrell would be called upon to create pre-production artwork that Hammer could use when trying to sell new projects to distributors. However, these mini-posters often bore little or no resemblance to the finished films. A selection of this preliminary artwork is shown on this page.

THE ART OF HORROR MOVIES

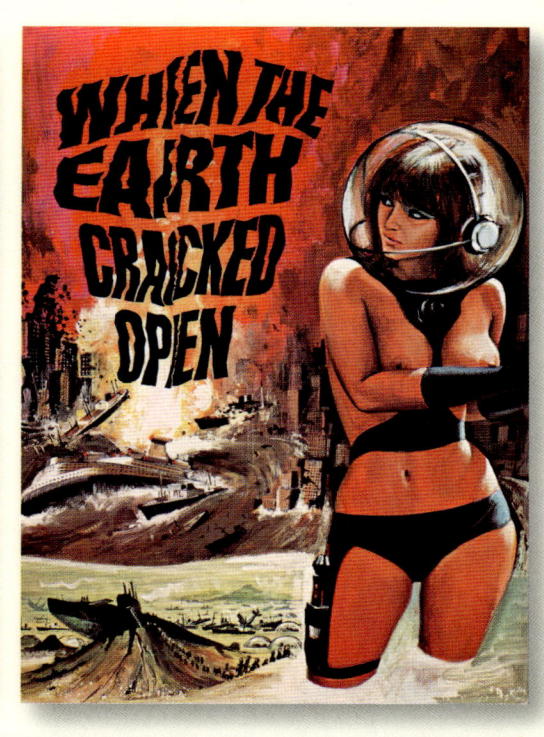

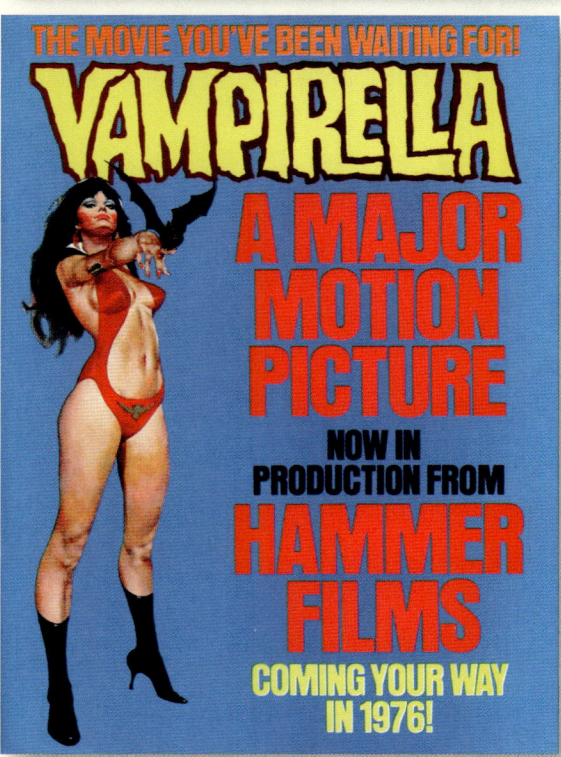

TOP LEFT: Many of these prospective projects from Hammer Films never made it past the preliminary poster stage in the early 1970s, as with Tom Chantrell's concept painting for *A Scent of New-Mown Hay*, based on the novel by John Blackburn.

TOP MIDDLE: Conceived in the early 1970s as a showcase for Jim Danforth's time-consuming stop-motion animation effects, *Zeppelin v Pterodactyls* was based on a story by David Allen, Dennis Muren, and Danforth, but proved to be too expensive.

TOP RIGHT: One of several pre-production posters produced by Tom Chantrell to try to sell *When the Earth Cracked Open*, an epic disaster movie that Hammer hoped might be distributed by American International Pictures in the US.

BOTTOM LEFT: In the mid-1970s Hammer teamed up with Warren Publishing Co. to bring the comic series *Vampirella* to the big screen, with various starlets touted for the title role. Despite multiple script drafts, it never happened.

BOTTOM RIGHT: *Nessie* was supposed to be an ambitious $7 million co-production between Hammer and Japan's Toho Company. However, when Columbia Pictures pulled out as distributor in 1977, the project collapsed.

THE SATANIC SEVENTIES

Women in Horror: 1970s

Polish-born Ingrid Pitt (1937–2010) became a genuine horror icon in the 1970s thanks to starring roles in Hammer's *The Vampire Lovers* (1970) and *Countess Dracula* (1971), and Amicus's portmanteau *The House That Dripped Blood* (1971). Former fashion model and later Bond girl Caroline Munro (b. 1949) displayed her ample charms in Hammer's *Dracula A.D. 1972* (1972) and *Captain Kronos Vampire Hunter* (1974). Jamaican-born Martine Beswick (b. 1941), another Bond girl, brought an exotic sensuality to her roles in *Dr. Jekyll & Sister Hyde* (1971) and *Seizure* (1974), while Stephanie Beacham (b. 1947) also encountered Christopher Lee's Count in 1972 Chelsea and a murderous crawling hand in *--And Now the Screaming Starts!* (1973).

ABOVE LEFT: Italian *locandina* by artist Renato Casaro for Hammer Films' *The Vampire Lovers* (Dir: Roy Ward Baker, 1970), based on J. Sheridan Le Fanu's influential novella "Carmilla" (1871–72).

TOP RIGHT: British quad for Hammer Films' *Dracula A.D. 1972* (Dir: Alan Gibson, 1972) by artist Tom Chantrell (1916–2001).

BOTTOM MIDDLE: 1975 French *grande affiche* for Hammer Films' *Dr Jekyll & Sister Hyde* (Dir: Roy Ward Baker, 1971) by Constantin Belinsky (1904–99). Brian Clemens's script combined Robert Louis Stevenson's novella with grave-robbers Burke and Hare.

BOTTOM RIGHT: Belgian *affiche* by artist Pascal Renard (1961–96) for Hammer Films' *Captain Kronos Vampire Hunter* (Dir: Brian Clemens, 1972).

OPPOSITE: *Dracula A.D. 1972* (2009), markers and colored pencil on paper by American artist Bruce Timm, done for the back cover of *Little Shoppe of Horrors* #22 (March, 2009). "Alex Toth, who designed all those wonderful Hanna-Barbera superhero cartoons in the 1960s, was a huge influence," admits Timm.

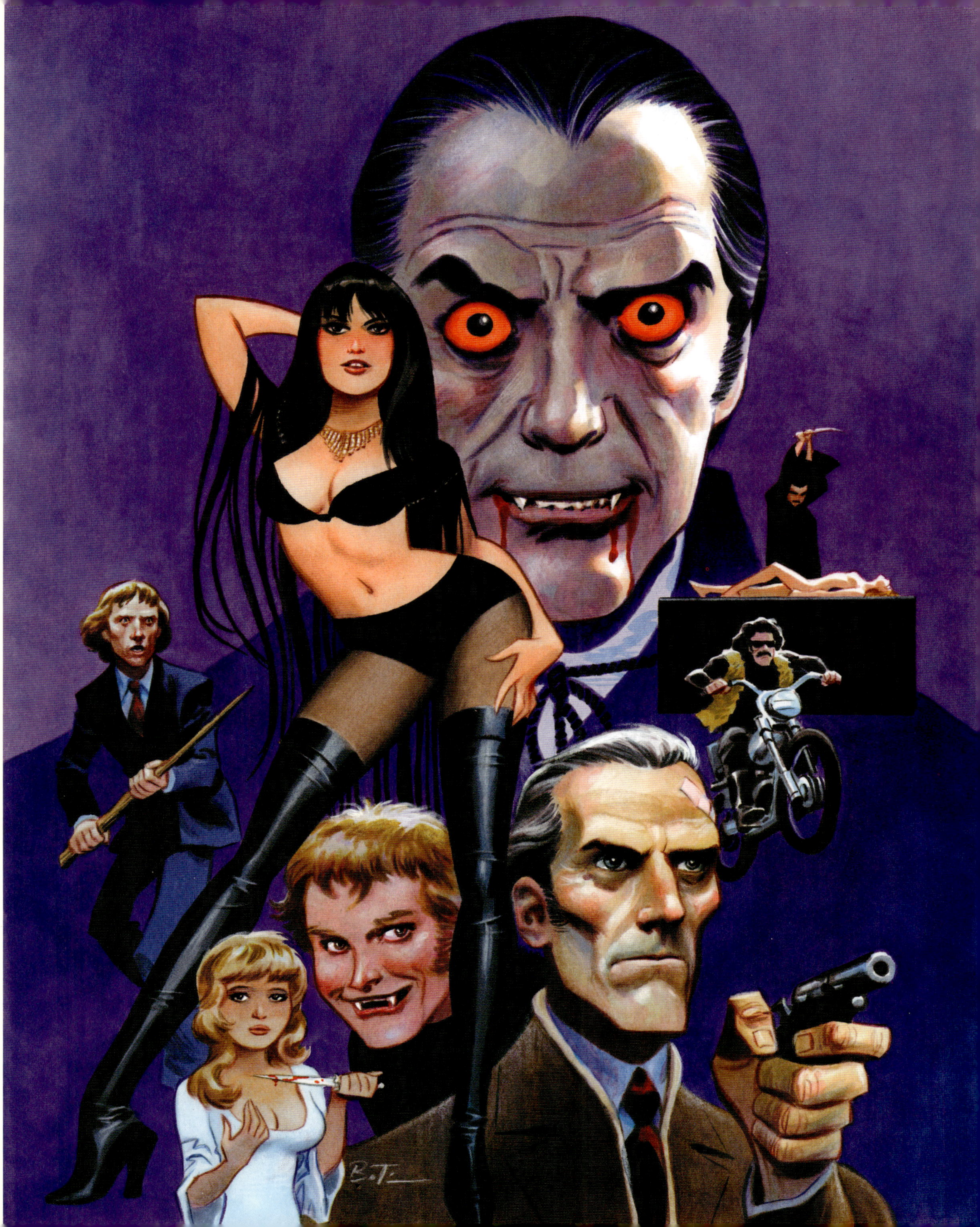

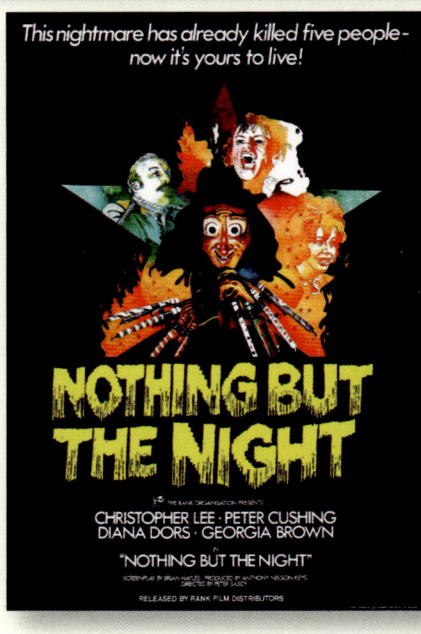

ABOVE LEFT: Italian *locandina* by Luca (Luciano) Crovato for *I, Monster* (Dir: Stephen Weeks, 1971) a failed attempt by Amicus to make the Dr. Jekyll and Mr. Hyde story in 3-D starring Christopher Lee, Peter Cushing, and Mike Raven. The production apparently ran out of money.

TOP RIGHT: British quad poster by Tom Chantrell for Eugino Martín's Spanish-made *Horror Express* (aka *Pánico en el Transiberiano* 1972), starring Christopher Lee, Peter Cushing, and Telly Savalas. The model train was left over from the same director's *Pancho Villa* (1972), also starring Savalas.

BOTTOM MIDDLE: Belgian poster for Tigon's *The Creeping Flesh* (1973), which starred Christopher Lee and Peter Cushing as rival Victorian scientists studying the essence of evil. Director Freddie Francis reportedly took over the production from Don Sharp at short notice.

BOTTOM RIGHT: Based on the novel by John Blackburn, Peter Sasdy's contemporary thriller *Nothing But the Night* (aka *The Resurrection Syndicate*, 1973) was produced by Christopher Lee's Charlemagne Films and co-starred Peter Cushing and Diana Dors. A pair of sequels never materialized.

THE ART OF HORROR MOVIES

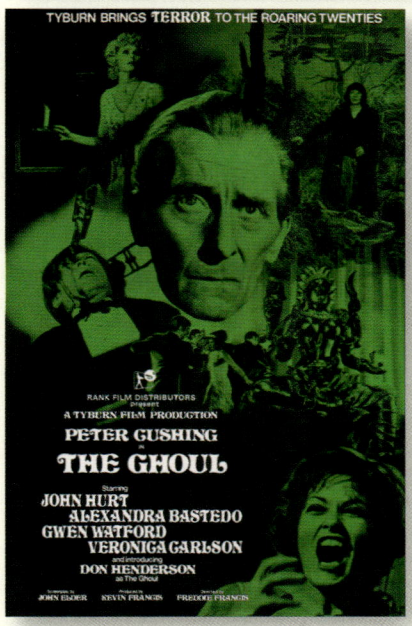

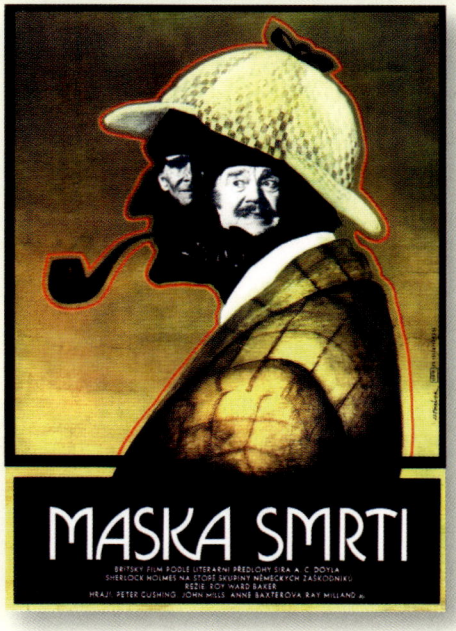

THIS PAGE: Tyburn Film Productions was founded in the early 1970s by producer Kevin Francis, the son of UK cinematographer and director Freddie Francis, to rival the output of those other great British studios, Hammer and Amicus. However, despite the talent involved, the horror boom was soon over.

ABOVE RIGHT: Italian *locandina* for *Persecution* (aka *The Terror of Sheba/The Graveyard*, 1974). Having dipped their toe in the water with *Tales That Witness Madness* (1973), this was the first "official" Tyburn movie. Directed by Don Chaffey, veteran Hollywood star Lana Turner reportedly hated it.

BOTTOM LEFT: *The Ghoul* (aka *Night of the Ghoul*, 1975) was much closer to the Hammer Gothic tradition that Tyburn was looking for, thanks to a script by John Elder (Anthony Hinds), direction by Freddie Francis, and the casting of Peter Cushing. It was filmed on *The Great Gatsby* sets.

TOP LEFT: British quad poster for Tyburn's *Legend of the Werewolf* (1975), which reunited the same creative trio from *The Ghoul*. David Rintoul played a young man raised by wolves, and the supporting cast included Ron Moody, Hugh Griffith, and Hammer veteran Michael Ripper.

BOTTOM MIDDLE: Czech poster by J.S. Tohánek for Tyburn's final film, *The Masks of Death* (Dir: Roy Ward Baker, 1984), again scripted by Elder/Hinds. Peter Cushing recreated his signature role of Sherlock Holmes one last time, aided by John Mills's faithful Doctor Watson.

THE SATANIC SEVENTIES

LEFT: *Kolchak: The Night Stalker* (2007), acrylic on board by American artist Douglas Klauba, painted for the cover of *The Kolchak Papers: The Original Novels* by Jeff Rice (Moonstone Books, 2007). "The 1972 made-for-television movie was a big influence on me," recalls the artist, "so painting this world was unbelievably rewarding."

RIGHT: *Trilogy of Terror* (2002), pastel on art board by Canadian-born American artist Harley Brown, done for the cover of *Filmfax* #89 (February–March 2002). "It was a real challenge to paint the wonderfully beautiful Karen Black as a monster," recalls Brown. "The fangs and knife helped, but she's still a marvelous looking demon."

THE SATANIC SEVENTIES

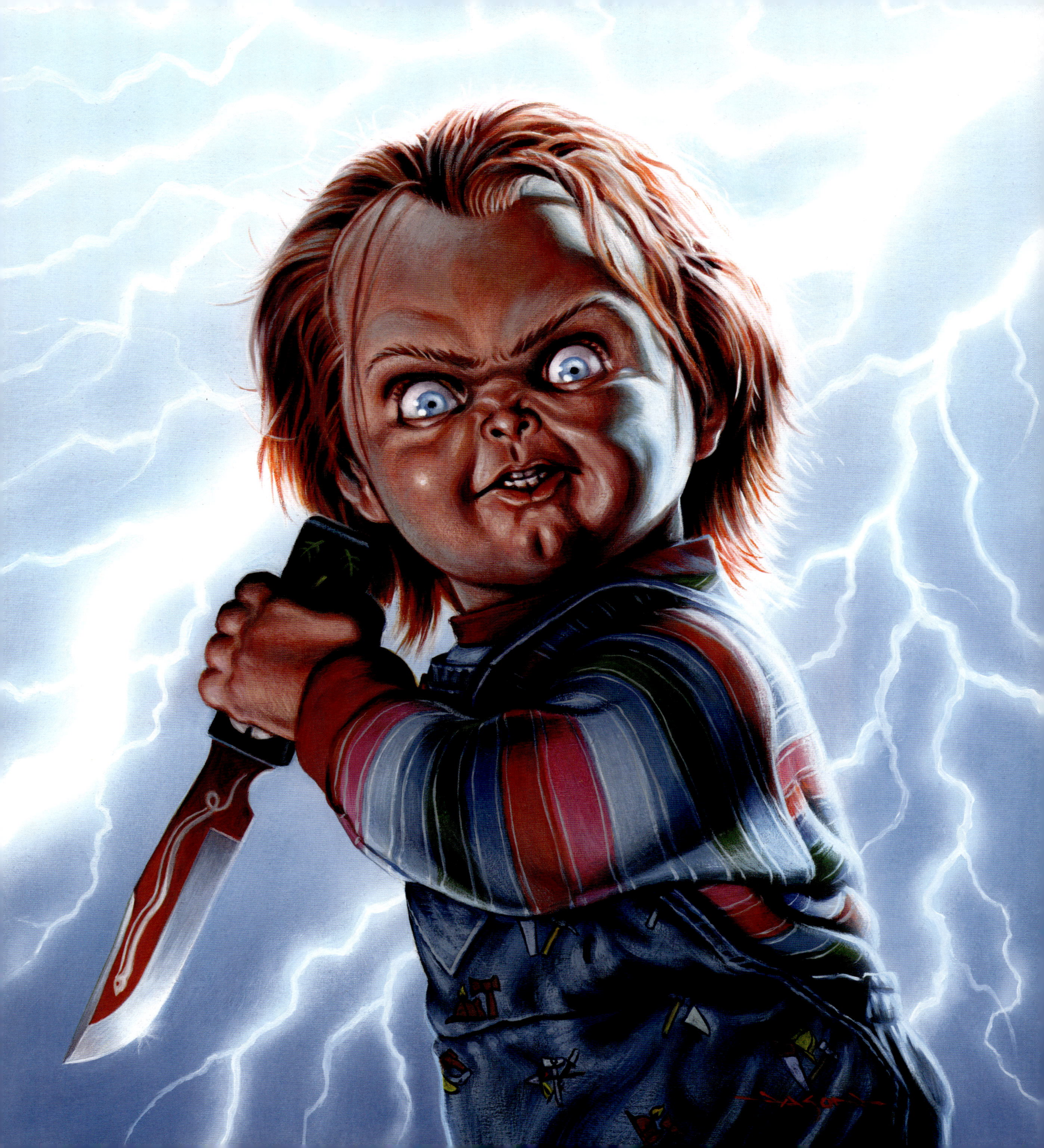

THE EVIL EIGHTIES

LISA MORTON

"It is not enough to have voluntary regulation.
We must bring in a ban to regulate the matter."

MARGARET THATCHER

> "If video censorship of the most stringent kind isn't brought in pretty damned quick we're going to have an upsurge in violence and terror and abuse in our land and homes the like of which we never suspected in our wildest terror."
>
> Lynda Lee Potter, *Daily Mail*, June 29, 1983

IF MOVIES IN the 1970s were defined by a new generation of filmmakers, the following decade belonged to a new generation of film*goers*. "Generation X" (also known as the "latchkey generation") was the first to lack full-time parental supervision—mothers had joined the workforce, and American divorce rates peaked in 1980. Add to that juvenile reactions to the sexual revolution—sociologists noted that children were sometimes confused or even frightened when parents introduced new partners into the home—and is it any wonder that the decade's movies seemed to be ruled by blade-wielding psychopaths who stalked parent-less, sexually agitated teens?

The runaway success of John Carpenter's *Halloween* (1978) had created a ready-made template that would virtually guarantee success with unsupervised youth, who became adept at sneaking into the R-rated thrillers that filled the theaters in the new multiplexes spreading across America. The *Halloween* model was simple: a storyline that mixed in an unstoppable killer, a group of teens, and a "final girl" who would, as academic Carol Clover later noted, serve as "abject terror personified."

First out of the gate in 1980 was *Friday the 13th*, which introduced the world to Jason Voorhees, originally presented as a drowned child whose crazed mother was really behind the murders, but later (in the third film) given his identity as a hockey-mask-wearing giant. The *Halloween* and *Friday the 13th* franchises were joined by stand-alone slashers with titles like *My Bloody Valentine* (1981), *Happy Birthday to Me* (1981), and *Graduation Day* (1981).

However, it wasn't until 1984 that Wes Craven injected genuine fresh blood into the genre with *A Nightmare on Elm Street*. Craven kept elements of the *Halloween* template—the circle of endangered teens, the final girl, the terrifying killer—but he cleverly flipped other tropes. In the story of Freddy Krueger, a horribly burned child-murderer who stalks his victims through their dreams, the parents weren't absent, but were instead to blame for the psycho's actions (they'd burned him alive after he escaped punishment for his crimes). Throughout the *Nightmare on Elm Street* series, Freddy Krueger (as played by Robert Englund) became more sarcastic and sardonic, a quotable anti-hero for "Generation X."

While adolescents devoured slasher films, adult horror lovers weren't forgotten in the movie theaters. The box office hits of the 1970s—*The Exorcist* (1973), *Jaws* (1975), *Carrie* (1976)—had shown that A-list directors were interested in horror, especially if it was based on a bestselling novel, and that trend was well represented in the 1980s.

In 1980, Stanley Kubrick released his film version of Stephen King's most acclaimed novel, *The Shining*. Kubrick's film borrowed the book's basic tale of Jack Torrance, a failed novelist who takes his wife and young son to an isolated resort hotel in the mountains, where he'll serve as caretaker during the snowy winter months . . . as he goes slowly mad while encountering the hotel's ghosts. Kubrick's trademark attention to set design and broad visuals was much on display, but the most surprising aspect of the film was the performance of Jack Nicholson

---

The box office hits of the 1970s had shown that A-list directors were interested in horror, especially if it was based on a bestselling novel, and that trend was well represented in the 1980s.

---

as Torrance, mugging with a demonic glee that gave the film its most famous moment—when Jack chops his way through a doorway in pursuit of his terrified wife and, sticking his face through the shattered wood, shouts out, "Heeeere's Johnny!"

Although other established directors also produced horror work in the 1980s (Ken Russell with *Altered States*, 1980, and *Lair of the White Worm*, 1988; Paul Schrader with *Cat People*, 1982; Jack Clayton with *Something Wicked This Way Comes*, 1983), there were others who rose to prominence during the decade. Most had started their careers with low-budget fare in the 1970s, but these directors all became genre superstars during the '80s.

John Carpenter directed his *Halloween* star Jamie Lee Curtis and his then-wife Adrienne Barbeau in *The Fog* (1980), about a coastal town beset by murderous spirits. Two years later, Carpenter helmed *The Thing*, a remake of *The Thing from Another World* (1951), about a team of scientists in a polar research station who encounter an identity-stealing alien. Carpenter's film, starring Kurt Russell, achieved enduring cult status thanks to its mix of existentialist horror and jaw-dropping special effects.

Carpenter's other contributions to '80s horror included an adaptation of Stephen King's killer-car ode *Christine* (1983); *Big Trouble in Little China* (1986), a comedy-adventure again starring Russell; *Prince of Darkness*

PREVIOUS SPREAD: *Child's Play* (2014), acrylic on wood panel by American artist Jason Edmiston, produced for a limited edition DVD and Blu-ray cover. "I wanted to show Chucky's maniacal character," explains the artist, "and tried to capture the killer doll in mid-chant, surrounded by crazy voodoo lightning."

TOP LEFT: Simple yet stylish one-sheet poster for PolyGram Pictures' horror-comedy *An American Werewolf in London* (Dir: John Landis, 1981), for which Rick Baker won the first official Oscar for Best Makeup.

BOTTOM LEFT: British poster for Universal's *The Thing* (Dir: John Carpenter, 1982) by artists Les Edwards and Jim Burns. "Originally the landscape was much more rugged," explains Edwards, "but the clients had it repainted by my chum Jim Burns as I had gone on holiday. That makes this the only Edwards-Burns collaboration in existence."

ABOVE RIGHT: *The Shining* (2014), signed and numbered screen print by American artist Brian Ewing. "These prints were all done originally as gig posters," explains the artist. "Having to do all the research and hunting for images from the movies, or finding new meaning in found images, has been a satisfying challenge."

THE EVIL EIGHTIES

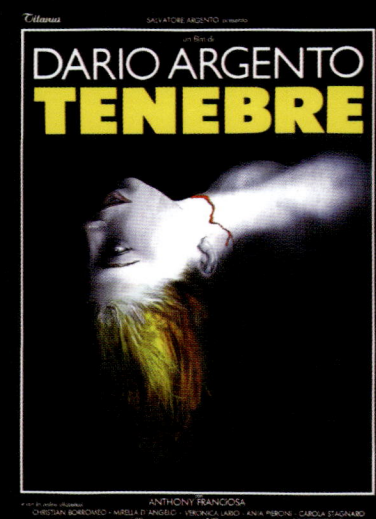

ABOVE LEFT: Colorful Italian poster for The Cannon Group's *Lifeforce* (Dir: Tobe Hooper, 1985), loosely based on the 1976 Lovecraftian novel *The Space Vampires* by British author Colin Wilson (1931–2013).

TOP MIDDLE: Japanese poster for Metro-Goldwyn-Mayer's box office hit *Poltergeist* (Dir: Tobe Hooper, 1982), for which it is widely believed that co-writer and producer Steven Spielberg supervised the shooting and editing.

TOP RIGHT: Stylish and subtle Italian poster for *Tenebre* (aka *Tenebrae*, 1982) by artist Renato Casaro (b. 1935). For the British quad poster, Casaro's art was changed so that the woman's bloody throat was covered by a red bow.

BOTTOM MIDDLE: 1992 German video poster for Ching Siu-Tung's spectacular Hong Kong production *Sien nui yau wan* (aka *A Chinese Ghost Story*, 1987) by Italian artist Renato Casaro. Heavily influenced by the vision of its Vietnamese-born producer, Tsui Hark (b. 1950), it was remade in 2011.

BOTTOM RIGHT: Japanese poster for New World Pictures' highly influential *Hellraiser* (1987), based on British writer-director Clive Barker's 1986 novella "The Hellbound Heart." It has been followed by nine sequels so far.

(1987), a Satanic thriller that bombed with critics, and *They Live* (1988), a horror sci-fi crossover in which wrestler Roddy "Rowdy" Piper discovered the truth about disguised aliens running our world.

Tobe Hooper, whose *The Texas Chain Saw Massacre* (1974) is credited by some scholars with being the real beginning of the slasher cycle, also produced some of the decade's most interesting horror. If *The Funhouse* (1981) came across as an entertaining but minor effort, Hooper's two mid-'80s offerings were among the genre's most unusual: *Lifeforce* (1985), based on Colin Wilson's novel *The Space Vampires*, was notable for a creature that mainly appeared as a comely and naked young woman (played by Mathilda May), and *The Texas Chainsaw Massacre 2*

> Thanks to the explosive growth of home video technologies, for the first time movie lovers could own their favorite films and watch them on their televisions whenever they wanted to.

(1986) was a black-humored descent into filmmaking madness, with a female disc jockey named Stretch (Caroline Williams) and a grudge-holding Texas Ranger (Dennis Hopper) taking on the first film's family of barbecue-loving maniacs.

However, Hooper's biggest hit was *Poltergeist* (1982). Produced by Steven Spielberg (who some cast members would later call "the *de facto* director"), *Poltergeist* moved the ghost story from its Gothic environs to a modern California suburb, and upped the ante considerably with state-of-the-art special effects. It became the year's top-grossing horror movie.

The potent combination of horror and humor was the driving force behind the cult status and commercial success of three breakout directors: Joe Dante, John Landis, and Tim Burton. Dante started the decade with *The Howling* (1981), a mostly serious werewolf film notable mainly for Rob Bottin's transformation makeup effects, but he hit big with *Gremlins* (1984), a frantic black comedy about cute little creatures with mean kin. Landis also established himself with a werewolf film, *An American Werewolf in London* (1981), ostensibly starring David Naughton as the title character, but really starring Rick Baker's werewolf effects. Tim Burton's *Beetle Juice* (1988) focused even more on the humor, with Michael Keaton taking center stage as a fast-talking demon who aids a pair of young ghosts, and the film had a major influence on Goth subculture.

But Hollywood horror wasn't all about big budgets in the 1980s. Thanks to the explosive growth of home video technologies, for the first time movie-lovers could own their favorite films and watch them on their televisions whenever they wanted to. The exploitation movies of the past, once intended mainly as supporting features for the Midwest drive-in circuit, now went direct to video, creating their own superstars and subgenres ("Video Nasties," anyone?) along the way. Although movies like Sam Raimi's *The Evil Dead* (1981), Frank Henenlotter's *Basket Case* (1982), Stuart Gordon's *Re-Animator* (1985), and John McNaughton's *Henry: Portrait of a Serial Killer* (1986) all achieved some success as theatrical midnight movies, they found their real homes in the videotape collections of horror fans.

Videotape also allowed hungry horror aficionados to discover horror from around the world, for indeed, horror was booming everywhere. Australia gave us Peter Jackson's gory debut *Bad Taste* (1987) and, two years later, his blood-drenched Muppets parody *Meet the Feebles*. In Hong Kong, Asian *auteur* Tsui Hark plundered martial arts films and Chinese folklore equally to create the frantic cannibal thriller *We're Going to Eat You* (*Di yu wu men*, 1980), the epic dark fantasy *Zu: Warriors from the Magic Mountain* (*Shu Shan–Xin Shu shan jian ke*, 1983), and the gorgeous (and crazed) *A Chinese Ghost Story* (*Sien nui yau wan*, 1987, directed by Ching Siu-Tung and produced by Tsui). Japan's Shinya Tsukamoto captured his country's anxieties about technology in *Tetsuo* (1989), while Dario Argento's elegant and stylish films from Italy, *Inferno* (1980), *Tenebrae* (1982), and *Opera* (1987), continued to explore the filmmaker's interest in art and architecture.

Also from Italy, but working with much lower budgets, Lucio Fulci's films like *The Beyond* and *The House by the Cemetery* (both 1981) gave fans low-budget zombie-driven gorefests. British novelist and filmmaker Clive Barker stunned audiences worldwide with the twisted sexuality of *Hellraiser* (1987, which also introduced another '80s horror icon, "Pinhead"); Canada's Guy Maddin injected surrealism and silent film technique into the genre with *Tales from the Gimli Hospital* (1988), and of course that country also offered up David Cronenberg, whose *Videodrome* (1983) was perhaps the only horror film of the decade to directly comment on the burgeoning home video industry.

It was a film directed by a woman, however, that would go on to be considered by some the finest horror film of the decade: Kathryn Bigelow's *Near Dark* (1987) was the director's second feature. With a script by Eric Red (who had also penned the 1986 Rutger Hauer vehicle *The Hitcher*), it wasn't the first vampire film of the decade (*Fright Night*, 1985, and *The Lost Boys*, 1987, had already put vampires into modern American small towns), but it recreated the vampire film as an erotically charged modern Western, with a young cowboy (Adrian Pasdar) falling in with a gang of murderous bloodsuckers who travel the back roads in a Winnebago.

Near Dark was released toward the end of the decade, as the slasher cycle and rise of hot young directors both seemed to be winding down, and it stands now as an elegiac conclusion to one of the horror genre's most exciting periods.

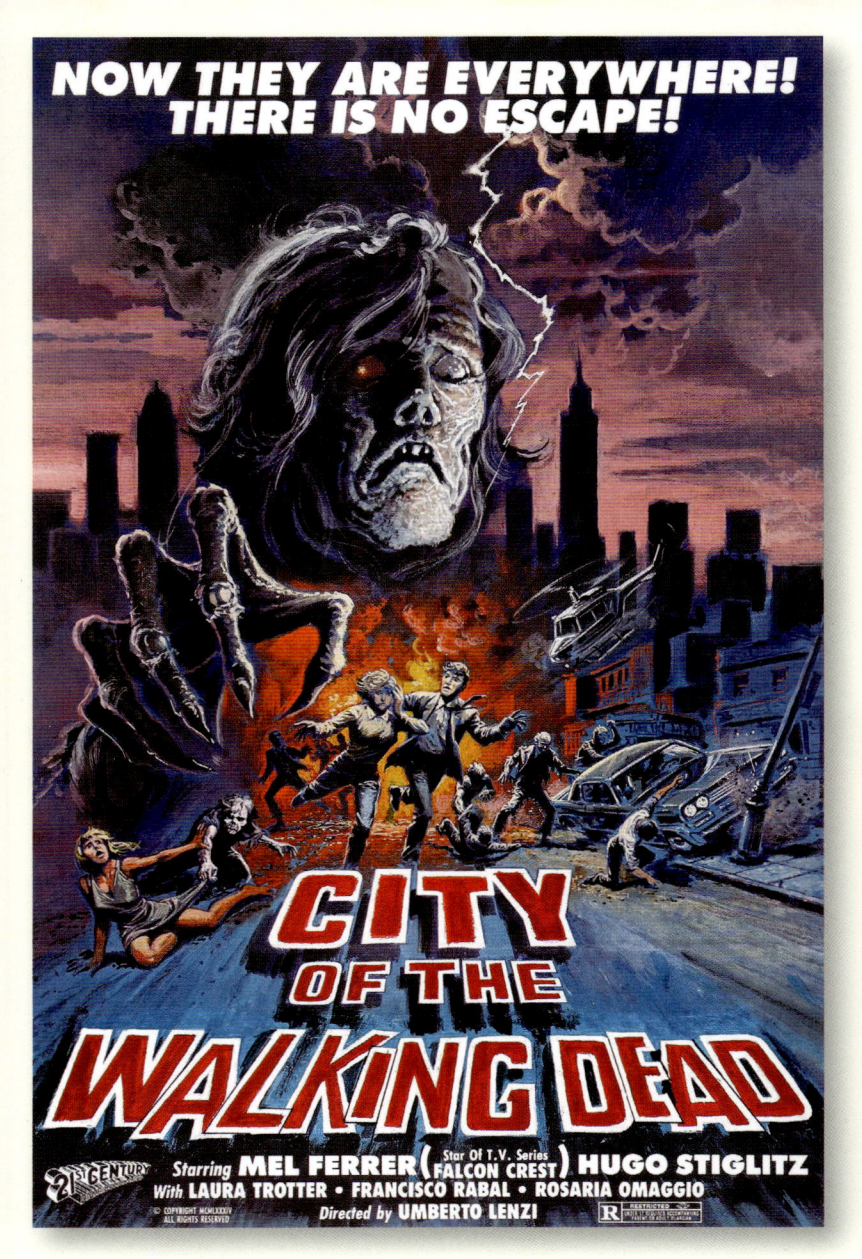

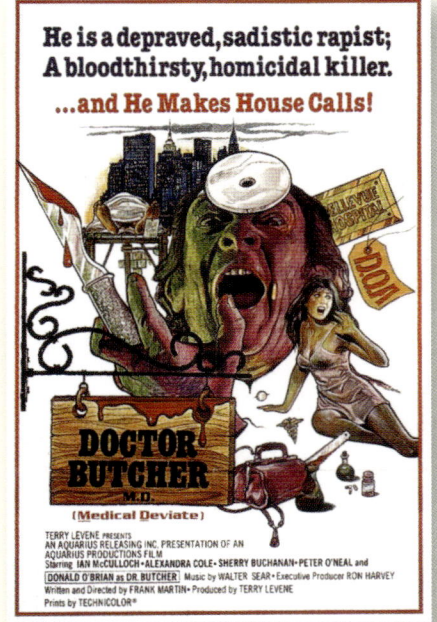

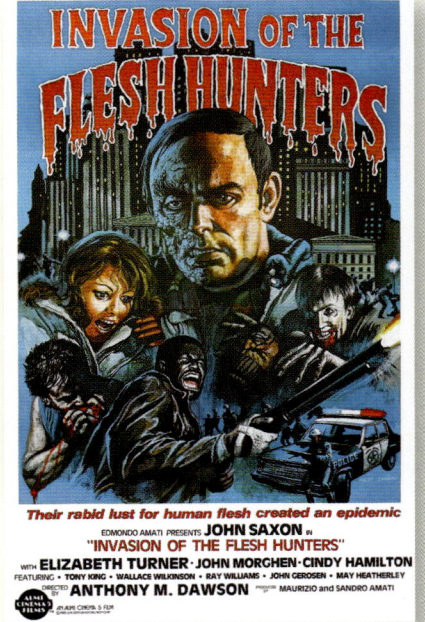

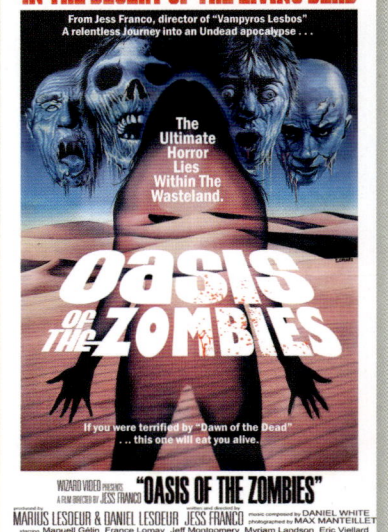

ABOVE LEFT: 1984 American one-sheet poster for Umberto Lenzi's Italian-Spanish co-production *Incubo sulla città contaminata/La invasión de los zombies atómicos* (aka *Nightmare City/City of the Walking Dead*, 1980).

TOP MIDDLE: 1982 one-sheet poster for the Italian *Zombi Holocaust* (Dir: Marino Girolami, 1980), released in America in a re-edited version as *Doctor Butcher M.D.*

TOP RIGHT: US one-sheet poster for the 1982 reissue of the Italian *Apocalypse Domani* (Dir: Antonio Margheriti, 1980) by artist Ken Barr (1933–2016).

BOTTOM MIDDLE: Colorful Thai poster for the Italian *L'aldila* (Dir: Lucio Fulci, 1981) by artist Noppadon. Released in America as *The Beyond*, it was included on the Video Nasties list in the UK.

BOTTOM RIGHT: 1986 American one-sheet poster for the French-Spanish co-production *L'Abîme des morts-vivants/La tumba de los muertos vivientes* (Dir: Jesús Franco, 1982) signed "C. Casaro."

OPPOSITE: *The Beyond* (2014), gouache on watercolor paper by British artist Graham Humphreys. "*The Beyond* is one of my favorite horror films," he reveals, "and this was designed as a cover for a soundtrack release by the Death Waltz Recording Co. My sympathies already lay with the artist who dies in the opening scene. I conceived this as his revenge!"

THE ART OF HORROR MOVIES

— 226 —

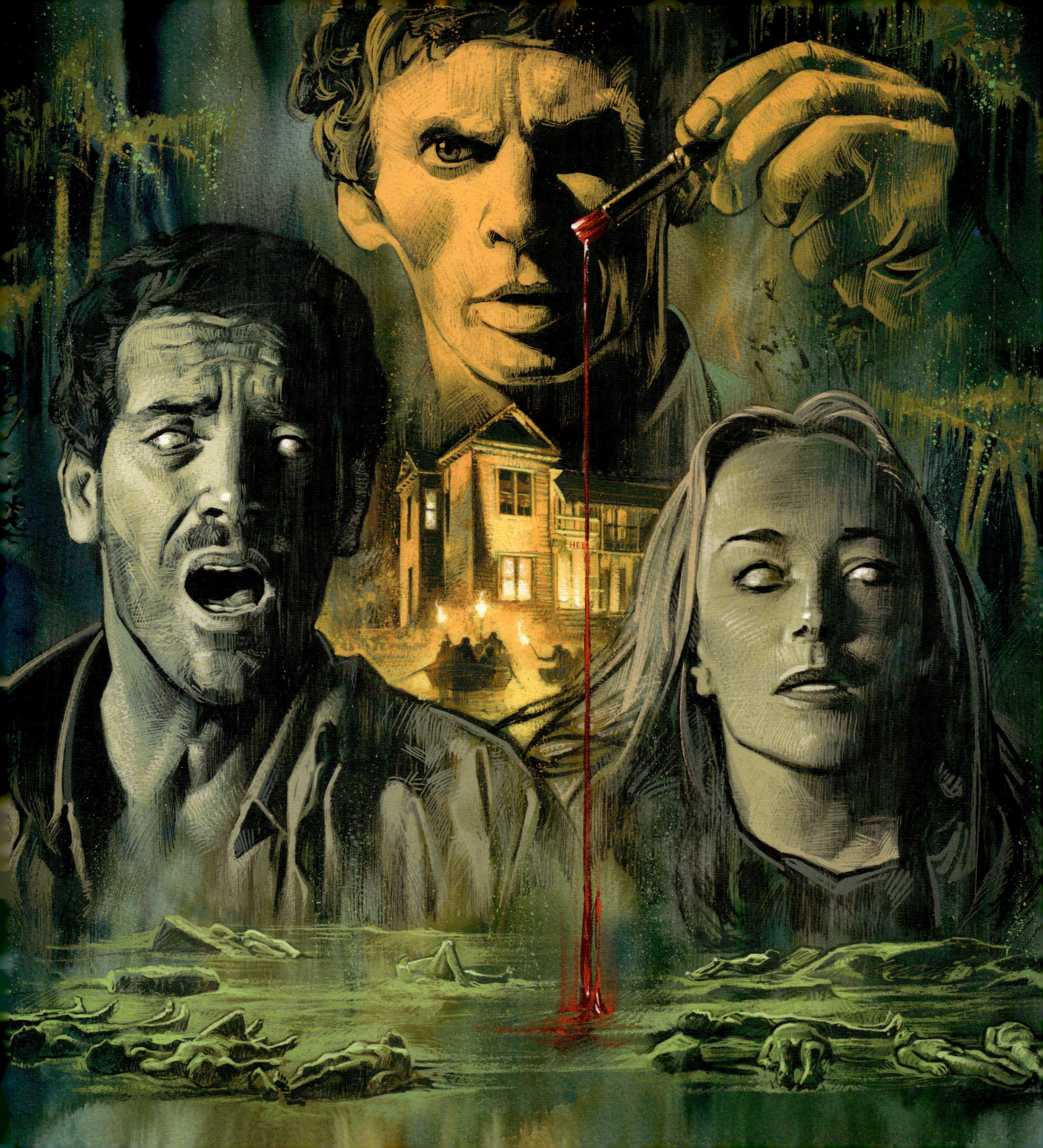

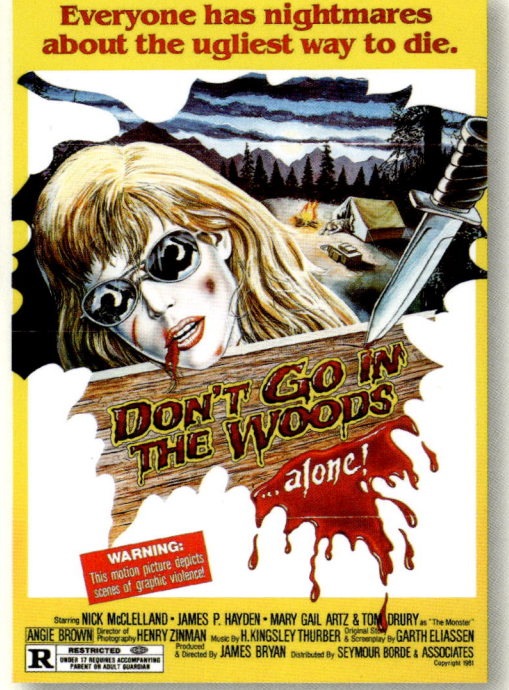

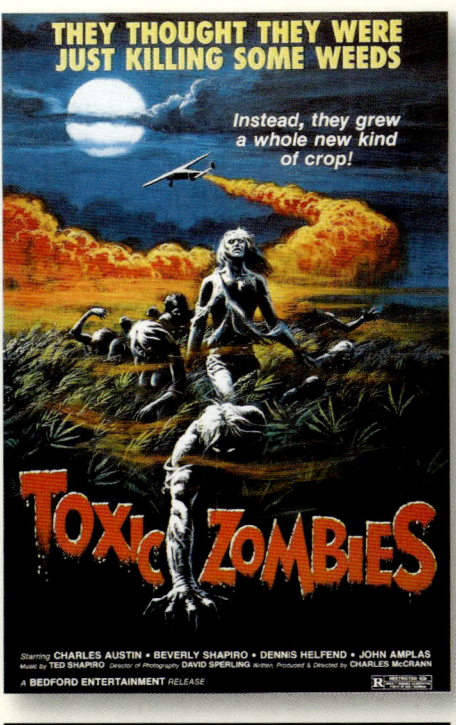

ABOVE LEFT: Spanish poster for *Cannibal Holocaust* (Dir: Ruggero Deodato, 1980), by "Mac" (Macario Gómez Quibus). An Italian precursor of "found footage" movies, it was initially accused of being a "snuff" film and banned in Italy and other countries for scenes of animal cruelty. In England it was put on the Video Nasties list.

TOP MIDDLE: German poster for *Don't Go in the House* (Dir: Joseph Ellison, 1980) by K. Dim which, despite its depiction of zombies, is actually a low-budget "slasher" movie about a psychopath who burns his female victims to death. No surprise that it ended up on the Video Nasties list in the UK.

TOP RIGHT: One-sheet poster for *Toxic Zombies* (Dir: Charles McCrann, 1980), an early example of the "redneck zombie" genre. As *Forest of Fear* it was soon added to the British Board of Film Classification's list of banned Video Nasties.

BOTTOM MIDDLE: One-sheet poster for the low budget *Don't Go in the Woods* (Dir: James Bryan, 1981), an independent "slasher" movie shot in ten days on a budget of just $20,000. It was banned as a Video Nasty in the UK until released uncut in 2007.

BOTTOM RIGHT: 1984 one-sheet poster for Lucio Fulci's *Quella villa accanto al cimitero* (aka *House by the Cemetery*, 1981), the third in the director's unofficial "Gates of Hell" trilogy. Originally issued in a cut version in England, it was subsequently banned as a Video Nasty.

THE ART OF HORROR MOVIES

RIGHT: *Freddy* (2014), a digital portrait of actor Robert Englund as claw-gloved serial killer Freddy Krueger from the *Nightmare on Elm Street* series by the British artist known as Godmachine. "I know Graham Humphreys, the artist who inspired the original," he explains, "and it was more of a hat-tip to him and his amazing work."

THE EVIL EIGHTIES

THE BASTARD SON OF A HUNDRED MANIACS

"I really know Freddy. He's like putting on a comfortable glove. No one else can double for me. There's a particular body language I use, a particular way I use my neck to make him a little unreal. He has some great lines too, with a bizarre sense of humor."
Robert Englund

WHEN A 36-YEAR-OLD character actor with eyes deepened by cigarette ash auditioned for director Wes Craven, he didn't say much... and yet he would wind up playing a killer whose tongue was as sharp as the blades on his clawed glove. Robert Barton Englund (b. 1947) was a Southern California native who'd been bitten early by the acting bug; he studied acting at both UCLA and Michigan's Oakland University before spending five years performing in regional productions of Shakespeare and Shaw.

His first major film role was in the 1974 romantic drama *Buster and Billie*, playing a rural Southern kid named "Whitey." He had small parts in *Eaten Alive* (1976) and *Dead & Buried* (1981), and a strong supporting role in the television miniseries *V* (1983). However, it took Wes Craven and *A Nightmare on Elm Street* (1984)—a role substantially different from the friendly hicks and surfers he'd usually played—to make him a star.

Although Freddy Krueger is a shadowy figure who rarely speaks (though he's often heard laughing offscreen) in the first *Elm Street*, Englund's performance was strong enough to make him irreplaceable, as the producers discovered when they tried to hire a stuntman for *A Nightmare on Elm Street 2: Freddy's Revenge* (1985), then swiftly scrapped the footage before bringing Englund back. In *A Nightmare on Elm Street 3: Dream Warriors* (1987), Freddy's gleefully macabre one-liners were finally placed front and center, although lines like the famous (and improvised), "Welcome to prime time, bitch!" also established a pattern of misogyny in Freddy's repartee that carried through the rest of the series.

As the amount of Freddy's dialogue increased in each film, so his appearance changed. Makeup artist David Miller had created Krueger's burned visage in the first *Nightmare*, but it was the redesigned (by Kevin Yagher) look in *Freddy's Revenge*, with more detailed burns and a more prominent, witch-like nose, that established the character's iconic image. Over seven sequels and a spin-off TV series, Freddy morphed into such oddities as a car, a motorcycle, a teenage hall monitor, an animated video-game character, a superhero, a television, a puppet, and a human nurse... played by Englund in drag.

Near the end of the series, Englund also got to show Freddy's human side: in *Freddy's Dead: The Final Nightmare* (1991), audiences were finally given the prequel story of Freddy as a human serial killer, before his transformation to dream-stalking spirit. Despite that film's title, Freddy still had two movies left to go: the postmodern *Wes Craven's New Nightmare* (1994), in which Englund appeared as himself, as Freddy Krueger, and as the ancient

> Robert Englund ties with Doug Bradley ("Pinhead" in the *Hellraiser* movies) for the most consecutive movie appearances as a horror character, and many fans and scholars alike considered him the first great horror actor to appear since Christopher Lee and Peter Cushing.

demon that had taken the fictional killer's form to stalk the real-life Heather Langenkamp; and lastly, in the mash-up *Freddy vs. Jason* (2003), Englund again appeared as both the human and dream versions of Freddy.

The actor also appeared in numerous other horror films, including *Galaxy of Terror* (1981) and *The Phantom of the Opera* (1989), as well as dozens of television appearances and animated voice-overs, but it was his work as Freddy Krueger that secured him a place in the pantheon of great horror actors. Robert Englund ties with Doug Bradley ("Pinhead" in the *Hellraiser* movies) for the most consecutive movie appearances as a horror character, and many fans and scholars alike considered him the first great horror actor to appear since Christopher Lee and Peter Cushing.

When *A Nightmare on Elm Street* received the inevitable reboot in 2010, Jackie Earle Haley took on the role of Freddy; but although the film performed well at the box office, critics blasted it, with many noting that (as Michael Rechtshaffen stated in *The Hollywood Reporter*) "there's just no replacing Englund." LM

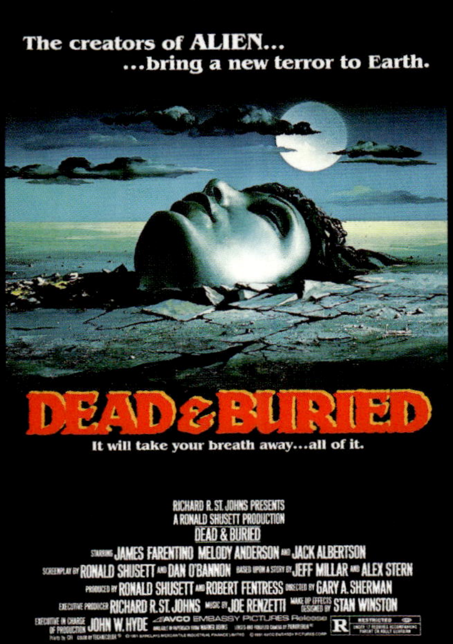

ABOVE LEFT: Japanese poster for New Line Cinema's *A Nightmare on Elm Street* (Dir: Wes Craven, 1984), which made a star out of Robert Englund who, as Fred (later Freddy) Krueger, murders teenagers through their dreams. The movie also marked the screen debut of Johnny Depp.

TOP RIGHT: This striking Thai poster for the sequel *A Nightmare on Elm Street 3: Dream Warriors* (Dir: Chuck Russell, 1987) by artist Kwow depicts future star Patricia Arquette's character being devoured by the nightmarish "Freddy Snake." This was co-writer Frank Darabont's first feature credit.

BOTTOM MIDDLE: One-sheet poster for Avco Embassy Pictures' *Dead & Buried* (Dir: Gary A. Sherman, 1981) by Italian artist Dario Campanile (b. 1948). Initially released uncut, it was later banned as a Video Nasty in the UK before being removed from the list.

BOTTOM RIGHT: One-sheet poster for 21st Century Film Corporation's *The Phantom of the Opera* (Dir: Dwight H. Little, 1989), the fifth "official" film version of Gaston Leroux's 1910 novel.

THE EVIL EIGHTIES

LEFT: *The Lost Boys* (2020), digital painting by Frederick Cooper. "Between the romanticism of vampires today and the movie's own comedy," observes the American artist, "it's not often mentioned how terrifying this film really is. Some of the most memorable monsters appear human."

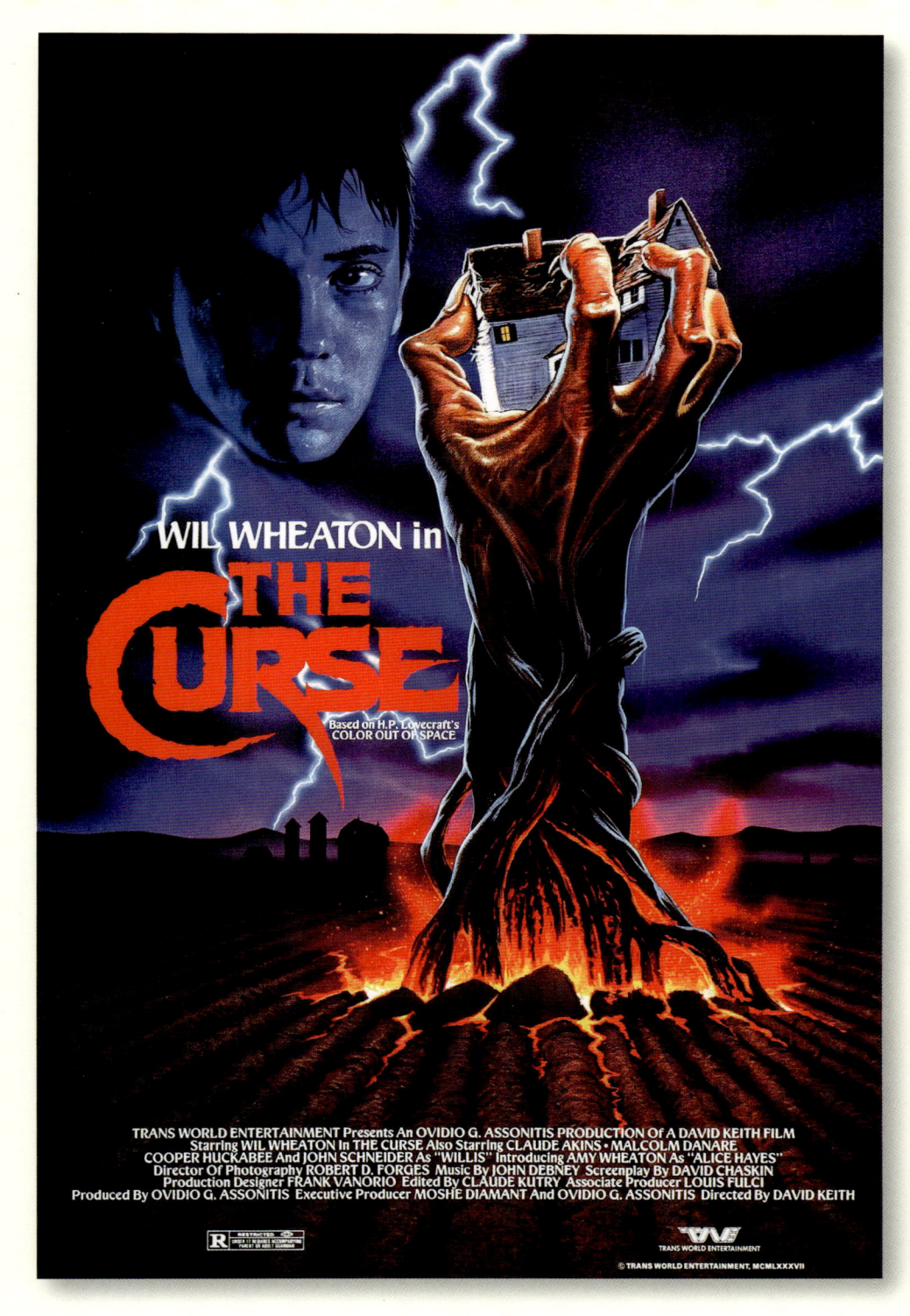

ABOVE LEFT: Although only acknowledged on the poster, Trans World Entertainment's Italian-made *The Curse* (David Keith, 1987) was the second film to be based on H.P. Lovecraft's 1927 story "The Colour Out of Space." Associate producer Lucio Fulci was miscredited as "Louis Fulci."

TOP RIGHT: Thai poster for Vidmark's direct-to-video *The Unnamable* (Dir: Jean-Paul Ouellette, 1988), inspired by a 1925 story by H.P. Lovecraft. Mark Kinsey Stephenson portrayed Randolph Carter in this film and *The Unnamable II: The Statement of Randolph Carter* (1992).

BOTTOM RIGHT: Based on a minor 1937 H.P. Lovecraft short story, a movie of *The Thing on the Doorstep* was announced in the trade magazines by New Age Entertainment as being in pre-production. It never happened, although they did make the direct-to-video sequel to *The Unnamable*.

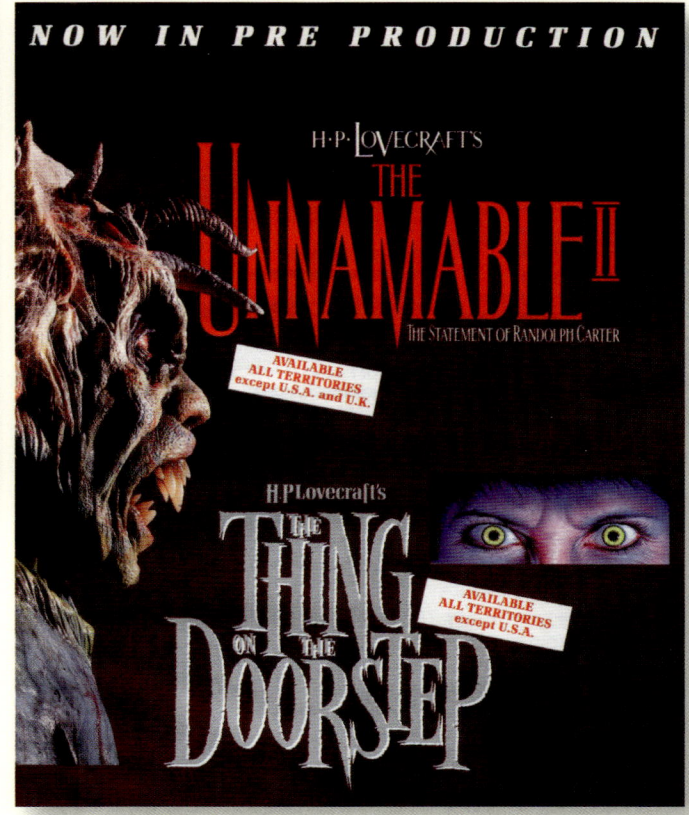

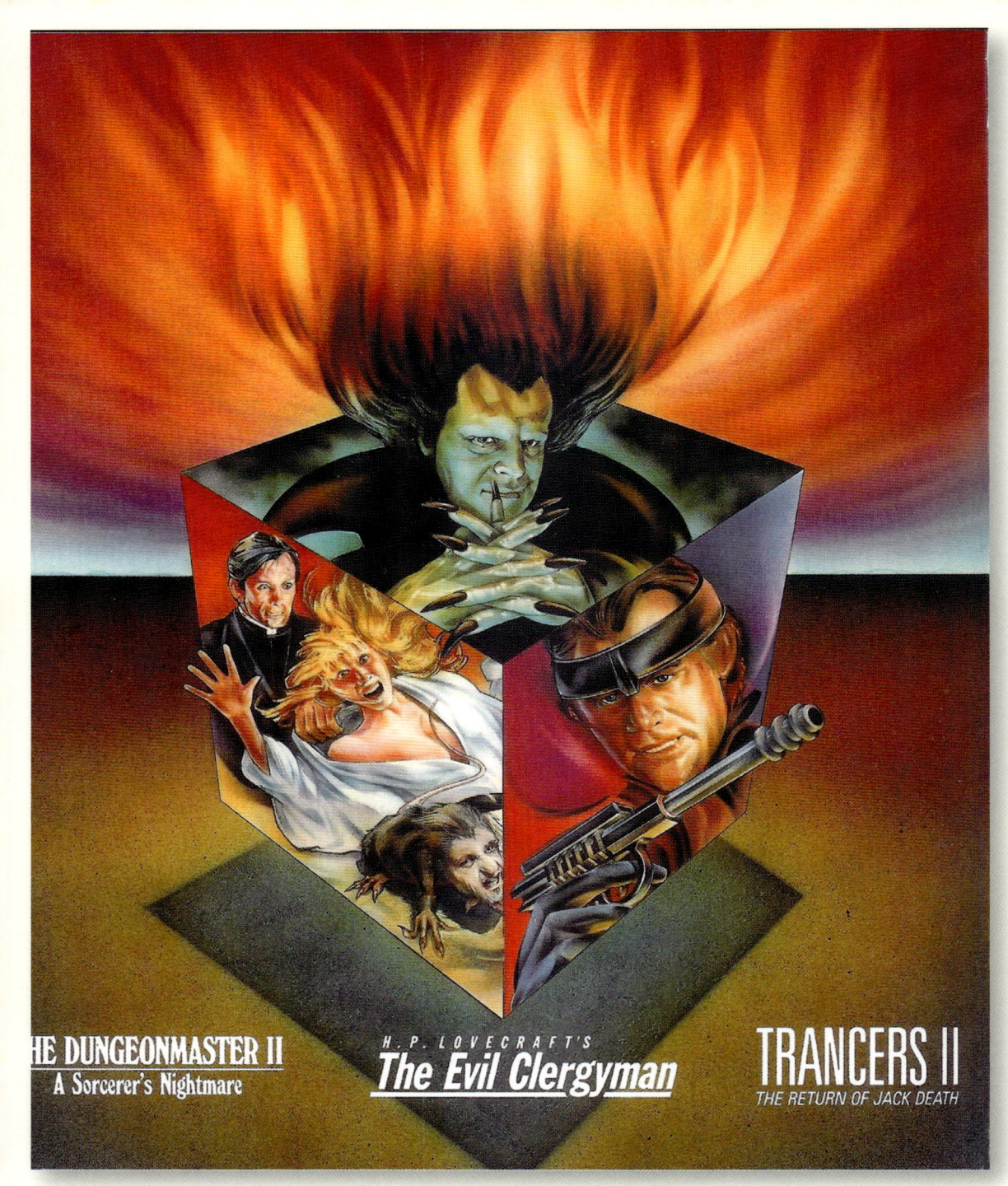

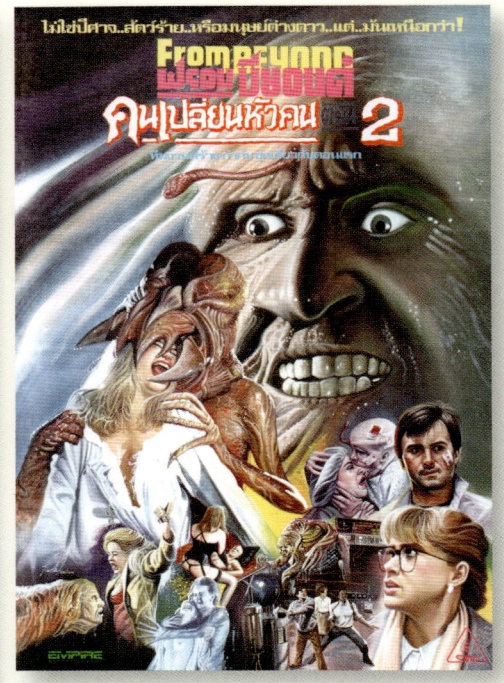

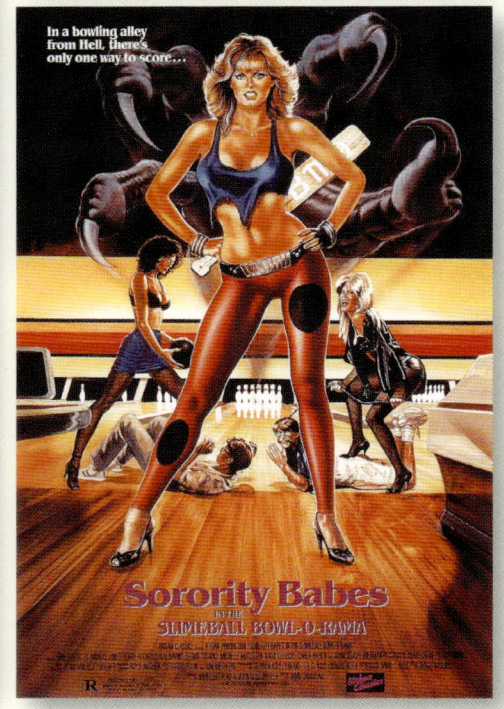

ABOVE LEFT: Trade advertisement for Empire Pictures' anthology movie *Pulse Pounders* (Dir: Charles Band, 1988), which was never released. It featured sequels to *Trancers* (1984) and *The Dungeonmaster* (1984), and a new adaptation of H.P. Lovecraft's posthumously published story "The Evil Clergyman" starring Jeffrey Combs.

TOP RIGHT: Thai poster by artist Jinda for Empire Pictures' *From Beyond* (Dir: Stuart Gordon, 1986), based on the H.P. Lovecraft story first published in 1934.

BOTTOM RIGHT: One-sheet poster for Empire Pictures' *Sorority Babes in the Slimeball Bowl-O-Rama* (Dir: David DeCoteau, 1988) by C.W. Taylor. It was released in the UK under its original title, *The Imp*.

THE ART OF HORROR MOVIES

RIGHT: *Lo Pan* (2015), a digital portrait of the villain from *Big Trouble in Little China* (1986) by American artist Lee Moyer. "I had great reference of James Hong in costume," he recalls, "and while I'd like to say I worked with wind, fire, all that kind of thing—it was Corel Painter as usual. It may not shake the pillars of Heaven, but I hope you like it."

ABOVE: *Jiangshi Attack* (2014), digital illustration by Malaysian artist Darren Tan, from the book *Vampires: A Hunter's Guide* by Steve White and Mark McKenzie-Ray (2014). "This was done for a book about various vampire species and the hunters who pursue them from different cultures around the world," reveals Tan.

RIGHT: *Mr. Vampire* (2016), pen and ink sketch by American artist Gary Gianni, who exclaims: "I wasn't aware that vampirism had spread east of the Carpathian Mountains until I saw . . . The Hopping Vampire!"

THE ART OF HORROR MOVIES

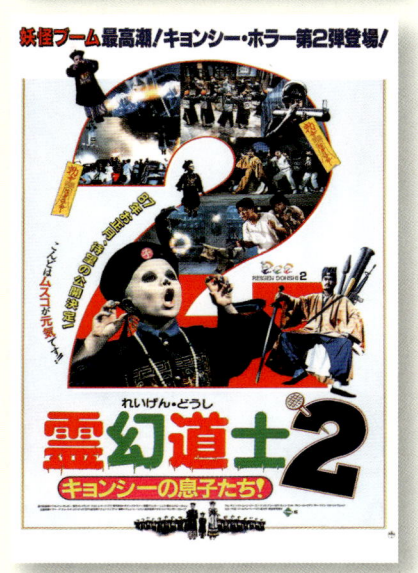

TOP MIDDLE: Poster for Golden Harvest's *Mr. Vampire* (*Geung si sin sang*, 1985), the first in the series of horror comedies directed by Ricky Lau (b. 1949) that kicked off the *jiangshi* ("hopping vampire") cinema boom in Hong Kong during the 1980s.

ABOVE LEFT: Poster for Golden Harvest's *Mr. Vampire II* (*Geung si ga zuk*, 1986), the second in a series of five Hong Kong *jiangshi* movies directed by Ricky Lau.

TOP RIGHT: Poster for the Taiwanese horror comedy *Aloha, the Little Vampire* (*Ling huan qi xiao bao*, 1987), directed by Yan-Chien Chuang and featuring a little vampire boy.

BOTTOM MIDDLE: Poster for *Hello Dracula 2* (*Ha luo jiang shi*, 1987), director Shi-Chen Wang's sequel to the 1985 Taiwanese *jiangshi* comedy.

BOTTOM RIGHT: Poster for the Hong Kong horror comedy *Vampire Buster* (*Zhuo gui da shi*, 1989), directed by Norman Law Man and Stanley Wing Siu under the name "Stanley K. W. Siu."

THE EVIL EIGHTIES

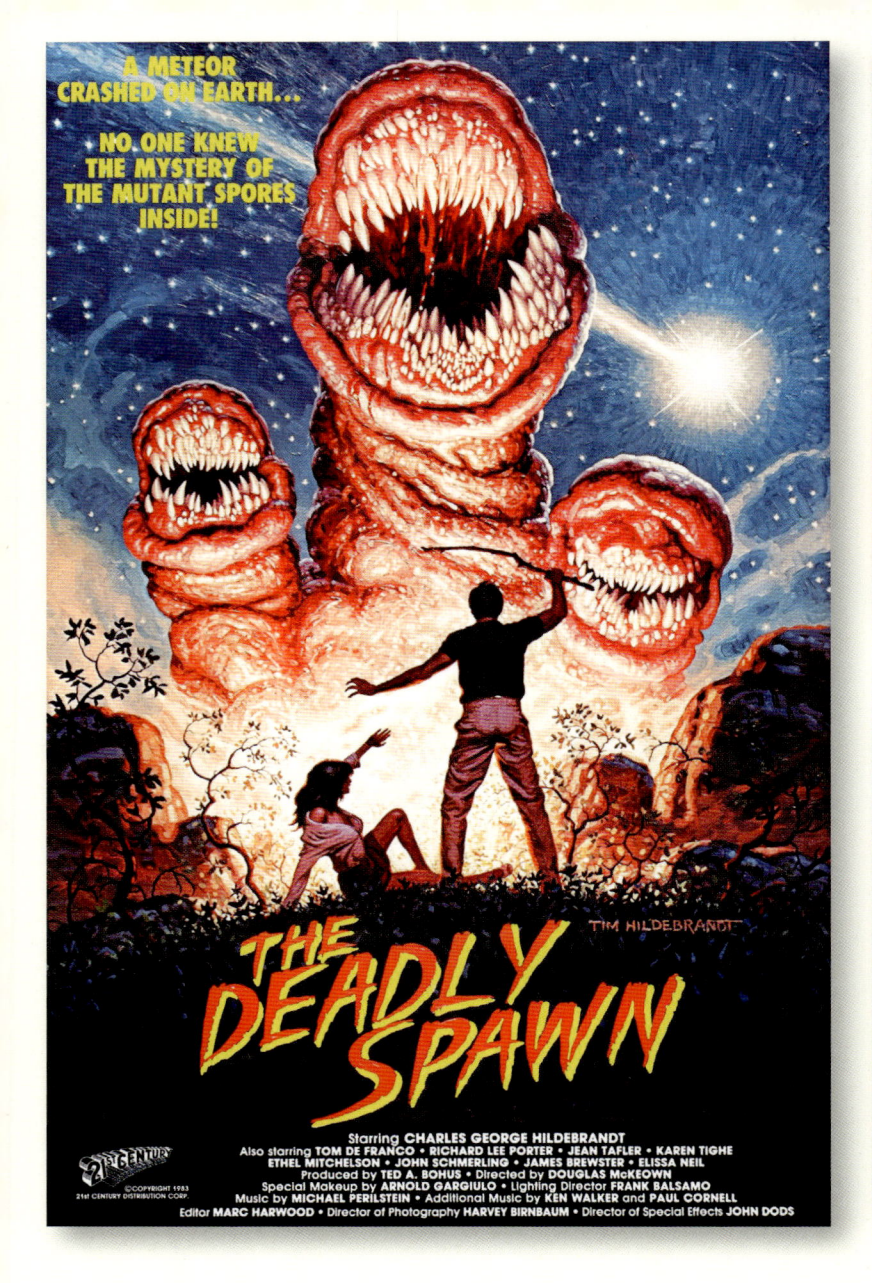

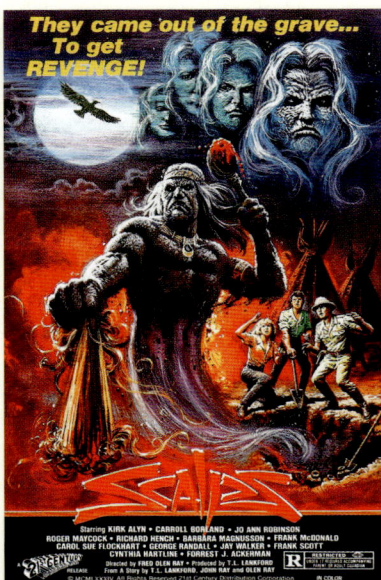

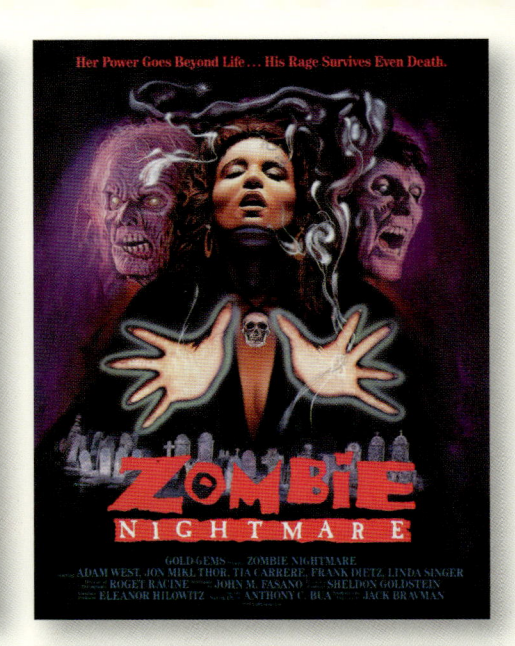

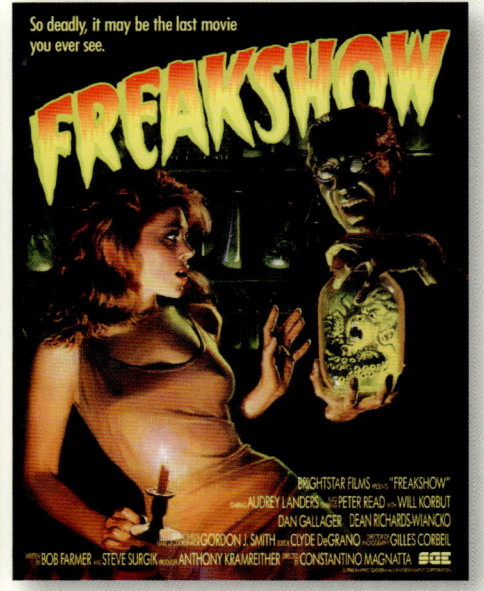

ABOVE LEFT: The one-sheet poster for 21st Century Distribution Corporation's *The Deadly Spawn* (Dir: Douglas McKeown, 1983) was painted by fantasy artist and executive producer Tim Hildebrandt, whose son Charles George Hildebrandt starred in this independent feature shot in New Jersey.

TOP MIDDLE: This one-sheet poster for 21st Century Distribution Corporation's *Scalps* (Dir: Fred Olen Ray, 1983), about a murderous Native American spirit taking revenge, is probably better than the movie itself. It featured old-timers Kirk Alyn and Carroll Borland, along with Forrest J Ackerman.

BOTTOM MIDDLE: Drew Struzan's original design underwent some changes on TMS Pictures' one-sheet for Tom Daley's *The Outing* (aka *The Lamp*, 1987). The artist's realistic depiction of the movie's evil genie was replaced on the final poster with just a pair of glowing green eyes.

TOP RIGHT: Trade advertisement by Frank Morris for Gold-Gem Ltd.'s *Zombie Nightmare* (Dir: Jack Bravman, 1987), which starred Adam West and Canadian heavy metal musician Jon Mikl Thor as a resurrected zombie seeking revenge upon the teenagers who killed him.

BOTTOM RIGHT: Wonderfully pulpy trade advertisement for Shapiro-Glickenhaus Entertainment's *Freakshow* (Dir: Constantino Magnatta, 1989), a Canadian anthology movie in which Audrey Landers's TV reporter stumbled upon a mysterious museum that had four frightening tales to tell.

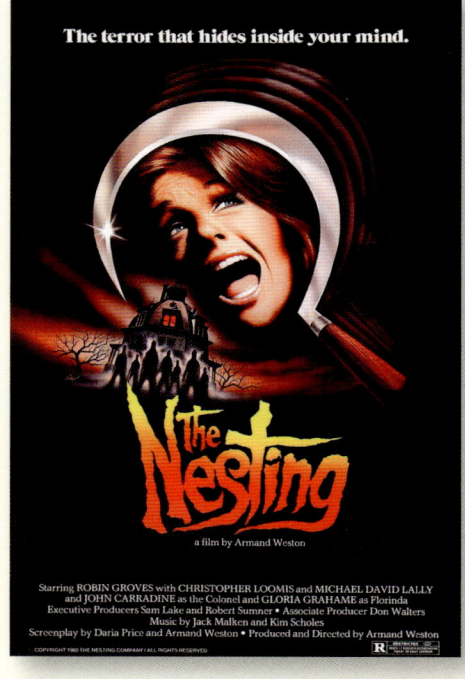

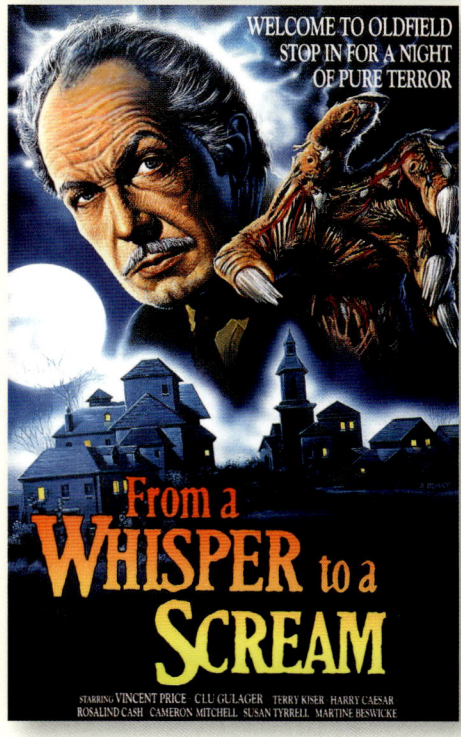

TOP RIGHT: Although the 1980s ushered in a new type of horror movie, there were still roles for the old stars. John Carradine never stopped working, and he turned up in the haunted house thriller *The Nesting* (Dir: Armand Weston, 1981), along with Gloria Grahame in her final movie.

ABOVE LEFT: Christopher Lee made a few clunkers in his time. One of these was Philippe Mora's shot-in-Czechoslovakia *Howling II: Stirba—Werewolf Bitch* (aka *Howling II… Your Sister is a Werewolf*, 1985). Graham Humphreys's 2016 gouache on watercolor paper art for Arrow Films' Blu-ray release makes it look classier than it actually is. "[the film was] not well-regarded at the time of its original release," recalls the British artist. "My cover was intended to establish strong female lead Sybil Danning with minimal gratuity and deliver werewolves and co-star Christopher Lee as supportive selling points."

BOTTOM RIGHT: UK video poster by "S. Dewey" for Jeff Burr's feature debut, *From a Whisper to a Scream* (aka *The Offspring*, 1987), which found poor Vincent Price playing the creepy narrator of a sleazy anthology movie. It also marked the final screen appearance of 83-year-old Angelo Rossitto.

THE EVIL EIGHTIES

BETELGEUSE BETELGEUSE

here lies
BETELGE

LEFT: *Beetlejuice* (2018), acrylics, gouache, dyes, and Prismacolor pencils on cold press illustration board by Christopher Franchi, who reveals: "Assembled and background-designed in Photoshop, this was a busy proposal for a pinball machine translite. Sadly, the manufacturer passed."

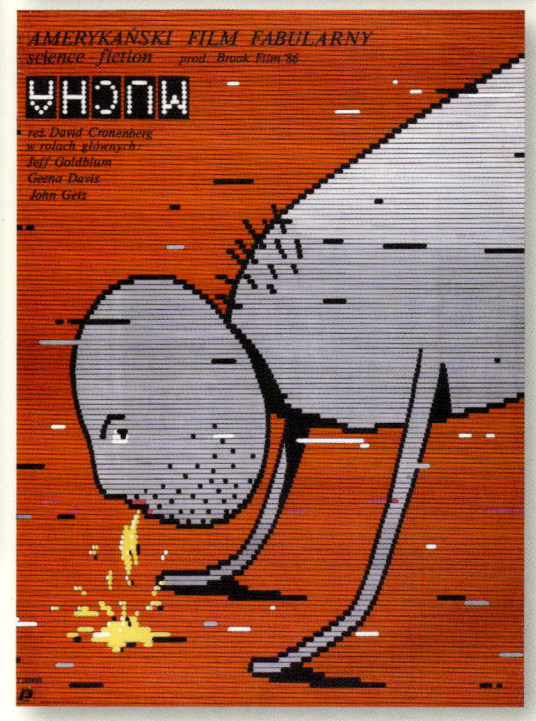

Long Live the New Flesh

After making several acclaimed low-budget Canadian movies, Toronto-based writer/director David Cronenberg (b. 1943) exploded (pun intended) into horror movie fame in 1981 with *Scanners*, about psychically gifted humans who could burst heads (an image that became one of the most defining icons of the decade). Cronenberg, whose work has defined "body horror," describes his aesthetic as "halfway between Hollywood and Europe." His five feature films from the 1980s—*Scanners*, *Videodrome* (1983), *The Dead Zone* (1983), *The Fly* (1986), and *Dead Ringers* (1988)—are frequently cited not just as superb horror from the time, but among the smartest and most disturbing horror films ever made. LM

ABOVE LEFT: Surreal French *grande* for *Videodrome* (Dir: David Cronenberg, 1983) by artist Laurent Melki (b. 1960), depicting Blondie singer Debbie Harry (who was billed as "Deborah" Harry).

TOP RIGHT: Thai poster for the Canadian movie *Scanners* (Dir: David Cronenberg, 1981), which did much to popularize exploding heads in the 1980s.

BOTTOM RIGHT: Polish poster for David Cronenberg's *The Fly* (1986) by acclaimed designer Eugeniusz Skorwider (b. 1954), who became Professor of Fine Arts at the University of Poznan, Poland.

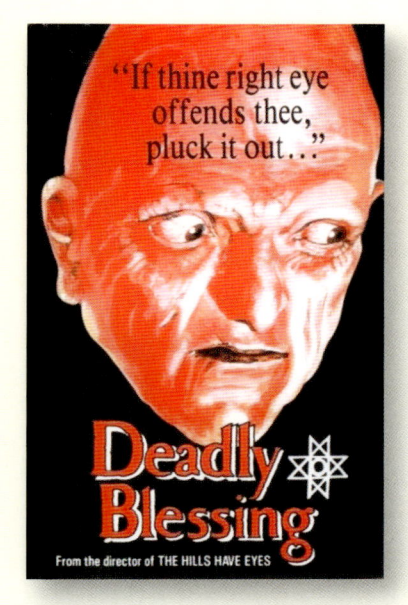

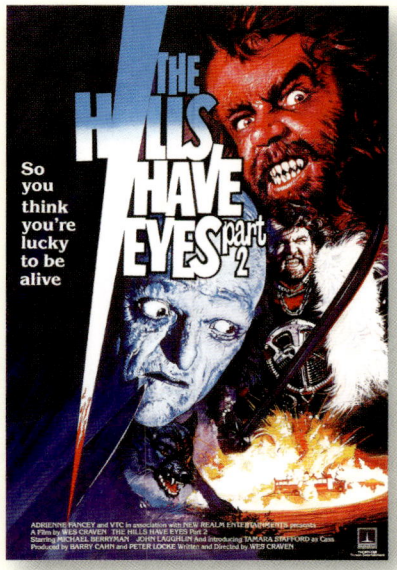

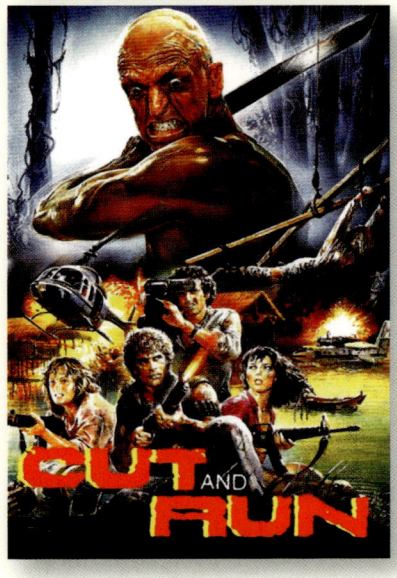

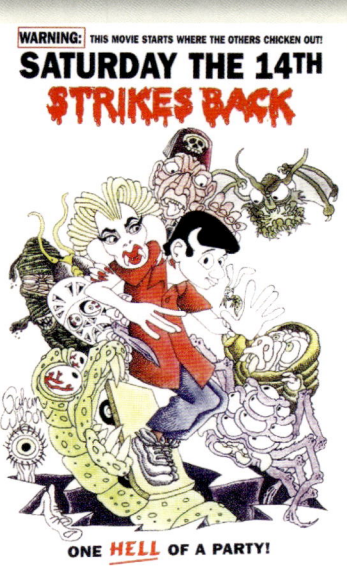

The New Rondo

Michael Berryman (b. 1948) was born with hypohidrotic ectodermal dysplasia, a rare medical condition leaving him with no sweat glands, hair, fingernails, or teeth. Discovered by producer George Pal, who gave him a part in *Doc Savage: The Man of Bonze* (1975), his big break came when Wes Craven cast him as the desert psycho "Pluto" in *The Hills Have Eyes* (1977), a role he repeated in the 1984 sequel, *The Hills Have Eyes Part II*. Craven also put him into *Deadly Blessing* (1981) and the TV movie *Invitation to Hell* (1984), before the actor began to turn up in such movies as *Weird Science* (1985) and *Teenage Exorcist* (1991) purely on the strength of his unusual appearance. More recently, Rob Zombie cast him in both *The Devil's Rejects* (2005) and *The Lords of Salem* (2012). As with Rondo Hatton more than seven decades ago, Berryman's unconventional looks continue to make him an iconic figure in horror movies, whether it's playing mutants, monsters, psychos, or evil undertakers.

TOP LEFT: DVD poster art for *Deadly Blessing* (Dir: Wes Craven, 1981), which starred Sharon Stone.

TOP MIDDLE: This British poster for *The Hills Have Eyes Part II* (Dir: Wes Craven 1984) uses the same image of Michael Berryman.

BOTTOM LEFT: Video poster for Ruggero Deodato's *Cut and Run* (*Inferno in diretta*, 1985).

BOTTOM MIDDLE: One-sheet poster for *Saturday the 14th Strikes Back* (Dir: Howard R. Cohen, 1988) by Gahan Wilson (b. 1930).

ABOVE RIGHT: *Michael Berryman* (2016), pen and ink and watercolor portrait by German artist Uli Meyer, who reveals: "The actor's amazing appearance inspired this sketch which, after sharing it on social media, was immediately acquired by a collector in Los Angeles."

THE EVIL EIGHTIES

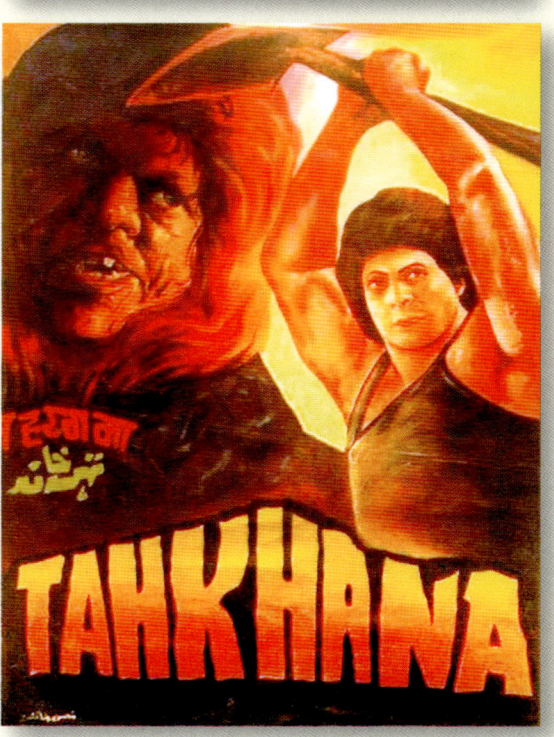

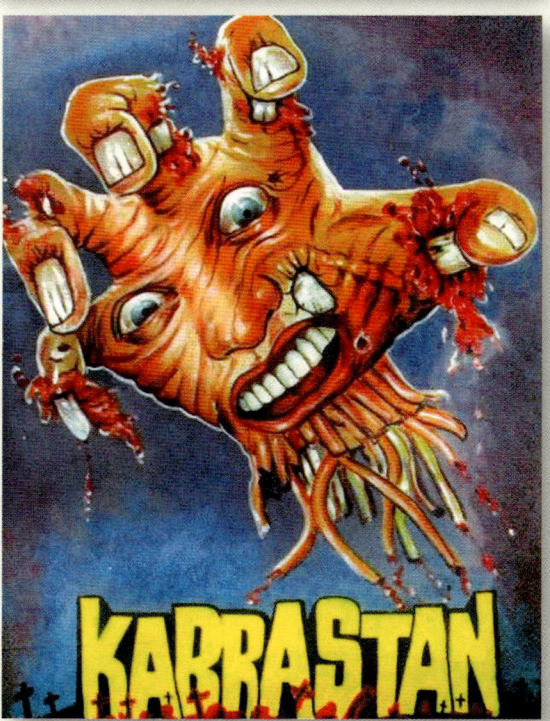

TOP LEFT: Indian poster for *Pyasa Shaitan* (Dir: Joginder [Shelly], 1984), a Hindi dubbed version of the Malayalam film *Vayanadan Thampan* (1978) which included added scenes of the director playing Satan.

TOP MIDDLE: Poster for *Purana Mandir* (Dir: Tulsi Ramsay and Shyam Ramsay, 1984), which was a huge hit and influenced many other Indian horror movies.

TOP RIGHT: Poster for the Bollywood old dark house comedy *Bhago Bhoot Aayaa* (Dir: Krishna Naidu, 1985).

BOTTOM LEFT: Indian poster for *Tahkhana* (Dir: Tulsi Ramsay and Shyam Ramsay, 1986).

BOTTOM MIDDLE: Indian poster for the *Kabrastan* (Dir: Mohan Bhakri, 1988), a Hindi movie in which a disfigured murder victim rises from the grave seeking revenge.

BOTTOM RIGHT: Poster for the Hindi horror movie *Purani Haveli* (Dir: Tulsi Ramsay and Shyam Ramsay, 1989), which sampled Ray Peterson's 1960 hit song "Tell Laura I Love Her."

THE ART OF HORROR MOVIES

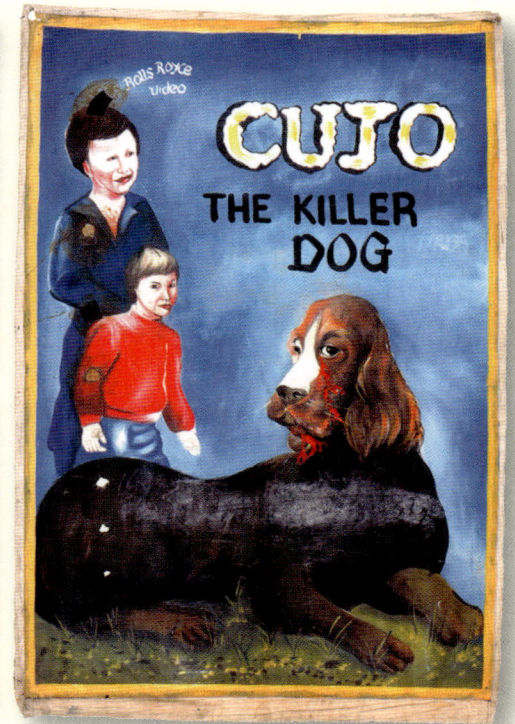

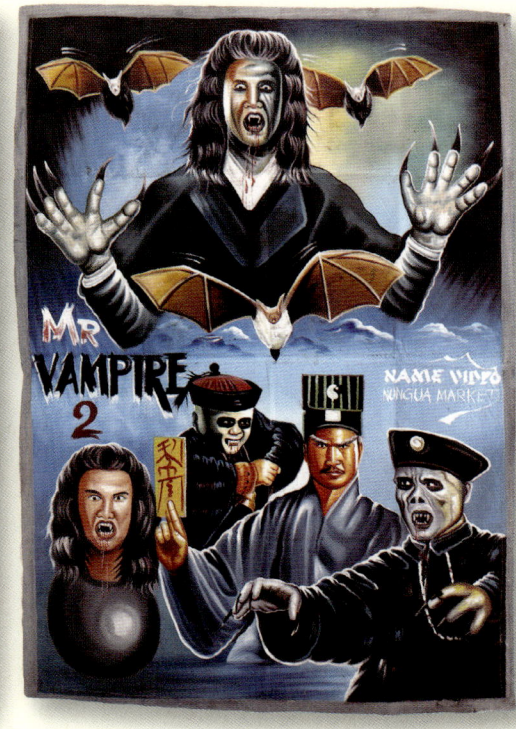

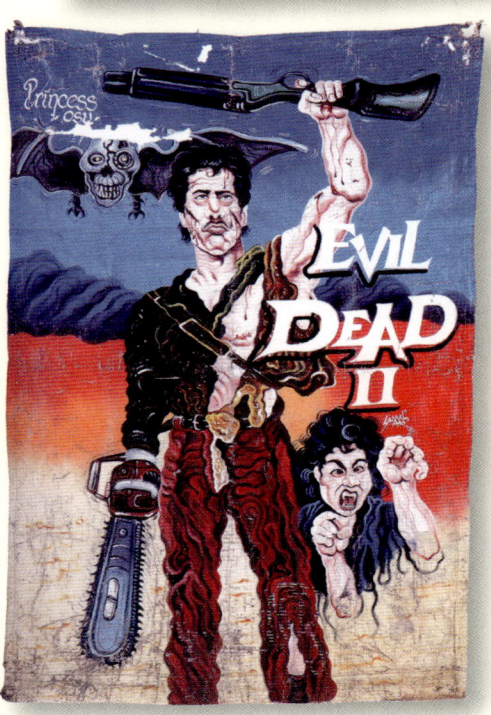

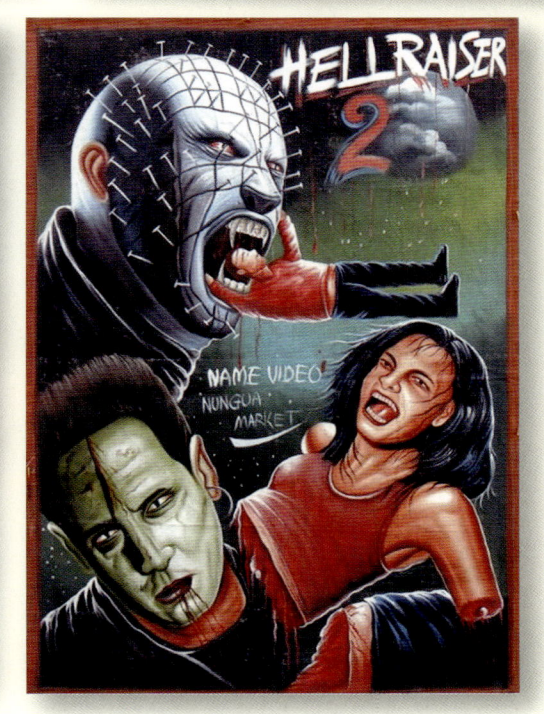

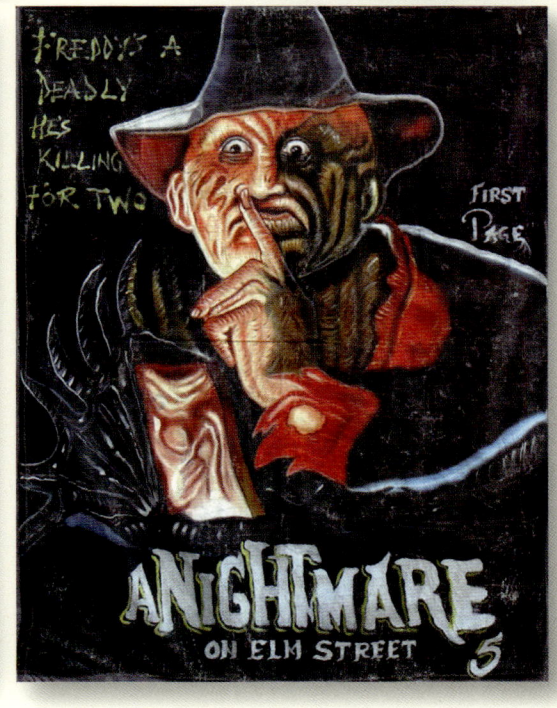

THIS PAGE: In the mid-1980s, video cassette technology made it possible for temporary "pop-up" cinemas to travel around the West African countries of Ghana and Nigeria, where local artists were hired to paint posters on split canvas flour sacks, often adding their own elements of folk art.

TOP LEFT: Flour-sack poster for *The Evil Dead* (Dir: Sam Raimi, 1981).

TOP MIDDLE: This poster adds its own subtitle to *Cujo* (Dir: Lewis Teague, 1983) for those unfamiliar with Stephen King's novel.

TOP RIGHT: Hand-painted poster for the Hong Kong–made *Mr. Vampire II* (Dir: Ricky Lau, 1986).

BOTTOM LEFT: The artist added his own skull-headed bat to this poster for *Evil Dead II* (Dir: Sam Raimi, 1987).

BOTTOM MIDDLE: An artist also embellished this flour-sack poster for the sequel *Hellbound: Hellraiser 2* (Dir: Tony Randel, 1988) by having a giant Pinhead apparently eat his victims.

BOTTOM RIGHT: The artist almost got the tagline correct for this West African flour-sack poster for *A Nightmare on Elm Street 5: The Dream Child* (Dir: Stephen Hopkins, 1989).

THE EVIL EIGHTIES

TOP LEFT: The Turkish poster for *Blood Beach* (Dir: Jeffrey Bloom, 1980) used the same photo-image as The Jerry Gross Organization's original US poster, but then added a funky head at the bottom that was probably supposed to represent one of the victims sucked under the sand by the monster.

BOTTOM LEFT: The Turkish poster for the United Film Distribution Company's *Day of the Dead* (1985), the third movie in George A. Romero's original zombie trilogy, appropriated the artwork for José Ramón Larraz's pseudonymously credited Spanish thriller *Rest in Pieces* (1987).

ABOVE RIGHT: This Turkish poster for United Artists' *Pumpkinhead* (Dir: Stan Winston, 1988), an effective slice of backwoods folk horror starring Lance Henriksen, simply ripped-off the pre-production artwork for Empire Pictures' *Breeders* (1986) and an unidentified slasher film.

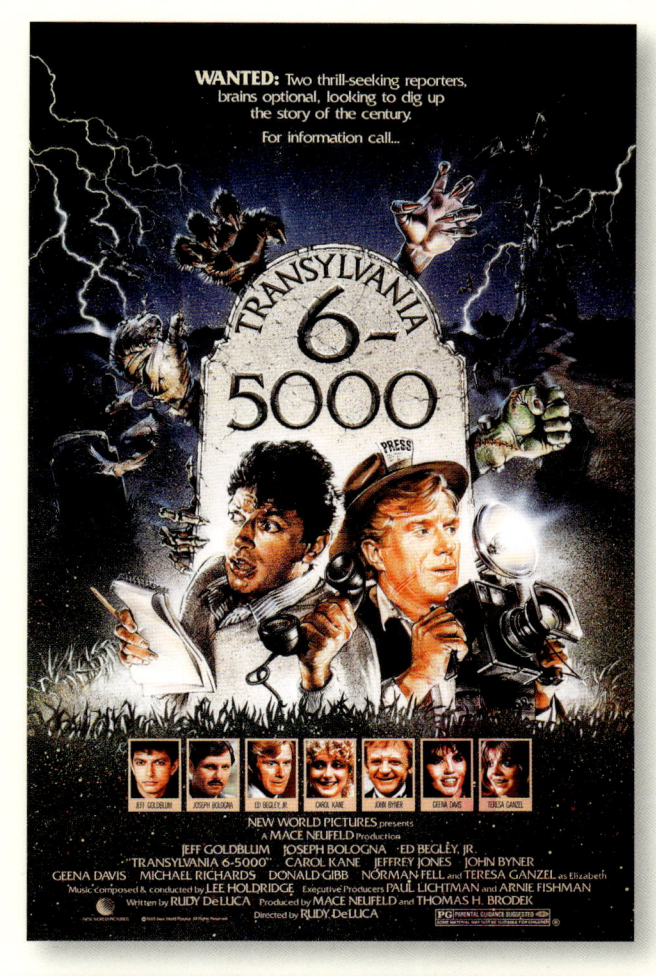

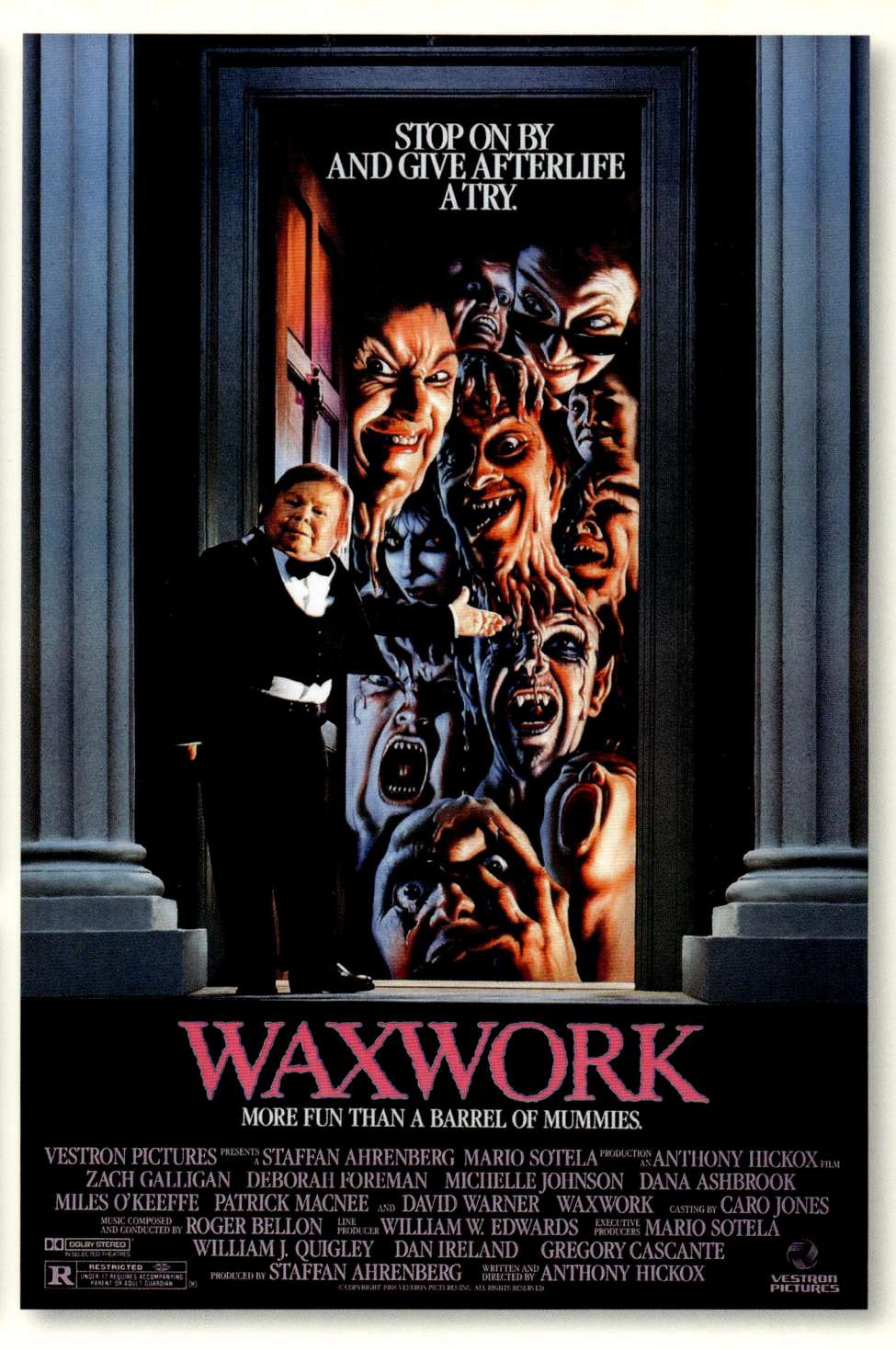

TOP LEFT: Rick Farrell's one-sheet poster, based on a concept by Morgan Weistling, for New World Pictures' horror-comedy *Transylvania 6-5000* (Dir: Rudy De Luca, 1985). Two tabloid newspaper reporters (Jeff Goldblum and Ed Begley, Jr.) set out to get a scoop on the monsters.

BOTTOM LEFT: Jumbo Mexican lobby card for *The Monster Squad* (Dir: Fred Dekker, 1987), the ultimate 1980s monster mash-up, as a group of kids try to save their hometown (and the world) from Count Dracula (Duncan Regehr), the Frankenstein Monster, a Wolfman, a Gillman, and a Mummy.

ABOVE RIGHT: The one-sheet poster for Vestron Pictures' *Waxwork* (Dir: Anthony Hickox, 1988) featured background art by future Disney artist Jim Warren (b. 1949). Six teens find themselves drawn into wax exhibits of a werewolf, a mummy, Count Dracula, and other classic monsters.

THE EVIL EIGHTIES

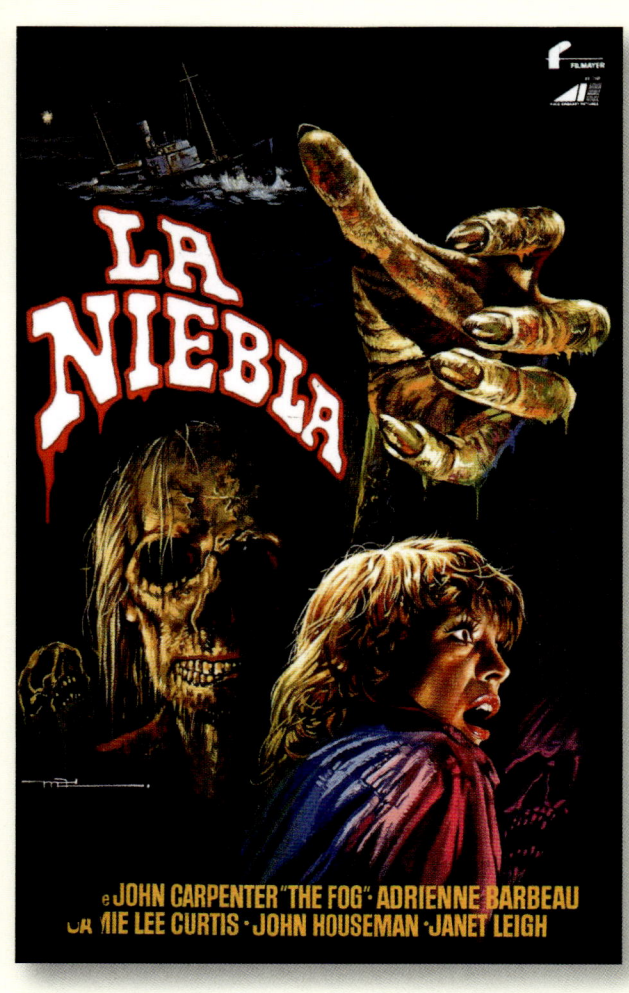

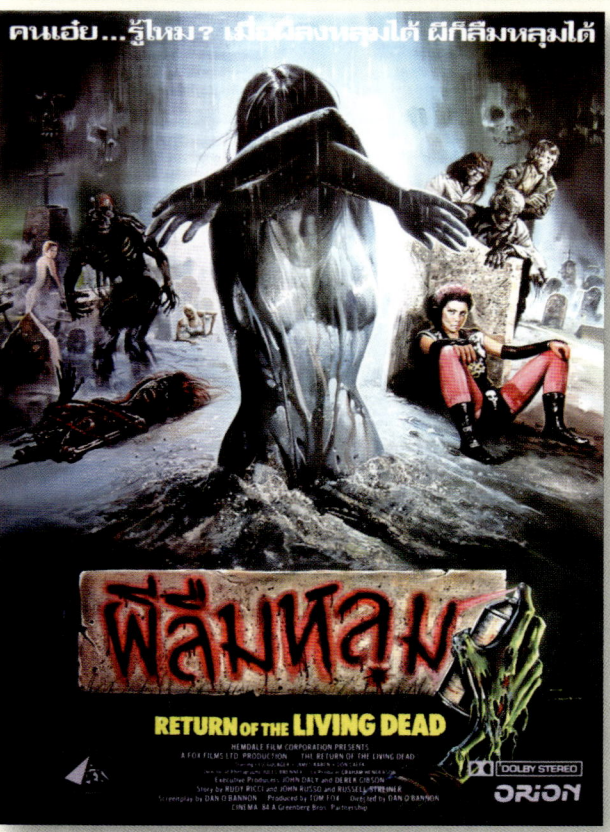

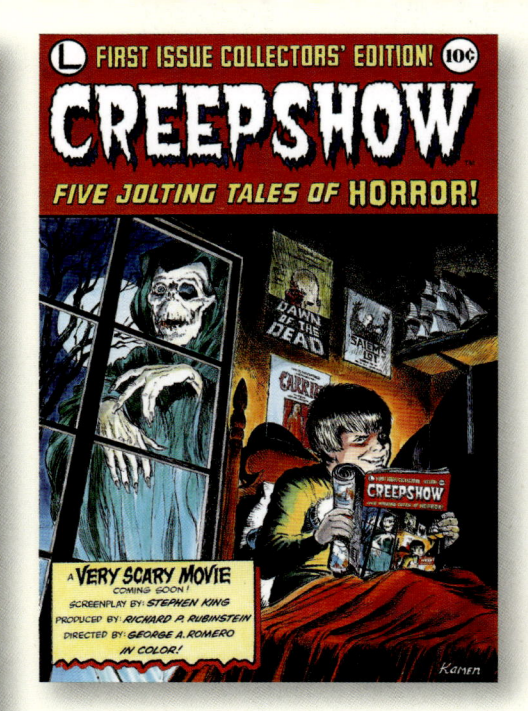

Women in Horror: 1980s

The daughter of legendary Hollywood actors Tony Curtis and Janet Leigh, Jamie Lee Curtis (b. 1958) achieved instant "scream queen" status with her role as put-upon babysitter Laurie Strode in John Carpenter's *Halloween* (1978), a role she reprised in three sequels. She co-starred with her mother in *The Fog* (1980) for the same director, and consolidated her status with *Prom Night* (1980), *Terror Train* (1980), and *Road Games* (1981). Adrienne [Jo] Barbeau (b. 1945) also starred in her then-husband John Carpenter's *The Fog* plus *Escape from New York* (1981), before going on to work with fellow genre *auteurs* Wes Craven (*Swamp Thing*, 1982) and George A. Romero (*Creepshow*, 1982). With her breakout role as a sexy zombie in *Return of the Living Dead* (1985), Linnea [Barbara] Quigley (b. 1958) quickly became the "Queen of the Bs" with such direct-to-video fare as *Silent Night, Deadly Night* (1984), *Creepozoids* (1987), *Sorority Babes in the Slimeball Bowl-O-Rama* (1988), *Hollywood Chainsaw Hookers* (1988), and *Night of the Demons* (1988), while Barbara Crampton (b. 1958) brought a more sophisticated sex appeal to the H.P. Lovecraft adaptations *Re-Animator* (1985), *From Beyond* (1986), and "The Evil Clergyman" sequence of *Pulse Pounders* (1988).

TOP LEFT: Spanish poster for *The Fog* (Dir: John Carpenter, 1980) by "Mac" (Macario Gómez Quibus), who seems to have "borrowed" Peter Cushing's zombie character Arthur Grimsdyke from *Tales from the Crypt* (1972).

BOTTOM LEFT: Thai poster by prolific artist Tongdee Panumas (b.1947) for *The Return of the Living Dead* (Dir: Dan O'Bannon, 1985), a belated comedy semi-sequel to *Night of the Living Dead* (1968).

TOP MIDDLE: Pre-release poster for *Creepshow* (Dir: George A. Romero, 1982) by famed EC Comics artist Jack Kamen (1920–2008) with Neal Adams (b. 1941).

TOP RIGHT: Japanese poster for *Re-Animator* (Dir: Stuart Gordon, 1985), based on the 1922 H.P. Lovecraft serial.

THE ART OF HORROR MOVIES

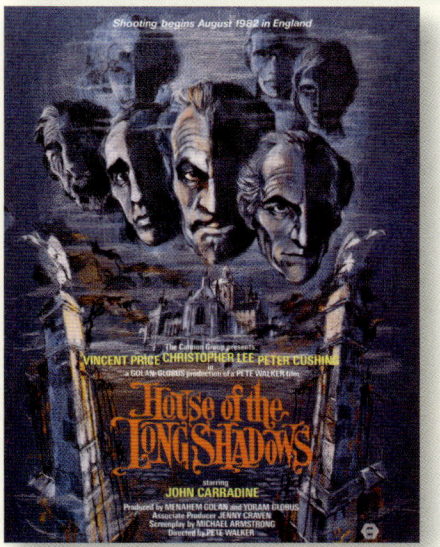

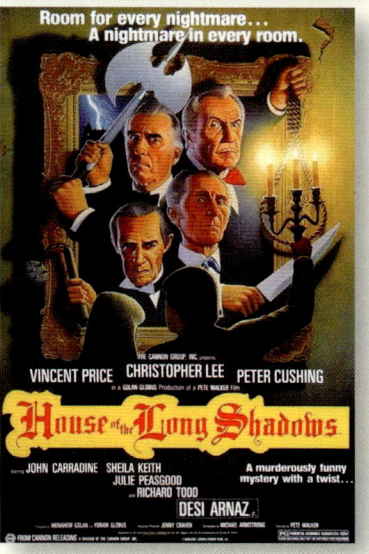

Cannon's Fodder

When plans to remake *The Old Dark House* (1932 and 1963) fell through, Cannon Films turned to the unlikely team of screenwriter Michael Armstrong and director Pete Walker to adapt Earl Derr Biggers's much-filmed 1913 novel and George M. Cohan's Broadway play *Seven Keys to Baldpate* into a genial vehicle for Vincent Price, Christopher Lee, Peter Cushing, and John Carradine (the only time these horror icons all worked together). *House of the Long Shadows* (1982) features Desi Arnaz, Jr. as a bestselling American author who, after making a bet with his publisher (Richard Todd), agrees to spend 24 hours in a creepy Welsh mansion writing a novel. Along the way he not only encounters the four horror stars (all apparently enjoying themselves), but also Sheila Keith, Julie Peasgood, and Norman Rossington. It marked the end of an era for this type of British horror film.

TOP LEFT: Limited to 1,500 copies, this British quad poster for *House of the Long Shadows* (1983) is by artist Robert Michael "Bob" Gibson (1938–2010), who was paid just £250 to paint it.

BOTTOM LEFT: 1982 pre-release trade advertisement for *House of the Long Shadows* (1983).

BOTTOM MIDDLE: US one-sheet poster for *House of the Long Shadows* (1983) signed "Batchelled."

ABOVE RIGHT: *House of the Long Shadows* (2016), mixed media on Fabriano paper by Argentinean artist Marcelo Neira. "I love painting portraits of movie and sports stars, and personalities from all over the world," he reveals.

THE EVIL EIGHTIES

— 249 —

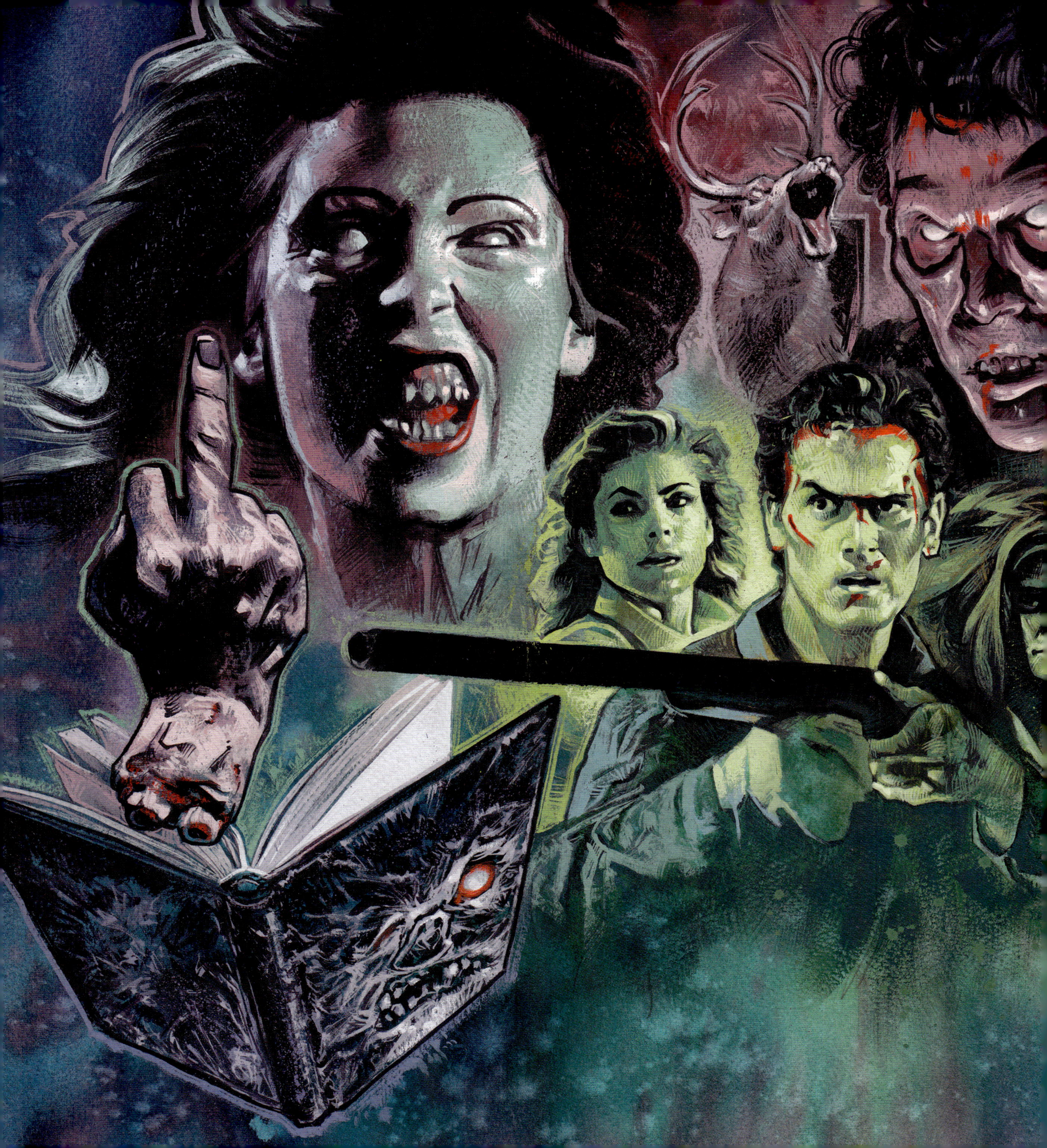

LEFT: *Evil Dead II* (2015), gouache on watercolor paper by British artist Graham Humphreys. "Not strictly an official film poster," he reveals, "this art formed the second in a trilogy of limited edition screen-print posters that paid direct homage to the *Evil Dead* films—providing a chance to revisit my own earlier artwork for the original releases in the 1980s, but employing skills and techniques since gained. The color scheme reflects the colorful action and keeps the image playful."

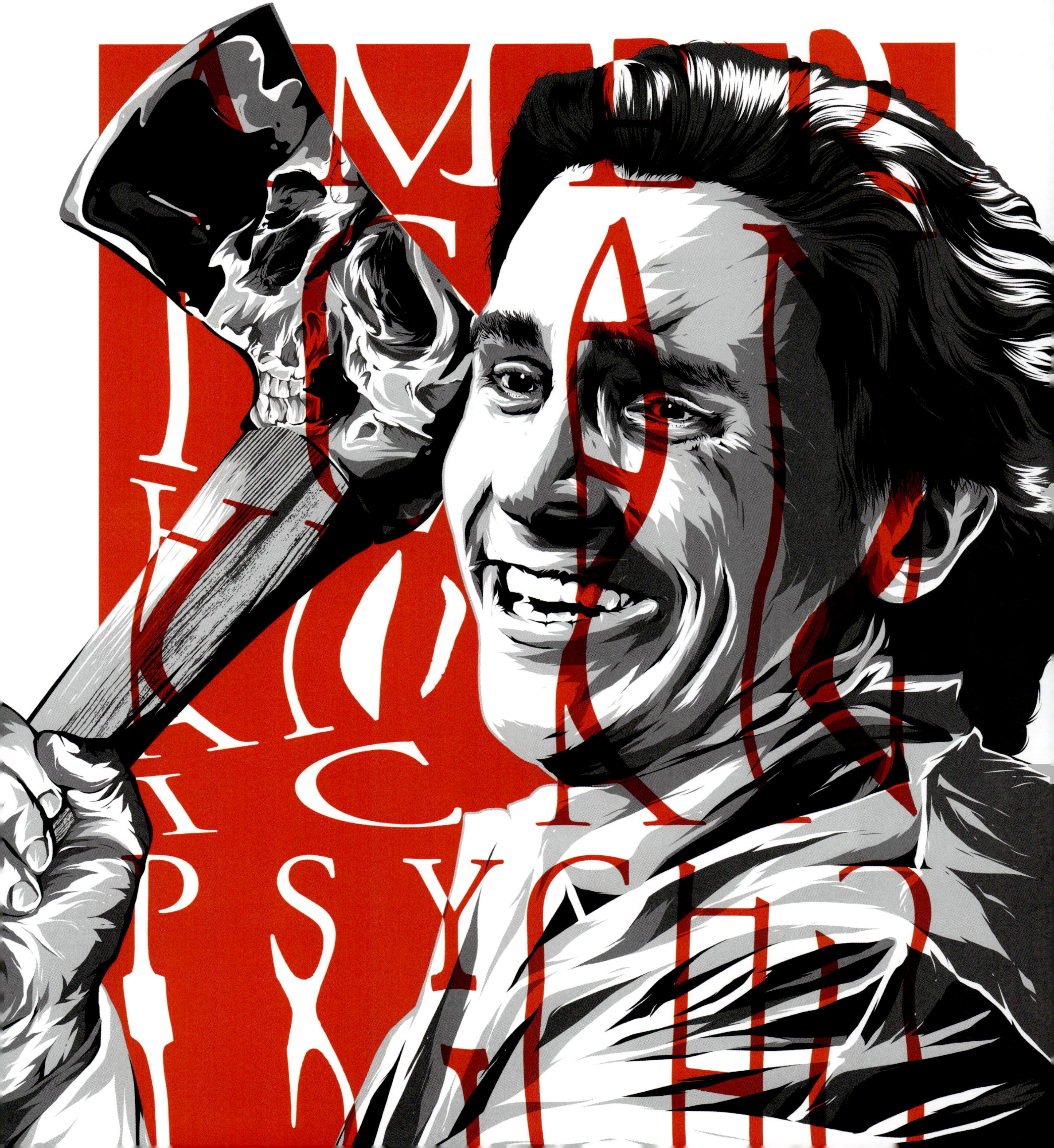

8

THE NASTY NINETIES

ANNE BILLSON

"No one in this world has ever lost money
by underestimating the intelligence
of the great masses of the plain people."

HENRY LOUIS MENCKEN

Phone Voice: "Do you like scary movies?"

Sidney Prescott (Neve Campbell): "What's the point? They're all the same. Some stupid killer stalking some big-breasted girl who can't act who is always running up the stairs when she should be running out the front door. It's insulting."
Scream (1996)

IN THE 1990s, horror movies went mainstream in a big way. Major Hollywood studios such as Columbia Pictures and Walt Disney Pictures teamed up with critically acclaimed directors to tackle what had previously been considered B-movie subjects, and cast them with A-list stars, though the results were usually more spectacular than scary.

Francis Ford Coppola reworked the most famous vampire story of them all as a supernatural romance in *Bram Stoker's Dracula* (1992), its lavish visual style enhanced by Eiko Ishioka's astonishing costume design. Mike Nichols brought office politics into the werewolf drama *Wolf* (1994), in which Jack Nicholson sprouted hair and urinated on his rival's shoes. Kenneth Branagh applied his Shakespeare-honed skills to *Mary Shelley's Frankenstein* (1994), in which he played the mad scientist, with Robert De Niro as his Creature. Tom Cruise and Brad Pitt flirted with undead homoeroticism in Neil Jordan's *Interview with the Vampire: The Vampire Chronicles* (1994), adapted from Anne Rice's bestseller.

David Lynch, whose films had always contained nightmarish elements, tipped all the way over into horror in *Twin Peaks: Fire Walk With Me* (1992), a big-screen prequel to his TV show *Twin Peaks* (1990–91), teased by a poster image of doomed homecoming queen Laura Palmer and a glimpse of the infamous red room.

Joss Whedon subverted a horror movie cliché by turning a cute blonde cheerleader into a vampire hunter in his screenplay for *Buffy the Vampire Slayer* (1992); unhappy with the film, he went on to explore the premise in a seven-season TV series (1997–2003), which suggested that vampires could also be boyfriends.

Elsewhere, vampires were undergoing a radical transformation from antagonist to protagonist, and migrated into art-house movies such as Michael Almereyda's *Nadja* (1994) and Abel Ferrara's *The Addiction* (1995), which further explored the creature's versatility as a metaphor for dependency and moral decay.

Jonathan Demme's *The Silence of the Lambs* (1991) introduced the term "serial killer" into pop culture and played up the thriller's horrific elements with a striking poster image of a death's-head moth on a young woman's mouth. The film won five Academy Awards, including Best Picture and Best Actor for Anthony Hopkins's iconic performance as Hannibal "the Cannibal" Lecter.

Psycho-thrillers such as *Copycat* (1995) and *Kiss the Girls* (1997) upgraded the "slasher" movie for mainstream audiences, with serial killers taking the place of bogeymen. The most horrific of them all was David Fincher's *Se7en* (1995), a grim tale of two detectives investigating a series of gruesome murders inspired by the Seven Deadly Sins.

Sam Raimi rounded off his 1980s "Evil Dead" trilogy with *Army of Darkness* (1992), which trapped its long-suffering hero in the Middle Ages and provided him with

---

Major Hollywood studios such as Columbia Pictures and Walt Disney Pictures teamed up with critically acclaimed directors to tackle what had previously been considered B-movie subjects, and cast them with A-list stars.

---

an evil alter ego, "Bad Ash." Tim Burton let his Gothic tendencies off the leash in *Sleepy Hollow* (1999), Washington Irving's headless horseman yarn reworked in Hammer horror mode and starring Johnny Depp as Ichabod Crane. Depp also starred, with sinister facial hair, in Roman Polanski's wickedly funny *The Ninth Gate* (1999) as a rare book collector scouring Europe for an ancient Lucifer-summoning text.

David Cronenberg's predilection for "body horror" mutated into the perverse sexuality of *Crash* (1996) and the multiple layers of *eXistenZ* (1999), which adopted the structure of role-playing computer games to dabble in the reality-is-not-what-you-think-it-is premise which permeated the 1990s and was first revitalized by Adrian Lyne's cult psychological horror story *Jacob's Ladder* (1990), in which a traumatized Vietnam veteran was haunted by demonic visions.

Dario Argento's *Trauma* (1993) and *The Phantom of the Opera* (1998) failed to recapture the flair of that director's earlier horror movies, though *The Stendhal Syndrome* (1996) offered some extraordinary fantasy sequences inspired by classical paintings.

George A. Romero had a low-key 1990s but directed *The Dark Half* (1993), about an author battling his evil alter ego, adapted from a novel by Stephen King, whose writings continued to provide filmmakers with rich pickings.

PREVIOUS SPREAD: *American Psycho* (2014), digital design for an unused poster by American artist Anthony Petrie, utilizing photocopier-manipulated typography. "This piece was meant to reflect the distorted reality experienced by the film's main protagonist, graphically and typographically," explains Petrie.

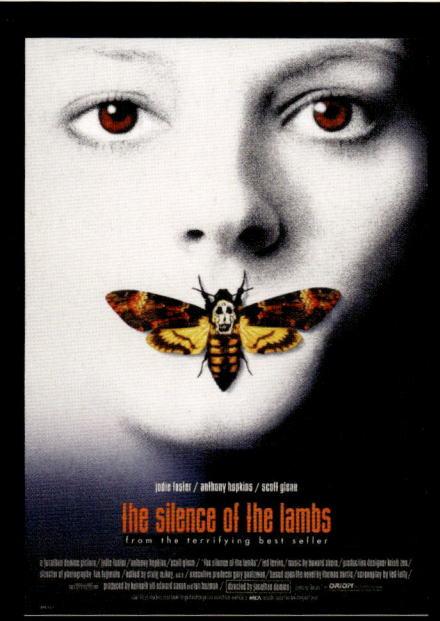

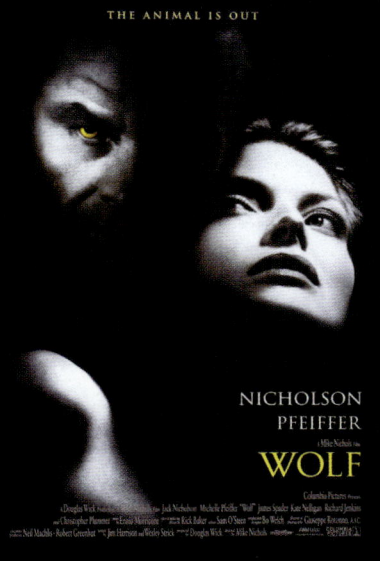

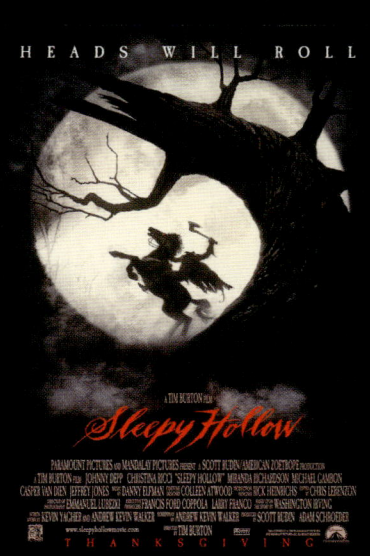

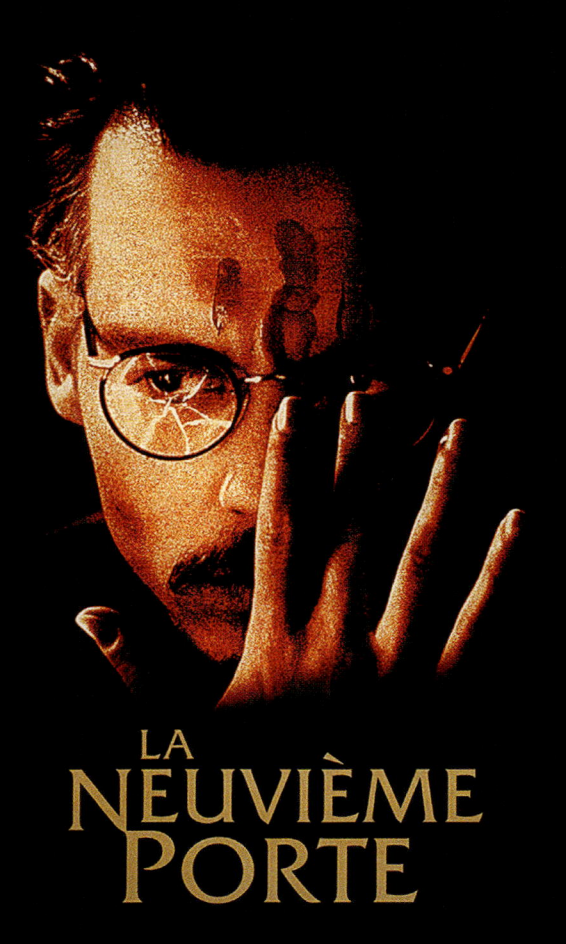

TOP LEFT: Created by advertising agency Dazu, the death's-head skull on the moth in Orion Pictures' one-sheet poster for *The Silence of the Lambs* (Dir: Jonathan Demme, 1991) is actually made up of seven naked bodies inspired by *In Voluptas Mors*, Philippe Halsman's 1951 photo portrait of Salvador Dali.

TOP MIDDLE: Jack Nicholson's subtle eye coloring is the only out of the ordinary touch in his otherwise romantic pose with Michelle Pfeiffer for Columbia Pictures' one-sheet poster for *Wolf* (Dir: Mike Nichols, 1994).

BOTTOM LEFT: Jennifer Jason Lee and Jude Law were literally linked in this Japanese poster for Alliance Atlantis Communications' *eXistenZ* (Dir: David Cronenberg, 1999), which is set inside a virtual reality game.

BOTTOM MIDDLE: This preview one-sheet poster for *Sleepy Hollow* (Dir: Tim Burton, 1999) focussed on the story's infamous Headless Horseman, while the final design was dominated by photo portraits of stars Johnny Depp and Christina Ricci.

ABOVE RIGHT: French *affiche* design for *The Ninth Gate* (Dir: Roman Polanski, 1999), in which Johnny Depp's rare book dealer sets out to track down a seventeenth century supernatural tome. It was loosely based on the 1993 novel *The Club Dumas* by Arturo Pérez-Reverte.

THE NASTY NINETIES

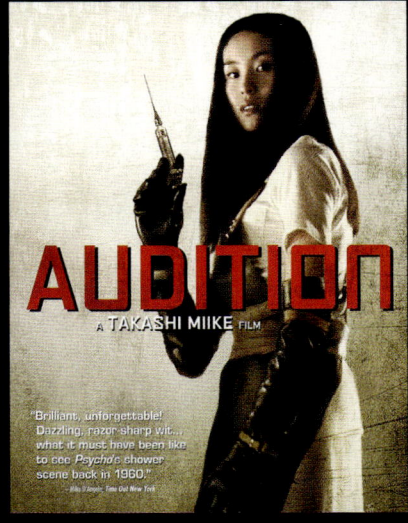

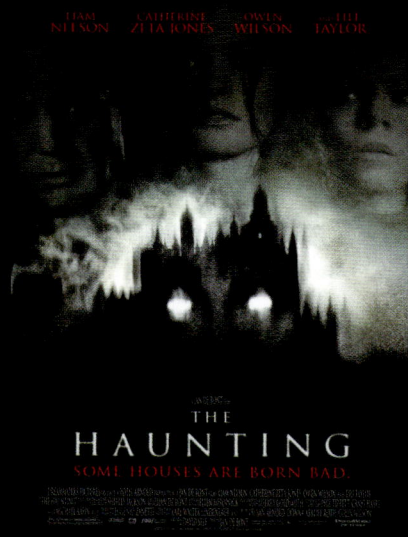

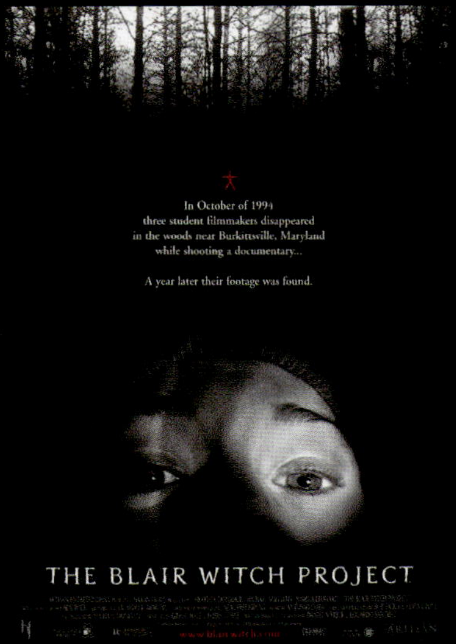

ABOVE LEFT: Striking Japanese poster for Peter Jackson's New Zealand gorefest *Braindead* (aka *Dead Alive*, 1992) by artist Hajime Sorayama (b. 1947), best known for his erotic biomechanoid portrayals of women.

TOP MIDDLE: Fetishistic poster of actress Eihi Shiina for Takashi Miike's *Audition* (aka *Ôdishon*, 1999), an early Japanese contribution to the "torture porn" subgenre of the 2000s.

TOP RIGHT: Kevin Bacon's character can see ghosts in Artisan Entertainment's *Stir of Echoes* (Dir: David Koepp, 1999), based on the 1958 "novel of menace" by Richard Matheson.

BOTTOM MIDDLE: One-sheet poster for DreamWorks' *The Haunting* (Dir: Jan de Bont, 1999), a remake of the 1963 movie which was also based on the 1959 novel by Shirley Jackson. Stephen King's unused first draft script eventually became the TV miniseries *Rose Red* (2002).

BOTTOM RIGHT: The iconic one-sheet poster for Artisan Entertainment's micro-budgeted *The Blair Witch Project* (Dir: Daniel Myrick and Eduardo Sánchez, 1999), which ushered in the "found footage" boom of the 2000s.

Among the most notable King adaptations were *Misery* (1990), which won Kathy Bates an Oscar for her performance as a psychotic fan; *Sleepwalkers* (1992), *Needful Things* (1993), and *Apt Pupil* (1998), as well as a steady trickle of TV movies and miniseries. The most successful King adaptations in the 1990s, however, were non-horror—*The Shawshank Redemption* (1994) and *The Green Mile* (1999), both scripted and directed by Frank Darabont.

John Carpenter directed the delirious meta-horror *In the Mouth of Madness* (1994), about a hunt for a missing Stephen King-type writer, as well as a remake (*Village of the Damned*, 1995) and dystopian sequel (*Escape from L.A.*, 1996), before tackling a vampire-Western hybrid with *Vampires* (1998).

The ubiquity of VHS (and later DVD) gave horror movies a longer life than they'd had in the past, and ensured the continuity of non-mainstream franchises.

Psycho-killers clashed with Tex-Mex vampires in another hybrid, *From Dusk Till Dawn* (1996), directed by Robert Rodriguez from a screenplay by Quentin Tarantino, whose own *Reservoir Dogs* (1992) and *Pulp Fiction* (1994) spearheaded a 1990s trend for gangster movies containing horrific ultra-violence, torture, and gore.

The most commercially successful of the horror directors who had revolutionized the genre in the 1970s was Wes Craven, who capped the franchise he himself had launched with the meta-horror *Wes Craven's New Nightmare* (1994) before breathing new life into the "slasher" subgenre again with *Scream* (1996)—Kevin Williamson's postmodern screenplay was set in a world where high school students discussed the "rules" of the horror genre and the best way to survive even as they were being stalked by a killer in a "Ghostface" mask.

Meanwhile, *Halloween* and *Friday the 13th* posted new entries in their long-running franchises, while *I Know What You Did Last Summer* (1997) and *Urban Legend* (1998) attempted to launch new ones.

The ubiquity of VHS (and later DVD) gave horror movies a longer life than they'd had in the past, and ensured the continuity of non-mainstream franchises such as *Puppet Master*, *Child's Play*, *Phantasm*, *Children of the Corn*, *Witchboard*, *Witchcraft*, *Hellraiser*, *Leprechaun*, *Wishmaster*, *Darkman*, and *The Dentist*.

A new generation of up-and-coming filmmakers from around the world injected fresh blood into the genre, with home video technology making old as well as new films more accessible to wider audiences.

In *Candyman* (1992), British-born Bernard Rose transposed a Clive Barker story about an urban legend from England to Chicago. New Zealander Peter Jackson evolved from the cheap and cheerful zombie splatter of *Braindead* (aka *Dead-Alive*, 1992) to a more disturbing real-life murder case in *Heavenly Creatures* (1994), before returning to horror-comedy with the ghostly effects-packed *The Frighteners* (1996). Mexican director Guillermo del Toro made a striking feature debut with *Cronos* (1993), a beguiling twist on vampire mythology, though his introduction to the Hollywood studio system ended badly when he failed to secure final cut of his creepy bug movie *Mimic* (1997). In Spain, Álex de la Iglesia peddled his personal brand of politically incorrect horror-satire with *The Day of the Beast* (1995).

Whispering Corridors (1998) launched a popular Korean franchise of chillers set in haunted schools. In Japan, Shinya Tsukamoto pushed cyberpunk body horror to extremes with *Tetsuo II: Body Hammer* (1992) and *Tokyo Fist* (1995). Takashi Miike's *Audition* (1999) began like a romance, but its poster, featuring a woman in black rubber gloves holding a syringe, offered fair warning of the ghastliness to come. Hideo Nakata's *Ringu* (1998), about a cursed videotape which doomed anyone who watched it to a terrible death, launched not just a franchise but an epidemic of films featuring creepy Asian ghosts with long black hair and a herky-jerky way of walking.

Ringu wasn't the only film to make ghosts scary again. M. Night Shyamalan's *The Sixth Sense* (1999) starred Bruce Willis as a child psychologist trying to help a small boy who sees dead people. Remakes such as *The Haunting* (1999), *House on Haunted Hill* (1999), and *The Mummy* (1999) reduced potentially horrific material to extravaganzas of flashy CGI effects, but Shyamalan's film prioritized creepy atmosphere and clever plotting. David Koepp's *Stir of Echoes* (1999), in which Kevin Bacon's telephone lineman was haunted by the specter of a murdered girl, was equally well-crafted, but overshadowed by the huge success of Shyamalan's film, with its mind-blowing narrative twist.

With the approach of the Millennium, there was a surge in religious-themed horror. Some films, such as *The Omega Code* (1999), were produced by Christian-backed companies, but Hollywood studios also played with hellfire. Al Pacino, as Satan, presided over a New York City law firm in *The Devil's Advocate* (1997), and Philadelphia detective Denzel Washington tracked a body-hopping demon in *Fallen* (1998). Pittsburgh hairdresser Patricia Arquette was afflicted by mysterious wounds in *Stigmata* (1999), while *End of Days* (1999) pitted Arnold Schwarzenegger against the Devil.

One of the first 1990s horror films to use "found footage" was *The Last Broadcast* (1998), in which a documentary filmmaker investigated the murder of two TV hosts. But it was *The Blair Witch Project* (1999) that would change forever the way horror movies were made. The film's phenomenal success also proved that a low-budget combination of dark woods, torch-lit faces, and ominous stick figures were able to terrify audiences at the sort of primal level that mainstream horror could never hope to reach.

**HITCHCOCK HA INVENTATO IL BRIVIDO
FULCI LO HA PERFEZIONATO**

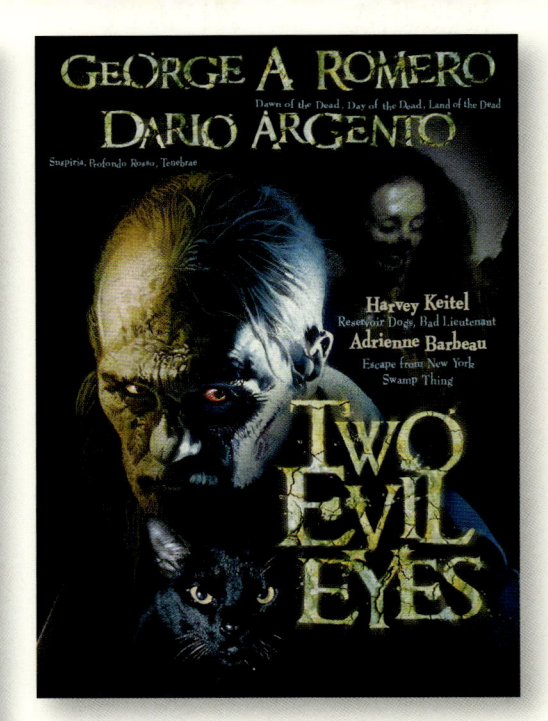

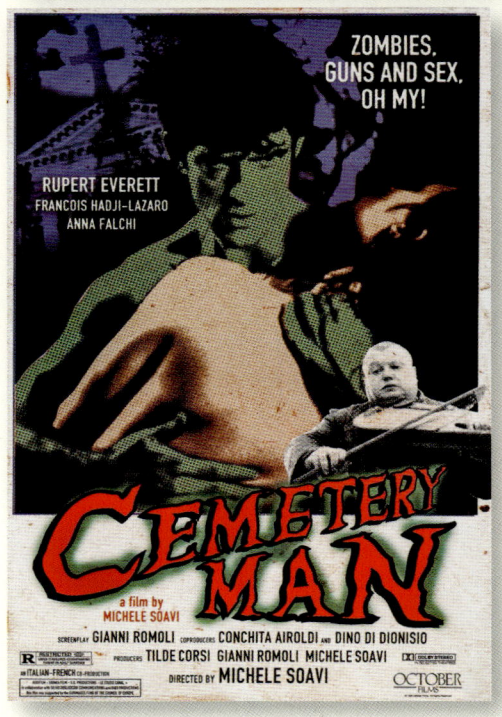

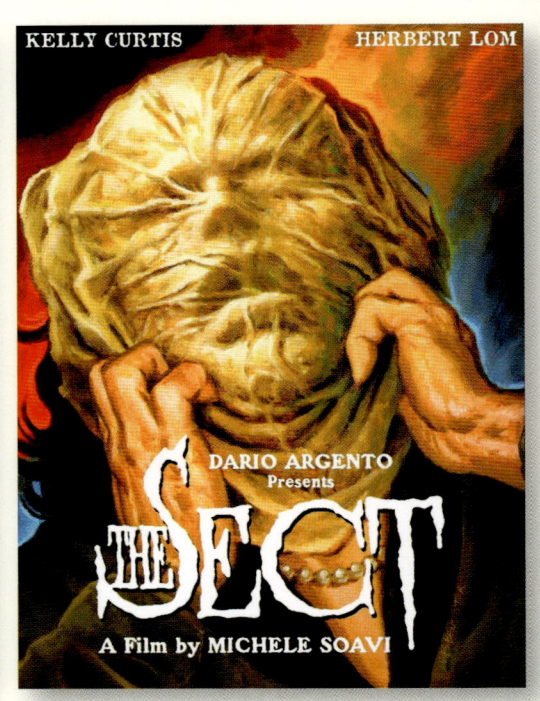

ABOVE LEFT: Enzo Sciotti's *locandina* for *A Cat in the Brain* (*Un gatto nel cervello*, 1990). Director Lucio Fulci's health was failing when he starred in this meta-horror film as a splatter movie director suffering from waking nightmares, whose problems are not helped by a crazed psychiatrist.

TOP MIDDLE: Enzo Sciotti (1944–2021) also did this poster for *Two Evil Eyes* (*Due occhi diabolici*, 1990), an Italian-American co-production that updated two classic tales by Edgar Allan Poe, directed by Dario Argento ("The Black Cat") and George A. Romero ("The Facts in the Case of M. Valdemar").

TOP RIGHT: Dario Argento co-scripted and produced Michele Soavi's *The Sect* (*La setta*, aka *The Devil's Daughter*, 1991). Herbert Lom played the mysterious leader of a Satanic cult that targets a young German schoolteacher (Kelly Curtis) who is destined to give birth to the Antichrist.

BOTTOM MIDDLE: Michele Soavi's *Cemetery Man* (*Dellamorte Dellamore*, 1994), starred British actor Rupert Everett as a cemetery caretaker who finds romance with a mysterious woman during a zombie outbreak. Martin Scorsese reportedly praised it as one of the best Italian movies of the '90s.

BOTTOM RIGHT: Japanese poster for Sergio Stivaletti's *The Wax Mask* (*M.D.C. Maschera di cera*, 1997). Loosely inspired by *House of Wax* (1953) and the work of Gaston Leroux, producer Dario Argento intended this film to be a comeback for co-writer Lucio Fulci, who died before filming began.

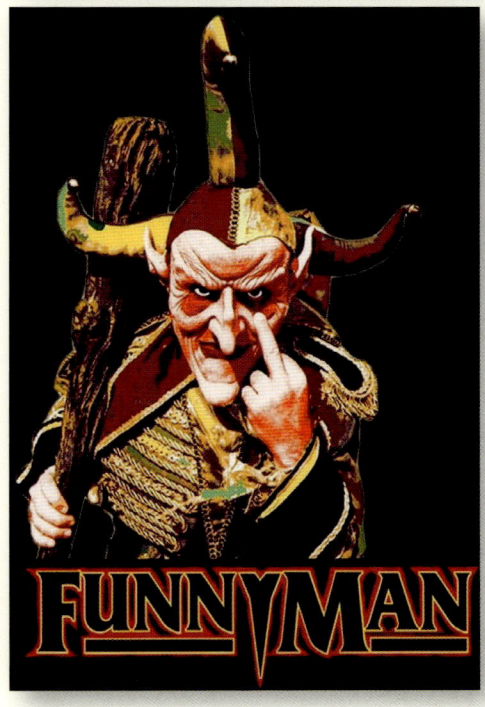

TOP LEFT: Shot in Spain, Juan Piquer Simón's *Cthulhu Mansion* (*La mansión de los Cthulhu*, 1991) had little to do with H.P. Lovecraft, as Frank Finlay's elderly magician and his daughter (Marcia Layton) are held captive by a gang of criminal teenagers in a house with powers of its own.

BOTTOM LEFT: Pinnacle Pictures' low-budget horror-comedy *Funny Man* (Dir: Simon Sprackling, 1994) benefited from Christopher Lee's cameo as the previous proprietor of an English stately home inhabited by a demonic jester (Tim James) who starts killing off the family of the new owner.

ABOVE RIGHT: Filmed on location around Europe, Hollywood Pictures' *An American Werewolf in Paris* (Dir: Anthony Waller, 1997) was a belated sequel to John Landis's 1981 original, in which Julie Delpy's suicidal lycanthrope turned out to be the daughter of the werewolf in the earlier movie.

THE NASTY NINETIES

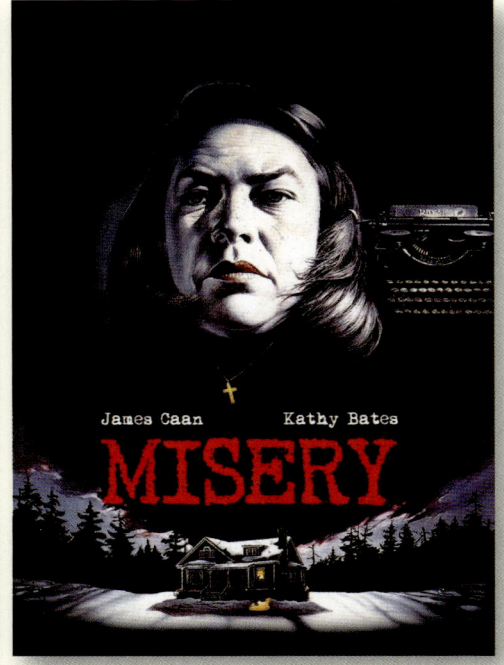

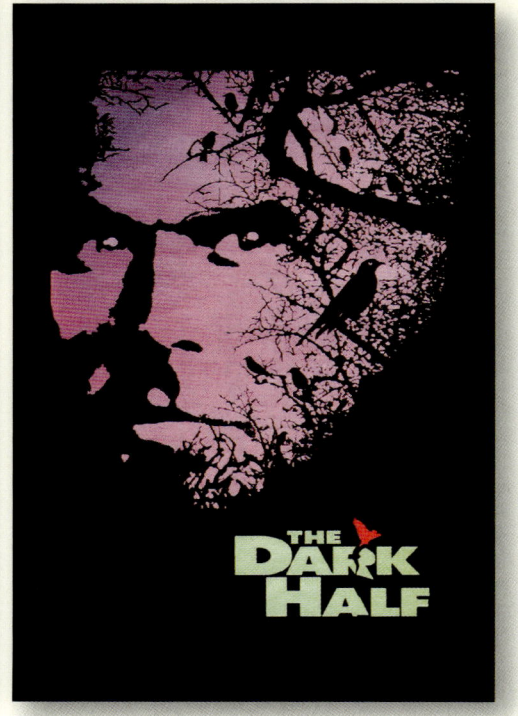

ABOVE LEFT: *Stephen King* (2011), digital portrait by French artist Jeff Stahl, produced for a caricature contest. "As a big fan of Stephen King, it was a lot of fun working on this piece," says the artist.

TOP RIGHT: German poster design for Columbia Pictures' *Misery* (Dir: Rob Reiner, 1990) by veteran Italian artist Renato Casaro (b. 1935). Based on the 1987 novel by Stephen King, Kathy Bates won the Best Actress Oscar for her role as the psychotic Annie Wilkes.

BOTTOM RIGHT: One-sheet poster design for Orion Pictures' *The Dark Half* (Dir: George A. Romero, 1993). Based on the 1989 autobiographical novel by Stephen King, the movie's release was delayed for two years.

THE ART OF HORROR MOVIES

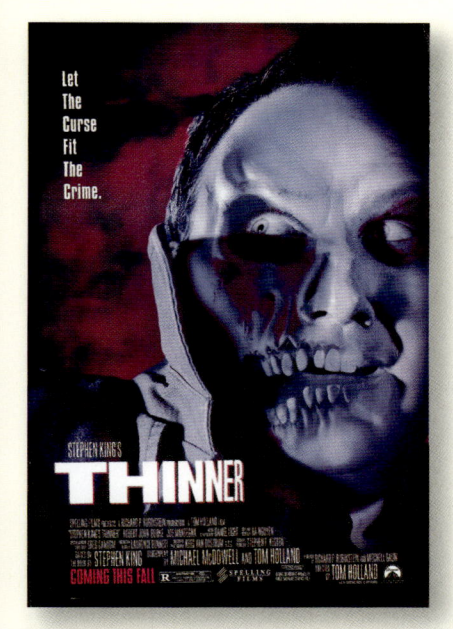

TOP LEFT: Pre-release poster for Paramount Pictures' *Thinner* (Dir: Tom Holland, 1996). Based on Stephen King's 1984 novel (published under his "Richard Bachman" pseudonym), the release was pushed back five months after it tested badly.

BOTTOM LEFT: One-sheet poster for United Artists' *The Rage: Carrie 2* (Dir: Katt Shea, 1999), a belated sequel to the 1976 movie which was based on Stephen King's first published novel in 1974.

ABOVE RIGHT: *Graveyard Shift* (1990), oils on hardboard by Les Edwards for the British quad poster [RIGHT] of the movie based on the 1970 Stephen King short story. "The art director wanted me to make the rats more and more cartoon-like," remembers the artist. "I resisted mightily, and fortunately we didn't actually come to blows."

THE NASTY NINETIES

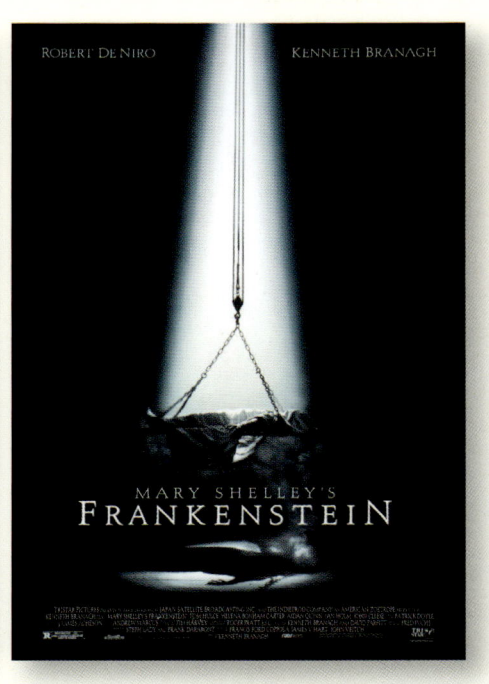

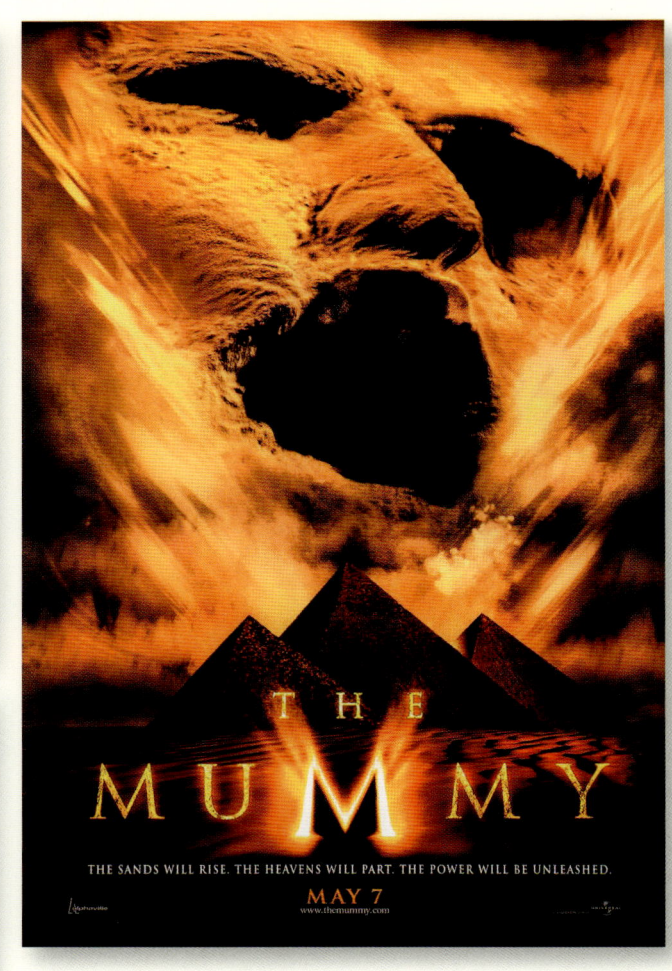

TOP LEFT: The 1990s were notable for Hollywood's big-budget regeneration of the classic monsters, beginning with Columbia Pictures' *Bram Stoker's Dracula* (Dir: Francis Ford Coppola, 1992). Despite the possessory credit, it was basically just an expensive reworking of Dan Curtis's 1974 TV movie.

TOP MIDDLE: Francis Ford Coppola went on to produce another possessory horror title—*Mary Shelley's Frankenstein* (1994)—for TriStar. Director Kenneth Branagh pulled double duty as Victor Frankenstein, while Robert De Niro brought Method to his portrayal of the tortured Creature.

BOTTOM LEFT: Although the Dr. Jekyll & Mr. Hyde story received a revisionist reboot with *Mary Reilly* in 1996, Jack Nicholson played the decade's most notable split personality in Columbia Pictures' *Wolf* (Dir: Mike Nichols, 1994), as his newly acquired lycanthropy brought out the animal in him.

BOTTOM MIDDLE: Roland Emmerich's $130 million re-imagining of *Godzilla* (1998) for TriStar Pictures was hardly an improvement over Toho's 1954 version. It also proved that no matter how expensive the CGI effects may be, they are sometimes no match for a man in a synthetic monster suit.

ABOVE RIGHT: Stephen Sommers rebooted Universal Pictures' *The Mummy* (1999) as an action-adventure franchise, while still paying homage to the story's horror origins. It was a box office hit that spawned two sequels (all starring Brendan Fraser as the archaeologist hero) and a five-movie spin-off series.

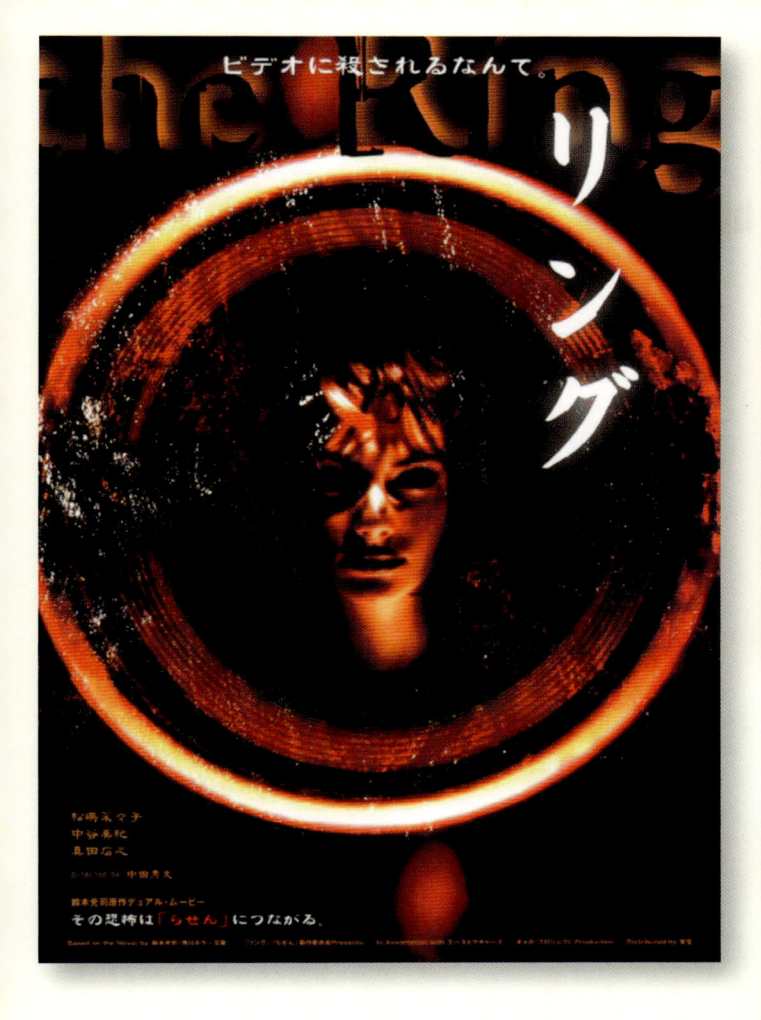

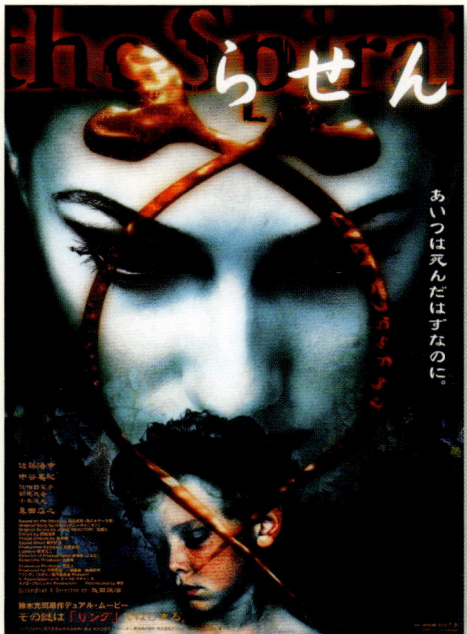

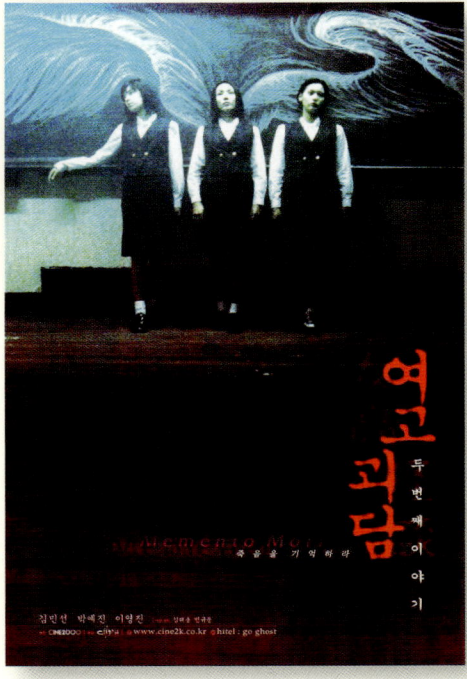

ABOVE LEFT: Rie Inō portrayed the creepy spirit of the girl-in-the-well who haunted a cursed video cassette in Hideo Nakata's influential *Ringu* (1998), based on the novel by Kōji Suzuki, which sparked a revival in Asian horror movies (and remakes) toward the end of the 1990s.

TOP MIDDLE: *Spiral* (*Rasen*, 1998), Jōji Iida's "forgotten" sequel to *Ringu*, was released in Japan at the same time, but did not do as well at the box office. Based more closely on the novel by Kōji Suzuki, Hinako Saeki took over the role of the vengeful spirit, Sadako Yamamura.

TOP RIGHT: Ki-hyeong Park's South Korean-made *Whispering Corridors* (*Yeogo goedam*, 1998) was set in a girls' school haunted by the malevolent spirit of a teenage suicide victim that attacks the members of staff. It spawned five in-name-only sequels and a 2019 Indonesian remake.

BOTTOM MIDDLE: South Korean directors Tae-yong Kim and Kyu-dong Min were forced by the producers to add ghosts to *Momento Mori* (*Yeogo goedam II*, 1999). The second entry in the connected-by-name only "Whispering Corridors" series revolved around a dead girl's strange diary.

BOTTOM RIGHT: Following the failure of *Spiral* (1998) at the Japanese box office, a replacement sequel to *Ringu* (1998) was hastily put together. *Ring 2* (*Ringu 2*, 1999) brought back director Hideo Nakata, screenwriter Hiroshi Takahashi, and Rie Inō as the vengeful spirit of Sadako.

THE NASTY NINETIES

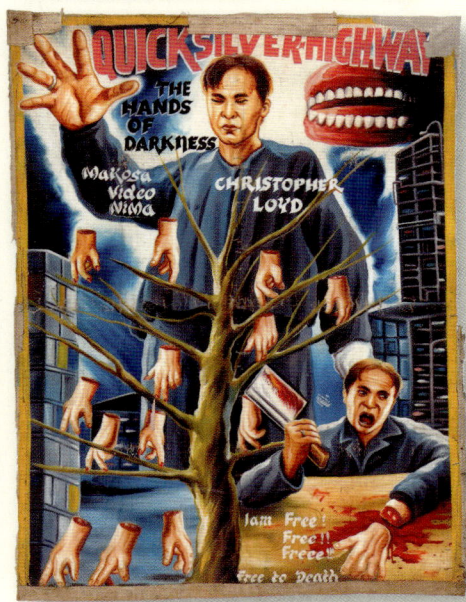

ABOVE LEFT: Hand-painted West African canvas flour-sack poster for a video screening of Dimension Films' *Hellraiser III: Hell on Earth* (Dir: Anthony Hickox, 1993), scripted by Peter Atkins and based on characters created by Clive Barker.

BOTTOM RIGHT: Split canvas sack poster for the Fox Network's TV movie *Quicksilver Highway* (Dir: Mick Garris, 1997), which adapted the 1985 short story "The Body Politic" by Clive Barker and Stephen King's 1992 story "Chattery Teeth."

TOP RIGHT: Ghanaian canvas sack poster for Twentieth Century Fox's *Nightbreed* (1990), based on the 1988 novella "Cabal," written by director Clive Barker.

OPPOSITE, BOTTOM LEFT: *Nightbreed* (1990), pencil on paper preliminary drawing by Les Edwards. "Clive hated the US poster for the movie," recalls Edwards, "so when it came to the UK version he suggested me."

OPPOSITE, TOP LEFT: *Nightbreed* (1990) oils on hardboard by Les Edwards. "The American poster represented the film as a 'slasher' movie," he explains. "A different approach was required for the UK. There are so many monsters in the film that I was spoiled for choice, although the real monster is actually David Cronenberg's Doctor Decker."

THE ART OF HORROR MOVIES

FAR RIGHT: *Swann, The Lord of Illusions* (2016), acrylic paint, colored pencils, and ink by American artist Douglas Klauba, produced as a limited edition poster by the Clive Barker Society. "My friend Kevin J. O'Connor, the actor who played the role of Swann in Clive Barker's 1995 movie, reprised his role in my studio to model for my painting," recalls the artist.

THE NASTY NINETIES

HIS NAME IS BRUCE

"I find it to be a very healthy, productive, one-with-the-universe-type thing to torment Bruce. And people love to watch his tormentation... they need to see him suffer. I think their entertainment is proportional to the amount of suffering Bruce does."

Sam Raimi

THE EXAGGERATEDLY SQUARE-JAWED handsomeness of Bruce Campbell (b. 1958) always made him look like a cartoon character sprung to life. It also earned him the nickname "The Chin"—*If Chins Could Kill! Confessions of a B Movie Actor* was the title of his 2002 autobiography.

One of his earliest acting gigs was in *Within the Woods* (1978), a horror short written and directed by friend and fellow Michigander Sam Raimi. It was used to raise backing for Raimi's low-budget feature debut, *The Evil Dead* (1981) in which Campbell played cult character Ashley J. Williams (popularly known as "Ash") for the first time. Ash is one of five college students whose weekend in an isolated cabin in the woods goes horribly wrong when they inadvertently summon demons that possess them one by one. Ash is forced to dismember his possessed friends in order to survive, but his own fate is left ambiguous.

Ash was brought back to battle demons all over again in *Evil Dead II* (1987)—part-remake, part-sequel, and just as splattery as the original, but with Campbell's aptitude for physical comedy and snappy one-liners now given free rein. In a slapstick (or "splatstick") *tour de force*, Ash is attacked by his own possessed hand and is forced to hack it off; afterward he fits a chainsaw to the stump for improved demon-battling capability.

In *Army of Darkness* (1992), Ash finds himself trapped in the Middle Ages, still fighting demons (or "Deadites" as they're now called) but exhibiting fresh levels of comic boorishness and forced to confront his own evil alter ego, "Bad Ash." Ash finally acquired equal title billing with his demonic foes in the TV series *Ash vs. Evil Dead* (2015–).

He is one of horror's most beloved characters, and a rarity among the genre's icons in that he's a hero (some of the time) rather than a monster. But—equally rare in a genre that tends toward one-dimensional archetypes—Ash has aged into a fully-realized character, a beer-bellied loser who refuses to grow up and is almost tragically devoid of self-awareness, with Campbell deftly piling on layers of stupidity and cynicism to make his demon-killing feats all the more entertaining.

Ash may be Campbell's signature role, but the actor is no one-trick pony. In the supernatural slasher movie *Maniac Cop* (1988), he played NYPD officer Jack Forrest; initially blamed for the murders, he survives the first film but gets stabbed through the neck in the 1990 sequel. He portrayed a sweet-natured descendant of legendary vampire-hunter Abraham Van Helsing in the horror comedy *Sundown: The Vampire in Retreat* (1989), and in *Bubba Ho-Tep* (2002) he gave a melancholy and rather moving performance as an aged Elvis Presley confronted by a soul-sucking Egyptian mummy.

In *Army of Darkness* (1992), Ash finds himself trapped in the Middle Ages, still fighting demons (or "Deadites" as they're now called) but exhibiting fresh levels of comic boorishness and forced to confront his own evil alter ego, "Bad Ash."

Campbell directed and starred in the horror comedies *Man with the Screaming Brain* (2005) and *My Name is Bruce* (2007); in the latter he appeared as a version of himself—a B-movie actor kidnapped by a fan who wants his help in driving a demon out of a small town in Oregon.

Campbell has worked extensively in television: he starred in *The Adventures of Brisco County, Jr.* (a Western with steampunk sci-fi elements, 1993–94), *and Jack of All Trades* (a *Wild Wild West*-style action-comedy about a nineteenth century secret agent, 2000). He had a recurring guest role (with dashing Douglas Fairbanks-style facial hair) as Autolycus, King of Thieves in *Hercules: The Legendary Journeys* (1995–99) and its sister show *Xena: Warrior Princess* (1996–99). Campbell's best-known non-genre work was his co-starring role in *Burn Notice* (2007–13) as Sam Axe, a slobby former Navy SEAL.

In a career bursting with B-movie greatness, the actor has also contributed memorable cameos to John Carpenter's *Escape from L.A.* (1996), Raimi's three *Spider-Man* movies (2002–07), assorted movies by the Coen Brothers, and—in an inspired piece of casting—played Ronald Reagan in the second season of the TV series *Fargo* (2015). AB

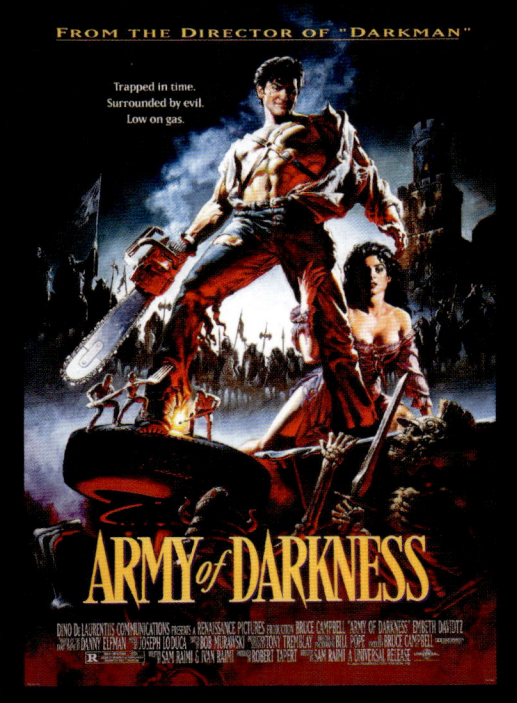

TOP LEFT: American one-sheet poster for Universal's second *Evil Dead* sequel *Army of Darkness* (Dir: Sam Raimi, 1992) by American artist Michael Hussar (b. 1964), clearly inspired by the work of Frank Frazetta.

BOTTOM LEFT: The surreal Japanese poster for *Army of Darkness* (1992) adapts Michael Hussar's key artwork for the movie that was re-titled *Kyaputen sûpâmâketto* (Captain Supermarket) in that country.

ABOVE RIGHT: *Ash* (2012), digital illustration by American artist Mark Hammermeister. "I painted this strictly for fun," he explains. "I've been a huge fan of the *Evil Dead* movies for many years. The colors were an experiment to create a mood that fit the insanity of the films."

THE NASTY NINETIES

ABOVE LEFT: *Edward Scissorhands* (2012), oils on canvas by Australian artist Nicky Barkla. "This artwork was inspired by the quote from the movie: 'I am not complete,'" explains the artist. "I painted Edward with a quirky kaleidoscopic hue to express the many colors of his character. He was never complete; there was much more to him than shades of black and white."

TOP RIGHT: *Edward Scissorhands* (2011), ink and watercolors on paper by Italian artist Roberto Ricci. "I created this drawing for 'The Movie Show' exhibition held at the Daniel Maghen Gallery in Paris, France (June–July, 2013)," recalls the artist. "The heart-shaped biscuit represents the love of the father towards his son. A father gone long ago, that Edward keeps holding with his scissor-hands."

BOTTOM RIGHT: One-sheet poster for Twentieth Century Fox's *Edward Scissorhands* (Dir: Tim Burton, 1990). Vincent Price made his final feature film appearance as the kindly inventor who dies before he can complete his creation, played by Johnny Depp.

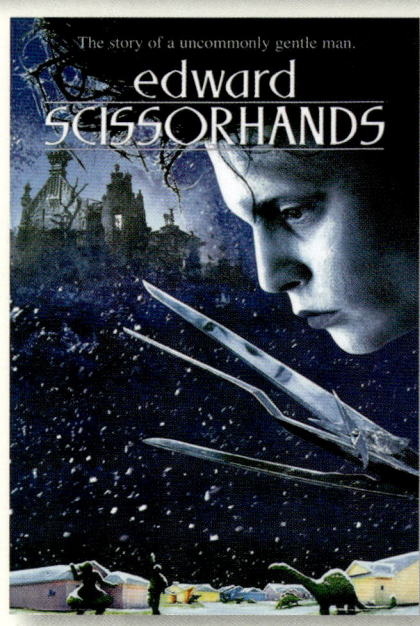

THE ART OF HORROR MOVIES

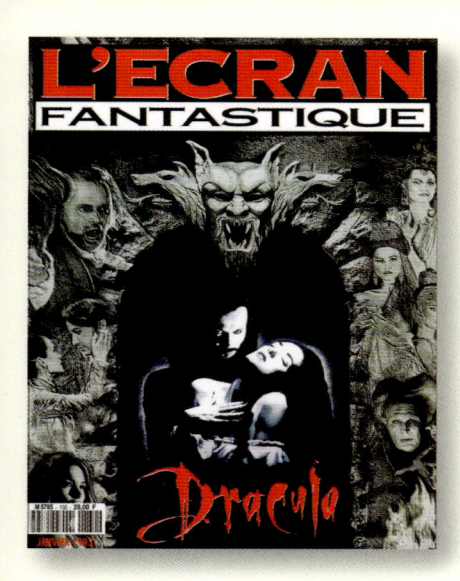

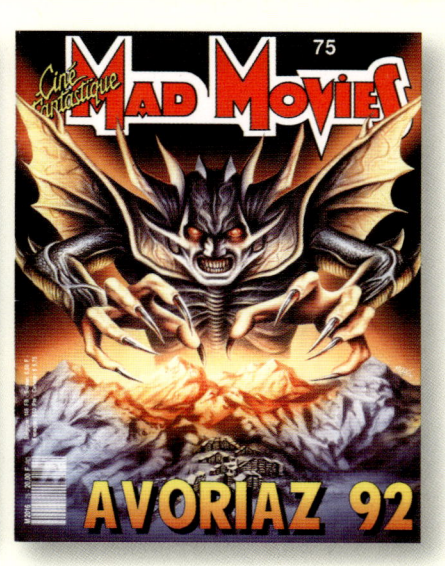

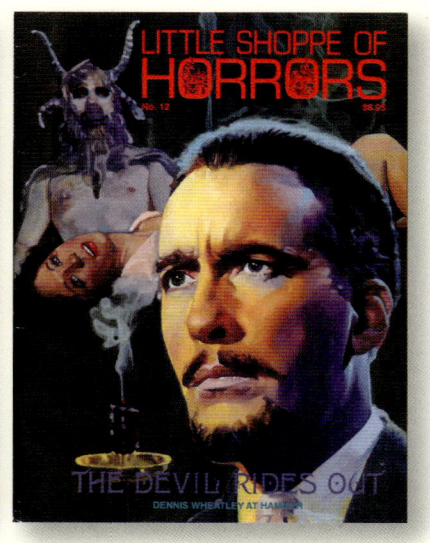

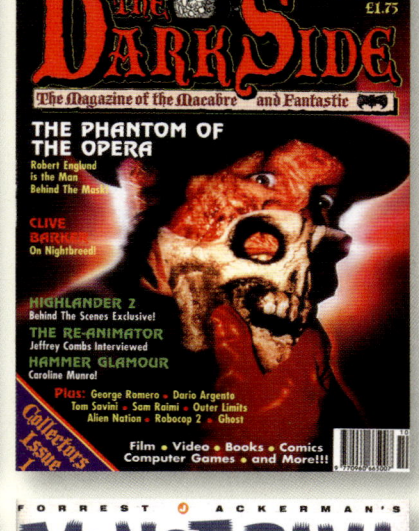

The Monster Kids Strike Back!

By the 1990s those "Monster Kids" who had grown up with the classic movie monster magazines over the previous three decades were now in a position to publish their own titles. *L'Ecran Fantastique* was actually founded as a French fanzine in 1969 by Alain Schlockoff, since when it has gone through multiple format changes. It was re-launched no less than four times during the early 1990s, eventually forcing Schlockoff to go off and create a new magazine, *Fantastyka*. Another French periodical, *Mad Movies*, was started by Jean-Pierre Putters as a fanzine in 1972. It went professional in the early 1980s, and celebrated its 300th issue in October 2016. Richard Klemensen founded his fanzine *Little Shoppe of Horrors* in 1972, shortly after his discharge from the US Army. Although published irregularly, by the time issue #12 appeared in 1994, with a cover of Christopher Lee from *The Devil Rides Out* by Steve Karchin, issues were regularly running over 100 pages. Allan Bryce launched *The Dark Side: The Magazine of the Macabre and Fantastic* in the UK in October 1990. Since then it has gone through a number of owners, but is still being published today. Visual Imagination's *Shivers* did not fare quite so well, despite a regular column by actress Ingrid Pitt, producing 138 issues between June 1992 and May 2008. Following the demise of *Famous Monsters of Filmland* in 1983 and his ill-fated involvement with *Monsterland* (1984–87), Forrest J Ackerman returned with *Monsterama* in Spring 1991. Unfortunately just one more issue appeared the following Spring. Co-publisher and Editor Stephen D. Smith launched *Monsterscene* in October 1992 and, from the second issue until it folded with #10 in 1997, regularly used acclaimed artist Basil Gogos on the cover. *Famous Monsters of Filmland* was revived in May 1993 with issue #200, featuring Kelly Freas's painting of reinstated editor Ackerman on the cover. The relationship didn't last long before Forry left the magazine and successfully sued its new publisher for breach of contract.

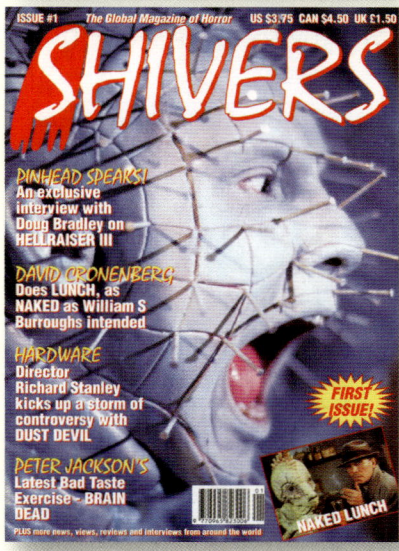

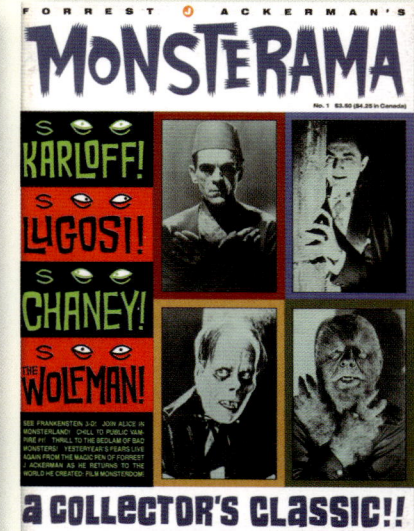

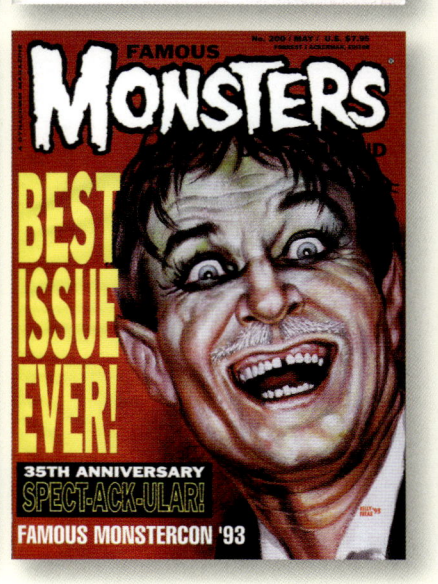

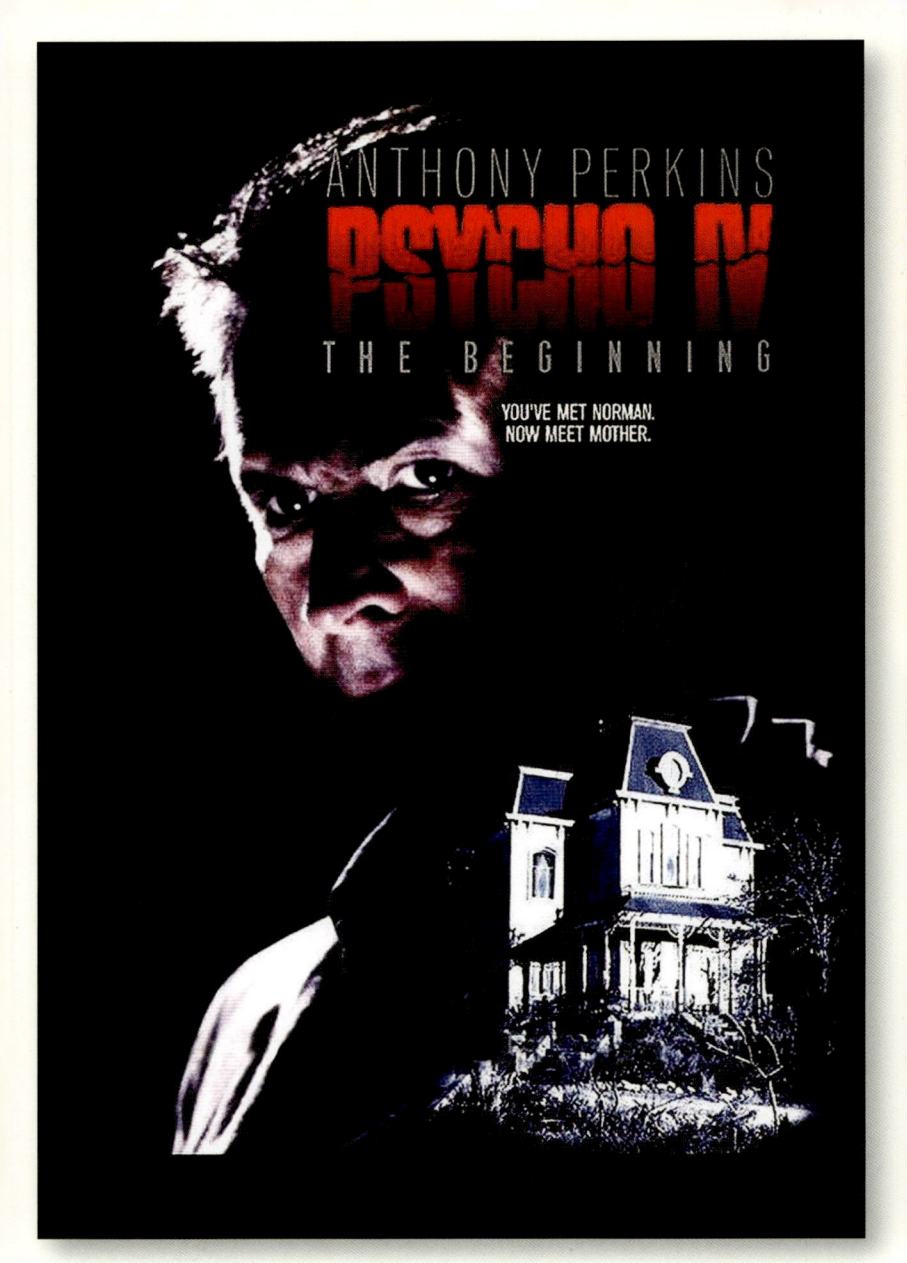

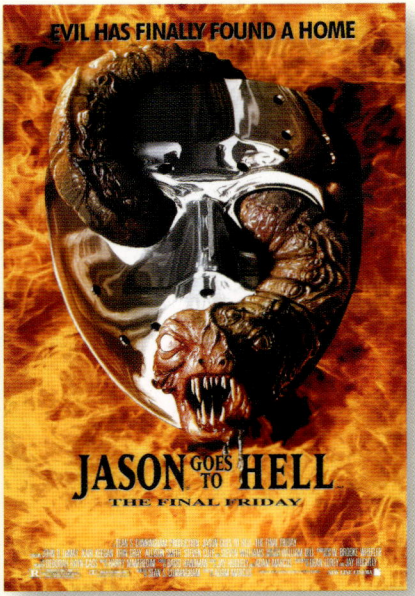

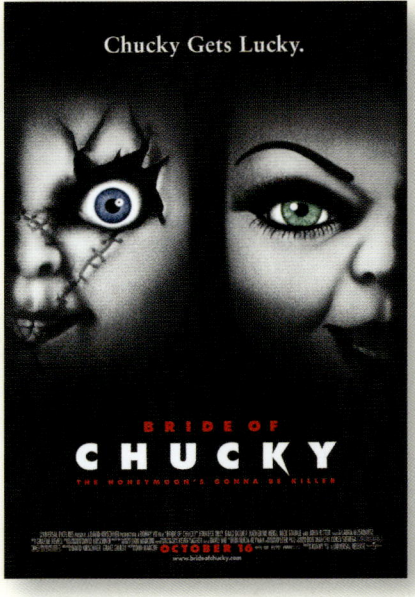

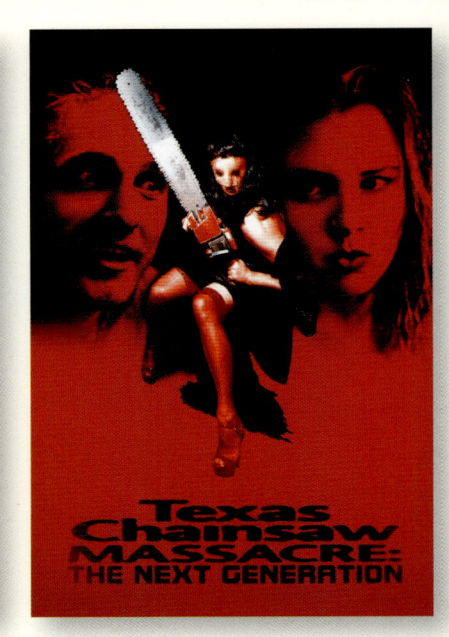

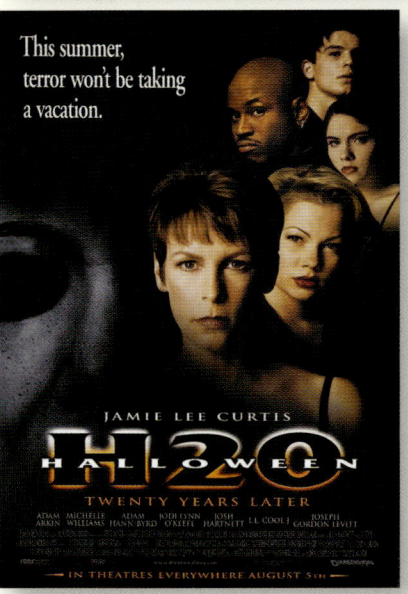

ABOVE LEFT: Anthony Perkins (1932–92) reprised his role as Norman Bates one final time for the Showtime Networks TV movie *Psycho IV: The Beginning* (Dir: Mick Garris, 1990).

TOP MIDDLE: Hockey-masked serial killer Jason Voorhees (Kane Hodder) encounters Freddy Krueger's glove at the climax of New Line Cinema's *Jason Goes to Hell: The Final Friday* (Dir: Adam Marcus, 1993), the eighth sequel to *Friday the 13th* (1980).

TOP RIGHT: Future stars Renée Zellwegger and Matthew McConaughey have to deal with Leatherface (Robert Jacks) and his cannibal family in New Line Cinema's *Texas Chainsaw Massacre: The Next Generation* (Dir: Kim Henkel, 1994).

BOTTOM MIDDLE: The murderous Chucky (voiced by Brad Dourif) finds a mate in mayhem with the bridal doll Tiffany (voiced by Jennifer Tilly) in Universal Pictures' third sequel, *Bride of Chucky* (Dir: Ronny Yu, 1998).

BOTTOM RIGHT: Jamie Lee Curtis returned as Laurie Strode to the series for the first time since *Halloween II* (1981) for Dimension Films' sequel/reboot *Halloween H20: 20 Years Later* (Dir: Steve Miner, 1998).

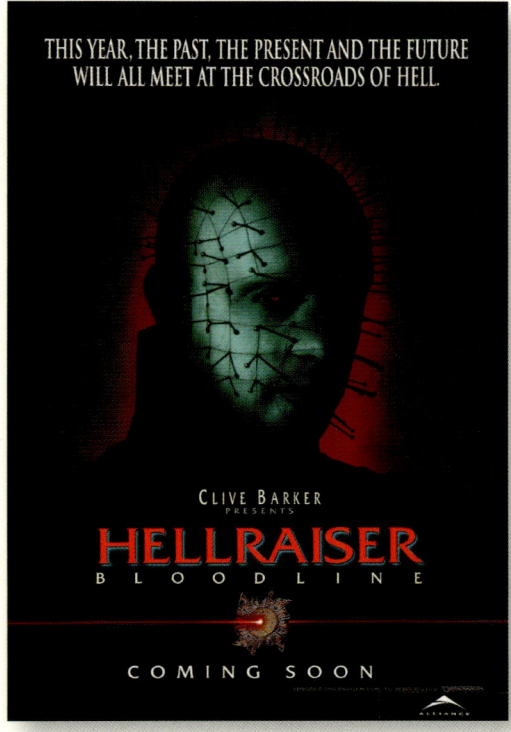

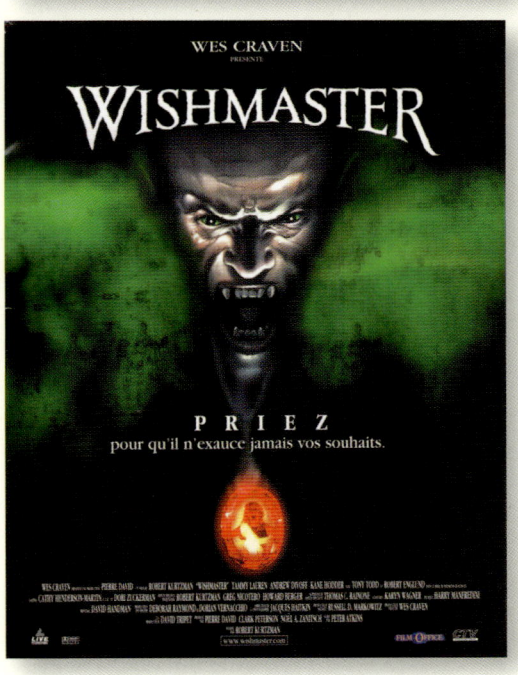

TOP LEFT: Scripted by Peter Atkins (b. 1955), Dimension Films' *Hellraiser Bloodline* (Dir: "Alan Smithee" aka Kevin Yagher, 1996), the third sequel to the 1987 original, takes the demonic Pinhead (Doug Bradley) into the twenty-second century.

BOTTOM LEFT: French *affiche* for Live Film & Mediaworks' *Wishmaster* (Dir: Robert Kurtzman, 1997), the first in the series about a demonic *djinn* (Andrew Divoff), created by British-born screenwriter Peter Atkins.

ABOVE RIGHT: *Peter Atkins* (2011), oils on canvas by Les Edwards. "This is a portrait of Peter Atkins with one of his creations keeping an eye on him," explains the artist. "It was done as a private commission, but was eventually used on the cover of a collection of Atkins's stories, *Rumours of the Marvellous* (2011)."

THE NASTY NINETIES

— 271 —

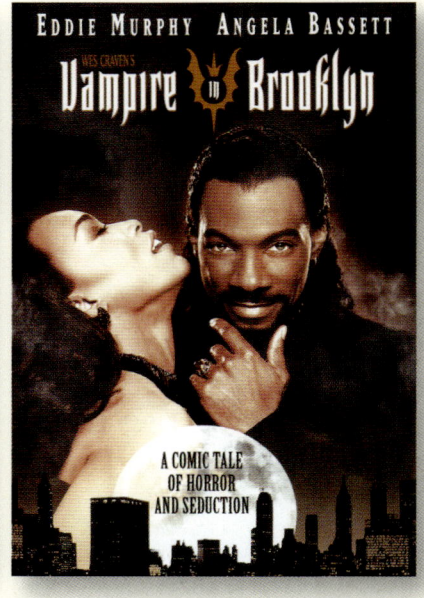

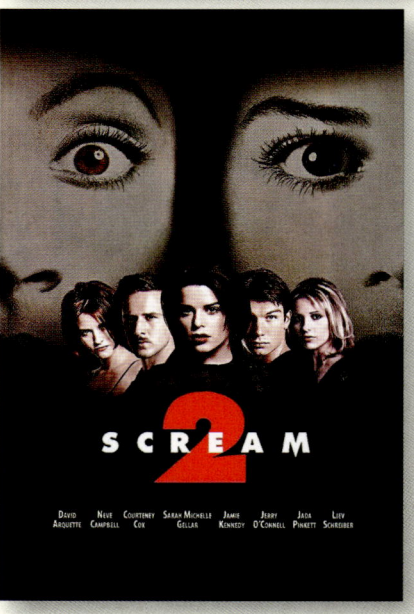

TOP LEFT: A trio of burglars find more than they expected in a suburban home in Universal Pictures' *The People Under the Stairs* (Dir: Wes Craven, 1991).

TOP MIDDLE: Eddie Murphy's bloodsucker goes looking for a mate in the Big Apple in Paramount Pictures' horror-comedy *Vampire in Brooklyn* (Dir: Wes Craven, 1995).

BOTTOM LEFT: A group of friends are menaced by a know-it-all serial killer in Dimension Films' *Scream* (Dir: Wes Craven, 1996), which reinvented the "slasher" genre.

BOTTOM MIDDLE: Another "Ghostface" serial killer menaces the survivors of the first movie in Dimension Film's sequel, *Scream 2* (Dir: Wes Craven, 1997).

ABOVE RIGHT: Freddy Krueger turns up in the real world to menace his creator and actors from the movie series in New Line Cinema's meta-sequel/reboot *Wes Craven's New Nightmare* (Dir: Wes Craven, 1994).

Reinventing the Genre

After a strict Baptist upbringing in Ohio, Wes [Wesley Earl] Craven (1939–2015) made his official directing debut with *The Last House on the Left* (1972), a grim rape-revenge drama loosely inspired by Ingmar Bergman's *The Virgin Spring* (1960) that he also wrote and edited. His second film, *The Hills Have Eyes* (1977), was a key entry in the psycho hillbilly subgenre. He added a supernatural element to "slasher" movies with *A Nightmare on Elm Street* (1984), gave it a meta-twist in *Wes Craven's New Nightmare* (1994), and reinvented the "slasher" subgenre yet again with *Scream* (1996). His other notable horror films include *Deadly Blessing* (1981), *Swamp Thing* (1982), *The Serpent and the Rainbow* (1988), *Shocker* (1989), *The People Under the Stairs* (1991), *Vampire in Brooklyn* (1995), and *Cursed* (2005). AB

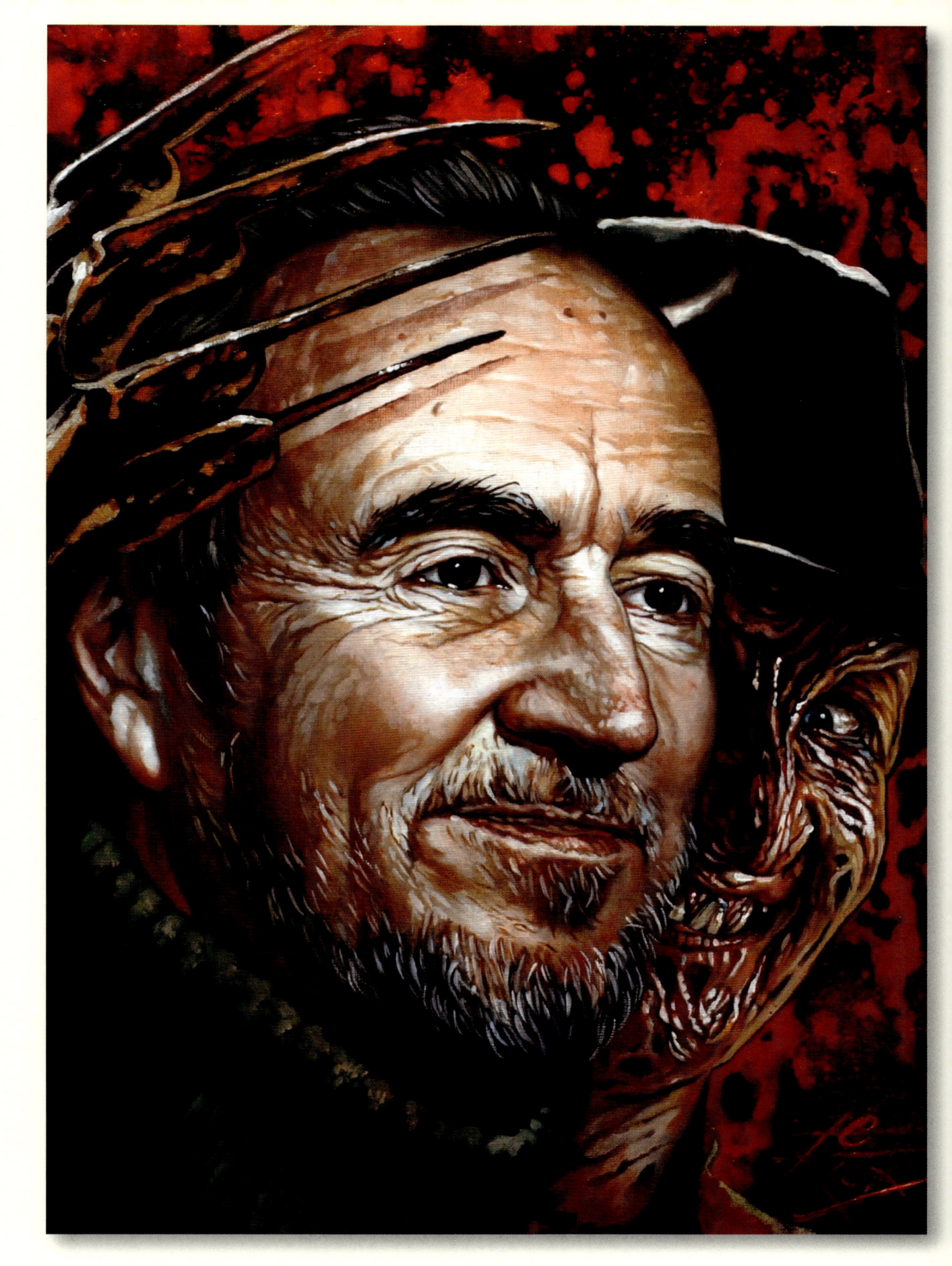

RIGHT: *Wes Craven* (2015), oils on board by British artist Rick Melton. "This was done as a magazine cover for *The Dark Side* #70," he reveals, "as a tribute to Wes Craven. Sadly I didn't read the job description properly—I was asked to make Freddy Krueger the main character, as the publishers thought casual browsers might not recognize Wes. D'oh!"

THE NASTY NINETIES

— 273 —

LEFT: *The Stendhal Syndrome* (2012), handmade silkscreen poster based on the 1996 movie, created by the Italian art collective Malleus Rock Art Lab. "This is one of a series of nine movie posters from Dark City Gallery celebrating the key films of Dario Argento," they explain. "We tried to represent the duality of the human mind."

Women in Horror: 1990s

Karen Black (1939–2013) was nominated for an Oscar in the early 1970s, but by the end of the decade was soon appearing in horror movies, a genre that she would eventually become most associated with thanks to such titles as *Haunting Fear* (1990) and *Aunt Lee's Meat Pies* (1992). Dee Wallace (b. 1948) also began acting in the '70s in films such as *The Hills Have Eyes* (1977), and has made a career out of playing strong matriarchal characters in movies like *I'm Dangerous Tonight* (1991) and *The Frighteners* (1996). Kristy Swanson (b. 1969) was the screen's first *Buffy the Vampire Slayer* (1992) and also appeared in *Deadly Friend* (1986) and *Highway to Hell* (1991) before personal problems temporarily derailed her career, while wild child Italian actress Asia Argento (b. 1975) starred in her father Dario's *Trauma* (1993), *The Stendhal Syndrome* (1996), and *The Phantom of the Opera* (1998).

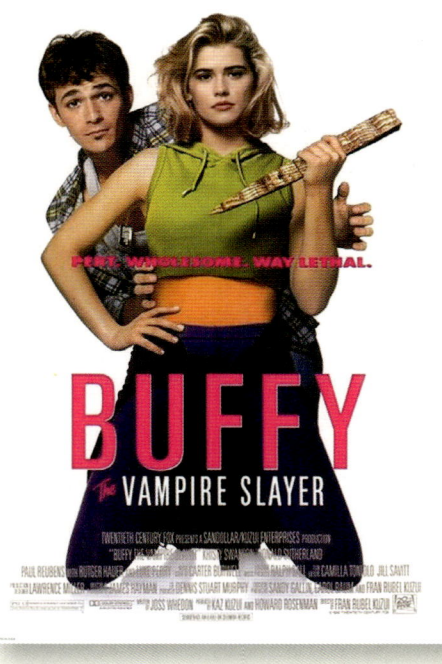

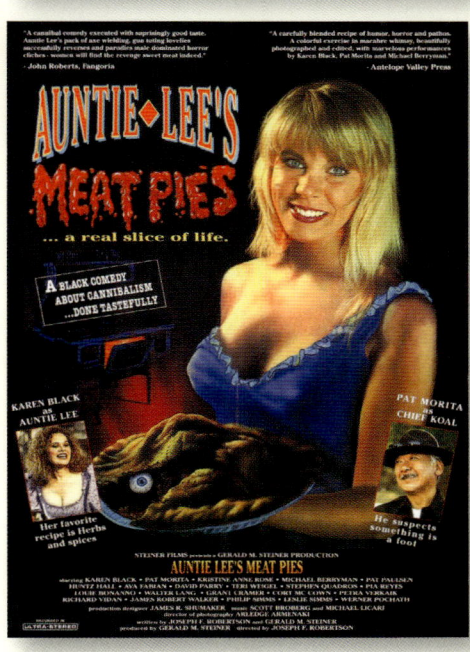

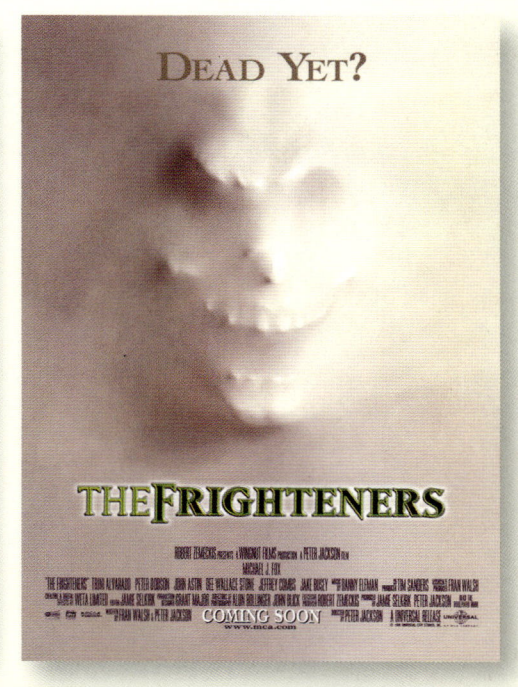

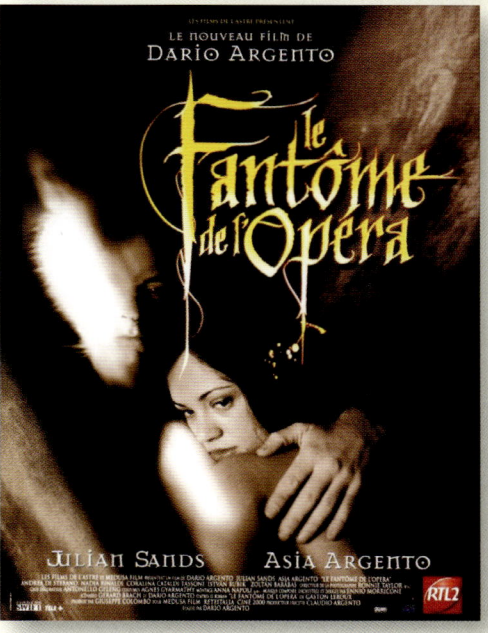

ABOVE LEFT: Original acrylic on board poster concept for *Highway to Hell* (Dir: Ate de Jong, 1991), one of two unused designs by American artist Frank Kelly Freas inspired by the tagline "The cops on this road don't take you to jail— they take you to Hell."

TOP MIDDLE: Before the 1997–2003 TV series starring Sarah Michelle Gellar, Kristy Swanson played the eponymous teenage slayer created by Joss Whedon in Twentieth Century Fox's *Buffy the Vampire Slayer* (Dir: Fran Rubel Kuzui, 1992).

TOP RIGHT: Michael J. Fox's ghost-buster can communicate with the dead in Universal Pictures' horror-comedy *The Frighteners* (Dir: Peter Jackson, 1996), filmed in New Zealand.

BOTTOM MIDDLE: Karen Black's devil worshipper used her seductive nieces to procure victims in Trans World Entertainment's horror-comedy *Aunt Lee's Meat Pies* (Dir: Joseph F. Robertson, 1992), which also featured Michael Berryman and Huntz Hall.

BOTTOM RIGHT: 1999 French *affiche* for Dario Argento's Italian version of *The Phantom of the Opera* (*Il fantasma dell'opera*, 1998), which didn't even bother to mask its Phantom (Julian Sands).

THE NASTY NINETIES

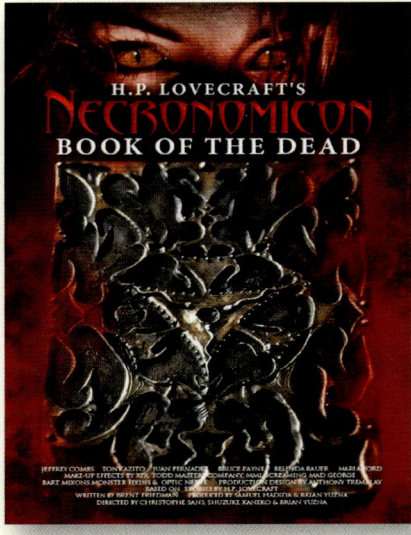

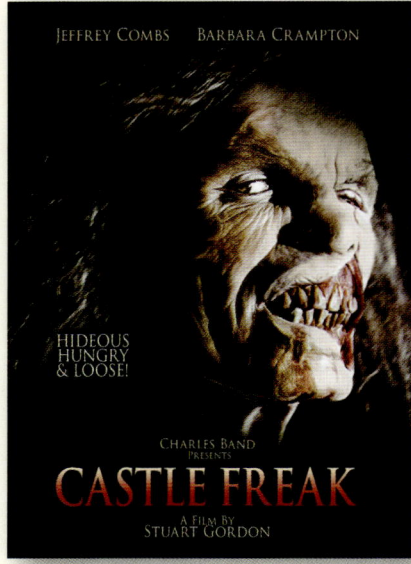

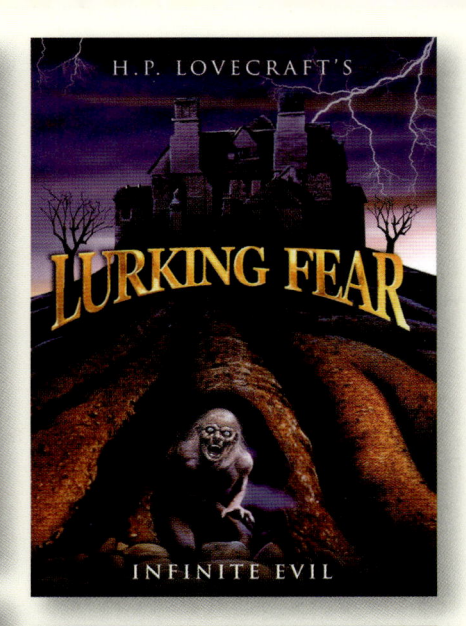

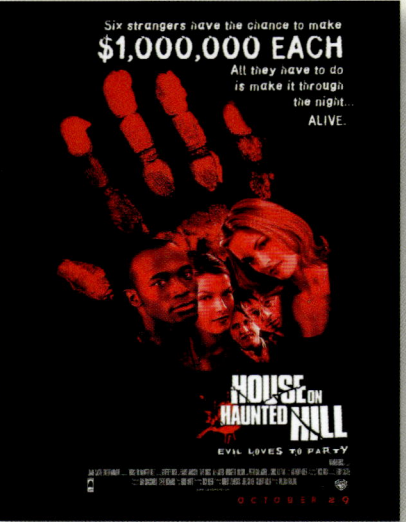

The Consummate Character Actor

Whether starring in direct-to-video titles such as *The Pit and the Pendulum* (1991) and *Doctor Mordrid* (1992), or appearing under makeup as various aliens in the *Star Trek* TV franchise, Jeffrey [Alan] Combs (b. 1954) is the consummate character actor. Along with his signature breakthrough role as Herbert West, a scientist obsessed with reviving the dead, in the H.P. Lovecraft-inspired *Re-Animator* (1985), *Bride of Re-Animator* (1989), and *Beyond Re-Animator* (2003), he portrayed the author himself for the anthology movie *Necronomicon: Book of the Dead* (1993) and turned up in other H.P.L. adaptations such as *From Beyond* (1986), "The Evil Clergyman" sequence in *Pulse Pounders* (1988), *Lurking Fear* (1994), *Castle Freak* (1995), and *The Dunwich Horror* (2009). As well as headlining low-budget films, Combs also provides strong support in such mainstream horror movies as *The Frighteners* (1996), *I Still Know What You Did Last Summer* (1998), and *House on Haunted Hill* (1999).

ABOVE LEFT: Full Moon Entertainment's *The Pit and the Pendulum* (Dir: Stuart Gordon, 1991) returned Edgar Allan Poe's 1842 story to its Spanish Inquisition setting, with Lance Henriksen as the torturer Torquemada.

TOP MIDDLE: Jeffrey Combs portrayed author H.P. Lovecraft himself in the wraparound segment of August Entertainment's anthology movie *Necronomicon: Book of the Dead* (Dir: Christophe Gans, Shûsuke Kaneko, and Brian Yuzna, 1993), which consisted of three Lovecraftian stories.

TOP RIGHT: Full Moon Entertainment's *Lurking Fear* (Dir: C. Courtney Joyner, 1994) was supposedly based on the 1923 short story by H.P. Lovecraft, as a group of townsfolk are attacked by ghouls.

BOTTOM MIDDLE: Apparently based on H.P. Lovecraft's 1926 story "The Outsider," Full Moon Entertainment's *Castle Freak* (Dir: Stuart Gordon, 1995) was filmed in Italy.

BOTTOM RIGHT: Warner Bros.' *House on Haunted Hill* (Dir: William Malone, 1999) was a remake of William Castle's 1959 movie starring Vincent Price, and the first of several horror remakes produced by Dark Castle Entertainment.

RIGHT: *Herbert West: Re-Animator* (2010), digital print by American artist Christopher Jones. "I was already a fan of the film when I got to draw the official comic book adaptation for it back in the day," he recalls. "I was really happy with how this turned out."

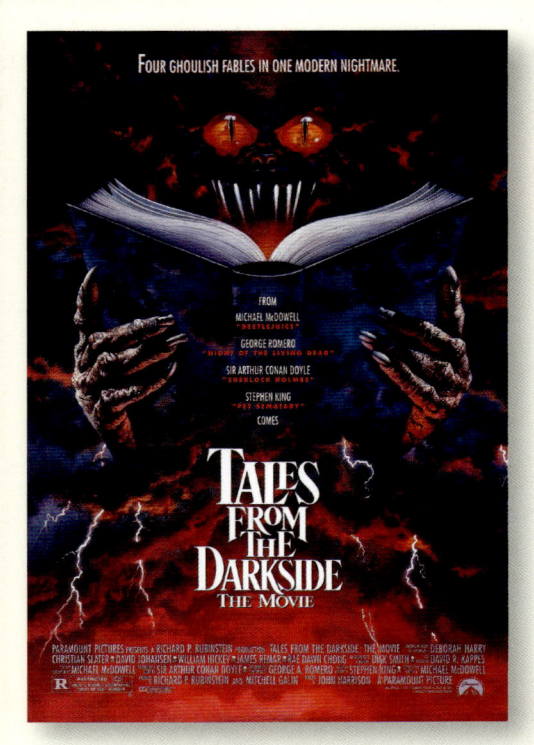

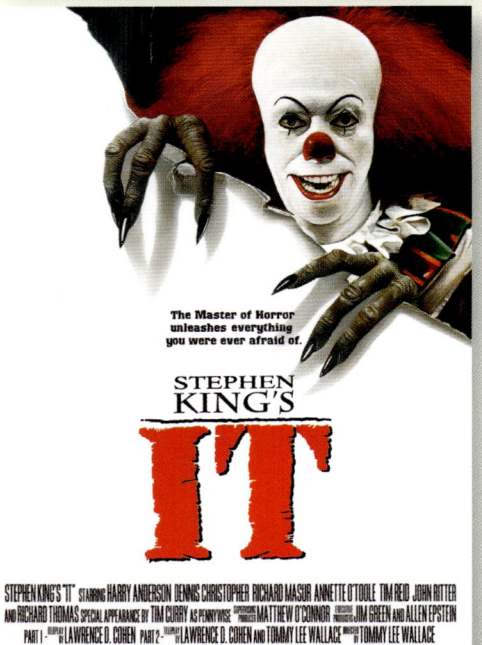

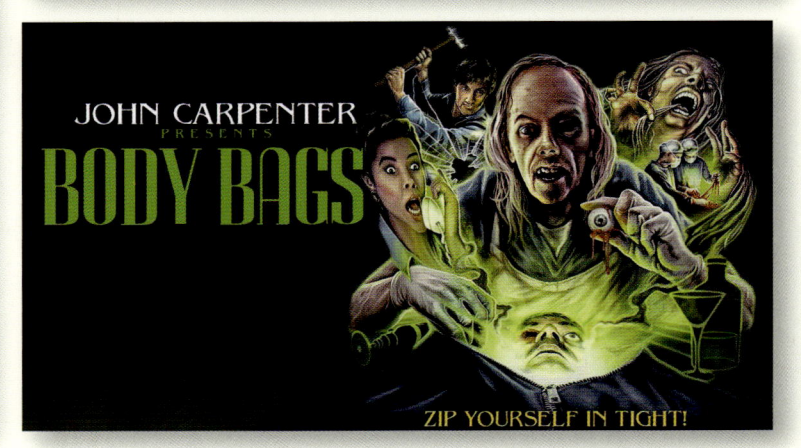

TOP LEFT: American one-sheet poster for Paramount Pictures' anthology film *Tales from the Darkside: The Movie* (Dir: John Harrison, 1990), inspired by Laurel Entertainment's 1983–88 syndicated TV series. It adapted stories by Michael McDowell, Sir Arthur Conan Doyle, and Stephen King.

BOTTOM LEFT: Initially broadcast by ABC-TV as a two-part miniseries in November 1990, Tommy Lee Wallace's *IT* was based on the 1986 novel by Stephen King. 30 million viewers tuned in over the two-night premiere, making it the network's highest-rated show of the year.

BOTTOM RIGHT: John Carpenter and Tobe Hooper not only directed, but also starred alongside fellow directors Wes Craven, Sam Raimi, and Roger Corman in the anthology movie *Body Bags* (1993) for Showtime Networks. It was supposed to be the pilot for a proposed series that never happened.

TOP RIGHT: NBC's *House of Frankenstein* (Dir: Peter Werner) was a two-part TV miniseries broadcast in November 1997 that revived the Universal franchise. While investigating a series of murders, Adrian Pasdar's LAPD detective encountered a werewolf, a vampire, and Frankenstein's Monster.

OPPOSITE: *Dr. Giggles* (2017), gouache on watercolor paper. "My job was to present this rather silly 1992 film's horror credentials to a new audience," explains artist Graham Humphreys. "The German distributor was unhappy with my choice of colour scheme, but this version is the original."

THE ART OF HORROR MOVIES

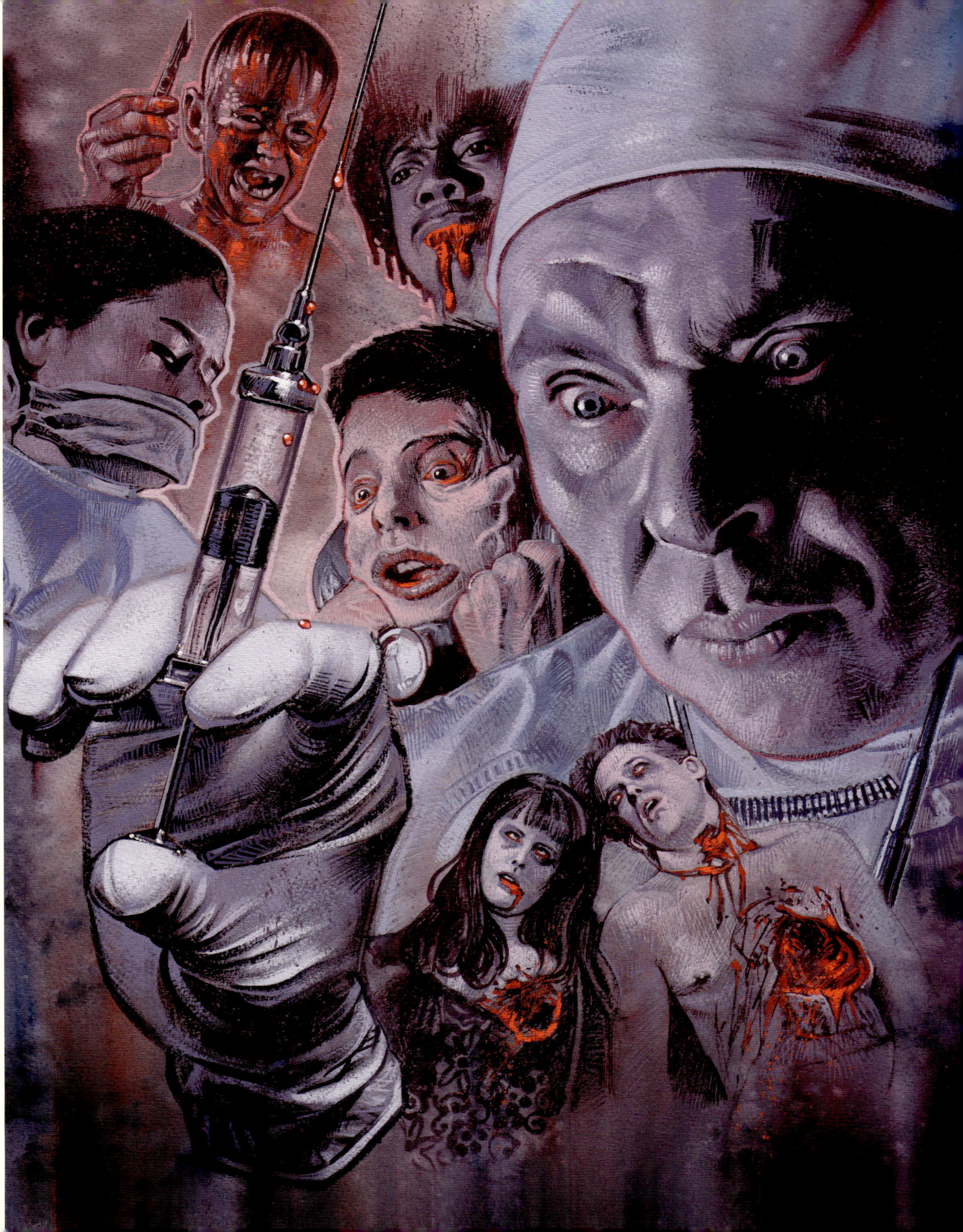

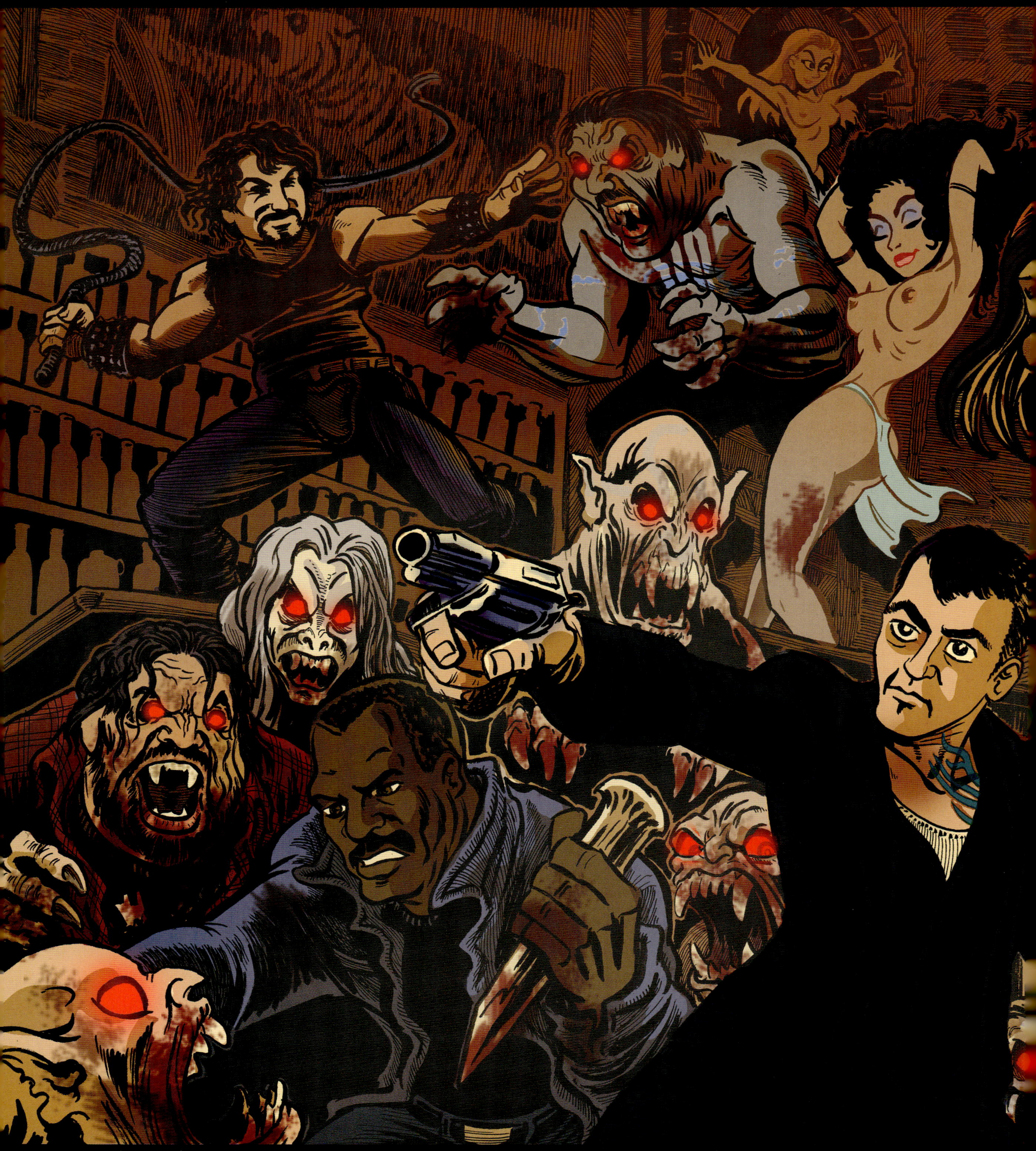

LEFT: *From Dusk Till Dawn* (2007), pen and ink drawing with digital coloring by American artist Bryan Baugh. "This was a private commission for one of my customers, who wanted to see my rendition of the movie," he explains. "The fun thing about this illustration was capturing the likenesses of the actors, as they slaughter all those hideous, bloodthirsty vampires."

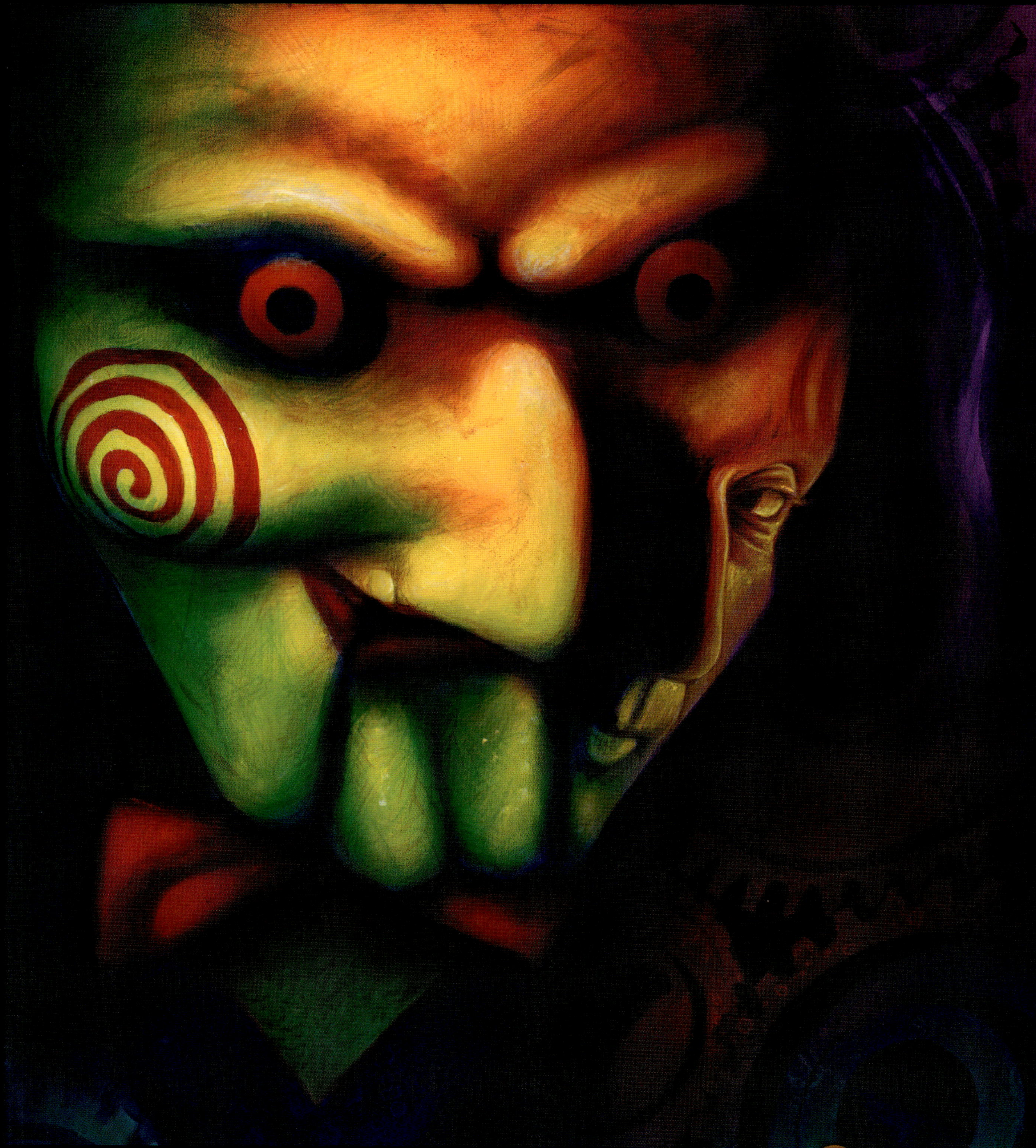

9
THE 2000s MANIACS

RAMSEY CAMPBELL

"Robert Pattinson should not take back Kristen Stewart.
She cheated on him like a dog & will do it again
—just watch. He can do much better!"

DONALD TRUMP

> "Good grief, we're getting offended by everything these days! People can't say anything without offending somebody."
> Hillary Clinton

THIS CENTURY SAW the rise of the horror film disguised as documentary, often "found footage." Although the trend began with *The Blair Witch Project* (1999), it really starts in prose with Edgar Allan Poe's "The Facts in the Case of M. Valdemar" (1845). Examples... *Lake Mungo* (2008) is an unusually restrained uncanny tale somewhat undermined by an irrelevant plot device. *The Last Exorcism* (2010) follows a fake exorcist as he ministers to the faithful, only to find he may be too incredulous himself. Two British films featuring psychic investigators—*The Casebook of Eddie Brewer* (2012) and *The Borderlands* (aka *Final Prayer*, 2013)—also confound skeptical characters to powerful effect, and the end of *The Borderlands* is gruesomely Lovecraftian.

Megan is Missing (2011) is a relentless cautionary tale about online grooming. *Creep* (2014) makes the documentarist himself the victim of a chilling plot. The Norwegian *Troll Hunter* (2010) balances humor and genuine monstrousness, while the Spanish *[Rec]* (2007) records a zombie epidemic in a Barcelona tenement and finds worse in the attic.

Apollo 18 (2011) brings back footage from a lunar expedition that reveals the existence of alien life (not unlike the film salvaged from the spaceship in *The Quatermass Xperiment*, 1955). In *Cloverfield* (2008) the characters use their phones to film a monstrous takeover of New York. *Cloverfield* is an extreme example of handheld filming, unwatchable by some.

V/H/S (2012) and *Hate Crime* (2012) take the tendency further, with little regard for the audience's viewing experience. *Sinister* (2012) is an effective variation on the basic form, in which a crime writer moves his family into a house where murder was committed, only to find more footage than he welcomes.

In *Final Destination* (2000) and its sequels Death (never seen) kills victims in set pieces increasingly close to silent slapstick. *Saw* (2004) developed into an elaborately constructed narrative, made up of eight feature films to date. *Hostel* (2005) and its sequels chronicle torture as recreation, which became a genre in itself. *Paranormal Activity* (2007) led to several sequels in which concealed cameras track a demon from family to haunted family.

It has also been a century for remakes. *Dawn of the Dead* (2004) is a slick but honorable reworking, while *The Texas Chainsaw Massacre* (2003) revives the relentlessness of the original. Though sometimes cited as a remake, *The Thing* (2011) is an effective prelude to John Carpenter's 1982 film. In 2009 *Friday the 13th* rose again from the lake. *Scream 3* (2000) and *Scream 4* (2011) had ingenious fun with "slasher" tropes. *Evil Dead* (2013) recalls the gruesomeness but not the humor of the original.

French horror came to the fore with a clinical yet confrontational treatment of erotic cannibalism, *Trouble Every Day* (2001), the ruthlessly grueling *Irréversible* (2002), and *Martyrs* (2008), the nightmare comedies *Calvaire* (2004) and—featuring Vincent Cassel as a man and his wife—*Sheitan* (2006), the suspenseful *High Tension* (2003) and *Them* (2006), the gleefully excessive *Inside* (2007), and the gory poetry of *Livid* (2011). *Caché* (2005) is by far the subtlest of the Gallic entries, and rewards repeated viewing. The Belgian co-production *Amer* (2009) refines *giallo* horror almost to abstraction.

From Sweden came *Let the Right One In* (2008), reinventing and reinvigorating the vampire film. Spanish horror included *The Orphanage* (2007), a psychological ghost story, while *Darkness* (2002) and *Fragile* (2005) involve ghostly children too.

Effective Japanese horrors of the period include *Spiral* (2000) where reality is deformed by a supernatural force; *Pulse* (2001), a paranoid vision of the afterlife; the atmospheric urban ghost story *Dark Water* (2002); the ruthlessly frightening *Ju-on: The Grudge* (2002) and its sequel. *Anime* produced Satoshi Kon's *Paprika* (2006), in which dreams and reality grow indistinguishable.

Korea's finest contributions were *A Tale of Two Sisters* (2003), an elaborate interleaving of the psychological and spectral; *The Eye* (2002), where a cornea transplant brings ghostly visions; *Into the Mirror* (2003), an inventive supernatural tale full of reflections; *The Host* (2006), a monster film enlivened by typically Korean shifts of tone.

Serbia was represented by the notoriously but defensibly excessive *A Serbian Film* (2010). Israel released two offbeat exercises in the macabre, *Rabies* (2010) and *Big Bad Wolves* (2013). Australia ranged from the gloating *Wolf Creek* (2005) to the supernatural metaphor of *The Babadook* (2014). Denmark released the bleak and confrontational *Antichrist* (2009), and Norway gave us *The Monitor* (aka *Babycall*, 2011), a psychological horror film that turns spectral—a trope also present in the American *Frailty* (2001) and the Irish-French co-production *Dorothy* (aka *Dorothy Mills*, 2008).

PREVIOUS SPREAD: *Want to Play a Game?* (2015), acrylic on canvas by American artist Scott Spillman, inspired by the *Saw* franchise. "I'm self-taught when it comes to the drawing and painting," he reveals.

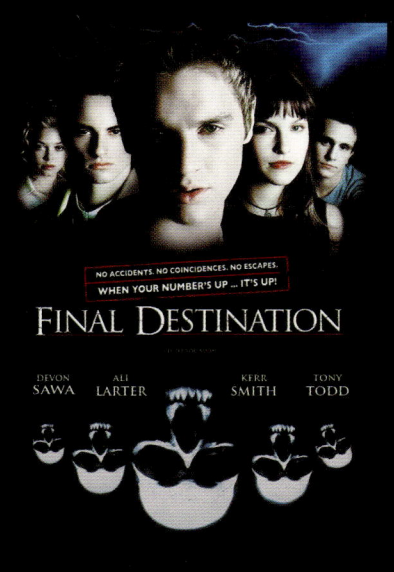

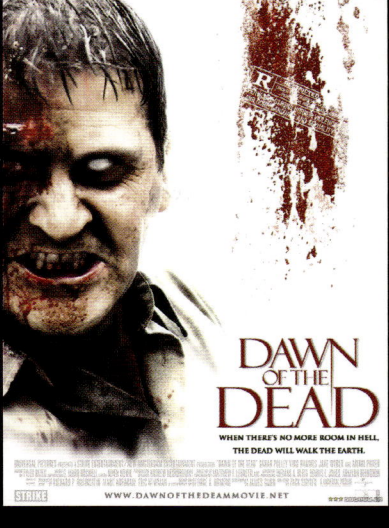

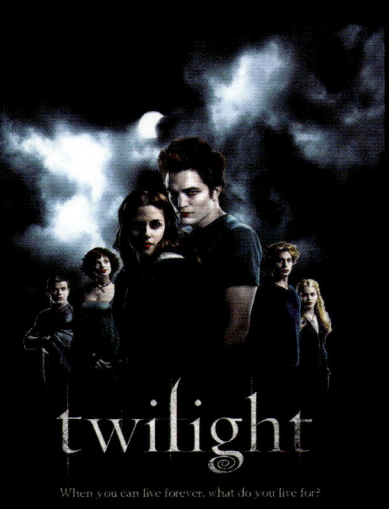

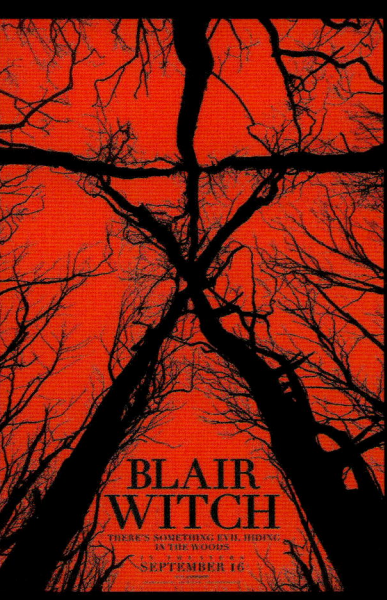

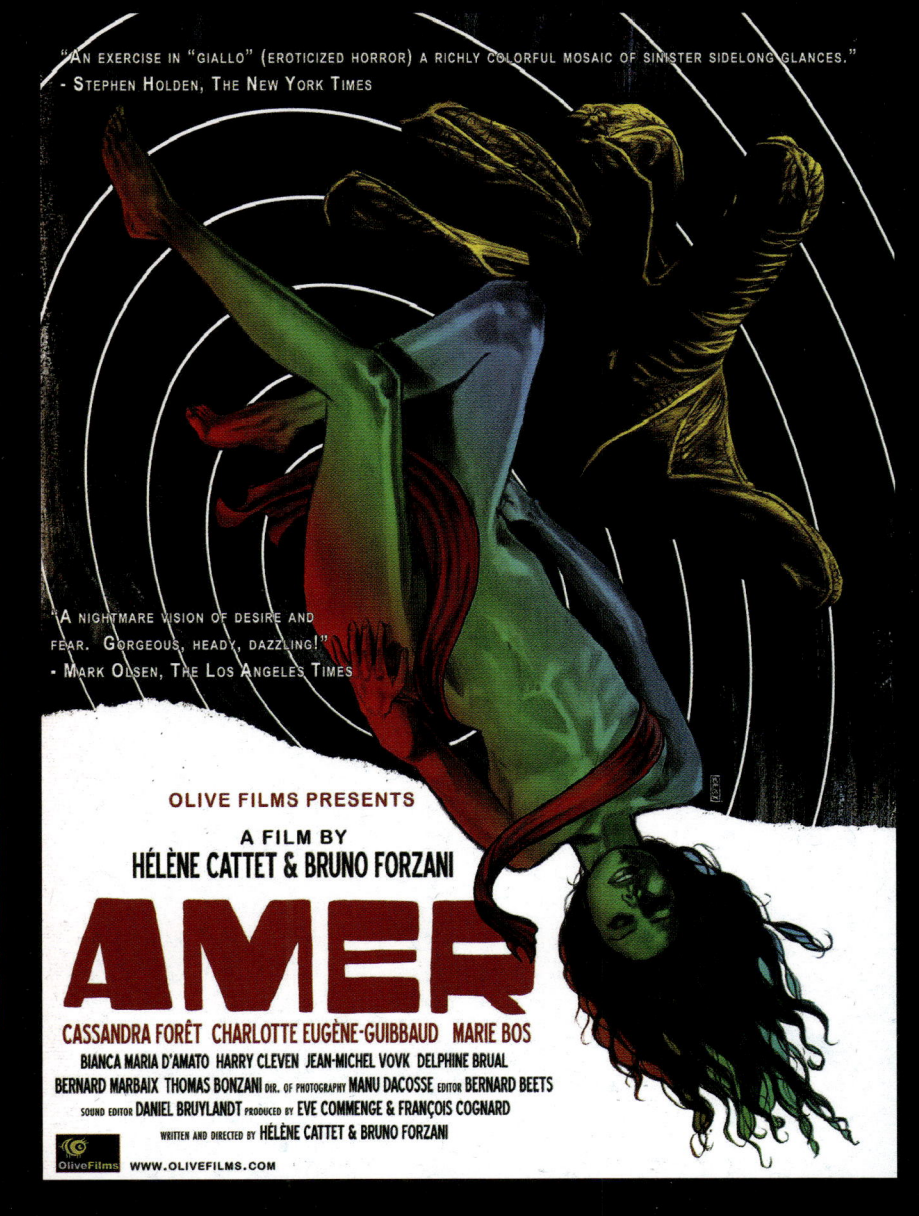

TOP LEFT: When a group of friends survive a plane crash, Death hunts them down in New Line Cinema's *Final Destination* (Dir: James Wong, 2000), the first in a successful horror movie franchise that began life as a proposed episode of TV's *The X Files*.

TOP MIDDLE: One-sheet poster for Universal Pictures' *Dawn of the Dead* (Zack Snyder, 2004), a remake of co-writer George A. Romero's 1978 zombie sequel.

BOTTOM LEFT: Kristen Stewart's Bella was torn between her romantic feelings for Robert Pattinson's vampire and Taylor Lautner's werewolf in Summit Entertainment's *Twilight* (Dir: Catherine Hardwicke, 2008), based on the series of young adult books by Stephenie Meyer.

BOTTOM MIDDLE: The "stickman" image is not so subtle on Lionsgate's pre-release one-sheet poster for *Blair Witch* (Dir: Adam Wingard, 2016), a belated second sequel/remake of the "found footage" phenomenon *The Blair Witch Project* (1999).

ABOVE RIGHT: Retro-style poster for Olive Films' 1970s *giallo* pastiche *Amer* (Dir: Hélène Cattet and Bruno Forzani, 2009), by Belgian artist Gilles Vranckx (b. 1975). The movie was a homage to the films of Dario Argento and Mario Bava.

THE 2000s MANIACS

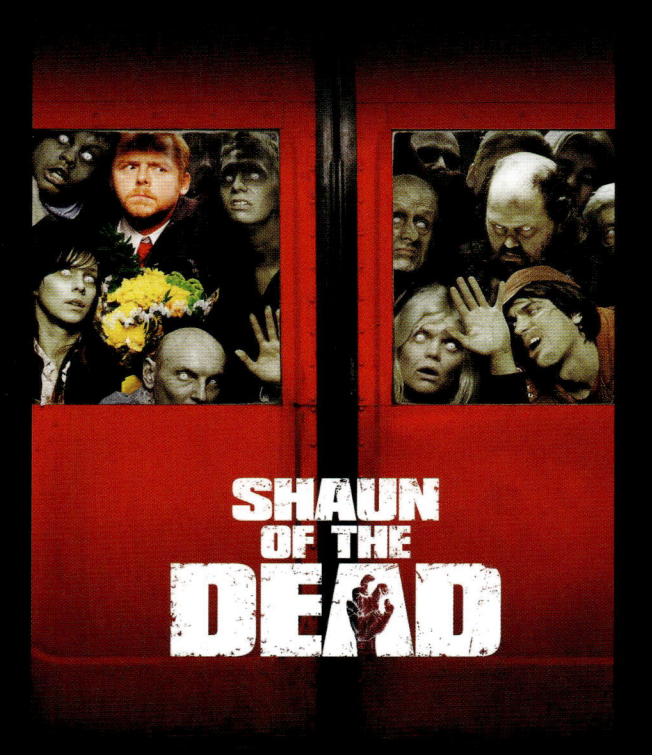

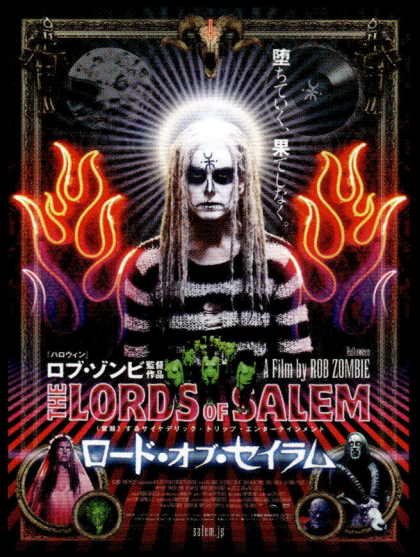

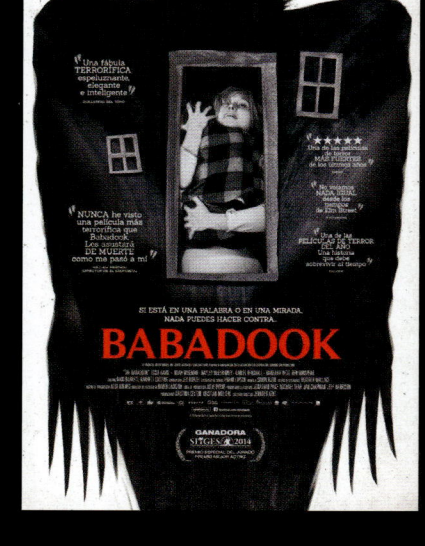

TOP LEFT: Clever pre-release poster designed by Creative Partnership for Universal Pictures' *Shaun of the Dead* (Dir: Edgar Wright, 2004), billed as "A romantic comedy. With zombies."

TOP RIGHT: British quad poster for the original Swedish version of *Let the Right One In* (*Låt den rätte komma in*, 2008), directed by Tomas Alfredson and based on John Ajvide Lindqvist's 2004 revisionist vampire novel.

BOTTOM LEFT: Striking German poster design for director Huan Vu's *The Color Out of Space* (*Die Farbe*, 2010), based on the 1927 short story by H.P. Lovecraft and set in the mid-1970s.

BOTTOM MIDDLE, LEFT: Japanese poster by graphic designer Yoshiki Takahashi (b. 1969) for Alliance's *The Lords of Salem* (Dir: Rob Zombie, 2012), which featured a host of veteran genre actors.

BOTTOM MIDDLE, RIGHT: French *affiche* based on the key design by American advertising agency Iconisus L&Y for Relativity Media's *Oculus* (Dir: Mike Flanagan, 2013), about a cursed antique mirror.

THE ART OF HORROR MOVIES

From Sweden came *Let the Right One In* (2008), reinventing and reinvigorating the vampire film. Spanish horror included *The Orphanage* (2007), a psychological ghost story, while *Darkness* (2002) and *Fragile* (2005) involve ghostly children too.

Elsewhere other traditional motifs were given new life. *30 Days of Night* (2007) looses feral vampires in protracted Alaskan darkness. While *The Wolfman* (2010) is an atmospheric tribute to the Universal Studios original (and best watched in the uncut version), *Ginger Snaps* (2000) developed lycanthropy as a symbol of adolescence (specifically, a female variation on *I Was a Teenage Werewolf* from the 1950s). *Dorian Gray* (2009) might almost be the Hammer film that studio neglected to make. Bernard Rose's

> Comedy overlaps with horror in *Shaun of the Dead* (2004), the satirical *Seed of Chucky* (2004), the suspenseful *Housebound* (2014), and the likeably deranged *The Voices* (2014). *Bubba Ho-Tep* (2002) captures the anarchic glee of Joe R. Lansdale's original tale.

Frankenstein (2015) reworks the Karloff original in gruesomely contemporary fashion. *The Human Centipede (First Sequence)* (2009) re-conceives the mad scientist in scatological terms. *The Descent* (2005) and *The Burrowers* (2008) concern degenerate humanoids living underground. *Bone Tomahawk* (2015) reinvents the horror Western.

In *The Children* (2008)—an intelligent treatment of the evil child motif—an unspecified infection turns children malevolent. In *Eden Lake* (2008) savage teenagers are the monsters, often disconcertingly human. *Mum & Dad* (2008) involves a peculiarly British monstrous family, frightening because banal. Realistic banality also underlies *Tony* (2009), a portrait of homicidal mania, and *A Horrible Way to Die* (2010), in which a serial killer attracts fans, not to mention *Snowtown* (aka *The Snowtown Murders*, 2011), where vigilantism gives its homophobic killers an excuse for their sadism. *Maniac* (2012) traps us behind the killer's eyes. *The Girl Next Door* (2007) is a troubling analysis of complicity in child abuse.

Psychic investigators figure in *Insidious* (2010) and its sequels, all of which show a flair for the uncanny image, as well as *The Conjuring* (2013). Ghosts show up delicately in *The Others* (2001), more aggressively in *The Woman in Black* (2012), and open a gateway to nightmare in *1408* (2007). Satanism proves vital in Rob Zombie's *The Lords of Salem* (2012)—which develops the occult images glimpsed in the same director's *Halloween II* (2009)—and in the somber revelations of *The Witch* (2015).

OPPOSITE, BOTTOM RIGHT: Spanish poster based on the key design for the Australian movie *The Babadook* (Dir: Jennifer Kent, 2014), in which a single mother tries to protect her young son from a storybook monster.

Effective films were based on tales by H.P. Lovecraft. *The Call of Cthulhu* (2005) and *The Whisperer in Darkness* (2011) are amateur in the best sense yet thoroughly professional. *Dagon* (2001) and the German *The Color Out of Space* (2011) capture Lovecraftian atmosphere too. *The Mist* (2007) brings Stephen King's monstrous siege to a cosmic conclusion.

More domestic terrors—specifically, home invasion—are central to the austere *Funny Games* (2007), as well as the witty *You're Next* (2011) and the gripping Spanish *Kidnapped* (2010). Insanity underlies the haunted asylum of *Session 9* (2001) and the inhospitable hospitals of *Shutter Island* (2010) and *Stonehearst Asylum* (2014), the crowded consciousnesses of *Identity* (2003) and *The Ward* (2010), and the lyrical nightmare of *Black Swan* (2010), not to mention the paranoid vision of *Anomalisa* (2015).

Comedy overlaps with horror in *Shaun of the Dead* (2004), the satirical *Seed of Chucky* (2004), the suspenseful *Housebound* (2014), and the likeably deranged *The Voices* (2014). *Bubba Ho-Tep* (2002) captures the anarchic glee of Joe R. Lansdale's original tale, and *The Cabin in the Woods* (2012) frolics through horror all the way to the cosmic. *Drag Me to Hell* (2009) rediscovers the vigorous excess of Sam Raimi's early work. *Tusk* (2014), planned as a horror comedy, ends up surprisingly poignant, and *Nina Forever* (2015) derives dark comedy as well as pathos from a stubborn revenant. *Grand Piano* (2013) is simultaneously thrilling and hilarious. The New Zealand *What We Do in the Shadows* (2014) is an amusingly straight-faced romp through vampirism.

Horror films engaging with contemporary developments include *My Little Eye* (2002) and *Unfriended* (2014), which find terror online. In the understated *Toad Road* (2012) drug use may open a path to Hell.

Science fiction generates horror in the extravagant *Prometheus* (2012), the invisible menace of *Hollow Man* (2000), the inexorably paradoxical *Triangle* (2009), the verbal virus of *Pontypool* (2008), the monstrous products of DNA experiments in *Splice* (2009), and the enigmatic alien invasion of *Under the Skin* (2013).

In *Jeepers Creepers* (2001) a serial killer proves to be literally inhuman. The dread pursuer in *It Follows* (2014) is conjured up by sex. In *Absentia* (2011) the uncanny inhabits an underpass, in *Oculus* (2013) an antique mirror. *Valhalla Rising* (2009) is a mystical journey into terror, *The Neon Demon* (2016) fashions horror from the fashion business. *Mulholland Drive* (2001) and *Inland Empire* (2006) convey the uncanny with insidious directness. *Kill List* (2011) has a hit man's mission ending in folk myth, territory *A Field in England* (2013) appears to inhabit. *Spring* (2014) is an unexpectedly touching monstrous romance.

That's by no means an exhaustive list, but these films and many other of this century demonstrate that horror movies can still disturb and surprise us. I believe they always will.

THE 2000s MANIACS

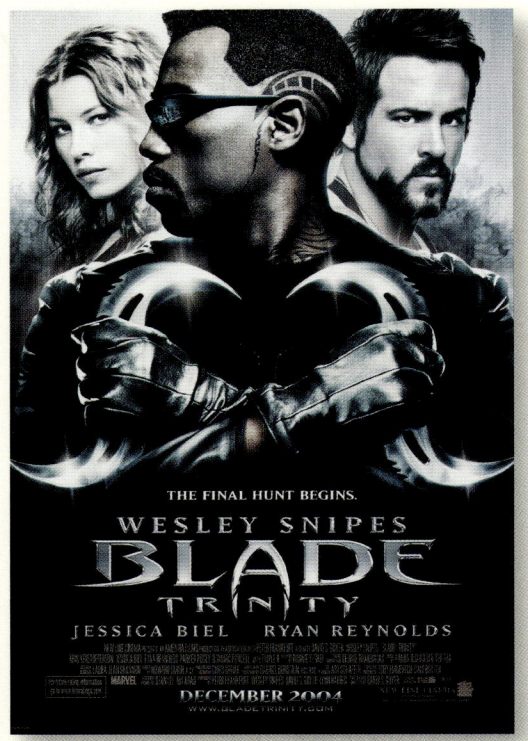

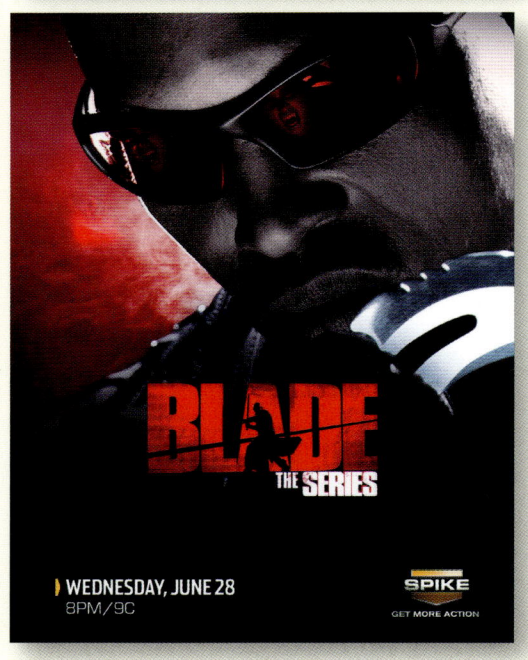

THIS PAGE: Created by writer Marv Wolfman and artist Gene Colan, hybrid half-human half-vampire hunter Blade made his debut as a supporting character in Marvel Comics' *The Tomb of Dracula* #10 (July, 1973). Since then, he has been featured in various other Marvel titles, along with issues of his own eponymous comics from 1994 onwards. After the character (voiced by J.D. Hall) appeared in episodes of the 1994–98 animated TV series *Spider-Man*, Wesley Snipes starred in New Line Cinema's *Blade* (Dir: Stephen Norrington, 1998). It was Marvel's first black superhero movie and the company's first box office success.

ABOVE LEFT: Stephen Norrington reportedly turned down directing the sequel, so Guillermo Del Toro was brought in to helm New Line Cinema's *Blade II* (2002), the highest-grossing entry in the trilogy. Wesley Snipes returned as the half-vampire "Daywalker," as did Kris Kristofferson as his human mentor, Abraham Whistler.

TOP RIGHT: David S. Goyer, who had written the first two movies, also took over the direction of New Line Cinema's troubled *Blade: Trinity* (2004). Wesley Snipes's human-vampire hybrid teamed up with Jessica Biel and Ryan Reynolds's vampire hunters, while Dominic Purcell portrayed a revived Dracula.

BOTTOM RIGHT: Co-created by David S. Goyer and taking place after the events in *Blade: Trinity*, *Blade: The Series* aired as a two-hour pilot and 11 weekly episodes on Spike TV in 2006. Rapper Kirk "Sticky Fingaz" Jones starred as Blade. Marvel Entertainment regained the movie rights to the character in 2012.

THE ART OF HORROR MOVIES

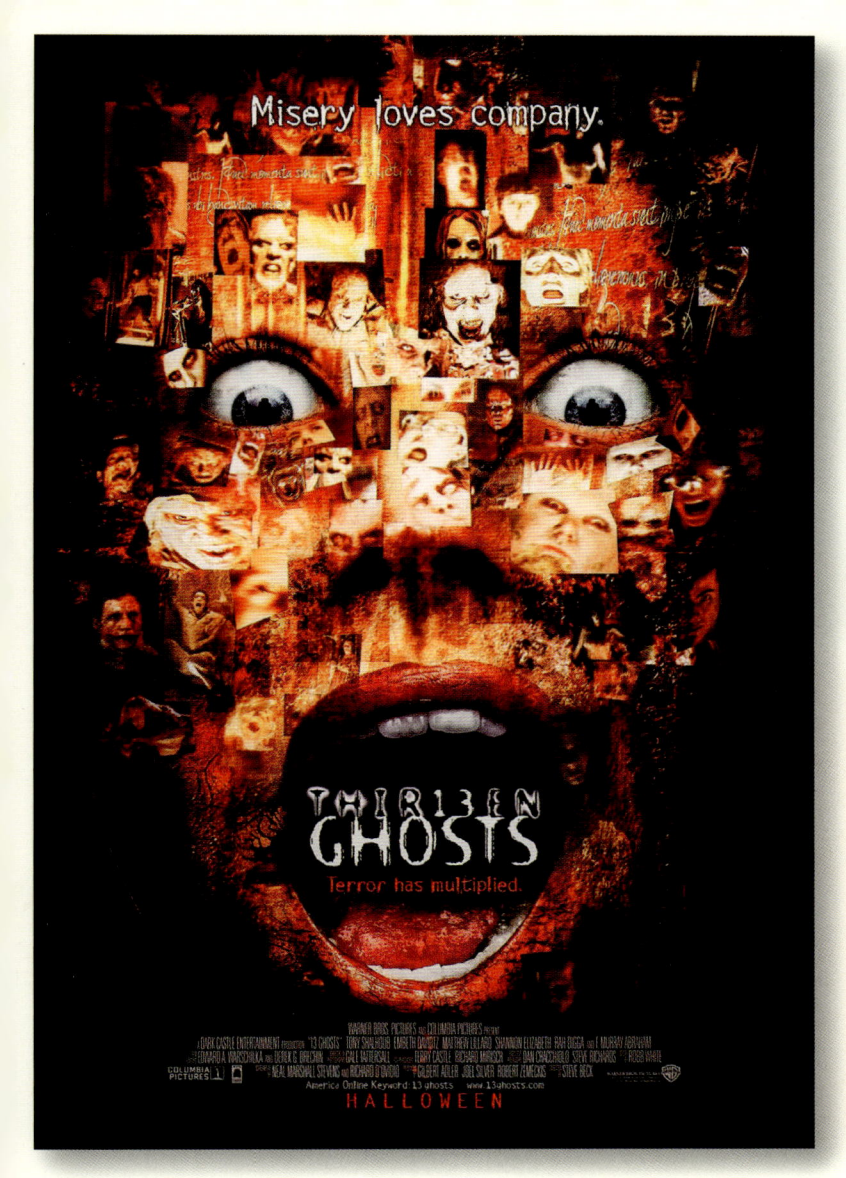

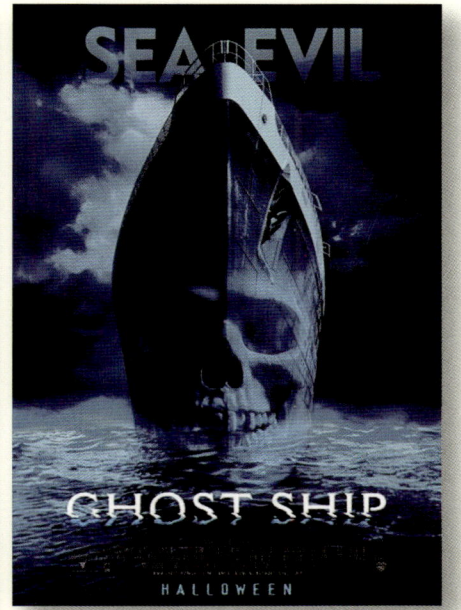

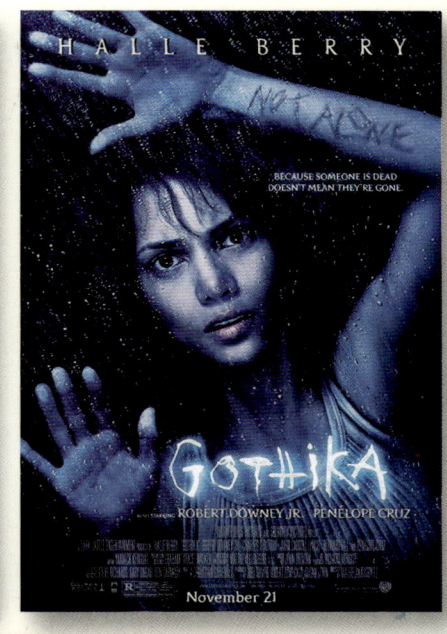

Castle Sinister

Dark Castle Entertainment was formed in 1999 by producers Joel Silver, Robert Zemeckis, and Gilbert Adler, initially to pay homage to the type of horror movies that William Castle used to make. To that end, their first two productions were updated remakes of Castle's *House on Haunted Hill* (1958) and *13 Ghosts* (1960), both co-produced with Castle's daughter, Terry Castle. Although *Ghost Ship* (2002) took its name from a 1952 British movie, it was the first Dark Castle project based on an original story. *Gothika* (2003) was also an original, and proved to be the production company's biggest box office hit to date. *House of Wax* (2005) was another updated remake, while *Return to House on Haunted Hill* (2007) was a direct-to-video sequel. Since then, Dark Castle's releases have included *The Reaping* (2007), *Orphan* (2009), *The Hills Run Red* (2009), and the distribution pick-up *Splice* (2009).

ABOVE LEFT: *Thir13en Ghosts* (Dir: Steve Beck, 2001), based on the 1960 movie *13 Ghosts*, was about a mechanized house filled with 12 angry spirits.

TOP MIDDLE: *Ghost Ship* (Dir: Steve Beck, 2002) was set aboard a haunted ocean liner that mysteriously disappeared in 1962.

TOP RIGHT: In *Gothika* (Dir: Mathieu Kassovitz, 2003), Halle Berry's possessed prison psychiatrist was accused of murder.

BOTTOM RIGHT: The search for a demonic statue was at the heart of the direct-to-video sequel *Return to House on Haunted Hill* (Dir: Victor Garcia, 2007).

THE 2000s MANIACS

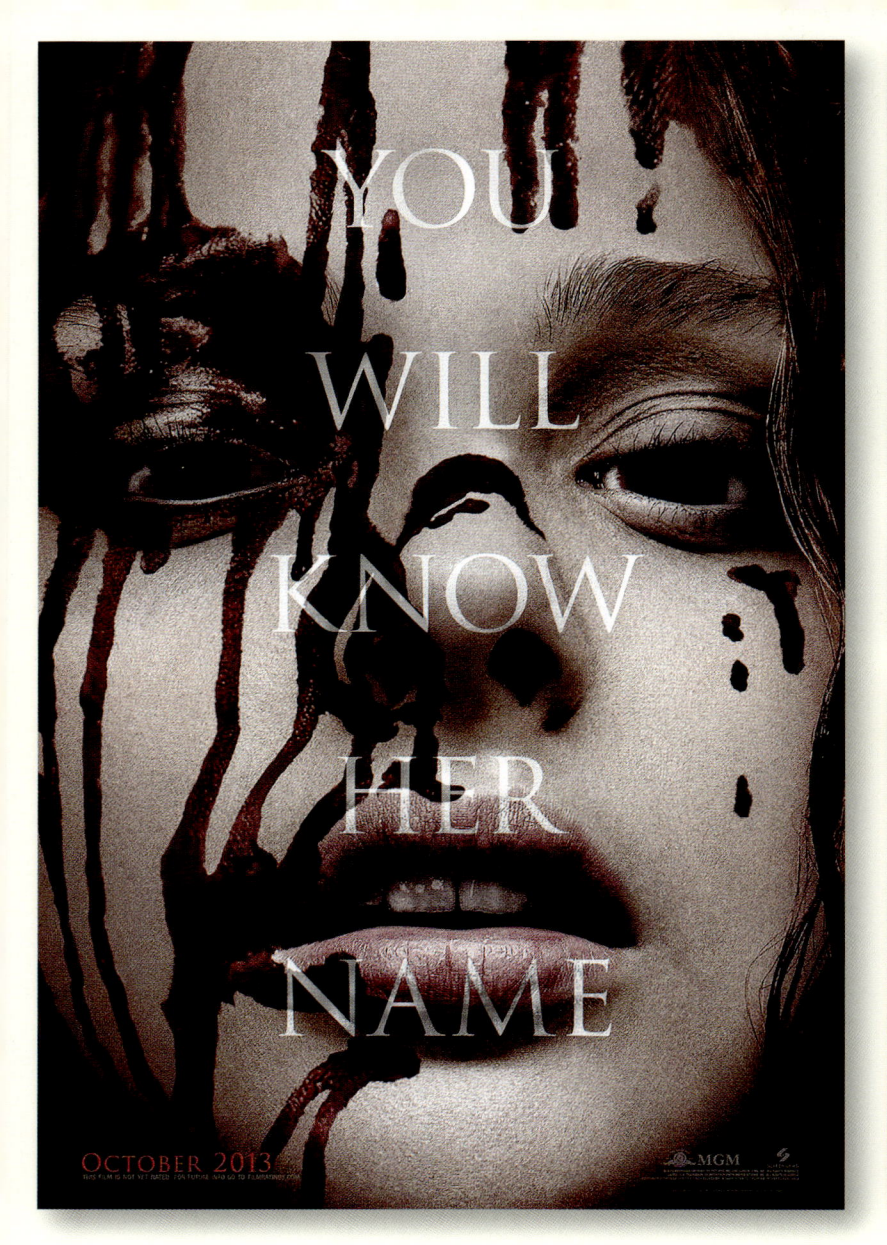

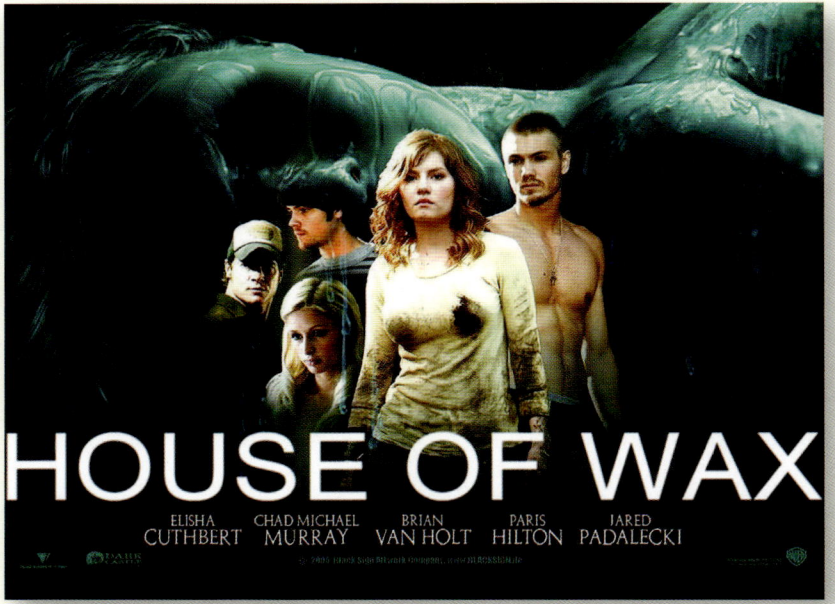

ABOVE LEFT: Teaser one-sheet poster for Metro-Goldwyn-Mayer's *Carrie* (Dir: Kimberly Peirce, 2013), a remake of the 1976 movie based on the 1974 novel by Stephen King. Chloë Grace Moretz played the telekinetic teen.

TOP RIGHT: Before co-starring in The CW's long-running TV series *Supernatural*, American actor Jared Padalecki appeared in Dark Castle Entertainment's Australian-made *House of Wax* (Dir: Jaume Collet-Serra, 2005), which was a "re-imagining" of the 1953 movie starring Vincent Price.

BOTTOM MIDDLE: Japanese poster for Lionsgate's *My Bloody Valentine* (Dir: Patrick Lussier, 2009), a 3-D remake of the 1981 Canadian movie. It starred Jensen Ackles, who appears with Jared Padalecki on The CW's *Supernatural* TV series.

BOTTOM RIGHT: Pre-release one-sheet poster created by advertising agency Ignition for Warner Bros.' 3-D *Godzilla* (Dir: Gareth Edwards, 2014), the second attempt by American filmmakers to remake the classic Japanese series which began in 1954.

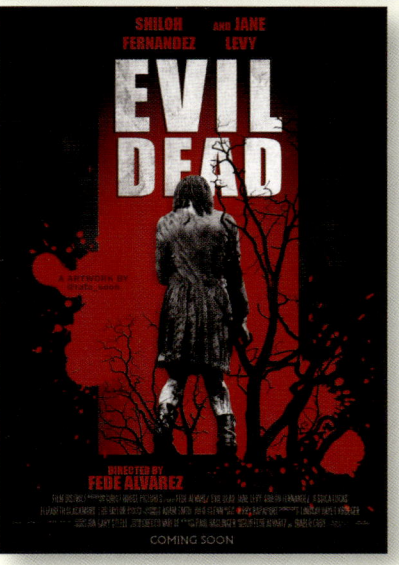

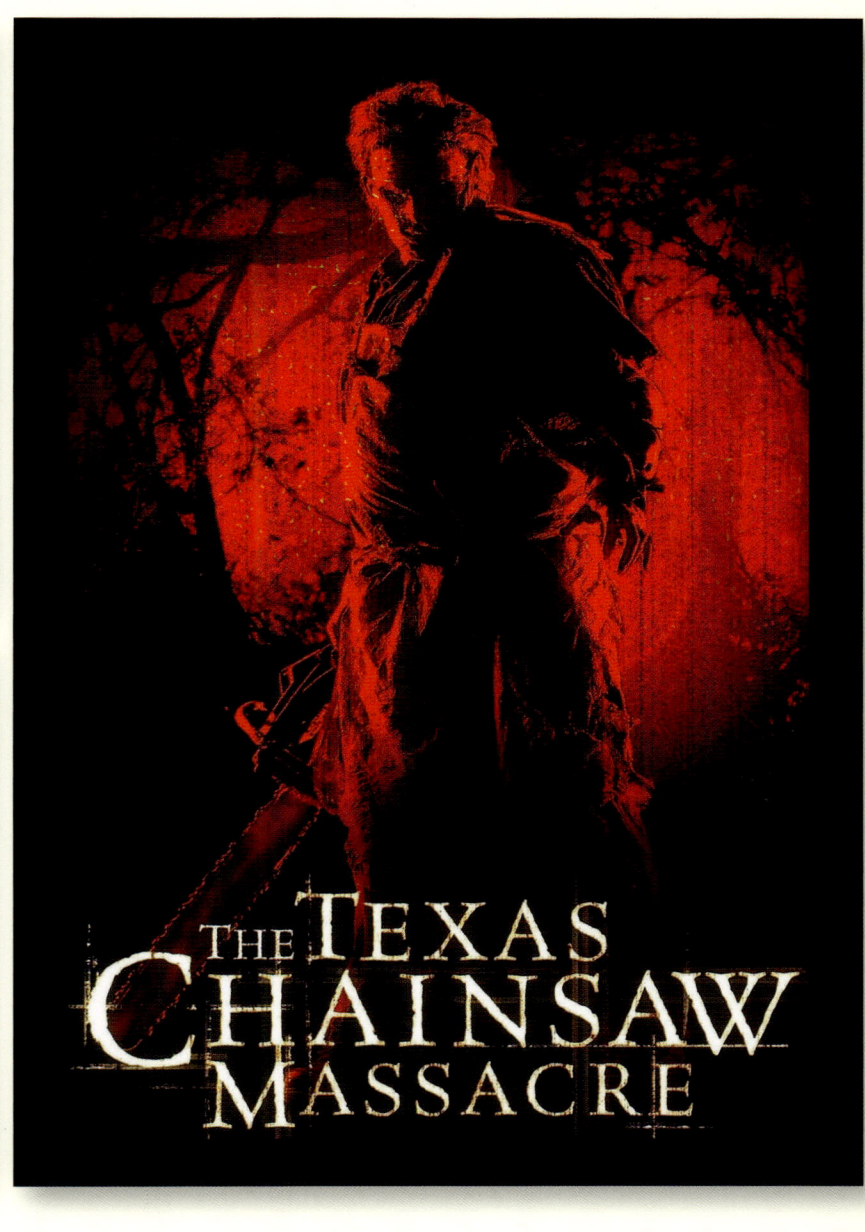

TOP LEFT: This pre-release poster for Dimension Films' *Halloween* (Dir: Rob Zombie, 2007), a remake of John Carpenter's 1978 movie, was apparently inspired by Reynold Brown's art for *The Masque of the Red Death* (1964).

BOTTOM LEFT: Pre-release poster for New Line Cinema's reboot of the 1980s movie franchise, *Friday the 13th* (Dir: Marcus Nispel, 2009), starring Jared Padalecki from the TV series *Supernatural*.

BOTTOM MIDDLE: Original director Sam Raimi and star Bruce Campbell (who has an uncredited cameo) were both producers on TriStar Pictures' *Evil Dead* (Dir: Fede Alvarez, 2013), a remake of the 1981 movie.

ABOVE RIGHT: Produced by Michael Bay, New Line Cinema's *The Texas Chainsaw Massacre* (Dir: Marcus Nispel, 2003) was a remake of the 1974 original and has so far spawned two sequels of its own.

THE 2000s MANIACS

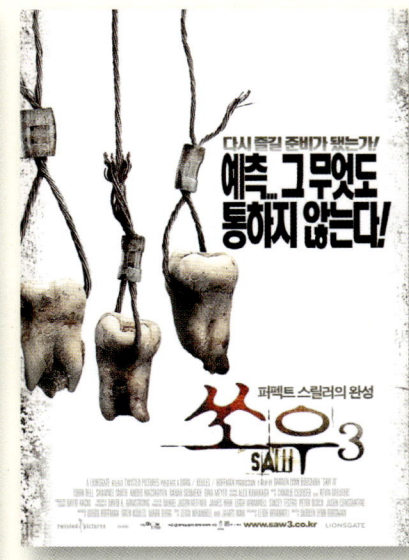

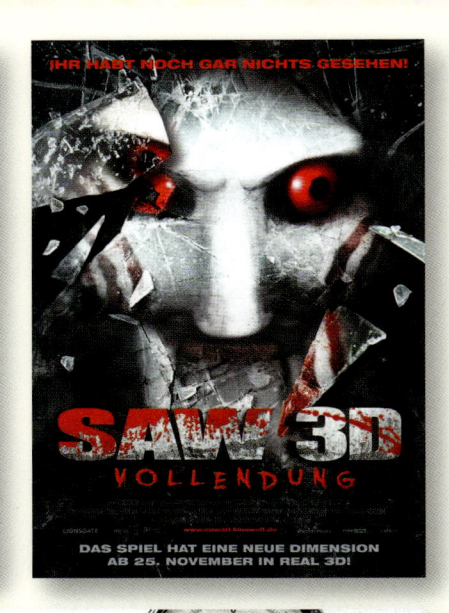

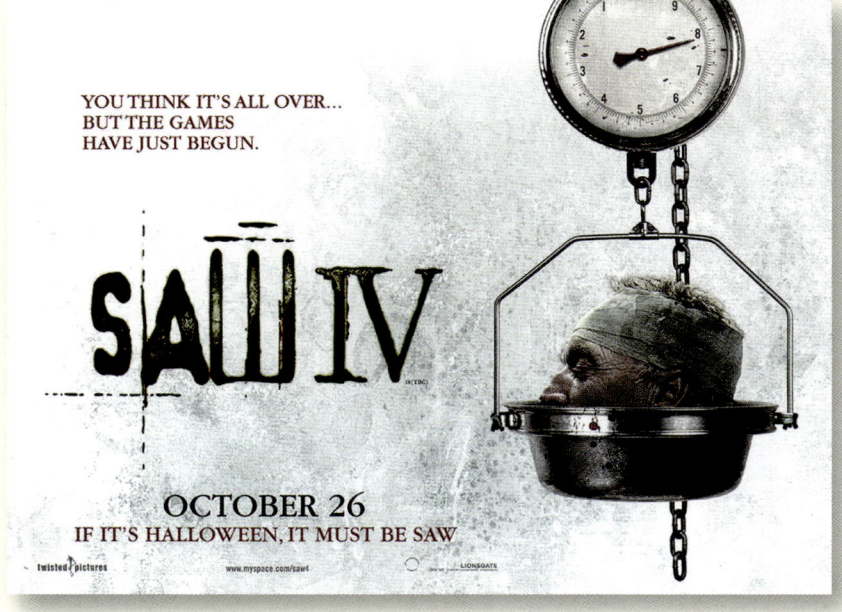

ABOVE LEFT: Tenth anniversary one-sheet poster by Jim Evans (b. 1950) for Lionsgate's *Saw* (Dir: James Wan, 2004), the first in the popular Halloween "torture porn" series which has so far run to eight movies.

TOP MIDDLE: Japanese poster for Lionsgate's *Saw III* (Dir: Darren Lynn Bousman, 2006), in which Shawnee Smith's crazed apprentice kidnaps a doctor to save Tobin Bell's serial killer Jigsaw from a terminal brain tumor.

BOTTOM RIGHT: Pre-release half-sheet poster for Lionsgate's *Saw IV* (Dir: Darren Lynn Bousman, 2007), in which Tobin Bell's Jigsaw/John Kramer sets a series of deadly traps from beyond the grave.

TOP RIGHT: German pre-release poster for Lionsgate's *Saw 3D* (Dir: Kevin Greutert, 2010), which was banned in that country until 2013. It was supposed to be the final chapter, but wasn't, as the filmmakers continue to play games with the audience.

THE ART OF HORROR MOVIES

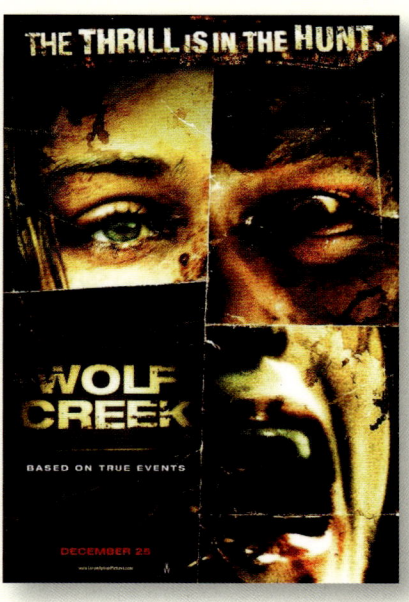

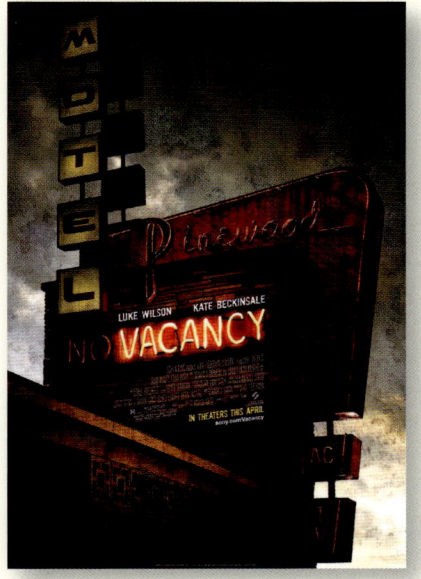

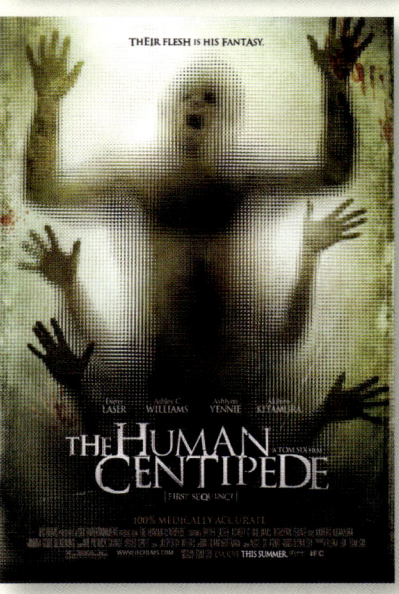

TOP LEFT: Italian poster for Lionsgate's *Hostel* (Dir: Eli Roth, 2005), a slice of xenophobic "torture porn" which was "presented" by Quentin Tarantino and has so far spawned two sequels.

TOP MIDDLE: John Jarratt's crazed bushman Mick Taylor hunts three backpackers across the Australian outback in Dimension Films' *Wolf Creek* (Dir: Greg McLean, 2005). Jarratt returned for the sequel and subsequent TV series.

BOTTOM LEFT: A married couple stranded at an isolated motel discover that they may become the subjects of a real-life "snuff" film in Screen Gems' *Vacancy* (Dir: Nimród Antal, 2007). It was followed by a prequel the following year.

BOTTOM MIDDLE: A mad scientist (Dieter Laser) kidnaps tourists and gruesomely stitches them together in the Dutch cult movie *The Human Centipede (First Sequence)* (Dir: Tom Six, 2009), which was followed by two postmodern sequels.

ABOVE RIGHT: Teaser poster for Universal Pictures' *The Purge: Election Year* (Dir: James DeMonaco, 2016), the third entry in the near-future franchise set on a night each year when any and all crime is considered legal.

THE 2000s MANIACS

HERE'S JOHNNY!

"With Johnny, people complain if I work with him, people complain if I don't work with him…"

Tim Burton

JOHNNY DEPP HAS appeared in more horror films than you might think. He made his first mark in *A Nightmare on Elm Street* (1984), falling foul of Freddy Krueger in bed and producing a famous geyser of blood. It's a debut he acknowledges with a cameo in *Freddy's Dead: The Final Nightmare* (1991), where (credited as "Oprah Noodlemantra") he warns television viewers against drugs and gets bopped in the face with a frying pan by Krueger.

Edward Scissorhands (1990) began his film relationship with Tim Burton, in a tale as dark and macabre as fairy tales frequently are, incidentally celebrating Vincent Price. *Ed Wood* (1994) continued the collaboration with his highly sympathetic portrait of the celebrated amateur filmmaker, which makes the point that creativity can be as heartfelt for an inept artist as a great one. Depp himself directed *The Brave* (1997), a restrained treatment of torture porn.

1999 confirmed his commitment to the macabre. In *The Ninth Gate* he's a book dealer whose search for a rare magical volume leads him into a narrative labyrinth riddled with occult symbols and references. In *The Astronaut's Wife* he's possessed by an alien and impregnates his wife on his return from space, a situation that conflates *Rosemary's Baby* with '50s science fiction cinema. While *Sleepy Hollow* indulges Tim Burton's eccentricities to an extent—Depp's investigator Ichabod Crane comes equipped with paraphernalia worthy of Heath Robinson—the film eloquently celebrates both Hammer Films and the glorious colors of Mario Bava.

Depp is a policeman in *From Hell* (2001) too—Inspector Abberline, would-be nemesis of Jack the Ripper, opium addict and clairvoyant. Less elaborate than the graphic novel by Alan Moore and Eddie Campbell, the film makes Freemasons its conspirators. *Pirates of the Caribbean: Curse of the Black Pearl* (2003) introduces Depp's Jack Sparrow, a pirate apparently in a constant state of intoxication from an unidentified substance. It's a persona he sustained throughout the extravagances of *Pirates of the Caribbean: Dead Man's Chest* (2006), *Pirates of the Caribbean: At World's End* (2007), *Pirates of the Caribbean: On Stranger Tides* (2011), and *Pirates of the Caribbean: Dead Men Tell No Tales* (2017). While the series derives from a Disneyland fairground ride, the fourth installment takes its title and some of its plot from a novel by the inventive fantasy writer Tim Powers.

Secret Window (2004) finds Depp playing a writer not wholly unlike Stephen King, author of the original tale. He's deranged not just by an imminent divorce but by writer's block and accusations of plagiarism too. In 2005 he provided just the voice of Victor Von Dort, spouse of Helena Bonham Carter's *Corpse Bride*, in Tim Burton's animated macabre romance. Although it's full of songs, Depp doesn't sing. He does in *Sweeney Todd: the Demon Barber of Fleet Street* (2007), Burton's spectacularly gory Stephen Sondheim musical, where Depp embodies all the pathos of the homicidal obsessed barber. He's among the actors who

---

Edward Scissorhands (1990) began his film relationship with Tim Burton.

---

helped Terry Gilliam turn his Satanic extravaganza *The Imaginarium of Doctor Parnassus* (2009) into a tribute to Heath Ledger, who died before filming was completed.

Despite their titles, *Alice in Wonderland* (2010) and *Alice Through the Looking Glass* (2016) are sequels to Lewis Carroll's tale. They favor the darker aspects of the original, not least in Depp's committed portrait of the crazed hatter, and resemble Tim Burton's own work as much as the original novel. In *Dark Shadows* (2012) Depp and Burton sought to pump new blood into the notably rickety television series. While the vampiric saga was serious as any television soap, the film is a camp parody, deriving its amusement from catapulting its eighteenth century vampire into the 1970s. All the same, Depp plays his undead nobleman as straight as Burton does his Gothic atmosphere.

In *Transcendence* (2014), a science fiction film imbued with quiet terror, he's uploaded halfway through the narrative but continues to dominate the plot, eventually the world. He's uncredited in *London Fields* (2016), turns up at the end of *Fantastic Beasts and Where to Find Them* (2016), and is a secondary character in *Tusk* (2014), hiding behind the name of his character Guy Lapointe, apparently so as not to steal the limelight from his fellow actors. Though the film was planned as a horror comedy, it ends up unnervingly touching, not to say reminiscent of Tod Browning's *Freaks* (1932). If you didn't know Depp was in the film you might not recognize him. His chameleonic qualities have graced our field for many years. Long may he continue. RC

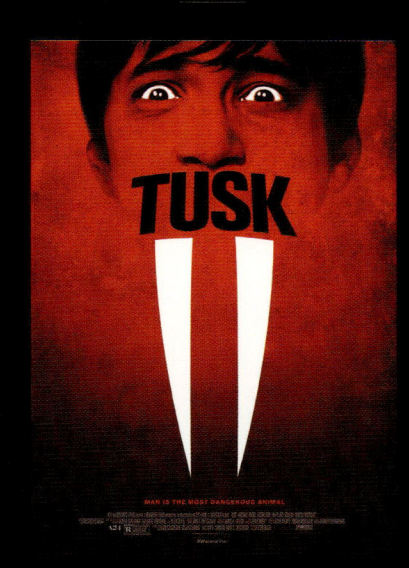

TOP LEFT: Johnny Depp's clairvoyant police inspector pursued Jack the Ripper through nineteenth century London in Twentieth Century Fox's *From Hell* (Dir: Albert Hughes and Allen Hughes, 2001), based on the serialized graphic novel (1989–96) by Alan Moore and Eddie Campbell.

TOP MIDDLE: Johnny Depp's successful author is menaced by a stranger (John Turturro) who claims that he stole his ideas in Columbia Pictures' *Secret Window* (Dir: David Koepp, 2004), based on the 1990 novella "Secret Window, Secret Garden" by Stephen King.

BOTTOM LEFT: Johnny Depp's singing barber supplies the fillings for the meat pies sold by Mrs. Lovett (Helena Bonham Carter) in DreamWorks' *Sweeney Todd: The Demon Barber of Fleet Street* (Dir: Tim Burton, 2007), based on Stephen Sondheim's smash-hit 1979 Broadway musical.

BOTTOM MIDDLE: Johnny Depp turned up in a supporting role in A24/Demarest Films' offbeat *Tusk* (Dir: Kevin Smith, 2014), in which Michael Parks's backwoods surgeon plans to turn a podcaster into a walrus.

ABOVE RIGHT: *Dark Shadows* (2012), pencil and digital portrait of Johnny Depp as vampire Barnabas Collins by American artist Mark Maddox, one of two covers produced by the artist for *Screem* #24 (May, 2012). "I really enjoyed painting this in terms of the color scheme," explains Maddox. "Tim Burton and Johnny Depp both own prints of the art."

THE 2000s MANIACS

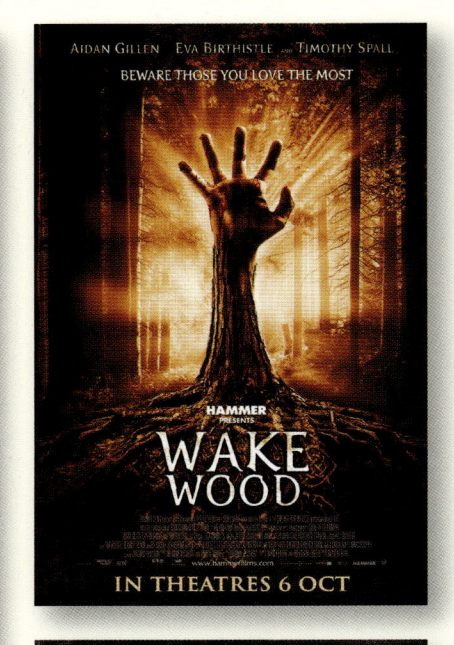

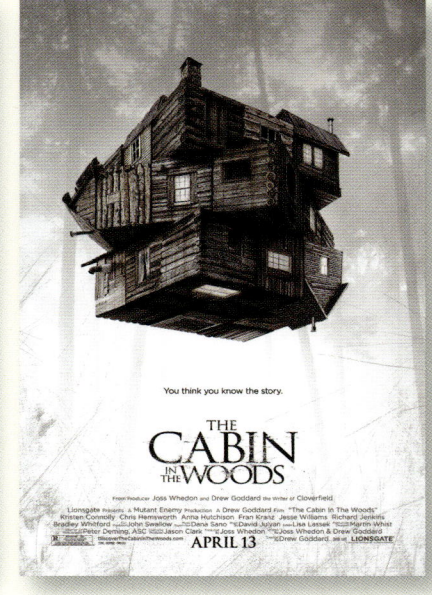

ABOVE LEFT: The one-sheet poster for Magnet Releasing's existential vampire movie *Kiss of the Damned* (Dir: Xan Cassavetes, 2012) by Akiko Stehrenberger, whose design was partly inspired by Ted Coconis's poster for *Dorian Gray* (1970).

TOP MIDDLE: American pre-release one-sheet for the supernatural thriller *Wake Wood* (Dir: David Keating, 2009), which marked the first theatrical release from Hammer Films for 30 years.

TOP RIGHT: Neil Kellerhouse's retro design for the one-sheet poster for Magnet Releasing's *The House of the Devil* (Dir: Ti West, 2009). "The only thing that was changed from the original poster presentation was making the word 'die' bold and red," reveals Kellerhouse.

BOTTOM MIDDLE: One-sheet poster for Magnet Releasing's *The Innkeepers* (Dir: Ti West, 2011) by Tim Hodge (aka The Dude Designs), who admits: "I have to take my hat off to Drew Struzan as a big inspiration."

BOTTOM RIGHT: Pre-release one-sheet created by design agency Ignition for Lionsgate's *The Cabin in the Woods* (2012). Co-scripted by Joss Whedon and director Drew Goddard as a postmodern tribute to classic horror films, it was actually filmed in 2009.

THE ART OF HORROR MOVIES

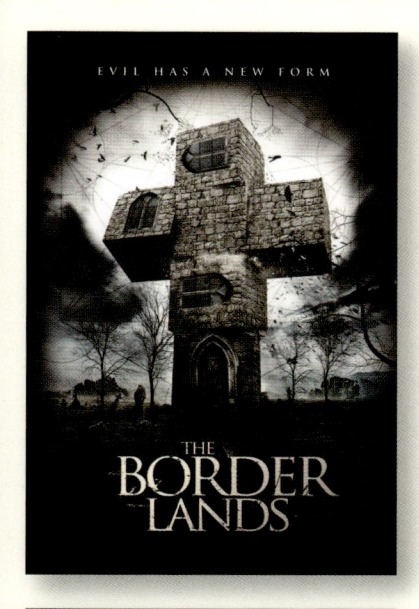

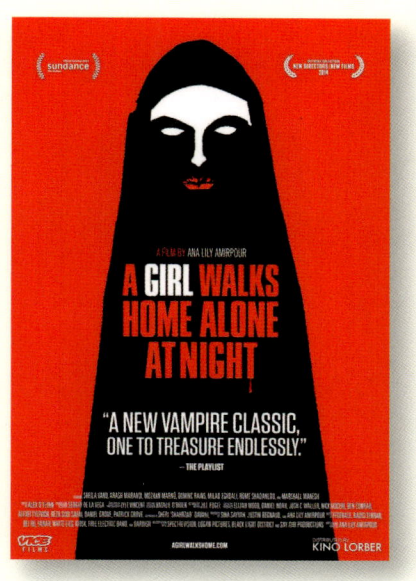

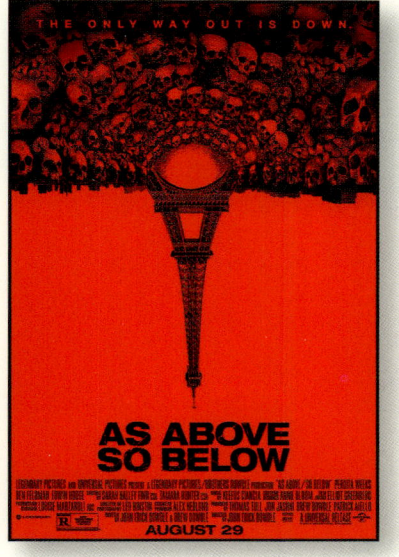

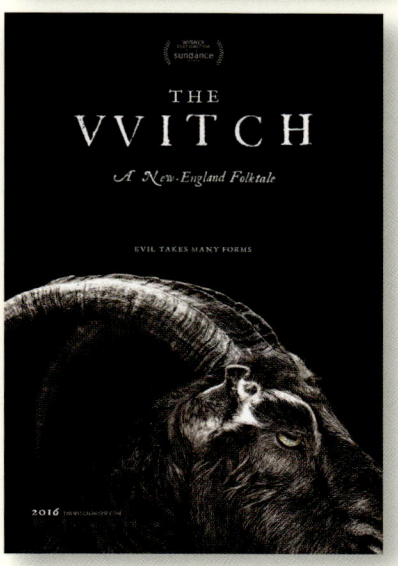

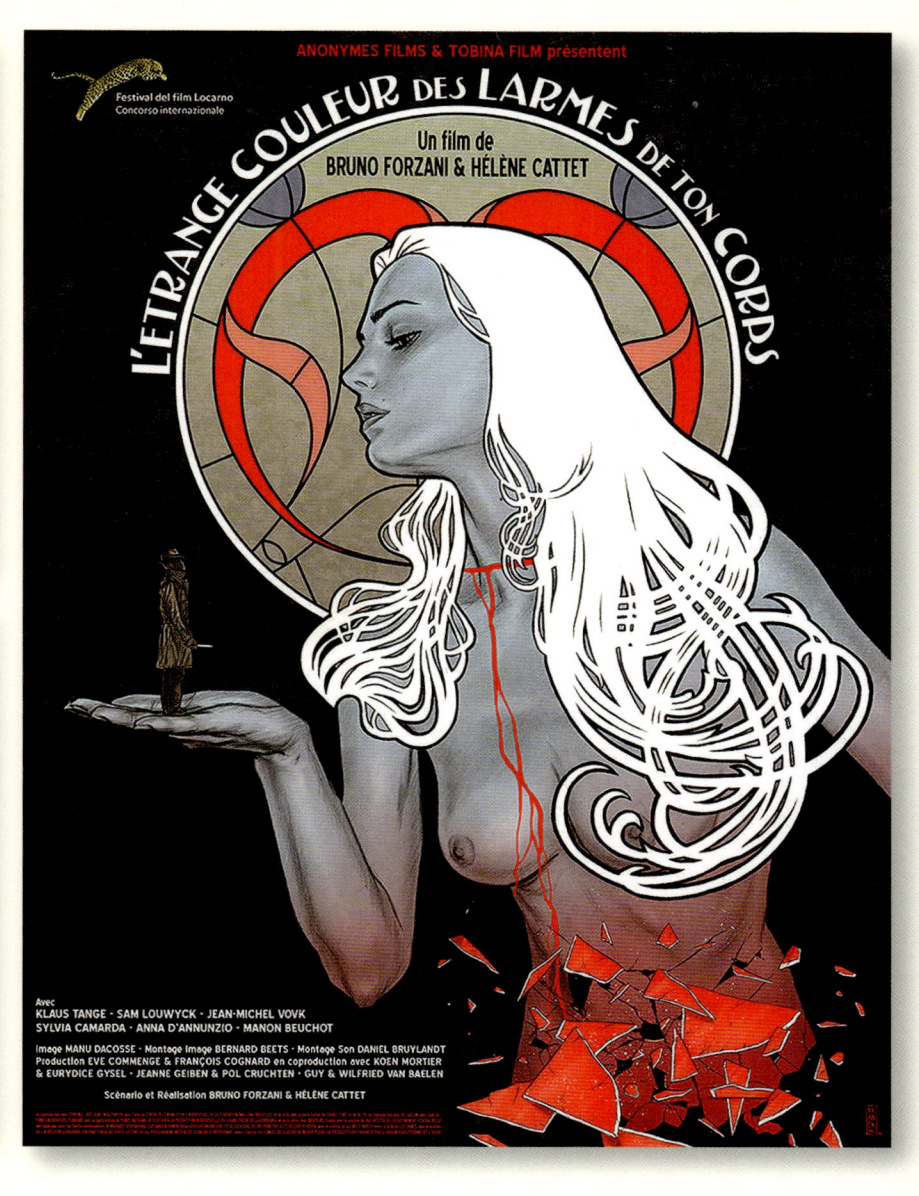

TOP LEFT: The British poster for Metrodome Distribution's "found footage" ghost story *The Borderlands* (Dir: Elliot Goldner, 2013) echoes the design for *The Cabin in the Woods* advertising. The movie was released as *Final Prayer* in America.

TOP MIDDLE: Stylish one-sheet poster design for Kino Lorber's *A Girl Walks Home Alone at Night* (Dir: Ana Lily Amirpour, 2014). Filmed in the Persian language in California, it is about a female Iranian vampire and included actor Elijah Wood among its producers.

BOTTOM LEFT: One-sheet poster created by design agency Ignition for Universal Pictures' *As Above, So Below* (Dir: John Erick Dowdle, 2014), a "found footage" exploration of the Paris catacombs that leads to Hell.

BOTTOM MIDDLE: One of three teaser poster designs by Gravillis, Inc. for A24's *The Witch: A New-England Folktale* (2015). Director Robert Eggers revisited many of the themes and images originally explored by Benjamin Christensen in *Häxan* (1922).

ABOVE RIGHT: Gilles Vranckx's Alphonse Mucha-inspired French poster for Hélène Cattet and Bruno Forzani's *L'étrange couleur des larmes de ton corps* (aka *The Strange Color of Your Body's Tears*, 2013), about a man searching for his missing wife in a strange apartment block.

THE 2000s MANIACS

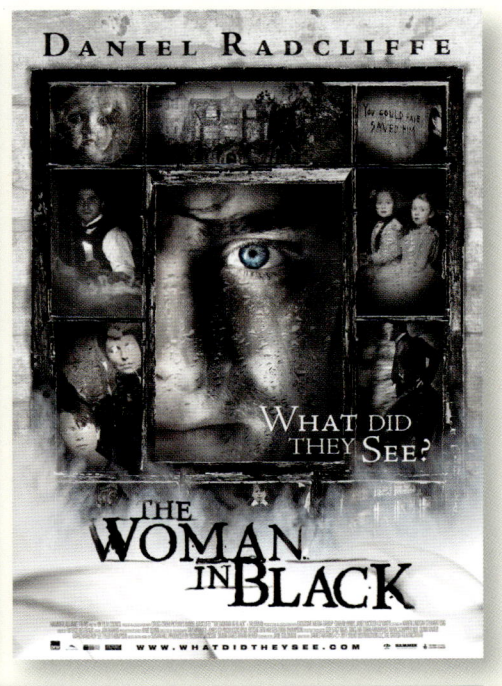

ABOVE RIGHT: Chloë Grace Moretz's child-vampire befriends a young boy (Kodi Smit-McPhee) in the new Hammer Films' *Let Me In* (Dir: Matt Reeves, 2010), an English-language remake of the 2008 Swedish film *Let the Right One In*, based on the bestselling novel by John Ajvide Lindqvist.

TOP LEFT: After 54 years, Sir Christopher Lee's final film for Hammer was the grim psychological thriller *The Resident* (Dir: Antti J. Jokinen, 2010). It starred Hilary Swank as a New York emergency doctor who is being stalked by her creepy new landlord (Jeffrey Dean Morgan).

TOP MIDDLE: Hammer's *The Woman in Black* (Dir: James Watkins, 2012), based on the 1983 novel by Susan Hill, was a remake of a 1989 made-for-TV film scripted by Nigel Kneale. Daniel Radcliffe starred as the young solicitor who travels to an isolated mansion and encounters a vengeful ghost.

BOTTOM LEFT: British quad poster for *The Woman in Black 2: Angel of Death* (Dir: Tom Harper, 2014). Hammer's sequel was set during World War II, as a group of children evacuated from London to the remote Eel Marsh House are stalked by the vengeance-seeking ghost from the earlier film.

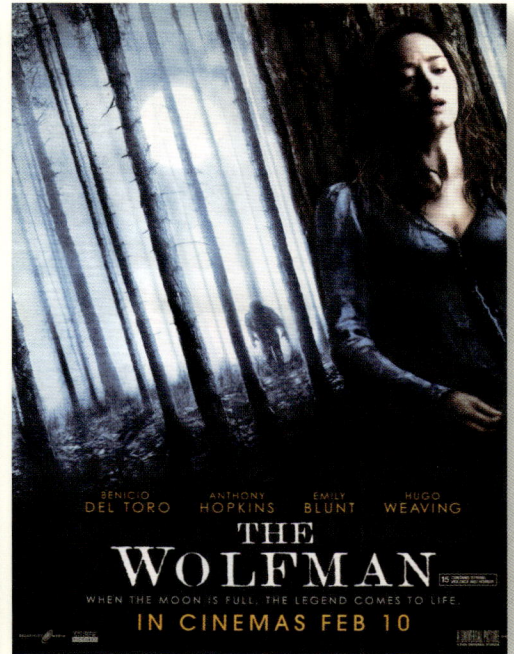

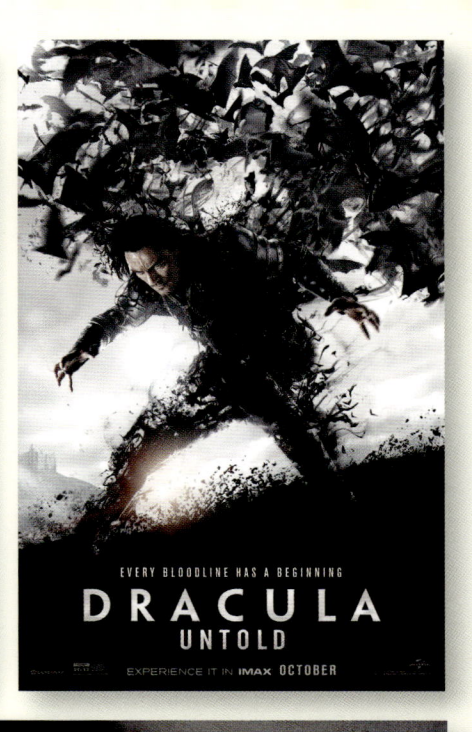

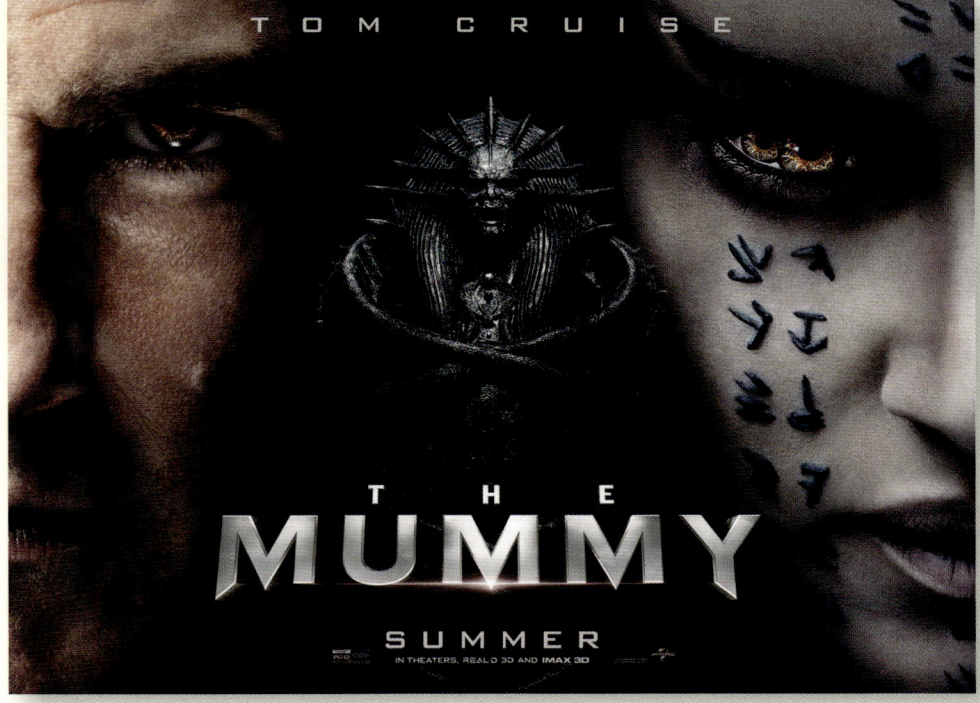

ABOVE LEFT: South Korean poster for *Van Helsing* (2004). After his success rebooting *The Mummy* franchise, Stephen Sommers attempted to turn the Universal Monsters into an action-adventure series with Hugh Jackman as the eponymous monster-hunter from *Dracula*.

TOP MIDDLE: British pre-release poster for Universal's *The Wolfman* (Dir: Joe Johnston, 2010), a remake of *The Wolf Man* (1941). Benicio del Toro stepped into the Lon Chaney, Jr. role as the reluctant lycanthrope, in Oscar-winning makeup created by Rick Baker and Dave Elsey.

TOP RIGHT: Universal Pictures decided to reboot Bram Stoker's story with a new action-adventure origin in *Dracula Untold* (Dir: Gary Shore, 2014), starring Luke Evans as the historical Vlad Drăculea. It was planned to retrospectively incorporate the film into the studio's "Dark Universe" series.

BOTTOM RIGHT: In 2014, Universal Pictures hired Alex Kurtzman and Chris Morgan to develop "Dark Universe," a shared world monster franchise. When Kurtzman's *The Mummy* (2017) flopped at the box office, despite starring Tom Cruise, the whole cinematic universe concept was scrapped.

THE 2000s MANIACS

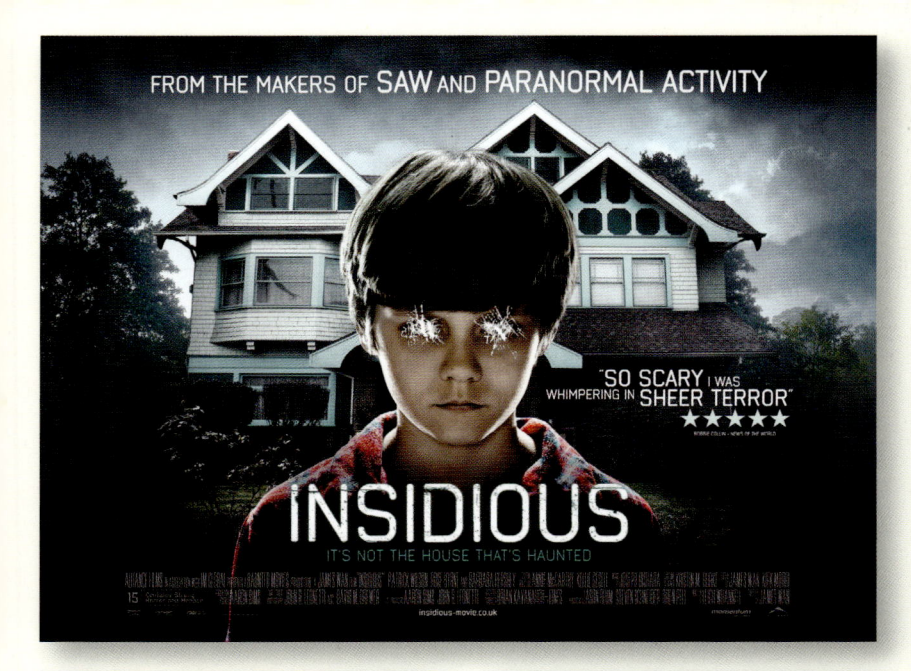

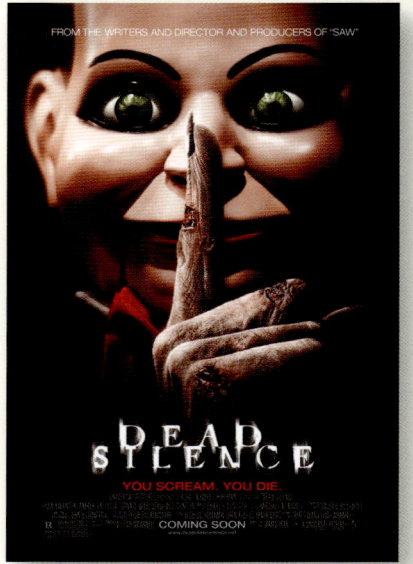

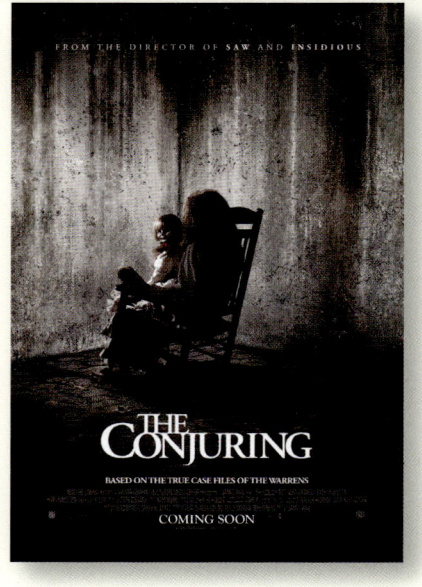

BOTTOM LEFT: One-sheet poster for Universal Pictures' *Dead Silence* (2007). This story of a cursed town and the dead ventriloquist who still haunts it marked the beginning of Malaysian-born director James Wan's hugely successful break from the *Saw* franchise.

TOP LEFT: British quad poster for Momentum Pictures' *Insidious* (Dir: James Wan, 2010), about a comatose boy whose soul is trapped in another dimension with evil spirits. It has spawned three sequels to date.

BOTTOM MIDDLE: Teaser one-sheet poster for New Line Cinema's *The Conjuring* (Dir: James Wan, 2013), which introduced Patrick Wilson and Vera Farmiga as the real-life married ghost-hunters who also investigated the "Amityville Horror" case.

ABOVE RIGHT: Advance one-sheet poster for Paramount Pictures' *Paranormal Activity: The Marked Ones* (Dir: Christopher Landon, 2014), the fifth entry in the popular franchise created by Oren Peli in 2007.

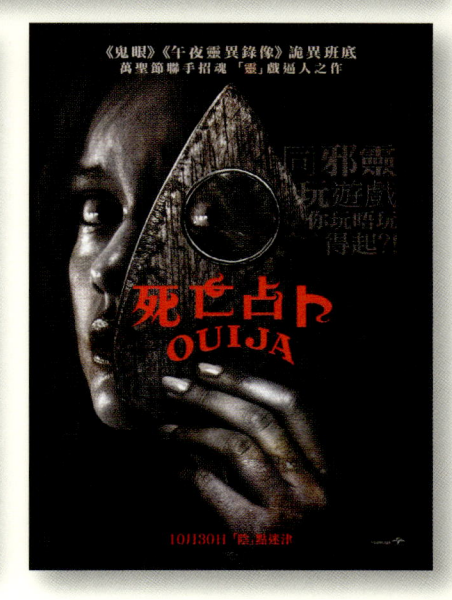

ABOVE LEFT: Teaser one-sheet poster for Warner Bros.' prequel *Annabelle* (Dir: John R. Leonetti, 2014), a demonic doll spin-off from *The Conjuring* series, co-produced by James Wan (b. 1977). A prequel of its own followed in 2017.

TOP RIGHT: British quad poster for Momentum Pictures' *Sinister* (Dir: Scott Derrickson, 2012), about a true crime author (Ethan Hawke) who finds his research coming back to haunt him. It was followed by a sequel in 2015.

BOTTOM MIDDLE: One-sheet pre-release poster for Open Road Films' comedy spoof of the recent "found footage" and "haunted house" movies, *A Haunted House* (Dir: Michael Tiddes, 2013), a revisionist take on the "race pictures" of the past.

BOTTOM RIGHT: Japanese pre-release poster for *Ouija* (Dir: Stiles White, 2014), about a cursed spirit-board that can really contact the dead. Co-produced by Michael Bay, a 1960s-set prequel was released two years later.

THE 2000s MANIACS

Blumhouse of Horror

Founded in 2000 by producer Jason Blum (b. 1969) to make low-budget movies that allow directors full creative control over their projects, Blumhouse Productions emerged as the dominant force in horror franchises during the first two decades of the twenty-first century. Beginning with Oren Peli's "found footage" *Paranormal Activity* in 2007, which was made for just $15,000 and grossed more than $193 million worldwide, Blumhouse went on to create such successful franchises as the *Sinister*, *The Purge*, *Insidious*, and *Ouija* series. In 2014, the company signed a first-look deal with Universal Pictures, which allowed it to expand into remakes or sequels of earlier movies such as *Halloween* (2018), *Black Christmas* (2019), and *The Invisible Man* (2020). Jeff Wadlow's *Fantasy Island* (2020) was a horror re-imagining and prequel to the ABC-TV series of the same name. In recent years, Blumhouse has also diversified into book publishing, television, and podcasts.

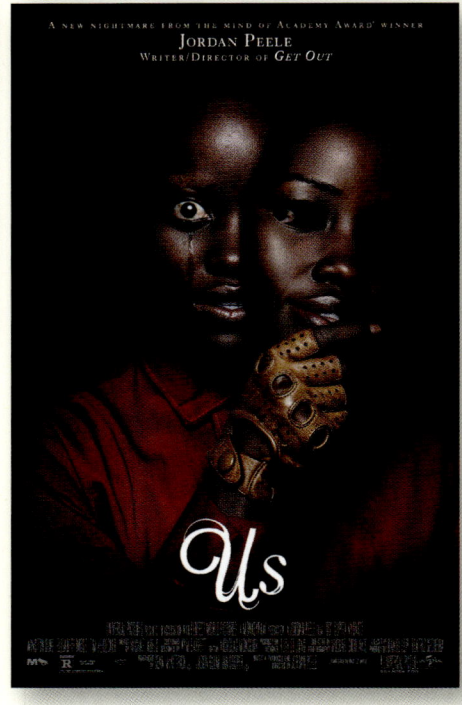

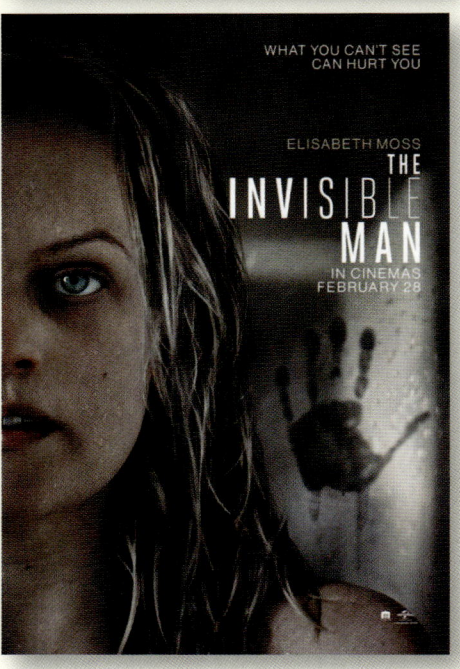

ABOVE LEFT: *Amityville: The Awakening* (Dir: Frank Khalfoun, 2017) was a failed attempt by Blumhouse to reboot the franchise.

TOP MIDDLE: *Get Out* (Dir: Jordan Peele, 2017) won an Oscar for Best Original Screenplay and garnered three other nominations.

TOP RIGHT: Blumhouse's *Halloween* (Dir: David Gordon Green, 2018) ignored most of the previous sequels and reboot attempts.

BOTTOM MIDDLE: Jason Blum was hired by Universal to produce Jordan Peele's second film, *Us* (2019), about a family of doppelgängers.

BOTTOM RIGHT: Initially developed as part of Universal's failed "Dark Universe" cinematic shared world, with Johnny Depp set to star, Blumhouse stepped in to revive *The Invisible Man* (Dir: Leigh Whannell, 2020). Shot in Australia on a budget of $7 million, it went on to gross more than 20 times that amount worldwide.

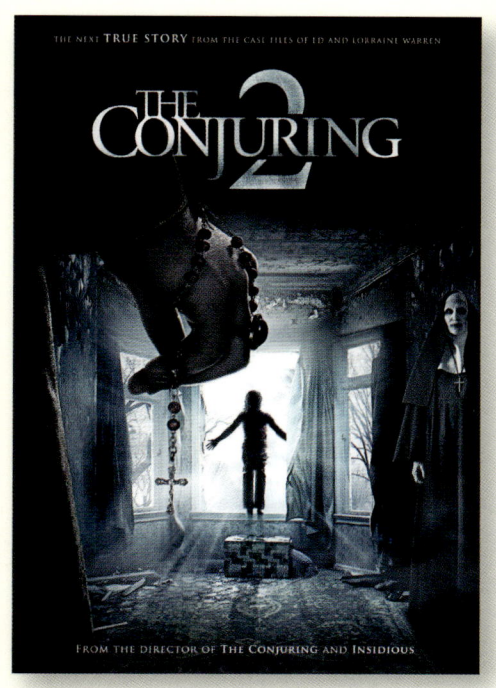

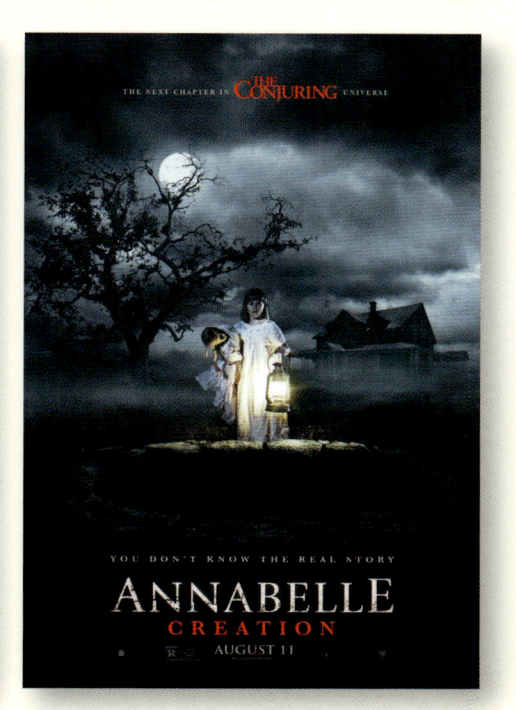

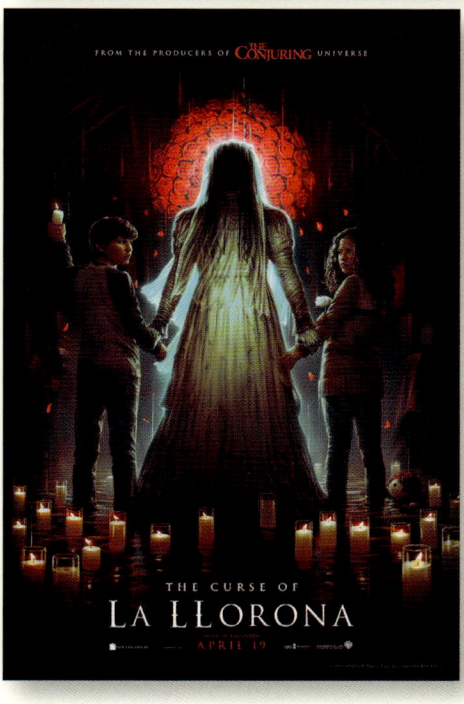

TOP LEFT: Patrick Wilson and Vera Farmiga reprised their roles as Ed and Lorraine Warren in James Wan's sequel *The Conjuring 2* (2016), based on the case of London's so-called "Enfield Poltergeist" in the late 1970s. This DVD poster added the image of The Nun, who got her own spin-off movie.

TOP MIDDLE: *Annabelle: Creation* (Dir: David F. Sandberg, 2017) was a prequel that revealed the origin of the possessed doll.

BOTTOM LEFT: Bonnie Aarons recreated her role of the demonic nun, Valak, in the spin-off *The Nun* (Dir: Corin Hardy, 2018).

BOTTOM MIDDLE: Father Perez (Tony Amendola) from *Annabelle* was the link in *The Curse of La Llorona* (Dir: Michael Chaves, 2019).

ABOVE RIGHT: *Annabelle Comes Home* (Dir: Gary Dauberman, 2019) was a sequel to the first two films in the series.

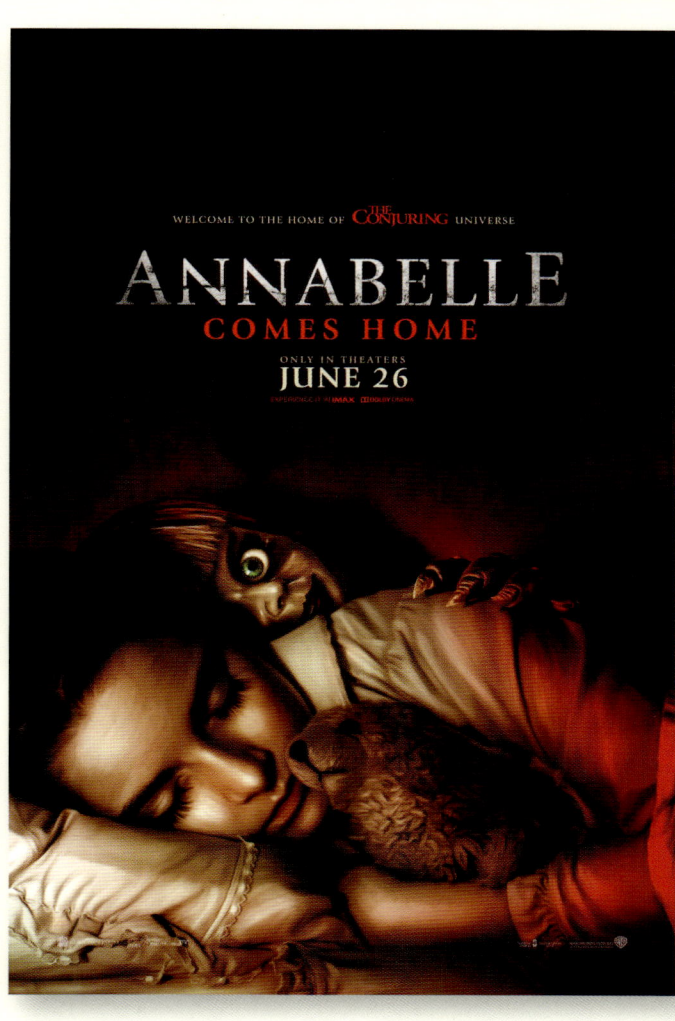

The Conjuring Universe

Giving Blumhouse Productions a close run in the horror franchise stakes, New Line Pictures' "The Conjuring Universe" began with James Wan's *The Conjuring* (2013), which fictionalized the supposedly real-life cases of paranormal investigators Ed and Lorraine Warren, who are best known for their dubious involvement in "The Amityville Horror." It was a box office hit and led to a sequel and the *Annabelle* spin-off series, which revolved around the origins of the eponymous demonic doll kept in the Warrens' occult museum. *The Nun* (2018) was the first in another prequel series, which was based on a character first introduced in *The Conjuring 2* (2018). Although *The Curse of La Llorona* (2019) was a stand-alone movie, it was linked to the shared world by a character that first appeared in *Annabelle* (2014). *The Conjuring* series has so far earned nearly $2 billion worldwide, making it one of the highest-grossing horror film franchises in cinema history.

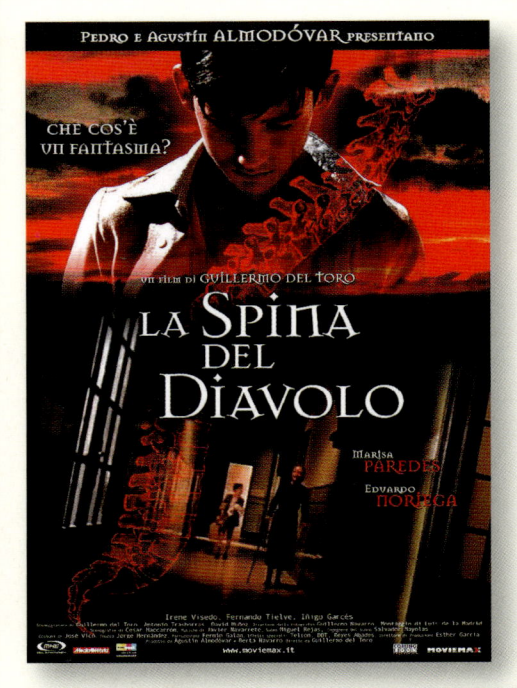

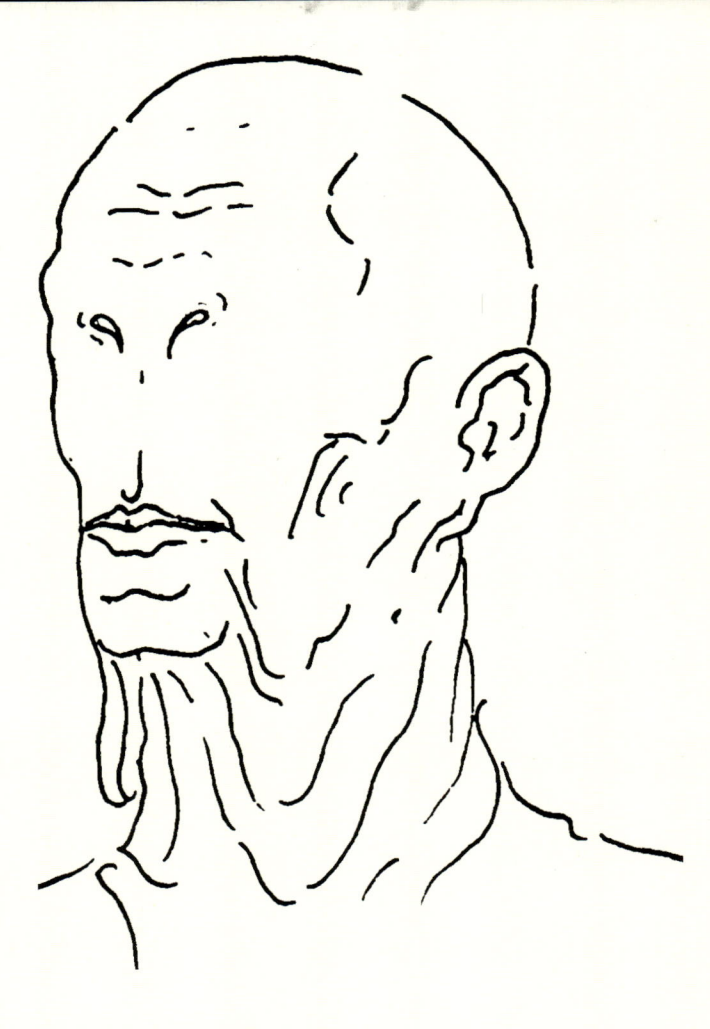

Del Toro's Terrors

Guillermo del Toro's films marry beauty and horror. They range from the political (*The Devil's Backbone*, 2001; *Pan's Labyrinth*, 2006) to the wryly superheroic (the *Hellboy* films) to a heady blend of religion and the monstrously macabre (*Cronos*, 1993; *Mimic*, 1997). All his films, including those based on comic books—the *Hellboy* series, the darker *Blade II* (2002)—include visionary images and concepts. *Pacific Rim* (2013) is a loving tribute to Ray Harryhausen and Japanese monster movies. *Crimson Peak* (2015) is the fullest expression so far of his Gothic and romantic tendencies, where the color and the sumptuous spectral mansion are among the stars of the film. RC

TOP LEFT: Italian poster for Guillermo del Toro's most personal movie, *El espinazo del diablo* (aka *The Devil's Backbone*, 2001), set in a haunted orphanage toward the end of the Spanish Civil War.

BOTTOM LEFT: Half-sheet poster for Universal Pictures' *Hellboy II: The Golden Army* (2008), Guillermo del Toro's sequel to his own 2004 movie, based on the Dark Horse Comics character created in 1993 by Mike Mignola (b. 1960).

TOP MIDDLE: Advance one-sheet poster designed by the Iconisus L&Y agency for Universal Pictures' *Crimson Peak* (2015), Guillermo del Toro's love letter to the movies of Roger Corman, as Mia Wasikowska's aspiring author goes to live in the titular haunted mansion.

ABOVE RIGHT: Original concept drawing by Guillermo del Toro of the "Pale Man," from *Pan's Labyrinth* (2006). Although DDT Efectos Especiales had sculpted the creature in clay, "I faxed them a drawing I did of the sculpture with all the face erased and only the nostrils on a flat Manta-ray surface," explains the writer-director.

OPPOSITE, TOP LEFT: Brazilian poster for the Spanish-Mexican *El laberinto del fauno* (aka *Pan's Labyrinth*, 2006), writer and director Guillermo del Toro's return to some of the themes he first explored in *The Devil's Backbone* (2001). The movie won three Academy Awards.

THE ART OF HORROR MOVIES

RIGHT: *Pan's Labyrinth* (2006), acrylic and oils on gessoed board poster design by American artist Drew Struzan. "The studio never used the painting because they thought it looked 'too much like art,'" recalls Struzan. "It did wind up on a special vinyl issue of the soundtrack album though."

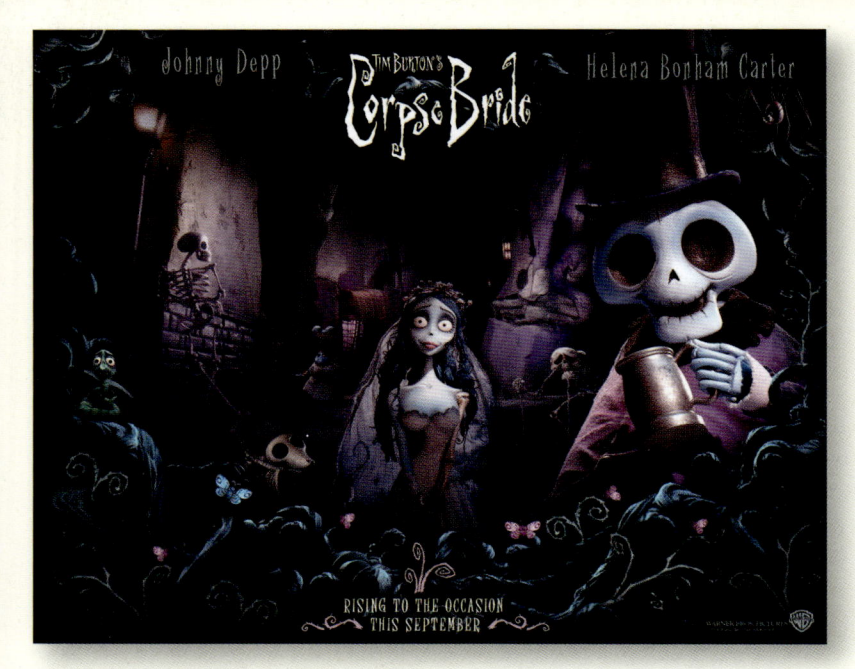

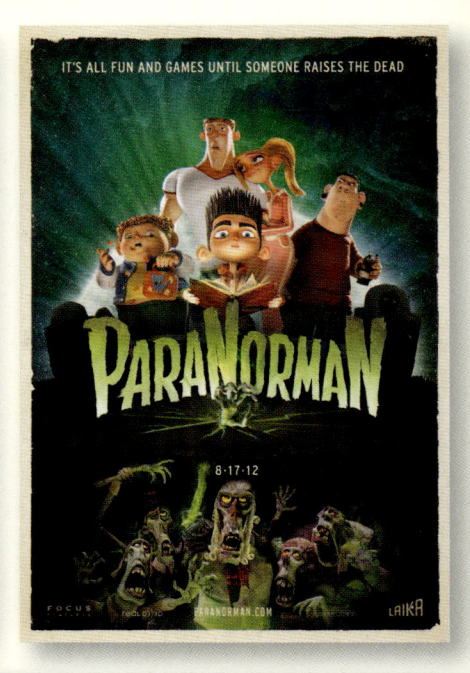

TOP LEFT: Advance half-sheet poster for Warner Bros.' *Corpse Bride* (Dir: Tim Burton and Mike Johnson, 2005), which used stop-motion puppet animation and featured the voices of Christopher Lee and Michael Gough.

TOP MIDDLE: Japanese poster for Focus Features' *Coraline* (Dir: Henry Selick, 2009), a 3-D stop-motion puppet movie about a young girl trapped in a frightening parallel world, based on the 2002 children's book by Neil Gaiman (b. 1960).

TOP RIGHT: One-sheet poster for Focus Features' *ParaNorman* (Dir: Chris Butler and Sam Fell, 2012), a 3-D stop-motion animated zombie comedy about a boy who can speak to the dead. It featured the first openly gay character in a mainstream animated movie.

BOTTOM LEFT: One-sheet poster for Columbia Pictures' 3-D animated *Monster House* (Dir: Gil Kenan, 2006).

BOTTOM MIDDLE: Teaser one-sheet poster for Columbia' Pictures' 3-D *Hotel Transylvania* (Dir: Genndy Tartakovsky, 2012).

BOTTOM RIGHT: Pre-release half-sheet poster for Twentieth Century Fox's *The Book of Life* (Dir: Jorge R. Gutiérrez, 2014), a 3-D animated musical inspired by the Mexican celebration of *Dia de Muertos* (Day of the Dead), co-produced by Guillermo del Toro.

THE ART OF HORROR MOVIES